Symbols and abbreviations used in the lists

(For full explanations, see the Guide to the lists of plants, pp.7–11.)

Sun and shade requirements

○ = sun

○ [◐] = sun (or partial shade)

○ ◐ = sun or partial shade

◐ [○] = partial shade (or sun)

◐ = partial shade

◐ [●] = partial (or full) shade

◐ ● = partial or full shade

Plant name

x = recognized hybrid

f. = forma (botanical form)

subsp. = subspecies

syn. = synonym

var. = varietas (botanical variety)

Many of the plants with an equals sign in their name (for example, *Rosa* Graham Thomas = "Ausmas") are protected by Plant Breeders' Rights.

Summaries of plant details

Figures in square brackets – for example [4–9] – at the end of the "type of plant" line of information refer to hardiness zones (see opposite).

The following symbol may appear immediately after the sun and shade symbols:

* = needs lime-free soil

Immediately below the "height" line of information, one or more of the following abbreviations may be used:

≈ = suitable for growing in shallow water (Damp and wet soils list only)

✔ = plants suitable for north-facing walls (Climbing plants list only)

✔✔ = plants suitable for north-facing and east-facing walls (Climbing plants list only)

✂ = foliage particularly useful for cutting (Variegated leaves; Grey, blue-grey or silver leaves; Purple, bronze or red leaves; Yellow or yellow-green leaves; and Decorative, green foliage lists only)

Dr = flowers or seed-heads suitable for drying (Flowers suitable for cutting list only)

RIGHT PLANT
RIGHT PLACE

FIRESIDE
Rockefeller Center
1230 Avenue of the Americas
New York, NY 10020

This revised edition first published in Great Britain in 2005
by Cassell Illustrated, a division of Octopus Publishing Group Limited

Published by arrangement with Cassell Illustrated

First Fireside revised edition 2005

FIRESIDE and colophon are registered trademarks of Simon & Schuster, Inc.

For information regarding special discounts for bulk purchases, please contact Simon & Schuster
Special Sales at 1-800-456-6798 or business@simonandschuster.com

Manufactured in China

10 9 8 7 6 5 4 3 2 1

ISBN 0 7432 7650 7

Editor: Joanna Chisholm
Project Editor: Joanne Wilson
American Consultant: Robert Herman
Americanizer: Kathy Fahey
Designers: Helen Taylor, Versha Jones
Design Manager: Jo Knowles
Publishing Manager: Anna Cheifetz

RIGHT PLANT
RIGHT PLACE

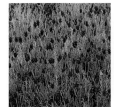

Over 1400 plants for every situation in the garden

Nicola Ferguson

A FIRESIDE BOOK
PUBLISHED BY SIMON & SCHUSTER
NEW YORK LONDON TORONTO SYDNEY

Contents

See Endpapers for symbols and abbreviations and plant hardiness zones

Introduction

IT IS TWENTY YEARS SINCE I wrote the introduction to the first edition of *Right Plant, Right Place*. In those intervening years, my garden, which inspired me to write the book, has changed and so too has the gardening world in general.

Not everything has altered, of course. Gardeners still need information to help them choose particular plants for particular places. And they need this information set out in a systematic way if the process of making their selection is not to be long-winded and complicated. *Right Plant, Right Place* has helped me and numerous other gardeners choose plants for our gardens, but a few years ago it became clear to me that the range of plants contained in the book no longer reflected the cultivars and species that were currently available in garden centers and nurseries.

So here is a new, comprehensively revised edition. As before, *Right Plant, Right Place* contains lists of plants for particular purposes in which all sorts of plants are mentioned and in which basic information (such as height and flower color) about actual species and varieties is set out in systematic form. It is still intended to help anyone—expert or beginner—who wants to produce a design for a whole garden or for part of a garden, or who wants to fill a particular place with a certain kind of plant.

Many plants are just as popular as they were in the early 1980s, and these have been retained in this edition. But there are also plenty of new introductions and newly appreciated "old" plants. In addition to the original twenty-seven lists, there are now two new ones: "Black" plants; and Perennial plants with a long, continuous flowering period. Some information—about flowering times, for example—has been made more precise, and in addition, to reflect the greatly increased range of plants available to gardeners, the comments on plants now often include information about other plants that may be of interest.

Shifts of emphasis in the gardening world have changed what plants we choose for our gardens. For example, interest in naturalistic styles of planting—including "prairie" and "matrix" planting—has drawn attention to robust perennials and large grasses and has led to an appreciation of the value of seedheads in the autumn and winter garden. Indeed, for some time now, and rather at the expense of shrubs, all sorts of perennials have been popular. On the other hand, certain plants, such as conifers, which were once much admired, are only now just beginning to be appreciated again.

There has also been the influence of climate change: with milder winters in many regions, half-hardy perennials, for example, are much more widely grown than they were when the first edition of *Right Plant, Right Place* was published. To some extent, these plants, bought as young specimens, have replaced the numerous annuals and biennials that many gardeners used to grow from seed.

Gardens are, on average, a good deal smaller than they were twenty years ago, and this change, too, has had effects. Fewer large trees are planted in private gardens now, but small trees with "extra" features, such as interesting bark or unusually colored foliage, are particularly favored. Reasons of space also account for the popularity of all sorts of plants that have decorative foliage as well as attractive flowers.

These and other changes mean that gardeners grow a different—although not completely different—range of plants than they did in the 1980s. The new edition of *Right Plant, Right Place* reflects this different range. So, whether you are a knowledgeable gardener needing to have your memory jogged or a complete beginner wanting plenty of basic information, these plant lists will be useful. The information does not amount to full-length description, and the lists will not design your garden for you, but they will make the whole business of choosing plants quicker and simpler than it might otherwise be.

GUIDE TO

Lists of plants

A<small>LL THE LISTS DEAL WITH</small> garden plants, rather than plants that are suitable only for growing under some sort of cover. The range of garden plants is, however, very large indeed and, in order to make these lists useful, a selection of plants has been made. Two main points have been borne in mind when choosing plants. First of all, the plants should be readily available to the ordinary gardener. (Although some slightly less usual plants appear in these lists, they should be as easily obtained from suppliers with a really wide range of general stock as from specialist nurseries.) Secondly, the selected plants should give a good idea of the range of height, flower color, and so on of all the plants both commonly offered by suppliers and frequently referred to in popular gardening books.

The titles and page numbers of all the lists are given on the Contents pages. Each list is preceded by a brief introduction and all the lists are organized in the same way. They are divided into a maximum of seven sun and shade categories, starting with "sun" and ending with "partial or full shade." Within each of these categories, there are illustrated and unillustrated sections.

In each illustrated section all the plants are arranged according to height, beginning with the tallest plant and ending with the smallest plant. This means that, when you are looking for a tall plant for a sunny place, you are not diverted by small plants that like cool, shady places. As well as photographs in the illustrated sections, there are several lines of basic information about each plant. These summaries of details are accompanied by short descriptions with additional information.

The unillustrated sections consist of the names and page numbers of other, relevant plants, which are illustrated and described elsewhere in the book. For example, in the unillustrated sections of the Climbing plants list you will find the names and page numbers of additional climbers. These plants will be illustrated and described in various other lists, such as Plants with variegated leaves and Plants with fragrant flowers. In all the unillustrated sections there is a very general indication of the heights of the plants, so that, if you are looking for a tree or large climber, you do not waste time turning to pages where all the plants shown are less than 12in/30cm tall.

The sun and shade requirements, the arrangement in order of height, the summaries of details, and so on are all further explained below.

Symbols for sun and shade

The seven symbols used in this book are:

○ = SUN. Plants in this category must receive sun during all or almost all of the day in the summer months. In some cases the sunniest possible position is needed and this sort of detail is mentioned in the descriptions of individual plants.

○[◐] = SUN (OR PARTIAL SHADE). Plants in this category prefer the conditions described under "sun," but they will also do reasonably well in partial shade. Some partially shaded sites do receive sunlight, but only for a relatively short period during the day. Other sites in partial shade are more consistently shaded but the light is dappled (as it is in fairly open woodland, for example). And, although some positions have unbroken shade cast on them during most of the day at least (if they are near buildings, for instance), these positions are still, in effect, partially shaded if they receive a good deal of light from above.

○◐ = SUN OR PARTIAL SHADE. Plants in this category do equally well in either position.

◐[○] = PARTIAL SHADE (OR SUN). This is the reverse of the situation described under "sun (or partial shade)," for which see above.

◐ = PARTIAL SHADE. For a description of partial shade, see under "sun (or partial shade)," above.

◐ [◐] = PARTIAL (OR FULL) SHADE. Plants in this category prefer partial shade, as described under "sun (or partial shade)" above, but they can be grown in fully shaded positions. A surprising number of plants do well without any direct sunlight. Indeed a site may receive no sunshine but still be reasonably light.

◐ ● = PARTIAL OR FULL SHADE. Plants in this category do equally well in either position. However, the symbol ◐ ● does not mean that all the plants in this category will grow in dark places, such as underneath dense, overhanging trees or very close to tall buildings. For plants that can tolerate full shade and very restricted light, see the list entitled "Plants tolerant of dense shade."

Some lists are so short that no plants appear in one or other of the sun and shade categories. Other lists deal with plants that are not suitable for growing in certain light conditions. In some lists, therefore, two or more categories have been combined, and the very shortest lists are divided simply into illustrated and unillustrated sections. In these cases, plants have been arranged in order of height alone, and no sun and shade symbols appear at the top of the pages. Throughout the book, the sun or shade requirements of individual plants are noted, so that it is always clear how much light a particular plant requires.

It is worth remembering that the sun and shade requirements of plants are sometimes affected by the ability of a particular soil to retain moisture. For instance, in consistently moisture-retentive soil, many plants will be able to withstand greater exposure to sun than they could if they were grown in light, free-draining, sandy soil.

Illustrations

Every plant that is fully described in this book is also illustrated once. Some plants appear in only one list; others are described in one list but are mentioned in several others. Plants that are included in several lists usually have a number of decorative features and they may be suitable for a variety of soils and sites. They are illustrated in what seems to be the most appropriate list and mentioned in the unillustrated sections of the other, relevant lists. Since some plants have several decorative features that are almost equally decorative, or they do almost equally well in more than one type of soil or site, it is important not to regard entries in the unillustrated sections of a list as necessarily less attractive than the plants that are illustrated in that list.

Arrangement in order of height

Within each illustrated section of every list, plants are arranged according to their height, with the tallest plant at the beginning of each section and the smallest plant at the end. Where there are several plants of the same height within a section, then those plants are placed in alphabetical order. Where several plants have the same minimum height but different maximum heights, then the plant with the greatest maximum height appears first: for example, if the height for plant A is estimated to be 12–24in/30–60cm and for plant B the estimate is 12–18in/30–45cm, then plant A appears before plant B. Individual specimens of both plants could be 18in/45cm high but, of the two plants, specimens of plant A are more likely to be taller.

Summaries of details

The summaries of details always take the same basic form, which generally consists of six separate items of information: name; sun and shade requirements; type of plant; flowering time; flower color; height. Where relevant, some other important characteristics are noted, usually after the information about height.

Name

In each case, the main, currently correct, botanical name of a plant appears first. If there are any alternative botanical names these appear, in parentheses, after the main botanical name. Any common names are placed in square brackets below the botanical name(s).

Main botanical name

The first word in the name of a plant denotes its genus (e.g. *Clematis* in *Clematis montana*); the second word often denotes the species of the plant (e.g. *montana* in *Clematis montana*).

If a species varies in the wild to the extent that it produces distinct variants, these botanical variants are referred to as subspecies—abbreviated to "subsp."—as in *Clematis alpina* subsp. *sibirica*. Varieties and forms are two further types of botanical variant. They are both less distinct than subspecies. In plant names, variety (or, technically, varietas) is abbreviated to "var." (as in *Clematis montana* var. *rubens*); and form (technically, forma) is shortened to "f." (as in *Clematis montana* f. *grandiflora*).

If a variety originated in cultivation, then the name of that variety appears in inverted commas (e.g. "Purpurea" in *Clematis recta* "Purpurea," and "Nelly Moser" in *Clematis* "Nelly Moser"). These cultivated varieties are often referred to as "cultivars." For legal reasons, the names of some cultivated varieties take the following form: *Rosa* Graham Thomas = "Ausmas;" *Choisya ternata* Sundance = "Lich." The name immediately preceding the equals sign is the plant's selling name or trade designation; the name following the equals sign is the name it has been registered under for the purposes of Plant Breeders' Rights.

A multiplication sign before or within the name of a plant denotes that the plant is a recognized hybrid. It may be a hybrid between two genera (e.g. x *Fatshedera lizei*) or between two species or varieites (e.g. *Camellia* x *williamsii*).

Some popular plants, such as roses, daffodils, and tulips, have very many cultivated varieties and these varieties have been divided into groups. In this book, if the group name is a useful piece of information for gardeners, it is placed, in parentheses, after the name of a plant: for example, *Rosa* "Albertine" (Rambler); and *Tulipa* "Red Riding Hood" (Greigii Group). In the case of some genera and species, at least two and sometimes dozens of cultivated varieties are readily available. To indicate this, the abbreviation "e.g." appears before the selected examples (for instance, *Crocus chrysanthus* e.g. "Cream Beauty," *Rhododendron* e.g. "Sappho" and Rosa e.g. "Ballerina"). If an "e.g." is omitted from a plant name in one list, although it appears in that same plant's name in other lists, this means that the plant is the only suitable variety—or the only readily available variety—in the context of that particular list.

Botanical synonym

A plant may have an alternative botanical name. Sometimes there are several alternative names. Any such names are preceded by the abbreviation "syn."—for synonym—and placed in parentheses after the main botanical name of the plant. These synonyms are names that botanical and horticultural research suggests are now incorrect. However, they will appear in older gardening books and they may still be used by some nurseries and garden centers.

Common name

If a plant has a common name this appears, in square brackets, below the plant's current botanical name and any synonyms it may have. Some plants have more than one common name. Other plants either have no common, English name, or their botanical names are better known—at least among gardeners—than their so-called common names. Where it seems that it would be useful, particularly to those gardeners who are unfamiliar with many botanical names, the common name of a species of plant appears along with cultivated varieties of that plant, too. There is an index of common names, as well as an index of botanical names and synonyms, at the end of the book.

Sun and shade requirements

How much sun or shade a plant requires is noted by means of a symbol or a set of symbols, which appears immediately beneath the name(s) of the plant. For a description of these symbols, see "Symbols for sun and shade" (above).

Type of plant (including hardiness)

Below the symbols denoting sun or shade requirements is a line of information stating whether a plant is, for instance, a shrub, a bulb, or a climber. This line also includes information about hardiness, in words and in international zone numbers. The zonal information is useful to gardeners in continental climates where there are large variations across the land masses. North America and parts of mainland Europe have continental climates. See the Endpapers at the back of the book for an explanation of these zones, as well as a map showing the extent of the relevant various zones, and temperature ranges for those zones.

Where a plant's habit of growth or hardiness varies according to, for instance, climate or maturity, this variability is indicated by the use of a virgule (for example, "hardy shrub/tree" and "slightly tender/hardy perennial"). Some plants are variably classified by botanists and horticulturists, sometimes being described as perennials, at other times being called shrubs, and so on. A virgule is used in these cases, too. When looking for a particular plant in books and catalogs, it can be very useful to know that it is worth searching under, for instance, chapters or sections on "Perennials" as well as those dealing with "Shrubs."

However it is expressed, hardiness depends, to a very considerable extent, on the site and the soil in a particular location, as well as the climate of a region and the genetic make-up of an individual plant. Tolerance of cold is a complex matter. It can also depend on, for instance, whether a plant has become well "ripened" after a hot summer or left vulnerably soft and sappy following a cool summer; whether periods of low temperatures are long or short; and whether soil conditions are wet or dry during periods of low temperatures (for example, some plants can survive very low temperatures, but only if their roots are dry). Generally speaking, however, in this book, variations in hardiness are defined as follows:

HARDY—This means that, unless there are prolonged periods of very low temperatures (5°F/-15°C), the plant needs no special protection in milder climates.

SLIGHTLY TENDER—This means that, in very cold weather, below 23°F/-5°C, superficial damage (such as browning of the leaves) will occur, but the plant is unlikely to die; in colder areas the plant may require some protection.

HALF-HARDY—This means that, once temperatures drop below freezing (32°F/0°C), damage will probably occur; in very cold weather (below 23°F/-5°C), all growth above ground level will be killed and the whole plant may die.

TENDER—This means that the plant will be damaged and quickly killed by frost.

Flowering time

Most summaries of details contain information about flowering time and flower color. Where no such information is given, then either the flowers are generally considered inconspicuous or the plant does not flower at all.

In some years particularly, the onset and the length of flowering time varies quite considerably. Therefore, throughout this book, the time of year is expressed as a season. This also makes the reference applicable to readers all over the world. In the cool-temperate areas of the northern hemisphere, the seasons may be translated into calendar months as follows:

early spring = March
mid-spring = April
late spring = May
early summer = June
midsummer = July
late summer = August
early autumn = September
mid-autumn = October
late autumn = November
early winter = December
midwinter = January
late winter = February

Flower color

If two or more colors are present in a single flower, then these colors are linked with an addition sign (for example, "white + green" for the two snowdrops featured in this book). If a plant is sold as a mixture of colors, this is noted and the various colors are listed. Certain plants are variable in their flower color and this information is included where relevant. Finally, if a flower color changes or fades with time, this, too, is noted.

Height

An estimate of the mature height of each plant is given in both imperial and metric measurements. Particularly in the case of many perennials, the flowers are held well above the leaves, so, where applicable, the measurements include the height of the plant when in flower. In the case of aquatic plants, the figures refer to the height of the plant above water.

The eventual height of a plant is subject to many variable factors such as temperature, rainfall, aspect, soil fertility, and drainage, and the care with which initial planting was carried out. Other factors such as pruning and the proximity of other, larger plants also have to be taken into consideration.

Even where a single figure is given, it must be taken only as an indication of mature height. However, it is possible to give estimates of the eventual height of plants grown in at least reasonably good conditions, and these are what the figures represent.

Other important characteristics

A few further characteristics are noted, where relevant, in the summaries of details. An asterisk after the sun and shade symbols denotes a plant that requires lime-free soil. Some plants marked in this way do, however, grow quite satisfactorily in a neutral soil (that is, soil that is neither acid nor alkaline); this is mentioned, where appropriate, in the descriptions of the plants.

Information about a small number of other characteristics is placed immediately below "height" in the summaries of details. All evergreen and semi-evergreen plants are marked "Evergreen" and "Semi-evergreen," respectively. (All other plants are deciduous.) Semi-evergreen plants normally retain some or all of their foliage through the year. Plants that are variably semi-evergreen or evergreen, or vary between being semi-evergreen and deciduous, are marked "Semi-evergreen/Evergreen" and "Semi-evergreen/Deciduous," respectively, with the predominant characteristic appearing first.

In a few of the lists, additional symbols or abbreviations are used to indicate, for instance, plants that are suitable for growing in shallow water, or climbers that can be grown against north-facing and east-facing walls. Foliage that is particularly useful for cutting, and flowers or seedheads that are suitable for drying, are also highlighted; and see also the Endpapers.

Descriptions of plants

As well as illustrations and summaries of details, the pictorial sections of lists contain short descriptions of plants. These provide information about, for instance, growing conditions, rates of growth, and related species and varieties. Features such as leaves, fruits, and bark are mentioned. The text also covers habit of growth: a plant may be described as, for instance, forming a wide, dense carpet of growth or as being very narrow and upright in shape. Some plants grow very slowly; others are vigorous; certain plants can, quite quickly, become invasive. Where relevant, information of this sort is included within the descriptions of individual plants.

In details about growing conditions, the word "humus" is used from time to time. Humus is decomposed organic material. Humus-rich soils retain moisture well and have a good, open structure. They may be fertile. Humus can be naturally present in a soil; it can also be added to soil—in the form of, for instance, garden compost and leaf mold.

Nearly all the plant descriptions include at least one measurement. Most often, this gives the length or the width of a plant's leaves or flowers. As well as being useful information in itself, this sort of measurement gives an idea of the scale of individual illustrations.

Occasionally, no such measurements are given: in the case of some conifers, for instance, where the leaves are very small and the overall outline of the plant is more important than leaf size, the descriptions mention simply that the leaves are "tiny."

After each plant description, any additional lists in which that plant appears are mentioned. The list headings are given in abbreviated form, and they are preceded by the words "Also for:." (For the full titles of lists, see the Contents pages.) These abbreviated list headings provide a quick summary of the decorative features, possible uses, and so on of each plant.

Unillustrated sections

In the unillustrated sections of lists, only the main botanical name of each plant is given. This is followed by a page number for an illustration and details of the plant. The plants in each section are arranged in general height categories. Usually, these categories are: minimum height 10ft/3m or more; minimum height between 3ft/90cm and 10ft/3m; and minimum height 3ft/90cm or less. A few plants appear twice in a single unillustrated section. Often, these plants are ivies or other climbers which, when grown vertically, will be "minimum height 10ft/3m or more" but, when grown horizontally and used as ground cover, will be "minimum height 3ft/90cm or less." Very adaptable plants appear in more than one sun or shade category (such plants will be happy in, for instance, ◐◑ sun or partial shade and ◑● partial or full shade).

Shallow soils over chalk

A SHALLOW SOIL OVER CHALK warms up quickly, is easy and pleasant to work, and problems with waterlogging and flooding are rare. It is potentially a very fertile soil. Adding really generous quantities of organic material that is acidic (such as leaf mold, garden compost, and well-rotted manure) improves not only the fertility of thin, chalky soil but also its texture and depth and its ability to retain moisture. Improvement will be gradual. Chalky soil is often described as "hungry," and in such soil organic material breaks down very quickly. It is therefore important to keep on applying organic materials—in the form of deep mulches, for instance.

Gardeners with very alkaline or limy soils have to contend with the unsuitability of their soils for growing all the acid-loving plants, such as rhododendrons and camellias. Those who garden on shallow soils over chalk have some additional problems, caused mainly by very fast drainage and the difficulty of excavating planting holes deep enough for large plants. Chalky soils are often thin and poor. Under very alkaline conditions, some nutrients are effectively "locked up" and so are unavailable to plants.

However, the main problem for many gardeners who live in areas of shallow, chalky soil is not rapid drainage or high alkalinity, but a wish to cultivate acid-loving plants. This longing can most easily be satisfied by growing otherwise prohibited plants in containers filled with lime-free potting compost (see "Trees, shrubs, and woody climbers suitable for growing in containers," pp.144–52, for a number of suggestions).

By far the most satisfactory solution is not to regard shallow, chalky soil as a problem at all, but to enjoy the plants that are adapted to growing well in such conditions. Unimproved soils of this sort are ideal for many rock-garden plants, such as *Dianthus*, stone cress (*Aethionema*) and numerous saxifrages. The majority of herbs thrive in light, alkaline soils: the marjorams, for example, are particularly at home there. Unimproved,

shallow, chalky soils also provide suitable conditions for creating wildflower meadows.

The plants in this list thrive in, rather than just tolerate, the alkalinity and the rather dry conditions of shallow soils over chalk. Many plants do not object to alkaline soils, but they develop problems when moisture is lacking: for example, most asters, including the familiar New York asters (varieties of *Aster novi-belgii*), are prone to mildew if they do not have a reliable source of moisture. Other plants, such as *Osmanthus delavayi*, grow well but may be short-lived on shallow, chalky soils.

The unillustrated section of this list includes a few plants that do not require alkaline soil but which are so adaptable that they prosper in a wide variety of soils, including shallow soils over chalk. Oregon grapeholly (*Mahonia aquifolium*), the purple-leaved filbert (*Corylus maxima* "Purpurea"), and the corkscrew hazel (*Corylus avellana* "Contorta") are all plants of this sort. There are also plants throughout this book that grow satisfactorily in virtually any soil. These plants include old favorites such as winter jasmine (*Jasminum nudiflorum*), the more vigorous varieties of ivy (*Hedera*), and the widely planted, variegated forms of *Euonymus fortunei*. Being evergreen, the euonymus and ivies are particularly useful, since the selection of evergreen plants suitable for thin, alkaline soils is rather limited.

Finally, it is worth remembering that some plants associated with woodlands and acid, humus-rich soils are not, in fact, averse to alkaline conditions. By incorporating large quantities of moisture-retentive material, the range of plants suitable for shallow soils over chalk can be widened very considerably indeed.

Almost all the plants that appear in the list entitled "Plants suitable for dry soils in hot, sunny sites," pp.51–63, also do well in alkaline conditions. They are particularly useful for very dry places in gardens with shallow soil over chalk.

Prunus e.g. "Taihaku"
[great white cherry]
○

type of plant: hardy tree [5–9]
flowering time: mid-spring
flower color: white
height: 30ft/9m

P. "Taihaku" gives a spectacular, although rather brief display of pure white blossom and coppery red, young foliage. The bowl-shaped flowers, each of which are more than 2in/5cm wide, are held in numerous, big, almost globular clusters. This vigorous Japanese cherry is upright when young, but in maturity it is flat-topped and very broad, with long sweeping branches. In autumn, its large, dark green, pointed leaves often turn yellow and orange. Other popular Japanese cherries with white flowers include P. "Shirotae" (syn. P. "Mount Fuji"). The low, spreading branches of this tree carry single and semi-double flowers, which are lightly fragrant. Both these plants can be grown in most soils of at least reasonable fertility and moderate drainage. They thrive, and flower well, in shallow, chalky soils.
also for: ■ Atmospheric pollution ■ Purple, bronze, or red leaves (young leaves only) ■ Colorful, autumn foliage

Cercis siliquastrum
[Judas tree]
○

type of plant: hardy tree/shrub [7–9]
flowering time: late spring
flower color: rose-lilac
height: 25–30ft/7.5–9m

This slow-growing plant typically makes a bushy-headed tree; less commonly, it is multi-stemmed. Although it is hardy, its numerous clusters of ½in/1cm-long pea-flowers may be damaged by late frosts. A sheltered position is therefore advisable and, in any case, warmth is needed to encourage profuse flowering. The flowers usually appear before the heart-shaped, blue-green leaves have fully emerged. Each leaf is up to 4in/10cm long. In some autumns the foliage turns a warm yellow. Particularly during hot summers, seed pods develop. These resemble snow peas or sugar peas, and ripen in late summer to rich reddish purple. Judas tree thrives on free-draining soils over chalk but it also does well on deep, moisture-retentive soils with good drainage.
also for: ■ Colorful, autumn foliage (see above) ■ Ornamental fruit (seed pods)

Prunus e.g. "Amanogawa"
[ornamental cherry]
○

type of plant: hardy tree [5–9]
flowering time: mid- to late spring
flower color: pale pink
height: 15–25ft/4.5–7.5m

The strikingly narrow, upright shape of this tree is its outstanding feature. With age, the branches become rather less erect. Clusters of semi-double, 1½in/4cm-wide, frilled flowers are freely produced. They are lightly and freshly fragrant, and they usually obscure most of the young, bronze-tinged foliage. In autumn, the tapering, deep green leaves generally color well in a mixture of reds, yellows and oranges. Most soils are suitable for this plant, as long as they are reasonably fertile and well drained. P. "Amanogawa" flourishes and often flowers especially well on shallow, chalky soils.
also for: ■ Atmospheric pollution ■ Purple, bronze, or red leaves (young leaves only) ■ Colorful, autumn foliage ■ Fragrant flowers

Fremontodendron "California Glory"
[flannel bush]
○

type of plant: slightly tender shrub [8–10]
flowering time: late spring to early autumn
flower color: yellow
height: 15–20ft/4.5–6m
Evergreen/Semi-evergreen

In colder climates, this vigorous, upright shrub needs a sheltered site against a sunny wall. Young plants may be killed in severe winters. Freely draining soil promotes good growth, and the plant does well in very alkaline conditions. The spectacular flowers are produced over a long period. They are about 2in/5cm wide, shallowly saucer-shaped and richly colored, and they look good among the lustrous, dark green, lobed leaves. The reverse of each leaf and the stems of the plant are densely covered with beige hairs. Even young plants flower well. F. "California Glory" grows quickly but is not long-lived.
also for: ■ Long, continuous flowering period

Buddleja alternifolia
○

type of plant: hardy shrub/tree [6–9]
flowering time: early summer
flower color: lilac
height: 10–12ft/3–3.6m

As long as drainage is good, buddlejas in general do well in a variety of soil types. However, a few – including B. alternifolia – seem to perform especially well on chalky soils. Even when this quick-growing shrub is not covered in strings of tiny, tubular, almond-scented flowers, its arching habit of growth makes it interesting. Trained as a standard, it makes an attractive, little, weeping tree, but for a sheltered garden only, since this buddleja is a shallow-rooted plant. Its narrow, rich green leaves are about 3in/8cm long. On the slightly less hardy variety, B.a. "Argentea," the foliage is pale gray.
also for: ■ Fragrant flowers

Prunus e.g. "Kiku-shidare-zakura"
(syn. *P.* "Cheal's Weeping")
[ornamental cherry]
○

type of plant: hardy tree [5–9]
flowering time: mid- to late spring
flower color: bright pink
height: 10–12ft/3–3.6m

The pendent branches of this slow-growing tree are long and arching. They become covered with a mass of very double flowers, each about 1½in/4cm wide. At about the same time, the slender, pointed leaves unfurl. The foliage is, briefly, bronze-tinged when young; it is mid-green and glossy in maturity. *P. x yedoensis* "Shidare-yoshino" is another weeping cherry; its pink-budded, white flowers open in early spring. Both these plants can be grown successfully in a wide range of soils, as long as drainage is at least reasonably good and fertility is not low. Flowering is usually especially good on shallow soils over chalk. For further examples of small, weeping trees, see pp.54, 65 and 96.
also for: ■ Atmospheric pollution

Xanthoceras sorbifolium
○

type of plant: slightly tender shrub/tree [6–9]
flowering time: late spring
flower color: white + carmine
height: 10–12ft/3–3.6m

This rather upright shrub or small tree produces rich green leaves up to 12in/30cm long. These are composed of numerous, slender, toothed leaflets. The foliage appears at about the same time as the star-shaped flowers which are borne in erect spikes, up to 8in/20cm long. As they age, the flowers develop carmine "eyes." Well-drained, alkaline soils are most suitable for *X. sorbifolium*. It needs shelter from cold winds, and from late frosts which can damage the flowers. Its flowers are most freely produced in regions with hot, dry summers.
also for: ■ Decorative, green foliage

Kolkwitzia amabilis
"Pink Cloud"
[beautybush]
○

type of plant: hardy shrub [5–8]
flowering time: late spring to early summer
flower color: soft pink + yellow
height: 10ft/3m

The main stems of this fast-growing shrub are erect; the upper growths are wide-spreading, arching and twiggy. This arrangement seems to emphasize the plant's abundance of flowers. Each pink-budded, bell-shaped bloom is about ½in/1cm wide. As additional attractions, there are bristly seed pods and, on the older stems and branches of mature specimens, conspicuously peeling, brown bark. Almost any soil is suitable but *K. amabilis* "Pink Cloud" is particularly successful on well-drained, alkaline soil. The rich green, tapered leaves are, briefly, tinged with bronze when young. *K. amabilis* itself has flowers of a less pronounced pink.
also for: ■ Ornamental fruit (seed pods) ■ Ornamental bark or twigs

Syringa meyeri "Palibin"
(syn. *S. palibiniana*)
[lilac]
○

type of plant: hardy shrub [4–8]
flowering time: late spring to early summer
flower color: lavender-pink or pale lilac
height: 4–5ft/1.2–1.5m

This miniature, slow-growing lilac produces numerous twiggy growths and little, light green leaves. These give a neat, rounded effect overall, even though the main branches of the plant are quite upright. From an early age *S. meyeri* "Palibin" becomes covered in dense, 4in/10cm-long flower heads. The little, tubular blooms open from purplish buds and exude a sweet, rather heavy fragrance. All well-drained, fertile soils are suitable for this shrub. Alkaline soil usually produces particularly good growth and a profusion of flowers. For another small lilac with fragrant flowers, see p.299.
also for: ■ Atmospheric pollution ■ Fragrant flowers

Perovskia "Blue Spire"
○

type of plant: hardy perennial/shrub [6–9]
flowering time: late summer to early autumn
flower color: blue
height: 4ft/1.2m

The several good qualities of this graceful, airy plant can be appreciated to the full either beside the sea, where it thrives, or in well-drained soil inland. It grows very successfully on dry and chalky soils. Gray-green, deeply cut leaves do not emerge completely until quite late in spring. They have a scent reminiscent of lavender. The little, tubular flowers are carried in numerous spikes, up to 12in/30cm long, which are held on upright but elegantly curving, gray-white stems, which look attractive even when leafless in winter.
also for: ■ Dry soils in hot, sunny sites ■ Gray, blue-gray, or silver leaves ■ Aromatic foliage ■ Ornamental bark or twigs

Cichorium intybus
[chicory]
○

type of plant: hardy perennial [4–9]
flowering time: midsummer to early autumn
flower color: blue
height: 3–4ft/0.9–1.2m (see description)

The clusters of daisy-like flowers produced by this plant open over a period of many weeks. Each cluster is 1½in/4cm wide. The flowers, which are attractive to bees, close after noon each day. They are usually an especially pretty blue, but white- and pink-flowered forms are also available. *C. intybus* consists of an open arrangement of strong, branching stems rising from a basal rosette of jagged, toothed, mid-green leaves. The plant is particularly at home in light, alkaline soil, but well-drained soils of most sorts are suitable. In poor, dry soil it may reach as little as 12in/30cm high.
also for: ■ Dry soils in hot, sunny sites ■ Long, continuous flowering period

Verbascum (Cotswold Group) e.g. "Gainsborough"
[mullein]
○

type of plant: hardy perennial [5–9]
flowering time: early to late summer
flower color: pale yellow
height: 3–4ft/0.9–1.2m
Semi-evergreen

Many hybrid verbascums are short-lived but they do produce eye-catching spires of saucer-shaped flowers that are attractive over a long period in summer. The branched flower stems of V. "Gainsborough" rise clearly above rosettes of gray-green foliage. The basal leaves are wrinkled and pointed, and each is about 10in/25cm long. The plant has a distinct preference for light, rather poor, alkaline soil. In any case, good drainage is essential, and this perennial is drought-tolerant. For an example of a popular, pink-flowered verbascum, see p.336.
also for: ■ Dry soils in hot, sunny sites ■ Gray, blue-gray, or silver leaves ■ Long, continuous flowering period

Pinus mugo e.g. "Mops"
[mountain pine, mugo pine]
○

type of plant: hardy conifer [3–8]
height: 36in/90cm
Evergreen

Especially when young, this plant grows very slowly. Its upright branches are covered in bright green, linear leaves, 2–3in/5–8cm long, which emerge from conspicuous, brown, winter buds. P. mugo "Mops" grows neatly and forms a symmetrical sphere of greenery. It is a very wind-resistant plant. P.m. "Ophir" resembles P.m. "Mops" in size and shape, but its green foliage turns golden-yellow in winter. P. mugo and its varieties grow well in a wide range of soil types, including shallow soils over chalk. They are at their best when drainage is good. If pruned from an early age, P. mugo and most of its varieties can be used to produce formal shapes, such as domes and cubes.
also for: ■ Windswept, seaside gardens ■ Growing in containers ■ Decorative, green foliage

Centranthus ruber
[Jupiter's beard, keys of heaven, red valerian]
○

type of plant: hardy perennial [5–9]
flowering time: early to late summer
flower color: pink or red or white
height: 30–36in/75–90cm

Apart from rather sweatily-scented foliage, this clump-forming plant has few faults. It is ideal for poor, dry, alkaline soil (where its growth is most compact), and it is often to be found flourishing in the mortar of a warm wall. Red valerian typically produces deep pink blooms. Funnel-shaped flowers, each less than ½in/1cm long, are borne in rounded heads and are attractive to butterflies. The plant self-sows, freely in ideal conditions. There is a red variety, C. ruber var. coccineus, and C.r. "Albus" has white flowers. The oval, pointed leaves of all these plants are slightly fleshy and gray-green.
also for: ■ Dry soils in hot, sunny sites ■ Gray, blue-gray, or silver leaves ■ Long, continuous flowering period

Caryopteris x clandonensis e.g. "Heavenly Blue"
○

type of plant: hardy shrub [6–9]
flowering time: late summer to early autumn
flower color: rich blue
height: 24–36in/60–90cm

All sorts of light, well-drained soils are suitable for varieties of C. x clandonensis. They thrive on chalk and in dry, sunny places. C. x c. "Heavenly Blue" (illustrated here with Lavatera x clementii "Rosea," see p.90) has gray-green foliage and a fairly erect habit of growth; it is usually as wide as it is tall. Its clusters of ½in/1cm-wide, tubular flowers have a whiskery appearance. C. x clandonensis "Kew Blue" is noted for its exceptionally dark flowers. C. x c. "Worcester Gold" (see p.212) has yellow foliage. The slender, toothed leaves of all these plants smell of varnish when bruised.
also for: ■ Dry soils in hot, sunny sites ■ Gray, blue-gray, or silver leaves ■ Aromatic foliage

Scabiosa caucasica e.g. "Clive Greaves"
[pincushion flower, scabious]
○

type of plant: hardy perennial [4–9]
flowering time: early summer to early autumn
flower color: lavender-blue
height: 24–30in/60–75cm

Although an alkaline soil with good drainage is ideal for this plant, well-drained soils of most kinds are suitable and quite dry conditions are tolerated. The lovely, long-stemmed flowers are produced in profusion, especially on young and frequently divided plants. S. caucasica "Clive Greaves" sometimes blooms from the very beginning of summer until quite late in autumn. The flowers, which are attractive to bees and butterflies, have pincushion-like centers and are each 3–4in/8–10cm wide. They last well in water. S.c. "Miss Willmott" has very pale cream flowers. The leaves of both these plants are light grayish green and lance-shaped; they form tight, basal clumps of growth.
also for: ■ Flowers suitable for cutting ■ Long, continuous flowering period

Chrysanthemum carinatum (syn. *C. tricolor*) e.g. "Court Jesters" ○

type of plant: slightly tender annual [8–10]
flowering time: midsummer to early autumn
flower color: mixed: pink, yellow, maroon, white + contrasting zones
height: 18–24in/45–60cm

The strikingly banded "daisies" of this plant remain fresh in water for about a week. They are borne on stiff, upright stalks above bright green, ferny foliage. Each flower is 2–3in/5–8cm wide. Ideally, varieties of *C. carinatum* should be given alkaline soil. Good drainage is essential. *C.c.* "Court Jester" has a fairly bushy habit of growth and is popular for summer bedding as well as for cutting. Some seed catalogs list a few varieties in separate colors, such as *C.c.* "Polar Star" which has white flowers with a yellow central zone.
also for: ■ Flowers suitable for cutting

Salvia x *sylvestris* e.g. "Mainacht" (syn. *S.* x *s.* May Night) ○

type of plant: hardy perennial [5–9]
flowering time: early to midsummer
flower color: dark violet
height: 18–24in/45–60cm

Numerous, richly colored, two-lipped flowers, each ½–1in/1–2.5cm long, are arranged around dark stems on *S.* x *sylvestris* "Mainacht." The plant is dense and sturdy with conspicuously upright flower-stalks. *S.* x *s.* "Rose Queen" bears pink flowers slightly later in summer; it is about 30in/75cm high. Of the same general appearance as *S.* x *s.* "Mainacht" are *S.* x *superba* (about 36in/90cm) and the smaller *S. nemorosa* "Ostfriesland" (syn. East Friesland), both of which produce rich violet-blue flower spikes on erect stems from about midsummer. (*S.* x *superba* has maroon bracts which remain decorative well into autumn.) All freely drained soils are suitable for these salvias and alkaline conditions give excellent results. The leaves are usually mid-green, medium-sized and hairy; they are often roughly oval. The flowers are very attractive to bees.

Erysimum cheiri (syn. *Cheiranthus cheiri*) e.g. "Blood Red" [wallflower] ○

type of plant: hardy biennial [7–10]
flowering time: mid- to late spring
flower color: deep red
height: 18in/45cm
Evergreen

Most seed catalogs list many varieties of biennial wallflowers. Some of these spicily fragrant plants—including *E. cheiri* "Blood Red"—are richly colored. Their four-petalled flowers are usually about 1in/2.5cm across and they are arranged in clusters. Other popular cultivars include *E.c.* "Cloth of Gold" (golden yellow flowers) and various dwarf varieties, such as the *E.c.* Bedder Series (suitable for an exposed, windy site). Siberian wallflower (*E.* x *allionii*), with its bright orange, fragrant flowers, is often listed, too. All these bushy, erect-stemmed plants bear slender, rich green leaves. They have a marked preference for well-drained, chalky or limy soil. In very cold districts they may need some winter protection but really good drainage increases the chances of survival.
also for: ■ Fragrant flowers

Filipendula vulgaris "Multiplex" (syn. *F. hexapetala* "Flore Pleno") [dropwort] ○

type of plant: hardy perennial [4–9]
flowering time: early to midsummer
flower color: white
height: 18in/45cm

From the bud stage onward, the flat, 4in/10cm-wide flower heads of *F. vulgaris* "Multiplex" look attractive. When dried, they form a haze of beige bobbles. The much-divided, ferny foliage is dark green and arranged in rosettes beneath slender, branching flower-stalks. The plant grows well and may increase quite quickly on fairly dry, chalky soil. It must have good drainage. In rich, moist soil it is inclined to flop and will usually need staking.
also for: ■ Decorative, green foliage ■ Flowers suitable for cutting (and drying)

Origanum laevigatum
e.g. "Herrenhausen"
○

type of plant: hardy perennial [5–8]
flowering time: midsummer to early autumn
flower color: lilac-pink + red-purple
height: 12–18in/30–45cm

The slender stems of *O. laevigatum* "Herrenhausen" carry 1in/2.5cm-wide clusters of lilac flowers. Each small, tubular flower is surrounded by conspicuous, red-purple bracts. The little, pointed leaves are very slightly aromatic. In spring, they are suffused with purple; later they mature to dark green and form a neat, dense mass. Stiff flower stems are upright early in the season but, as summer progresses, they tend to splay outward. The plant thrives in well-drained, preferably alkaline soil and a really sunny site. *O.l.* "Hopleys" bears pinkish flowers and purple bracts; it flowers slightly later than *O.l.* "Herrenhausen."
also for: ■ Purple, bronze, or red leaves (young leaves only)

Pulsatilla vulgaris
[pasque flower]
○

type of plant: hardy perennial [5–7]
flowering time: mid- to late spring
flower color: violet-purple
height: 9–12in/23–30cm (see description)

Pasque flower needs excellent drainage. Its tufts of grayish green, finely divided, hairy leaves are at their largest and densest after the 2in/5cm-wide, bell-shaped flowers have faded. At flowering time, the stems of these plants are only 4–6in/10–15cm high. Attractive, silvery, wispy seedheads develop during early summer. Readily available variants of pasque flower include white-flowered *P. vulgaris* "Alba" and red-flowered *P.v.* var. *rubra*.
also for: ■ Decorative, green foliage ■ Ornamental fruit (seedheads)

Origanum "Kent Beauty"
○

type of plant: slightly tender perennial [8–10]
flowering time: mid- to late summer
flower color: green changing to rose-pink
height: 8in/20cm
Semi-evergreen

Even though it is not entirely hardy, particularly if it has to contend with winter wet, this subshrub grows well in a range of soil types. It thrives in alkaline soil with really good drainage. Its light green, rounded leaves are a pretty accompaniment to the numerous, hanging clusters of bracts. Each cluster is up to 2in/5cm long. The pale green bracts soon change to soft rose-pink and are much more conspicuous than the tiny, partially hidden, pink flowers. Slender, trailing stems form a mound of growth some 8in/20cm wide.
also for: ■ Dry soils in hot, sunny sites

Scutellaria scordiifolia
[helmet flower, skullcap]
○

type of plant: hardy perennial [5–8]
flowering time: mid- to late summer
flower color: bright violet-blue
height: 6–8in/15–20cm
Evergreen

S. scordiifolia has a preference for alkaline conditions. In fertile soil, this robust plant can sometimes become invasive; growth is less vigorous and the plant is more floriferous in light, gritty, rather poor soil. Its erect stems and pointed, wrinkled, bright green leaves form a dense, bushy mass, above which the slender, hooded flowers are carried in short spikes. Each flower is usually about 1in/2.5cm long.

Aethionema "Warley Rose"
[rock cress]
○

type of plant: hardy perennial [5–8]
flowering time: late spring to early summer
flower color: lilac-pink
height: 6in/15cm
Evergreen/Semi-evergreen

By the beginning of summer, nearly all the stems of this bushy subshrub are topped with clusters of pretty, ¼in/0.5cm-wide, four-petalled flowers. Light, preferably alkaline soil with good drainage and a position in full sun usually produce excellent results. The thin, little leaves of this stone cress are bluish gray, and this coloring complements the lilac-pink of the flowers. *A.* "Warley Rose" is normally short-lived. It tends to be rather open when newly planted and to become bushier as it establishes.
also for: ■ Dry soils in hot, sunny sites ■ Crevices in paving ■ Gray, blue-gray, or silver leaves

Dianthus gratianopolitanus
(syn. *D. caesius*)
[carnation, pink]
○

type of plant: hardy perennial [5–8]
flowering time: early to midsummer
flower color: rich pink
height: 6in/15cm
Evergreen

This outstandingly simple and beautiful plant is also one of the longest-lived species of *Dianthus*. Its very sweetly scented, 1in/2.5cm-wide, fringed flowers cover a dense carpet of narrow, gray-green leaves which spreads about 12in/30cm wide. Although this carnation is most at home in alkaline soil that is very well-drained, chalk or lime is not essential. Good drainage, however, *is* important and this plant thrives in a dry wall and between paving stones.
also for: ■ Dry soils in hot, sunny sites ■ Ground cover ■ Crevices in paving ■ Gray, blue-gray, or silver leaves ■ Fragrant flowers

Iris reticulata
○

type of plant: hardy bulb [4–8]
flowering time: late winter to early spring
flower color: deep violet-purple + yellow
height: 6in/15cm at flowering time

Some of the small, bulbous irises are very difficult to grow but *I. reticulata* is a most attractive exception. It does, however, need a really sunny position and also sharply drained soil that, for preference, contains some chalk or lime. It is most likely to continue flowering from year to year if the bulbs have been planted deeply and if they can be rather dry in summer. The petals are held in an elegant, open arrangement. The flowers are up to 3in/8cm wide and violet-scented. They are obscured a little by the thin, upright leaves which lengthen in spring. For a related, hybrid iris see p.316.
also for: ■ Fragrant flowers ■ Winter-flowering plants

Iris "Katharine Hodgkin" (Reticulata)
○

type of plant: hardy bulb [5–8]
flowering time: late winter to early spring
flower color: pale gray-blue + yellow
height: 4–6in/10–15cm at flowering time

This charming, delicately colored iris increases happily in ideal conditions. It should be planted deeply in light, well-drained soil, and it needs a sunny position where it can be warm and dry during the dormant season in summer. *I.* "Katherine Hodgkin" has a preference for alkaline conditions. At flowering time the flower-stalks are quite short and the flowers—at about 3in/8cm wide—are relatively large. The thin, rush-like, soft green leaves lengthen considerably after the flowers have faded.
also for: ■ Winter-flowering plants

Lobularia maritima (syn. *Alyssum maritimum*) e.g. "Oriental Night" [sweet alyssum]
○

type of plant: hardy annual [7–10]
flowering time: early to late summer
flower color: rich purple
height: 4in/10cm

Light, chalky soils are suitable for *L. maritima* "Oriental Night," but they should not be too fertile or else growth becomes thin, rather than cushiony and spreading. The grayish leaves are small and narrow and often obscured by the little, four-petalled flowers. These are held in rounded heads 1–1½in/2.5–4cm wide. For a fragrant, white-flowered variety of *L. maritima*, see p.59. Seed catalogs often list mixtures, and pink- and lilac-flowered cultivars are available, too. All these plants respond well to dead-heading. As their species name would suggest, they thrive by the sea.
also for: ■ Dry soils in hot, sunny sites ■ Crevices in paving

---

ADDITIONAL PLANTS, featured elsewhere in this book, that are suitable for shallow soils over chalk

○ **sun**

minimum height 10ft/3m or more
Acer platanoides "Crimson King," see p.198
Corylus maxima "Purpurea," see p.199
Fagus sylvatica Atropurpurea Group, see p.198
Laburnum x *watereri* "Vossii," see p.96
Populus alba, see p.183
Prunus "Kanzan," see p.95
Sophora japonica, see p.94
Syringa x *josiflexa* "Bellicent," see p.40
Syringa vulgaris "Charles Joly," see p.96
Syringa vulgaris "Katherine Havemeyer," see p.297
Syringa vulgaris "Madame Lemoine," see p.269
Thuja plicata "Zebrina," see p.161

minimum height between 3ft/90cm and 10ft/3m
Buddleja davidii "Harlequin," see p.162
Buddleja davidii "Royal Red," see p.96
Buddleja davidii "White Profusion," see p.298
Chimonanthus praecox, see p.316
Colutea arborescens, see p.253
Euonymus japonicus "Ovatus Aureus," see p.162
Olearia x *haastii*, see p.96
Olearia macrodonta, see p.90
Rhamnus alaternus "Argenteovariegata," see p.162
Sambucus nigra f. *porphyrophylla* "Gerda," see p.329
Spartium junceum, see p.52

Syringa pubescens subsp. *microphylla* "Superba," see p.299
Taxus baccata "Standishii," see p.145
Verbascum olympicum, see p.183

minimum height 3ft/90cm or less
Arabis ferdinandi-coburgi "Old Gold," see p.167
Aubrieta "Red Carpet," see p.109
Aurinia saxatilis "Citrina," see p.108
Caragana arborescens "Walker," see p.54
Caryopteris x *clandonensis* "Worcester Gold," see p.212
Cistus x *argenteus* "Silver Pink," see p.56
Cistus x *hybridus*, see p.55
Cistus x *purpureus*, see p.91
Coronilla valentina subsp. *glauca* "Citrina," see p.335
Coronilla valentina subsp. *glauca* "Variegata," see p.164
Dianthus alpinus, see p.156
Dianthus deltoides, see p.154
Dianthus "Doris," see p.283
Dianthus "Haytor White," see p.283
Dianthus "Inchmery," see p.302
Dianthus "Mrs Sinkins," see p.302
Dianthus "Pike"s Pink," see p.60
Erodium chrysanthum, see p.190
Erodium manescaui, see p.338
Erysimum "Bowles' Mauve," see p.337
Erysimum cheiri "Harpur Crewe," see p.302

Erysimum linifolium "Variegatum," see p.166
Gypsophila elegans "Covent Garden," see p.281
Gypsophila repens "Rosea," see p.60
Hebe ochracea "James Stirling," see p.212
Hedysarum coronarium, see p.300
Helichrysum italicum subsp. *serotinum*, see p.247
Helichrysum "Schwefellicht," see p.282
Helictotrichon sempervirens, see p.184
Hermodactylus tuberosus, see p.324
Hyssopus officinalis, see p.246
Iberis sempervirens, see p.107
Iris "Harmony," see p.316
Iris unguicularis, see p.316
Juniperus x *pfitzeriana* "Pfitzeriana Aurea," see p.211
Juniperus squamata "Blue Carpet," see p.107
Juniperus squamata "Blue Star," see p.188
Leontopodium alpinum, see p.154
Lilium candidum, see p.300
Lobularia maritima "Snow Crystals," see p.59
Origanum vulgare "Aureum," see p.213
Origanum vulgare "Country Cream," see p.248
Salvia argentea, see p.55
Scabiosa atropurpurea "Chile Black," see p.330
Teucrium x *lucidrys*, see p.138
Verbascum chaixii "Album," see p.55
Verbascum "Helen Johnson," see p.336
Xerochrysum bracteatum "Summer Solstice," see p.272

Sorbus aria "Lutescens"
[whitebeam]
○[◐]

type of plant: hardy tree [4–9]
flowering time: late spring to early summer
flower color: creamy white
height: 30–40ft/9–12m

When they are young, the veined, oval leaves of this whitebeam are completely covered in a dense, creamy white down; the upper surfaces of mature leaves are gray-green. This is a tough tree that grows well in a variety of soils and situations. It is remarkably tolerant of atmospheric pollution, coastal winds and extreme alkalinity. It has a fairly upright, rounded to pyramidal habit of growth. In late summer to early autumn, the 3in/8cm-wide clusters of little flowers are replaced by bunches of dark red berries. Before falling, the foliage turns an attractive yellow-buff.
also for: ■ Windswept, seaside gardens ■ Atmospheric pollution ■ Gray, blue-gray, or silver leaves (young leaves particularly) ■ Autumn foliage ■ Ornamental fruit

Juniperus communis
e.g. "Hibernica"
[common juniper]
○[◐]

type of plant: hardy conifer [3–8]
height: 15–20ft/4.5–6m
Evergreen

During much of its life this slow-growing conifer forms a neat and narrow column of tiny, pointed, slightly blue-gray leaves. The foliage is arranged in numerous, dense, little sprays. As J. communis "Hibernica" matures, it becomes quite tall and much less compact. It is popular for formal plantings. J.c. "Compressa" (see p.149) is, in effect, a miniature version of this juniper. Most well-drained soils are suitable for these plants, which are at home on thin, chalky soil though they also thrive in light, acid soil. They grow well in a dry, sunny place.
also for: ■ Dry soils in hot, sunny sites

Deutzia x elegantissima
e.g. "Rosealind"
○[◐]

type of plant: hardy shrub [6–9]
flowering time: late spring to early summer
flower color: rose-pink fading to pale pink
height: 4ft/1.2m

This easily grown shrub bears large quantities of clustered, starry flowers among its pointed, mid-green leaves. Each cluster is up to 3in/8cm wide. For a deutzia with flowers of an altogether paler, more lilac-like pink, there is D. x hybrida "Mont Rose." D. gracilis "Nikko" grows only 24–36in/60–90cm high; its flowers are white, and it is of a more spreading shape overall than D. x elegantissima "Rosealind" which has upright main stems and arching branches. All well-drained soils, including those that are very alkaline, are suitable for these plants. They do not, however, perform well in very dry conditions. The flowers can become damaged by spring frosts and, in cold districts, a sheltered position is advisable.
also for: ■ Atmospheric pollution

Fritillaria imperialis
e.g. "Maxima Lutea"
[crown imperial]
○[◐]

type of plant: hardy bulb [5–9]
flowering time: mid-spring
flower color: yellow
height: 36in/90cm

Some of the varieties of F. imperialis, including the example shown here, are more readily available than the species (which has reddish orange flowers on dark stems). As well as F.i. "Maxima Lutea," there are varieties with deep orange-red flowers (e.g. F.i. "Prolifera"), while F.i. "Aureomarginata" has rich orange flowers and cream-edged leaves. All these plants like alkaline soils and they appreciate fertile conditions. Good drainage is essential. Crown imperials are best planted in a site where there is shelter from wind and where the bulbs can be left undisturbed from year to year. Their whorled, bright green foliage and leafy topknots add to the dramatic effect of the pendent flowers (each of which is about 2½in/6cm long). Most people find the smell of the blooms unpleasant at close range.

Philadelphus
e.g. "Manteau d'Hermine"
[mock orange]
○[◐]

type of plant: hardy shrub [5–8]
flowering time: early to midsummer
flower color: white
height: 30–36in/75–90cm

Many of the popular mock oranges make shrubs that are too big for a small garden, but the densely twiggy, rounded variety shown here is quite suitable for a restricted space. It is normally only slightly wider than it is tall. Its numerous, double, bowl-shaped flowers, each about 1½in/4cm wide, have a very sweet, slightly fruity fragrance. They look good against the conspicuous light green of the plant's pointed, oval leaves. Almost any soil with reasonable drainage is suitable for this easily grown shrub. Light, alkaline soils give good results. For an example of a taller mock orange, see p.99.
also for: ■ Atmospheric pollution ■ Fragrant flowers

Dictamnus albus
[burning bush, dittany, gas plant]
○[◑]

type of plant: hardy perennial [3–8]
flowering time: early summer
flower color: white
height: 24–36in/60–90cm

Burning bush is a long-lived plant of great beauty. It bears graceful, 1in/2.5cm-wide flowers, which have distinctively long and wispy stamens. In warm weather, as the seed capsules begin to ripen, the vaporized oil surrounding the whole plant can be ignited. Both the leaves and the flowers are freshly and strongly aromatic. The upright stems and deep green, divided leaves create a clump of bushy growth. *D. albus* is at its best in light, fairly fertile, alkaline soil but most soils with good drainage are suitable. This plant grows well in a dry, sunny place.

also for: ■ Dry soils in hot, sunny sites ■ Aromatic foliage ■ Fragrant flowers

Knautia macedonica
(syn. *Scabiosa rumelica*)
○[◑]

type of plant: hardy perennial [5–9]
flowering time: mainly mid- to late summer
flower color: deep crimson
height: 24in/60cm

K. macedonica's long-lasting "pincushion" flowers are held on slender, branched, somewhat curving stems. Each flower is about 1¼in/3cm across. Flowers may start to appear in early summer and continue into early autumn. Bees are attracted to the blooms. In light, well-drained soil the whole plant remains neat, but in richer, moister conditions it is larger and lax and the slim stems may need staking. The stems and grayish green, variably shaped leaves form a fairly loose clump of growth. The plant thrives in alkaline soil and it tolerates short periods of drought.

Centaurea montana
[mountain bluet]
○[◑]

type of plant: hardy perennial [3–8]
flowering time: late spring to midsummer
flower color: violet-blue
height: 18in/45cm

This familiar, cottage-garden perennial sprawls rather untidily, but its cornflower-like blooms are prettily colored and quite large (often more than 2in/5cm wide). They are attractive to bees and butterflies. Slender leaves form loose, open masses of growth. This vigorous plant flourishes in well-drained soils of all sorts, including those that are moist and those that are thin, chalky and rather dry. The white-flowered form, *C. montana* "Alba," is readily available, and there are also varieties with pink, blue or violet blooms.

Saxifraga "Southside Seedling"
[saxifrage]
○[◑]

type of plant: hardy perennial [4–8]
flowering time: late spring to early summer
flower color: white + crimson
height: 12in/30cm
Evergreen

The numerous, little, open-faced flowers of this vigorous and long-lived saxifrage are carried in sprays up to 12in/30cm long. These sprays arch over light green leaf rosettes, which form mats of rather fleshy growth. Leaf edges are encrusted with beads of silvery lime. The whole plant looks especially attractive in crevices in a drystone wall. Really well-drained, preferably alkaline soil is required, and the roots must be kept cool and moist. In warm districts the plant needs to be protected from the drying effects of strong sun. *S.* "Southside Seedling" is a Ligulate or Silver saxifrage. *S.* "Whitehill" is another popular saxifrage of this type; it bears white flowers.

ADDITIONAL PLANTS, featured elsewhere in this book, that are suitable for shallow soils over chalk

○[◑] sun (or partial shade)

minimum height 10ft/3m or more
Acer pseudoplatanus "Brilliantissimum,"
    see p.203
Crataegus x lavallei "Carrierei," see p.256
Crataegus monogyna, see p.142
Crataegus phaenopyrum, see p.98
Thuja plicata, see p.139
Viburnum opulus "Xanthocarpum," see p.68

minimum height between 3ft/90cm and 10ft/3m
Euonymus alatus, see p.238
Euonymus europaeus "Red Cascade,"
    see p.257
Jasminum humile "Revolutum,"
    see p.304
Osmanthus delavayi, see p.304
Philadelphus "Silberregen," see p.305
Viburnum opulus "Compactum,"
    see p.257

minimum height 3ft/90cm or less
Dictamnus albus var. purpureus, see p.249
Euonymus alatus "Compactus," see p.239
Geranium dalmaticum, see p.111
Geranium pratense "Mrs Kendall Clark," see p.224
Geranium renardii, see p.225
Geranium sanguineum, see p.111
Juniperus communis "Compressa," see p.149
Malcolmia maritima Mixed, see p.157
Saxifraga paniculata, see p.195

Fagus sylvatica
e.g. "Pendula"
[European beech]
○◑

type of plant: hardy tree [4–9]
height: 50–70ft/15–21m

European beech (*F. sylvatica*) and its numerous varieties, including weeping beech with its very broad, rounded head of drooping branches, are trees for well-drained soil. They flourish in alkaline conditions. Typically, their leaves are wide, wavy-edged, pointed ovals, each 3–4in/8–10cm long. The foliage is bright green in spring, rich green in summer and orange-russet in autumn. Small plants and trees that have been clipped retain their russet foliage through winter. Weeping beeches with purple leaves include *F.s.* "Purpurea Pendula" (10–15ft/3–4.5m high) and slender *F.s.* "Purple Fountain" (60ft/18m high). These plants need sun for good leaf color. In contrast, *F.s.* "Dawyck" (syn. "Fastigiata") makes a narrow, green spire some 80ft/24m high.
also for: ■ Atmospheric pollution ■ Colorful, autumn foliage

Acer campestre
[hedge maple]
○◑

type of plant: hardy tree [5–9]
height: 30ft/9m; sometimes 50ft/15m+

This tough and adaptable tree thrives on light, alkaline soil but can be grown successfully on a wide range of other soils, including clay. Its fairly upright, twiggy branches and attractive, three-lobed, 2½in/6cm-long leaves create a rounded crown of growth. It may sucker. Summer foliage color is light to mid-green; autumn leaves are yellow and usually long-lasting. Field maple can be pruned hard and can be used for hedging (plants should be 18in/45cm apart).
also for: ■ Heavy, clay soils ■ Atmospheric pollution ■ Hedging plants ■ Colorful, autumn foliage

Taxus baccata
e.g. "Fastigiata"
[English yew]
○◑●

type of plant: hardy conifer [6–8]
height: 30ft/9m
Evergreen

Pairs of this erect, columnar tree are often used as sombre sentinels in formal gardens. English yew is a slow-growing and remarkably long-lived plant which, with age, can become very wide-girthed. Its linear leaves, each about 1in/2.5cm long, are dark green; on *T. baccata* "Fastigiata Aureomarginata" (which makes a dense column of growth up to 15ft/4.5m high) the young leaves have bright yellow margins. (For *T. baccata* itself, see p.140; for yellow-leaved *T.b.* "Standishii," see p.145.) *T. baccata* and its varieties grow in all well-drained soils, including those that are very alkaline. They tolerate considerable dryness and also deep shade (although yellow-leaved varieties need sun for good leaf color). Most Irish yews are female. Pollinated female plants bear small, red, berry-like fruits. The seeds of these fruits, like most other parts of English yew, are toxic.
also for: ■ Acid soils ■ Dry soils in hot, sunny sites ■ Dry shade ■ Dense shade ■ Ornamental fruit

Forsythia x *intermedia*
e.g. "Lynwood Variety"
○◑

type of plant: hardy shrub [6–9]
flowering time: early to mid-spring
flower color: yellow
height: 8–10ft/2.4–3m

Few soils or sites deter the growth of forsythias and they do well even in shallow, chalky conditions. *F.* x *intermedia* "Lynwood Variety" has large, four-petalled flowers, 1½in/4cm wide, which, even in a partially shaded position, are freely produced along the erect branches. (When used for informal hedging, the plants should be about 24in/60cm apart.) The flowers appear before the leaves. When out of flower, the mid- to dark green, oval or pointed leaves, and the often slightly unruly shape of these shrubs, make most forsythias rather dull. Hence the increasing popularity of varieties such as *F.* "Fiesta," which has leaves irregularly marked in yellow and lime-green.
also for: ■ Heavy, clay soils ■ Atmospheric pollution ■ Hedging plants ■ Flowers suitable for cutting

Buxus sinica var. insularis
(syn. B. microphylla var. koreana)
[boxwood]
○◑

type of plant: hardy shrub [5–9]
height: 24–36in/60–90cm
Evergreen

This is a rather loose, spreading shrub with small, thick, rounded leaves, ½in/1cm or so long, which turn olive-green in winter. In cold weather, the foliage may become entirely rust-coloued. *B. sinica* var. *insularis* is long-lived, slow-growing and tolerant of greater cold than common or English box (*B. sempervirens;* see p.140) but, like it, it grows in most soils, including those that are limy or chalky. Particularly in dry conditions, the foliage benefits from some shade. The yellowish spring flowers are not very noticeable except for their sweet fragrance. Cultivated varieties of *B. sinica* var. *insularis* are hardier than the species itself and they tend to stay green in winter—in milder climates at least. *B.s.* var. *i.* "Winter Gem" forms a fairly open mass of shiny foliage that is rich soft green, and reaches about 5ft/1.5m tall after ten years.
also for: ■ Fragrant flowers

Campanula glomerata
e.g. "Superba"
[clustered bellflower]
○◑

type of plant: hardy perennial [3–8]
flowering time: early to late summer
flower color: rich purple-violet
height: 24–30in/60–75cm

The "superb" feature of *C. glomerata* "Superba" is the strikingly deep color of its dense, rounded, 2in/5cm-wide heads of bell-shaped flowers. These are borne on dark, upright, leafy stems (the leaves are rich green and pointed). This vigorous, clump-forming plant grows strongly and self-sows in all fertile, well-drained soils that retain moisture easily, but it is also at home on shallow, chalky soils. It can be invasive. *C.g.* var. *alba* has white flowers. Some lower-growing varieties are available too.
also for: ■ Long, continuous flowering period

Lathyrus vernus
[spring vetchling]
○◑

type of plant: hardy perennial [5–9]
flowering time: mid- to late spring
flower color: purple + blue fading to blue
height: 15in/38cm

This bushy little plant is easily grown in all well-drained soils, including quite dry soils, but it revels in alkaline conditions. Its slender, pointed leaflets and erect stems create a dense clump of bright greenery over which the numerous, ½in/1cm-wide pea-flowers open. The less vigorous *L. vernus* "Alboroseus" bears bicolored, pink-and-white flowers.

Saxifraga "Gregor Mendel"
(syn. S. x apiculata)
[saxifrage]
○◑

type of plant: hardy perennial [4–6]
flowering time: early to mid-spring
flower color: primrose-yellow
height: 4–6in/10–15cm
Evergreen

Although Porphyrion saxifrages, of which *S.* "Gregor Mendel" is an example, need gritty, alkaline soil and can be grown in a sunny site, they must not be allowed to become hot and dry. In warmer districts, therefore, it is advisable to plant them in partial shade. The vigorous hybrid shown here is easier to grow than some Porphyrion saxifrages. Its tiny, linear leaves form a dense cushion of pale greenery below the erect-stemmed sprays of cup-shaped, ¼in/0.5cm-wide flowers. Other popular saxifrages of this type include pink-flowered, gray-leaved *S.* "Jenkinsiae" and white-flowered *S.* "Alba."
also for: ■ Crevices in paving

Anemone blanda
e.g. "White Splendor"
[Grecian windflower]
○◑

type of plant: hardy tuber [6–9]
flowering time: early to mid-spring
flower color: white
height: 4in/10cm

The neat, daisy-like flowers of this plant are up to 2½in/6cm wide. They contrast most attractively with the deep soft green of the ferny foliage. *A. blanda* and its varieties thrive on free-draining, chalky soil, and in other soils and sites where drainage is good (including, for example, the loose, humus-rich soils of light woodland). They do well beneath deciduous shrubs and trees. *A.b.* "White Splendor," in time, increases into sizeable patches of growth. There are some pink varieties of *A. blanda*, and sky-blue cultivars include *A.b.* "Ingramii." *A. blanda* itself usually has deep blue flowers.

Asplenium trichomanes
[maidenhair spleenwort]
○◐

type of plant: hardy fern [3–8]
height: 3–6in/8–15cm
Evergreen/Semi-evergreen

This little fern's tendency to establish
itself in the mortar of an old wall shows
its liking for alkaline conditions. It seems
particularly at home in cool crevices
and the bright, olive-tinged green of
its young fronds can be an appealing
embellishment to a shady wall and steps.
However, this is a very adaptable plant
that tolerates dry, shaded conditions and
also grows well in sun. In sun, the tufts
of dark stems and numerous, rounded
leaflets are smaller and denser than in
a moist, shady place.
also for: ■ Dry shade ■ Crevices in paving
■ Decorative, green foliage

Crocus tommasinianus
○◐

type of plant: hardy corm [5–8]
flowering time: late winter to early spring
flower color: pale lavender or pale lilac
height: 3–4in/8–10cm

Its free-flowering nature, its hardiness and its cheapness all contribute
to this crocus's popularity. It self-sows, and it increases rapidly in rather
gritty, alkaline soils. In heavier soils it multiplies much less quickly.
C. tommasinianus is suitable for naturalizing in grass—as are most of its
varieties, including violet-purple *C.t.* "Whitewell Purple" and deep red-
purple *C.t.* "Ruby Giant." The slender-budded, 2in/5cm-long flowers of all
these plants are accompanied by slim, grassy leaves which are dark green
with pale, central stripes.
also for: ■ Winter-flowering plants

ADDITIONAL PLANTS, featured elsewhere in this book, that are suitable for shallow soils over chalk

○◐ sun or partial shade

minimum height 10ft/3m or more
Acer platanoides "Drummondii," see p.170
Buxus sempervirens, see p.140
Carpinus betulus, see p.143
Carpinus betulus "Fastigiata," see p.44
Cornus mas, see p.318
Fagus sylvatica, see p.143
Ligustrum lucidum, see p.100
Prunus lusitanica, see p.140
Taxus baccata, see p.140
Viburnum rhytidophyllum, see p.226

minimum height between 3ft/90cm and 10ft/3m
Acer negundo "Flamingo," see p.171
Buxus sempervirens "Aureovariegata," see p.172
Corylus avellana "Contorta," see p.267
Forsythia ovata, see p.319
Prunus lusitanica "Variegata," see p.171
Sambucus nigra f. laciniata, see p.226
Sambucus racemosa "Plumosa Aurea,"
   see p.215
Taxus cuspidata, see p.63
Viburnum x bodnantense "Dawn," see p.319

minimum height 3ft/90cm or less
Buxus sempervirens "Suffruticosa," see p.141
Corydalis lutea, see p.347
Hesperis matronalis, see p.309
Juniperus sabina "Tamariscifolia," see p.113

◐|○| partial shade (or sun)

minimum height between 3ft/90cm and 10ft/3m
Sarcococca confusa, see p.321

minimum height 3ft/90cm or less
Helleborus foetidus, see p.82
Iris foetidissima, see p.261
Iris foetidissima "Variegata," see p.180
Mahonia aquifolium, see p.122
Sarcococca hookeriana var. humilis, see p.314

◐ partial shade

minimum height 3ft/90cm or less
Anemone nemorosa, see p.50
Asplenium scolopendrium, see p.232
Asplenium scolopendrium Undulatum Group,
   see p.232

◐● partial or full shade

minimum height 10ft/3m or more
Buxus sempervirens, see p.140
Taxus baccata, see p.140
Taxus baccata "Fastigiata," see p.21

minimum height between 3ft/90cm and 10ft/3m
Buxus sempervirens "Aureovariegata,"
   see p.172
Sarcococca confusa, see p.321
Taxus cuspidata, see p.63

minimum height 3ft/90cm or less
Buxus sempervirens "Suffruticosa,"
   see p.141
Helleborus foetidus, see p.82
Iris foetidissima, see p.261
Iris foetidissima "Variegata," see p.180
Mahonia aquifolium, see p.122
Polystichum aculeatum, see p.233
Polystichum setiferum Divisilobum Group,
   see p.233
Sarcococca hookeriana var. humilis,
   see p.314

Acid soils

THE PLANTS IN THE following list require or have a decided preference for acid soil. Almost all plants will grow in moderately acid soil, and moist, humus-rich, woodland soil of moderate acidity is many gardeners' idea of perfection.

However, extreme acidity does present problems. This is because very acid soils are infertile: even the more sheltered parts of peaty moorlands support a very limited range of plants. Plants in this list that are suitable for infertile, acid soils include a variety of bog rosemary (*Andromeda polifolia* "Compacta") and one of the summer-flowering heaths, *Erica cinerea* "C.D. Eason." Among the other plants suitable for these conditions are varieties of *Calluna vulgaris* (for page numbers, see the index of botanical names) and the double-flowered form of gorse, *Ulex europaeus* "Flore Pleno." Brooms such as the varieties of *Cytisus* x *praecox* shown on pp.53 and 97 can be grown in many soils, including poor, acid soils.

Extremely acid soils can have their fertility boosted by the addition of materials such as well-rotted farmyard manure and garden compost. In certain cases, the application of lime in some form may be necessary. (Simple kits for testing soil acidity are readily available from stockists of horticultural supplies.)

Many of the plants on the following pages are woodland in origin. They therefore appreciate soil that is cool, moist, and well drained. Quite a few acid-loving plants come from the wetter regions of the world (since rain can wash away basic elements in soil, conditions of extreme acidity are often found in areas of high rainfall). The fact that many acid-loving plants are woodlanders is reflected in the high proportion of entries in the various shade categories in this list.

As well as cool, moist, woodland soil, there are dry, sandy soils and heavy, clay soils that are acid. Plants such as the gorse and the brooms mentioned above prosper in acid soils that are light, dry and free draining, while *Magnolia* x *soulangeana* and its varieties, the bald or

swamp cypress (*Taxodium distichum*) and the pin oak (*Quercus palustris*) all prefer to grow in acid soils that are moister and heavier.

However, not everyone wishes to have a little bit of heathery moorland in their back garden, and the many rather strident hybrid rhododendrons convince some gardeners that recreating a part of the Himalayas is an equally unattractive proposition. Even if these plants do seem desirable, planting some acid-loving plants that are not rhododendrons, camellias, or heathers adds variety to a woodland or heather garden.

Choosing these alternative acid-lovers also extends the season of interest of such gardens. The peak flowering period for acid-loving plants is spring to early summer, and gardens on acid soil can seem decidedly subdued for the rest of the year. Yet there are beautiful, late-flowering plants for these gardens: tiger lilies (*Lilium lancifolium* and its varieties) and *Eucryphia*, for example, and fragrant shrubs or trees, such as the sweet pepperbush (*Clethra alnifolia*) and the winter-flowering witch hazels (*Hamamelis*).

Autumn foliage is an additional source of late-season interest and there are many acid-lovers with leaves that color well. Indeed, on acid soils that are rather infertile, autumn color tends to be especially brilliant.

Finally, this list of plants suitable for acid soils is a source of suggestions for gardeners in areas of alkaline soil who want to grow lime-hating plants. In peat walls and beds and in containers filled with a lime-free potting compost, these gardeners can grow tempting, otherwise-forbidden plants such as camellias and rhododendrons, blue poppies (*Meconopsis*), and autumn gentians (*Gentiana sino-ornata*, for example). They may even be able to accommodate, in their main beds and borders, plants such as the winter-flowering heathers (*Erica carnea*, for example), which tolerate a certain degree of alkalinity, provided a good depth of moisture-retentive soil is available as well.

Larix kaempferi
(syn. L. leptolepis)
[Japanese larch]
○

type of plant: hardy conifer [5–8]
height: 80–100ft/24–30m

Although its size restricts its use to a large area, this fast-growing, deciduous conifer is valuable for a number reasons: it is tolerant of poor soils (as long as they are not alkaline or wet); it makes a good windbreak inland; its young shoots create an attractive, red-brown haze in winter sunshine; and, in autumn, its tufts of needle-like leaves turn soft russet (having emerged, in spring, bright fresh green). Each little tuft of leaves is about 1¼in/3cm wide. The cones, which resemble miniature roses, are small and brown and attractive at close quarters. There are varieties of this conically shaped tree that have pendulous branches and others that produce blue-green foliage.
also for: ■ Colorful, autumn foliage ■ Ornamental bark or twigs

Picea glauca var. albertiana
"Conica"
[white spruce]
○

type of plant: hardy conifer [2–7]
height: 6–10ft/1.8–3m
Evergreen

Even when grown in the sheltered sites and the acid or neutral, moisture-retentive soils that are most suitable for them, specimens of this plant reach their ultimate height only after many years. However, their strikingly neat, triangular outline, their very dense growth and the bright green of their young foliage are all evident from an early age. The soft, needle-like leaves mature to mid-green during summer; they are arranged in sprays about 1¼in/3cm long. Other popular, slow-growing spruces include the extremely slow, bun-shaped P. mariana "Nana," and P. abies "Nidiformis," which is more or less nest-shaped and eventually wide-spreading.
also for: ■ Growing in containers

Callistemon citrinus "Splendens"
[bottlebrush]
○

type of plant: half-hardy shrub [10–11]
flowering time: mid- to late summer
flower color: brilliant red
height: 6ft/1.8m
Evergreen

The arching and spreading branches of this shrub are clothed with slender, leathery leaves that give off a lemon-like scent when crushed. Dense "bottlebrush" flowers appear at the ends of the branches and are 3–4in/8–10cm long. They are followed by cylinder-shaped clusters of persistent but not very decorative seeds. Other red-flowered bottlebrushes include C. rigidus. All bottlebrushes need moisture-retentive, neutral to acid soil that has good drainage. A sheltered site is advisable for C. citrinus "Splendens," even in a mild area.
also for: ■ Aromatic foliage

Leptospermum scoparium
e.g. "Red Damask"
[manuka, New Zealand tea tree]
○

type of plant: slightly tender shrub [8–10]
flowering time: late spring to early summer
flower color: deep soft crimson
height: 5–7ft/1.5–2.1m
Evergreen

Except in very mild districts, this upright, open and rather twiggy shrub must be given the shelter of a warm wall. There, its richly colored, ½in/1cm-wide, double flowers – which look like little, frilly buttons – are freely borne among the contrastingly dark foliage. The tiny, slender leaves emit a slightly medicinal smell when crushed. Although L. scoparium "Red Damask" likes well-drained soil that is, preferably, neutral to acid, it does not thrive in dry conditions. L.s. (Nanum Group) "Kiwi" is a dwarf variety with deep crimson-pink flowers.
also for: ■ Growing in containers ■ Aromatic foliage

Lilium lancifolium var. splendens
(syn. L. tigrinum)
[tiger lily]
○

type of plant: hardy bulb [4–9]
flowering time: late summer to early autumn
flower color: salmon-orange
height: 4–5ft/1.2–1.5m

This variety of tiger lily grows more strongly than the species. Although it is prone to viral diseases, it seems to tolerate them well. Each dark, upright stem is clothed with slender, pointed leaves and carries about twenty-five "turk's cap" flowers. Individual blooms are about 5in/12cm wide. Full sun and good drainage are the essential ingredients for success with tiger lilies, and moist, acid conditions are preferable. L. lancifolium "Flore Pleno" bears double flowers. Other easily grown lilies with "turk's cap" flowers include L. martagon (purplish pink flowers), L.m. var. album (white) and L. henryi (orange). These last three plants do well in alkaline conditions. See also L. speciosum var. rubrum on p.33.

Baptisia australis
[false indigo, wild indigo]
○

type of plant: hardy perennial [3–9]
flowering time: early summer
flower color: violet-blue
height: 4ft/1.2m

The loose spikes of pea-flowers produced by B. australis are borne on grayish, upright stems. The individual blooms are 1–1¼in/2.5–3cm long. With the sun shining through the petals, the flower color is almost royal-blue. Leaves are divided into three leaflets and, when young, the bushy mass of foliage has a blue tinge. This long-lived plant resents disturbance. It likes neutral to acid soil that is deep, fertile and well drained. Its clusters of dark gray, inflated seed pods are suitable for use in dried arrangements.
also for: ■ Decorative, green foliage ■ Ornamental fruit (seed pods)

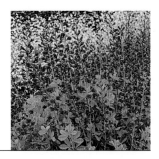

Iris ensata (syn. I. kaempferi)
e.g. "Moonlight Waves"
[Japanese iris]
○ ✳

type of plant: hardy perennial [5–9]
flowering time: midsummer
flower color: white + green-yellow
height: 36in/90cm

The rather flat flowers of *I. ensata* "Moonlight Waves" appear above slender, upright, mid-green leaves. Each bloom is 5–6in/12–15cm wide. The plant thrives in fertile, humus-rich, acid soil with plenty of moisture. It flourishes in damp and wet positions. The margins of ponds and streams are suitable sites, but only if the roots of the plant are not submerged in winter, since this leads to rot. There are numerous varieties of *I. ensata* including, for example, *I.e.* "Rose Queen," which has pale rose-pink flowers, and *I.e.* "Variegata," which has big, violet flowers and white-striped foliage.
also for: ■ Damp and wet soils

Erica vagans
e.g. "Mrs D.F. Maxwell"
[Cornish heath]
○

type of plant: hardy shrub [7–9]
flowering time: late summer to mid-autumn
flower color: rose-cerise
height: 15–18in/38–45cm
Evergreen

When the dense, upright flower spikes of this heath have faded, russet seedheads develop and these are decorative throughout the winter months. The cone-shaped flowers, each about 2⅓in/6cm long, are good for cutting. *E. vagans* "Mrs D.F. Maxwell" is a notably neat and dense variety, with tiny, dark green, needle-like leaves, but the Cornish heaths in general form tidy, spreading hummocks of growth. They make efficient ground-cover. As long as there is plenty of humus, they tolerate slightly limy soil, and they grow better in heavyish soils than most ericas. *E.v.* "Lyonesse" bears attractive, white flowers; *E.v.* "Valerie Proudley" is small and has yellow leaves.
also for: ■ Ground-cover ■ Ornamental fruit (seedheads) ■ Flowers suitable for cutting ■ Long, continuous flowering period

Erica cinerea
e.g. "C.D. Eason"
[bell heather]
○ ✳

type of plant: hardy shrub [5–9]
flowering time: midsummer to early autumn
flower color: magenta-pink
height: 9–12in/23–30cm
Evergreen

Of the commoner types of heath or heather, varieties of *E. cinerea* are the ones most likely to succeed in the drier sorts of acid soil, such as those containing a high proportion of sand. The plants should not, however, be allowed to dry out completely. Little, bell-shaped blooms are carried in short spikes, each usually about 2in/5cm long. Many varieties are richly colored: *E.c.* "Velvet Night," for example, has very dark purple flowers. Also popular is low-growing *E.c.* "Pink Ice," with its bright rose-pink flowers. Not all varieties of bell heather form dense hummocks of weed-suppressing growth but *E.c.* "C.D. Eason" does and it makes good ground-cover, spreading 18in/45cm or so wide. All the above varieties have tiny, thin, dark green leaves and they flower over many weeks.
also for: ■ Ground-cover ■ Long, continuous flowering period

Erica tetralix
e.g. "Alba Mollis"
[cross-leaved heath]
○ ✳

type of plant: hardy shrub [4–8]
flowering time: early summer to early autumn
flower color: white
height: 9in/23cm
Evergreen

All the readily available varieties of *E. tetralix* have grayish foliage but some, like *E.t.* "Alba Mollis," are downy and particularly silvery. The leaves are arranged around erect shoots in a series of crosses. At the ends of the shoots are small clusters of flowers that open over a period of many weeks. Each flower is just over ¼in/0.5cm wide. Lime-free soil is essential and cross-leaved heaths have a preference for damp conditions. *E.t.* "Con Underwood" is another popular variety; it has magenta flowers and gray-green leaves. For a gray-leaved heather, see p.188.
also for: ■ Damp and wet soils ■ Gray, blue-gray, or silver leaves ■ Long, continuous flowering period

---

ADDITIONAL PLANTS, featured elsewhere in this book, that are suitable for acid soils

○ sun

minimum height 10ft/3m or more
Acacia dealbata, see p.297
Acer rubrum, see p.235
Picea pungens "Koster,"
   see p.183
Pinus radiata, see p.89
Pinus sylvestris, see p.263
Quercus palustris, see p.235
Quercus rubra, see p.235

minimum height between 3ft/90cm and 10ft/3m
Astelia chathamica, see p.184
Erica arborea "Albert's Gold," see p.211
Physocarpus opulifolius "Diabolo," see p.199
Taxus baccata "Standishii," see p.145

minimum height 3ft/90cm or less
Calluna vulgaris "Gold Haze," see p.212
Calluna vulgaris "H.E. Beale," see p.106
Calluna vulgaris "Robert Chapman," see p.237
Calluna vulgaris "Silver Knight," see p.188

Erica x darleyensis "Darley Dale," see p.106
Erica x darleyensis "Silberschmelze,"
   see p.316
Erica erigena "Brightness," see p.138
Eriophorum angustifolium, see p.67
Eucalyptus gunnii, see p.184
Lilium formosanum var. pricei, see p.302
Lilium "Star Gazer," see p.272
Lithodora diffusa "Heavenly Blue," see p.109
Stokesia laevis, see p.282
Ulex europaeus "Flore Pleno," see p.54

Nothofagus antarctica
[Antarctic beech]
○【◐】

type of plant: hardy/slightly tender
tree/shrub [7–9]
height: 30–40ft/9–12m

The little, crinkled leaves of this plant are, at first, light green; as they mature, they become dark and glossy; in autumn, they turn yellow. Each leaf is about 1¼in/3cm long and delicately toothed and veined. Moist but well-drained soil is most suitable for this plant. It dislikes alkaline conditions. Except in a sheltered site, Antarctic beech tends to grow slowly. It usually produces an open, distinctly twiggy, sometimes lopsided crown of growth and develops into either a large shrub or a small tree.

also for: ■ Colorful, autumn foliage

Rhododendron
e.g. "Sappho"
○【◐】✻

type of plant: hardy shrub [5–8]
flowering time: early summer
flower color: white + dark purple
height: 10–12ft/3–3.6m
Evergreen

This old but very useful rhododendron hybrid remains popular, partly because of its toughness and partly because of the distinctive coloring of its flowers. Each funnel-shaped bloom is about 3in/8cm long. The slender leaves are medium-sized, dark and leathery. Unless grown in sun, this rounded plant tends to be rather open and leggy. Moisture-retentive, well-drained, humus-rich soil and a sheltered position are the ideal growing conditions. However, R. "Sappho" and the two large rhododendron hybrids shown on pp.29 and 101 are easily pleased, as long as they have soil that is lime-free. R. "Cunningham's White" is another very hardy hybrid with white flowers; it grows about 6ft/1.8m tall.

also for: ■ Atmospheric pollution

Exochorda x macrantha
"The Bride"
○【◐】

type of plant: hardy shrub [5–7]
flowering time: late spring
flower color: white
height: 5–6ft/1.5–1.8m

The lax, arching branches on this shrub form a spreading mound of growth that becomes covered in flowers. Each flower resembles a little, single rose and is about 1¼in/3cm wide. The leaves are medium-sized, rounded and, at flowering time, rather pale, grayish green. Although this plant prefers acid soil, most soils are suitable, as long as they have reasonable drainage and do not dry out easily. To encourage the production of large numbers of flowers, a sheltered, sunny site should be chosen. As it ages, E. x macrantha "The Bride" tends to become rather untidy.

Rhododendron
e.g. Blue Diamond Group
○【◐】✻

type of plant: hardy shrub [6–9]
flowering time: mid- to late spring
flower color: lavender-blue
height: 3–5ft/ 0.9–1.5m
Evergreen

Rhododendrons in the Blue Diamond Group are dense, rounded, slow-growing plants with fairly upright branches. Like many small-leaved rhododendrons they do well in sun, provided they have moist, well-drained, lime-free soil and a site that protects their flowers from possible frost damage. The broadly funnel-shaped flowers are each about 2in/5cm long and of a remarkably clear blue for a rhododendron. They are arranged in small trusses, with up to five flowers in each truss. The small, oval leaves emit a slight, astringent scent when bruised.

Iris forrestii
○【◐】

type of plant: hardy perennial [6–9]
flowering time: early summer
flower color: yellow + purple-brown
height: 15–18in/38–45cm

The flowers of this iris appear for only a rather brief period but they are elegant and their gentle coloring is attractive. They are about 2½in/6cm wide and only slightly scented. The leaves are long and narrow and are shiny mid-green on their upper surface. They form a clump of growth. I. forrestii is best in neutral to slightly acid soil that is moist or damp, and a period of dryness in late summer is beneficial.

also for: ■ Damp and wet soils

ADDITIONAL PLANTS, featured elsewhere in this book, that are suitable for acid soils

○【◐】 sun (or partial shade)

minimum height 10ft/3m or more
Crataegus monogyna, see p.142
Nyssa sylvatica, see p.238

minimum height between 3ft/90cm and 10ft/3m
Fothergilla major, see p.238
Physocarpus opulifolius "Dart's Gold,"
 see p.214
Rhododendron luteum, see p.238

minimum height 3ft/90cm or less
Erica carnea "King George," see p.317
Erica carnea "Springwood White," see p.111
Erica carnea "Vivellii," see p.344
Iris x robusta "Gerald Darby," see p.69

Sciadopitys verticillata
[Japanese umbrella pine]
◯◗✳

type of plant: hardy conifer [5–8]
height: 50–70ft/15–21m
Evergreen

This conifer's tufts of glossy, 5in/12cm-long, needle-like leaves are arranged radially, like the ribs of an umbrella—hence the plant's common name. When young, Japanese umbrella pine grows very slowly (after ten years it may well be only 20in/50cm tall). As it matures, it grows more rapidly and it eventually makes a large but slender pyramid of dark greenery. It may occasionally be shrub-like with several main stems. Fairly rich, moist, acid soil is most suitable.
also for: ■ Decorative, green foliage

Sorbus aucuparia
[mountain ash, rowan]
◯◗

type of plant: hardy tree [3–9]
flowering time: late spring
flower color: creamy white
height: 30–50ft/9–15m

Mountain ash is most at home on various kinds of acid soils; it tends to be short-lived on shallow, chalky soils. Its clustered, saucer-shaped flowers are arranged in heads about 5in/12cm wide. They are followed, from late summer, by bunches of orange-red berries which are enjoyed by birds. The numerous, toothed, dark green leaflets, up to 2in/5cm long, turn red and yellow in mid-autumn. especially in cold regions. The central branches of this tree are strikingly upright. In maturity, the overall outline is rounded or broadly conical. *S. aucuparia* "Sheerwater Seedling" is a slender, upright tree.
also for: ■ Damp and wet soils ■ Atmospheric pollution ■ Colorful, autumn foliage ■ Ornamental fruit

Cornus kousa var. chinensis
[Kousa dogwood]
◯◗

type of plant: hardy tree/shrub [5–9]
flowering time: late spring to early summer
flower color: cream fading to pink
height: 20–25ft/6–7.5m

Spreading branches and dense, rich green foliage create a rounded head of growth on *C. kousa* var. *chinensis*. Along the branches appear numerous, upward-facing flowers, each flower surrounded by four conspicuous, 2in/5cm-long bracts. Pimply, red, strawberry-like fruits ripen in early autumn. A little later, the broad, slightly curved leaves turn a striking purplish crimson. *C. kousa* itself has rather smaller "flowers" and a more layered habit of growth, while *C.k.* "Satomi" produces deep pink bracts. All these plants perform best in rich, moisture-retentive soil that is acid to neutral. They need shelter from spring frosts.
also for: ■ Colorful, autumn foliage ■ Ornamental fruit

Magnolia x soulangeana
◯◗

type of plant: hardy shrub/tree [5–9]
flowering time: mainly mid- to late spring
flower color: usually palest pink + rose-purple
height: 20–25ft/6–7.5m

It may take about five years for this popular magnolia to produce its 5in/12cm-wide, goblet-shaped flowers in large quantities. Each year, the first flowers appear before the large, broad-ended leaves emerge. There may be a second flush of flowers in late summer. *M. x soulangeana* makes a spreading shrub or tree, with fairly upright branches; it is often as wide as it is high. Ideally, it should be given fertile, moisture-retentive, humus-rich soil that is acid to neutral, but it tolerates some alkalinity. Cold winds may damage its developing flowers. *M.* "Elizabeth" has yellow flowers. See also p.100.
also for: ■ Heavy, clay soils ■ Atmospheric pollution ■ Flowers suitable for cutting

Eucryphia x nymansensis
"Nymansay"
◯◗

type of plant: slightly tender tree [8–9]
flowering time: late summer to early autumn
flower color: white
height: 15–30ft/4.5–9m
Evergreen

This narrow and erect tree becomes clothed in cup-shaped flowers, each about 3in/8cm wide, although it may be at least five years before it produces a really eye-catching display. (Smaller, shrubby *E. milliganii* can flower profusely after a shorter time.) The flowers, which resemble single roses, shine out from among glossy, dark green, serrated leaves. *E. x nymansensis* "Nymansay" tolerates some lime but is at its best in light, moist soil that is acid or neutral. It needs protection from cold winds and hot sun. In mild, maritime districts this plant may eventually reach 50ft/15m.

Amelanchier canadensis
[Juneberry, shadbush, snowy mespilus]
◯◗

type of plant: hardy shrub/tree [5–9]
flowering time: mid- to late spring
flower color: white
height: 15–20ft/4.5–6m

Loose, 2in/5cm-long clusters of small, starry flowers appear in very large numbers on this plant. At first, the leaves, which emerge with the flowers, have a bronzed coppery tinge; later they are mid-green; in autumn, they turn red, orange and yellow. *A. canadensis* forms an erect, suckering shrub or a dome-headed tree. Although it prefers acid conditions, it is easily grown in any well-drained soil that remains moist or damp. Its edible, purple-black fruits are not very decorative, but they are enjoyed by birds as well as humans. *A. lamarckii* is taller and has brighter autumn foliage than *A. canadensis*.
also for: ■ Damp and wet soils ■ Atmospheric pollution ■ Purple, bronze, or red leaves (young leaves only) ■ Colorful, autumn foliage

Halesia carolina
(syn. *H. tetraptera*)
[silver bell, snowdrop tree]
○◐✱

type of plant: hardy shrub/tree [5–8]
flowering time: mid- to late spring
flower color: white
height: 12–18ft/3.6–5.4m

The wide-spreading branches of this plant come into leaf quite late in spring and this helps to show the lovely, pendent, bell-shaped flowers to advantage. The flowers are small (less than 1in/2.5cm long) but very numerous, although plants need to be several years old before they bloom freely. Strange, oval, green fruits with "wings" follow the flowers and, in autumn, the mid-green, tapering leaves often turn yellow. *H. carolina* grows best in moist, humus-rich soil and in a site which is sheltered from cold winds. It needs lime-free conditions.
also for: ■ Colorful, autumn foliage ■ Ornamental fruit

Chamaecyparis obtusa
e.g. "Nana Gracilis"
[Hinoki cypress]
○◐

type of plant: hardy conifer [5–9]
height: 12–15ft/3.6–4.5m
Evergreen

After ten years this conifer will probably be only 36in/90cm tall. However, its fans of deep green foliage can be enjoyed even when the plant is quite small. When crushed, the tiny, scale-like, blunt-ended leaves emit a sweet, resinous scent. In maturity, *C. obtusa* "Nana Gracilis" forms a generous pyramid of growth. *C.o.* "Nana" is an even slower-growing plant; it makes a flat-topped mound of growth less than 24in/60cm high after many years. *C.o.* "Nana Aurea" and *C.o.* "Nana Lutea" have golden yellow foliage (both these varieties are smaller than *C.o.* "Nana Gracilis"). All these plants prefer acid to neutral soil; they thrive in well-drained, moisture-retentive conditions.
also for: ■ Decorative, green foliage ■ Aromatic foliage

Rhododendron
e.g. "Cynthia"
○◐✱

type of plant: hardy shrub [5–8]
flowering time: late spring
flower color: rich crimson-pink
height: 12–15ft/3.6–4.5m
Evergreen

Some older hybrid rhododendrons such as *R.* "Cynthia" remain popular because of their hardiness and their general toughness. *R.* "Cynthia" is widely dome-shaped, rather open and has fairly upright branches. Its large flower heads are made up of funnel-shaped blooms, each about 3in/8cm long. Especially in a sheltered site, this rhododendron flowers freely. Its dark green, leathery leaves are oval. As long as the soil is lime-free, this plant tolerates a wide range of conditions but growth is best in moisture-retentive, well-drained, humus-rich soils. *R.* "Cynthia" becomes leggy in full shade. *R.* "Britannia" has large, scarlet flowers; it is about 6ft/1.8m high. See also pp.27 and 101.
also for: ■ Atmospheric pollution

Camellia x williamsii
e.g. "Donation"
○◐✱

type of plant: hardy shrub [7–10]
flowering time: early to late spring
flower color: pink
height: 10–12ft/3–3.6m
Evergreen

This outstanding camellia produces its flowers in profusion every year, even in colder regions. Each semi-double bloom is 4–5in/10–12cm across. In some years, the plant begins to flower in late winter. As with other *williamsii* varieties, the faded flowers do not remain on the branches but drop to the ground. Pointed, oval leaves create a dense mass of lustrous, dark greenery on upright branches. Vigorous, robust *C. x williamsii* "Donation" needs lime-free soil and ideally cool, deep, humus-rich soil and shelter from early morning sun. *C. x w.* "Anticipation" has deep rose-pink flowers; *C. x w.* "Debbie" is mid-pink. For a single-flowered variety, see the following illustration.
also for: ■ Decorative, green foliage ■ Long, continuous flowering period

Camellia x williamsii
e.g. "J.C. Williams"
○◐✱

type of plant: hardy shrub [7–10]
flowering time: mainly early to mid-spring
flower color: pale pink
height: 8–10ft/2.4–3m
Evergreen

The single blooms on this camellia are freely borne against broad, gleaming, deep green leaves. Each flower is 3–4in/8–10cm wide. In ideal conditions, the first flowers may appear in late winter and flowering can continue into late spring. The *williamsii* camellias have the advantage over their *japonica* counterparts of shedding their flowers when the petals have faded. *C. x williamsii* "J.C. Williams" is vigorous and has an open, spreading habit of growth. It thrives in deep, rich, acid soil that retains moisture easily. Though it does well in cool regions, it needs a lighter position in those areas to flower well. Another popular *williamsii* variety is shown above.
also for: ■ Decorative, green foliage ■ Long, continuous flowering period

Magnolia liliiflora "Nigra"
(syn. *M.* x *soulangeana* "Nigra")
○◐✱

type of plant: hardy shrub [6–9]
flowering time: late spring to early summer and intermittently into autumn
flower color: purple-red, pale purplish pink within
height: 8–10ft/2.4–3m

M. liliiflora "Nigra" is a small and bushy plant compared to many popular magnolias and its elegant, 5in/12cm-long, goblet-shaped flowers are of an unusually rich yet soft color; they are only slightly fragrant. Its deep green leaves are tapered and glossy. The plant grows slowly and its branches are fairly upright; it is eventually wider than it is tall. Well-drained, moisture-retentive soil is most suitable for this magnolia, which should be given a position that is sheltered from cold winds. It must have lime-free conditions. *M.l.* "Nigra" is the parent of a number of hybrids, including *M.* "Susan," which produces fragrant, deep purplish pink flowers in mid- and late spring.

Tropaeolum speciosum
[flame nasturtium, Scottish flame flower]
○◑

type of plant: hardy perennial climber [7–9]
flowering time: mainly mid- to late summer
flower color: bright red
height: 8–10ft/2.4–3m

Flame flower grows vigorously in areas with cool summers and high rainfall. Provided its roots can be shaded, it is suitable for walls of any aspect, but it does not do well in a hot, dry place. It needs cool, moisture-retentive soil that is, ideally, neutral to acid. Its slender stems are decorated with lobed, mid-green leaves and vividly colored, trumpet-shaped flowers, 1½in/4cm long. Flowering may begin in early summer and, in cool regions particularly, it can continue into autumn. From late summer, bright blue berries develop. This climber looks especially attractive growing through other plants.
also for: ■ Climbing plants ■ Decorative, green foliage ■ Ornamental fruit ■ Long, continuous flowering period (see above)

Kalmia latifolia
[calico bush, mountain laurel]
○◑✽

type of plant: hardy shrub [5–9]
flowering time: late spring to early summer
flower color: pale to deep pink
height: 6–10ft/1.8–3m
Evergreen

Although sometimes shy-flowering, this slow-growing, rounded shrub produces spectacular flower clusters among glossy, dark greenery. Each cluster can be up to 6in/15cm wide. The leaves are large, leathery and pointed. General growth benefits from some shade, but for plenty of flowers to appear, mountain laurel needs good light. As long as there is sufficient moisture, the plant can be grown in sun. In any case, the soil should be lime-free, cool and moist with plenty of organic matter. Varieties of this plant include K. latifolia "Ostbo Red," which has conspicuous red buds and pale pink flowers.

Rhododendron
e.g. "Berryrose"
[azalea]
○◑✽

type of plant: hardy shrub [5–9]
flowering time: late spring
flower color: salmon pink + yellow
height: 5–7ft/1.5–2.1m

Knaphill-Exbury azaleas, of which R. "Berryrose" is an example, are upright plants noted for their large flower trusses, 4–6in/10–15cm wide. The slightly scented, funnel-shaped flowers of R. "Berryrose" accompany bronze, young foliage. Many Knaphill-Exbury azaleas produce good autumn leaf color: on R. "Berryrose," the light green, pointed, oval leaves turn yellowish before falling, but for a variety with richer autumn color, see p.102. All these plants need well-drained, moisture-retentive, lime-free soil. R. "Persil" has white blooms; there are yellow- and orange-flowered varieties, too.
also for: ■ Atmospheric pollution ■ Purple, bronze, or red leaves (young leaves only)

Pieris japonica
e.g. "Valley Rose"
○◑✽

type of plant: hardy shrub [6–9]
flowering time: early to mid-spring
flower color: pink fading to white
height: 5–6ft/1.5–1.8m
Evergreen

Some pieris—including P. japonica "Valley Rose"—are grown principally for their graceful clusters of tiny (¼in/0.5cm-long), bell-shaped flowers, rather than their young foliage. The flower buds and stalks of "Valley Rose" are showy from mid-autumn onward (the illustration shows the plant in midwinter). Pointed, deep green leaves are pale green on first emerging. Free-flowering varieties of P. japonica with white blooms include P.j. "Grayswood" and P.j. "Purity." A few varieties, such as P.j. "Valley Valentine," produce crimson flowers. All these plants need shelter from cold winds and cool, moist but well-drained, lime-free soil. Their blooms last well in indoor arrangements.
also for: ■ Flowers suitable for cutting

Hydrangea macrophylla
(Hortensia) e.g. "Générale Vicomtesse de Vibraye"
○◑

type of plant: hardy/slightly tender shrub [6–9]
flowering time: midsummer to early autumn
flower color: light blue or rose (see description)
height: 4–6ft/1.2–1.8m

As with so many hydrangeas, the flower color of this variety is affected by soil: in acid soil, the globular flower heads, 6–8in/15–20cm wide, are light blue; in alkaline soil, they are pale pink. They fade to sea-green and are then suitable for drying (they are less good as fresh cut flowers). This rounded shrub needs good drainage, fertile, moist, humus-rich soil and, in colder areas, a fairly sheltered site. In mild, maritime areas it thrives in an open position. Its broadly oval, pointed leaves are light to mid-green. See also p.150.
also for: ■ Windswept, seaside gardens ■ Atmospheric pollution ■ Growing in containers ■ Ornamental fruit (seedheads) ■ Flowers suitable for cutting (mainly drying) ■ Long, continuous flowering period

Rhododendron
e.g. "Dopey"
○◑✽

type of plant: hardy shrub [6–9]
flowering time: late spring to early summer
flower color: rich red
height: 4–6ft/1.2–1.8m
Evergreen

There are numerous popular hybrids of R. yakushimanum (for this species, see p.227). They include red-flowered varieties, such as R. "Dopey" (illustrated here) and R. "Titian Beauty," pinks such as R. "Percy Wiseman" and R. "Surrey Heath," yellows like R. "Golden Torch" and creams such as R. "Grumpy." All these slow-growing plants require acid soil that is open-textured, moisture-retentive and rich in humus. In a very sunny site, the flower color of some varieties fades quickly but R. "Dopey" tends to retain its rich color well. It is a fairly upright plant with dark green, pointed, oval leaves. Its bell-shaped flowers are 2–3in/5–8cm long.
also for: ■ Growing in containers

Rhododendron
e.g. Elizabeth Group
○◐✻

type of plant: slightly tender/hardy shrub [7–9]
flowering time: mid- to late spring
flower color: bright scarlet-red
height: 3–5ft/0.9–1.5m
Evergreen

Although *R.* Elizabeth Group plants vary a little, they all produce numerous, trumpet-shaped flowers from an early age. Individual blooms are usually at least 3in/8cm wide. Each plant slowly forms a spreading and fairly flat-topped dome of growth with leaves that are small, pointed and of a soft, dark green. As long as their roots are cool and moist and in lime-free soil, these plants can be grown in a sunny site, though they do need shelter from frost and wind. In a cold garden, *R.* "Scarlet Wonder" [zones 5–9] is an alternative to *R.* Elizabeth Group plants; it has bright red, bell-shaped flowers.

Lupinus e.g. "My Castle"
[lupine]
○◐

type of plant: hardy perennial [3–9]
flowering time: early to midsummer
flower color: brick-red
height: 36in/90cm

The flower spikes of hybrid lupines such as *L.* "My Castle" are long—on average, about 18in/45cm—and strikingly upright. They rise above clumps of soft, mid-green leaves that are divided into slender "fingers" of foliage. Some varieties, including *L.* "The Governor (shown in the following illustration) have conspicuously bicolored blooms. *L.* "The Chatelaine" bears pink-and-white flowers. Other popular hybrids include *L.* "Chandelier" (yellow) and *L.* "Noble Maiden" (creamy white). Due to disease problems, Russell hybrids are now best raised from seed. Seed catalogs usually list 24in/60cm-high *L.* "Lulu," too. Both the Russell hybrids and *L.* "Lulu" are normally offered as mixtures of colors. All the plants mentioned here are rather short-lived, but growing them in light, acid to neutral soil and dead-heading them regularly extends their life-span. For the tree lupine (*L. arboreus*), see p.91.

Lupinus e.g. "The Governor"
[lupine]
○◐

type of plant: hardy perennial [3–9]
flowering time: early to midsummer
flower color: blue + white
height: 36in/90cm

See preceding plant.

Bulbinella hookeri
○◐

type of plant: slightly tender/half-hardy perennial [8–10]
flowering time: late spring to early summer
flower color: yellow
height: 18–24in/45–60cm

The upright stems of this perennial are topped with "poker heads" of densely packed, starry flowers. Each flower head is approximately 3in/8cm long. The stems rise from tufts of grass-like leaves that form thick clumps of olive-tinged greenery. The leaves often have red tips. In order to grow well, *B. hookeri* needs neutral to acid soil that is moisture-retentive and humus-rich. The slightly fleshy foliage may be retained in winter.

Luzula nivea
[snowy woodrush]
○◐

type of plant: hardy perennial [4–9]
flowering time: late spring to midsummer
flower color: pale ivory
height: 8in/45cm
Evergreen

When several of these grass-like plants are grown together, their fluffy flower heads create a strikingly pale and delicate haze. Each of these 2in/5cm-long flower heads is carried well clear of the plant's loose tufts of slim, hairy, bright green leaves. The flowers dry well. Humus-rich soils that are acid to neutral and moist give the best results. Snowy woodrush spreads slowly.
also for: ■ Flowers suitable for cutting (mainly drying)

Iris Californian Hybrids
(syn. *I.* Pacific Coast Hybrids)
○◑

type of plant: hardy perennial [7–10]
flowering time: late spring to early summer
flower color: mixed: blue, yellow, cream, mauve, purple, bronze, white
height: 10–20in/25–50cm
Evergreen/Semi-evergreen

In fertile, sandy soil that does not dry out, the narrow, arching leaves of these plants form sizeable clumps. The elegantly shaped and delicately marked flowers, each 2–3in/5–8cm wide, are available in a remarkable range of colors. Specialist nurseries also stock numerous varieties of separate colors. As well as good drainage and soil that is moisture-retentive and neutral to acid, these plants need warmth and shelter in order to thrive. They often do well in the dappled shade cast by trees. *I.* Californian Hybrids are often referred to collectively as Pacific Coast irises.
also for: ■ Ground cover

Narcissus cyclamineus
[daffodil]
○◑

type of plant: hardy bulb [6–9]
flowering time: early spring
flower color: yellow
height: 4–8in/10–20cm

As long as it has moisture during the growing season, this lovely little daffodil is quite easy to grow. *N. cyclamineus* is most at home in open-textured, humus-rich soil that is acid to neutral. Its fully swept-back flowers are about 2in/5cm long. They are held on slender stems above bright green leaves. Hoop-petticoat daffodil (*N. bulbocodium*) has funnel-shaped flowers and enjoys similar but slightly less damp conditions. Both species are suitable for naturalizing. For an example of a hybrid daffodil derived from *N. cyclamineus*, see p.293.
also for: ■ Damp and wet soils

ADDITIONAL PLANTS, featured elsewhere in this book, that are suitable for acid soils

○◑ sun or partial shade

minimum height 10ft/3m or more
Cercidiphyllum japonicum, see p.240
Eucryphia glutinosa, see p.241
Magnolia x *soulangeana* "Lennei," see p.100
Parrotia persica, see p.241
Rhododendron "Fastuosum Flore Pleno," see p.101
Stachyurus praecox, see p.318
Stewartia pseudocamellia Koreana Group, see p.266
Taxodium distichum, see p.71

Taxus baccata, see p.140
Taxus baccata "Fastigiata," see p.21

minimum height between 3ft/90cm and 10ft/3m
Clethra alnifolia, see p.308
Hamamelis x *intermedia* "Pallida," see p.318
Magnolia stellata, see p.101
Osmunda regalis, see p.72
Rhododendron "Daviesii," see p.309
Rhododendron "Gibraltar," see p.102
Rhododendron "Praecox," see p.319
Taxus cuspidata, see p.63
Zenobia pulverulenta, see p.309

minimum height 3ft/90cm or less
Begonia Cocktail Series, see p.207
Deschampsia cespitosa "Bronzeschleier," see p.289
Deschampsia flexuosa "Tatra Gold," see p.216
Liriope muscari, see p.83
Liriope muscari "Variegata," see p.176
Persicaria vacciniifolia, see p.117
Rhododendron impeditum, see p.151
Rhododendron "Wee Bee," see p.151
Rhododendron williamsianum, see p.112
Rhododendron yakushimanum, see p.227

Styrax japonicus
[Japanese snowbell]
◑[○]✻

type of plant: hardy tree [6–9]
flowering time: early summer
flower color: white
height: 20–25ft/6–7.5m

Because Japanese snowbell's numerous, bell-shaped flowers hang from the undersides of its slender branches, they are most conspicuous when viewed from below. Each ½in/1cm-long flower ripens into a dangling, oval, green fruit that lasts into winter. In autumn, pointed leaves turn from glossy, rich green to yellow and sometimes red. Japanese snowbell slowly forms a very graceful tree. Its symmetrical arrangement of spreading, almost tiered branches creates an open pyramid of airy growth. The plant thrives in a sheltered, woodland site and in moist, lime-free soil with good drainage. There are varieties of *Styrax japonica,* such as *S.j.* Benibana Group "Pink Chimes," with pink flowers.
also for: ■ Colorful, autumn foliage ■ Ornamental fruit

Camellia japonica
e.g. "Adolphe Audusson"
◑[○]✻

type of plant: hardy shrub [7–10]
flowering time: early to mid-spring
flower color: blood-red
height: 8–10ft/2.4–3m
Evergreen

The large, semi-double flowers of this vigorous camellia are produced in profusion on a narrow pyramid of bushy growth. Each flower is up to 5in/12cm wide. Tapering, oval leaves provide a glossy, dark green background for these blooms. All *japonica* camellias thrive in well-drained, moisture-retentive, humus-rich, acid soil. Although the plants are hardy, their flowers—even the relatively weatherproof reds—need a site sheltered from wind, frost and early morning sun. In cool regions, *japonica* varieties may need quite a sunny position to flower well; *williamsii* varieties (for examples, see p.29) are often a better choice in these areas. There are hundreds of *japonica* varieties to choose from: *C.j.* "Jupiter" has single, red flowers.
also for: ■ Atmospheric pollution ■ Growing in containers ■ Decorative, green foliage

Rhododendron augustinii
◑[◎] ✳ (see description)

type of plant: hardy shrub [6–9]
flowering time: mid- to late spring
flower color: variable—light to dark violet-tinged blue
height: 6–10ft/1.8–3m
Evergreen

The upright branches of this bushy rhododendron become smothered in clustered, funnel-shaped flowers, each about 1½in/4cm wide. Even young plants bloom freely. Flower color is variable but some specimens are almost true blue. The leaves are mid-green to dark green, small and pointed. Although R. augustinii grows in neutral to slightly alkaline soil, better growth is produced in acid conditions. In any case, it is important that the roots of the plant remain cool and moist. A sheltered site is also advisable since the flowers that open first in spring can be damaged by frost.

Hydrangea macrophylla (Lacecap) e.g. "Mariesii Perfecta" (syn. H.m. "Blue Wave")
◑[◎]

type of plant: hardy/slightly tender shrub [6–9]
flowering time: late summer to mid-autumn
flower color: rich blue + pale blue or mauve *or* pink (see description)
height: 4–6ft/1.2–1.8m

Less formal than the familiar mophead or Hortensia hydrangeas, Lacecap varieties such as H. macrophylla "Mariesii Perfecta" produce flat flower heads made up of tiny, fertile flowers surrounded by larger, showier, sterile flowers. For H.m. "Mariesii Perfecta" to be really blue flowered, the soil must be acid; on neutral to alkaline soil the blooms are lilac to pink. Each stout-stemmed flower head is about 6in/15cm wide. The plant is dense and often wider than it is high, and it is a notably hardy variety; some Lacecaps are reliably hardy only to zone 7. H.m. "Mariesii Grandiflora" (syn. "White Wave") bears white flowers. Both varieties have mid- to light green, pointed leaves. They thrive in rich, moist soil with good drainage. H.m. "Quadricolor" and H.m. "Tricolor" are Lacecap hydrangeas with variegated foliage.
also for: ■ Atmospheric pollution ■ Long, continuous flowering period

Rhododendron e.g. "Palestrina" [azalea]
◑[◎]✳

type of plant: hardy shrub [6–10]
flowering time: late spring
flower color: white
height: 3½–4ft/1.05–1.2m
Evergreen/Semi-evergreen

The neat, little, oval leaves on this rather upright plant are almost obscured by flowers in late spring. Most evergreen azaleas have intensely colored blooms (see, for instance, below and p.152), but the cool, shapely flowers of R. "Palestrina" are an attractive alternative, especially since they are enhanced by the fresh green of the plant's foliage. Each of the funnel-shaped flowers, about 2½in/6cm long, has a light green center. Like most evergreen azaleas, R. "Palestrina" grows slowly. Provided there is adequate moisture in lime-free, well-drained soil, this azalea can be given a position in sun. Shelter from cold winds is important whether the site is sunny or shaded.
also for: ■ Growing in containers

Lilium speciosum var. rubrum [lily]
◑[◎]✳

type of plant: hardy bulb [5–9]
flowering time: late summer to early autumn
flower color: deep pink + white
height: 3–4ft/0.9–1.2m

L. speciosum var. rubrum needs a warm, sheltered position if it is to flower well. It also requires moist, free-draining, acid soil. When well suited, it produces a dozen or more, 4in/10cm-wide "turk's cap" flowers on each of its dark stems. L. speciosum itself has red-spotted, white or pink flowers. L.s. var. album is pure white. All three plants are richly and very sweetly fragrant. They make excellent cut flowers. Unfortunately, these lilies are prone to viral diseases and, when infected, they produce few flowers. Their leaves are slender, pointed and rather leathery.
also for: ■ Flowers suitable for cutting ■ Fragrant flowers

Rhododendron e.g. "Blue Danube" [azalea]
◑[◎]✳

type of plant: hardy shrub [6–10]
flowering time: late spring to early summer
flower color: violet
height: 3–4ft/0.9–1.2m
Evergreen

R. "Blue Danube" produces a mass of funnel-shaped flowers, which—at up to 2in/5cm across—are large for an evergreen azalea. It grows slowly and makes a rather flat-topped plant with slender, dark green, glossy leaves. It needs lime-free soil that is both well drained and moisture-retentive, and it is advisable to provide shelter from cold winds. In regions with cool summers, most evergreen azaleas, including this example, can be given a sunny position. R. "Hatsugiri" is another popular evergreen azalea with similarly vivid purplish flowers. For a cooler colored evergreen azalea, see above.
also for: ■ Growing in containers

Skimmia japonica "Rubella"
◐[○]

type of plant: hardy shrub [7–9]
flowering time: early to mid-spring
flower color: white *or* pinkish
height: 3–4ft/0.9–1.2m
Evergreen

This is a male skimmia and it therefore produces no berries, yet its dark red flower buds are almost as conspicuous as fruit. They decorate this dense, hummocky plant during autumn and winter and then open out into 3in/8cm-long heads of sweetly fragrant, starry flowers. The gleaming, leathery leaves are sleek, pointed ovals of rich green. *S. japonica* "Rubella" grows slowly. It needs neutral to acid soil and flourishes in cool, moist, shady positions.
also for: ■ Atmospheric pollution ■ Ground cover ■ Growing in containers ■ Fragrant flowers

Gillenia trifoliata
[bowman's root, Indian physic]
◐[○]

type of plant: hardy perennial [4–9]
flowering time: early to midsummer
flower color: white from pink buds
height: 36in/90cm

The airy flower sprays of *G. trifoliata* make very attractive material for cutting. Each little, wispy bloom, 1in/2.5cm or so wide, is pink in bud and has red outer parts that are persistent and decorative. The stems are dark, upright and wiry, and clothed with deep green, narrow leaflets. Ideally, this plant should be given a cool, shady site and well-drained but moisture-retentive soil. Although it has a preference for neutral to slightly acid soils, it is easy to grow and, provided it has moisture, it can be given a sunny site. In sunny positions the foliage turns orange, red and russet in autumn.
also for: ■ Colorful, autumn foliage (see above) ■ Flowers suitable for cutting

Rhododendron
e.g. Cilpinense Group
◐[○] ✱

type of plant: hardy/slightly tender shrub [7–9]
flowering time: early spring
flower color: pale pink
height: 36in/90cm
Evergreen

These lovely, bell-shaped flowers are produced so early in spring that they are particularly susceptible to frost damage. A sheltered site is, therefore, essential in all but the mildest areas. *R.* Cilpinense Group plants have a fairly open habit of growth and deep green, hairy leaves, which are small and slender. Their flowers are 1½in–2in/4–5cm long. For examples of pale pink rhododendrons that bloom later in spring, see pp.112 and 227. Well-drained soil that is moisture-retentive—and lime-free, of course—is suitable for all these plants.
also for: ■ Growing in containers

Primula pulverulenta
◐[○]

type of plant: hardy perennial [6–8]
flowering time: late spring to early summer
flower color: deep red-purple
height: 30–36in/75–90cm

Extreme acidity is not suitable for most primulas but they thrive on substantial, moisture-retentive soils that are either neutral or slightly acid. Opulently colored, pale-stemmed *P. pulverulenta* needs fertile soil and grows especially well in damp ground near water. (In consistently damp conditions, this primula can generally be planted in sun.) Its large, crinkled, light green leaves form rosettes at the base of its sturdy flower-stalks. The rather flat-faced, tubular flowers of this so-called Candelabra primula are about 1in/2.5cm across. They are arranged in a series of whorls on each stem. *P.p.* "Bartley Pink" has soft pink flowers. Both plants are free-flowering. For other Candelabra primulas, see right and pp.78 and 79.
also for: ■ Damp and wet soils

Rhododendron
e.g. "Carmen"
◐[○] ✱

type of plant: hardy shrub [6–9]
flowering time: mid- to late spring
flower color: dark red
height: 24–36in/60–90cm
Evergreen

The luxurious coloring of this plant's numerous, waxy flowers is enhanced by the rich green of its shiny foliage. Each bell-shaped bloom is about 2in/5cm long. The oval leaves are of about the same length. *R.* "Carmen" slowly forms a hummock of growth that is usually wider than it is tall and that is particularly dense in sun. In sun, however, it may be difficult to ensure that the roots of the plant stay cool and moist and, in many gardens, a position with some shade is more practical. The ideal soil is humus-rich and both well drained and moisture-retentive. Conditions must be lime-free.

Primula beesiana
◗[◯]

type of plant: hardy perennial [5–8]
flowering time: late spring to early summer
flower color: magenta-pink + yellow
height: 24in/60cm
Deciduous/Semi-evergreen

All the so-called Candelabra primulas, of which P. beesiana is an example, have flower-stalks that are encircled by whorls of primrose-like blooms. Each of P. beesiana's flowers is about ¾in/2cm across. Light green, finely toothed leaves, shaped like elongated tongues, form rosettes of growth at the base of the sturdy flower stems. The plant is happiest in humus-rich, acid to neutral soils that are either damp or, at least, consistently moist. This primula can be grown in a sunny position, but then really moist soil conditions are essential. For a further example of a Candelabra primula, see left.
also for: ■ Damp and wet soils

Rhododendron
e.g. "Curlew"
◗[◯]✱

type of plant: hardy shrub [7–9]
flowering time: mid- to late spring
flower color: clear light yellow
height: 18–24in/45–60cm
Evergreen

This free-flowering rhododendron grows slowly and neatly. It forms a spreading mass of little, pointed, oval leaves. When R. "Curlew" is in full flower, its dark, shiny foliage is almost covered in trusses of funnel-shaped, 2in/5cm-wide blooms. It needs a sheltered position, as well as the usual moist, well-drained, lime-free soil. R. "Princess Anne" is a somewhat similar, yellow-flowered hybrid of neat, dense growth, to about 30in/75cm high. One of the hardiest, readily available rhododendrons with yellow flowers is R. "Patty Bee" [zones 6–9]; it prefers a sunny site.
also for: ■ Growing in containers

Primula vialii
◗[◯]

type of plant: hardy perennial [7–9]
flowering time: midsummer
flower color: lilac + red buds
height: 12–18in/30–45cm

The distinctive flower heads of this primula are dense, two-tone spikes about 4in/10cm long. They are carried on pale stems well above rosettes of fairly slender, mid- to light green leaves. Individual leaves may be up to 12in/30cm long. In autumn, the cylindrical seedheads can be quite attractive en masse. P. vialii is at its best in climates with cool summers. It appreciates soil that is neutral to acid and also moist and fertile. This usually short-lived plant thrives in damp places.
also for: ■ Damp and wet soils

Begonia
e.g. Non Stop Series
◗[◯]

type of plant: half-hardy tuber [9–11]
flowering time: early summer to early autumn
flower color: mixed—red, orange, pink, white, yellow, apricot
height: 10–12in/25–30cm

Compared with the Semperflorens begonias (see p.207), Tuberhybrida begonias such as B. Non Stop Series have much larger flowers and larger, pointed, mid-green leaves. They are popular for bedding. Their numerous flowers are 3–4in/8–10cm wide and, to look their best, these double blooms need a position that is sheltered and not too sunny. The plants require neutral to acid soil that has good drainage and that retains moisture easily. Non Stop Series begonias are fairly upright and bushy. They are available in separate colors as well as in mixtures. B. "Pin-up" is another popular Tuberhybrida variety; its white flowers have pink edges.

Andromeda polifolia
e.g. "Compacta"
[bog rosemary]
◗[◯]✱

type of plant: hardy shrub [2–7]
flowering time: late spring to early summer
flower color: pale pink
height: 9–12in/23–30cm
Evergreen

Nurseries that specialize in heaths and heathers or in rhododendrons probably list this plant. It is particularly suitable for lime-free soil that is damp or at least fairly moist, and it copes well with poor, very acid conditions. A. polifolia "Compacta" forms a stiff little bush, densely twiggy and with narrow, bluish green leaves and numerous, 1¼in/3cm-wide, bell-shaped flowers. Other varieties, such as white-flowered A.p. "Alba," have an almost prostrate habit of growth. In areas with cool summers, A. polifolia and its varieties tolerate some sun.
also for: ■ Damp and wet soils

Polygala chamaebuxus var. grandiflora (syn. *P.c.* "Purpurea," *P.c.* "Rhodoptera")
◑[○]

type of plant: hardy shrub [5–8]
flowering time: mainly late spring to early summer
flower color: purple-pink + yellow
height: 6in/15cm
Evergreen

This creeping shrub produces numerous, ½in/1cm-long, pea-flowers among its neat, pointed, rich green leaves. It thrives in moist, preferably acid soil that is well drained and humus-rich. Although sometimes slow to establish, *P. chamaebuxus* var. *grandiflora* may eventually spread 24–36in/60–90cm wide. It is often especially successful when grown in a dry stone wall in a cool, shaded site.

Gentiana sino-ornata
[gentian]
◑[○] ✳

type of plant: hardy perennial [5–9]
flowering time: early to mid-autumn
flower color: rich intense blue
height: 3–4in/8–10cm
Semi-evergreen

Given lime-free soil that is well drained and humus-rich, and that never dries out, *G. sino-ornata* is easy to grow. In ideal conditions, its stems spread—rooting as they go—until they and their little tufts of bright green, grassy leaves cover an area at least 12in/30cm wide. The shapely, trumpet-flowers, with their luminous coloring and subtle stripings, are usually about 2in/5cm long. Related varieties of gentian include the rather smaller, slightly earlier-flowering *G.* x *macaulayi* "Kingfisher." In cool, damp regions these autumn-flowering gentians can be given a position in full sun.

ADDITIONAL PLANTS, featured elsewhere in this book, that are suitable for acid soils

◑[○] **partial shade (or sun)**

minimum height between 3ft/90cm and 10ft/3m
Camellia japonica "Alba Simplex," see p.152
Camellia japonica "Lavinia Maggi,"
see p.103

Enkianthus campanulatus, see p.243
Pieris japonica "Variegata," see p.177

minimum height 3ft/90cm or less
Gaultheria procumbens, see p.123
Primula bulleyana, see p.78

Primula japonica, see p.78
Primula japonica "Postford White," see p.79
Rhododendron "Mother's Day," see p.152
Rhododendron "Rosebud," see p.152
Skimmia japonica subsp. *reevesiana*,
see p.260

Crinodendron hookerianum (syn. *Tricuspidaria lanceolata*)
[lantern tree]
◧ ✳

type of plant: slightly tender shrub [9–10]
flowering time: late spring to early summer
flower color: crimson
height: 10–15ft/3–4.5m
Evergreen

In mild districts, this magnificent, upright, densely foliated shrub eventually becomes tree-like and as much as 30ft/9m high. Elsewhere, lantern tree is considerably smaller but still very striking. It has dark, slender, glossy leaves, and its long-stalked, pendent flowers—each about 1in/2.5cm long—look like little lanterns. It needs shelter from cold winds, and it also requires acid soil that is moisture-retentive and well drained. In moist soil and a really sheltered position, this plant can be grown in sun.

Desfontainia spinosa
◑ ✳

type of plant: slightly tender shrub [8–9]
flowering time: midsummer to early autumn
flower color: red + yellow
height: 4–6ft/1.2–1.8m
Evergreen

The holly-like, little leaves of this slow-growing shrub make a good, glossy, dark green background for the bright, tubular flowers, each of which is about 1¼in/3cm long. Overall, the rather upright shoots of *D. spinosa* create a dense, bushy mass. The plant must have moist, lime-free soil that is also well drained and fertile. Some shelter is required, too. It thrives in mild, moist areas, where it can be grown in sun, but it is not so easy to grow well in warmer, drier regions. In ideal conditions, *D. spinosa* will still be in flower in mid-autumn in many years.
also for: ■ Long, continuous flowering period

Meconopsis betonicifolia (syn. *M. baileyi*)
[Himalayan blue poppy, Tibetan blue poppy]
◑

type of plant: hardy perennial [7–9]
flowering time: early summer
flower color: rich sky- to lavender-blue
height: 3–4ft/0.9–1.2m

A cool atmosphere and moist, open-textured, acidic soil are needed to produce the most strikingly colored specimens of Himalayan blue poppy. Except in ideal conditions, with shelter and rich soil, this poppy is short-lived and dies once it has flowered. Its clusters of 3–4in/8–10cm-wide flowers are borne on stiff, bristly stems above rosettes of large, light green, hairy leaves. Plants sold as *M.* x *sheldonii* are usually longer-lived and often have flowers of a very clear blue. *M. betonicifolia* var. *alba* has white flowers.

Blechnum spicant
[hard fern]
◗✳

type of plant: hardy fern [4–8]
height: 12–18in/30–45cm
Evergreen (see description)

This tough and amenable fern tolerates some dryness but its ground-covering clumps of dark green, leathery fronds will be largest in moist soil. Beneath the conspicuous, upright, fertile fronds lie rosettes of fronds that are broader, sterile and up to 18in/45cm long. The sterile fronds are evergreen. *B. spicant* is at home in damp woodland and similar, cool, shady places. It needs acid soil.
also for: ■ Damp and wet soils ■ Ground cover ■ Decorative, green foliage

Trillium erectum
[purple trillium, stinking Benjamin]
◗

type of plant: hardy perennial [4–9]
flowering time: mid- to late spring
flower color: reddish maroon
height: 12–15in/30–38cm

Each stem of this vigorous plant bears a whorl of three broad, pointed leaves and a single, often slightly nodding flower. Each bloom, with its three broad, recurving petals, is about 2in/5cm wide. The flowers are rather variable in color but they are commonly a deep red of some sort, although white forms are not unusual. The smell given off by the flowers is sometimes likened to rotting meat or wet dogs (but see p.313 for a wood lily with pleasantly fragrant flowers). *T. sessile* [zones 5–9] bears its dark wine-colored, stalkless flowers face upward and its leaves are marbled with gray and dark purplish green. The foliage of both these trilliums dies down during summer. Acid to neutral soil that is light, humus-rich and moist is ideal for these plants.

Lewisia Cotyledon Hybrids
◗

type of plant: hardy perennial [6–9]
flowering time: late spring to midsummer
flower color: various—red, salmon, pink, cream, white
height: 6–9in/15–23cm
Evergreen

If these lovely plants are to grow outdoors, rather than in an alpine house, they must be given very well-drained soil. Positioning them in crevices or on slopes also helps insure that moisture disperses quickly. These precautions are necessary since wetness in winter leads to rotting of the roots. Humus-rich and preferably acid soil produces the best results. However, even in ideal conditions, *L.* Cotyledon Hybrids tend to be fairly short-lived. Their flowers, up to 1½in/4cm wide, are borne in clusters on erect stems. The mid- to dark green, often strap-shaped leaves form rosettes of rather fleshy foliage. Numerous named forms of *L. cotyledon* are available from nurseries specializing in alpine plants.

Thalictrum kiusianum
[meadow rue]
◗

type of plant: hardy perennial [5–8]
flowering time: early to midsummer
flower color: mauve-pink
height: 4in/10cm

A haze of tiny, clustered flowers hovers, on reddish stems, over this little plant's fern-like foliage. Each little flower is usually less than ½in/1cm wide and its attractive, fluffy appearance is due to its conspicuous stamens and its slender "petals." Moist, humus-rich, acid soil and a cool, shaded place provide ideal growing conditions for *T. kiusianum*, which spreads slowly to form a mat of dark, often purple-tinged, bluish-green leaves.
also for: ■ Decorative, green foliage

ADDITIONAL PLANTS, featured elsewhere in this book, that are suitable for acid soils

◗ partial shade

minimum height 10ft/3m or more
Berberidopsis corallina, see p.136
Rhododendron "Loderi King George,"
  see p.313

minimum height between 3ft/90cm and 10ft/3m
Corylopsis pauciflora,
  see p.313
Dicksonia antarctica, see p.231
Pieris floribunda, see p.49
Pieris "Forest Flame," see p.208

minimum height 3ft/90cm or less
Athyrium niponicum var. *pictum,* see p.196
Blechnum penna-marina, see p.121
Fritillaria camschatcensis, see p.332
Luzula sylvatica "Marginata," see p.121
Reineckea carnea, see p.121

Kirengeshoma palmata
◐● ✳

type of plant: hardy perennial [5–9]
flowering time: late summer to early autumn
flower color: pale yellow
height: 3–4ft/0.9–1.2m

The large, lobed, tree-like leaves, the dark stems and the pale, thick-petalled flowers of K. palmata combine to produce an overall effect of distinct elegance. The flower buds appear in early summer and need a fairly sheltered site to encourage them to develop later. They dangle gracefully, in loose sprays, but tend not to open widely, remaining as slender bells or tubes of creamy yellow. Cool, moist, peaty soil is most suitable for this perennial, which forms a clump of growth, with the largest of the light green leaves—which can be up to 8in/20cm long—at the base of the plant.
also for: ■ Decorative, green foliage

Leucothoe Scarletta = "Zeblid"
◐● ✳

type of plant: hardy shrub [5–8]
flowering time: early summer
flower color: white
height: 18–24in/45–60cm
Evergreen

L. Scarletta creates a dense, spreading mound of arching stems and lustrous foliage, which is usually as wide as it is high. When young, the slender, pointed leaves are rich red; they then turn dark green and in autumn and winter they are bronzed wine-red. The flowers resemble those of lily of the valley and are borne, not very freely, in drooping bunches. Humus-rich, moist but well-drained soil and a cool site are needed. L. fontanesiana (syn. L. walteri) "Rainbow" has cream-variegated leaves that are flushed pink when young; it is an arching shrub, around 4ft/1.2m high. Both plants require acid soil.
also for: ■ Ground cover ■ Decorative, green foliage ■ Purple, bronze, or red leaves (young leaves only) ■ Colorful, autumn foliage (winter color, too)

Uvularia grandiflora
[large merrybells]
◐●

type of plant: hardy perennial [4–9]
flowering time: mid- to late spring
flower color: yellow
height: 18–24in/45–60cm

Both the slender, fresh green leaves and the pointed petals of U. grandiflora are slightly twisted and this adds to their charm. When the 2in/5cm-long, bell-shaped flowers first appear, their stems are quite short; they lengthen as spring progresses. The flowers are rather short-lived. U. grandiflora is at its best in a cool, shady place and in humus-rich, acid to neutral soil that is moist but well drained. U.g. var. pallida is less widely available; its flowers are a paler yellow than those of the species. Both the species and its variety form clumps of growth and increase fairly slowly. When these plants begin to die back, in late summer, their foliage briefly turns soft shades of yellow and buff.

ADDITIONAL PLANTS, featured elsewhere in this book, that are suitable for acid soils

◐● **partial or full shade**

minimum height 10ft/3m or more
Rhododendron "Fastuosum Flore Pleno," see p.101
Taxus baccata, see p.140
Taxus baccata "Fastigiata," see p.21

minimum height between 3ft/90cm and 10ft/3m
Taxus cuspidata, see p.63

minimum height 3ft/90cm or less
Cornus canadensis, see p.125
Gaultheria procumbens, see p.123

Liriope muscari, see p.83
Pachysandra terminalis, see p.123
Pachysandra terminalis "Variegata,"
  see p.181
Phlox stolonifera "Blue Ridge,"
  see p.125

PLANTS SUITABLE FOR

Heavy, clay soils

HEAVY, CLAY SOILS ARE DENSE, especially if they have become compacted. Their very fine-particled structure means that they incorporate little air, and water does not easily pass through them. In almost airless, semi-waterlogged conditions many plants suffocate, begin to rot, and finally die; others form roots only slowly. Yet clay soils are intrinsically fertile. If heavy clay has plenty of organic matter such as strawy manure, leaf mold, and garden compost dug into it, to open it up and to improve it generally, and if it can be regularly mulched to augment and maintain the process of improvement, then a wide range of plants will grow in it—often very much more luxuriantly than in a light, fast-draining soil.

However, it can take some time before any improvements are completed, and the following list consists of plants that are prepared to tolerate soil that is heavy and slow draining. Some of these plants might be seen at their very best in soil with better drainage, and many would become established more quickly in well-drained conditions, but all these plants should grow quite satisfactorily in heavy clays.

Virtually every plant in this list is hardy. A few plants are very slightly tender, but even they will be successful on heavy, clay soils, particularly in warmer regions. Often it is a combination of wetness and low temperatures, rather than low temperatures alone, that kills plants. Heavy clays are both wet and cold and plants grown in them become, in effect, less hardy. Whenever possible, planting on heavy clays should be carried out in spring and not in autumn. Spring planting means that young plants spend relatively little time trying to contend with cold, wet soil.

Certain groups of plants tend not to thrive on heavy clay. The majority of annuals and biennials have fine, shallow roots and they are, therefore, ill-equipped to cope with heavy soils, although the biennial, common foxglove grows well on clay, and its lovely white form, *Digitalis purpurea* f. *albiflora*, is included in this list.

Relatively few evergreens prosper on heavy clay. Examples of those that do, include some barberries (*Berberis* x *stenophylla* and *B. darwinii*), *Viburnum rhytidophyllum,* and *V. tinus*, and some firethorns (see *Pyracantha* "Soleil d'Or" in this list, and also p.258). Smaller evergreen or semi-evergreen plants suitable for heavy clays include most *Bergenia, Ajuga,* and *Lamium.*

Most bulbous plants tend not to do well on heavy clay but the more robust daffodils (*Narcissus*), many snowdrops (*Galanthus*), and *Camassia*, and the lovely snowflakes (*Leucojum*) are all suitable.

The plants that really revel in heavy clay include hearty perennials, such as *Eupatorium purpureum* subsp. *maculatum* "Atropurpureum," *Rudbeckia laciniata* "Herbstsonne," and the Japanese anemone *Anemone* x *hybrida* "Honorine Jobert," all of which are illustrated in this list. Many handsome foliage plants thrive in heavy clay: see, for example, the *Rodgersia, Hosta* and *Acanthus* in the unillustrated sections of this list. Combined with substantial grasses such as *Calamagrostis arundinacea* and various *Miscanthus* (for examples of which, see pp. 169 and 239), these plants produce the bold, naturalistic look that so many gardeners find attractive.

Heavy, clay soils that have been lightened and improved, even partially, are able to support an even wider range of plants. In addition to those plants that grow more or less anywhere, such as winter jasmine (*Jasminum nudiflorum*), *Kerria japonica* "Pleniflora," and most privets (*Ligustrum*), many shrubs that are basically very easy-going, but that object to being waterlogged, are suitable for heavy clays that have been improved. Cotoneasters, barberries (*Berberis*), and the more vigorous roses are just a few of the plants that thrive in the fertile, moisture-retentive conditions of improved clay.

For additional plants suitable for heavy clay, see also the following list in particular: "Plants suitable for damp and wet soils," pp.64–79.

Quercus robur
(syn. *Q. pedunculata*)
[English oak, pedunculate oak]
○

type of plant: hardy tree [6–8]
height: 80–100ft/24–30m

Ideally, this tree should be grown in deep, moist loam but similar soils, including stiff and heavy clays, also give good results. common oak is very long-lived. Its crown is eventually wide, rounded and fairly open. Lobed and oblong leaves appear fairly late in spring. They are each 4–5in/10–12cm long. The acorns, although abundant, are inconspicuous from a distance. Cypress oak (*Q. robur* f. *fastigiata*) makes a tapering column of growth that can be more than 80ft/24m high. It and other oak varieties, such as those with golden or cut leaves, are available from specialist nurseries.

Alnus cordata
[Italian alder]
○

type of plant: hardy tree [7–9]
flowering time: late winter to early spring
flower color: yellowish
height: 50–80ft/15–24m

Bright green, glossy foliage is the principal feature of this narrow, pyramidal tree, but the early catkins are also attractive and the plant itself is tough and grows quickly, even on poor soil. Except in a very cold, exposed position, it makes a good windbreak. Italian alder"s little, woody "cones" ripen from green to brown in summer. After the heart-shaped, 4in/10cm-long leaves fall, these "cones" become conspicuous but they are not especially decorative. In some colder gardens Italian alder may reach only 30–40ft/9–12m high. Although it prefers moist growing conditions, it tolerates quite dry soils. For wet—rather than damp—soil, the common alder (*A. glutinosa*; zones 4–9) is a better choice.
also for: ■ Damp and wet soils ■ Atmospheric pollution ■ Decorative, green foliage ■ Winter-flowering plants

Fraxinus excelsior
e.g. "Pendula"
[European ash]
○

type of plant: hardy tree [4–9]
height: 40–50ft/12–15m

The pendent branches and numerous, slender leaflets on this tree create a humped dome of growth. Each leaf, up to 12in/30cm long, is composed of about a dozen dark green leaflets. The foliage unfurls, from black winter buds, rather late in spring. Robust and vigorous European ash (*F. excelsior*) and its familiar varieties—including weeping ash (*F.e.* "Pendula") —grow well in any soil of reasonable fertility, although they have a preference for deep, moisture-retentive soil. *F.e.* "Jaspidea" is another popular variety; it resembles the species in its open-branched, round-headed outline but its winter twigs are yellow and, in late spring and again in autumn, its leaves too are yellow. All these ashes are tolerant of wind in coastal as well as inland gardens. However, the species is the most practical choice for a very exposed site; it is less decorative but considerably cheaper than the varieties.
also for: ■ Windswept, seaside gardens ■ Atmospheric pollution

Syringa x *josiflexa* "Bellicent"
[lilac]
○

type of plant: hardy shrub [5–9]
flowering time: late spring to early summer
flower color: rose-pink
height: 10–12ft/3–3.6m

This vigorous and healthy shrub produces numerous 9in/23cm-long, plume-like flower clusters on dark, slightly arching stalks. When the flowers are fully expanded, they emit a sweet, heavy scent that not everyone finds attractive. *S.* x *josiflexa* "Bellicent" has a rather upright habit of growth when young; it becomes more spreading with age. Its leaves are dark, oval and pointed. Chalky clays are particularly suitable but growth is good in a wide range of fertile soils, including those that are light and drain quite quickly.
also for: ■ Shallow soils over chalk ■ Atmospheric pollution ■ Flowers suitable for cutting ■ Fragrant flowers (see above)

Spiraea "Arguta"
(syn. S. x arguta "Bridal Wreath")
[bridal wreath, foam of May]
○

type of plant: hardy shrub [5–9]
flowering time: mid- to late spring
flower color: white
height: 6ft/1.8m

Each of the arching stems of this dense, rounded shrub becomes covered with tightly packed clusters of flowers. The clusters are each about 2in/5cm wide and they almost obscure the slender, fresh green leaves. Together, the mass of blossom and the habit of growth make this a spectacular shrub during its flowering season. S. "Arguta" is easily pleased, although it has a preference for good, deep, moisture-retentive soil and open sites. S. nipponica "Snowmound" is also very free-flowering. Its white blossom appears in early summer on a shrub that is slightly smaller and more spreading than S. "Arguta".
also for: ■ Atmospheric pollution

Abelia x grandiflora
○

type of plant: slightly tender shrub [7–9]
flowering time: late summer to early autumn
flower color: pink-tinged white
height: 1.5–1.8m/5–6ft
Semi-evergreen/Evergreen

The slightly fragrant flowers of this graceful shrub have persistent, reddish pink outer parts that remain decorative long after the petals have fallen. There are normally large quantities of the ¾in/2cm-long, bell-shaped blooms. When A. x grandiflora is young, its brittle stems are upright; as it matures, they become more arching. The neat, little, pointed leaves are glossy and rich deep green. Less vigorous A. x g. "Francis Mason" and A. x g. Confetti produce yellow-edged and cream-edged foliage, respectively. A. "Edward Goucher" has flowers that are purplish pink. All these plants need a sheltered site. A. x grandiflora can be grown in most soils and, especially in warmer districts, it is very successful on clay.

Salix hastata "Wehrhahnii"
[willow]
○

type of plant: hardy shrub [6–9]
flowering time: early spring
flower color: silver-gray changing to yellow
height: 4–6ft/1.2–1.8m

The upright branches of this shrub are dark purple-brown and they contrast strikingly with the numerous, very pale catkins. As they mature, these catkins—which are up to 3in/8cm long—become more brightly colored. The rounded, dark green leaves do not develop fully until after flowering time. S. hastata "Wehrhahnii" slowly forms a dense, spreading clump of stems. It is suitable for most garden soils, including heavy clays, and it does well in damp and wet areas of ground. S. gracilistyla "Melanostachys" is another dark-twigged, medium-sized willow; it has intriguing, black catkins in early spring.
also for: ■ Damp and wet soils ■ Ornamental bark or twigs

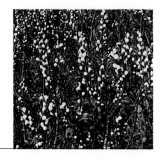

Prunus glandulosa "Alba Plena"
[Chinese bush cherry, dwarf flowering almond]
○

type of plant: hardy shrub [5–8]
flowering time: late spring
flower color: white
height: 4–5ft/1.2–1.5m

Many-petalled, ¼in/2cm-wide flowers appear in profusion all along this shrub"s thin, upright stems. The pale green leaves are small and slender and develop at about the same time as the flowers. For there to be plenty of blossom, the plant needs a sheltered site in full sun. Most reasonably fertile, moisture-retentive soils, including heavy clay, are suitable. P. glandulosa "Sinensis" (syn. "Rosea Plena") has pale pink, double flowers, but it is not so readily available as P.g. "Alba Plena".

Helenium e.g. "Butterpat"
[sneezeweed]
○

type of plant: hardy perennial [4–9]
flowering time: late summer to early autumn
flower color: yellow
height: 36in/90cm

The two varieties of sneezeweed illustrated here and below are easily grown in most soils and they are good for cutting. They thrive in moisture-retentive conditions. Like all the popular varieties, H. "Butterpat" is floriferous but needs regular division to keep it flowering freely. Its daisy-like flowers are 2–3in/5–8cm wide and attractive to bees. If dead-headed and regularly divided, H. "Moerheim Beauty" in particular will continue to produce a significant number of blooms into autumn. Bicolored cultivars include H. "Wyndley" (yellow-and-orange flowers). All these plants form clumps of growth with upright stems and slender, mid-green leaves.
also for: ■ Flowers suitable for cutting

Helenium
e.g. "Moerheim Beauty"
[sneezeweed]
○

type of plant: hardy perennial [4–9]
flowering time: mid- to late summer
flower color: bronze-red
height: 36in/ 90cm

See preceding plant.

Hemerocallis
e.g. "Stafford"
[daylily]
○

type of plant: hardy perennial [5–9]
flowering time: midsummer to early autumn
flower color: mahogany-red + yellow
height: 30–36in/75–90cm
Semi-evergreen

There is a huge range of hybrid daylilies. The vigorous, hardy varieties, such as H. "Stafford," grow well in all sorts of moisture-retentive soils; they are often at their best in damp places. Individually, the flowers of daylilies are short-lived but the numerous buds open, more or less continuously, over several weeks. H. "Stafford" has fairly upright, branching stems with 4in/10cm-wide flowers of an elegant, sculpted, star shape (other hybrids produce double or rounder-"petalled" or more spidery blooms). The flower stems rise above a dense, ground-covering clump of arching, strap-shaped, light green leaves. Further examples of readily available, richly colored daylilies include H. "Sammy Russell" (dark red), H. "Black Magic" (deep maroon) and H. "Little Wine Cup" (see p.44).
also for: ■ Damp and wet soils ■ Ground cover ■ Decorative, green foliage

Lythrum salicaria
e.g. "Blush"
[purple loosestrife]
○

type of plant: hardy perennial [4–9]
flowering time: midsummer to early autumn
flower color: pale pink
height: 30in/75cm

Purple loosestrife and most of its varieties have erect spikes of very brightly colored flowers (for an example, see p.66); L. salicaria "Blush," however, is gentle in coloring. Its pale, starry flowers open, in succession, over a long period. The plant forms stiff-stemmed clumps of growth with slim, pointed leaves, above which rise slender spires of flowers, each spire approximately 12in/30cm long. All moisture-retentive soils are suitable but this loosestrife does really well in damp and wet conditions.
also for: ■ Damp and wet soils ■ Long, continuous flowering period

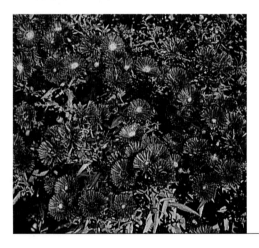

Aster novi-belgii
e.g. "Jenny"
[New York aster]
○

type of plant: hardy perennial [4–8]
flowering time: early to mid-autumn
flower color: purplish red
height: 12–18in/30–45cm

Dwarf hybrid asters are available in shades of blue, pink, red and white. A. novi-belgii "Jenny" is typically tidy and free-flowering. Its richly colored, 1in/2.5cm-wide, double flowers are carried, in open clusters, on branching stems. These stems are covered in little, slender leaves. To grow well, these clump-forming perennials need fertile soil and constant moisture (a reliable source of moisture also helps reduce their susceptibility to an attack of mildew). Other popular, dwarf varieties include A.n.-b. "Little Pink Beauty," A.n.-b. "Kristina" (white) and A.n.-b. "Audrey" (lavender-blue). They are all excellent for cutting. For an example of a taller aster, see p.271.
also for: ■ Flowers suitable for cutting

ADDITIONAL PLANTS, featured elsewhere in this book, that are suitable for heavy clay soils

○ sun

minimum height 10ft/3m or more
Acer platanoides "Crimson King," see p.198
Catalpa bignonioides, see p.95
Catalpa bignonioides "Aurea," see p.210
Catalpa x erubescens "Purpurea," see p.198
Corylus maxima "Purpurea," see p.199
Ginkgo biloba, see p.235
Metasequoia glyptostroboides, see p.65
Platanus x hispanica, see p.94
Populus alba, see p.183
Populus x jackii "Aurora," see p.161
Populus nigra "Italica," see p.94

Quercus palustris, see p.235
Salix alba subsp. vitellina "Britzensis," see p.264
Salix babylonica var. pekinensis "Tortuosa," see p.263

minimum height between 3ft/90cm and 10ft/3m
Aster novae-angliae "Harrington"s Pink," see p.270
Berberis x stenophylla, see p.138
Colutea arborescens, see p.253
Inula magnifica, see p.65
Salix caprea "Kilmarnock," see p.65
Salix fargesii, see p.220
Sambucus nigra f. porphyrophylla "Gerda," see p.329

Syringa pubescens subsp. microphylla "Superba," see p.299
Thuja occidentalis "Rheingold," see p.210

minimum height 3ft/90cm or less
Abies balsamea Hudsonia Group, see p.147
Aster novi-belgii "Marie Ballard," see p.271
Ilex crenata "Golden Gem," see p.211
Lythrum salicaria "Robert," see p.66
Salix lanata, see p.185
Spiraea japonica "Anthony Waterer," see p.141
Spiraea x vanhouttei Pink Ice, see p.164
Weigela florida "Foliis Purpureis," see p.200

Rudbeckia laciniata "Herbstsonne" (syn. *R.* Autumn Sun) [black-eyed Susan, coneflower]
○【●】

type of plant: hardy perennial [5–9]
flowering time: midsummer to early autumn
flower color: yellow + green
height: 6–7ft/1.8–2.1m

This imposing plant produces numerous, bold flowers, up to 5in/12cm wide and each with a prominent central cone. Flowers are carried on branched, upright stems above large, veined leaves, and the plant forms a clump of growth. For other, smaller coneflowers with long flowering seasons, see p.343. All these plants need moderately fertile, moisture-retentive soil to perform well. They may take a little while to establish in heavy, poorly drained soil but, once established there, they thrive.
also for: ■ Long, continuous flowering period

Weigela e.g. "Bristol Ruby"
○【●】

type of plant: hardy shrub [5–8]
flowering time: late spring to early summer
flower color: deep red
height: 5–8ft/1.5–2.4m

Weigelas are easily grown shrubs that do well in almost all soils. However, they have a preference for moisture-retentive conditions and they thrive on clay. *W.* "Bristol Ruby" is a fairly erect variety which, especially in full sun, produces large quantities of its bell-shaped flowers, each of which is 1½in–2in/4–5cm long. Its leaves are oval, pointed and of a deep green that complements the flower color very satisfactorily. Other hybrid weigelas produce flowers mostly in reds and pinks; some whites are available, too. *W. middendorffiana* has pale yellow, spring flowers and is usually best in a sheltered site. Weigelas with decorative foliage are shown on pp.172, 200 and 216.
also for: ■ Atmospheric pollution

Eupatorium purpureum subsp. *maculatum* "Atropurpureum" [Joe Pye weed]
○【●】

type of plant: hardy perennial [4–9]
flowering time: late summer to mid-autumn
flower color: purplish pink
height: 5ft/1.5m

This is the sort of rather coarse—but impressive—plant that is well able to cope with the exigencies of heavy clay. Its size and general nature make it suitable either for a wild garden or for a large border. The stiff, upright, purplish stems are clothed in pointed leaves, which are arranged in whorls. *E. purpureum* subsp. *maculatum* "Atropurpureum" forms clumps of growth. Its richly colored flowers are carried in heads up to 6in/15cm wide. They are attractive to butterflies. *E. purpureum* itself is rather taller than this variety, with flowers and stems of lighter coloring. Both plants thrive in any moist soil and have a preference for alkaline conditions.
also for: ■ Damp and wet soils

Camassia leichtlinii subsp. *leichtlinii* (syn. *C.l.* "Alba") [quamash]
○【●】

type of plant: hardy bulb [4–9]
flowering time: late spring to early summer
flower color: green-tinged, creamy white
height: 30–36in/75–90cm

There are various forms of *C. leichtlinii*. As well as some with deep blue flowers and others with paler blue or lilac flowers, there is this attractive, white-flowered form. They all produce numerous, starry flowers in erect spikes that are up to 12in/30cm long. They make good cut flowers. By late summer, the flowering stems, with their tufts of untidy, strap-shaped leaves, have usually died down completely. Rather heavy, rich, moist soils give the best results. The plants are suitable for naturalizing in grass.
also for: ■ Flowers suitable for cutting

Solidago
e.g. "Goldenmosa"
[goldenrod]
○◖●◗

type of plant: hardy perennial [4–9]
flowering time: late summer to early autumn
flower color: bright yellow
height: 30in/75cm

The whole of *S.* "Goldenmosa" has a yellowish cast to it: the clusters of tiny flowers are yellow; the stiff, upright, leafy flower stems are yellow; and the foliage is light yellowish green. Heavy, moisture-retentive soils are, perhaps, most suitable, but this robust plant is not fussy. The flower plumes, which are 9–12in/23–30cm long, can be dried as well as used fresh in indoor arrangements. They are attractive to butterflies. Other popular goldenrods include *S.* "Goldkind" (syn. Golden Baby), which is about 18in/45cm tall, and 12in/30cm-high *S.* "Queenie" (syn. "Golden Thumb"). The taller goldenrods tend to be too vigorous for most gardens.
also for: ■ Flowers suitable for cutting (and drying)

Hemerocallis
e.g. "Little Wine Cup"
[daylily]
○◖●◗

type of plant: hardy perennial [5–9]
flowering time: mid- to late summer
flower color: soft wine-red
height: 18in/45cm
Semi-evergreen

In recent years shorter-growing daylilies with small flowers have become popular. The trumpet-shaped, yellow-throated flowers of *H.* "Little Wine Cup" are often not much more than 2in/5cm wide. They are carried, on rather short stems, above the plant"s dense clump of slender, bright green leaves. Although individual flowers last only one day, there are numerous buds that open in succession. Other readily available dwarf hemerocallis include *H.* "Stella de Oro," which produces its yellow flowers over many weeks in summer and early autumn, and *H.* "Cream Drop," which has creamy yellow flowers from midsummer. To perform well, all these varieties of daylily need fertile soil that retains moisture. Flowering is particularly profuse in a sunny position.
also for: ■ Damp and wet soils

ADDITIONAL PLANTS, featured elsewhere in this book, that are suitable for heavy clay soils

○◖●◗ sun (or partial shade)

minimum height 10ft/3m or more
Abies koreana, see p.255
Acer pseudoplatanus "Brilliantissimum," see p.203
Crataegus laevigata "Paul"s Scarlet," see p.99
Crataegus x lavallei "Carrierei," see p.256
Crataegus monogyna, see p.142
Crataegus phaenopyrum, see p.98
Malus tschonoskii, see p.238
Tilia "Petiolaris," see p.98
Viburnum opulus "Xanthocarpum," see p.68

minimum height between 3ft/90cm and 10ft/3m
Acanthus mollis, see p.110
Acanthus spinosus, see p.223
Berberis darwinii, see p.257

Cornus alba "Elegantissima," see p.68
Cornus alba "Kesselringii," see p.331
Cornus alba "Sibirica," see p.265
Cornus alba "Spaethii," see p.169
Cornus sericea "Flaviramea," see p.265
Miscanthus sinensis "Gracillimus," see p.239
Miscanthus sinensis "Zebrinus," see p.169
Philadelphus "Virginal," see p.99
Potentilla fruticosa "Vilmoriniana,"
   see p.142
Rheum palmatum, see p.223
Viburnum opulus "Compactum," see p.257

minimum height 3ft/90cm or less
Ajuga reptans "Atropurpurea," see p.205
Aster pilosus var. *pringlei* "Monte Cassino,"
   see p.286

Calamagrostis arundinacea, see p.111
Caltha palustris "Flore Pleno," see p.70
Hemerocallis fulva "Flore Pleno," see p.68
Hemerocallis "Golden Chimes," see p.224
Hemerocallis "Pink Damask," see p.110
Iris sibirica "Perry"s Blue," see p.69
Iris sibirica "White Swirl," see p.69
Ligularia dentata "Desdemona," see p.204
Lysimachia nummularia "Aurea," see p.112
Mentha suaveolens "Variegata," see p.170
Potentilla fruticosa "Elizabeth," see p.110
Potentilla fruticosa "Tangerine," see p.343
Rheum "Ace of Hearts," see p.224
Rudbeckia fulgida var. *sullivantii* "Goldsturm,"
   see p.343
Solidago flexicaulis "Variegata," see p.169
Spiraea japonica "Goldflame," see p.214

Carpinus betulus "Fastigiata"
(syn. *C.b.* "Pyramidalis")
[hornbeam]
○◖

type of plant: hardy tree [5–9]
height: 40ft/12m

The erect twigs and branches of this hornbeam form a dense, narrow head of growth that broadens into a strikingly symmetrical flame shape. The mid-green, pointed, oval leaves are pleated and each around 3in/8cm long. They turn rich yellow in autumn, when there are also dangling, tassel-like clusters of yellow-brown, winged seeds. Any soil is suitable but growth is especially good on heavy clay. On older specimens, the bark is gray and craggily fluted.
also for: ■ Shallow soils over chalk
■ Atmospheric pollution ■ Colorful, autumn foliage ■ Ornamental fruit
■ Ornamental bark or twigs

Aesculus x carnea "Briotii"
[red horse chestnut]
◯◑

type of plant: hardy tree [6–9]
flowering time: late spring to early summer
flower color: rose-red
height: 30–40ft/9–12m; up to 80ft/24m in areas of hot summers

This dome-headed tree grows in most soils and tolerates very alkaline conditions, but the best specimens are those planted in deep, moist, fertile loams and clays. In full flower, its large spikes of brightly colored flowers make A. x carnea "Briotii" an impressive sight. Its leaves are rich, glossy green and composed of 5–7 leaflets, each about 9in/23cm long. There is usually at least some yellow autumn color but there are no fruits. The larger, wider-spreading and more vigorous common horse chestnut (A. hippocastanum) is only suitable for a really large garden.
also for: ■ Atmospheric pollution

Pyracantha e.g. "Soleil d'Or"
(syn. P. "Golden Sun," P. "Yellow Sun")
[firethorn]
◯◑

type of plant: hardy shrub [7–10]
flowering time: early summer
flower color: white
height: 10ft/3m
Evergreen

While many pyracanthas have red or orange berries (for an example, see p.258), there are several, popular varieties with yellow fruits. P. "Soleil d'Or" is a fairly upright shrub with spreading growths and numerous, 3in/8cm-wide bunches of yellow berries. These are conspicuous among its dark green, glossy, tongue-shaped leaves. The berries are preceded by flattish clusters of five-petalled flowers that have a rather unpleasant scent. This pyracantha can be used to make a thorny hedge (individual plants should be about 24in/60cm apart). It can also be grown freestanding, or it can be trained against a wall of any aspect. Most soils, including clay, are suitable for P. "Soleil d'Or," although it does not do well in very alkaline conditions.
also for: ■ Atmospheric pollution ■ Ornamental fruit

Viburnum plicatum f. tomentosum e.g. "Mariesii"
◯◑

type of plant: hardy shrub [5–9]
flowering time: late spring
flower color: white
height: 6–8ft/1.8–2.4m

The outstanding feature of this shrub is its widely spreading, horizontally arranged branches. During the flowering season this interesting, tiered habit of growth is accentuated by the "lacecap" flowers, each of which is 3–4in/8–10cm wide. Although fruiting is not usually regular or prolific, the flowers may be followed by red berries. In autumn, the veined, tapering leaves turn from light green to a rich wine-maroon. Moisture-retentive, fertile soils, including clays, are most suitable for V. plicatum f. tomentosum "Mariesii" but most soils produce good specimens. V.p. f. t. "Lanarth" is a similar variety; V.p. f. t. "Pink Beauty" has pink flowers.
also for: ■ Colorful, autumn foliage

Chaenomeles x superba e.g. "Pink Lady"
[flowering quince]
◯◑

type of plant: hardy shrub [5–9]
flowering time: early spring to early summer
flower color: rich rose-pink
height: 5–6ft/1.5–1.8m

There are few soils and sites with which varieties of C. x superba cannot cope. For preference, however, shallow, chalky soils should be avoided and it should be remembered that deep shade diminishes the number of flowers and subsequent fruits. C. x s. "Pink Lady" has dark, spreading branches. Its cup-shaped blooms, up to 2in/5cm wide, open both before and with the glossy, approximately oval leaves and make good material for cutting. In a sheltered site C. x s. "Pink Lady" may start flowering in late winter. Its yellow, apple-like, autumn fruits are richly aromatic. A white-flowered chaenomeles is shown on p.101. Other popular, pink-flowered varieties include C. speciosa "Geisha Girl" and C.s. "Moerloosei" (syn. "Apple Blossom").
also for: ■ Atmospheric pollution ■ Ornamental fruit ■ Flowers suitable for cutting ■ Long, continuous flowering period

Anemone x *hybrida*
(syn. *A. japonica*)
e.g. "Honorine Jobert"
[Japanese anemone]
○◑

type of plant: hardy perennial [5–9]
flowering time: late summer to mid-autumn
flower color: white
height: 4ft/1.2m

Japanese anemones are tough and adaptable plants with a preference for substantial, moisture-retentive soils, including clay. They are especially long-flowering on moist soils. At first, the plants increase slowly but, once established, their suckering shoots can spread quite widely. *A.* x *hybrida* "Honorine Jobert" has 2½in/6cm-wide, single flowers of a characteristic elegance and simplicity. Semi-doubles such as *A.* x *h.* "Whirlwind" (white) and *A.* x *h.* "Königin Charlotte" (pink; see p.112) are also popular. The flowers of all these varieties are held on branched stems well above the ground-covering, lobed leaves.
also for: ■ Ground cover ■ Long, continuous flowering period

Persicaria amplexicaulis e.g. "Atrosanguinea" (syn. *Polygonum amplexicaule* "Atrosanguineum") [bistort, mountain fleece]
○◑

type of plant: hardy perennial [5–9]
flowering time: midsummer to early autumn
flower color: deep red
height: 3–4ft/0.9–1.2m
Semi-evergreen

Especially in rich soils that are damp or that retain moisture easily, *P. amplexicaulis* "Atrosanguinea" can spread fairly quickly into generous, weed-suppressing clumps of growth up to 4ft/1.2m wide. It is easily robust enough to cope well with heavy clay. Its slim spikes of flowers, 3–4in/8–10cm long, are strikingly numerous and they are produced over a period of many weeks. They make an effective contrast to the plant"s broad, bright green leaves. *P.a.* "Inverleith" is a readily available variety that is smaller than *P.a* "Atrosanguinea; it is about 18in/45cm high and wide.
also for: ■ Damp and wet soils ■ Ground cover ■ Long, continuous flowering period

Digitalis grandiflora
(syn. *D. ambigua*)
[yellow foxglove]
○◑

type of plant: hardy biennial/perennial [4–8]
flowering time: early to midsummer
flower color: pale yellow
height: 24–36in/60–90cm
Evergreen

Each of the softly colored "bells" of this foxglove is about 2in/5cm long and delicately marked in brown inside. The flowers are carried above clumps of soft green, veined leaves that become progressively smaller and narrower up the stout stalks. *D. grandiflora* grows well in a variety of moisture-retentive soils, including clay, but it is not, in any case, a long-lived plant. Although it survives in dryish shade, flowering is rather limited there. *D. lutea* is another, popular, yellow-flowered foxglove; it has smaller "bells" in slender spires and self-sows freely.

Ilex crenata e.g. "Helleri" [Japanese holly]
○◑

type of plant: hardy shrub [6–8]
height: 24–36in/60–90cm
Evergreen

Used frequently in the United States, where English holly (*I. aquifolium*) is usually unsatisfactory, *I. crenata* and its varieties are tolerant of both winter cold and summer heat. Numerous varieties are available. *I.c.* "Helleri," shown here, has layers of horizontal branches that are crowded with dark, spineless leaves, about ½in/1cm long. It slowly develops a ground-covering dome of growth about twice as wide as it is high. Eventually, it may exceed 4ft/1.2m in height. It rarely flowers or fruits. *I. crenata* itself makes a good topiary plant; *I.c.* "Convexa" is useful for hedging. All these hollies can be grown in a variety of moisture-retentive soils, including clay. They have a preference for acid to neutral conditions.
also for: ■ Ground cover

Inula hookeri
○◐

type of plant: hardy perennial [4–8]
flowering time: late summer to mid-autumn
flower color: yellow
height: 24–30in/60–75cm

This bushy, spreading plant grows well on clay and on other soils that retain moisture easily. Its very narrow-rayed, slightly fragrant flowers, up to 3in/8cm wide, emerge from strikingly hairy buds. The pointed, mid-green leaves, each up to 6in/15cm long, are also hairy. Although the slender stems of *I. hookeri* are basically upright, they tend to be rather lax. In rich, moist soil, this plant often increases rapidly.

Polemonium caeruleum
[Jacob's ladder]
○◐

type of plant: hardy perennial [4–8]
flowering time: late spring to midsummer
flower color: lavender-blue (see description)
height: 24in/60cm

The mid-green leaves of this plant are feathery and charmingly in keeping with its numerous, dainty flowers. Each little, cup-shaped bloom is only about ½in/1cm wide and dozens of buds open over several weeks. *P. caeruleum* tends to vary: *P.c.* subsp. *caeruleum* f. *album* is white-flowered (a white-flowered seedling is just visible in the illustration); there is also cream-variegated *P.c.* Brise d'Anjou, which has blue flowers. All moist, fertile soils—including heavy ones—produce good specimens of these clump-forming, erect-stemmed plants. Although they are short-lived, the plants self-sow, often very freely.
also for: ■ Long, continuous flowering period

Narcissus
e.g. "Mount Hood" (Trumpet)
[daffodil]
○◐

type of plant: hardy bulb [4–9]
flowering time: mid-spring
flower color: white + cream, fading to white
height: 18in/45cm

Many of the taller hybrid daffodils are vigorous plants that do well in almost any soil that is reasonably fertile and that stays moist during spring. Heavy clay soils are suitable, as long as they do not become waterlogged. *N.* "Mount Hood" has large, more or less white flowers, 4in/10cm wide. It is often used for mass planting. The white flowers of another vigorous Trumpet daffodil, *N.* "Empress of Ireland," are even larger. Popular, yellow-flowered, Trumpet daffodils include robust *N.* "Dutch Master". Both *N.* "Dutch Master" and *N.* "Mount Hood" are excellent for naturalizing in grass. All these daffodils have green or blue-green, strap-shaped, basal leaves.

Anemone sylvestris
[snowdrop anemone]
○◐

type of plant: hardy perennial [4–9]
flowering time: late spring to early summer
flower color: white
height: 12–15in/30–38cm

Snowdrop anemone is suitable for a wide range of soils, including heavy clay. In light soils the plant tends to spread, rather too rapidly, into large, dense, suckering colonies. Its drooping flower buds are carried well clear of the dark green, much-divided foliage. They open out into slightly fragrant, yellow-stamened blooms which, at 2in/5cm wide, are like miniature versions of Japanese anemone flowers. These are followed by fluffy, "cotton wool" seedheads.
also for: ■ Ornamental fruit (seedheads)

Polemonium "Lambrook Mauve" (syn. *P. reptans* "Lambrook Manor")
○◑

type of plant: hardy perennial [4–8]
flowering time: late spring to early summer
flower color: lilac-blue
height: 12–15in/30–38cm

The flowers of this spreading, clump-forming plant are carried in open sprays above mounds of numerous, small, mid-green leaflets. Each little, cup-shaped flower is not much more than ½in/1cm across. Moist, fertile soils produce good growth but, as long as conditions are not dry, this is an adaptable, easily grown plant. Though it is related to prolifically self-sowing Jacob's ladder (*P. caeruleum*, see the previous page), *P.* "Lambrook Mauve" does not self-sow.

Narcissus
e.g. "W.P. Milner" (Trumpet) [daffodil]
○◑

type of plant: hardy bulb [4–9]
flowering time: early to mid-spring
flower color: pale yellow
height: 9in/23cm

Popular Trumpet daffodils tend to produce large blooms (see, for example, *N.* "Mount Hood" on the previous page). This charming, shorter-stemmed variety has nodding flowers that are only about 2½in/6cm wide and, although it is small, it is robust and naturalizes well in grass. *N.* "W.P. Milner" succeeds in most soils that remain moist during the growing season, including heavy clay. *N.* "Little Beauty" (pale cream + yellow) and *N.* "Little Gem" (all yellow) are two further examples of sturdy, miniature, Trumpet daffodils. All these plants have strap-shaped, basal leaves which are blue- or grayish green or mid-green.

ADDITIONAL PLANTS, featured elsewhere in this book, that are suitable for heavy clay soils

○◑ sun or partial shade

minimum height 10ft/3m or more
Acer campestre, see p.21
Acer pensylvanicum, see p.266
Acer platanoides "Drummondii," see p.170
Carpinus betulus, see p.143
Magnolia x soulangeana, see p.28
Magnolia x soulangeana "Lennei," see p.100
Pyracantha "Orange Glow," see p.258
Taxodium distichum, see p.71
Viburnum rhytidophyllum, see p.226

minimum height between 3ft/90cm and 10ft/3m
Acer negundo "Flamingo," see p.171
Aconitum volubile, see p.134
Aesculus parviflora, see p.242
Aruncus dioicus, see p.72
Aucuba japonica "Variegata," see p.150
Carex pendula, see p.73
Chaenomeles speciosa "Nivalis," see p.101
Chaenomeles x superba "Knap Hill Scarlet,"
  see p.345
Choisya ternata, see p.289

Corylus avellana "Contorta," see p.267
Darmera peltata, see p.73
Dipsacus fullonum, see p.259
Forsythia x intermedia "Lynwood Variety," see p.21
Forsythia ovata, see p.319
Kerria japonica "Pleniflora," see p.289
Ligularia "The Rocket," see p.72
Magnolia stellata, see p.101
Ribes sanguineum "Pulborough Scarlet," see p.81
Salix integra "Hakuro-nishiki," see p.172
Sambucus nigra f. laciniata, see p.226
Sambucus racemosa "Plumosa Aurea," see p.215
Viburnum x bodnantense "Dawn," see p.319
Viburnum x burkwoodii, see p.308
Viburnum x carlcephalum, see p.308
Viburnum sargentii "Onondaga," see p.206
Viburnum tinus, see p.318
Viburnum tinus "Variegatum," see p.172
Weigela "Florida Variegata," see p.172

minimum height 3ft/90cm or less
Ajuga reptans "Burgundy Glow," see p.176
Ajuga reptans "Catlin's Giant," see p.116
Alchemilla conjuncta, see p.326

Alchemilla mollis, see p.114
Anemone x hybrida "Königin Charlotte," see p.112
Bergenia "Bressingham Ruby," see p.242
Bergenia cordifolia, see p.228
Bergenia "Silberlicht," see p.115
Camassia quamash, see p.292
Chelone obliqua, see p.74
Hedera helix "Congesta," see p.228
Hemerocallis lilioasphodelus, see p.310
Leucojum aestivum "Gravetye Giant," see p.75
Lysimachia punctata, see p.74
Lysimachia punctata "Alexander," see p.173
Mentha spicata, see p.251
Narcissus "Carlton," see p.292
Narcissus "Salome," see p.292
Persicaria bistorta "Superba," see p.74
Prunella grandiflora "Loveliness," see p.117
Ranunculus acris "Flore Pleno," see p.291
Ranunculus ficaria "Brazen Hussy," see p.207
Rodgersia pinnata "Superba," see p.73
Rodgersia podophylla, see p.206
Sasa veitchii, see p.113
Symphytum x uplandicum "Variegatum," see p.173
Viburnum davidii, see p.259

Digitalis purpurea f. albiflora
[common foxglove]
◑[○]

type of plant: hardy biennial [5–8]
flowering time: early to midsummer
flower color: white
height: 4–5ft/1.2–1.5m

In the dappled shade of woodland the tall, pale spires of white foxgloves look strikingly elegant. Although moisture-retentive soil and cool, shaded places provide ideal growing conditions, *D. purpurea* f. *albiflora* is an adaptable plant and a wide range of soils and sites is suitable. Each tubular flower is about 2½in/6cm long and variably spotted inside. The thick flower-stalks rise from rosettes of big, downy, pointed leaves. Other pale-flowered forms of the common foxglove include *D.p.* "Sutton's Apricot," which has creamy apricot-pink flowers. A mixed-color strain of foxgloves is shown on p.294. *D. purpurea* itself usually has purplish pink flowers.
also for: ■ Flowers suitable for cutting

Aconitum
e.g. "Bressingham Spire"
[aconite, monkshood]
◐◧

type of plant: hardy perennial [4–8]
flowering time: midsummer to early autumn
flower color: deep violet-blue
height: 36in/90cm

A. "Bressingham Spire" has strikingly upright flower spikes that, together with the darkness of the hooded, 1in/2.5cm-long blooms and the deep divisions of the glossy leaves, make it an imposing plant. A. "Spark's Variety" has similarly colored flowers on taller, branching stems; A. "Stainless Steel" bears long spikes of pale blue-gray blooms; for pale cream flowers see p.294. Fertile, moisture-retentive soils, including clays, are most suitable for these monkshoods. They may need to be watered in dry weather, if they are grown in sun. All parts of these plants are toxic if eaten and, when they are handled, they may cause skin irritation.
also for: ■ Flowers suitable for cutting

Primula vulgaris
[primrose]
◐◧

type of plant: hardy perennial [5–8]
flowering time: early to late spring
flower color: pale yellow
height: 4–6in/10–15cm
Semi-evergreen

This well-loved plant thrives in moist, heavy soils and in cool places such as open woodland. In sheltered sites, the flat, 1in/2.5cm-wide flowers may begin to appear at the end of winter. They often have a fresh, sweet fragrance. When well suited, primroses form ground-covering clumps of crinkled, bright green foliage and they sow themselves freely. There are numerous primrose cultivars, including double-flowered forms such as P. "Miss Indigo" (deep purple) and P. "Dawn Ansell" (white). P. vulgaris subsp. sibthorpii has single flowers in various shades of purplish pink.
also for: ■ Ground cover

Eranthis hyemalis
[winter aconite]
◐◧

type of plant: hardy tuber [5–9]
flowering time: late winter to early spring
flower color: yellow
height: 3–5in/8–12cm

Winter aconite is one of those tantalizing plants that can make large and beautiful carpets of color once established, or it can disappear without trace a couple of years after planting. Two factors that make the former state of affairs more likely are plenty of moisture (in a fairly heavy loam or clay, for example) and the use of freshly lifted tubers. Winter aconites often grow successfully beneath deciduous shrubs and trees. Their buttercup-like flowers emerge from globular buds that "sit" on ruffs of bright green, deeply divided leaves. Each flower is about 1in/2.5cm wide. The whole plant dies back by late spring.
also for: ■ Winter-flowering plants

ADDITIONAL PLANTS, featured elsewhere in this book, that are suitable for heavy clay soils

◐◧ partial shade (or sun)

minimum height between 3ft/90cm and 10ft/3m
Digitalis purpurea Excelsior Group, see p.294
Weigela Briant Rubidor, see p.216

minimum height 3ft/90cm or less
Aconitum "Ivorine," see p.294

Ajuga reptans "Variegata," see p.178
Digitalis x mertonensis, see p.295
Dryopteris filix-mas, see p.81
Hosta sieboldiana var. elegans, see p.196
Kerria japonica "Picta," see p.177
Mahonia aquifolium, see p.122
Pulmonaria longifolia, see p.180

Saxifraga x urbium, see p.230
Scrophularia auriculata "Variegata," see p.177
Symphytum ibericum, see p.123
Tellima grandiflora, see p.119
Tellima grandiflora Rubra Group, see p.243
Trachystemon orientalis, see p.83

Pieris floribunda
◐✳

type of plant: hardy shrub [5–8]
flowering time: early to mid-spring
flower color: white
height: 4–6ft/1.2–1.8m
Evergreen

Although it is much less colorful than varieties of pieris that have brilliant new leaf growth (for an example, see p.208), P. floribunda is a hardier plant. It grows quite slowly and has a more or less rounded outline. Its little, bell-shaped flowers are carried in erect sprays, about 5in/12cm long. They last well on the shrub and when cut and used in arrangements. Glossy, fairly slender leaves provide a good, dark background for these pale blooms. Lime-free soil that is moist and humus-rich is most suitable for this shrub but, as long as these ideal soil conditions are provided in the initial planting area, then P. floribunda grows well in heavy soil once established. A site sheltered from cold winds is advisable and this is a handsome shrub for a woodland garden.
also for: ■ Acid soils ■ Flowers suitable for cutting

Leucojum vernum
[spring snowflake]
◑

type of plant: hardy bulb [4–8]
flowering time: late winter to early spring
flower color: white + green
height: 6–8in/15–20cm

Spring snowflake does well in almost any moisture-retentive soil; it thrives in woodland conditions. Some people find that the flowers smell unattractively like hawthorn blossom, while to others the fragrance seems sweet and pure. Each 1in/2.5cm-long, bell-shaped bloom has pretty, green tips to its petals. There is usually just one flower to each stem. The strap-like leaves are glossy and a brighter, yellower green than this illustration would suggest. They lengthen after the flowers have faded.
also for: ■ Fragrant flowers (see above) ■ Winter-flowering plants

Anemone nemorosa
[anemone]
◑

type of plant: hardy tuber [5–9]
flowering time: mid- to late spring
flower color: white or pink-flushed white
height: 6in/15cm

Moist, humus-rich soils are ideal, but this vigorous and remarkably adaptable little plant grows well in heavy soils and it tolerates quite dry conditions, too. It prefers alkaline conditions and succeeds on shallow, chalky soils. It is, perhaps, especially attractive when naturalized in grass among deciduous trees and shrubs. By midsummer the ferny, divided leaves have died down completely. Popular varieties include *A. nemorosa* "Robinsoniana" and *A.n.* "Allenii," both of which have lavender-blue flowers (*A.n.* "Allenii" is the more vigorous of the two plants and better in dry shade). There are also some double-flowered varieties. The flowers of all these plants are not usually more than about 1in/2.5cm wide.
also for: ■ Shallow soils over chalk ■ Dry shade

Pulmonaria angustifolia
[blue cowslip, blue lungwort]
◑●

type of plant: hardy perennial [3–8]
flowering time: early to late spring
flower color: bright royal-blue
height: 9in/23cm

This pulmonaria's clumps of foliage, each 12–18in/30–45cm wide, form substantial, spreading patches of growth in a cool, moist spot. Clusters of ½in/1cm-wide, funnel-shaped flowers, reddish in bud, open in succession and the plant is in bloom for almost all of spring. Slender, dark green leaves lengthen to approximately 9in/23cm after flowering time. Though it is a tolerant and robust plant, *P. angustifolia* needs moisture-retentive soil and some shade in order to grow well. *P.a.* subsp. *azurea* has flowers of a particularly intense blue, while those of *P.a.* "Munstead Blue" are slightly deeper in color than the flowers of the species.
also for: ■ Ground cover ■ Long, continuous flowering period

ADDITIONAL PLANTS, featured elsewhere in this book, that are suitable for heavy clay soils

◑ partial shade

minimum height 3ft/90cm or less
Brunnera macrophylla "Hadspen Cream," see p.179
Galanthus nivalis, see p.320
Hosta undulata var. *albomarginata*, see p.79

◑[◐]/◑● partial shade (or full shade)/partial or full shade

minimum height between 3ft/90cm and 10ft/3m
Astilboides tabularis, see p.232

minimum height 3ft/90cm or less
Aegopodium podagraria "Variegatum," see p.122
Bergenia cordifolia, see p.228
Bergenia "Silberlicht," see p.115
Brunnera macrophylla, see p.122
Dryopteris filix-mas, see p.81
Hedera helix "Congesta," see p.228
Hosta sieboldiana var. *elegans*, see p.196
Lamium galeobdolon "Hermann's Pride," see p.83
Lamium maculatum "Aureum," see p.217
Lamium maculatum "Beacon Silver," see p.84
Lamium maculatum "Roseum," see p.124

Lamium maculatum "White Nancy," see p.181
Mahonia aquifolium, see p.122
Pachyphragma macrophyllum, see p.122
Polygonatum x hybridum, see p.295
Pulmonaria longifolia, see p.180
Pulmonaria rubra "David Ward," see p.181
Pulmonaria rubra "Redstart," see p.321
Pulmonaria saccharata Argentea Group, see p.181
Pulmonaria "Sissinghurst White," see p.123
Sasa veitchii, see p.113
Symphytum ibericum, see p.123
Trachystemon orientalis, see p.83

Dry soils in hot, sunny sites

MANY PLANTS APPRECIATE a position in sunshine, but not all sun-loving plants can withstand hot, dry conditions and periods of drought. Fast-draining sandy soils, shallow soils over chalk, and poor, stony soils can all be sufficiently hot and dry to cause serious problems for some plants. Steep, south-facing slopes, beds at the foot of sunny, sheltered walls, and some windy sites, for example, are all potential trouble spots, and any problems with heat and dryness tend to be exacerbated in sites such as these.

However, there are numerous plants that revel in hot, dry conditions. When appropriately planted, dry, sunny sites can be very floriferous places where plants become established remarkably quickly and where they often flower earlier than usual each year. For example, many grasses and most gray-leaved plants are at their very best in dry, sunny sites.

Plants that do well in hot, dry sites have adapted themselves, in various ways, to cope with the exigencies of heat and drought. Many of these adaptations are highly decorative. For instance, some plants have hairy leaves. The hairs help to protect the surface of the leaf from becoming desiccated and they also produce various, attractive textures: hairy leaves can be woolly, felted or silky. In the present list, the large, woolly leaves of silver sage (*Salvia argentea*) are outstanding. There are numerous, additional examples of hairy-leaved plants in "Plants with gray, blue-gray, or silver leaves" (pp.182–96), including woolly thyme (*Thymus pseudolanuginosus*) and the familiar lambs' ears (*Stachys byzantina*).

Some plants have developed thick, fleshy leaves in order to retain moisture and to prevent desiccation: houseleeks (*Sempervivum*), which do so well in dry stone walls, are examples of plants with this sort of foliage. Some popular, little stonecrops, such as *Sedum spathulifolium* "Cape Blanco," produce succulent foliage, and *Euphorbia myrsinites* is a particularly stylish, small plant with fleshy leaves.

The development of tiny or narrow leaves is another moisture-conserving adaptation. When only very limited areas of leaf surface are exposed to sun and wind, relatively little evaporation can take place. Small- or narrow-leaved plants in this list include *Lavandula angustifolia* "Loddon Pink," *Penstemon pinifolius*, and *Gypsophila repens* "Rosea." Some plants carry this survival strategy one stage further by having few leaves at all (see *Spartium junceum* on the following page).

Finally, most plants with aromatic foliage can withstand strong sun and lack of moisture. This is because the oils contained in their leaves become volatile in heat and produce a protective haze around the vulnerable leaf surfaces, thereby preventing the whole plant from becoming desiccated. Aromatic plants in this list include lavender (*Lavandula*), rosemary (*Rosmarinus*), and *Artemisia*; the "Aromatic foliage" list (see pp.244–51) also contains numerous plants that thrive in hot, dry conditions.

If large quantities of moisture-retaining materials, such as garden compost and leaf mold, are added to the soil, then hot and rather arid sites can support a wider range of plants than appears here. However, a better, long-term approach—especially in areas of consistently low rainfall—is to use plants that are tolerant of these conditions.

It is also worth bearing in mind that a good covering of foliage can do much to reduce the loss of moisture from soil (as well as this list, see also the "Ground Cover" list, pp.104–25, for various dense, leafy plants that are suitable for hot, dry soils). For inspiring accounts of making and maintaining dry and gravel gardens, see *The Dry Garden* (Dent, 1978) and *Beth Chatto's Gravel Garden* (Frances Lincoln, 2000), both by Beth Chatto.

Plants that thrive in fast-draining soil and a sunny site beside the sea are not always suitable for hot, dry sites inland, where the level of ambient humidity may be considerably lower.

Genista aetnensis
[Mount Etna broom]
○

type of plant: slightly tender/hardy shrub/tree [8–10]
flowering time: mid- to late summer
flower color: bright yellow
height: 15–20ft/4.5–6m

This plant's open structure of pendulous branches and rush-like, green twigs is filled, from midsummer, with masses of hanging, vanilla-scented blossom. Each pea-flower is only about ½in/1cm long. Light, rather poor soil that drains quickly is ideal; on richer soils this shrub does not flower very freely. Older specimens are often particularly interesting and idiosyncratic in shape but they may also be unstable. Such instability is most likely to be a problem on really light, sandy soil, and mature plants there may need support. Mount Etna broom has virtually no leaves.
also for: ■ Atmospheric pollution ■ Fragrant flowers

Elaeagnus "Quicksilver"
(syn. *E. angustifolia* Caspica Group)
[oleaster, Russian olive]
○

type of plant: hardy shrub/tree [3–9]
flowering time: early summer
flower color: creamy yellow
height: 10–15ft/3–4.5m

The silvery green, matt-textured foliage of this fast-growing plant is its most obvious attraction. Each elegantly tapering leaf is about 4in/10cm long. The starry flowers, though only ½in/1cm long and subdued in coloring, exude a wonderfully rich and sweet scent. *E.* "Quicksilver" produces a fairly loose, bushy, pyramidal head of growth. The plant can be trained on a single stem. It sometimes suckers. It thrives in hot, dry soils, provided they are not very alkaline. *E.* "Quicksilver" is one of the hardiest gray-leaved plants, and its resistance to wind and salt spray makes it useful in an exposed, seaside garden.
also for: ■ Windswept, seaside gardens ■ Gray, blue-gray, or silver leaves ■ Fragrant flowers

Spartium junceum
[Spanish broom]
○

type of plant: slightly tender/hardy shrub [8–11]
flowering time: early summer to early autumn
flower color: yellow
height: 7–10ft/2.1–3m

Spanish broom grows quickly and has a tendency to become lanky with age. Sharply draining soil, full sun and an annual trimming of the upright, rush-like twigs all help to produce bushy plants. Strong winds, including salty sea gales, also encourage dense growth. The plant thrives in chalky soils. Its numerous pea-flowers, each about 1in/2.5cm long, open in succession over a period of many weeks. They exude a rich, sweet scent. The tiny leaves are only very sparsely produced.
also for: ■ Shallow soils over chalk ■ Windswept, seaside gardens ■ Atmospheric pollution ■ Ornamental bark or twigs ■ Fragrant flowers ■ Long, continuous flowering period

Stipa gigantea
[giant feather grass, golden oats]
○

type of plant: hardy perennial (grass) [6–9]
flowering time: early to late summer
flower color: purplish ripening to golden yellow
height: 6–8ft/1.8–2.4m
Evergreen/Semi-evergreen

Despite its impressive size, this magnificent grass does not need staking. Ideally, giant feather grass should have a dark background to ensure that its haze of oat-like seed heads is conspicuous. These erect-stemmed inflorescences are up to 18in/45cm long. They remain attractive well into winter in the garden, and they can also be dried for indoor decoration. The thin, lax, mid-green leaves create a weed-proof clump of growth about 24in/60cm high. Medium to fairly light soil with good drainage is most suitable for this grass, which tolerates periods of drought.
also for: ■ Ground cover ■ Ornamental fruit (seedheads) ■ Flowers suitable for cutting (and drying)

Ceanothus x delileanus "Gloire de Versailles"
[California lilac]
○

type of plant: hardy shrub [7–10]
flowering time: midsummer to mid-autumn
flower color: soft powder-blue
height: 5–7ft/1.5–2.1m

In milder climates, deciduous California lilacs do not need the protection of a sunny wall—although, given such shelter, they flourish and grow 10–12ft/3–3.6m high. Provided the site is not exposed, they are quite suitable for an open bed or border. *C.* x *delileanus* "Gloire de Versailles" produces a lengthy succession of slightly fragrant flower clusters, about 4in/10cm long, among large, mid-green, oval leaves. It has an open, fairly upright habit of growth. Well-drained soils of most sorts are suitable, although growth is not good on shallow, chalky soils. Light, dry soil produces good results, as long as young plants are watered in their first season. Similar, deciduous California lilacs include *C.* x *d.* "Topaze," which has dark blue flowers, and pale pink *C.* x *pallidus* "Marie Simon."
also for: ■ Atmospheric pollution ■ Long, continuous flowering period

Lespedeza thunbergii
[bush clover]
○

type of plant: hardy shrub/perennial [6–9]
flowering time: late summer to early autumn
flower color: rose-purple
height: 5ft/1.5m

The long, loose branches of this subshrub bear tripartite, bright blue-green leaves and numerous, hanging sprays of pea-flowers. Each flower is very small but the sprays can be up to 6in/15cm long. *L. thunbergii* has a slightly ungainly habit of growth, and often looks best when grown on a sunny bank. It is, typically, nearly twice as wide as it is tall. In cold climates, the plant dies back in winter and new shoots do not appear until late spring. *L. thunbergii* grows best in light, well-drained soil, and it flourishes in a dry, sunny site.

Asphodeline lutea
(syn. *Asphodelus luteus*)
[Jacob's rod, king's spear, yellow asphodel]
○

type of plant: hardy perennial [6–8]
flowering time: late spring to early summer
flower color: yellow
height: 3–4ft/0.9–1.2m

Long, thin, blue-green leaves clothe the erect stems of *A. lutea* and also form grassy, basal clumps. Each stem is topped with numerous, densely packed, starry flowers, about 1¼in/3cm across. They have a slight, sweet scent and are followed by large, globular, shiny green seed pods, which make interesting material, either fresh or dried, for cutting. The plant needs well-drained soil and a warm position. It flourishes in a dry, sunny site. Although this plant should not be parched at flowering time, it is able to withstand periods of drought later. *A. liburnica* has paler yellow flowers that are produced slightly later; it is about 36in/90cm tall.
also for: ■ Gray, blue-gray, or silver leaves ■ Ornamental fruit (seed pods) ■ Flowers suitable for cutting (and drying)

Yucca filamentosa
[Adam's needle]
○

type of plant: hardy shrub [4–9]
flowering time: mid- to late summer
flower color: creamy white
height: 24–30in/60–75cm foliage height; 4–6ft/1.2–1.8m flower height
Evergreen

Adam's needle is at its best in dry climates and in really well-drained soil. It is a good deal more free-flowering than many other yuccas. To prevent its magnificent, 36in/90cm spikes of tulip-shaped flowers from damage, a site sheltered from strong winds should be chosen. Its green or bluish green leaves are almost as dramatic as its flowers: they are stiff and sword-shaped and arranged in a bold, dense clump. Their edges are decorated, to a greater or lesser extent, with numerous, curly threads. *Y. filamentosa* "Bright Edge" has leaves with bright yellow margins; it flowers less reliably than the species and is a smaller plant. *Y.f.* "Ivory" is another readily available, green-leaved yucca that flowers freely.
also for: ■ Growing in containers ■ Decorative, green foliage

Leymus arenarius
(syn. *Elymus arenarius*)
○

type of plant: hardy perennial (grass) [4–9]
flowering time: mid- to late summer
flower color: blue-gray ripening to buff
height: 4–5ft/1.2–1.5m

This "blue" grass is quite different from the stiff, tufted fescues (see, for example, *Festuca glauca*, p.188). Its pale blue-gray leaves are broader and they arch. The flower spikes, each about 12in/30cm long, stand clear of the loose, 24in/60cm-high clumps of foliage; they dry well. *L. arenarius* is a native of the seashore and at home in light, sandy soil. In these conditions, it is very vigorous indeed and too invasive for a small garden. Its running roots are, however, useful for stabilizing light soil in a hot, dry position. In most garden settings it is best to confine the roots to a pot.
also for: ■ Gray, blue-gray, or silver leaves ■ Flowers suitable for cutting (and drying)

Cytisus x *praecox*
e.g. "Warminster"
[Warminster broom]
○

type of plant: hardy shrub [6–9]
flowering time: mid- to late spring
flower color: pale yellow
height: 4ft/1.2m

The slender, green branches of quick-growing Warminster broom create an attractive, rounded, spreading shape throughout the year, but when they become covered with ½in/1cm-long pea-flowers, the effect is quite spectacular. Unfortunately, this great arching sheaf of blossom has a heavy, acrid smell. *C. x praecox* and its varieties are easily grown in quite a wide range of soils, although very alkaline conditions are not suitable. They are particularly successful in really well-drained, rather infertile soil. Unless they are pruned lightly after flowering, they soon become gaunt and lanky. Their thin, light green leaves are short-lived. For a low-growing broom with pale yellow flowers, see p.107. *C. x p.* "Allgold" is shown on p.97.
also for: ■ Atmospheric pollution ■ Ornamental bark or twigs

Caragana arborescens "Walker"
[Siberian pea tree]
○

type of plant: hardy tree [3–8]
flowering time: late spring
flower color: pale yellow
height: 3–6ft/0.9–1.8m (see description)

The light green, feathery leaves of this tree do not develop fully until late spring but, even when it is leafless, this is a striking plant. Its stiffly pendulous branches form an unusually neat and narrow "bell" of weeping growth. Except in climates with hot, dry summers, the clusters of pale yellow pea-flowers are not very numerous. Each flower is about ¾in/2cm long. As well as being very hardy, this little tree is wind-resistant, tolerant of poor and very alkaline soils and able to withstand drought. It thrives on all soils with good drainage. *C. arborescens* "Walker" may be grafted on to a clear stem, and its height then depends on the size of the stem used when grafted. For other, small, weeping trees see pp.14, 65 and 96.
also for: ■ Shallow soils over chalk ■ Growing in containers

Teucrium fruticans
[shrubby germander, tree germander]
○

type of plant: slightly tender shrub [7–10]
flowering time: early summer to early autumn (see description)
flower color: pale blue
height: 3–5ft/0.9–1.5m
Evergreen

Only in mild areas can this rather sparsely branched shrub be grown in an open position. Elsewhere it needs shelter and warmth. Its neat, pointed, gray leaves and its 1in/2.5cm-long, lipped flowers are carried on pale gray stems. The foliage has a sharp but attractive scent when crushed. Flowering takes place in a series of flushes with scatterings of blooms in between. Both *T. fruticans* and darker-flowered *T.f.* "Azureum" require light, rather dry soil. In warm climates, shrubby germander is used for hedging; young plants should be about 30in/75cm apart.
also for: ■ Hedging plants (see above) ■ Gray, blue-gray, or silver leaves ■ Aromatic foliage

Ulex europaeus "Flore Pleno"
(syn. *U.e.* "Plenus")
[gorse, furze, whin]
○

type of plant: hardy shrub [7–9]
flowering time: usually early to late spring; intermittently during rest of year
flower color: yellow
height: 3–4ft/0.9–1.2m
Evergreen

When difficult, arid sites need to be planted, this free-flowering, tough plant is a good choice. Its ferociously spined, thorny-leaved branches are fairly upright. The plant has a rounded outline overall. Especially on warm days, the little, double pea-flowers, each about ¾in/2cm long, emit a coconut-like fragrance. Rich and very alkaline soils are not suitable for this shrub but it thrives in sandy soil in a windswept, seaside garden. With young plants set about 24in/60cm apart, it makes a dense, impenetrable hedge. Unlike the species, this double-flowered variety does not self-sow.
also for: ■ Acid soils ■ Windswept, seaside gardens ■ Atmospheric pollution ■ Hedging plants ■ Fragrant flowers ■ Long, continuous flowering period

Eryngium giganteum
[Miss Willmott's ghost, sea holly, eryngo]
○

type of plant: hardy biennial [6–9]
flowering time: late summer to early autumn
flower color: blue
height: 36in/90cm

From a rosette of heart-shaped, green leaves, *E. giganteum* produces stiff, branching stems that are almost white. The stems carry barrel-shaped flower heads, each about 2½in/6cm high, surrounded by impressively jagged, pale gray bracts. The whole ensemble looks striking right from when the immature, silvery green flower heads first take shape until the plant turns into an eye-catching "skeleton" in autumn. Though this plant dies after flowering once, it often self-sows freely—particularly in the fast-draining soils and dry, sunny places it likes best. It makes excellent, long-lasting material for cutting and it dries well, too.
also for: ■ Flowers suitable for cutting (and drying)

Stipa calamagrostis
[feather grass, needle grass, spear grass]
○

type of plant: hardy perennial (grass) [6–10]
flowering time: midsummer to early autumn
flower color: pale green ripening to buff
height: 36in/90cm

Since they are denser than the flower heads of many other grasses, the feathery plumes of *S. calamagrostis* are impressive, even in small numbers, in a mixed planting. The plumes, each up to 12in/30cm long, remain decorative, as seedheads, during the winter months. They sway above a thick but rather untidy clump of thin, bluish green leaves. If they are cut when fully ripened, the flower heads last well when dried. This is one of the most attractive and free-flowering grasses for light, well-drained soils.
also for: ■ Ornamental fruit (seedheads) ■ Flowers suitable for cutting (and drying)

Cistus x hybridus
(syn. *C.* x *corbariensis*)
[rock rose, sun rose]
○

type of plant: slightly tender/hardy shrub [7–10]
flowering time: early to midsummer
flower color: white + yellow
height: 30–36in/75–90cm
Evergreen

When grown in light soil that drains rapidly and given an open and really sunny position, C. x hybridus quickly forms a broad hummock of soft green, felted, wavy leaves. Its numerous, crimson-budded flowers, each about 1½in/4cm across, open in succession over several weeks. The toughest rock rose in cultivation is generally considered to be C. laurifolius [zones 7–10]; it has pure white flowers, up to twice the size of those of C. x hybridus. It may grow up to 6ft/1.8m tall. Both these shrubs thrive in windy, seaside gardens and, as long as conditions are not extremely alkaline, they do well on shallow, chalky soils, too. They are not long-lived plants.
also for: ■ Shallow soils over chalk ■ Atmospheric pollution ■ Ground cover

Eryngium x tripartitum
[sea holly, eryngo]
○

type of plant: hardy perennial [5–8]
flowering time: mid- to late summer
flower color: violet-blue
height: 30–36in/75–90cm

E. x tripartitum tends to sprawl untidily in fertile and moist soils. General growth is much more satisfactory, and flower color is often especially good, in soils that are light and well drained. The plant flourishes in dry conditions and tolerates periods of drought well. Its slender, branching flower stems rise from basal rosettes of dark green, wedge-shaped leaves. Although the globular flowers are small (about ½in/1cm in diameter), they are numerous and each flower is made more conspicuous by the long, thin bracts surrounding it. E. planum also produces numerous, little flowers, and several especially well-colored varieties of this species are available, including, for example, E.p. "Blaukappe." All these plants are useful for cutting and they may also be dried.
also for: ■ Flowers suitable for cutting (and drying)

Salvia argentea
[silver sage]
○

type of plant: hardy perennial/biennial [5–9]
flowering time: mid- to late summer
flower color: white
height: 30–36in/75–90cm

Before this plant produces its little, lipped flowers on their wide-branching stems, its leaves are particularly silvery and woolly. After the flowers have faded, the foliage is less remarkable. Each broad, toothed basal leaf is up to 8in/20cm long, and the foliage can build into a mounded rosette more than 24in/60cm wide. S. argentea often dies once it has flowered, but its life can be prolonged by pinching out the flowering shoots before they develop. The plant thrives in very well-drained soil and a really sunny site.
also for: ■ Shallow soils over chalk ■ Gray, blue-gray, or silver leaves

Verbascum chaixii "Album"
[nettle-leaved mullein]
○

type of plant: hardy perennial [5–9]
flowering time: mid- to late summer
flower color: white + maroon
height: 30–36in/75–90cm
Semi-evergreen

The strikingly upright flower spikes of this verbascum are densely packed with 1in/2.5cm-wide, saucer-shaped blooms. The spires of flowers rise above hairy, rather dark green leaves that are long and pointed. The foliage is arranged in rosettes. V. chaixii itself has yellow flowers with purple "eyes." Both the species and V.c. "Album" self-sow readily in the well-drained, preferably alkaline and rather infertile soils that they like best. Both plants are drought-tolerant. For a pink-flowered verbascum, see p.336, and for a verbascum with all-yellow flowers, see p.15.
also for: ■ Shallow soils over chalk

Halimium lasianthum
○

type of plant: slightly tender/half-hardy shrub [8–9]
flowering time: late spring to early summer
flower color: golden yellow + dark chocolate-maroon
height: 24–36in/60–90cm
Evergreen

H. lasianthum displays a lovely, warm combination of yellow and dark chocolate-maroon in its petals. It flowers freely, especially in hot, dry climates. Each saucer-shaped bloom is about 1in/2.5cm across. The leaves are gray-green with paler undersides and the overall effect is soft and grayish. H. lasianthum is a branching, spreading plant, often more than twice as wide as it is high. H. ocymoides is similar but more upright in its habit of growth. Both plants need very well-drained soil and full sun. They thrive on dry, sunny banks and in seaside gardens.
also for: ■ Ground cover ■ Growing in containers ■ Gray, blue-gray, or silver leaves

Artemisia "Powis Castle"
○

type of plant: slightly tender perennial/shrub [6–10]

height: 24–30in/60–75cm

Evergreen/Semi-evergreen

Since this artemisia flowers only rarely, its wide mound of deeply cut, silvery foliage remains neat and its stems stay tidy. The leaves, each 2½in/6cm long, have an attractive, pungent scent and they create an elegant tracery of pale gray that flatters many other plants. A. "Powis Castle" flourishes and is hardiest in sharply drained soil and a really sunny site, but most well-drained soils are suitable. In areas with cold winters, its top growth may be damaged.

also for: ■ Ground cover ■ Gray, blue-gray, or silver leaves ■ Aromatic foliage

Cistus x argenteus "Silver Pink"
(syn. C. "Silver Pink")
[rock rose, sun rose]
○

type of plant: slightly tender shrub [8–10]

flowering time: early to midsummer

flower color: soft pale pink

height: 24–30in/60–75cm

Evergreen

Against its dark, grayish, slender leaves, the pale flower sprays of this shrub look especially pretty. Each saucer-shaped flower is about 3in/8cm wide and, although individual blooms only last one day, numerous buds open in succession. C. x argenteus "Silver Pink" is bushy but fairly open in habit of growth; it is usually a little wider than it is tall. Like all rock roses, it appreciates really good drainage, rather poor soil and plenty of sun. It withstands salty winds well. Other popular rock roses with light pink flowers include C. "Grayswood Pink" (with which the larger-flowered C. x a. "Silver Pink" is often confused); there are also white- and bright pink-flowered forms (see pp.55 and 91).

also for: ■ Shallow soils over chalk ■ Atmospheric pollution

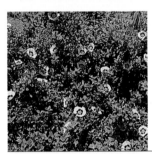

x Halimiocistus wintonensis
(syn. Cistus wintonenis, Halimium wintonensis)
"Merrist Wood Cream"
○

type of plant: slightly tender/hardy shrub [8–9]

flowering time: late spring to early summer

flower color: creamy yellow + dark maroon + yellow

height: 18–24in/45–60cm

Evergreen

Each delightfully delineated, 2in/5cm-wide flower produced by this shrub lasts only a very short time but, especially in regions with hot, dry summers, there are very numerous buds that open in succession. x H. wintonensis "Merrist Wood Cream" revels in dry, rather infertile soil and full sun. It makes a spreading hummock of growth, typically rather wider than it is high. The young leaves in particular are soft and gray; the older foliage is darker and gray-green. x H. wintonensis is also readily available; its flowers are white with maroon markings. For the long-flowering x H. sahucii, see p.339.

also for: ■ Gray, blue-gray, or silver leaves

Tulbaghia violacea
[pink agapanthus, society garlic, sweet garlic]
○

type of plant: slightly tender perennial [8–10]

flowering time: midsummer to early autumn

flower color: pale lilac-mauve to lilac

height: 18–24in/45–60cm

Semi-evergreen

Once established in a really warm, sunny position and in soil that drains sharply, this drought-resistant plant forms substantial clumps. Its elegant, slightly scented, trumpet-shaped flowers, arranged in heads about 4in/10cm wide, are carried on strong stems. The slender, grayish leaves of T. violacea smell strongly of onions when bruised. T.v. "Silver Lace" (syn. "Variegata") has gray foliage that is striped in palest cream. Since these plants have corm-like underground stems, they are often available from bulb specialists.

Lavandula angustifolia
e.g. "Loddon Pink"
[lavender]
○

type of plant: hardy shrub [6–9]

flowering time: midsummer

flower color: soft pink

height: 18in/45cm

Evergreen

As well as the familiar blue- and purple-flowered lavenders, there are varieties—such as L. angustifolia "Loddon Pink"—with pink flowers. A few white-flowered forms (e.g. L.a. "Nana Alba") are also available. L.a. "Loddon Pink" grows quickly and forms a neat, rounded mass of long stems, narrow leaves and short flower spikes. Both the foliage and the flowers have the typical, "clean" scent of lavender, and the flowers are very attractive to bees. The leaves have a grayish cast to them. Sharply drained soil and hot, dry situations are especially suitable for all these lavenders. They can be used to make dwarf hedges (young plants should be about 12in/30cm apart).

also for: ■ Hedging plants ■ Gray, blue-gray, or silver leaves ■ Aromatic foliage ■ Fragrant flowers

Allium cristophii
(syn. A. albopilosum)
○

type of plant: hardy/slightly tender bulb [7–9]
flowering time: early summer
flower color: pale mauve
height: 12–24in/30–60cm

The stout-stalked, globular flower heads of A. cristophii can be up to 10in/25cm in diameter. Individual flowers are star-shaped. When dried, some purplish coloring is retained in the stalks of the individual florets and the whole head keeps its shape well. The leaves are gray-green and strap-shaped. Usually, they have more or less completely withered by flowering time. A. cristophii is easily grown in all fertile, well-drained soils and it thrives in hot, dry conditions.
also for: ■ Flowers suitable for cutting (and drying)

Antirrhinum majus
e.g. "Sweetheart"
[snapdragon]
○

type of plant: grown as half-hardy annual [8–10]
flowering time: midsummer to mid-autumn
flower color: mixed—white, yellow, orange, pink, red
height: 12in/30cm

Dwarf varieties of snapdragon, including double-flowered A. majus "Sweetheart," are quite suitable for light, dry soil. Under such conditions, their flowers may be rather small (not much more than ³⁄₄in/2cm long), but they will be numerous and they will appear over a long period. Rust disease affects many snapdragons but A.m. "Sweetheart" is a particularly resistant variety. It is bushy and its deep green leaves are slim, pointed and glossy. For an example of a tall snapdragon, see p.275.

Dimorphotheca sinuata Hybrids
[star of the veldt]
○

type of plant: half-hardy/hardy annual [8–10]
flowering time: midsummer to early autumn
flower color: mixed—white, lemon, orange, salmon, cream
height: 12in/30cm

In warm gardens, D. sinuata Hybrids can be treated as hardy annuals and sown, in late spring, where they are to flower. They need light, dryish soil, and they flourish in sandy soil. Their flowers are carried on upright stems well above the bushy, spreading mass of slender, pungently scented leaves. The 1½in/4cm-wide daisies close in shade and during dull weather. It is, therefore, best to give the plants as sunny a position as possible. In some seed catalogs D. sinuata Hybrids may be incorrectly listed under D. aurantiaca.

Osteospermum jucundum
(syn. Dimorphotheca barberae, O. barberae)
○

type of plant: slightly tender perennial [8–10]
flowering time: early summer to mid-autumn
flower color: variable—pink to magenta-purple, purplish on reverse
height: 12in/30cm
Evergreen

The numerous daisies of this long-flowering perennial are each about 2in/5cm wide. They are carried on fairly upright stems above spreading clumps of slender, often grayish leaves. The foliage is strongly and rather unpleasantly scented. O. jucundum grows especially densely in light soil and in a warm, sunny, sheltered site. In these conditions it survives almost all winters in milder regions. O. "Lady Leitrim" is another popular Osteospermum that is reasonably hardy [zones 9–10], given favorable conditions; its flowers are white with pink markings. For a yellow-flowered variety, see p.339. A variety with variegated foliage is shown on p.166. Osteospermum need full sun for their flowers to open wide. They often flower particularly well by the sea.
also for: ■ Ground cover ■ Long, continuous flowering period

Iris e.g. "Cherry Garden"
(Standard Dwarf Bearded)
○

type of plant: hardy perennial [4–9]
flowering time: mid- to late spring
flower color: maroon-plum
height: 10–12in/25–30cm

Among the widely grown bearded irises, it is the smaller cultivars—such as I. "Cherry Garden," and also I. "Blue Denim" (see following page)—that most appreciate hot, dry conditions. These charming, sturdy, little plants are at home in sharply drained soil and really sunny sites. Their flowers are 2–3in/5–8cm wide and they are usually held just above the grayish or light green, sword-shaped leaves. I. "Cherry Garden" is a popular variety with richly colored blooms. As a further example of a variety with this sort of coloring, there is I. "Little Blackfoot" (very dark purple flowers). I. "Blue Denim" produces blue flowers, as do I. "Austrian Sky" and I. "Tinkerbell." In addition, there are dozens of standard dwarf bearded irises in shades of yellow, violet, purple-red and pale green, as well as white. Their flowers frequently have attractive markings or their petals are of contrasting colors.

Iris e.g. "Blue Denim"
(Standard Dwarf Bearded)
○

type of plant: hardy perennial [4–9]
flowering time: mid- to late spring
flower color: mid-blue
height: 10in/25cm

See preceding plant.

Tropaeolum
e.g. Whirlybird Series
[nasturtium]
○

type of plant: grown as hardy annual [10–11]
flowering time: early summer to mid-autumn
flower color: mixed—shades of red, yellow, orange, cream
height: 10in/25cm

Poor, dry soil encourages nasturtiums to flower well and to grow densely. In richer, moister conditions there can be a preponderance of foliage and the stems can be long and lax. *T.* Whirlybird Series produce single and semi-double, approximately funnel-shaped flowers, each about 2in/5cm wide. The flowers are held well above the bushy mound of pale, almost circular leaves. (The flowers of some varieties of nasturtium are partially hidden by foliage.) As well as mixtures of *T.* Whirlybird Series, some seed catalogs list separate colors of these very easily grown plants.
also for: ■ Ground cover

Penstemon pinifolius
○

type of plant: slightly tender/hardy perennial/shrub [8–10]
flowering time: early to late summer
flower color: bright orange-red
height: 9–12in/23–30cm
Evergreen

In really well-drained, gritty soil and full sun this little subshrub is very probably reliably hardy. Its crowd of fine, upright stems carries light green, needle-like leaves and loose spikes of narrow, tubular flowers, each about 1in/2.5cm long. *P. pinifolius* "Mersea Yellow" is slightly smaller and has bright yellow flowers. Both plants have an attractive, airy delicacy about them.
also for: ■ Long, continuous flowering period

Zauschneria californica "Dublin"
(syn. *Z.c.* "Glasnevin")
[California fuschia]
○

type of plant: slightly tender perennial [8–10]
flowering time: late summer to early autumn
flower color: bright red
height: 9–12in/23–30cm

The flowers of this popular variety of Californian fuschia are elegantly slender tubes of brilliant color. Each flower is about 1in/2.5cm long. Given a position in full sun and sharply drained soil, *Z. californica* "Dublin" flowers profusely and makes substantial clumps of growth above spreading, underground shoots. It looks particularly attractive in a dry stone wall. The little, hairy leaves of *Z. californica* "Dublin" are rich green; those of *Z.c.* "Olbrich Silver" are silvery gray.
also for: ■ Long, continuous flowering period

Eschscholzia californica
e.g. Thai Silk Series
[California poppy]
○

type of plant: grown as hardy annual [8–11]
flowering time: early summer to early autumn
flower color: mixed—yellow, red, orange, pink, cream
height: 9in/23cm

Apart from their masses of bright, silky blooms on erect stems, California poppies have decorative foliage which is blue-green or blue-gray and finely divided. *E. californica* Thai Silk Series produces single and semi-double flowers with fluted petals. They emerge from characteristically slender, long-pointed buds and, when fully open, are about 2½in/6cm wide. The largest number of flowers appear on plants grown on poor, fast-draining soil. In dull weather the flowers close up and, even on fine days, they are open during the lightest part of the day only.
also for: ■ Gray, blue-gray, or silver leaves

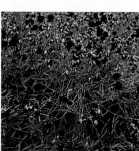

Helianthemum
e.g. "Mrs C.W. Earle"
(syn. *H.* "Fireball")
[rock rose, sun rose]
○

type of plant: hardy shrub [6–9]
flowering time: late spring to midsummer
flower color: deep red
height: 9in/23cm
Evergreen

Double-flowered varieties of sun rose, such as *H.* "Mrs C.W. Earle," retain their petals until evening, while the blooms of single-flowered varieties have normally disintegrated by early afternoon. All sun rose flowers are small—usually about 1in/2.5cm wide—but they are very numerous and they open in succession. In full sun and very well-drained soil most of these plants make dense, spreading hummocks of growth that are effective ground cover. *H.* "Mrs C.W. Earle" has very narrow, deep green leaves. Some varieties produce gray leaves (see, for example, p.189). Other double-flowered varieties include *H.* "Jubilee" (yellow) and *H.* "Rose of Leeswood" (pink).
also for: ■ Ground cover ■ Crevices in paving

Linaria maroccana
e.g. "Fairy Bouquet"
[toadflax]
○

type of plant: hardy annual [6–10]
flowering time: early summer to early autumn
flower color: mixed—violet, blue, red, pink, yellow + contrasting colors on "lips"
height: 9in/23cm

This upright, branching plant flowers freely in most well-drained soils. However, L. maroccana "Fairy Bouquet" is at its best where drainage is really good, and it is quite suitable for hot and rather dry conditions. It can be grown in crevices in a wall. Its numerous flowers are like miniature versions of snapdragons (Antirrhinum); each one is only about ½in/1cm long. The narrow little leaves are light green. This easy plant grows quickly and usually self-sows freely.

Rosmarinus officinalis Prostratus Group (syn. R. lavandulaceus)
[rosemary]
○

type of plant: half-hardy/slightly tender shrub (herb) [9–10]
flowering time: late spring to early summer
flower color: lavender-blue
height: 6–18in/15–45cm (see description)
Evergreen

Plants in the R. officinalis Prostratus Group are variable. Typically, their arching branches and masses of narrow, warmly aromatic leaves form mounds of growth, but these can be quite loose or very dense. The plants look especially attractive growing on steep slopes, or spilling down walls from a raised bed (as in this illustration). Light, dry soil and plenty of sun encourages dense growth and the production of numerous ½in/1cm-long, lipped flowers. In these conditions the plants may well survive short periods of temperatures just below freezing point. R.o. "McConnell's Blue" is another readily available, prostrate rosemary.
also for: ■ Ground cover (see above) ■ Aromatic foliage

Lobularia maritima
(syn. Alyssum maritimum)
e.g. "Snow Crystals"
[sweet alyssum]
○

type of plant: hardy annual [7–10]
flowering time: early to late summer
flower color: white
height: 6in/15cm

Only the white-flowered varieties of L. maritima are quite as sweetly honey-scented as the species; the darker varieties have little or no fragrance. All varieties bloom profusely and those with pale flowers, in particular, are attractive to butterflies. These plants grow well in a sunny place and in light soil; they are particularly at home in a seaside garden. L.m. "Snow Crystals" makes a neat mound of narrow, grayish leaves and 1½in/4cm-wide flower heads. For an example of a dark-flowered variety, see p.18.
also for: ■ Shallow soils over chalk ■ Crevices in paving ■ Fragrant flowers

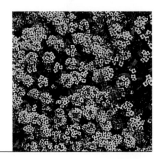

Portulaca grandiflora
e.g. Sundial Series
[rose moss, purslane]
○

type of plant: half-hardy/tender annual [10–11]
flowering time: midsummer to early autumn
flower color: mixed—yellow, white, red, pink, orange, cream, apricot
height: 6in/15cm

Dry, rather poor soil and a warm site are suitable for this drought-resistant plant. Its spreading stems are dark soft red and, with the slim, fleshy, bright green leaves, they form mats of growth about 6in/15cm wide. The flowers, each 1½–2in/4–5cm or more wide, are like little, semi-double roses. They close, at least partially, in dull weather. Even though P. grandiflora Sundial Series plants perform better in cool climates than most varieties, they produce relatively few flowers in cool, wet summers.

Silene uniflora
(syn. S. maritima, S. vulgaris subsp. maritima)
e.g. "Robin Whitebreast"
(syn. "Flore Pleno")
[campion, catchfly]
○

type of plant: hardy perennial [4–9]
flowering time: mainly early to midsummer
flower color: white
height: 6in/15cm
Semi-evergreen

The lower growths of S. uniflora "Robin Whitebreast" are prostrate and clothed in neat, pointed, gray-green leaves. The flowering stems are upright and branching. When the deeply cut petals of the 1in/2.5cm-wide, double flowers have faded, the intriguing, little, inflated parts beneath them remain. S. uniflora "Druett's Variegated" is a smaller, less vigorous, single-flowered variety that has leaves that are edged in cream. These deep-rooted plants are well adapted to dry, sharply drained soil, but they grow in almost any soil with good drainage.
also for: ■ Gray, blue-gray, or silver leaves

Tulipa linifolia
[tulip]
○

type of plant: hardy bulb [5–9]
flowering time: mid- to late spring
flower color: scarlet
height: 6in/15cm

The bright flowers of this tulip begin to open when they are still nestling among the slim, gray-green leaves of the plant. As they develop, they rise above the foliage and then, if it is sunny, they open wide—to about 3in/8cm across—and the black base of each conspicuously shining petal is revealed. Even half-open, as shown here, or in green-tinged bud, the flowers are beautifully and precisely shaped. *T. linifolia* is at its very best in dry, stony soil and where it can receive plenty of summer warmth.

Tulipa tarda
[tulip]
○

type of plant: hardy bulb [5–9]
flowering time: mid-spring
flower color: yellow + white
height: 6in/15cm

Each of this tulip's stems may carry as many as six flowers. When fully expanded from their cream-and-green buds, the distinctively marked, star-shaped blooms are usually about 2in/5cm wide. The leaves are long and slender and a soft, slightly gray green. Full sun and sharply drained soil give the best results but *T. tarda* persists and spreads in a wide range of soils.

Dianthus
e.g. "Pike's Pink"
[carnation, pink]
○

type of plant: hardy perennial [4–8]
flowering time: early to late summer
flower color: pale pink + pink
height: 4in/10cm
Evergreen

Hybrid alpine pinks, such as *D.* "Pike's Pink," like really good drainage and they have a preference for alkaline soils. They are short-lived but very floriferous plants. *D.* "Pike's Pink" produces masses of double to semi-double flowers, each about 1in/2.5cm wide and deliciously clove-scented. The largest number of flowers are borne in early to midsummer, but there are always some flowers toward the end of the season as well. The crowded, gray-green leaves are narrow and pointed. They form mats of growth. Other hybrid alpine pinks include short-stemmed *D.* "Little Jock" (mauve-pink), *D.* "Dewdrop" (white with yellow-green edges) and *D.* "Fusilier" (red). *D.* "Little Jock" and *D.* "Dewdrop" are fragrant.
also for: ■ Shallow soils over chalk ■ Crevices in paving ■ Gray, blue-gray, or silver leaves ■ Fragrant flowers ■ Long, continuous flowering period (see above)

Geranium (Cinereum Group)
e.g. "Ballerina"
(syn. *G. cinereum* "Ballerina")
[cranesbill]
○

type of plant: hardy perennial [5–8]
flowering time: late spring to late summer
flower color: pale lilac-pink
height: 4in/10cm
Semi-evergreen/Evergreen

These dark-eyed flowers, each about 1in/2.5cm wide, are produced over many weeks. Each petal is beautifully veined in deep red but, from a distance, the overall effect is quite pale. The foliage is gray-green and deeply lobed. *G.* (Cinereum Group) "Ballerina" forms fairly loose mats of tufted growth. Most really well-drained soils are suitable for this drought-tolerant plant, and a warm site encourages the production of plenty of flowers. *G. subcaulescens* (see p.155) is similar except it has bright magenta-pink flowers.
also for: ■ Gray, blue-gray, or silver leaves ■ Long, continuous flowering period

Gypsophila repens
e.g. "Rosea"
○

type of plant: hardy perennial [4–9]
flowering time: late spring to midsummer
flower color: pale pink
height: 3–6in/8–15cm
Semi-evergreen

If placed in the crevice of a wall, this trailing plant not only has its clouds of tiny flowers displayed to advantage but it also obtains the warmth and good drainage it needs. However, *G. repens* "Rosea" may be grown with equal success in any sunny spot where there is light, really well-drained soil. It thrives in alkaline soil and tolerates drought. Its thick cushion of thin, little leaves is usually about 18in/45cm wide. The five-petalled flowers are each ¼–½in/0.5–1cm across.
also for: ■ Shallow soils over chalk ■ Ground cover ■ Crevices in paving ■ Long, continuous flowering period

Crocus chrysanthus
e.g. "Blue Pearl"
○

type of plant: hardy corm [4–9]
flowering time: late winter to early spring
flower color: pale lilac-blue
height: 3–4in/8–10cm

Hybrids derived from *C. chrysanthus* have flowers which are earlier and also smaller than the blooms of the so-called Dutch crocuses (for examples of which, see p.63). Their long-tubed flowers are not usually more than about 1in/2.5cm wide and 1½in/4cm long. Most varieties are yellow or, like *C.c.* "Blue Pearl," they have blue blooms; however, *C.c.* "Snow Bunting," for example, has white flowers and there are bicolored varieties, such as dark mauve-and-white *C.c.* "Ladykiller." For a cream-flowered Chrysanthus crocus, see p.317. All these crocuses grow best in really well-drained soil and their flowers open early in a warm, sunny site. Their narrow, grassy leaves have pale, central stripes.
also for: ■ Winter-flowering plants

Dorotheanthus bellidiformis
(syn. *Mesembryanthemum criniflorum*) Mixed
[Livingstone daisy, ice plant]
○

type of plant: half-hardy annual [9–11]
flowering time: midsummer to early autumn
flower color: mixed—pink, red, pale mauve, yellow, buff, white
height: 3–4in/8–10cm

The succulent leaves and stems of dorotheanthus are indications of the plant's ability to withstand quite long periods of drought. In the light, sharply drained soils it likes best, it grows densely and makes good, temporary ground cover (each spreading, sprawling plant is about 12in/30cm wide). It copes well with poor and shallow soils. Unless light conditions are bright, the 1in/2.5cm-wide daisies remain closed, and therefore a really sunny site should be chosen. The leaves of the plant are light green and usually rather slender.
also for: ■ Ground cover ■ Crevices in paving

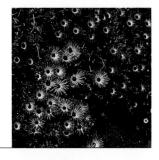

Sempervivum tectorum
[hens and chicks, houseleek]
○

type of plant: hardy perennial [5–9]
flowering time: early to midsummer
flower color: deep pink
height: 3in/8cm
Evergreen

Common houseleek and cobweb houseleek (see p.191) are widely available, but specialist nurseries offer a very wide range of these and other sempervivums. Common houseleek produces thick, succulent, basically blue-green leaves in rosettes 4–6in/10–15cm wide. Its bristly-edged foliage is often flushed with reddish purple tints or it may be completely purple. Clusters of starry flowers are carried on stout, leafy stems up to about 12in/30cm high. Infertile soil with sharp drainage suits this plant best and, in these sorts of conditions, its dense mats of attractive foliage are often about 18in/45cm wide. It thrives even where the depth of soil is very limited—in, for example, a dry stone wall and crevices of various sorts.
also for: ■ Ground cover ■ Crevices in paving ■ Purple, bronze, or red leaves (see above)

Sedum spathulifolium
e.g. "Cape Blanco"
[stonecrop]
○

type of plant: hardy perennial [5–8]
flowering time: early to midsummer
flower color: yellow
height: 2in/5cm
Evergreen

This little plant produces a mat of succulent, gray foliage that consists of numerous, tightly packed rosettes of white-dusted leaves. Each leaf is spoon-shaped and up to ¾in/2cm long. *S. spathulifolium* "Cape Blanco" grows well in a warm position, where it may spread about 12in/30cm wide. Red stems support starry flowers that are borne in clusters, each usually less than 1in/2.5cm across. Any well-drained or dryish soil is suitable for this plant. A purple-leaved variety of *S. spathulifolium* is shown on p.203.
also for: ■ Ground cover ■ Crevices in paving ■ Gray, blue-gray, or silver leaves

ADDITIONAL PLANTS, featured elsewhere in this book, that are suitable for dry soils in hot, sunny sites

○ sun

minimum height 10ft/3m or more
Cytisus battandieri, see p.297
Gleditsia triacanthos "Rubylace," see p.198
Gleditsia triacanthos "Sunburst," see p.210
Hippophae rhamnoides, see p.89
Juniperus scopulorum "Skyrocket," see p.145
Koelreuteria paniculata, see p.219
Robinia pseudoacacia "Frisia," see p.210
Sophora japonica, see p.94
Tamarix tetrandra, see p.89

minimum height between 3ft/90cm and 10ft/3m
Achillea filipendulina "Gold Plate," see p.270
Berberis x stenophylla, see p.138
Colutea arborescens, see p.253
Cytisus x praecox "Allgold," see p.97
Foeniculum vulgare "Purpureum," see p.200
Hibiscus syriacus "Oiseau Bleu," see p.334
Hibiscus syriacus "Woodbridge," see p.145
Indigofera heterantha, see p.334
Lupinus arboreus, see p.91
Perovskia "Blue Spire," see p.14
Pittosporum tobira, see p.298
Rosmarinus officinalis, see p.245
Taxus baccata "Standishii," see p.145
Tropaeolum majus Tall Mixed, see p.129
Verbascum olympicum, see p.183

minimum height between 12in/30cm and 3ft/90cm
Artemisia absinthium "Lambrook Silver," see p.185
Artemisia arbrotanum, see p.245
Artemisia ludoviciana "Valerie Finnis," see p.185
Ballota pseudodictamnus, see p.186
Caryopteris x clandonensis "Heavenly Blue," see p.15
Caryopteris x clandonensis "Worcester Gold,"
    see p.212
Centranthus ruber, see p.15
Cichorium intybus, see p.14
Cistus x purpureus, see p.91
Convolvulus cneorum, see p.188
Cytisus x kewensis, see p.107
Dianthus "Doris," see p.283
Dianthus "Haytor White," see p.283
Eryngium bourgatii, see p.165
Erysimum linifolium "Variegatum," see p.166
Euphorbia characias subsp. wulfenii, see p.184
Festuca glauca, see p.188

Festuca glauca "Golden Toupee," see p.213
Gaillardia "Burgunder," see p.277
Genista hispanica, see p.105
Genista lydia, see p.97
Gladiolus communis subsp. byzantinus, see p.276
Gypsophila elegans "Covent Garden," see p.281
Gypsophila paniculata "Bristol Fairy," see p.272
x Halimiocistus sahucii, see p.339
Hebe pimeleoides "Quicksilver," see p.188
Helichrysum "Schwefellicht," see p.282
Helictotrichon sempervirens, see p.184
Hermodactylus tuberosus, see p.324
Hordeum jubatum, see p.281
Hyssopus officinalis, see p.246
Iris unguicularis, see p.316
Juniperus x pfitzeriana "Pfitzeriana Aurea," see p.211
Juniperus squamata "Blue Carpet," see p.107
Juniperus squamata "Blue Star," see p.188
Lavandula angustifolia "Hidcote," see p.138
Lavandula angustifolia "Munstead," see p.247
Lavandula stoechas subsp. pedunculata, see p.246
Lilium candidum, see p.300
Limonium platyphyllum, see p.280
Linaria purpurea "Canon Went," see p.336
Lotus hirsutus, see p.187
Lychnis coronaria, see p.186
Lychnis coronaria "Alba," see p.186
Mentzelia lindleyi, see p.301
Nepeta x faassenii, see p.107
Osteospermum "Buttermilk," see p.339
Pennisetum orientale, see p.280
Phlomis fruticosa, see p.185
Ruta graveolens "Jackman's Blue," see p.187
Salvia officinalis "Icterina," see p.247
Salvia officinalis "Purpurascens," see p.201
Salvia officinalis "Tricolor," see p.166
Santolina chamaecyparissus, see p.138
Santolina pinnata subsp. neapolitana, see p.186
Satureja montana, see p.247
Stachys byzantina, see p.187
Stipa tenuissima, see p.278
Teucrium x lucidrys, see p.138
Verbascum "Gainsborough," see p.15
Verbascum "Helen Johnson," see p.336
Veronica spicata subsp. incana, see p.189
Yucca gloriosa "Variegata," see p.164

minimum height 12in/30cm or less
Acaena saccaticupula "Blue Haze," see p.191

Achillea tomentosa, see p.108
Aethionema "Warley Rose," see p.17
Alyssum spinosum "Roseum," see p.154
Antennaria microphylla, see p.108
Arabis alpina subsp. caucasica "Flore Pleno,"
    see p.108
Arabis ferdinandi-coburgi "Old Gold," see p.167
Armeria maritima "Alba," see p.109
Artemisia schmidtiana "Nana," see p.191
Aubrieta "Red Carpet," see p.109
Aurinia saxatilis "Citrina," see p.108
Chamaemelum nobile "Treneague," see p.109
Crocus chrysanthus "Cream Beauty," see p.317
Dianthus deltoides, see p.154
Dianthus gratianopolitanus, see p.17
Dianthus "Inchmery," see p.302
Dianthus "Mrs Sinkins," see p.302
Euphorbia cyparissias "Fens Ruby," see p.203
Euphorbia myrsinites, see p.191
Geranium subcaulescens, see p.155
Helianthemum "Rhodanthe Carneum," see p.189
Helianthemum "Wisley Primrose," see p.107
Helichrysum italicum subsp. serotinum,
    see p.247
Iberis sempervirens, see p.107
Lobularia maritima "Oriental Night," see p.18
Lychnis flos-jovis "Hort's Variety," see p.189
Oenothera macrocarpa, see p.341
Origanum "Kent Beauty," see p.17
Osteospermum "Silver Sparkler," see p.166
Othonna cheirifolia, see p.190
Pelargonium "L'Elégante," see p.167
Phlox douglasii "Boothman's Variety," see p.156
Saponaria ocymoides, see p.109
Sedum kamtschaticum var. floriferum
    "Weihenstephaner Gold," see p.342
Sedum spathulifolium "Purpureum," see p.203
Sedum spurium "Variegatum," see p.156
Sempervivum arachnoideum, see p.191
Stachys byzantina "Silver Carpet," see p.191
Tanacetum haradjanii, see p.190
Thymus Coccineus Group, see p.157
Thymus herba-barona, see p.248
Thymus pseudolanuginosus, see p.192
Thymus pulegioides "Bertram Anderson," see p.213
Thymus serpyllum var. albus, see p.157
Thymus vulgaris "Silver Posie," see p.248
Tropaeolum majus Alaska Series, see p.167
Tulipa "Red Riding Hood," see p.167

Crocus speciosus
e.g. "Albus"
○[○]

type of plant: hardy corm [5–9]
flowering time: early to mid-autumn
flower color: white
height: 4–6in/10–15cm

C. speciosus and all its readily available varieties, such as C.s. "Albus," are vigorous, easily grown plants that are ideal for naturalizing in grass or among deciduous shrubs. When grown in grass, their large, long-tubed flowers are supported and remain upright; in bare ground some of the blooms may collapse, especially in rough weather. These crocuses thrive in sharply drained, gritty soil but they increase quickly in most well-drained soils. In sunny weather their flowers open completely and are up to 3in/8cm wide. Their thin, grass-like leaves appear after the flowers have faded, and they are longest in spring. C. speciosus itself varies in color from lilac-blue to blue-purple.

Crocus vernus
e.g. "Purpureus Grandiflorus"
○【◐】

type of plant: hardy corm [4–9]
flowering time: early to mid-spring
flower color: dark purple
height: 4–6in/10–15cm

So-called Dutch crocuses are available mainly in shades of blue and purple. Some white and striped varieties are listed (for an example, see *C. vernus* "Striped Beauty," below). They are also sold as mixtures. Their grassy foliage lengthens as their large flowers fade. *C.v.* "Purpureus Grandiflorus" is floriferous and easy to grow. Each of its dark blooms is about 2½in/6cm long. All well-drained soils are suitable, but the plants thrive and multiply in sites where the drainage is really good and where the corms remain dry during summer. Positions in full sun encourage early flowering. Dutch crocuses can be naturalized in short grass, either beneath deciduous trees or in more open sites. The flowers need sunny weather in order to open fully.

Crocus vernus
e.g. "Striped Beauty"
○【◐】

type of plant: hardy corm [4–9]
flowering time: early to mid-spring
flower color: white + purple
height: 4–6in/10–15cm

See preceding plant.

Taxus cuspidata
[Japanese yew]
○◐●

type of plant: hardy conifer [4–7]
height: 5–20ft/1.5–6m (see description)
Evergreen

Japanese yew is widely grown and numerous varieties are available. It thrives in well-drained soil of all types. Although a moisture-retentive soil is ideal, this conifer copes admirably with hot, dry soil, dry shade, and shallow, chalky soil. Depending on the variety, Japanese yew is a small, pyramidal tree with fairly upright branches or an erect to spreading shrub of varying height and width. Dark green, sharp-ended, narrow leaves, 1in/2.5cm long, are arranged in rows. Colored foliage varieties are available. Female plants produce red, berry-like fruits.
also for: ■ Shallow soils over chalk ■ Acid soils ■ Dry shade ■ Dense shade ■ Atmospheric pollution ■ Hedging plants ■ Ornamental fruit (female plants)

Oenothera biennis
[evening primrose, sundrops]
○◐

type of plant: grown as hardy biennial [4–9]
flowering time: early summer to mid-autumn
flower color: yellow
height: 3–5ft/0.9–1.5m

This plant produces so many self-sown seedlings that it is suitable only for informal and wildflower gardens. However, evening primrose does have its attractions: the 2in/5cm-wide, bowl-shaped flowers open, from numerous slender buds, over an exceptionally long period; the 24in/60cm-wide rosettes of foliage, from which the upright flower stems rise, make useful, short-term ground cover; the flowers are sweetly fragrant; and, finally, the plant is well able to cope with dry and infertile soils (indeed, it grows in almost any soil with good drainage). Each flower is very short-lived, opening in late afternoon and lasting until the middle of the following day.
also for: ■ Ground cover ■ Fragrant flowers

Allium moly
○◐

type of plant: hardy bulb [7–9]
flowering time: early to midsummer
flower color: yellow
height: 8–12in/20–30cm

In most soils, and especially in soils with sharp drainage, *A. moly* increases prolifically. It can be naturalized beneath shrubs or at the edge of woodland. Its bright, starry flowers are borne in loose clusters, about 2in/5cm across. They last well in water, but the whole plant has an oniony smell that can become rather too noticeable indoors. Its long, broad, grayish leaves begin to wither as the flowers fade. *A.m.* "Jeannine" has larger flower clusters than the species. *A. flavum* is another readily available allium with yellow flowers; it is usually rather taller than *A. moly* and its flowers are pendent.

ADDITIONAL PLANTS, featured elsewhere in this book, that are suitable for dry soils in hot, sunny sites

○【◐】 **sun (or partial shade)**

minimum height 10ft/3m or more
Juniperus communis "Hibernica," see p.19

minimum height between 3ft/90cm and 10ft/3m
Corokia cotoneaster, see p.265
Juniperus virginiana "Grey Owl," see p.194

minimum height 3ft/90cm or less
Acaena microphylla, see p.111
Dictamnus albus, see p.20
Dictamnus albus var. *purpureus*, see p.249
Juniperus communis "Compressa," see p.149
Melissa officinalis "Aurea," see p.250

○◐ **sun or partial shade**

minimum height 10ft/3m or more
Taxus baccata, see p.140
Taxus baccata "Fastigiata," see p.21

minimum height 3ft/90cm or less
Erinus alpinus, see p.158
Hypericum calycinum, see p.82
Juniperus sabina "Tamariscifolia," see p.113

Damp and wet soils

including plants suitable for shallow water

WATERFALLS AND FOUNTAINS may catch the eye, but it is relatively still expanses of water—ponds, lakes, and slow-moving streams—that set off plants so well. The following list includes plants that grow in shallow water, those that thrive in really wet, boggy soil, and those that are suitable for damp soil. These plants can transform the appearance of sodden areas of ground, and they can make various "water features," natural or artificial, look serene and composed as well as decorative.

Gardeners who consider that leaves are just as attractive as flowers will find that selecting plants for a water or bog garden is a particularly enjoyable exercise. Some of the largest-leaved plants grow in damp and watery places. Illustrated in this list are plants such as *Darmera peltata*, which produces big, rounded leaves, *Hosta undulata* var. *albomarginata* with its bold, variegated foliage, and magnificent ferns such as *Osmunda regalis* and *Matteuccia struthiopteris*. Additional large-leaved plants that enjoy moist growing conditions include *Gunnera manicata*, with its vast, veined leaves. (The "Decorative, green foliage" list, pp.218–33, in which this most impressive plant is illustrated, also contains a considerable number of other moisture-loving plants.)

Even when plants have small leaves, plenty of moisture tends to produce strikingly generous quantities of growth. The little, yellow leaves of *Lysimachia nummularia* "Aurea" and slender-leaved Bowles' golden sedge (*Carex elata* "Aurea") are produced most prolifically when the plants are constantly damp.

Some plants may not have particularly ornamental leaves but they create bold shapes overall, and for this reason they look attractive beside water. Plants that provide good, vertical contrast to horizontal stretches of water include the various forms of redtwig dogwood (*Cornus alba*), the winter twigs of which create thickets of strikingly upright, colored growth. Some smaller,

moisture-loving plants in this list provide upright shapes: there are, for example, irises, such as *Iris sibirica* "White Swirl," and also shallow-water plants such as pickerel weed (*Pontederia cordata*) and the strangely marked club rush (*Schoenoplectus lacustris* subsp. *tabernaemontani* "Zebrinus").

Plants with arching stems or leaves also look good beside water: angel's fishing rod (*Dierama pulcherrimum*) and the pendulous or weeping sedge (*Carex pendula*), both of which are illustrated here, arch gracefully and they look their very best when reflected in water.

As well as handsome foliage plants, there are plenty of decorative flowering plants for damp and wet soils. These include *Astilbe*, daylilies (*Hemerocallis*), *Primula* and assorted *Iris*, globeflowers (*Trollius*), and knotweed (*Persicaria amplexicaulis*). Big, stout perennials such as *Inula magnifica*, *Aruncus dioicus* and *Ligularia* "The Rocket" thrive where there is a good supply of moisture. However, some smaller flowering plants also enjoy these conditions. This list includes such charming plants as *Dodecatheon meadia* and *Myosotis scorpioides* "Mermaid," both of which are usually less than 18in/45cm tall.

With a constant supply of moisture (or, at least, plenty of moisture during the growing season), flowering plants such as *Astilbe* and *Primula* can be grown in full sun, and this encourages them to produce especially large numbers of blooms. So often, in the absence of really moist growing conditions, moisture-loving plants have to be given a shaded site in order to conserve what moisture is available. In water or bog gardens, where such shading is not necessary, these plants can be seen at their most lush and floriferous.

For additional plants suitable for damp and wet soils, see also the following list in particular: "Plants suitable for heavy, clay soils," pp.39–50. Many of the plants in the following list are adaptable and will grow quite satisfactorily in ordinary, moisture-retentive soils.

Metasequoia glyptostroboides
[dawn redwood]
○

type of plant: hardy conifer [5–10]
height: 60–80ft/18–24m

Although most soils, including those that are wet, are quite suitable for this narrowly conical tree, growth is especially fast (as much as 36in/90cm a year initially) on deep, fertile soil that is damp and well drained. A site sheltered from strong winds is needed for good growth in maturity. The soft, feathery foliage of this deciduous conifer comprises sprays of ½in/1cm-long, narrow leaves. These are bright green when young; quite late in autumn, they turn red-gold or pinkish russet. The dark, red-brown, peeling bark is often conspicuous on mature trees.
also for: ■ Heavy, clay soils ■ Atmospheric pollution ■ Colorful, autumn foliage

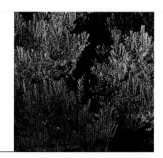

Salix caprea "Kilmarnock"
(syn. *S.c.* var. *pendula*)
[Kilmarnock willow]
○

type of plant: hardy tree [5–8]
flowering time: early to mid-spring
flower color: pale gray turning to yellow
height: 6–9ft/1.8–2.7m (see description)

Kilmarnock willow has a neat, dense head of conspicuously weeping branches. Its oval catkins, up to 1¼in/3cm long, are at first silky-soft and pale gray; as they mature they turn fuzzy and yellow. They appear before the dark green foliage emerges. When fully expanded, the leaves are broad, pointed and up to 4in/10cm long. This little tree needs good, deep, moisture-retentive soil to grow well and it thrives in damp and even in wet soil. The height of individual specimens depends on the height of the stems on to which they have originally been grafted. For other, small, weeping trees, see pp.14, 54 and 96.
also for: ■ Heavy, clay soils

Inula magnifica
○

type of plant: hardy perennial [4–8]
flowering time: mid- to late summer
flower color: yellow
height: 6ft/1.8m

Everything about *I. magnifica* is big and bold: its spidery daisies, each of which is up to 6in/15cm across; its huge, rough, dark green leaves; and its stout, upright stems. The basal leaves—which can be well over 24in/60cm long—form such an impressive clump of growth that the plant looks striking even before the branching heads of big, purple-brown flower buds develop. Vigorous and robust *I. magnifica* thrives in most fertile, moisture-retentive soil, including damp soil near water. In very windy situations its large leaves may become damaged.
also for: ■ Heavy, clay soils ■ Decorative, green foliage

Salvia uliginosa
[bog sage]
○

type of plant: slightly tender/half-hardy perennial [8–10]
flowering time: late summer to mid-autumn
flower color: sky-blue
height: 5–6ft/1.5–1.8m

Even in mild areas, this clump-forming perennial needs a warm site to perform well. Individually, the lipped flowers, at about ¾in/2cm long, are fairly small, but they are striking because of their gloriously clear coloring. They are arranged, in spike-like heads, at the ends of branched stems that are slender and curving and that often need support. The mid-green leaves are long, slim and toothed, and they have a pungent, not very pleasant scent. In the rich, moist soils it likes best, bog sage spreads quite widely; when really well suited, it can be invasive. In cold areas the roots should be protected in winter.
also for: ■ Long, continuous flowering period

Dierama pulcherrimum
[angel's fishing rod, wand flower]
○

type of plant: slightly tender corm [7–9]
flowering time: mid- to late summer
flower color: usually deep pink
height: 4–5ft/1.2–1.5m
Semi-evergreen/Evergreen

The wiry flower stems of *D. pulcherrimum* arch elegantly and sway in the slightest breeze. They are strung, at first, with silver buds, and then with hanging, bell-shaped flowers that are each around 2in/5cm long. Light, rich soil that stays moist during summer is ideal, and the plant looks attractive growing near water. It resents disturbance. *D. dracomontanum* [zones 8–9] is about half the height of *D. pulcherrimum*; it has flowers that vary in color from light pink to red. Both plants produce tufts of rather untidy, mid-green, grass-like leaves.

Butomus umbellatus
[flowering rush, water gladiolus]
○

type of plant: hardy perennial (aquatic) [6–9]
flowering time: mid- to late summer
flower color: pink
height: 4ft/1.2m
≈

Flowering rush can be grown in fertile, boggy ground and in water up to 10in/25cm deep. However, it is most floriferous when planted either in rich mud at the edges of a pond or slow-moving river or in shallow water (no more than 6in/15cm deep). Its thin, twisted, rush-like leaves are bronze when young and rich green when mature. Its slightly fragrant, cup-shaped flowers, up to 1in/2.5cm across, are arranged in open heads, on top of erect stems.

Lobelia
e.g. "Queen Victoria"
○

type of plant: hardy perennial [6–9]
flowering time: late summer to mid-autumn
flower color: blood-red
height: 30–36in/75–90cm

There are a number of hybrid, perennial lobelias with vividly or richly colored flowers. Some varieties, including *L.* "Queen Victoria" and the more recent, hardier *L.* "Dark Crusader" [zones 4–8], also have leaves and stems that are deep red-purple or maroon. All these clump-forming plants need shelter and rich, damp soil. The emerging shoots of the less hardy varieties are susceptible to frost damage. *L.* "Queen Victoria" tends to be short-lived. Its tubular flowers, each about ¼in/3cm long, are carried in long spikes above slim, pointed leaves that are deep purple-red.
also for: ■ Purple, bronze, or red leaves ■ Long, continuous flowering period

Zantedeschia aethiopica "Crowborough"
[calla lily]
○

type of plant: hardy/slightly tender perennial [8–11]
flowering time: late spring to midsummer
flower color: white + yellow
height: 30–36in/75–90cm
≈

This particular variety of calla lily is almost fully hardy. Nevertheless, if it is planted either in rich, moisture-retentive soil in a border or in fertile, boggy ground, *Z. aethiopica* "Crowborough" usually needs to have its roots covered in winter, at least for the first few years. Growing it as a marginal aquatic, in water up to 12in/30cm deep, helps it to survive low temperatures. Its supremely elegant, trumpet-like blooms, each 4–6in/10–15cm long, make magnificent and long-lasting cut flowers. The accompanying, arrow-shaped leaves are also very handsome. They form a clump of lush, glossy, rich green growth. For a green-flowered variety of calla lily, see p.323.
also for: ■ Decorative, green foliage ■ Flowers suitable for cutting

Lythrum salicaria
e.g. "Robert"
[purple loosestrife]
○

type of plant: hardy perennial [4–9]
flowering time: midsummer to early autumn
flower color: bright clear pink
height: 30in/75cm

L. salicaria and most of its varieties are strongly colored. Each erect flower spike is 12in/30cm or so long. The numerous, small flowers are shaped like shallow funnels; they open over a long period. Purple loosestrife is easily grown in any moisture-retentive soil, and it thrives in damp or wet conditions. *L.s.* "Robert" has flowers of typically bright color; for a variety with pale pink flowers, see p.42. The leaves of these clump-forming plants are long and narrow and they cover the lower parts of the stems. The mid-green foliage sometimes turns yellow in autumn. Flower spikes of *L. virgatum* cultivars, such as *L.v.* "Rosy Gem," are more slender.
also for: ■ Heavy, clay soils ■ Long, continuous flowering period

Carex elata "Aurea"
(syn. C. stricta "Bowles' Golden")
[Bowles' golden sedge]
○

type of plant: hardy perennial [5–9]
height: 24–30in/60–75cm

These very slender leaves, each of which is up to about 24in/60cm long, are so narrowly margined in green that the overall effect is of an arching spray of plain, strong yellow. Although its variegation and bright coloring fade substantially by late summer, Bowles' golden sedge retains its elegant shape. When compared with the foliage, the little, brown, "rat-tail" flowers are not particularly decorative. This sedge can be grown in moisture-retentive, border soil but it really prospers in damp soil or in wet ground near water.
also for: ■ Variegated leaves

Pontederia cordata
[pickerel weed]
○

type of plant: hardy perennial (aquatic) [4–10]
flowering time: late summer
flower color: blue
height: 24in/60cm
≈

Pickerel weed produces a mass of crowded, upright stems, each of which is topped with a dense flower spike about 4in/10cm long. An inch or so below every flower head there is—usually—just one arrow-shaped leaf. With its bright green coloring and its smooth, glossy texture, the bold and stylish foliage contrasts well with the numerous, little, lipped flowers that are packed into each flower head. Pickerel weed is an easy, fairly vigorous plant for the edges of a pond or slow-moving stream. It can be grown in water up to 5in/12cm deep.
also for: ■ Decorative, green foliage

Schizostylis coccinea e.g. "Major"
(syn. S.c. "Grandiflora")
[Kaffir lily]
○

type of plant: hardy perennial [6–9]
flowering time: early to mid-autumn
flower color: orange-tinted rich red
height: 18–24in/45–60cm

Particularly in mild regions with high rainfall, *S. coccinea* "Major" spreads freely when it is grown in rich soil that is moderately moist to damp. The opulently colored blooms, each 2–2½in/5–6cm across, have a silky sheen. They open in succession on stiff, strong stems and they are very long-lasting when cut. There are sheaves of narrowly sword-shaped, bright green leaves. An example of a pale pink variety of Kaffir lily is shown on p.282. The species itself has small, scarlet flowers, and *S.c.* f. *alba* is white-flowered.
also for: ■ Flowers suitable for cutting

Eriophorum angustifolium
[common cotton grass]
○

type of plant: hardy perennial (aquatic) [4–9]
flowering time: late spring to early summer
flower color: white
height: 12–18in/30–45cm
Evergreen ≈

Too vigorous for most garden settings, this rush-like perennial looks appropriately natural and informal in a wild or bog garden. As it needs plenty of moisture, common cotton grass thrives in boggy ground and open positions and it is particularly at home in acid, peaty soils. It can be grown in up to 2in/5cm of water. Its very narrow, sharply pointed leaves form a clump of mid-green growth beneath the flower stalks. The tufted, white flower heads, each 1–2in/2.5–5cm across, last well when dried.
also for: ■ Acid soils ■ Flowers suitable for cutting (and drying)

Ranunculus constantinopolitanus "Plenus" (syn. R. bulbosus "Speciosus Plenus," R. speciosus "Flore Pleno")
[buttercup, crowfoot]
○

type of plant: hardy perennial [4–8]
flowering time: late spring to early summer
flower color: rich yellow + green
height: 12in/30cm

The shiny petals of R. constantinopolitanus "Plenus" are tightly packed into flower heads in which the sharp green, central parts emphasize the rich, clear yellow of the outer petals. The flowers are up to 2in/5cm wide. Their attractive coloring is enhanced by the deep green of the plant's lobed and toothed leaves. The foliage forms clumps of growth. As well as being happy in all fertile, moisture-retentive soils, this non-invasive buttercup grows well in damp places.

Acorus gramineus
e.g. "Ogon"
[Japanese rush]
○

type of plant: hardy perennial (aquatic) [5–10]
height: 10in/25cm
Evergreen/Semi-evergreen ≈

The glossy, grass-like leaves of A. gramineus "Ogon" are generously striped in greenish yellow and cream. They retain their color well, and, in regions where they are evergreen, they are brightly colored even in winter. Each slender, pointed leaf is 8–12in/20–30cm long and the foliage is arranged in gracefully arching fans. In summer, fleshy spikes of tiny, greenish flowers are produced but these are inconspicuous. A.g. "Variegatus" is also readily available; its rich green leaves are striped with cream. Both these plants can be grown in damp or wet soils, as well as water up to about 2in/5cm deep.
also for: ■ Variegated leaves

Menyanthes trifoliata
[bogbean, marsh trefoil]
○

type of plant: hardy perennial (aquatic) [3–10]
flowering time: late spring to early summer
flower color: white
height: 9in/23cm
≈

Since this creeping plant spreads widely, it is generally suitable only for growing in or near a large pond. Bogbean is at home either in wet mud or in water up to 6in/15cm deep. Its sprays of starry, wispy-edged flowers and tripartite leaves are carried on dark, upright stems. Each pink-budded flower is about ¾in/2cm across. Even when not in flower, this plant is attractive because of the arrangement and the smooth glossiness of its light green foliage.
also for: ■ Decorative, green foliage

ADDITIONAL PLANTS, featured elsewhere in this book, that are suitable for damp and wet soils

○ sun

minimum height 10ft/3m or more
Alnus cordata, see p.40
Hippophae rhamnoides, see p.89
Populus alba, see p.183
Populus x jackii "Aurora," see p.161
Populus nigra "Italica," see p.94
Quercus palustris, see p.235
Salix alba subsp. vitellina "Britzensis," see p.264
Salix babylonica var. pekinensis "Tortuosa," see p.263

minimum height between 3ft/90cm and 10ft/3m
Cortaderia selloana "Pumila," see p.269
Phormium tenax, see p.221
Phormium tenax Purpureum Group, see p.199
Physocarpus opulifolius "Diabolo," see p.199
Salix fargesii, see p.220
Salix hastata "Wehrhahnii," see p.41
Sambucus nigra f. porphyrophylla "Gerda," see p.329

minimum height 3ft/90cm or less
Achillea ptarmica The Pearl Group, see p.275

Erica tetralix "Alba Mollis," see p.26
Glyceria maxima var. variegata, see p.165
Hemerocallis "Stafford," see p.42
Iris ensata "Moonlight Waves," see p.26
Liatris spicata, see p.276
Lythrum salicaria "Blush," see p.42
Pleioblastus viridistriatus, see p.164
Salix lanata, see p.185
Schizostylis coccinea "Mrs Hegarty," see p.282
Zantedeschia aethiopica "Green Goddess," see p.323

Viburnum opulus
e.g. "Xanthocarpum"
[European cranberry bush, guelder rose]
○[◖]

type of plant: hardy shrub [4–8]
flowering time: early summer
flower color: white
height: 10–12ft/3–3.6m

Viburnum and its varieties make good plants for permanently damp ground, although they do well in almost any soil—including those that are shallow and chalky. The 3in/8cm-wide, lacecap flowers of V. opulus "Xanthocarpum" are followed, from early autumn, by bunches of long-lasting berries. As these ripen fully, to a beautiful, translucent apricot-yellow, the lobed leaves—each of which is up to 4in/10cm long—change from mid-green to yellow. The plant is vigorous, dense and fairly upright. The species itself is also popular; it has bright red, shiny berries and crimson-pink autumn color. V.o. "Aureum" produces yellow leaves and some red berries. For a very free-fruiting, red-berried variety, see p.257.
also for: ■ Shallow soils over chalk ■ Heavy, clay soils ■ Colorful, autumn foliage ■ Ornamental fruit

Cornus alba
e.g. "Elegantissima"
[redtwig dogwood]
○[◖]

type of plant: hardy shrub [3–8]
height: 6–7ft/1.8–2.1m

Throughout the year the redtwig dogwood is interesting: in winter there are shiny, upright, bright plum-red to maroon stems (these are most colorful when young and at least some of the growths should be cut right back each year); in spring and summer the stems carry tapering, gray-green, irregularly white-edged leaves, up to 4in/10cm long (among which the white flower clusters are inconspicuous); finally, in autumn the foliage turns soft shades of pink and orange. Almost any soil is suitable for C. alba "Elegantissima." This tough, fast-growing dogwood is most lush and vigorous in damp and wet conditions. For other varieties of C. alba, see p.169, 265 and 331.
also for: ■ Heavy, clay soils ■ Atmospheric pollution ■ Variegated leaves ■ Colorful, autumn foliage ■ Ornamental bark or twigs

Cirsium rivulare
"Atropurpureum"
○[◖]

type of plant: hardy perennial [4–8]
flowering time: early summer to early autumn
flower color: crimson
height: 4ft/1.2m

The neat, 1¼in/3cm-wide "thistles" produced by C. rivulare "Atropurpureum" are carried, usually in clusters, on upright, branching stems. These rise well clear of long, dark, jagged leaves that form a basal clump of growth. The main flowering period is early and midsummer, but significant numbers of blooms continue to appear during late summer and early autumn. Damp soils with good drainage produce especially satisfactory growth, but this an adaptable plant that does well in almost any soil, provided conditions are reasonably fertile and moisture-retentive. It may spread quite vigorously when well suited.
also for: ■ Long, continuous flowering period (see above)

Euphorbia palustris
[milkweed, spurge]
○[◖]

type of plant: hardy perennial [5–8]
flowering time: late spring to early summer
flower color: bright green-yellow
height: 36in/90cm

In common with many milkweeds, E. palustris has flower heads that are decorative well before they open fully and which, even in their faded state, are quite attractive. The clusters of cupped flowers are large, up to 5in/12cm across, and together with the stout, leafy, upright stems they create an impression of fresh and robust bushiness. In autumn, slender, pointed leaves turn from bright green to yellow and sometimes orange, too; the stems turn pink. E. palustris grows best in soil that is consistently damp (where it may be more than 4ft/1.2m tall), but it flourishes in ordinary, garden soil, as long as it retains moisture. E. schillingii [zones 7–9] also appreciates moist soil; its bright, long-lasting, yellow-green flowers appear from midsummer until well into autumn. The cut stems of these plants exude a milky juice which can irritate skin.
also for: ■ Colorful, autumn foliage

Hemerocallis fulva "Flore Pleno"
[daylily]
○[◖]

type of plant: hardy perennial [4–9]
flowering time: mid- to late summer
flower color: tawny orange
height: 36in/90cm
Semi-evergreen

Thick, upright stems on H. fulva "Flore Pleno" carry sumptuous, double flowers, up to 5in/12cm across. Below these, the long, arching, mid-green leaves form a clump of growth, about 36in/90cm wide, which is rather untidy but which acts as effective ground cover. A variegated, double-flowered form, H.f "Kwanso Variegated," bears light green leaves that are variably striped in white. These plants are easy to grow in any moisture-retentive soil but they are particularly successful in rich and damp conditions. They flower especially well in sun.
also for: ■ Heavy, clay soils ■ Ground cover

Iris sibirica
e.g. "White Swirl"
○[◐]

type of plant: hardy perennial [4–9]

flowering time: early summer

flower color: white

height: 36in/90cm

I. sibirica and its varieties look especially attractive beside water. They thrive in a sunny place and in fertile soil that is moist to damp. However, they are adaptable plants and they grow quite satisfactorily in slightly drier and shadier conditions. Compared with older varieties, such as *I.s.* "Perry's Blue" (see below), *I.s.* "White Swirl" has flowers of a more spreading but perhaps less graceful shape. There are several flowers to a stem, and each flower is about 4in/10cm across. The stems are erect, rising clearly above the clump of narrow, rather upright, mid-green leaves. Other varieties bear lilac, cream, purple or bicolored flowers. Many more recent introductions have fuller flowers or flowers with ruffled petals.

also for: ■ Heavy, clay soils ■ Flowers suitable for cutting

Schoenoplectus lacustris
subsp. *tabernaemontani*
(syn. *Scirpus tabernaemontani*)
"Zebrinus"
[club rush]
○[◐]

type of plant: hardy perennial (aquatic) [4–9]

height: 36in/90cm

Evergreen ≈

The quill-like, leafless stems of club rush have curious, horizontal bands of bright green and white. These markings tend to fade as the erect stems age and, unless the roots are divided frequently, plain green stems may outnumber those that are variegated. This rush can be grown either in still or slow-moving water—up to 12in/30cm deep—or in boggy ground where the soil is fertile. In summer there are spikes of brown flowers but these are small and inconspicuous. For another plant with horizontal stripes, see p.169.

also for: ■ Variegated leaves

Monarda
e.g. "Croftway Pink"
[bee balm]
○[◐]

type of plant: hardy perennial [4–9]

flowering time: midsummer to early autumn

flower color: rose-pink

height: 30–42in/75–105cm

M. "Croftway Pink" and related varieties such as *M.* "Cambridge Scarlet" (see p.249) need moist, fertile soil. They do not do well, however, in soils that are wet in winter, and mildew can be a problem in dry summers. At their best, they produce numerous, spidery-looking whorls of flowers over many weeks and their pointed leaves and erect stems form thick clumps of growth. The slender, tubular flowers, up to 2in/5cm long, are attractive to bees. Most varieties spread to about 18in/45cm wide but some, including *M.* "Croftway Pink," can become invasive in really rich, damp soil. The tapering leaves of these plants emit a smell of fresh oranges when bruised. Other pale-flowered varieties include *M.* "Schneewittchen" (white blooms) and mildew-resistant *M.* "Aquarius" (light mauve).

also for: ■ Aromatic foliage ■ Flowers suitable for cutting ■ Long, continuous flowering period

Iris x robusta "Gerald Darby"
(syn. *I.* "Gerald Darby")
○[◐]

type of plant: hardy perennial [5–9]

flowering time: late spring to early summer

flower color: blue-violet

height: 30–36in/75–90cm

≈

All moist to wet soils that are deep and fertile are suitable for *I. x robusta* "Gerald Darby" and it also grows well in very shallow water at the margins of a pond. It prefers neutral to acid conditions. Its bright green, upright, sword-shaped leaves arch at their tips and are marked purple at their bases. They are flushed with mauve-blue when they emerge; in late autumn they turn yellowish. There are several elegant blooms, 2½–3in/6–8cm across, on each dark purplish stem. They make good cut flowers. Other popular irises for shallow water and for damp to wet soils include purple-flowered *I. ensata* (syn. *I. kaempferi*) and its varieties (for a white-flowered example of which, see p.26) and the blue-flowered *I. laevigata* and its varieties.

also for: ■ Acid soils ■ Flowers suitable for cutting

Iris sibirica
e.g. "Perry's Blue"
○[◐]

type of plant: hardy perennial [4–9]

flowering time: late spring to early summer

flower color: rich sky-blue

height: 30–36in/75–90cm

This adaptable plant flourishes in sunshine and in all fertile soils that are moist to damp; it also grows well in drier and slightly shadier conditions. There are several, readily available, blue-flowered varieties of *I. sibirica*, including *I.s.* "Perry's Blue." Its graceful, delicately marked flowers are about 3in/8cm across; there are several blooms to each erect stem. *I. sibirica* itself is also popular; its flowers are violet-blue. Other varieties have lilac, cream, purple or bicolored flowers. A white-flowered variety is shown above. Some more recent introductions have blooms that are fuller or have ruffled petals. All these plants hold their flowers well above grass-like clumps of slender, rather upright, mid-green leaves. These irises look particularly attractive growing beside water.

also for: ■ Heavy, clay soils ■ Flowers suitable for cutting

Acorus calamus
"Argenteostriatus"
[sweet flag]
○[◐]

type of plant: hardy perennial (aquatic) [4–10]
height: 24–36in/60–90cm
≈

All parts of this plant have a warm, spicy scent. The rich green leaves are cleanly and conspicuously striped— on one edge only—with creamy white, and this variegation is long-lasting. In spring the emerging shoots are pink and some of this coloring is retained, for a while, at the base of each narrow, upright leaf. Individual leaves can be more than 36in/90cm long. *A. calamus* "Argenteostriatus" is at its best in shallow water (up to 9in/23cm deep) but damp and wet soils are also suitable. Fleshy spikes of greenish flowers are produced in summer, but these are inconspicuous among the plant's leaves.
also for: ■ Variegated leaves ■ Aromatic foliage

Lychnis flos-cuculi
[ragged robin]
○[◐]

type of plant: hardy perennial [3–8]
flowering time: late spring to early summer
flower color: variable—shades of pink
height: 24in/60cm

Ragged robin is a plant for damp and boggy ground and really moist borders. Its pretty, wispy flowers, with their deeply cut petals, are each 1¼–1½in/ 3–4cm wide. They are perched on top of upright, openly branched stems. These rise well clear of the basal leaves which are mid-green, and long and thin. The whole plant is slender and has a charming, informal air about it. *L. flos-cuculi* "Jenny" is a recently introduced variety which has fully double, lilac-pink flowers.

Caltha palustris "Flore Pleno"
[kingcup, marsh marigold]
○[◐]

type of plant: hardy perennial (aquatic) [4–8]
flowering time: mid- to late spring
flower color: golden yellow
height: 10in/25cm
≈

C. palustris "Flore Pleno" grows well in wet and very moist ground or in a few inches of water (no more than 6in/15cm deep). Its double flowers are densely petalled, glistening "pompoms," each about 1in/2.5cm across. These are carried on branching stems above creeping, ground covering clumps of foliage. The leaves are shining, dark green and kidney-shaped. *C. palustris* itself has single flowers of a beautiful simplicity. The single-flowered, white variety, *C.p.* var. *alba*, is shown right.
also for: ■ Heavy, clay soils ■ Ground cover

Mentha aquatica
[watermint]
○[◐]

type of plant: hardy perennial (aquatic) [6–9]
flowering time: late summer to mid-autumn
flower color: lilac
height: 9–18in/23–45cm; sometimes up to 36in/90cm
≈

Watermint hybridizes readily with other mints and individual plants are apt to vary a good deal, in height as well as in other respects. It can be grown either in wet soil or, at the edges of a stream or pond, in water up to 4in/10cm deep. Its dark green leaves, which are usually no more than 2½in/6cm long, may be either oval or quite slender and pointed. They are pungently mint-scented. The foliage is often tinged with purple and, on the younger growths especially, the veins and stalks of the leaves may also be purple. Rounded, fluffy flower heads appear at the ends of erect, often maroon-purple, leafy stems. This is a very vigorous, potentially invasive plant.
also for: ■ Purple, bronze, or red leaves ■ Aromatic foliage

Oenanthe javanica "Flamingo"
○[◐]

type of plant: slightly tender/half-hardy perennial [9–11]
flowering time: late summer
flower color: white
height: 8–12in/20–30cm

Although it is particularly at home in damp and wet soils, this vigorous plant does well in ordinary, moisture-retentive conditions, too. The spreading, rooting stems of *O. javanica* "Flamingo" carry ferny leaves, up to 6in/15cm long when fully expanded. The numerous, slender, light green leaflets are edged in white and flushed with pink. Leaf color is best in a sunny site. Clusters of tiny flowers, each with their own stalk, are carried in flattish heads. If the flowers are either pinched out before they develop or removed as soon as they fade, then the foliage quality is especially good. Some shelter is also beneficial.
also for: ■ Ground cover ■ Variegated leaves

Primula rosea
○◖

type of plant: hardy perennial [6–8]
flowering time: early to mid-spring
flower color: bright pink + yellow
height: 8in/20cm

This plant requires a constant supply of moisture to do well. It is suitable for quite boggy ground and for the banks of a stream or natural pond. Its slender, mid-green leaves are bronze-tinted when they first emerge. They form rosettes of growth and lengthen fully only after *P. rosea* has finished flowering. The ¾in/2cm-wide flowers are arranged in clusters that begin to open almost as soon as the stalks have emerged above ground level. *P.r.* "Grandiflora" has larger flowers and is more vigorous.

Caltha palustris var. alba
[kingcup, marsh marigold]
○◖

type of plant: hardy perennial [4–8]
flowering time: early to late spring
flower color: white + yellow
height: 6–8in/15–20cm

Although the individual flowers of *C. palustris* "Flore Pleno" (see left) are longer-lasting, the charming, single blooms of *C.p.* var. *alba* are produced over a longer period (indeed, flowering sometimes continues into summer). Like the double-flowered variety, *C.p.* var. *alba* thrives in boggy ground but it is not at its best in shallow water. Its simple flowers, each about 1in/2.5cm across, may start to open before the shiny, kidney-shaped leaves have expanded fully. Bright green foliage and creeping roots create small clumps of growth, and the plant is usually only a little wider than it is tall.
also for: ■ Long, continuous flowering period

ADDITIONAL PLANTS, featured elsewhere in this book, that are suitable for damp and wet soils

○◖ **sun (or partial shade)**

minimum height 10ft/3m or more
Liquidambar styraciflua, see p.237
Nyssa sylvatica, see p.238
Pseudosasa japonica, see p.223

minimum height between 3ft/90cm and 10ft/3m
Actaea simplex Atropurpurea Group, see p.204
Cornus alba "Kesselringii," see p.331
Cornus alba "Sibirica," see p.265
Cornus alba "Spaethii," see p.169

Cornus sericea "Flaviramea," see p.265
Eupatorium purpureum subsp. *maculatum* "Atropurpureum," see p.43
Physocarpus opulifolius "Dart's Gold," see p.214
Rheum palmatum, see p.223
Viburnum opulus "Compactum," see p.257

minimum height 3ft/90cm or less
Aronia melanocarpa, see p.239
Astrantia major "Sunningdale Variegated," see p.169

Hemerocallis "Golden Chimes," see p.224
Hemerocallis "Little Wine Cup," see p.44
Hemerocallis "Pink Damask," see p.110
Houttuynia cordata "Chameleon," see p.170
Iris chrysographes black-flowered, see p.331
Iris forrestii, see p.27
Ligularia dentata "Desdemona," see p.204
Lobelia x gerardii "Vedrariensis," see p.343
Lysimachia nummularia "Aurea," see p.112
Monarda "Cambridge Scarlet," see p.249
Primula veris, see p.306
Rheum "Ace of Hearts," see p.224

Taxodium distichum
[bald cypress, swamp cypress]
○◑

type of plant: hardy conifer [6–10]
height: 60–80ft/18–24m

Patient gardeners can contemplate planting this tree, rather than the somewhat similar, faster-growing dawn redwood (*Metasequoia glyptostroboides,* see p.65). They will be rewarded with more graceful foliage (although it emerges—a bright pale green—very late in spring), summer foliage of a fresher green and brighter russet autumn color. The leaves are narrow, ¾in/2cm long and arranged in feather-like sprays. Although conical when young, in maturity *T. distichum* is columnar and its fibrous, red-brown bark is striking. Old trees sometimes look rather uneven and sparse. Any moisture-retentive soil is suitable but growth is best in wet and swampy sites, where prominent aerial roots, known as "knees," often develop. This tree has a preference for acid conditions. It grows most successfully in regions with hot summers.
also for: ■ Acid soils ■ Heavy, clay soils ■ Colorful, autumn foliage
■ Ornamental bark or twigs

Filipendula rubra
[queen of the prairie]
○◑

type of plant: hardy perennial [3–9]
flowering time: early to midsummer
flower color: bright mid-pink fading to pale pink
height: 6–7ft/1.8–2.1m

Despite its great height, this vigorous, clump-forming perennial usually needs staking only if it is grown in a windy site. *F. rubra* thrives—and its roots may spread rapidly—in wet or damp soil; in slightly drier conditions, a partially shaded site is needed to conserve moisture. The branched flower heads, which can be as much as 8in/20cm across, are frothy masses of tiny blooms. Lower down the upright stems there are large, handsome, dark green leaves, up to 8in/20cm long, with deeply cut lobes. *F. rubra* "Venusta" (syn. "Venusta Magnifica") has darker rose-pink flowers. However, plants sold under this name are often no deeper in coloring than the specimen illustrated here.
also for: ■ Decorative, green foliage

Neillia sinensis
○◐

type of plant: hardy shrub [6–8]
flowering time: early summer
flower color: pale pink
height: 6ft/1.8m

This easily grown and adaptable shrub produces tiny, tubular flowers in slender sprays at the ends of its twiggy growths. Each spray is about 2½in/6cm long. *N. sinensis* creates a thicket of upright main stems that then arch and branch into slightly zigzagging twigs near their tips. The leaves are rich green, veined and jagged, with long, central points. Most soils are suitable but growth is especially good on moist, fertile soil and soil that is permanently damp. *N. thibetica* has longer sprays of rose-pink flowers but is otherwise quite similar.

Aruncus dioicus
(syn. *A. sylvestris*)
[goatsbeard]
○◐

type of plant: hardy perennial [3–8]
flowering time: early to midsummer
flower color: creamy white or greenish white
height: 4–6ft/1.2–1.8m

Damp conditions are ideal for this big, handsome plant. However, goatsbeard is vigorous enough to grow well in most reasonably fertile soils, as long as they do not dry out easily. Long, mid-green leaves are divided into tapering leaflets. They create large clumps of weed-proof growth, above which rise strong, upright stems carrying the plumes of tiny flowers, each plume up to 18in/45cm long. Nurseries often stock both male and female plants. On female plants, the plumes are less feathery but they are followed by attractive seedheads—and numerous self-sown seedlings. (The plant illustrated here is female.) *A. dioicus* "Kneiffii" is a cut-leaved variety and is only about 36in/90cm high.
also for: ■ Heavy, clay soils ■ Ground cover ■ Decorative, green foliage

Ligularia
e.g. "The Rocket"
○◐

type of plant: hardy perennial [4–8]
flowering time: mid- to late summer
flower color: bright yellow
height: 4–6ft/1.2–1.8m

An overall impression of handsome vigor is created by the great, black-stemmed flower spikes and the big, jagged leaves of *L.* "The Rocket." The spikes, with their numerous, wispy "daisies," are often about 24in/60cm long. They rise erectly above the clumps of long-stalked, rounded leaves, which are rich bright green. *L. przewalskii* has deeply cut as well as jagged leaves, and its flowers are a less bright yellow. Both these plant thrive in damp and wet soils. In less moist conditions, shelter from drying winds and hot sun is especially important since exposed plants quickly wilt.
also for: ■ Heavy, clay soils ■ Decorative, green foliage

Osmunda regalis
[royal fern, flowering fern]
○◐✳

type of plant: hardy fern [3–9]
height: 4–6ft/1.2–1.8m
≈

As long as it has acid or neutral soil that is permanently damp, this imposing fern forms a large, dense clump. Royal fern is especially lush on the banks of a river or pond or right at the water's edge. The new growths are erect and orange-brown (on *O. regalis* "Purpurascens" the youngest growths are maroon-purple and some of this coloring is retained through summer). Mature fronds are bright green until autumn, when they turn yellow and yellowish brown. Each broad, finely divided frond can be well over 36in/90cm long. Most specimens of *O. regalis* produce a few upright, fertile fronds that ripen to a rust color and that resemble plumes of flowers.
also for: ■ Acid soils ■ Decorative, green foliage ■ Colorful, autumn foliage

Angelica gigas
○◐

type of plant: hardy biennial/perennial [5–9]
flowering time: late summer to early autumn
flower color: maroon-plum
height: 4–5ft/1.2–1.5m

Although *A. gigas* is happy in drier conditions, this short-lived plant grows well in rich, damp soil. Its handsome, divided leaves form a clump of rather bright greenery beneath the thick, upright flower-stalks. These branching flower-stalks, their surmounting flower heads and the leaf sheaths are all deeply and opulently colored. Each hemispherical flower head is about 5in/12cm wide.

Carex pendula
[drooping sedge, pendulous sedge, weeping sedge]

○◑

type of plant: hardy perennial [5–9]
flowering time: late spring to early summer
flower color: green turning to brown
height: 4–5ft/1.2–1.5m
Evergreen

As they mature, the flower spikes of this grass-like plant become pendulous. They then dangle, like very large catkins, from gracefully arching stems. Each spike is up to 6in/15cm long. *C. pendula* forms substantial clumps of slender, pointed, bright green leaves. It is most suitable for cool soil that is damp or wet; it grows well in heavy soil. This robust plant looks imposing and appropriate in woodland gardens. It is suitable for naturalizing.
also for: ■ Heavy, clay soils ■ Ground cover

Darmera peltata (syn. Peltiphyllum peltatum)

○◑

type of plant: hardy perennial [5–9]
flowering time: mid-spring
flower color: pink
height: 3½ft/1.05m

Each of these rounded, lobed leaves is usually at least 12in/30cm in diameter. The foliage has a glossy, crinkled surface and is deep green in maturity. Beside water or in boggy ground, or in rich soil that is reliably moist, this vigorous, creeping, occasionally invasive plant makes good ground cover. In ideal conditions, *D. peltata* can be 6ft/1.8m high with leaves 24in/60cm wide. The flowers appear before the foliage and are susceptible to frost damage. Each dense, rounded head of tiny blooms, up to 5in/12cm wide, is perched on top of a long, bare stem. In moist soil and full sun the leaves may turn coppery red in autumn.
also for: ■ Heavy, clay soils ■ Ground cover ■ Decorative, green foliage ■ Colorful, autumn foliage (see above)

Senecio tanguticus
(syn. *Ligularia tangutica*, *Sinacalia tangutica*)
[Chinese groundsel]

○◑

type of plant: hardy perennial [6–9]
flowering time: late summer to mid-autumn
flower color: bright yellow
height: 3–5ft/0.9–1.5m

This handsome perennial is probably best grown in a large area of informal planting since its spreading clumps of growth are often invasive. Chinese groundsel is especially vigorous in fertile soil that is moist or damp; in drier places its growth is restricted but then, in sun, its dark green, jagged leaves may wilt—at least temporarily. Conical flower heads, with numerous wispy "daisies," are carried on upright stems and are each about 12in/30cm long; they ripen into fluffy seedheads. Older stems are almost black. Many of the flowers illustrated here are in bud.
also for: ■ Decorative, green foliage ■ Ornamental fruit (seedheads)

Rodgersia pinnata "Superba"

○◑

type of plant: hardy perennial [5–8]
flowering time: mid- to late summer
flower color: bright pink
height: 3–4ft/0.9–1.2m

Although seen here as impressive, coppery pink seedheads, the stout-stemmed flowers of this bold, clump-forming plant look magnificent earlier in the year, too. Then the branched heads, each 12–18in/30–45cm long, are filled with starry, pink flowers. The bold, wrinkled foliage is just as striking: when young, each slender leaflet is suffused with bronze, and the mature foliage is dark green. Open-textured soil that is moist or boggy is ideal. *R. pinnata* "Superba" also does well in fertile, moisture-retentive soil, though in these less damp conditions it may need a more shaded position. Shelter from cold and drying winds is always beneficial. *R. aesculifolia* has somewhat similar foliage but its flowers are creamy colored.
also for: ■ Heavy, clay soils ■ Ground cover ■ Purple, bronze, or red leaves (young leaves only) ■ Decorative, green foliage ■ Ornamental fruit (seedheads)

Lysimachia clethroides
[loosestrife]

○◑

type of plant: hardy perennial [4–9]
flowering time: late summer to early autumn
flower color: white
height: 36in/90cm

L. clethroides flowers usefully late in the gardening year, and it remains interesting well into autumn, when its slim, pointed leaves turn from light green to red. The graceful, arching flower spikes are up to 8in/20cm long and good for cutting. They are carried at the ends of erect stems. Damp or, at least, fairly moist soil is needed to grow this plant well. If the soil is also rich, growth can be quite rapid and individual plants can form patches at least 24–36in/60–90cm wide.
also for: ■ Colorful, autumn foliage ■ Flowers suitable for cutting

Lysimachia punctata
[loosestrife]

○◑

type of plant: hardy perennial [4–8]
flowering time: mid- to late summer
flower color: bright yellow
height: 36in/90cm

Appropriately robust and unpretentious for an informal or wildflower garden, this loosestrife has a more invasive habit than its relation on the previous page. *L. punctata* spreads widely in damp or reliably moist soil, and it grows at least adequately in any ordinary soil. Its cup-shaped flowers, each about ¾in/2cm across, are interspersed with pointed leaves on the erect stems and the clear, bright yellow of the flowers looks well with the fresh green of the foliage. A less vigorous, variegated form of *L. punctata* is shown on p.173.
also for: ■ Heavy, clay soils

Mimulus cardinalis
[scarlet monkey flower]

○◑

type of plant: hardy/slightly tender perennial [7–10]
flowering time: early to late summer
flower color: scarlet
height: 36in/90cm

The tubular blooms of scarlet monkey flower appear in succession throughout the summer months. They are carried in leafy spikes on erect stems. Each flower is up to 2in/5cm long. The leaves are hairy, toothed and light green. Scarlet monkey flower is at home in damp soil that is open-textured and fertile, but it also thrives in ordinary garden soil, as long as it is reasonably moisture-retentive and fertile. The plant needs a position sheltered from wind if it is not to become very untidy by late summer. Smaller, hybrid mimulus with red flowers include short-lived but showy *M.* "Wisley Red" and *M.* "Highland Red" [both zones 8–10].
also for: ■ Long, continuous flowering period

Persicaria bistorta "Superba"
(syn. *Polygonum bistorta* "Superbum")
[bistort]

○◑

type of plant: hardy perennial [4–8]
flowering time: late spring to early summer and usually repeating until mid-autumn
flower color: pink
height: 30–36in/75–90cm

The light green foliage of this robust perennial is, perhaps, a little too weed-like for some gardeners' tastes but it is arranged in substantial, ground-covering clumps and it does not look at all out of place in "natural" plantings. Growing well in any fertile and at least reasonably moisture-retentive soil, *P. bistorta* "Superba" flourishes and is particularly free-flowering in damp ground (though in damp conditions it may become invasive). The 3in/8cm-long cylinders of densely packed flowers are carried well above broad, pointed leaves.
also for: ■ Heavy, clay soils ■ Ground cover

Trollius chinensis
(syn. *T. ledebourii*)
"Golden Queen"
[globe flower]

○◑

type of plant: hardy perennial [4–8]
flowering time: early to midsummer
flower color: orange-yellow
height: 30–36in/75–90cm

A distinctive feature of *T. chinensis* itself and of this popular variety is the bunch of upright stamens in the center of each 2in/5cm-wide flower. Other commonly grown globe flowers have much more rounded blooms (see, for example, *T. europaeus*, right). Damp, boggy soil is not essential for growing *T.c.* "Golden Queen" well, but the soil should be rich and deep and it must not dry out. The deeply divided and toothed leaves form a clump of bright green, weed-suppressing growth beneath the upright flower stems. *T. chinensis* and its varieties are good for cutting.
also for: ■ Ground cover ■ Flowers suitable for cutting

Chelone obliqua
[turtle head]

○◑

type of plant: hardy perennial [4–9]
flowering time: late summer to early autumn
flower color: lilac-pink to rose-purple
height: 30in/75cm

C. obliqua's rigid, upright stems are generously clothed in veined and toothed, deep green leaves which have tapering points. There are usually at least six flowers crowded around the tip of each stem. The flowers, each about 1¼in/3cm long, resemble the open-mouthed heads of turtles (hence the common name). *C. obliqua* is particularly at home in fertile soil that is wet or damp, but it also does well in most soils of reasonable fertility and it can cope with heavy clays. Its mass of stems grows densely enough to exclude weeds. This plant spreads slowly, often into substantial patches of growth. *C. glabra* (syn. *C. obliqua* var. *alba*) is also widely available; its flowers are white or very pale pink.
also for: ■ Heavy, clay soils ■ Ground cover

Sanguisorba obtusa
[Japanese burnet]
○◑

type of plant: hardy perennial [4–8]
flowering time: midsummer to early autumn
flower color: bright pink fading to pale pink
height: 30in/75cm

These dark-stemmed burnets are often up to 3in/8cm long and, although their shape and coloring make them immediately eye-catching, the foliage of this vigorous plant is just as interesting and decorative in its own way. In the constantly moist conditions Japanese burnet enjoys most, individual leaves can be more than 15in/38cm long. Each leaf is divided into numerous, rounded, grayish green leaflets that have serrated edges. Rising well clear of this rather loose mass of foliage are the branching, slightly arching flower stems. These are fairly lax and often need some support. In autumn, the leaves may take on pink and orange tones.
also for: ■ Decorative, green foliage

Cyperus longus
[galingale]
○◑

type of plant: hardy perennial [4–8]
flowering time: late summer to early autumn
flower color: reddish brown
height: 24–48in/60–120cm
Evergreen ≈

Galingale can be grown either in marshy ground or in shallow water (up to 12in/30cm deep). It usually creates quite large masses of grassy-looking growth. The stems are upright and each stem carries two or three long, narrow leaves that are glossy, bright green. Small spikes of flowers (seen here as seedheads in mid-autumn) are arranged in openly branched heads, each head about 3in/8cm across. Just below the flowers are several long, leaf-like bracts. Since these bracts, as well as the leaves, arch elegantly and widely, the overall effect is one of swirling wispiness. The seedheads persist through winter.
also for: ■ Decorative, green foliage ■ Ornamental fruit (seedheads)

Leucojum aestivum "Gravetye Giant"
[summer snowflake]
○◑

type of plant: hardy bulb [4–9]
flowering time: mid- to late spring
flower color: white + green
height: 24–36in/60–90cm

Few bulbous plants grow well in wet and damp soils but *L. aestivum* and this excellent variety are outstandingly attractive exceptions. *L.a.* "Gravetye Giant" is larger and more robust than the species, and its flowers are displayed more conspicuously above and among the clumps of upright, rich green, strap-shaped leaves. The hanging bells have tiny touches of green on the tips of their petals. There are usually about five bells, each around 1¼in/3cm long, to a stem. *L.a.* "Gravetye Giant" likes humus-rich soils. It can be grown successfully in ordinarily moisture-retentive soil, but damp and even wet conditions produce especially impressive results.
also for: ■ Heavy, clay soils

Chaerophyllum hirsutum "Roseum"
○◑

type of plant: hardy perennial [5–8]
flowering time: late spring to early summer
flower color: lilac-pink
height: 24–30in/60–75cm

This light and airy plant has 2½in/6cm-wide heads of tiny flowers on erect, branching stems. The mid-green foliage is also attractive: its numerous, deeply cut, toothed leaflets create a ferny effect that complements the delicate shape and coloring of the flowers. Humus-rich soil that is either damp or, at least, reasonably moist is most suitable for *C. hirsutum* "Roseum," but it is easily grown in quite a wide range of soils. Its modest elegance seems particularly appealing in the surroundings of an informal garden.
also for: ■ Decorative, green foliage

Trollius europaeus
[globeflower]
○◑

type of plant: hardy perennial [4–8]
flowering time: late spring to early summer
flower color: lemon-yellow
height: 24–30in/60–75cm

T. europaeus makes a lovely cut flower and a beautiful garden plant. Its 2in/5cm-wide flowers are of a satisfying rotundity; they contrast well with the clump of bright green, deeply divided and toothed leaves. The flowers are perched on top of almost leafless, upright stems. This rather variable perennial grows densely and flowers freely in any soil that stays moist during warm weather, but performs particularly well in rich, damp soil. *T.* x *cultorum* "Superbus" (syn. *T. europaeus* "Superbus") is a closely related, free-flowering plant with slightly deeper yellow blooms, while *T.* x *cultorum* "Lemon Queen" and *T.* x *c.* "Alabaster" have pale yellow and pale creamy yellow flowers respectively.
also for: ■ Ground cover ■ Flowers suitable for cutting

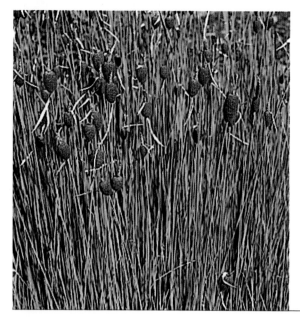

Typha minima
[dwarf cattail, least cattail]
○◑

type of plant: hardy perennial (aquatic) [6–9]
flowering time: mid- to late summer
flower color: rich yellowish brown
height: 24–30in/60–75cm
≈

Although not aggressively invasive like some cattails, T. minima is still quite vigorous and it is not a good choice for a very small area of water. The plant is suitable for growing in fertile mud under water up to 12in/30cm deep. Its more or less egg-shaped flower heads, each about 1in/2.5cm long and topped with a small spike, can be used in dried flower arrangements. The leaves and the flower stems, which are light grayish green, are very thin and conspicuously upright.
also for: ■ Flowers suitable for cutting (mainly drying)

Astilbe e.g. "Deutschland"
○◑

type of plant: hardy perennial [4–8]
flowering time: early to midsummer
flower color: white
height: 18–24in/45–60cm

When given plenty of moisture, the numerous hybrid astilbes such as A. "Deutschland" grow well in full sun—where they often flower very freely; in drier conditions, some shade is needed. A. "Deutschland" bears tiny flowers in plumes 5–6in/12–15cm long. The flower heads rise above thick clumps of shining, rich green leaves that are divided into toothed leaflets. Red-brown seedheads ripen after the flowers have faded. There are also many red- and pink-flowered varieties of astilbe (for examples, see pp.112, 116, 228 and 229). To flourish, these plants generally need fertile, humus-rich soil.
also for: ■ Ground cover ■ Decorative, green foliage ■ Ornamental fruit (seedheads)

Dodecatheon meadia
[shooting stars]
○◑

type of plant: hardy perennial [5–7]
flowering time: mid- to late spring
flower color: variable—magenta-pink, mauve-pink
height: 12–18in/30–45cm

Damp, open-textured soil and cool, woodland conditions are ideal for this perennial. D. meadia also does well near a pond or stream (although it does not like waterlogged soil). The bare flower stems rise erectly, well above low clumps of smooth, pointed, pale green leaves. Each stem carries several delicately shaped, cyclamen-like flowers, about ¾in/2cm long. D. meadia f. album has white flowers. Both plants die down and become dormant after flowering.

Geum rivale
e.g. "Leonard's Variety"
[purple avens, Indian chocolate]
○◑

type of plant: hardy perennial [3–8]
flowering time: late spring to midsummer
flower color: coppery pink
height: 12–18in/30–45cm
Semi-evergreen

Purple avens and its varieties can be grown in damp and in ordinarily moist soils, but their rounded and lobed, bright green, hairy leaves grow most thickly in rather boggy ground. G. rivale "Leonard's Variety" produces numerous, broadly bell-shaped flowers which hang prettily from reddish stalks. Each flower is about 1½in/4cm across. G. rivale itself is also popular but its slightly smaller flowers are usually a less conspicuous, brownish pink; G.r. "Album" has white flowers, and closely related G. "Lionel Cox" produces very pale apricot-yellow flowers.
also for: ■ Ground cover

Juncus effusus f. spiralis
[corkscrew rush]
○◑

type of plant: hardy perennial [4–9]
flowering time: early to late summer
flower color: brown
height: 12–18in/30–45cm
Evergreen ≈

The extraordinary stems of this rush form a rather loose and untidy tangle of twists and curls. New growth is rich green and shiny; older, desiccated, brown stems persist for some time, unless removed. There are no leaves but little brown flowers appear in clusters, about 2in/5cm long, and these are held close to the smooth, cylindrical stems. Corkscrew rush can be grown in an inch or two of water or in soil that is either wet or permanently moist. It does not require lime-free conditions, but it prefers acid soils.

Lysichiton americanus
[yellow skunk cabbage]
○◑

type of plant: hardy perennial (aquatic) [6–9]
flowering time: early to mid-spring
flower color: bright yellow
height: 12–18in/30–45cm; leaves lengthen
after flowering to 24–42in/60–105cm
≈

When lit by low sun early in the year, the musky scented "flowers" of yellow skunk cabbage look splendid, but some gardeners consider that there is a price to pay when the massive, oblong, weed-suppressing leaves lengthen fully later. In an informal, waterside setting, however, the bold clumps of glossy, rich green foliage look very striking. Each "flower" consists of a column of true flowers which is surrounded by a cowl-shaped spathe, about 10in/25cm long. The less vigorous *L. camtschatcensis* has sweetly scented flowers and white spathes. Both plants need deep, rich soil and constant moisture and should be grown in damp or boggy ground.
also for: ■ Ground cover ■ Decorative, green foliage

Fritillaria meleagris
[snake's head fritillary, checkered lily]
○◑

type of plant: hardy bulb [4–9]
flowering time: mid- to late spring
flower color: variable—usually purple but
also purple-pink or white
height: 12in/30cm

Snake's head fritillary is widely admired: its broad, pendent bells, each about 1½in/4cm long, hang from slender stems that also bear a few thin, gray-green leaves. The petals of the darker colored forms are marked with a strange but beautiful checkering. Snake's head fritillary is suitable for naturalizing in grass. However, it is sometimes difficult to establish: not only does it like coolness and moisture but it also requires good drainage. Conditions must remain damp or, at the very least, reasonably moist during the growing season. *F. acmopetala* (see p.324) is often easier to grow.

Houttuynia cordata
"Flore Pleno" (syn. *H.c.* "Plena")
○◑

type of plant: hardy perennial [5–9]
flowering time: midsummer
flower color: white
height: 9–12in/23–30cm
≈

Even in its double-flowered form, *H. cordata* is vigorous enough to be invasive sometimes—especially if it is grown in rich, damp soil or in fertile mud along the edge of a pond or stream. The heart-shaped, red-edged leaves, each about 3in/8cm long and orange-scented, have a purplish, metallic sheen that is slightly more pronounced in sun. Tiny flowers, interspersed with conspicuous, pure white bracts, are arranged in small spikes. *H.c.* "Flore Pleno" can be grown in a wide range of conditions, from very shallow water to ordinary, moisture-retentive soil, but the hotter the climate, the greater the need for some shade. The spreading roots and leafy, upright stems of this plant make good ground cover. *H.c.* "Chameleon" (see p.170) produces variegated foliage.
also for: ■ Ground cover ■ Decorative, green foliage ■ Aromatic foliage

Cardamine pratensis "Flore Pleno"
[cuckoo flower, lady's smock]
○◑

type of plant: hardy perennial [3–8]
flowering time: mid-spring to early summer
flower color: pale lilac
height: 9in/23cm

This slender, little plant is at its most vigorous in fertile soil that is damp or even wet, and it is ideal for growing in an informal or wild garden. It thrives on the banks of a stream or pond but also does well in any soil that remains consistently moist during the growing season. *C. pratensis* "Flore Pleno" produces rosettes of leaves with numerous, rounded leaflets. From these rosettes rise rather fleshy, upright stems that carry sprays of charming, frilly-looking flowers. Each flower is roughly ¾in/2cm across. The foliage is often grayish green.

Myosotis scorpioides
(syn. *M. palustris*) "Mermaid"
[water forget-me-not]
○◑

type of plant: hardy perennial [4–10]
flowering time: early to late summer
flower color: blue
height: 6–9in/15–23cm
Evergreen ≈

The flowers of this water forget-me-not are very small—little more than ¼in/0.5cm across—but they are produced in large numbers from the very beginning of summer. As the season progresses, the stems of the flower sprays elongate and rise above the foliage. This plant is most at home in 2–3in/5–8cm of water, but it also prospers in wet soil or in ground that is, at least, dependably moist. Its slender, pointed leaves are shiny, rich green. They are arranged in tufts that create mats of growth.
also for: ■ Long, continuous flowering period

Primula florindae
[giant cowslip]
◑[○]

type of plant: hardy perennial [6–8]
flowering time: mid- to late summer
flower color: yellow
height: 30–42in/75–105cm

Sweetly and freshly fragrant, pendent flowers on this vigorous, long-lived plant are arranged in big, stylish heads. Individual flowers are up to 1in/2.5cm long and a single head may be hung with as many as eighty flowers. The seedheads, which are dusted in a pale powder, are also attractive. In fertile soil that is damp or wet, the pale flower stems are especially tall and the rosettes of big, long-stalked, broadly heart-shaped leaves form dense, weed-excluding patches of rich green growth. When well suited, giant cowslip self-sows freely.
also for: ■ Ground cover ■ Ornamental fruit (seedheads) ■ Fragrant flowers

Primula bulleyana
◑[○]

type of plant: hardy perennial [6–8]
flowering time: early to midsummer
flower color: orange
height: 24–30in/60–75cm

This primula's ½in/1cm-wide, more or less flat-faced flowers are carried, in a distinctive "candelabra" arrangement, on thick stems, above rosettes of large, rich green, crinkled leaves. In a sunny position, these tiered blooms may well begin to emerge from their red buds in late spring. However, if P. bulleyana is grown in sun, then it is especially important to ensure that the soil remains cool and moist. Its ideal growing conditions are a partially shaded site and deep, humus-rich, damp soil that is neutral to slightly acid. For other so-called Candelabra primulas, see below and right.
also for: ■ Acid soils

Mertensia pulmonarioides
(syn. M. virginica)
[Virginia bluebells, Virginia cowslip]
◑[○]

type of plant: hardy perennial [4–9]
flowering time: mid- to late spring
flower color: rich sky-blue
height: 18in/45cm

No doubt this perennial's sprays of prettily colored, pendent, 1in/2.5cm-long flowers would be seen more commonly in woodland and wild flower gardens if it were not for the fact that, by late summer, not only the flowers but also the smooth, bluish green leaves and the branching stems have died back. Virginia bluebells forms rather loose clumps of more or less upright growth. It is easily grown in any moisture-retentive, humus-rich soil, and it thrives in a damp place near water and in cool woodland.
also for: ■ Gray, blue-gray, or silver leaves

Primula japonica
[Japanese primrose]
◑[○]

type of plant: hardy perennial [6–8]
flowering time: late spring to early summer
flower color: purplish red
height: 18in/45cm

P. japonica and its varieties such as P.j. "Postford White" are easily grown but not especially long-lived perennials. They flourish in acid to neutral soil that is humus-rich and either damp or, at least, reliably moisture-retentive. Japanese primroses can be grown in sun if soil conditions are consistently moist, although the flower color tends to change and fade more quickly in sunshine. The rather flat-faced flowers, each ¾in/2cm across, are arranged in tiers up stout stems that rise clearly above rosettes of light green, blunt-nosed leaves. P.j. "Miller's Crimson" has flowers of a less purple-red; for white-flowered P.j. "Postford White," see right. These are all so-called Candelabra primulas; for further examples, see above and pp.34 and 35.
also for: ■ Acid soils

Primula japonica
e.g. "Postford White"
[Japanese primrose]
◗[◯]
type of plant: hardy perennial [6–8]
flowering time: late spring to early summer
flower color: white + red
height: 18in/45cm

See preceding plant.

ADDITIONAL PLANTS, featured elsewhere in this book, that are suitable for damp and wet soils

◗[◯] **partial shade (or sun)**

minimum height between 3ft/90cm and 10ft/3m
Angelica archangelica, see p.327

minimum height 3ft/90cm or less
Andromeda polifolia "Compacta," see p.35

Filipendula ulmaria "Aurea," see p.216
Hosta fortunei var. *albopicta,*
   see p.177
Hosta sieboldiana var. *elegans,*
   see p.196
Hosta undulata var. *undulata,*
   see p.178

Primula beesiana, see p.35
Primula pulverulenta,
   see p.34
Primula sikkimensis, see p.312
Primula vialii, see p.35
Scrophularia auriculata "Variegata,"
   see p.177

Actaea matsumurae
(syn. *Cimicifuga simplex* var.
matsumurae) e.g. "White Pearl"
[bugbane, baneberry, cohosh,
autumn snakeroot]
◗
type of plant: hardy perennial [4–8]
flowering time: early to mid-autumn
flower color: white
height: 36in/90cm

Above clumps of pale green, ferny foliage, these wands
of pure white flowers appear late in the gardening
year. At first, the slender "bottle-brushes," each
6–8in/15–20cm long, are composed of greenish
buds. These open out into tiny flowers with prominent
stamens—and a rather unpleasant scent. *A. matsumurae*
"White Pearl" is happiest in cool, moisture-retentive
soil and some shade. It thrives in damp, rich soils.
A. racemosa is a taller, summer-flowering species.
For a purple-leaved bugbane, see p.204.
also for: ■ Decorative, green foliage

Hosta undulata var.
albomarginata
(syn. *H.* "Thomas Hogg")
[plantain lily]
◗
type of plant: hardy perennial [3–9]
flowering time: early to midsummer
flower color: lilac
height: 36in/90cm

Most hostas luxuriate in rich, damp soil, although they do not like wet or
waterlogged conditions. *H. undulata* var. *albomarginata* is readily available,
vigorous and easy to grow. Once established, it thrives in heavy clay. Its
bold, pointed, rich green leaves, each about 8in/20cm long, are irregularly
margined in white. They create dense, weed-excluding mounds of growth,
about 18in/45cm high and as much as 36in/90cm wide. The tall spires of
funnel-shaped flowers are carried well clear of the foliage. Other popular
white- or cream-edged hostas include *H.* "Francee," *H.* "Patriot," *H.* "Shade
Fanfare" and *H. crispula* (for the last plant, see p.179).
also for: ■ Heavy, clay soils ■ Ground cover ■ Variegated leaves

Matteuccia struthiopteris
[ostrich fern]
◗
type of plant: hardy fern [2–8]
height: 30–48in/75–120cm

The beautifully symmetrical, sterile fronds of this fern are arranged in
striking "shuttlecocks" of vibrant green. Each frond is made up of numerous,
slender, toothed leaflets, about 4in/10cm long. In winter, the previously
inconspicuous, inner, fertile fronds, each at least 12in/30cm long, persist in
their withered, brown state. Their strange, upright shapes are surprisingly
decorative. Once established, *M. struthiopteris* spreads quite widely,
especially in the damp, boggy or moist conditions that it finds most
congenial. It is handsome near water and in woodland. This fern needs
a sheltered site to look its best.
also for: ■ Decorative, green foliage

ADDITIONAL PLANTS, featured elsewhere in this book, that are suitable for damp and wet soils

◗ **partial shade**

minimum height 3ft/90cm or less
Athyrium filix-femina, see p.231
Blechnum penna-marina, see p.121
Blechnum spicant, see p.37
Hosta crispula, see p.179
Hosta fortunei var. *albopicta* f. *aurea,* see p.217

Hosta lancifolia, see p.121
Onoclea sensibilis, see p.231

◗[◖]/◗◖ **partial shade (or full shade)/partial
or full shade**

minimum height between 3ft/90cm and 10ft/3m
Astilboides tabularis, see p.232

minimum height 3ft/90cm or less
Geranium phaeum, see p.86
Geranium phaeum var. *phaeum* "Samobor,"
   see p.180
Hosta "Halcyon," see p.196
Hosta sieboldiana var. *elegans,*
   see p.196
Sasa veitchii, see p.113

Dry shade

THE VERY MENTION OF DRY SHADE makes normally enthusiastic gardeners become dejected. Even a little preliminary digging in a dry, shady site can be a very depressing exercise, particularly when all that is achieved is the excavation of some pieces of tree root from a shallow layer of dusty soil. However, do not underestimate the satisfaction to be gained from overcoming the problems presented by dry shade.

Areas of dry shade are often created by large trees, although they may also exist at the base of a wall or tall building, particularly if these structures shelter the site from rain-bearing winds. In addition, hedge bottoms are shady places that are notoriously dry with impoverished soil, and some very fast-draining soils can be almost as dry in a little shade as they are in sunshine. Whatever the cause of dry shade, the single factor most likely to solve the problem is the provision of moisture-retaining material. (In the case of hedges, some lessening of the overall size also helps to reduce dryness. The same is true of trees, although any large-scale tree pruning is best left to professional tree surgeons.)

Suitable, moisture-retaining materials include leaf mold, garden compost, and well-rotted manure. All these substances increase the amount of organic matter and thereby improve the ability of soil to retain moisture. At the very least, plants that are to be grown in a dry, shady site should be provided with generously sized planting holes, and these holes should be filled with plenty of the type of organic material mentioned above.

In the case of particularly dry sites that contain a mass of tree roots, it is often worth not only filling the planting holes with plenty of organic matter but also placing a generous layer of moisture-retentive material over the whole area. This new layer—and any subsequent top-dressings and mulches—will, in time, be amalgamated into the existing soil. The process of integration can be speeded up by loosening the soil, as far as possible, before applying the new layer. Until any

newly planted specimen is well established in dry, shaded conditions, it needs to be watched carefully for signs of drought. In certain circumstances, it may be worth considering the installation of an irrigation system.

Growth can become slightly patchy in dry shade, and it is often advisable to restrict planting to several specimens of a single species or variety of plant that really can tolerate the conditions, rather than trying to grow a wide range of different plants.

In the inhospitable conditions of a dry, shaded place, many plants are less vigorous than normal. They may flower and fruit less freely and be rather smaller than usual. Perhaps the best effect to aim for in these difficult sites is plenty of healthy foliage. Neither the ivy (*Hedera*) in this list nor Atlantic ivy (*H. hibernica*) in the following list is especially decorative, but each produces quantities of healthy, rich green foliage. *H. hibernica*, in particular, is very useful for creating extensive sweeps of ground cover beneath large trees. Other, tough ground cover plants that cope well with dry shade include rose of Sharon (*Hypericum calycinum*), *Liriope muscari,* and lesser periwinkle (*Vinca minor*) in this list, as well as, for example, the variegated woodrush *Luzula sylvatica* "Marginata," *Rubus tricolor,* and *Pachysandra terminalis.*

Most of these plants form carpets of growth, but there are plants in this list with different habits of growth. The male fern (*Dryopteris filix-mas*), for example, produces erect to arching fronds, and giant bellflower (*Campanula latifolia* var. *macrantha*) has stiff, upright stems. Taller-growing plants that are tolerant of dry shade include English holly (*Ilex aquifolium*), Oregon grape (*Mahonia aquifolium*) and Japanese laurels such as *Aucuba japonica* "Variegata." Finally, two very attractively scented plants— lily of the valley (*Convallaria*) and Christmas or sweet box (*Sarcococca*)—appear in the "Fragrant flowers" list, pp.296–314, and both tolerate dry shade.

Plants in this list are arranged in order of height alone.

Ribes sanguineum
e.g. "Pulborough Scarlet"
[flowering currant]
◯◑

type of plant: hardy shrub [6–9]
flowering time: mid-spring
flower color: deep red
height: 6–9ft/1.8–2.7m

R. sanguineum and its varieties thrive in well-drained, fertile soil, but they are very tolerant plants that also grow—with remarkable success—in a dry, shady position. Indeed, they are so adaptable that they cope admirably with heavy clay, too. R.s. "Pulborough Scarlet" is a vigorous, upright variety; it is useful for hedging (plants should be about 24in/60cm apart). Other popular varieties include white-flowered R.s. White Icicle and R.s. "Brocklebankii," which has yellow leaves and pink flowers. (R.s. "Brocklebankii" grows slowly and needs a partially shaded site and reasonably moist soil to produce good-quality foliage.) The pendent flower clusters of these plants are 2–3in/5–8cm long. The leaves are neat, three-lobed and usually rich green.
also for: ■ Heavy, clay soils ■ Atmospheric pollution ■ Hedging plants

Hedera helix
e.g. "Green Ripple"
[ivy]
◑●[◯]

type of plant: hardy climber [5–10]
height: 4–6ft/1.2–1.8m; 6in/15cm as ground cover
Evergreen

Among the very many varieties of H. helix are numerous, attractive forms with green foliage, such as H.h. "Green Ripple." The rich green leaves of this variety are up to 3in/8cm long, with sharply pointed lobes and prominent veins. They are held at various angles, giving a lively effect. This very hardy ivy climbs by means of aerial roots. It also makes excellent, carpeting ground cover, about 6in/15cm high. It grows almost anywhere, including dry shade. It is not quite so successful in a sunny place and it is unsuitable for a hot, dry site or waterlogged soil. See also H.h. "Ivalace" (p.150).
also for: ■ Dense shade ■ Atmospheric pollution ■ Ground cover ■ Climbing plants ■ Growing in containers ■ Decorative, green foliage

Campanula latifolia
var. macrantha
[bellflower]
◯◑

type of plant: hardy perennial [4–8]
flowering time: mid- to late summer
flower color: dark violet-blue
height: 36in/90cm

This bellflower is a vigorous perennial that can compete with the roots of other plants in conditions that are quite dry, but not parched. Its bell-shaped flowers are about 2in/5cm long. They are carried on stiff, upright stems above basal clumps of rich green, long-stalked leaves. The plant is at its best—and self-sows—in soil that is moisture-retentive and at least reasonably well drained. There are various white-flowered forms of C. latifolia as well as other varieties with deep blue and with pale blue flowers.

Dryopteris filix-mas
[male fern]
◑●[◯]

type of plant: hardy fern [3–9]
height: 24–48in/60–120cm
Semi-evergreen

Even thoroughly discouraging conditions, such as dry shade, seem to produce quite large and luxuriant specimens of this vigorous, rather erect fern. Male fern "seeds" itself in places where few other plants could be coaxed to survive. Infertile soil and a sunny position inhibit its growth only a little. The mature fronds remain rich green until well into winter and, with the thick roots of the plant, they make good ground cover. There are many varieties of male fern. D. filix-mas "Crispa Cristata" has crested and crisped fronds, and is so decorative that it deserves a cool position and moist soil; it is slightly smaller than the species.
also for: ■ Heavy, clay soils ■ Ground cover ■ Decorative, green foliage

Campanula trachelium
e.g. "Bernice"
[bats-in-the-belfy, nettle-leaved bellflower, throatwort]
◯◑

type of plant: hardy perennial [4–8]
flowering time: mid- to late summer
flower color: rich violet-blue
height: 20in/50cm

Any well-drained soil is suitable for C. trachelium "Bernice" and it thrives in dry soil. Its upright, leafy stems carry clusters of double flowers. Each bell-shaped flower is about 1in/2.5cm long. The leaves are bright mid-green, bristly, toothed and, especially toward the base of the plant, distinctly nettle-like. There are white-flowered forms of this bellflower, with single and with double flowers. C. trachelium itself has blue or mauve blooms; it usually self-sows prolifically.

Helleborus foetidus
[stinking hellebore, bear's foot, dungwort]
◗●[○]

type of plant: hardy perennial [6–9]
flowering time: late winter to mid-spring
flower color: pale green; often + maroon
height: 18–24in/45–60cm
Evergreen

The very dark green, spidery leaves of stinking hellebore contrast strikingly with its pale-stalked, light green flowers. Branched flower heads consist of about a dozen pendent, bell-shaped blooms, each ½–1in/1–2.5cm wide. *H. foetidus* Wester Flisk Group plants have distinctly red-rimmed flowers and leaf-stalks, and their flower stems are reddish, too. All these self-sowing plants are most at home in cool, neutral to alkaline, humus-rich soil, but they also grow in quite dry places. In drier conditions, however, their overlapping fans of foliage form less dense clumps of growth and are less effective as ground cover. For another example of a green-flowered hellebore, see p.327. The cut flowers of these hellebores should be treated in the same way as those of *H. niger* (see p.321). Incidentally, stinking hellebore hardly seems to deserve its off-putting common names.
also for: ■ Shallow soils over chalk ■ Ground cover ■ Decorative, green foliage ■ Flowers suitable for cutting ■ Winter-flowering plants ■ Green flowers ■ Long, continuous flowering period

Symphoricarpos x chenaultii "Hancock"
[snowberry]
○◗●

type of plant: hardy shrub [5–8]
height: 18–24in/45–60cm

This easily-grown, dense and suckering shrub makes effective ground cover almost anywhere, even in a dry, shady place. Over time, it creates a sprawling mass of growth up to 10ft/ 3m wide. Its long-lasting, purplish pink, spherical fruits are about ¼in/0.5cm wide. They ripen from early autumn onward and are most profuse and colorful in a sunny or only lightly shaded site. In shade, they are almost white. Inconspicuous, pink, summer flowers are attractive to bees. The little, oval leaves are bright green and can last well into winter; in cold weather, they may become purple or orange tinted.
also for: ■ Dense shade ■ Atmospheric pollution ■ Ground cover ■ Ornamental fruit

Dicentra eximia
[fringed bleeding heart, turkey corn]
◗[○]

type of plant: hardy perennial [4–10]
flowering time: late spring to early summer and intermittently until autumn
flower color: pink
height: 15in/38cm

The ferny, often grayish green foliage of this spreading perennial makes neat clumps of growth. Fringed bleeding heart nearly always produces a few more of its nodding, bell-shaped blooms after the main flush of flowers. It is easily grown and tolerates dry shade well, but it performs best, self-sowing freely, in humus-rich, woodland soil. *D.* "Luxuriant" has deeper pink blooms. *D. formosa* is very similar to fringed bleeding heart (and may be sold incorrectly under the name *D. eximia*); it, too, is suitable for a dry, shady site. *D. formosa* var. *alba* bears white flowers. The individual blooms on all these plants are ½–1in/1–2.5cm long.
also for: ■ Decorative, green foliage

Geranium nodosum
[cranesbill]
◗●

type of plant: hardy perennial [5–8]
flowering time: late spring to early autumn
flower color: light purplish pink
height: 12–18in/30–45cm

G. nodosum spreads and self-sows in all but the most inhospitable of dry, shaded places. Its veined and lobed leaves are very variable in size. They form fairly loose, spreading clumps of shiny, bright green growth. Over and among this greenery are carried the 1¼in/3cm-wide, funnel-shaped flowers on thin stems. *G. phaeum* and *G. macrorrhizum* and most of their variants can also cope with dry shade, as long as they are given a good start at planting time. (See the index of botanical names for these additional hardy *Geranium*.)
also for: ■ Dense shade ■ Ground cover ■ Long, continuous flowering period

Hypericum calycinum
[rose of Sharon, Aaron's beard]
○◗●

type of plant: hardy shrub [6–9]
flowering time: midsummer to early autumn
flower color: bright yellow
height: 12–18in/30–45cm
Evergreen/Semi-evergreen

Rose of Sharon is such a tough and vigorous shrub that it can compete with the roots of much larger plants and it copes with poor and dry soils in a variety of unpromising places. It makes a mass of erect stems and creeping roots that suppresses weeds very effectively. Even in a difficult site, it may be expected to spread about 5ft/1.5m wide and it is often invasive. Its saucer-shaped flowers have conspicuous stamens and are each about 3in/8cm across. They are carried just above the rich green, pointed, oval leaves.
also for: ■ Dry soils in hot, sunny sites ■ Dense shade ■ Atmospheric pollution ■ Ground cover ■ Long, continuous flowering period

Trachystemon orientalis
◑●◐

type of plant: hardy perennial [5–9]
flowering time: early spring
flower color: bright blue
height: 12–18in/30–45cm

This vigorous, often invasive plant spreads especially quickly and densely in moist, shaded conditions but it makes effective ground cover almost anywhere. In a windy position, however, the leaves—which are arranged in overlapping layers—may rub against each other and become bruised and damaged. When fully expanded, these rough, heart-shaped, rich green leaves are around 10in/25cm long. The little flowers have reflexed petals; they appear just as the leaves begin to unfurl.

also for: ■ Heavy, clay soils ■ Dense shade ■ Ground cover

Epimedium x rubrum
[red barrenwort]
◑◐

type of plant: hardy perennial [4–9]
flowering time: mid- to late spring
flower color: crimson + cream
height: 12in/30cm

E. x rubrum seems to grow adequately almost anywhere, forming spreading, ground covering clumps of foliage about 12in/ 30cm wide. However, it is at its best in fertile, humus-rich, moisture-retentive soil. Its shapely, pointed leaflets are 3–4in/8–10cm long. They are coppery red when young and mid-green in summer; in autumn, the foliage turns pink-tinged deep red and then copper-bronze. The leaves remain on E. x rubrum until spring. Its little, nodding flowers are carried on thin stems.

also for: ■ Ground cover ■ Purple, bronze, or red leaves (young leaves only) ■ Decorative, green foliage ■ Colorful, autumn foliage

Liriope muscari
[lilyturf]
◐◑●

type of plant: hardy perennial [6–10]
flowering time: late summer to late autumn
flower color: violet-mauve
height: 12in/30cm
Evergreen

L. muscari is often used as ground cover for dry soil, especially in shaded sites. It grows slowly and forms dense clumps of growth about 45cm/18in wide. Among the slim, arching, rich green leaves rise erect spikes of tiny, bead-like flowers. Each spike is 5in/12cm or more long. Although this lilyturf is very tolerant, it grows especially well in a cool spot where the soil is light but also moisture-retentive. It has a preference for acid conditions. L. muscari "Munroe White" is a readily available, white-flowered variety. A variegated variety is shown on p.176.

also for: ■ Acid soils ■ Ground cover ■ Long, continuous flowering period

Polypodium vulgare
[wall polypody]
◑◐

type of plant: hardy fern [3–8]
height: 12in/30cm
Evergreen

Wall polypody is very drought-tolerant and it creeps widely over large areas of well-drained or dry soil. It can also be planted in crevices in a wall and, in damper regions particularly, it flourishes on an old tree stump. Its dark green, often leathery fronds are arranged on long, wiry stems. The foliage is less lacy and rather bolder than that of some ferns. It stays green in winter and withers in spring; the new foliage emerges in early summer. P. interjectum "Cornubiense" is another drought-tolerant polypody; it has especially attractive, much-divided fronds.

also for: ■ Ground cover ■ Decorative, green foliage

Lamium galeobdolon
(syn. Galeobdolon luteum,
Lamiastrum galeobdolon)
"Hermann's Pride"
[yellow archangel] ◑●

type of plant: hardy perennial [6–9]
flowering time: early to midsummer
flower color: yellow
height: 6in/15cm
Evergreen/Semi-evergreen

Although in a really difficult, dry, shaded place, the notoriously invasive L. galeobdolon "Florentinum" (syn. "Variegatum") can be useful, a safer choice for most gardens is the less vigorous and more floriferous variety shown here. L.g. "Hermann's Pride" has neat, pointed leaves, about 1¼in/3cm long and precisely patterned with a network of silver markings. Its small, two-lipped flowers are arranged in little whorls. In moist, fertile, well-drained soil, this plant grows densely and forms a carpet at least 18in/45cm wide. In poorer, drier soil it is less vigorous, but it should still perform well.

also for: ■ Heavy, clay soils ■ Dense shade ■ Ground cover ■ Variegated leaves

Vinca minor
[lesser periwinkle, creeping myrtle]
◐◑●

type of plant: hardy shrub [5–9]
flowering time: mainly mid-spring to early summer
flower color: blue
height: 6in/15cm
Evergreen

Lesser periwinkle quickly makes a dense carpet of long, rooting stems and little, glossy, pointed leaves. It tolerates dense shade and dryness, although sunshine and ordinary, well-drained soil encourage it to flower well. There are many varieties of V. minor including, for instance, some with reddish purple flowers, others with white flowers and some that are double-flowered. The varieties with variegated foliage (for an example of which, see p.118) tend to be less vigorous than the species and some of its plain-leaved variants, which can be invasive. The starry flowers of these plants open to about 1in/2.5cm wide from slim, little buds.

also for: ■ Dense shade ■ Atmospheric pollution ■ Ground cover

Cyclamen hederifolium
(syn. C. neapolitanum)
◑[○]

type of plant: hardy tuber [6–9]
flowering time: late summer to mid-autumn
flower color: pink
height: 4–6in/10–15cm

The ivy-like, marbled leaves of this plant appear in autumn and die down in late spring. If the plant is grown under deciduous trees or shrubs, its foliage can, therefore, receive light, even if the larger plants cast dense shade in summer. The flowers, with their gracefully reflexed petals, are up to 1in/2.5cm long. *C. hederifolium* and its variants need good drainage and like light, humus-rich soil. They cope well with dry shade. When well suited, they form thick clumps of foliage and produce numerous self-sown seedlings. These cyclamen are suitable for naturalizing. *C.h.* var. *hederifolium* f. *albiflorum* has pure white flowers and is readily available, though often rather expensive.
also for: ■ Variegated leaves

Lamium maculatum
"Beacon Silver"
[spotted deadnettle]
◑●

type of plant: hardy perennial [4–9]
flowering time: late spring to early summer
flower color: purplish pink
height: 4–6in/10–15cm
Semi-evergreen

This vigorous, carpeting plant has leaves, about 1½in/4cm long, which are almost completely silver, except for a thin green margin. *L. maculatum* "Beacon Silver" grows nearly anywhere, provided there is some shade, but it is at its best in soil that retains moisture easily. Its foliage creates a silvery carpet of growth at least 24in/60cm wide, and this is particularly useful for giving a light effect in deeply shaded areas. The whorled flowers are very small and hooded; they are arranged in spikes. *L. maculatum* itself is also tolerant of dry shade, but most of its other cultivars are not.
also for: ■ Heavy, clay soils ■ Dense shade ■ Ground cover ■ Variegated leaves

Waldsteinia ternata
◑●

type of plant: hardy perennial [4–8]
flowering time: late spring to early summer
flower color: yellow
height: 4in/10cm
Semi-evergreen

W. ternata looks rather like a strawberry plant with yellow flowers. It is a vigorous perennial that soon makes an impenetrable carpet of creeping roots and pretty, three-lobed leaves. It does well in most soils and it tolerates dry shade. It may become invasive in moist, well-drained, fertile conditions. Saucer-shaped flowers, up to ½in/1cm across, are carried in clusters just above the 2½in/6cm-long leaves. The combination of bright yellow flowers and glossy green foliage is most attractive. The leaves are fresh green when young, rich green when mature and they may become bronzed in winter.
also for: ■ Ground cover ■ Decorative, green foliage

ADDITIONAL PLANTS, featured elsewhere in this book, that are tolerant of dry shade

Dense shade

IN NEARLY EVERY GARDEN there is an area that is not only sunless but also so darkened by high walls or by overhanging trees that it is densely shaded. Many plants that would grow well in a site that receives little or no sun will not tolerate the complete lack of light in such very heavily shaded places.

Whether the garden is new or established, these places of barren gloominess can be very discouraging. Often the easiest solution seems to be to treat them as outdoor storage areas and to abandon all hopes of growing anything. Yet, as the illustrated and unillustrated sections of the following list show, the range of plants that tolerate dense shade is actually quite wide.

Between them, the plants described here have several features that will brighten a gloomy corner. Flowers—and any subsequent fruits—are usually rather sparse in positions of poor light. However, it is not only flowers and fruits that lighten a dark place, but also leaves. Several of the plants in the list have shiny foliage, often of a particularly rich green, and glossiness enlivens densely shaded areas. The leaf size of these plants varies considerably: the lobed leaves of x *Fatshedera lizei*, for example, can be as much as 10in/25cm across, while the highly polished, rounded leaves of European wild ginger (*Asarum europaeum*) are 3–4in/8–10cm wide, and the leaf-like, modified shoots of butcher's broom (*Ruscus aculeatus*) are only 1in/2.5cm or so long.

Variegated foliage can lighten and enliven dense shade, but in general the markings on such foliage tend to become very subdued in low light. This is because plants do their best to maximize the chlorophyll-containing, energy-producing, green areas of their leaves when light is very limited. However, there are some plants that manage to remain conspicuously variegated, even in dense shade. Such plants include the variegated form of bishop's weed or goutweed (*Aegopodium podograria* "Variegatum"), a variety of the greater periwinkle (*Vinca major* "Variegata") and almost all the deadnettles

(*Lamium*) in this book. The variegated forms of boxwood (*Buxus*), such as *B. sempervirens* "Aureovariegata," also seem to keep their leaf markings remarkably well in densely shaded places.

Another way to enliven a gloomy spot is to introduce plants that contrast with one another. Differences between plants can be based on leaf size, shape, texture and color, or they may involve variety in habit of growth. *Iris foetidissima* and Solomon's seal (*Polygonatum* x *hybridum*) are two distinctively shaped plants that can add considerable style to gloomy places. They contrast well with plants, such as lesser periwinkle (*Vinca minor*) and wild ginger, that produce low carpets of growth.

Certain densely shaded sites may require tall and medium-sized plants. As well as the ivy (*Hedera*) and x *Fatshedera* at the beginning of this list, suitable, taller-growing plants include shrubs such as boxwood (*Buxus sempervirens* and its forms), Japanese aralia (*Fatsia japonica*), Oregon grape (*Mahonia aquifolium*), Christmas or sweet box (*Sarcococca confusa*) and the cherry laurel *Prunus laurocerasus* "Otto Luyken."

Many plants described here are woodland in origin and have adapted to dry, shaded growing conditions beneath trees. In densely shaded sites that are also dry, this "Dense shade" list can therefore be used in conjunction with the preceding "Dry shade" list, on pp.80–84.

In dense shade, plants may become taller and lankier than usual, as they reach upward toward available light.

NB: Plants in this list are arranged in order of height alone.

Hedera hibernica
(syn. *H. helix* subsp. *hibernica*)
[Atlantic ivy]
◐●[○]

type of plant: hardy climber [5–10]
height: 25ft/7.5m; 9–12in/23–30cm as
ground cover
Evergreen

This vigorous, fast-growing ivy climbs by means of aerial roots and is
suitable for walls of all aspects. It also makes excellent, carpeting ground
cover, at least 6ft/1.8m wide. Atlantic ivy grows in almost any soil, as long as
it is not waterlogged, and in any site, provided it is not hot and dry. This is
an especially useful plant for dry, shaded areas beneath trees. The medium
to large (about 4in/10cm wide), five-lobed leaves are rich green and glossy.
They become darker in winter. Variegated ivies tend to lose their variegation
in densely shaded places, but there are interesting, green-leaved ivies which
succeed in dense shade (for examples, see pp.81 and 150).
also for: ■ Dry shade ■ Atmospheric pollution ■ Ground cover ■ Climbing
plants

x *Fatshedera lizei*
◐●[○]

type of plant: slightly tender shrub [8–11]
height: 3–5ft/0.9–1.5m; to about 12ft/3.6m
when trained against a wall
Evergreen

x *F. lizei* can be grown either as a sprawling, ground covering shrub or,
given support, as a rather loose-limbed "climber." It is tolerant of difficult
conditions, including dry shade and dense shade. Its shapely, lobed, leathery
leaves, up to 10in/25cm across, are a glossy rich green. Rounded heads
of pale green flowers appear in autumn, but they tend not to be freely
produced outdoors in cooler climates. Ideally, this plant should have well-
drained, fertile soil. It needs moist soil if grown in sun. Treated as a sprawling
shrub, it is likely to be more than 10ft/3m wide in maturity.
also for: ■ Dry shade ■ Windswept, seaside gardens ■ Atmospheric pollution
■ Ground cover ■ Climbing plants ■ Growing in containers ■ Decorative,
green foliage

Ruscus aculeatus
[butcher's broom]
◐●[○]

type of plant: hardy shrub [7–9]
height: 2–3ft/60–90cm
Evergreen

Any soil—poor or fertile, heavy or light—is suitable for this stiff, upright,
slow-growing subshrub. It succeeds under a tree and in other dry, shaded
places. The hard, spiny-tipped "leaves" are, in fact, modified shoots; they
are a gleaming dark green and each about 1in/2.5cm long. Tiny flowers are
followed by bright red, shiny berries, just under ½in/1cm in diameter, for
the production of which both male and female plants are needed. (There
are self-fertile plants, but these are not widely available.) The fruit normally
lasts from autumn well into winter, and sometimes persists until late spring.
Danae racemosa is a rather similar plant, with dark green "leaves" and red
berries; it, too, is good in a densely shaded place, although it prefers moister
soil than butcher's broom.
also for: ■ Dry shade ■ Ornamental fruit (see above)

Geranium phaeum
[dusky cranesbill, mourning widow]
◐●

type of plant: hardy perennial [4–8]
flowering time: late spring to early summer
flower color: very dark purple
height: 24–30in/60–75cm
Semi-evergreen

G. phaeum thrives in soil that is cool and moist and at least reasonably well
drained. However, it is adaptable enough to cope with dry shade, too,
although its clumps of light green, veined and lobed leaves may be sparser
and therefore less efficient as ground cover in such conditions. In any case,
the plant does well in a deeply shaded place. Its numerous, nodding flowers,
each ¾in/2cm wide, are carried on erect stems, and they are very attractive
to bees. Among the varieties of *G. phaeum*, white-flowered *G.p.* "Album" is
one of the most readily available; for a variegated form, see p.180.
also for: ■ Damp and wet soils ■ Dry shade ■ Ground cover ■ Decorative,
green foliage ■ "Black" plants

Euphorbia amygdaloides
var. *robbiae* (syn. *E. robbiae*)
[wood spurge]
○◐●

type of plant: hardy/slightly tender perennial [7–9]
flowering time: mid-spring to early summer
flower color: yellow-green
height: 18–24in/45–60cm
Evergreen

This tough, leathery-leaved plant grows in all sorts of
difficult conditions, including dense shade, dry shade
and poor soils. Its upright stems are clothed with
handsome rosettes of narrow, dark green leaves, above
which rise loose, 7in/18cm-long heads of little, cup-
shaped flowers. The flower heads remain decorative
over a long period but, if they are removed as soon as
they begin to fade, the plant grows especially densely
and the foliage is particularly handsome. Even beneath
a tree, *E. amygdaloides* var. *robbiae* makes good,
carpeting ground cover. It is, however, quite often
invasive. If grown in sun it needs moisture-retentive soil.
The flowers and the foliage make attractive cut material
(although care should be taken with the cut stems
since they exude a milky juice that may irritate skin).
also for: ■ Dry shade ■ Ground cover ■ Decorative,
green foliage ■ Flowers suitable for cutting ■ Green
flowers

Rubus tricolor
[ornamental bramble, blackberry]
◐●[○]

type of plant: hardy shrub [7–9]
flowering time: midsummer
flower color: white
height: 12–18in/30–45cm, sometimes to 30in/75cm
Evergreen/Semi-evergreen

Like its relative the bramble or blackberry, *R. tricolor* is an extremely vigorous plant. However, it is a good deal more decorative and useful. Its spreading, rooting stems are bristly and often red-tinged. They are clothed in deeply veined, approximately heart-shaped leaves, up to 4in/10cm long, which are glossy and an excellent, rich dark green. The little, saucer-shaped flowers are usually rather sparse; they are sometimes followed by red, raspberry-like, edible fruits. *R. tricolor* grows almost anywhere but has a preference for shaded places and moist soil. It can expand at a rate of 36in/90cm a season and forms a dense carpet of growth that mounds up with age, until it is sometimes about 30in/75cm high.
also for: ■ Dry shade ■ Ground cover ■ Decorative, green foliage

Asarum europaeum
[European wild ginger]
◐●

type of plant: hardy perennial [4–8]
height: 4–6in/10–15cm
Evergreen

These smooth and very glossy, rounded leaves form quite wide carpets of rich deep green, even in densely shaded places. Each leaf is 3–4in/8–10cm across; in winter the foliage may become slightly burnished. The small, spring flowers are hidden by the leaves. Wild ginger is most at home in moisture-retentive, humus-rich soil that is well drained and neutral to acid, but it is accommodating and prospers in most soils in shade (although it is only moderately tolerant of dry shade).
also for: ■ Ground cover ■ Decorative, green foliage

Ramonda myconi
(syn. *R. pyrenaica*)
◐●

type of plant: hardy perennial [6–8]
flowering time: late spring to early summer
flower color: variable—lavender to violet
height: 4in/10cm
Evergreen

A cool, damp, shady site and light, humus-rich soil provide the ideal growing conditions for this plant. *R. myconi* is able to survive periods of complete dryness. It is more at home growing in a vertical rather than a horizontal position, and so is often planted in wall crevices. Here, its rosettes of wrinkled, red-fringed, dark green leaves as well as its ¾in/2cm-wide flowers are shown to advantage. The flowers are carried, in small sprays, on stiff stems.
also for: ■ Decorative, green foliage

ADDITIONAL PLANTS, featured elsewhere in this book, that are tolerant of dense shade

minimum height 10ft/3m or more
Buxus sempervirens, see p.140
x Fatshedera lizei, see p.86
Ligustrum ovalifolium, see p.140
Rhododendron "Fastuosum Flore Pleno," see p.101
Taxus baccata, see p.140
Taxus baccata "Fastigiata," see p.21

minimum height between 3ft/90cm and 10ft/3m
Fatsia japonica, see p.149
Hedera helix "Green Ripple," see p.81
Sarcococca confusa, see p.321
Taxus cuspidata, see p.63

minimum height 3ft/90cm or less
Aegopodium podagraria "Variegatum," see p.122
Buxus sempervirens "Suffruticosa," see p.141
Convallaria majalis, see p.314
Cornus canadensis, see p.125
Geranium nodosum, see p.82
Geranium phaeum var. *phaeum* "Samobor," see p.180
Hedera helix "Green Ripple," see p.81
Hedera helix "Ivalace," see p.150
Hedera hibernica, see p.86
Helleborus x hybridus, see p.321
Helleborus x hybridus black-flowered, see p.332
Hypericum calycinum, see p.82
Iris foetidissima, see p.261

Lamium galeobdolon "Hermann's Pride," see p.83
Lamium maculatum "Beacon Silver," see p.84
Lamium maculatum "Roseum," see p.124
Lamium maculatum "White Nancy," see p.181
Mahonia aquifolium, see p.122
Maianthemum bifolium, see p.124
Pachysandra terminalis, see p.123
Polygonatum x hybridum, see p.295
Prunus laurocerasus "Otto Luyken," see p.113
Sarcococca hookeriana var. *humilis*, see p.314
Symphoricarpos x chenaultii "Hancock," see p.82
Trachystemon orientalis, see p.83
Vinca major "Variegata," see p.175
Vinca minor, see p.83

Windswept, seaside gardens

THOSE WHO GARDEN INLAND may imagine, as they drive along some coastal road during their summer vacation, that a garden beside the sea must be an entirely trouble-free possession, a place where exotica flourish and familiar plants become almost unrecognizably large and luxuriant. If they could see the same area in autumn and winter, they might change their minds. An exposed, coastal garden, although lovely on a calm day in summer, can be dispiritingly windswept and salt-encrusted during stormy weather. Nevertheless, it is true that the mild, moist climate of the seaside can provide an exceptionally favorable environment in which to grow plants, but only after the problem of salt-laden wind has been dealt with.

All the plants listed below withstand high winds and salt spray. By doing so, not only do they themselves survive but they also shelter and protect other, more vulnerable plants. Once a barrier is established in the face of salt, wind and blown sand, it is possible to grow a very wide range of plants in a seaside garden.

Much the most satisfactory forms of shelter are those that filter wind; solid barriers create turbulence on the leeward side, and this can cause as much damage as winds straight from the sea. In very exposed positions, plants that are intended to form the first line of defence will themselves need the shelter of netting or sacking screens when they are young. Some of the plants in this list are too decorative—and too expensive—to use as part of the first barrier between garden and sea. Usually, plants that are exposed to the full brunt of wind, salt and sand become battered and bent, and their leaves may be scorched and torn. Trees in this position are often little more than misshapen shrubs, yet they perform a very important function.

Practical choices for the first line of defence include the Monterey and Corsican pines (*Pinus radiata* and *P. nigra* var. *laricio*), holm oak (*Quercus ilex*), singleseed hawthorn (*Crataeagus monogyna*) and *Populus alba*.

Other suitable plants include the following species: sycamore maple (*Acer pseudoplatanus*), Monterey cypress (*Cupressus macrocarpa*) and white willow (*Salix alba*). Some decorative varieties of these last three plants are included in this book, but these should be saved for more protected and tranquil positions.

Once a barrier against salt- and sand-laden winds has become established, choosing small and medium-sized plants for a seaside garden presents relatively few problems. Therefore this list concentrates on trees and shrubs 3ft/90cm or more high. Indeed, small plants that naturally hug the ground have a habit of growth that acts as built-in protection against high winds.

When choosing plants for coastal gardens, it is worth bearing in mind some of the other ways in which plants defend themselves against wind and salt spray. Comparatively little damage can be done to leaves that are tough and leathery (see, for example, *Griselinia littoralis*) or to very small or very narrow leaves (see *Tamarix tetrandra* and *Pinus radiata*). Some plants have virtually no leaves (see *Spartium junceum*) or their leaves are very reduced (see *Ulex europaeus* "Flore Pleno").

Certain plants that succeed by the sea have foliage that is partially or completely covered in tiny hairs. These hairs protect the leaf surface from being damaged by salt and blown sand and they also reduce the loss of moisture caused by wind. The two daisy bushes (*Olearia*) illustrated in this list have foliage that is densely hairy beneath and leathery on top. Many gray-leaved plants do well by the sea. *Brachyglottis* (Dunedin Group) "Sunshine", for example, has foliage that is entirely white-felted when young and gray-green with white undersides in maturity. This shrub also has flexible stems, which are invaluable in windy sites.

In windswept, seaside gardens the height of some plants may be lower than average, particularly if the plants are used to provide shelter.

Pinus radiata
[Monterey pine]
○

type of plant: slightly tender conifer [7–10]
height: 80–110ft/24–33m
Evergreen

Monterey pine is at first conical, then broadly dome-headed. It grows very rapidly in most regions and a number of young specimens can soon form an effective shelter belt, especially near the sea. The thin, needle-like leaves, each 4–6in/10–15cm long, are bright green but, in the dense crown of the plant, they appear quite dark. All well-drained soils are suitable for this conifer, although it prefers fairly acid soil; it is short-lived on shallow, chalky soils. Corsican pine (*P. nigra* var. *laricio*, syn. *P.n.* subsp. *maritima*) also makes an excellent, maritime windbreak; it is lime-tolerant, and has attractive, deeply fissured bark.
also for: ■ Acid soils

Quercus ilex
[holm oak]
○

type of plant: slightly tender tree [7–10]
height: 60–80ft/18–24m
Evergreen

When fully exposed to salt-laden winds holm oak grows well, but it is usually quite small and shrub-like. In more tranquil surroundings, it forms a very substantial, leafy, dome-headed tree. The new foliage emerges pale gray in early summer and soon becomes glossy dark green on its upper surface. The leaves, up to 3in/8cm long, are usually oval and pointed. Holm oak can be used for topiary, and it makes an attractive formal hedge (plants should be about 24in/60cm apart). It grows slowly, especially when young. Its yellowish catkins are short-lived. Since very cold winds and late frosts are apt to "burn" the foliage, this tree is more commonly planted in mild regions. Most soils are suitable, but those that are deep, fertile and well drained give the best results.
also for: ■ Atmospheric pollution ■ Hedging plants

Hippophae rhamnoides
[sea buckthorn]
○

type of plant: hardy shrub [4–8]
height: 12ft/3.6m; sometimes up to 25ft/7.5m

Once established, this vigorous, often suckering shrub tends to sow itself liberally in its own shelter. It can be invasive. If plants of both sexes are grown, then dense clusters of numerous, long-lasting, bright yellow-orange berries develop. Each globular berry is just over ¼in/0.5cm in diameter. Narrow, silvery gray leaves, to 2½in/6cm long, help disguise the stiff and rather coarse growth of this thorny plant. Although sea buckthorn thrives on sandy and other light and dry soils, it tolerates a wide range of conditions, including damp soil. If it is used for hedging, young plants should be about 30in/75cm apart. It is a very wind- and salt-tolerant plant.
also for: ■ Dry soils in hot, sunny sites ■ Damp and wet soils ■ Hedging plants ■ Gray, blue-gray or silver leaves ■ Ornamental fruit

Tamarix tetrandra
[tamarisk]
○

type of plant: hardy shrub/tree [6–9]
flowering time: late spring to early summer
flower color: light pink
height: 10–12ft/3–3.6m

Provided it is cut back hard after flowering, *T. tetrandra* maintains its graceful, arching habit and does not become too open and gangling. Its tiny, overlapping, light green leaves, which give a feathery appearance to the whole plant, resist damage from both salt spray and polluted air. They are almost completely obscured at flowering time by the thickly clustered masses of very small, four-petalled flowers. Light, well-drained soils of all types are suitable for this fast-growing plant but very shallow, limy soil is usually best avoided. This tamarisk and the much later-flowering, rose-pink *T. ramosissima* (syn. *T. pentandra*) make good informal hedges in seaside gardens. Young plants for hedging should be about 24in/60cm apart.
also for: ■ Dry soils in hot, sunny sites ■ Atmospheric pollution ■ Hedging plants

Buddleja globosa
[orange ball tree]
○

type of plant: slightly tender/hardy shrub [7–9]
flowering time: early summer
flower color: orange-yellow
height: 8–12ft/2.4–3.6m
Semi-evergreen

The bright pompoms of this rounded and rather open shrub are sweetly scented. There are several dense, globular flower heads, about ¾in/2cm across, at the end of each stiff, more or less erect branch. The veined and pointed leaves, dark green above and pale beige-felted beneath, are large – up to 8in/20cm long. This fast-growing shrub needs good drainage and, ideally, deep, fertile soil. Dry, shallow soil should be avoided. Although orange ball tree is not suitable for a position that is fully exposed to salt-laden winds, it does well in a seaside garden.
also for: ■ Fragrant flowers

Olearia macrodonta
[daisy bush, arorangi]
○

type of plant: slightly tender shrub [8–10]
flowering time: early to midsummer
flower color: white + yellow
height: 8–12ft/2.4–3.6m; up to 20ft/6m in
very mild areas
Evergreen

Like many *Olearia*, this vigorous, upright species is tolerant of strong, salt-laden winds. Its attractive, sage-green, holly-like leaves, each about 3in/8cm long, have the double protection of leathery and glossy upper surfaces and white-felted undersides. Though the numerous "daisies," arranged in heads up to 6in/15cm across, are sweetly fragrant, the musky scent of the foliage tends to dominate. *O. macrodonta* needs well-drained soil and, in inland gardens, a warm, sheltered site. It thrives on chalk. The plant grows quickly and makes a good hedge or screen in maritime areas (young plants should be about 36in/90cm apart).
also for: ■ Shallow soils over chalk ■ Hedging plants ■ Decorative, green foliage ■ Fragrant flowers

Escallonia rubra
"Crimson Spire"
○

type of plant: slightly tender shrub [7–9]
flowering time: midsummer to early autumn
flower color: deep crimson
height: 6–8ft/1.8–2.4m
Evergreen

Many of the hybrid escallonias are valuable plants by the sea since they are so tolerant of salt-laden winds. Because it has an upright habit of growth, *E. rubra* "Crimson Spire" is especially useful for hedging and screening. Its glossy, pointed leaves, each about 1½in/4cm long, form a dense, deep green background for the numerous clusters of ½in/1cm-wide, tubular flowers. In mild areas, this shrub grows quickly; inland, it is slower and needs shelter from frost and cold winds. Almost any soil with reasonable drainage is suitable. Vigorous, red-flowered *E.r.* var. *macrantha* [zones 8–10] grows less erectly than *E.r.* "Crimson Spire," but it too makes an excellent seaside hedge. When used for hedging, both these escallonias should be about 30in/75cm apart. The flowers of these shrubs are attractive to butterflies.
also for: ■ Atmospheric pollution ■ Hedging plants

Lavatera x clementii
e.g. "Rosea"
[mallow]
○

type of plant: slightly tender shrub/
perennial [7–10]
flowering time: early summer to mid-autumn
flower color: rose-pink
height: 6–8ft/1.8–2.4m

This very fast-growing but fairly short-lived subshrub produces numerous, 3in/8cm-wide, cup-shaped blooms over an unusually long period. The dark, upright stems are clothed in lobed, slightly gray leaves. Other popular shrubby *Lavatera* include *L. x clementii* "Barnsley" (see p.334), darker pink *L. x c.* "Burgundy Wine" and mauve-pink *L. x c.* "Bredon Springs". All these plants need a warm site and they are longest-lived in light, well-drained soil. Although they prosper in a seaside garden, they are not suitable for a position that is fully exposed to salt-laden winds.
also for: ■ Long, continuous flowering period

Escallonia
e.g. "Apple Blossom"
○

type of plant: slightly tender shrub [7–9]
flowering time: early to midsummer
flower color: pink-tinged white
height: 6ft/1.8m
Evergreen/Semi-evergreen

Although this dense, rather stiffly branched shrub grows well in coastal regions, it is not quite so suitable for full exposure to sea winds as *E. rubra* and its varieties (for an example of which, see above). However, many gardeners would consider that its pretty sprays of larger flowers make *E.* "Apple Blossom" a more decorative plant (each cupped flower is up to 1in/2.5cm across). The glossy leaves are slender, pointed ovals of dark green. *E.* "Apple Blossom" makes an attractive hedge (young plants should be about 30in/75cm apart). *E.* "Donard Seedling" is rather taller, with smaller, pale pink flowers and is slightly hardier. Both plants prosper in any well-drained soil. Their flowers are attractive to butterflies.
also for: ■ Atmospheric pollution ■ Hedging plants ■ Flowers suitable for cutting

Bupleurum fruticosum
[shrubby hare's ear]
○

type of plant: slightly tender shrub [7–10]
flowering time: midsummer to early autumn
flower color: greenish yellow
height: 5–8ft/1.5–2.4m
Evergreen

A loose structure of slightly curving, reddish brown stems shows both the flower heads and the tongue-shaped leaves of this shrub to advantage. The smooth and gleaming, dark green foliage has a bluish cast to it and the mid-rib of each 3in/8cm-long leaf is distinctly pale. Domed heads of little, starry flowers ripen to pretty seedheads. Inland, *B. fruticosum* needs a warm, sheltered site; in mild, coastal regions, it can be grown in an exposed position. It is tolerant of salty winds. Any well-drained soil is suitable.
also for: ■ Decorative, green foliage

Lupinus arboreus
[tree lupine]
○

type of plant: slightly tender shrub [8–10]
flowering time: early to late summer
flower color: usually pale yellow
height: 5–8ft/1.5–2.4m
Evergreen/Semi-evergreen

Part of the attraction of tree lupine is its ephemeral nature. It quickly makes a spreading mass of upright stems and deeply divided, grayish green leaves. For a few years only, it produces numerous spikes of pea-flowers, each spike up to 12in/30cm long. The flowers are sweetly scented, with a smell reminiscent of clover. The plant's preference is for slightly acid conditions and it is at its best in light, rather poor soil. It is salt- and wind-resistant and does well beside the sea. It often self-sows. There are forms of this plant with white, blue and purple flowers.

also for: ■ Dry soils in hot, sunny sites ■ Fragrant flowers ■ Long, continuous flowering period

Atriplex halimus
[tree purslane, sea orache]
○

type of plant: slightly tender/hardy shrub [7–9]
height: 4–6ft/1.2–1.8m
Semi-evergreen

The arching, pale gray stems of this often loose-growing shrub are clothed in silvery gray, diamond-shaped leaves, up to 2½in/6cm long. The foliage lasts well when cut. Tree purslane is exceptionally resistant to salty, sea winds. It is neatest and densest when grown on light, free-draining, rather poor soils. When young plants are set about 24in/60cm apart they make an attractive, informal hedge. The flowers of *A. halimus* are tiny, and the fruits rarely ripen.

also for: ■ Hedging plants ■ Gray, blue-gray or silver leaves

Hebe
e.g. "Midsummer Beauty"
○

type of plant: slightly tender shrub [8–10]
flowering time: mainly midsummer to mid-autumn
flower color: lilac-purple fading to near-white
height: 4–5ft/1.2–1.5m
Evergreen

The large-leaved hebes are, generally, very floriferous but not very hardy plants. Since they can cope with coastal winds, and since severe frosts are rare in maritime regions, the seaside is a particularly appropriate place for these shrubs. They also grow well in urban areas. *H.* "Midsummer Beauty" produces elegantly tapering spikes of wispy, sweetly scented flowers, each spike 6in/15cm or more long. The blooms, which are attractive to butterflies, usually appear in two main flushes. The bright green leaves are slender and pointed; when young, they are reddish purple beneath. This fast-growing, rounded, fairly erect plant needs well-drained but reasonably moisture-retentive soil. Other popular hebes with large- to medium-sized leaves include *H.* "Great Orme," which has bright pink flower spikes.

also for: ■ Atmospheric pollution ■ Fragrant flowers

Cistus x *purpureus*
[rock rose, sun rose]
○

type of plant: slightly tender shrub [8–10]
flowering time: early to midsummer
flower color: mauve-tinged pink + crimson
height: 3–4ft/0.9–1.2m
Evergreen

Although each of these tissue-thin flowers, up to 3in/8cm across, is very short-lived, there are numerous buds which open in succession. *C.* x *purpureus* is an excellent seaside plant. It thrives in light, dry soils that are not too fertile and it grows well in shallow, chalky soils. It is bushy and rounded with upright stems that are clothed in narrow leaves. In maturity, the foliage is a slightly somber, dark grayish green. The young growths are resinous and fragrant. *C.* x *pulverulentus* "Sunset" has magenta flowers that are even more brightly colored than those of *C.* x *purpureus*.

also for: ■ Shallow soils over chalk ■ Dry soils in hot, sunny sites ■ Atmospheric pollution ■ Aromatic foliage

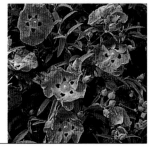

ADDITIONAL SHRUBS (3ft/90cm and over) **AND TREES**, featured elsewhere in this book, that are suitable for windswept, seaside gardens

○ **sun**

minimum height 10ft/3m or more
Elaeagnus "Quicksilver," see p.52
Eucalyptus pauciflora subsp. *niphophila*, see p.264
Fraxinus excelsior "Pendula," see p.40
Populus alba, see p.183

minimum height between 3ft/90cm and 10ft/3m
Brachyglottis "Sunshine," see p.184

Colutea arborescens, see p.253
Escallonia "Iveyi," see p.298
Euonymus japonicus "Ovatus Aureus," see p.162
Griselinia littoralis "Variegata," see p.162
Laurus nobilis "Aurea," see p.211
Lavatera x *clementii* "Barnsley," see p.334
Luma apiculata "Glanleam Gold," see p.162
Myrtus communis, see p.298

Myrtus communis subsp. *tarentina*, see p.146
Olearia x *haastii*, see p.96
Ozothamnus rosmarinifolius, see p.299
Pinus mugo "Mops," see p.15
Pittosporum tobira, see p.298
Rosmarinus officinalis, see p.245
Spartium junceum, see p.52
Ulex europaeus "Flore Pleno," see p.54
Yucca gloriosa "Variegata," see p.164

Griselinia littoralis
[broadleaf]
○[◑]

type of plant: slightly tender shrub [8–10]
height: 10–15ft/3–4.5m; up to 25ft/7.5m
in very mild regions
Evergreen

In really mild, coastal regions, this dense, upright shrub can form a small tree. Its copious, leathery leaves, of an attractive, gleaming apple green, are highly resistant to damage from salt-laden winds. Each leaf is 3–4in/8–10cm long and broadly oval. *G. littoralis* grows quite quickly and makes an excellent hedge or windbreak beside the sea. (Young plants for hedging should be about 24in/60cm apart.) Inland, a sunny, sheltered site is needed. Any fertile and at least reasonably well-drained soil is suitable for this shrub. There are several, even less hardy, variegated varieties of *G. littoralis* (for an example of which, see p.162).
also for: ■ Hedging plants ■ Decorative, green foliage

Rosa
e.g. "Fru Dagmar Hastrup"
(Rugosa)
[rose]
○[◑]

type of plant: hardy shrub [4–9]
flowering time: early summer to mid-autumn
(almost continuously)
flower color: silvery pink
height: 4–5ft/1.2–1.5m

Leathery leaves and thickets of stout stems equip this healthy rose to withstand the effects of salty winds. In addition, the plant thrives in the light, sandy soils so often found in seaside gardens (although it prospers in most soils, including those that are infertile). Its tapering buds open to sweetly scented, 3½in/9cm-wide flowers. The later blooms are accompanied by crimson, tomato-shaped hips. Both the flowers and the fruits are shown to advantage by gleaming, rich green, wrinkled leaves that turn yellow in autumn. Vigorous, prickly *R.* "Fru Dagmar Hastrup," with its rather spreading habit of growth, is suitable for large-scale ground cover. It can also be used for informal hedging (plants should be about 36in/90cm apart).
also for: ■ Atmospheric pollution ■ Ground cover ■ Hedging plants ■ Colorful, autumn foliage ■ Ornamental fruit ■ Fragrant flowers

---

ADDITIONAL SHRUBS (3ft/90cm and over) **AND TREES**, featured elsewhere in this book, that are suitable for windswept, seaside gardens

○[◑] **sun (or partial shade)**

minimum height 10ft/3m or more
Arbutus unedo, see p.257
Cordyline australis, see p.223
Crataegus laevigata "Paul's Scarlet," see p.99
Crataegus monogyna, see p.142
Ilex x altaclerensis "Golden King," see p.168
Ilex aquifolium "Argentea Marginata,"
see p.168
Ilex aquifolium "Ferox Argentea," see p.168
Laurus nobilis, see p.249
Pittosporum tenuifolium, see p.222
Sorbus aria "Lutescens," see p.19

**minimum height between 3ft/90cm
and 10ft/3m**
Berberis darwinii, see p.257
Cordyline australis "Torbay Dazzler,"
see p.148

Elaeagnus pungens "Maculata," see p.169
Laurus nobilis, see p.249
Potentilla fruticosa "Elizabeth," see p.110
Potentilla fruticosa "Vilmoriniana,"
see p.142
Rosa "Blanche Double de Coubert,"
see p.142
Rosa "Roseraie de l'Haÿ," see p.343

○◑ **sun or partial shade**

minimum height 10ft/3m or more
Elaeagnus x ebbingei, see p.140
Ilex aquifolium, see p.139
Ilex aquifolium "Bacciflava," see p.258
Ilex aquifolium "J.C. van Tol," see p.258

**minimum height between 3ft/90cm
and 10ft/3m**
Cotoneaster franchetii, see p.259

Fatsia japonica, see p.149
Fuchsia "Mrs Popple," see p.346
Fuchsia "Riccartonii," see p.143
Garrya elliptica, see p.325
Hydrangea macrophylla "Générale Vicomtesse
de Vibraye," see p.30
Hydrangea macrophylla "Madame Emile
Mouillère," see p.150
Viburnum tinus, see p.318

◑[◐]/◐● **partial shade (or sun)/partial
or full shade**

minimum height 10ft/3m or more
x *Fatshedera lizei,* see p.86

**minimum height between 3ft/90cm
and 10ft/3m**
x *Fatshedera lizei,* see p.86
Fatsia japonica, see p.149

Atmospheric pollution

COMPARED WITH A HUNDRED or even fifty years ago, there are relatively few urban gardeners who have to contend with the problem of growing plants in a dirty, smoky atmosphere. Polluted air is not, however, entirely a thing of the past, and plants need to be carefully chosen for sites near large groups of factories or beside very busy roads.

Some plants are especially well equipped to withstand dirt and grime. A considerable number of these are also tolerant of salt spray, and this makes them useful not only by the seaside but also near roads that are regularly salted in winter. As well as the daisy bush (*Olearia* x *haastii*) and the hawthorn (*Crataegus laevigata* "Paul's Scarlet") in this list, there are numerous other plants in the book that thrive both at the seaside and in polluted air. Holm oak (*Quercus ilex*) and both *Escallonia* illustrated in the "Windswept, seaside gardens" list, pp.88–92, all do well in polluted air, too.

Other salt- and pollution-tolerant plants include various hollies (*Ilex*). Typically, holly leaves are tough and shiny, and many plants that tolerate atmospheric pollution have foliage of this sort. Grime and dust cause relatively little damage to hard or leathery leaves, and rain will wash any dirt off these leaves quickly. Other plants protect themselves by having very few leaves (see, for example, the two different kinds of broom illustrated in this list: *Cytisus* x *praecox* "Allgold" and *Genista lydia*).

In areas in which the atmosphere has been polluted over many years, the soil will have become soured, and possibly impoverished. Many plants with flowers that resemble those of the edible pea can succeed in poor, polluted soils. This is because plants in the pea family can enrich soil with nitrogen themselves. Several plants in this family are illustrated in this list, including Japanese pagoda tree (*Sophora japonica*) and *Laburnum* x *watereri* "Vossii." Other suitable plants of this type include Spanish broom (*Spartium junceum*) and double-flowered gorse (*Ulex europaeus* "Flore Pleno").

Most plants in this list are tolerant of atmospheric pollution because they are inherently vigorous and undemanding. Many are familiar, long-term stalwarts of numerous gardens, but this does not mean that all pollution-tolerant plants are humdrum and uninteresting. There are many stylish plants described in this list. They include magnificent trees, such as weeping silver linden (*Tilia* "Petiolaris") and handkerchief tree (*Davidia involucrata*), as well as glorious flowering shrubs such as *Camellia* and *Magnolia*. Other possible examples range from impressive foliage plants, such as *Fatsia japonica*, to elegant, winter-flowering shrubs such as *Garrya elliptica* and robust roses with wonderfully scented flowers (for example, see *Rosa* "Roseraie de l'Haÿ").

In really poor and very polluted soils only the most vigorous and undemanding plants grow satisfactorily, but if the soil is improved through the addition of large quantities of organic material a much wider range of plants can be cultivated. Such materials include well-rotted manure and garden compost, both of which not only raise fertility but also ameliorate what will almost certainly be very poor soil structure.

Those who deal with the planting and maintenance of sites in areas of atmospheric pollution are often particularly interested in long-lived, woody plants, and this list concentrates on plants of this sort. However, there are perennials, bulbs, annuals and biennials that tolerate atmospheric pollution. Plants in the genera *Coreopsis*, *Dianthus* and *Iberis* are particularly suitable, as are most Japanese anemones (*Anemone* x *hybrida*), lupines (*Lupinus*) and *Aster*. In addition, many African lilies (*Agapanthus*) and bearded iris hybrids grow remarkably well in polluted air, and all the more vigorous ferns and *Bergenia* also prosper in these conditions.

In very polluted areas, some plants will be smaller than they would be under more favorable conditions, and some evergreens may be semi-evergreen or deciduous.

Populus nigra "Italica"
[Lombardy poplar]
○

type of plant: hardy tree [6–9]
height: 80–100ft/24–30m

Even when this fast-growing tree has reached its ultimate height, it is unlikely to be much more than 15ft/4.5m wide. Despite its very slender shape, however, Lombardy poplar is unsuitable for planting near a building, since it has a very extensive root system. Its triangular leaves, up to 4in/10cm long, are—briefly—bronze when young; they mature to glossy, bright green and in autumn they turn yellow. Several specimens can be used to form a windbreak or screen. Most soils, including damp soils and heavy clays, are suitable but growth is best in deep, fertile, moisture-retentive soil with reasonable drainage.
also for: ■ Heavy, clay soils ■ Damp and wet soils ■ Colorful, autumn foliage

Platanus x *hispanica*
(syn. *P.* x *acerifolia*)
[London plane]
○

type of plant: hardy tree [5–8]
height: 70–100ft/21–30m

The mottled trunks, sinuous branches and high, domed crowns of London planes are familiar sights in many European cities. The handsome, lobed leaves, as much as 12in/30cm across, are variable in shape but more or less maple-like. In autumn they turn from bright green to yellow or yellow-orange. Spherical, brown fruits, about 1in/2.5cm in diameter, persist until spring and dangle conspicuously from the leafless branches. Thriving in deep, moist soil and doing well in a range of other moisture-retentive soils, too, London plane is less successful on dry or shallow soil. In regions with hot summers, this very long-lived tree grows especially fast and often achieves heights in excess of 100ft/30m.
also for: ■ Heavy, clay soils ■ Decorative, green foliage ■ Colorful, autumn foliage ■ Ornamental fruit ■ Ornamental bark or twigs

Sophora japonica
[Japanese pagoda tree]
○

type of plant: hardy tree [5–8]
flowering time: late summer to early autumn
flower color: creamy white
height: 60–75ft/18–22.5m

Although upright and growing quickly when young, *S. japonica* spreads into a wide vase shape as it matures. Well-established specimens bear pea-flowers in showy clusters, about 8in/20cm long. In cooler regions, flowering is good only after long, hot summers. In regions where hot summers are the norm, the flowers are followed by persistent, green fruits that look like strings of beads. (When they finally fall, in late winter, these seed pods are slippery underfoot.) The ash-like leaves, to 10in/25cm long, emerge late in spring. They are divided into numerous, slender, rich green leaflets. All well-drained soils are suitable, and this tree thrives in a sunny place and in dry and infertile soil.
also for: ■ Shallow soils over chalk ■ Dry soils in hot, sunny sites ■ Decorative, green foliage ■ Ornamental fruit (seed pods)

Picea omorika
[Serbian spruce]
○

type of plant: hardy conifer [5–8]
height: 50–70ft/15–21m
Evergreen

Serbian spruce is a variable plant. The best forms are very narrowly spire-shaped with curved branches that have upswept tips. The thin, flattened leaves, up to ¾in/2cm long, are dark green above and cream below. Although the pointed cones are quite small, they are a beautiful dark purple when young. This is a very adaptable plant: unusually for a conifer, it tolerates moderately polluted air; it also copes with infertile soils and with both very alkaline and very acid conditions. Serbian spruce is at its best, however, in deep, moist, preferably neutral to acid soil. It does not do well on shallow and dry soil.
also for: ■ Ornamental fruit

Catalpa bignonioides
[Indian bean tree, southern catalpa]
○

type of plant: hardy tree [5–10]
flowering time: mid- to late summer
flower color: white + purple
height: 40–50ft/12–15m

C. bignonioides and its yellow-leaved variety (see p.210) thrive in sheltered sites in urban areas. Their bold, heart-shaped leaves, up to 10in/25cm long and mid-green on the species, do not unfold until early summer. Mature specimens produce loose, upright heads of 2in/5cm-wide, bell-shaped flowers. These are often followed by long, thin, hanging seed pods that are brown when ripe. Both the species and its variety are wide-spreading, rounded trees. They grow best in fertile, moisture-retentive soil, and they perform particularly well in regions with hot summers.
also for: ■ Heavy, clay soils ■ Decorative, green foliage ■ Ornamental fruit (seed pods)

Prunus avium "Plena"
[gean, bird cherry]
○

type of plant: hardy tree [4–9]
flowering time: late spring
flower color: white
height: 35–40ft/10.5–12m

The long-stalked, fully double flowers of this round-headed tree are very freely produced. They appear as the pointed, oval leaves emerge, and they are arranged in generous, hanging bunches. Each flower is about 1½in/4cm across. Being double, the flowers last longer than the slightly earlier, single blooms of P. avium itself. In autumn, the dark green foliage becomes tinged with red. Both the species and P.a. "Plena" grow in most soils; ideally, they should have moist, fertile, well-drained, alkaline soil. The species, which is up to 70ft/21m high, is useful as a fast-growing windbreak inland.
also for: ■ Colorful, autumn foliage

Pyrus calleryana "Chanticleer"
[ornamental pear]
○

type of plant: hardy tree [5–9]
flowering time: mid-spring
flower color: white
height: 30–40ft/9–12m

The upswept, often thorny branches of this tough, pollution-tolerant tree create a neat pyramid of growth—a convenient shape for street plantings. The numerous, clustered, saucer-shaped flowers, each about ¾in/2cm across, are, at first, unaccompanied by any foliage. When fully expanded, the leaves are 3–4in/8–10cm long, rounded with a distinct point, and of a soft, gleaming, dark green. In late autumn or early winter, they turn purplish and deep red; they may be retained on the tree through most of the winter months. P. calleryana "Chanticleer" is suitable for planting in almost any soil. It is tolerant of infertile and moderately dry conditions.
also for: ■ Colorful, autumn foliage

Prunus e.g. "Kanzan"
(syn. P. "Sekiyama")
[ornamental cherry]
○

type of plant: hardy tree [5–9]
flowering time: mid- to late spring
flower color: bright purplish pink fading to pale pink
height: 25–30ft/7.5–9m

The frothy, pink blossom of this ornamental cherry is, briefly, an eye-catching, springtime sight. Fully double flowers, each 2in/5cm across, hang in bunches alongside the emerging, reddish bronze foliage. The tapering leaves mature to deep green, and there is some yellow autumn color. Upright at first, the stiff branches of this short-lived tree spread with age and eventually P. "Kanzan" is rather wider than it is tall. P. "Pink Perfection" is another popular ornamental cherry with pink, double flowers of a less purplish hue than those of P. "Kanzan." As long as they are reasonably fertile and well drained, most soils are suitable for these trees. They flourish and often flower especially well on shallow, chalky soils.
also for: ■ Shallow soils over chalk ■ Purple, bronze or red leaves (young leaves only)

Morus nigra
[black mulberry]
○

type of plant: hardy tree [5–9]
height: 20–30ft/6–9m

Mature specimens of M. nigra bear small, edible, raspberry-like fruits, which are red-black when fully ripe in late summer. Although these mulberries taste good, they are not particularly decorative and it is the spreading dome of stout branches, the large leaves and the eventually gnarled appearance of the often-leaning trunk that make this tree interesting. Its leaves are heart-shaped and up to 6in/15cm long. In autumn they turn from rich green to pale yellow, and they are finally bright yellow. This very long-lived tree needs a sheltered site and deep, fertile soil to produce good crops of fruit. It does not grow successfully on badly drained soil.
also for: ■ Colorful, autumn foliage

Laburnum x watereri "Vossii"
○

type of plant: hardy shrub [4–9]
flowering time: late spring to early summer
flower color: yellow
height: 20–25ft/6–7.5m

Showers of slightly fragrant pea-flowers drape this laburnum. Some of the tapering tassels of blossom are as much as 24in/60cm long, although 12–18in/30–45cm is more usual. They are followed by small quantities of grayish brown seed pods. The main branches of this tree are erect, but the subsidiary growths are arching and spreading and clothed in mid- to dark green, tripartite leaves. Each pointed, oval leaflet is 2–3in/5–8cm long. The small-scale foliage prevents the tree from looking solid and heavy when out of flower. Any well-drained soil is suitable, and this laburnum tolerates very alkaline conditions. All parts of the plant are highly poisonous if eaten.
also for: ■ Shallow soils over chalk

Morus alba "Pendula"
[white mulberry]
○

type of plant: hardy tree [6–9]
height: 10–15ft/3–4.5m

The stiff branches and hanging shoots of this little tree usually form a mushroom of growth, which is clothed to the ground in broad, sometimes lobed, glossy, light green leaves of variable shape and size; some leaves may be up to 7in/18cm long. The foliage turns yellow in autumn. In late summer, raspberry-like fruits, up to 1in/2.5cm long, ripen from white to red. They are generally considered to taste rather insipid compared with the fruits of the black mulberry (for which, see the previous page). A warm, sheltered site and deep, moisture-retentive soil are most suitable for M. alba "Pendula." Good drainage is important. M. alba itself is a quick-growing, low-branching tree, about 30ft/9m high, with a spreading crown.

Syringa vulgaris
e.g. "Charles Joly"
[common lilac, French lilac]
○

type of plant: hardy shrub [4–8]
flowering time: late spring to early summer
flower color: dark purple
height: 10–12ft/3–3.6m

The popular varieties of common lilac are tough, vigorous plants which grow well in most urban and industrial districts. S. vulgaris "Charles Joly" has erect branches with smooth, rich green, pointed leaves and double flowers which are arranged in dense heads, at least 6in/15cm long. These flowers are richly and heavily scented. S.v. "Andenken an Ludwig Späth" (syn. "Souvenir de Louis Spaeth") is a single-flowered variety of deep purplish red coloring. Common lilac and its varieties all have a fairly short flowering season. Their greedy roots need fertile soil and good drainage to grow well. They thrive on shallow, chalky soils and, once established, they also do well on chalky clays.
also for: ■ Shallow soils over chalk ■ Heavy, clay soils (see above) ■ Flowers for cutting ■ Fragrant flowers

Buddleja davidii
e.g. "Royal Red"
[butterfly bush, summer lilac]
○

type of plant: hardy shrub [6–9]
flowering time: mid- to late summer
flower color: deep purplish red
height: 7–10ft/2.1–3m

Varieties of B. davidii are robust, free-flowering shrubs with richly and sweetly scented blooms that are very attractive to butterflies. The varieties vary in color from dark reds and purples (such as B.d. "Royal Red," illustrated here, and B.d. "Black Knight" with its very deep violet flowers), through mid-blues and pinks (such as B.d. "Empire Blue") to whites (see p.298). A variegated cultivar is shown on p.162. B.d. "Royal Red" has especially large—up to 20in/50cm long—flower spikes at the ends of its arching growths. It leaves are spear-shaped and mid-green. All these plants thrive in a wide range of well-drained soils. They tolerate quite dry conditions.
also for: ■ Shallow soils over chalk ■ Fragrant flowers

Olearia x haastii
[daisy bush]
○

type of plant: slightly tender/hardy shrub [8–10]
flowering time: mid- to late summer
flower color: white + yellow
height: 5–6ft/1.5–1.8m
Evergreen

Pollution-tolerant and also well-equipped to succeed in a fully exposed position by the sea, this dense, rounded shrub is very floriferous. Its little, yellow-centered "daisies" have a sweet, but not entirely pleasant scent. They are arranged in clusters, up to 3in/8cm wide. The leathery leaves, no more than 1in/2.5cm long, have white-felted undersides and smooth, sage-green upper surfaces. In towns and by the sea, O. x haastii is a good hedging or screening plant (plants should be about 36in/90cm apart). Any well-drained soil is suitable, and growth on shallow, chalky soils is usually good.
also for: ■ Shallow soils over chalk ■ Windswept, seaside gardens ■ Hedging plants

Cytisus x praecox
e.g. "Allgold"
[broom]
○

type of plant: hardy shrub [6–9]
flowering time: mid- to late spring
flower color: yellow
height: 4–5ft/1.2–1.5m

This fast-growing but rather short-lived shrub has numerous, slender, green twigs. These become less upright and more arching as the plant matures, and they are quite a feature of established specimens. They remain green through winter and add considerably to the general appearance of the plant, since only a few narrow, little leaves are produced. The heavily and pungently scented pea-flowers, each about ½in/1cm long, appear in profusion. Although it is satisfactory on quite a wide range of soils, *C. x praecox* "Allgold" is most successful in really well-drained, rather infertile soil. It does not do well in very alkaline conditions, and it tends to get leggy unless pruned lightly after flowering. Other popular varieties of *C. x praecox* include white-flowered *C. x p.* "Albus," and *C. x p.* "Warminster" (see p.53) which has pale yellow flowers.
also for: ■ Dry soils in hot, sunny sites ■ Ornamental bark or twigs

Rosa e.g. Peace
= "Madame A. Meilland"
(Hybrid Tea or Large-flowered)
[rose]
○

type of plant: hardy shrub [6–9]
flowering time: early summer to mid-autumn
flower color: pale to mid-yellow, flushed with pink
height: 4–5ft/1.2–1.5m

This famous rose is tough, vigorous and bushy. Its pink-edged, double blooms are weather-resistant and, despite their lack of a pronounced fragrance, they are popular for cutting. Each bloom is often more than 4in/10cm wide. The leaves are dark green, glossy and leathery. Ideally, *R.* Peace should have well-cultivated soil but, like most strong-growing varieties, it copes with a wide range of soils, including quite poor soils. Other pollution-tolerant roses in this book include Floribundas such as *R.* Iceberg (see p.346), Rugosas such as *R.* "Roseraie de l'Haÿ" (see p.343) and Ground-cover roses such as *R.* Surrey (see p.105).
also for: ■ Flowers for cutting ■ Long, continuous flowering period

Genista lydia
[broom]
○

type of plant: hardy/slightly tender shrub [7–9]
flowering time: late spring to early summer
flower color: yellow
height: 18–24in/45–60cm

This very floriferous shrub looks especially attractive hanging over the edge of a low wall or covering a steep, sunny bank. It produces masses of ½in/1cm-long pea-flowers that are arranged in short sprays on its dense, arching, gray-green twigs. *G. lydia* is especially free-flowering in sharply drained and rather infertile soil, but it is easily grown in any soil—acid or alkaline—with good drainage. In time, the semi-prostrate branches and arching twigs form hummocks of growth more than 5ft/1.5m wide. The leaves are small and narrow and only sparsely produced, but the twigs give an evergreen effect.
also for: ■ Dry soils in hot, sunny sites ■ Ground cover ■ Ornamental bark or twigs

ADDITIONAL TREES, SHRUBS, AND WOODY CLIMBERS, featured elsewhere in this book, that are tolerant of atmospheric pollution

○ sun

minimum height 10ft/3m or more
Acer platanoides "Crimson King," see p.198
Alnus cordata, see p.40
Catalpa bignonioides "Aurea," see p.210
Catalpa x erubescens "Purpurea," see p.198
Eucalyptus pauciflora subsp. niphophila, see p.264
Fagus sylvatica Atropurpurea Group, see p.198
Fraxinus angustifolia "Raywood," see p.236
Fraxinus excelsior "Pendula," see p.40
Genista aetnensis, see p.52
Ginkgo biloba, see p.235
Gleditsia triacanthos "Rubylace," see p.198
Gleditsia triacanthos "Sunburst," see p.210
Liriodendron tulipifera, see p.219
Liriodendron tulipifera "Aureomarginata," see p.161
Magnolia grandiflora "Exmouth," see p.297
Malus "Royalty," see p.198
Metasequoia glyptostroboides, see p.65
Paulownia tomentosa, see p.219
Populus alba, see p.183
Populus x jackii "Aurora," see p.161
Prunus "Amanogawa," see p.13
Prunus cerasifera "Pissardii," see p.198
Prunus "Kiku-shidare-zakura," see p.14
Prunus x subhirtella "Autumnalis," see p.316
Prunus "Taihaku," see p.13
Pyrus salicifolia "Pendula," see p.183
Quercus ilex, see p.89

Quercus palustris, see p.235
Quercus rubra, see p.235
Rhus typhina, see p.236
Robinia pseudoacacia "Frisia," see p.210
Rosa "Albertine," see p.127
Salix alba subsp. vitellina "Britzensis," see p.264
Syringa x josiflexa "Bellicent," see p.40
Syringa vulgaris "Katherine Havemeyer," see p.297
Syringa vulgaris "Madame Lemoine," see p.269
Tamarix tetrandra, see p.89

minimum height between 3ft/90cm and 10ft/3m
Berberis x stenophylla, see p.138
Berberis thunbergii f. atropurpurea, see p.200
Berberis thunbergii f. atropurpurea "Rose Glow," see p.163
Buddleja davidii "Harlequin," see p.162
Buddleja davidii "White Profusion," see p.298
Ceanothus x delileanus "Gloire de Versailles," see p.52
Colutea arborescens, see p.253
Cytisus x praecox "Warminster," see p.53
Escallonia "Apple Blossom," see p.90
Escallonia "Iveyi," see p.298
Escallonia rubra "Crimson Spire," see p.90
Euonymus japonicus "Ovatus Aureus," see p.162
Hebe "Midsummer Beauty," see p.91
Hedera helix "Buttercup," see p.211
Hibiscus syriacus "Oiseau Bleu," see p.334
Hibiscus syriacus "Woodbridge," see p.145

Phormium tenax, see p.221
Phormium tenax Purpureum Group, see p.199
Rhamnus alaternus "Argenteovariegata," see p.162
Sambucus nigra f. porphyrophylla "Gerda," see p.329
Spartium junceum, see p.52
Spiraea "Arguta," see p.41
Symphoricarpos orbiculatus "Foliis Variegatis," see p.163
Syringa meyeri "Palibin," see p.14

minimum height 3ft/90cm or less
Berberis thunbergii f. atropurpurea "Atropurpurea Nana," see p.202
Brachyglottis "Sunshine," see p.184
Ceratostigma willmottianum, see p.337
Cistus x argenteus "Silver Pink," see p.56
Cistus x hybridus, see p.55
Cistus x purpureus, see p.91
Eucalyptus gunnii, see p.184
Genista hispanica, see p.105
Hebe rakaiensis, see p.106
Hebe "Silver Queen," see p.147
Hebe "Youngii," see p.108
Phormium "Yellow Wave," see p.164
Rosa Surrey, see p.105
Rosa Whisky Mac, see p.301
Spiraea japonica "Anthony Waterer," see p.141
Ulex europaeus "Flore Pleno," see p.54
Weigela florida "Foliis Purpureis," see p.200

Tilia "Petiolaris"
[weeping silver linden]
○[◐]

type of plant: hardy tree [5–8]
height: 60–80ft/18–24m

Even in winter, this big, bold, very long-lived tree looks magnificent. It forms a very broad column of growth (60ft/18m or more wide) with weeping branches, hanging shoots, and dense masses of foliage that touch the ground. The rounded leaves, up to 4in/10cm long, are gleaming dark green above, pale and white-felted below; they turn light yellow in autumn. They are long-stalked and flutter in the breeze. In late summer, T. "Petiolaris" bears hanging clusters of tiny, pale yellow flowers; these are not very conspicuous but they have a strong, rich, sweet fragrance. The nectar is poisonous to bumble bees. T. "Petiolaris" prefers but does not require alkaline soil. Most soils, including heavy clays, are suitable, and the tree thrives in fertile, moisture-retentive soil with good drainage. It dislikes dry soil.
also for: ■ Heavy, clay soils ■ Colorful, autumn foliage ■ Fragrant flowers

---

Crataegus phaenopyrum
(syn. C. cordata)
[Washington hawthorn]
○[◐]

type of plant: hardy tree [4–8]
flowering time: early summer
flower color: white
height: 25ft/7.5m

In autumn, the foliage of Washington hawthorn turns from mid-green to shades of red and orange with some purplish undertones. Each maple-like leaf is deeply lobed, glossy and about 2½in/6cm long. Small, bowl-shaped flowers last only about two weeks and, although they look pleasing, they have a pungent and unpleasant smell. The main attraction of Washington hawthorn is its shiny scarlet fruit. These spherical berries, each about ¼in/0.5cm long, hang in generous bunches and usually last right through winter. In outline the tree is broadly rounded to oval. It is very twiggy, and the branches and trunk are thorny. This tough and adaptable plant can be grown in a wide range of soils, though moist, well-drained conditions produce the best results.
also for: ■ Shallow soils over chalk ■ Heavy, clay soils ■ Colorful, autumn foliage ■ Ornamental fruit

Malus floribunda
[Japanese flowering crabapple, showy crabapple]
○[◑]

type of plant: hardy tree [5–8]
flowering time: mid- to late spring
flower color: pink changing to white
height: 20–25ft/6–7.5m

As its botanical name indicates, this tree flowers abundantly. Individually, the saucer-shaped, slightly fragrant blooms are small—about 1in/2.5cm across—yet the young foliage is almost hidden each spring by the mass of blossom that emerges from deep pink buds. Numerous, tiny, yellow fruits follow the flowers. Semi-pendulous branches, with their deep green, pointed, oval leaves, create a broad crown of growth, and the plant is often wider than it is tall. Japanese floweing crabapple is easy to grow in most soils, including moderately heavy clays, but it dislikes waterlogged conditions. It flowers and fruits especially well when planted in full sun.
also for: ■ Heavy, clay soils (see above) ■ Ornamental fruit

Betula pendula
e.g. "Youngii"
[Young's weeping birch]
○[◑]

type of plant: hardy tree [2–8]
height: 18–25ft/5.4–7.5m

The lower branches of B. pendula "Youngii" touch the ground, and so it is not until autumn, when the foliage drops, that the silvery white trunk and branches are really conspicuous. In spring and summer, the triangular, 1½in/4cm-long leaves of this dome-shaped birch are dark green; they turn greenish gold in autumn. B. pendula itself (see p.264) is a graceful tree with pendulous branchlets; B.p. "Tristis" (40–50ft/12–15m high) is narrow and upright with hanging growths. Almost any soil is suitable for these tough and adaptable but short-lived trees. They cope well with poor and dry soils, but they are at their best on neutral to slightly acid soils. For other, small, weeping trees, see pp.14, 54, 65 and 96.
also for: ■ Colorful, autumn foliage ■ Ornamental bark or twigs

Crataegus laevigata
(syn. C. oxyacantha)
e.g. "Paul's Scarlet"
(syn. "Coccinea Plena")
[English hawthorn]
○[◑]

type of plant: hardy tree [5–9]
flowering time: late spring
flower color: deep pink
height: 15–20ft/4.5–6m

The double-flowered forms of C. laevigata such as C.l. "Paul's Scarlet" are more decorative than singleseed hawthorn (see p.142) and they are nearly as robust and hardy. They grow well in towns and cities, and also beside the sea and in exposed gardens inland. Almost any soil is suitable, although they have a preference for the heavier sorts. C.l. "Paul's Scarlet" produces masses of clustered, double flowers, each about ½in/1cm across, and few, if any, dark red berries. Its moderately thorny branches make a round, spreading, often pleasingly asymmetrical head of growth. The lobed leaves are glossy, mid-green and about 2in/5cm long. C.l. "Rosea Flore Pleno" bears double, pale pink flowers; C.l. "Plena" has double, white flowers.
also for: ■ Heavy, clay soils ■ Windswept, seaside gardens

Philadelphus
e.g. "Virginal"
[mock orange]
○[◑]

type of plant: hardy shrub [5–8]
flowering time: early to midsummer
flower color: white
height: 8–10ft/2.4–3m

This tall, vigorous mock orange has a rather ungainly, upright habit of growth. The double or semi-double flowers, 1½–2in/4–5cm across, of P. "Virginal" are held in numerous, large clusters, and they exude an exceptionally sweet and aromatic fragrance. They shine out from among dark green, pointed leaves. There are smaller mock oranges (for an example of which, see p.19), and several varieties have single rather than double flowers—P. "Belle Etoile" and P. "Beauclerk," for example; see also p.305. All these plants are easy to grow. They prosper in fertile, well-drained soil of most sorts and are usually very successful on shallow, chalky soils. P. "Virginal," however, performs best in rich, moist soil, and it can cope with heavy clay.
also for: ■ Heavy, clay soils (see above)
■ Flowers for cutting ■ Fragrant flowers

ADDITIONAL TREES, SHRUBS, AND WOODY CLIMBERS, featured elsewhere in this book, that are tolerant of atmospheric pollution

○[◐] sun (or partial shade)

minimum height 10ft/3m or more
Acer pseudoplatanus "Brilliantissimum," see p.203
Arbutus unedo, see p.257
Betula pendula, see p.264
Crataegus x lavallei "Carrierei," see p.256
Crataegus monogyna, see p.142
Ilex x altaclerensis "Golden King," see p.168
Ilex aquifolium "Argentea Marginata," see p.168
Ilex aquifolium "Ferox Argentea," see p.168
Ilex opaca, see p.254
Jasminum officinale, see p.304
Malus "John Downie," see p.255
Malus tschonoskii, see p.238

Malus x zumi "Golden Hornet," see p.255
Rhododendron "Sappho," see p.27
Rosa "Wedding Day," see p.129
Sorbus aria "Lutescens," see p.19

minimum height between 3ft/90cm and 10ft/3m
Berberis darwinii, see p.257
Cornus alba "Elegantissima," see p.68
Cornus alba "Kesselringii," see p.331
Cornus alba "Sibirica," see p.265
Cornus alba "Spaethii," see p.169
Cornus sericea "Flaviramea," see p.265
Deutzia x elegantissima "Rosealind," see p.19
Elaeagnus pungens "Maculata," see p.169
Jasminum humile "Revolutum," see p.304

Osmanthus delavayi, see p.304
Philadelphus "Silberregen," see p.305
Rhododendron luteum, see p.238
Rosa "Blanche Double de Coubert," see p.142
Rosa "Fru Dagmar Hastrup," see p.92
Rosa "Roseraie de l'Haÿ," see p.343
Weigela "Bristol Ruby," see p.43

minimum height 3ft/90cm or less
Aronia melanocarpa, see p.239
Hebe pinguifolia "Pagei," see p.194
Philadelphus "Manteau d'Hermine," see p.19
Sorbus reducta, see p.224
Spiraea japonica "Goldflame," see p.214

Davidia involucrata
[dove tree, ghost tree, handkerchief tree]
○◐
type of plant: hardy tree [7–9]
flowering time: late spring
flower color: white
height: 40–50ft/12–15m

Specimens of D. involucrata are usually about ten years old before they begin to produce sizeable quantities of the spectacular, petal-like bracts that earn the plant its various common names. A pair of these bracts surrounds each of the true flowers, which are quite small; in contrast, the bracts can be up to 8in/20cm long. Young trees are cone-shaped; mature trees have domed heads of upright to spreading branches. The broad, pointed leaves, each 4–6in/10–15cm long, are mid-green and conspicuously veined. Deep, fertile, moisture-retentive soil produces the best growth, and young trees in particular benefit from some shelter. Red-brown, egg-shaped fruits are often numerous, but they are not especially decorative.

Ligustrum lucidum
[Chinese privet]
○◐
type of plant: slightly tender shrub/tree [8–11]
flowering time: late summer to early autumn
flower color: creamy white
height: 20–30ft/6–9m
Evergreen/Semi-evergreeen

Any well-drained soil is suitable for this vigorous, glossy-leaved privet. Although L. lucidum does not require alkaline soil, it is useful as a large evergreen for rather dry, chalky soils. It is at its best in regions with warm summers, where it will flower very freely and form a large, billowing dome of glinting greenery. In these warmer climates it grows more than 30ft/9m high. Each shining leaf is a sleek, pointed oval, up to 6in/15cm long, of rich deep green. Even in bud, the large, open clusters of little flowers are decorative. Once open, the flowers, which are attractive to butterflies, exude a very sweet, heavy scent which not everyone likes. There are variegated forms of this plant, including L.l. "Excelsum Superbum," which has light green leaves edged in yellow.
also for: ■ Shallow soils over chalk ■ Decorative, green foliage ■ Fragrant flowers (see above)

Magnolia x soulangeana "Lennei"
○◐
type of plant: hardy shrub/tree [5–9]
flowering time: mid- to late spring
flower color: rose-purple + white
height: 20–25ft/6–7.5m

There are a number of varieties of M. x soulangeana with flowers that are rather darker than usual. These include M. x s. "Lennei" (shown here) and deep pink-flowered M. x s. "Rustica Rubra." M. x s. "Lennei" produces its rotund, 4in/10cm-wide goblets mainly in late spring. This slightly later than usual flowering season helps to reduce the likelihood of the developing blooms being damaged by frosts and cold winds. The plant is vigorous, wide-spreading—30ft/9m or more in maturity—and it nearly always remains shrub-like. Its light green, broad-ended leaves are up to 12in/30cm long; they begin to emerge after the first flowers have opened. Ideally, this magnolia should be given deep, fertile, humus-rich soil that is moisture-retentive and acid to neutral, but it tolerates some alkalinity and is successful on heavy clays. It should have a sheltered site. For M. x soulangeana itself, see p.28. M. x s. "Brozzonii" has white flowers late in spring.
also for: ■ Acid soils ■ Heavy, clay soils ■ Flowers for cutting

Rhododendron
e.g. "Fastuosum Flore Pleno"
○●● ✳

type of plant: hardy shrub [5–8]
flowering time: late spring to early summer
flower color: mauve
height: 10–12ft/3–3.6m
Evergreen

As long as they have a lime-free soil that is fairly well drained and reasonably moisture-retentive, some of the older and very hardy, hybrid rhododendrons grow almost anywhere. Many of them are successful in full sun and dense shade, as well as enjoying partial shade, and they make successful town plants. *R.* "Fastuosum Flore Pleno" has large heads of long-lasting, semi-double flowers. The individual blooms are funnel-shaped and 2–3in/5–8cm long. The plant has a rounded outline, with upright branches and medium-sized, dark green, leathery, pointed leaves. Other examples of large, very hardy hybrids are shown on pp.27 and 29.
also for: ■ Acid soils ■ Dense shade

Magnolia stellata
[star magnolia]
○●

type of plant: hardy shrub [5–9]
flowering time: early to mid-spring
flower color: white
height: 8–10ft/2.4–3m

Unusual among magnolias for producing its slim-petalled, slightly fragrant flowers from a very early age, this sturdily twigged, rounded species is a popular choice for a small garden. Its velvety, sage-green buds begin to open early in spring and the flowers are therefore liable to damage unless the plant has a site sheltered from frosts, cold winds and the effects of too-rapid thawing by early morning sun. The abundant flowers are each about 4in/10cm across. Narrow, mid- to light green leaves appear after the flowers. *M. stellata* grows slowly and is best in deep, fertile soil that is well drained but moisture-retentive and ideally contains little or no lime. However, this is not a demanding plant. *M.s.* "Royal Star" has flowers with more numerous petals; *M.* x *loebneri* "Leonard Messel" is a tree magnolia (up to 25ft/7.5m high) with pale pink, starry flowers.
also for: ■ Acid soils ■ Heavy, clay soils

Chaenomeles speciosa
(syn. *C. lagenaria*) e.g. "Nivalis"
[Flowering quince]
○●

type of plant: hardy shrub [5–9]
flowering time: early spring to early summer
flower color: white
height: 6–8ft/1.8–2.4m

Although the many popular varieties of *Chaenomeles* grow in almost any soil and site, they flower and fruit better in sunny positions and in reasonably fertile, well-drained soil (very alkaline conditions should be avoided). *C. speciosa* "Nivalis" is a vigorous variety with a rather open network of erect, dark branches. It looks best when trained against a wall (any aspect is suitable) and it may then exceed the heights given here. Often particularly early to flower, it produces its 1½in/4cm-wide, cup-shaped blooms over a long period. These are popular for cutting. The first flowers appear before the glossy, oval leaves; they are followed by apple-like fruits, which are greenish yellow and aromatic and which ripen in late summer and early autumn. Popular *C. speciosa* "Geisha Girl" bears peach-colored flowers; varieties with red blooms include low-growing *C.s.* "Simonii."
also for: ■ Heavy, clay soils ■ Ornamental fruit ■ Flowers for cutting ■ Long, continuous flowering period

Rhododendron
e.g. "Gibraltar"
[azalea]
○◑✳

type of plant: hardy shrub [5–9]
flowering time: late spring
flower color: bright orange + yellow
height: 5–7ft/1.5–2.1m

The stout, upright shoots of this vigorous azalea carry numerous, dense trusses of bright flowers. These trusses are often 6in/15cm in diameter. The funnel-shaped flowers, soft crimson in bud, have frilly edges to their petals. In autumn the medium-sized, pointed leaves of *R.* Gibraltar" turn a mixture of bronze, red and orange. Other popular, deciduous azaleas with flowers of this sort of warm color include *R.* "Klondyke," which has bright orange-gold flowers. For a hybrid of much paler, softer coloring, see p.309. All these plants need soil that is lime-free and it should also be well drained and moisture-retentive.

also for: ■ Acid soils ■ Colorful, autumn foliage

ADDITIONAL TREES, SHRUBS, AND WOODY CLIMBERS, featured elsewhere in this book, that are tolerant of atmospheric pollution

○◑ **sun or partial shade**

minimum height 10ft/3m or more
Acer campestre, see p.21
Acer griseum, see p.266
Acer platanoides "Drummondii," see p.170
Aesculus x carnea "Briotii," see p.45
Amelanchier canadensis, see p.28
Aralia elata, see p.225
Buxus sempervirens, see p.140
Carpinus betulus, see p.143
Carpinus betulus "Fastigiata," see p.44
Cotoneaster frigidus "Cornubia," see p.258
Elaeagnus x ebbingei, see p.140
Euonymus fortunei "Emerald Gaiety," see p.113
Euonymus fortunei "Silver Queen," see p.151
Fagus sylvatica, see p.143
Fagus sylvatica "Pendula," see p.21
Hedera colchica "Dentata Variegata," see p.171
Hydrangea anomala subsp. petiolaris, see p.131
Ilex aquifolium, see p.139
Ilex aquifolium "Bacciflava," see p.258
Ilex aquifolium "J.C. van Tol," see p.258
Ligustrum ovalifolium, see p.140
Magnolia x soulangeana, see p.28
Osmanthus heterophyllus, see p.141
Parthenocissus quinquefolia, see p.240
Parthenocissus tricuspidata, see p.240
Pyracantha "Orange Glow," see p.258
Pyracantha "Soleil d'Or," see p.45
Rhododendron "Cynthia," see p.29

Rosa "Madame Alfred Carrière," see p.133
Sorbus aucuparia, see p.28

minimum height between 3ft/90cm and 10ft/3m
Acer negundo "Flamingo," see p.171
Aesculus parviflora, see p.242
Aucuba japonica "Variegata," see p.150
Buxus sempervirens "Aureovariegata," see p.172
Chaenomeles x superba "Knap Hill Scarlet,"
  see p.345
Chaenomeles x superba "Pink Lady," see p.45
Cotoneaster franchetii, see p.259
Cotoneaster horizontalis, see p.267
Cotoneaster salicifolius "Exburyensis," see p.259
Cotoneaster simonsii, see p.143
Euonymus fortunei "Emerald 'n' Gold," see p.174
Fatsia japonica, see p.149
Forsythia x intermedia "Lynwood Variety," see p.21
Forsythia ovata, see p.319
Garrya elliptica, see p.325
Hedera helix "Oro di Bogliasco," see p.133
Hydrangea macrophylla "Générale Vicomtesse
  de Vibraye," see p.30
Hydrangea macrophylla "Madame Emile
  Mouillère," see p.150
Hypericum "Hidcote," see p.345
Kerria japonica "Pleniflora," see p.289
Ligustrum ovalifolium "Aureum," see p.171
Lonicera nitida "Baggesen's Gold," see p.215
Mahonia x media "Charity," see p.318
Photinia davidiana "Palette," see p.172

Rhododendron "Berryrose," see p.30
Ribes sanguineum "Pulborough Scarlet," see p.81
Rosa Iceberg, see p.346
Taxus cuspidata, see p.63
Viburnum tinus, see p.318
Viburnum tinus "Variegatum," see p.172
Weigela "Florida Variegata," see p.172

minimum height 3ft/90cm or less
Buxus sempervirens "Suffruticosa," see p.141
Cotoneaster dammeri, see p.118
Cotoneaster horizontalis, see p.267
Euonymus fortunei "Emerald Gaiety," see p.113
Euonymus fortunei "Emerald 'n' Gold," see p.174
Euonymus fortunei "Silver Queen," see p.151
Hedera colchica "Dentata Variegata," see p.171
Hedera helix "Congesta," see p.228
Hedera helix "Ivalace," see p.150
Hydrangea "Preziosa," see p.346
Hypericum calycinum, see p.82
Lonicera nitida "Silver Beauty," see p.172
Lonicera pileata, see p.113
Parthenocissus quinquefolia, see p.240
Parthenocissus tricuspidata, see p.240
Prunus laurocerasus "Otto Luyken," see p.113
Skimmia x confusa "Kew Green," see p.310
Stephanandra incisa "Crispa," see p.114
Symphoricarpos x chenaultii "Hancock," see p.82
Vinca major "Variegata," see p.175
Vinca minor, see p.83
Vinca minor "Argenteovariegata," see p.118

Camellia japonica
e.g. "Lavinia Maggi"
◑[◯] ✳

type of plant: hardy shrub [7–10]
flowering time: early to mid-spring
flower color: white or pale pink + carmine + pink
height: 6–8ft/1.8–2.4m
Evergreen

The numerous varieties of *C. japonica* are some of the most elegant plants for a city garden. Their rather formal flowers are in shades of red (see, for example, p.32), white (see p.152) or pink (for instance, *C.j.* "Debutante" has light pink flowers and *C.j.* "Elegans" produces deep rose-pink blooms). Some plants, such as double-flowered *C.j.* "Lavinia Maggi" (shown here) and semi-double *C.j.* "Lady Vansittart," have striped flowers (each 3–4in/8–10cm wide). *C.j.* "Lavinia Maggi" is a vigorous, fairly upright plant with broad, pointed leaves. All *japonica* camellias produce handsome, leathery foliage that is glossy and usually dark green. They need moisture-retentive, humus-rich, acid soil and a sheltered site to perform well. Exposure to early morning sun after frost can result in serious damage to the flowers. In cooler regions, *williamsii* camellias (for examples of which, see p.29) are often more satisfactory.

also for: ■ Acid soils ■ Growing in containers ■ Decorative, green foliage

Hydrangea macrophylla
(Hortensia) e.g. "Ayesha"
◑[◯]

type of plant: hardy/slightly tender shrub [6–9]
flowering time: midsummer to early autumn
flower color: gray- or blue-lilac or pink (see description) fading to lilac-tinged pale green
height: 4ft/1.2m

Just as popular as mophead (or Hortensia) hydrangeas that have more conventionally shaped flowers (for examples, see pp.30 and 150) is bushy, glossy-leaved *H. macrophylla* "Ayesha" with its distinctive, lilac-like, cupped flowers. Each of its dense, rather flat flower heads is about 6in/15cm wide and very slightly fragrant. The rich green leaves are broad with tapering points. A sheltered site and fertile, moisture-retentive soil with good drainage give the most satisfactory results. Acid soil produces the bluest coloring; in alkaline conditions the flowers are pinkish.
also for: ■ Growing in containers ■ Long, continuous flowering period

ADDITIONAL TREES, SHRUBS, AND WOODY CLIMBERS, featured elsewhere in this book, that are tolerant of atmospheric pollution

◑[◯] / ◑ partial shade (or sun)/partial shade

minimum height 10ft/3m or more
x *Fatshedera lizei*, see p.86
Hedera canariensis "Gloire de Marengo," see p.136
Hedera hibernica, see p.86
Parthenocissus henryana, see p.180

minimum height between 3ft/90cm and 10ft/3m
Camellia japonica "Adolphe Audusson," see p.32
Camellia japonica "Alba Simplex," see p.152
Hedera helix "Glacier," see p.124
Hedera helix "Green Ripple," see p.81
Hydrangea macrophylla "Mariesii Perfecta," see p.33
Mahonia japonica, see p.312
Philadelphus coronarius "Aureus," see p.217
Sarcococca confusa, see p.321
Weigela Briant Rubidor, see p.216

minimum height 3ft/90cm or less
Berberis thunbergii "Aurea, see p.216
x *Fatshedera lizei*, see p.86
Hedera canariensis "Gloire de Marengo," see p.136
Hedera helix "Glacier," see p.124
Hedera helix "Green Ripple," see p.81

Hedera hibernica, see p.86
Mahonia aquifolium, see p.122
Sarcococca hookeriana var. *humilis*, see p.314
Skimmia japonica subsp. *reevesiana*, see p.260
Skimmia japonica "Rubella," see p.34

◑● partial or full shade

minimum height 10ft/3m or more
Buxus sempervirens, see p.140
Euonymus fortunei "Emerald Gaiety," see p.113
Euonymus fortunei "Silver Queen," see p.151
x *Fatshedera lizei*, see p.86
Hedera canariensis "Gloire de Marengo," see p.136
Hedera hibernica, see p.86
Ligustrum ovalifolium, see p.140
Parthenocissus henryana, see p.180
Parthenocissus quinquefolia, see p.240
Parthenocissus tricuspidata, see p.240
Rhododendron "Fastuosum Flore Pleno," see p.101

minimum height between 3ft/90cm and 10ft/3m
Buxus sempervirens "Aureovariegata," see p.172
Fatsia japonica, see p.149
Hedera helix "Glacier," see p.124

Hedera helix "Green Ripple," see p.81
Sarcococca confusa, see p.321
Taxus cuspidata, see p.63

minimum height 3ft/90cm or less
Buxus sempervirens "Suffruticosa," see p.141
Euonymus fortunei "Emerald Gaiety," see p.113
Euonymus fortunei "Silver Queen," see p.151
x *Fatshedera lizei*, see p.86
Hedera canariensis "Gloire de Marengo," see p.136
Hedera helix "Congesta," see p.228
Hedera helix "Glacier," see p.124
Hedera helix "Green Ripple," see p.81
Hedera helix "Ivalace," see p.150
Hedera hibernica, see p.86
Hypericum calycinum, see p.82
Lonicera pileata, see p.113
Mahonia aquifolium, see p.122
Parthenocissus quinquefolia, see p.240
Parthenocissus tricuspidata, see p.240
Prunus laurocerasus "Otto Luyken," see p.113
Sarcococca hookeriana var. *humilis*, see p.314
Skimmia x *confusa* "Kew Green," see p.310
Symphoricarpos x *chenaultii* "Hancock," see p.82
Vinca major "Variegata," see p.175
Vinca minor, see p.83

Ground cover

THE TERM "GROUND COVER" seems rather dated now, but this does not mean that low-maintenance, weed-excluding plants have gone out of fashion or that they are no longer regarded as useful. We do not use the term "ground cover" so much today, mainly because we now take it for granted that covering the ground more or less densely with plants is a sensible idea. Obviously, ground cover plants save labor because they greatly reduce weeding, but they have other advantages too. They save water by reducing evaporation (an important consideration where soils are dry and where desiccating winds may exacerbate difficulties). Some ground cover plants are useful for binding loose soils on sites such as steep slopes, where erosion can be a serious problem. Finally, many gardeners like the natural look that collections of hummock-forming or carpeting plants produce.

Unless a gently undulating carpet of very similarly sized plants is the effect actually aimed at, however, it is best to avoid the temptation to plant only the quickest-maturing material, which tends to be hummock-forming or carpeting. Trees and larger shrubs introduce variety to ground cover. Even in plantings made up entirely of fast-maturing material, the effect need not be monotonous if careful attention has been paid to contrasts in, for example, the color and shape, and the texture and pattern of leaves.

There are considerable differences in the foliage of the many hummock- and carpet-forming plants that are suitable for ground cover. The rich green, deeply cut foliage of bloody cranesbill (*Geranium sanguineum*) and the woolly, gray leaves of cat's ears (*Antennaria microphylla*) are both quite different from the tiny, dark green needles produced by many ground covering heathers. And all these leaves differ from the rounded, white-edged leaves of *Euonymus fortunei* "Emerald Gaiety" and the unusually large, glossy, purplish brown leaves of *Ajuga reptans* "Catlin's Giant."

As well as hummock- and carpet-forming plants, this list features plants with other habits of growth too: the very first plant in the list—*Prunus tenella* "Fire Hill"—produces a slowly spreading thicket of upright stems, as does Oregon grape (*Mahonia aquifolium*). The list also includes plants with, for example, long leaves that arch conspicuously, such as pheasant's tail grass (*Calamagrostis arundinacea*) and various daylilies (*Hemerocallis*).

When planning any ground cover scheme, it is important to remember that some weed-suppressing plants spread very rapidly. Any plant that increases quickly may, at first, seem attractive, especially to the owner of a new garden. However, after a few years, attempts to limit the expansion of plants such as *Trachystemon orientalis* and the bamboo *Pleioblastus argenteostriatus* f. *pumilus* can prove difficult and time-consuming. Any reference, in the comments on each plant, to "rampant" or "invasive" tendencies should be noted, and the long-term implications taken into account. Despite these warnings, most ground cover plants are neither invasive nor difficult to grow, and there are plants of this sort for every soil and site. Indeed, since many woodland plants have a carpeting habit of growth, the choice of ground cover for shady sites—so often regarded as difficult places—is encouragingly large.

Just how successful a particular ground cover scheme turns out to be depends not only on choosing plants appropriate to the soil and site but also on careful preparation. A weed-proof layer of growth can establish rapidly in soil that has been cleared of perennial weeds, thoroughly dug over and, if necessary, enriched.

A particularly useful source of information about ground cover plants is Graham Stuart Thomas" *Plants for Ground Cover* (Dent, 1977). This authoritative work discusses general topics, such as preparation and maintenance, as well as giving details of a wide range of plants of all types, including plants that are suitable for really large areas.

Prunus tenella "Fire Hill"
[dwarf Russian almond]

○

type of plant: hardy shrub [4–9]
flowering time: mid- to late spring
flower color: pink
height: 3–4ft/0.9–1.2m

Clustered along the slender, upright stems of this shrub are numerous bright-budded, bowl-shaped blooms, each 1in/2.5cm or so across. Long, slim leaves, dark green and glossy, unfurl after the airy flowers have faded. *P. tenella* "Fire Hill" prevents weed growth by forming a suckering thicket that increases, in a fairly restrained manner, until the plant is at least as wide as it is tall. Well-drained, moderately fertile soil of most sorts is suitable for this plant, but it does not perform well in dry or very alkaline conditions.

Phlomis russeliana
(syn. *P. samia, P. viscosa*)

○

type of plant: hardy perennial [4–9]
flowering time: mainly early to midsummer
flower color: pale yellow
height: 30–36in/75–90cm
Evergreen

The stout stems of *P. russeliana* are set with whorls of hooded flowers and soft green, rough-textured leaves. In winter the stems and seedheads persist and they are dark and decorative. The basal leaves, which are heart-shaped, 8in/20cm or more long and evergreen, create clumps of weed-smothering growth. This is a vigorous plant, rooting as it spreads, sometimes forming large patches but more often with a spread of about 24in/60cm. It is easily grown in any well-drained soil.
also for: ■ Ornamental fruit (seedheads)

Ceanothus thyrsiflorus
var. *repens* (syn. *C. repens*)
[blueblossom]

○

type of plant: hardy/slightly tender shrub [8–10]
flowering time: late spring to early summer
flower color: mid-blue
height: 24–36in/60–90cm
Evergreen

This fast-growing but not very long-lived ceanothus makes a mounded carpet of spreading growth, which is usually twice as wide as it is high. The abundant flower clusters are tufted cylinders about 1¼in/3cm long. Their attractive coloring is enhanced by the rich glossy green of the approximately oval leaves. Flowering and general growth are best in sheltered sites. Most well-drained, fertile soils are suitable and, once established, this vigorous ceanothus can cope with quite dry conditions. However, *C. thyrsiflorus* var. *repens* does not grow well on shallow, chalky soils.
also for: ■ Dry soils in hot, sunny sites (see above)

Genista hispanica
[Spanish gorse]

○

type of plant: hardy/slightly tender shrub [7–9]
flowering time: late spring to early summer
flower color: bright yellow
height: 24–36in/60–90cm

G. hispanica makes a dense and tidy cushion of prickly growth and is up to 5ft/1.5m wide when mature. It is a very drought-tolerant and wind-resistant plant, which is excellent in a seaside garden and on fast-draining soil. Its narrow leaves are deciduous and only sparsely produced but, because the upright stems are green, the overall effect is evergreen. This is normally a very free-flowering plant. It produces particularly large numbers of its clustered, ½in/1cm-long pea-flowers on light and poor soils.
also for: ■ Dry soils in hot, sunny sites ■ Atmospheric pollution
■ Ornamental bark or twigs

Rosa e.g. Surrey = "Korlanum"
(Ground cover)
[rose]

○

type of plant: hardy shrub [5–9]
flowering time: early summer to mid-autumn
flower color: mid-pink
height: 24–36in/60–90cm

Among the so-called County Series ground cover roses (which also include white-flowered *R.* Kent and yellow-flowered *R.* Gwent), *R.* Surrey is a rather larger plant than most. It forms a mound of dark, glossy, leafy growth about 4ft/1.2m wide. The frilly, double flowers, each approximately 2½in/6cm wide, are carried in clusters. County Series roses are disease-resistant and they flower almost continuously over a long period. They are vigorous enough to cope with poor soils, although they prefer fertile, well-drained, moisture-retentive soil. For illustrations of other roses that make effective ground cover, see *R.* "The Fairy" (p.275) and *R.* "Ballerina" (p.146).
also for: ■ Atmospheric pollution

Achillea millefolium
e.g. "Cerise Queen"
[yarrow]

○

type of plant: hardy perennial [3–8]
flowering time: mid- to late summer
flower color: cerise
height: 24–30in/60–75cm

The pale-eyed flowers of this rather invasive plant are arranged in flat heads, each 3–4in/8–10cm wide. They are carried on upright stems and are useful both for cutting and for drying. Bees and butterflies also find the blooms attractive. In all fertile, well-drained soils the roots and the feathery, dark green foliage of *A millefolium* "Cerise Queen" form a weed-excluding mat of growth about 24in wide/60cm.
also for: ■ Flowers suitable for cutting (and drying)

Hebe rakaiensis
○

type of plant: hardy/slightly tender shrub [7–10]
flowering time: early to midsummer
flower color: white
height: 24–30in/60–75cm
Evergreen

H. rakaiensis is a dense "bun" of tidy, tapering leaves, each of which is ½–¾in/1–2cm long. The plant is, typically, at least a little wider than it is tall. In summer, the apple-green foliage receives a rather uneven dusting of pale, 1½in/4cm-long flower spikes. As well as being useful ground cover, the naturally neat shape of this hebe means it looks good in rather formal settings. It can be lightly clipped. It needs well-drained but not dry soil, and some shelter from cold winds. Other neat, dense, rounded hebes include *H. cupressoides* "Boughton Dome" and *H. topiaria*.
also for: ■ Atmospheric pollution ■ Growing in containers ■ Decorative, green foliage

Centaurea hypoleuca
"John Coutts"
[knapweed, hardheads]
○

type of plant: hardy perennial [4–8]
flowering time: early to late summer
(see description)
flower color: bright clear pink
height: 24in/60cm

This sturdy and vigorous plant makes good ground cover on sunny, well-drained ground. Its clumps of foliage are usually about 24in/60cm wide. Although it has spreading roots, it increases quite slowly and is not invasive. The long, many-lobed leaves are light grayish green above and pale gray beneath. Especially when *C. hypoleuca* "John Coutts" is growing well, its 2½in/6cm-wide flowers are borne almost continuously during summer and sometimes into autumn too. These bright pink, ruff-like blooms are carried on strong stems, which are only a little taller than the clumps of foliage. The flowers last well in water, and they are attractive to bees and butterflies.
also for: ■ Flowers suitable for cutting

Bidens ferulifolia
○

type of plant: grown as half-hardy annual [8–10]
flowering time: early summer to mid-autumn
flower color: yellow
height: 18–24in/45–60cm

The slender stems and finely divided, bright green leaves of this very free-flowering plant create a mass of trailing growth that is at least as wide as it is high. *B. ferulifolia* is a popular ingredient of hanging baskets but it also makes good, short-term ground cover. There are varieties of this plant with slightly larger flowers and with a more prostrate habit of growth. The starry flowers of the species are 1¼–1½in/3–4cm across, and are carried in little sprays. Although these plants tolerate some dryness, they are best in well-drained soil that retains moisture.

Sedum "Herbstfreude"
(syn. S. Autumn Joy)
[stonecrop]
○

type of plant: hardy perennial [3–10]
flowering time: early to mid-autumn
flower color: rose-pink changing to salmon-pink, then deep terracotta
height: 18–24in/45–60cm

S. "Herbstfreude" is attractive from spring onward, when its rosettes of fleshy, blue-green leaves first appear. The foliage and upright stems develop into a ground covering clump of growth. Even when green and in bud, the big, flat flower heads are striking: they are often 6in/15cm wide. Once fully colored, the flowers are useful for cutting, and they attract bees; they ripen into rich red-brown seedheads. Any well-drained soil is suitable, as long as it is not parched in summer. *S. spectabile* "Brilliant" bears vividly colored, pink flowers of similar shape. *S.s.* "Iceberg" (see p.283) has white flowers.
also for: ■ Gray, blue-gray, or silver leaves ■ Ornamental fruit (seedheads) ■ Flowers suitable for cutting (and drying)

Calluna vulgaris
e.g. "H.E. Beale"
[heather, ling]
○ ✳

type of plant: hardy shrub [5–8]
flowering time: early to late autumn
flower color: shell-pink
height: 18in/45cm
Evergreen

Its tall sprays of double, tubular flowers, its vigor and its late flowering season all account for this plant's long-standing popularity. The flower sprays may be up to 12in/30cm long and they are useful for cutting. The plant forms a dense, spreading hummock of erect stems and tiny, overlapping, dark green leaves. Many of the numerous cultivars of *C. vulgaris*, such as *C.v.* "H.E. Beale" and deeper pink *C.v.* "Peter Sparkes," make very effective ground cover. They are typically a little wider than they are tall. They all need an open position and lime-free, rather infertile soil that is well drained and moisture-retentive.
also for: ■ Acid soils ■ Flowers suitable for cutting ■ Long, continuous flowering period

Erica x darleyensis
e.g. "Darley Dale"
[heath]
○

type of plant: hardy/slightly tender shrub [7–9]
flowering time: early winter to early spring
flower color: pale lilac-pink fading to purplish pink
height: 12–18in/30–45cm
Evergreen

Tiny, narrow, dark green leaves and numerous stems on this hummock-forming heath make excellent ground cover. The plant usually spreads to about 18in/45cm wide. Its little, cylindrical blooms are carried in spikes 2–3in/5–8cm long. Other ground covering varieties of *E. x darleyensis* include white-flowered *E. x d.* "Silberschmelze" (see p.316), *E. x d.* "Arthur Johnson" (pink flowers) and *E. x d.* "Kramer's Rote" (red flowers). Ideally, all these plants should have well-drained, moisture-retentive, acid to neutral soil, though they tolerate some alkalinity. They are intolerant of drought.
also for: ■ Acid soils ■ Winter-flowering plants ■ Long, continuous flowering period

Nepeta x faassenii
(syn. N. mussinii)
[catmint]

○

type of plant: hardy perennial [4–9]
flowering time: early summer to early autumn
(see description)
flower color: lavender-blue
height: 12–18in/30–45cm
Semi-evergreen

Provided its rather curving stems are cut back hard in spring and it is given really well-drained soil, N. x faassenii forms a thick clump of growth and one that is at least as wide as it is tall. Its wrinkled, fairly slender, gray-green leaves, each about 1¼in/3cm long, are hairy. They emit a minty, slightly musty scent when bruised. Cats seem to find this smell attractive and they may roll in the plant. Flower spikes are borne over many weeks—especially if the plant is trimmed again in midsummer. N. "Six Hills Giant" grows up to 36in/90cm tall; it tolerates more soil moisture than N. x faassenii does.
also for: ■ Dry soils in hot, sunny sites ■ Gray, blue-gray, or silver leaves ■ Aromatic foliage

Cytisus x kewensis
[broom]

○

type of plant: hardy shrub [6–9]
flowering time: late spring to early summer
flower color: pale yellow
height: 12–15in/30–38cm

Spreading up to 5ft/1.5m wide, the long, arching, grayish green branches of C. x kewensis grow densely enough to smother most weeds, particularly if the plant is given really well-drained soil and a site in full sun. However, most reasonably well-drained soils are suitable for this more or less prostrate plant. It is good in infertile conditions. There are always very large numbers of ½in/1cm-long pea-flowers, but the small, tripartite leaves are only sparsely produced. C. x beanii is another low-growing broom suitable for ground cover. Its golden yellow flowers cover a dense hummock of erect, green twigs. Both these brooms are short-lived.
also for: ■ Dry soils in hot, sunny sites ■ Growing in containers

Juniperus squamata
"Blue Carpet"
[juniper]

○

type of plant: hardy conifer [5–8]
height: 12–15in/30–38cm
Evergreen

Although the wide-spreading branches of this vigorous juniper may need pruning to keep the plant prostrate, J. squamata "Blue Carpet" does make very good ground cover. It grows slowly, becoming over 4ft/1.2m wide. Its tapering, sharp-pointed leaves, ¼in/0.5cm-long, are blue-gray in summer; the foliage may become tinged with purple. Other "blue" junipers suitable for ground cover include J. horizontalis. "Blue Chip" and J.h. "Bar Harbor" [zones 4–9]. All these plants thrive in well-drained soil and on sunny banks. J. squamata "Blue Carpet" is particularly suitable for shallow, chalky soils.
also for: ■ Shallow soils over chalk ■ Dry soils in hot, sunny sites ■ Gray, blue-gray, or silver leaves

Geum "Borisii"
[avens]

○

type of plant: hardy perennial [5–8]
flowering time: late spring to early summer
flower color: orange-red
height: 12in/30cm
Semi-evergreen

Smaller than some of the other familiar varieties of avens, G. "Borisii" also has a denser clump of bright green foliage beneath its open-faced, 1¼in/3cm-wide flowers. Between them, the lobed basal leaves and the rounded stem leaves cover the ground thickly. Individual plants usually spread about 12in/30cm wide, and branched flower stems rise well above the foliage. Moisture-retentive soil of moderate fertility is most suitable for this plant. It flowers well if divided frequently.

Helianthemum
e.g. "Wisley Primrose"
[sun rose]

○

type of plant: hardy shrub [6–9]
flowering time: late spring to midsummer
flower color: yellow
height: 9–12in/23–30cm
Evergreen

In general, sun roses make good ground cover, especially if they are cut back hard after flowering. H. "Wisley Primrose" is a dense, vigorous variety with slender, gray-green leaves. It forms a hummock of spreading growth about 18in/45cm wide. Although its 1in/2.5cm-wide, saucer-shaped flowers shed their petals in the afternoon, numerous buds provide a succession of blooms. Sun roses thrive in well-drained and dry soil and in warm, sunny sites. They are fairly short-lived plants. For two further hybrid sun roses, see pp.58 and 189.
also for: ■ Dry soils in hot, sunny sites ■ Crevices in paving ■ Gray, blue-gray, or silver leaves

Iberis sempervirens
(syn. I. commutata)
[candytuft]

○

type of plant: hardy perennial/shrub [4–9]
flowering time: late spring to early summer
flower color: white
height: 9–12in/23–30cm
Evergreen

Candytuft creates a trailing carpet, at least 18in/45cm wide, of little, narrow, dark green leaves. The foliage is more or less obscured when all the dazzling white, layered flower clusters are open. Individual clusters are up to 2in/5cm wide. After flowering, the plant should be trimmed to ensure it grows densely. Candytuft thrives in most well-drained soils: it is useful for poor, dry and shallow chalky conditions. I. sempervirens "Weisser Zwerg" (syn. "Little Gem") is smaller and neater than the species. There are also annual candytufts, such as I. umbellata Fairy Series [zones 7–10].
also for: ■ Shallow soils over chalk ■ Dry soils in hot, sunny sites ■ Crevices in paving

Aurinia saxatilis
(syn. *Alyssum saxatile*)
e.g. "Citrina"
[gold dust, cloth of gold,
basket of gold]
○

type of plant: hardy perennial [3–8]
flowering time: mid- to late spring
flower color: pale yellow
height: 9in/23cm
Evergreen

Once highly popular, and still as useful, robust and easily grown as ever, *A. saxatilis* and its varieties form carpeting mounds of foliage beneath masses of tiny flowers. The plants look especially attractive in paving or in walls or along border edges. They thrive in light, well-drained soils, including ones that are shallow and chalky, and they cope admirably with hot, dry conditions. They tend to be rather short-lived. *A.s.* "Citrina" has flowers that are paler than those of the species; they are arranged in numerous little sprays, each about 1¼in/3cm wide. Its slender, pointed leaves are gray-green and covered in short hairs. The plant is usually about 15in/38cm wide. It needs to be cut back hard after flowering to keep its sprawling growth from becoming too loose and untidy.
also for: ■ Shallow soils over chalk ■ Dry soils in hot, sunny sites ■ Crevices in paving ■ Gray, blue-gray, or silver leaves

Hebe "Youngii"
(syn. *H.* "Carl Teschner")
○

type of plant: hardy/slightly tender shrub [7–10]
flowering time: midsummer
flower color: violet-blue
height: 9in/23cm
Evergreen

These little, tapering leaves and their dark stems form tidy, mounded carpets of growth. The shining foliage is a fairly bright, rich green. Typically, *H.* "Youngii" is covered in buds and 1¼in/3cm-long spikes of bowl-shaped flowers. In the well-drained, not too dry soils that are most suitable, this shrub often spreads about 24in/60cm wide. Its neat and floriferous habit makes it a good plant for growing in containers.
also for: ■ Atmospheric pollution ■ Growing in containers

Achillea tomentosa
[yarrow]
○

type of plant: hardy perennial [4–9]
flowering time: mainly early to midsummer
flower color: yellow
height: 6–9in/15–23cm
Evergreen

Smaller than the familiar border achilleas, *A. tomentosa* produces flat-topped flower clusters that are only about 3in/8cm wide. These are held well clear of the neat, rooting mat of narrow and much-divided leaves. The foliage is downy and grayish. As long as it has good drainage, this is an easily grown plant and it tolerates poor and dry soils. It usually spreads to about 12in/30cm wide.
also for: ■ Dry soils in hot, sunny sites

Arabis alpina subsp. *caucasica*
(syn. *A. albida*, *A. caucasica*)
e.g. "Flore Pleno"
[rock cress]
○

type of plant: hardy perennial [4–9]
flowering time: mid- to late spring
flower color: white
height: 6–8in/15–20cm
Evergreen

The tufted mat of foliage produced by *A. alpina* subsp. *caucasica* "Flore Pleno" can be appreciated both as efficient ground cover and as an attractive setting for the loose sprays of ½in/1cm-wide, double flowers. The toothed leaves are softly hairy and gray-green. Easily grown in any soil with good drainage, this tough plant thrives in dry and poor soils. However, it is not a plant for very small spaces, since given enough room it will probably spread to at least 18in/45cm wide. There are pink-flowered forms of this rock cress, and *A.a.* subsp. *c.* "Variegata" has cream edges to its leaves.
also for: ■ Dry soils in hot, sunny sites ■ Crevices in paving ■ Gray, blue-gray, or silver leaves

Antennaria microphylla
(syn. *A. macrophylla*)
[cat's ears]
○

type of plant: hardy perennial [3–8]
flowering time: late spring to early summer
flower color: rose-pink
height: 6in/15cm
Semi-evergreen

The papery blooms of this plant retain their shape well and remain decorative, even in their pale, dried state. They are borne in small clusters on stiff, upright stems, and are illustrated here just after most of their pink coloring has faded. Each fluffy-looking flower is about ½in/1cm across. Little, white-backed, rounded leaves create a tight, gray, woolly mat, up to 24in/60cm wide, which roots as it spreads. To grow well, *A. microphylla* needs light, gritty soil but, as long as there is good drainage, it is quite easily pleased. The flowers dry well but are useful only for very small arrangements.
also for: ■ Dry soils in hot, sunny sites ■ Crevices in paving ■ Gray, blue-gray, or silver leaves

Armeria maritima "Alba"
[sea pink, thrift]
○

type of plant: hardy perennial [4–9]
flowering time: late spring to midsummer
flower color: white
height: 6in/15cm
Evergreen

A. maritima "Alba" holds its stiff-stemmed, long-lasting flower heads well above its bright green foliage. Each "pincushion" flower head is about 1in/2.5cm across. The leaves form a dense cushion of grassy growth at least 12in/30cm wide. Other varieties include A.m. "Splendens," which bears deep purple flowers. The blooms of the species are usually mid-pink. All these plants look especially attractive growing near stone—either on a rock garden, between paving stones or on a dry stone wall. They thrive in poor, dry soil in full sun but succeed in all well-drained soils.
also for: ■ Dry soils in hot, sunny sites ■ Crevices in paving ■ Long, continuous flowering period

Phlox subulata
e.g. "McDaniel's Cushion"
[moss phlox, creeping phlox]
○

type of plant: hardy perennial [3–8]
flowering time: late spring to early summer
flower color: bright pink
height: 5in/12cm
Evergreen

Phlox subulata "McDaniel's Cushion" is floriferous and vigorous, and it is especially useful for ground cover. Its dense cushion of tiny, bright green leaves spreads up to 24in/60cm wide. Numerous little, slim buds open out into starry flowers which are unusually large—up to 1½in/4cm wide. The flowers are arranged in small sprays. For a slower-growing, smaller-flowered variety of moss phlox see p.155. There are dozens of other varieties in various shades of red, purple, lilac and pink: P.s. "Maischnee" (syn. May Snow) is a popular white. Any reasonably fertile, well-drained soil is suitable for these plants.
also for: ■ Crevices in paving

Lithodora diffusa
(syn. Lithospermum diffusum)
"Heavenly Blue"
○✻

type of plant: hardy shrub [6–8]
flowering time: mainly late spring to early summer
flower color: vivid blue
height: 4–6in/10–15cm
Evergreen

In ideal conditions—well-drained, humus-rich, acid soil and a really sunny site—the spreading stems and neat, slender, deep green leaves of L. diffusa "Heavenly Blue" create a weed-proof carpet at least 24in/60cm wide. If necessary, density of growth can be improved by a light clipping after flowering. The funnel-shaped flowers, ½in/1cm wide, are arranged in clusters. They appear in large quantities in the main flowering season and in smaller numbers throughout summer. L.d. "Star," which is a newer variety than L.d. "Heavenly Blue," has blue petals edged in white.
also for: ■ Acid soils ■ Crevices in paving ■ Long, continuous flowering period (see above)

Aubrieta
e.g. "Red Carpet"
○

type of plant: hardy perennial [5–8]
flowering time: mid-spring to early summer
flower color: deep red
height: 3–4in/8–10cm
Evergreen

The more vigorous varieties of aubrieta make very floriferous, although rather short-lived cover for sunny banks. They also look well on walls and in the crevices between paving stones. Like most varieties, A. "Red Carpet" has soft, pointed, grayish green leaves on somewhat sprawling stems. Its dense cushion of growth is usually at least 12in/30cm wide. Loose sprays of single flowers, about 1¼in/3cm across, attract butterflies. The plant flourishes in well-drained, preferably alkaline soil and full sun. Other varieties bear flowers in pink, purple and violet. A few aubrieta have variegated foliage.
also for: ■ Shallow soils over chalk ■ Dry soils in hot, sunny sites ■ Crevices in paving

Chamaemelum nobile
(syn. Anthemis nobilis)
"Treneague"
[chamomile]
○

type of plant: hardy perennial [6–9]
height: 3–4in/8–10cm
Evergreen

Non-flowering chamomile is sometimes used to produce a lawn or path in a really dry place. (It cannot, however, tolerate the very heavy wear and tear that some grasses can withstand.) Creeping stems and rich green, feathery leaves, each 1–1½in/2.5–4cm long, create a dense, rooting carpet, which emits a fruity fragrance when trodden on. Individual plants spread to about 12in/30cm wide. Light, preferably sandy soil is suitable for this plant which, once established, is drought-tolerant. Unless it is clipped once or twice a year, it becomes patchy and bare and is rather short-lived. C. nobile "Flore Pleno" is also popular; it produces white, double, daisy-like flowers.
also for: ■ Dry soils in hot, sunny sites ■ Crevices in paving ■ Aromatic foliage

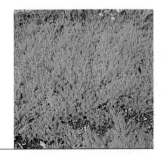

Saponaria ocymoides
[rock soapwort]
○

type of plant: hardy perennial [4–9]
flowering time: early summer
flower color: bright pink
height: 3–4in/8–10cm

S. ocymoides is a vigorous, trailing plant with branched stems and little, bright green leaves that create a weed-suppressing mat of growth. It becomes covered in sprays of open-faced flowers. Each flower is about ½in/1cm across and its outer parts are purplish. Although this plant spreads, sometimes up to 30in/75cm wide, it is easily controlled. It may be restrained, to some extent, by planting it between paving stones or in the crevices of a wall—where it looks very attractive. This is not a long-lived perennial but it does self-sow. It grows well in dry, sunny places and anywhere there is really good drainage.
also for: ■ Dry soils in hot, sunny sites ■ Crevices in paving

ADDITIONAL PLANTS, featured elsewhere in this book, that are suitable for ground cover

○ sun

minimum height 36in/90cm or more
Brachyglottis "Sunshine," see p.184
Campsis x tagliabuana "Madame Galen," see p.127
Juniperus x pfitzeriana "Pfitzeriana Aurea,"
    see p.211
Rosa "Ballerina," see p.146
Salix lanata, see p.185
Spiraea japonica "Anthony Waterer," see p.141
Stipa gigantea, see p.52

minimum height between 12in/30cm and 36in/90cm
Artemisia "Powis Castle," see p.56
Ballota pseudodictamnus, see p.186
Brachyglottis monroi, see p.221
Calluna vulgaris "Gold Haze," see p.212
Calluna vulgaris "Silver Knight," see p.188
Cistus x hybridus, see p.55
Erica vagans "Mrs D.F. Maxwell," see p.26
Genista lydia, see p.97
Glyceria maxima var. variegata, see p.165
Halimium lasianthum, see p.55
Hebe "Mrs Winder," see p.201
Hemerocallis "Stafford," see p.42
Hyssopus officinalis, see p.246
Limonium platyphyllum, see p.280
Lotus hirsutus, see p.187

Pennisetum alopecuroides "Hameln," see p.277
Rosa "The Fairy," see p.275
Salvia officinalis "Purpurascens," see p.201
Santolina chamaecyparissus, see p.138
Santolina pinnata subsp. neapolitana, see p.186
Sedum telephium "Matrona," see p.280
Stachys byzantina, see p.187

minimum height 12in/30cm or less
Acaena saccaticupula "Blue Haze," see p.191
Alyssum spinosum "Roseum," see p.154
Anthemis punctata subsp. cupaniana, see p.189
Arabis ferdinandi-coburgi "Old Gold," see p.167
Arenaria montana, see p.155
Berberis thunbergii f. atropurpurea "Atropurpurea
    Nana," see p.202
Calluna vulgaris "Robert Chapman," see p.237
Centaurea bella, see p.190
Ceratostigma plumbaginoides, see p.237
Convolvulus cneorum, see p.188
Dianthus deltoides, see p.154
Dianthus gratianopolitanus, see p.17
Dorotheanthus bellidiformis Mixed, see p.61
Erica cinerea "C.D. Eason," see p.26
Erica x darleyensis "Silberschmelze," see p.316
Festuca glauca, see p.188
Festuca glauca "Golden Toupee," see p.213
Geranium x riversleaianum "Russell Prichard,"
    see p.341

Gypsophila repens "Rosea," see p.60
Helianthemum "Mrs C.W. Earle," see p.58
Helianthemum "Rhodanthe Carneum," see p.189
Hypericum olympicum, see p.155
Origanum vulgare "Aureum," see p.213
Osteospermum jucundum, see p.57
Phlox douglasii "Boothman's Variety," see p.156
Phlox subulata "Tamaongalei," see p.155
Rosmarinus officinalis Prostratus Group, see p.59
Satureja montana, see p.247
Sedum kamtschaticum var. floriferum
    "Weihenstephaner Gold," see p.342
Sedum "Ruby Glow," see p.190
Sedum spathulifolium "Cape Blanco," see p.61
Sedum spathulifolium "Purpureum," see p.203
Sedum spectabile "Iceberg," see p.283
Sempervivum tectorum, see p.61
Stachys byzantina "Silver Carpet," see p.191
Tanacetum haradjanii, see p.190
Thymus pseudolanuginosus, see p.192
Thymus pulegioides "Bertram Anderson,"
    see p.213
Trifolium repens "Purpurascens Quadrifolium,"
    see p.168
Tropaeolum majus Alaska Series, see p.167
Tropaeolum majus Tall Mixed, see p.129
Tropaeolum Whirlybird Series, see p.58
Veronica prostrata, see p.156
Veronica spicata subsp. incana, see p.189

Acanthus mollis
[bear's breeches]
○ [◐]

type of plant: hardy perennial [7–10]
flowering time: late summer to early autumn
flower color: mauve-purple + white
height: 4ft/1.2m
Semi-evergreen

This plant's spikes of hooded, spiny flowers are 24–36in/60–90cm long. They are not freely produced, but the large size and strong shape of the dark, glossy, lobed leaves are more than adequate compensation. Individual leaves of A. mollis are about 24in/60cm long. They are even longer and more dramatic on the freer-flowering A. spinosus (see p.223), and broader on plants in A. mollis Latifolius Group. The foliage of all these plants rises from tight rosettes and forms mounds of growth. The plants prefer deep, fertile, well-drained soil but, once established, they spread and even self-sow almost anywhere. A.m. "Hollard's Gold" has yellow-green leaves.
also for: ■ Heavy, clay soils ■ Decorative, green foliage

Potentilla fruticosa
e.g. "Elizabeth" (syn. P. arbuscula)
[shrubby cinquefoil]
○ [◐]

type of plant: hardy shrub [3–7]
flowering time: early summer to mid-autumn
flower color: bright primrose-yellow
height: 36in/90cm

P. fruticosa "Elizabeth" has an unusually long flowering season and a neat, dense, weed-smothering habit of growth. It forms a bushy mass, about 4ft/1.2m wide, of crowded twigs and narrow, little leaflets. The mid-green foliage makes an effective background for the bright flowers, each of which is up to 1½in/4cm wide. Other ground covering varieties include P.f. "Abbotswood" (white flowers), P.f. "Tilford Cream" (cream) and P.f. Princess (pink); for a variety with red to orange flowers, see p.343. As long as conditions are not wet or very dry, most soils are suitable for these adaptable plants.
also for: ■ Heavy, clay soils ■ Windswept, seaside gardens ■ Long, continuous flowering period

Hemerocallis
e.g. "Pink Damask"
[daylily]
○ [◐]

type of plant: hardy perennial [4–9]
flowering time: mid- to late summer
flower color: dusky rose-pink
height: 30–36in/75–90cm

There are now literally thousands of hybrid daylilies in cultivation. Most of the popular varieties produce handsome, weed-proof clumps of arching, slender, strap-shaped and usually bright green leaves. H. "Pink Damask" is a vigorous variety and it is free-flowering, especially when planted in a sunny site. Its yellow-throated, 5in/12cm-wide flowers are elegantly star-shaped and have attractive, pale midribs. Though each flower is very short-lived, numerous buds open in succession. H. "Catherine Woodbery" is a pink-flowered, fragrant hybrid of paler, lilac-tinged coloring. Fertile, moisture-retentive soil is most suitable for these daylilies and they grow lushly in damp ground, although they are generally tolerant of quite a wide range of conditions. For additional Hemerocallis see the index of botanical names.
also for: ■ Heavy, clay soils ■ Damp and wet soils ■ Decorative, green foliage

Calamagrostis arundinacea
(syn. *Stipa arundinacea*)
[feather reed grass]
○[◑]

type of plant: hardy perennial (grass) [6–10]
flowering time: midsummer to early autumn
flower color: purplish bronze
height: 30in/75cm
Evergreen

C. arundinacea produces masses of long, thin, arching leaves that form an elegant fountain of dark green growth about 4ft/1.2m wide. As autumn approaches, the foliage assumes tones of russet, orange and yellow. These colors are most pronounced when the plant is grown in well-drained soil and a sunny position. The tiny flowers, which are carried in drooping, 24in/60cm-long heads on very slim stems, create a hazy cloud above the dense sheaves of foliage. Fertile, moisture-retentive soil is most suitable for this plant, but it is easily grown and reasonably adaptable. It usually self-sows freely.

also for: ■ Heavy, clay soils ■ Colorful, autumn foliage (winter color, too)

Stachys macrantha
(syn. *S. grandiflora*)
○[◑]

type of plant: hardy perennial [5–8]
flowering time: early to midsummer
flower color: mauve-pink
height: 18–24in/45–60cm

The wrinkled and scalloped, 3in/8cm-long leaves of *S. macrantha* form a dense clump of growth up to 12in/30cm wide. Above these rich green leaves, sturdy-looking whorls of hooded flowers are borne on erect stems. Bishop's wort or wood betony (*S. officinalis*) is a somewhat similar plant and it too makes good ground cover. It has dense heads of flowers which may be pink, white or red-purple. Any well-drained, fertile soil is suitable for these perennials but conditions need to be reasonably moisture-retentive if the plants are to make effective ground cover. *S. macrantha* "Superba" is a more vigorous and richly colored variety.

Geranium sanguineum
[bloody cranesbill]
○[◑]

type of plant: hardy perennial [4–8]
flowering time: early summer to early autumn
flower color: magenta-pink
height: 9in/23cm

G. sanguineum makes a dense, spreading hummock of growth, usually to about 12in/30cm wide, in any moderately fertile, well-drained soil, including soil that is shallow and chalky. Vividly colored, cup-shaped flowers, up to 1½in/4cm across, are produced over a period of many weeks. In autumn the very deeply cut, rich green leaves often take on red and orange tints. Popular varieties of *G. sanguineum* include the taller, white-flowered *G.s.* "Album" and the shorter *G.s.* var. *striatum* (syn. var. *lancastrense*) with its pretty, pale pink flowers.

also for: ■ Shallow soils over chalk ■ Decorative, green foliage ■ Colorful, autumn foliage ■ Long, continuous flowering period

Erica carnea
e.g. "Springwood White"
[heath, heather]
○[◑]

type of plant: hardy shrub [5–8]
flowering time: midwinter to early spring
flower color: white
height: 8–12in/20–30cm
Evergreen

The tight carpets of growth created by *E. carnea* and its varieties make very effective ground cover. *E.c.* "Springwood White" spreads densely and vigorously, rooting as it goes, to at least 24in/60cm wide. It is consistently free-flowering, with generous spikes of ¼in/0.5cm-long, cylindrical flowers. Its tiny, needle-like leaves are rich bright green and carried on upright stems. *E. carnea* varieties all tolerate some alkalinity and a little shade, but are at their best in an open position and in neutral to acid, humus-rich soil that is well drained and moisture-retentive.

also for: ■ Acid soils ■ Winter-flowering plants ■ Long, continuous flowering period

Geranium dalmaticum
[cranesbill]
○[◑]

type of plant: hardy perennial [5–8]
flowering time: early to midsummer
flower color: soft pink
height: 4–6in/10–15cm
Evergreen/Semi-evergreen

Spreading slowly, to about 18in/45cm wide, this cranesbill forms dense cushions of glossy, light green foliage. Each little leaf is almost circular in outline but deeply divided into several, scalloped lobes. Gently colored, flat-faced flowers, each 1–1½in/2.5–4cm across, are arranged in loose clusters. The foliage turns red in autumn. Provided it has good drainage, this is an easily grown plant. White-flowered *G. dalmaticum* "Album" is less vigorous than the species.

also for: ■ Crevices in paving ■ Decorative, green foliage ■ Colorful, autumn foliage

Acaena microphylla
[New Zealand burr, bidi-bidi]
○[◑]

type of plant: hardy perennial [6–8]
height: 1–2in/2.5–5cm
Semi-evergreen

A. microphylla's tiny leaves, with their numerous, rounded leaflets, knit together into a dense, prostrate mat of bronzed greenery. The suffusion of bronze on the foliage is most pronounced in spring. Small, crimson burrs, spiny and each 1–1¼in/2.5–3cm wide, ripen in late summer, having succeeded inconspicuous flowers. This New Zealand burr spreads fairly rapidly, especially in really well-drained soil and a sunny site; it often reaches 24in/60cm or more across. It copes well with hot, dry conditions and poor soils.

also for: ■ Dry soils in hot, sunny sites ■ Crevices in paving ■ Purple, bronze, or red leaves ■ Ornamental fruit

Lysimachia nummularia "Aurea"
[golden creeping Jenny]
○[◐]

type of plant: hardy perennial [4–8]
flowering time: early to midsummer
flower color: bright yellow
height: 1–2in/2.5–5cm
Evergreen

The ideal growing conditions for this creeping, carpeting plant are full sun and moist, fertile soil. In shadier places the almost circular, ¾in/2cm-diameter leaves are lime-green rather than sharp yellow, and the plant grows less densely. Drier conditions result in patchy growth and less attractive foliage. When well suited, *L. nummularia* "Aurea" is vigorous and spreads widely, to at least 36in/90cm, its long stems rooting as they go. This yellow-leaved variety does not flower as freely as the green-leaved species (which is also useful for ground cover). The flowers of both plants are saucer-shaped and up to ¾in/2cm across.
also for: ■ Heavy, clay soils ■ Damp and wet soils ■ Yellow or yellow-green leaves

---

ADDITIONAL PLANTS, featured elsewhere in this book, that are suitable for ground cover

○[◐] **sun (or partial shade)**

minimum height 36in/90cm or more
Acanthus spinosus, see p.223
Hemerocallis fulva "Flore Pleno," see p.68
Juniperus virginiana "Gray Owl," see p.194
Pseudosasa japonica, see p.223
Rheum "Ace of Hearts," see p.224
Rheum palmatum, see p.223
Rosa "Fru Dagmar Hastrup," see p.92

minimum height between 12in/30cm and 36in/90cm
Anaphalis triplinervis, see p.194

Anthericum liliago, see p.286
Astrantia major "Sunningdale Variegated," see p.169
Geranium x magnificum, see p.239
Hemerocallis "Golden Chimes," see p.224
Heuchera micrantha var. diversifolia "Palace Purple," see p.205
Lathyrus latifolius "White Pearl," see p.130
Melissa officinalis "Aurea," see p.250
Potentilla fruticosa "Tangerine," see p.343
Spiraea japonica "Goldflame," see p.214

minimum height 12in/30cm or less
Ajuga reptans "Atropurpurea," see p.205

Caltha palustris "Flore Pleno," see p.70
Dryas octopetala, see p.157
Erica carnea "King George," see p.317
Erica carnea "Vivellii," see p.344
Geranium renardii, see p.225
Hebe pinguifolia "Pagei," see p.194
Houttuynia cordata "Chameleon," see p.170
Mentha suaveolens "Variegata," see p.170
Oenanthe javanica "Flamingo," see p.70
Phuopsis stylosa, see p.344
Teucrium scorodonia "Crispum Marginatum," see p.170

Astilbe chinensis var. taquetii "Superba"
○◐

type of plant: hardy perennial [5–9]
flowering time: late summer to early autumn
flower color: mauve-pink
height: 4ft/1.2m

This plant flowers a good deal later and is rather taller than some of the more commonly seen varieties of astilbe. Its rich green foliage, divided into several pointed leaflets, makes good ground cover in moisture-retentive or damp soils that are also fertile (though the plant does well in slightly drier conditions, too). Clumps of foliage are usually about 36in/90cm wide. Above them rise densely packed, upright spikes, 18in/45cm or so long, of fluffy flowers, which are followed by brown seedheads. *A. chinensis* var. *taquetii* "Purpurlanze" (syn. Purple Lance) has flowers of pinkish magenta.
also for: ■ Damp and wet soils ■ Decorative, green foliage ■ Ornamental fruit (seedheads)

Rhododendron williamsianum
○◐✳

type of plant: hardy shrub [7–9]
flowering time: mid- to late spring
flower color: pale pink
height: 3–5ft/0.9–1.5m
Evergreen

The outstandingly pretty, bell-shaped blooms of this rhododendron are each about 1½in/4cm long. As the flowers fade, the new foliage emerges. At first, the neat, rounded leaves are richly brown-bronze; in maturity, they are slightly glaucous green. The plant slowly forms a dense dome of growth that may be up to 5ft/1.5m wide. As long as its root-run is moist, cool and lime-free, and the site is fairly sheltered, *R. williamsianum* thrives in sun as well as partial shade. Plants in R. Bow Bells Group include *williamsianum* hybrids that resemble *R. williamsianum* itself and have bell-shaped flowers in shades of light pink; the leaves are reddish bronze when young.
also for: ■ Acid soils ■ Purple, bronze, or red leaves (young leaves only)

Anemone x hybrida
(syn. *A. japonica*)
e.g. "Königin Charlotte"
(syn. Queen Charlotte)
[Japanese anemone]
○◐

type of plant: hardy perennial [5–9]
flowering time: late summer to mid-autumn
flower color: soft pink
height: 3–4ft/0.9–1.2m

Particularly in fairly heavy soils, this erect, suckering plant eventually spreads widely. Even in lighter, moisture-retentive soil, *A. x hybrida* "Königen Charlotte" is soon about 24in/60cm wide. Its large, dark green, lobed leaves create good ground cover. Semi-double, 3in/8cm-wide flowers are carried, on branched stems, well clear of the foliage. Lower-growing varieties with pink flowers include *A. hupehensis* "Hadspen Abundance" and *A.h.* var. *japonica* "Bressingham Glow" (both 24–30in/60–75cm high). For a popular, white-flowered variety, see p.46. All these plants flower over a period of several weeks, especially if they are grown in consistently moist ground.
also for: ■ Heavy, clay soils ■ Long, continuous flowering period

Sasa veitchii

type of plant: hardy perennial (bamboo) [8–11]
height: 3–4ft/0.9–1.2m
Evergreen

Intriguingly, the variegation on these large, dark green, oblong leaves is caused by withering of the leaf margins. As each 10in/25cm-long leaf matures, its edges become parchment-colored. *S. veitchii* is a vigorous, spreading bamboo that is happy in most reasonably moisture-retentive soils. (Moisture is especially important if a sunny position is chosen.) The plant itself is hardy but general growth—and the quality of the foliage—is best in warm, humid climates and sheltered sites. Dense thickets of slender, purplish canes can soon cover areas several metres wide and the plant may become invasive. It is, therefore, most suitable for large areas.
also for: ■ Heavy, clay soils ■ Damp and wet soils ■ Variegated leaves

Juniperus sabina "Tamariscifolia"
[juniper]

type of plant: hardy conifer [4–8]
height: 36in/90cm
Evergreen

In time, the overlapping, spreading branches of *J. sabina* "Tamariscifolia" build up into a mound 5–6ft/1.5–1.8m wide. The dense, prickly, needle-like leaves are bright green or slightly blue-green. Other readily available, green-leaved junipers that are useful for ground cover include the vigorous *J. communis* "Repanda" [zones 3–8], which ultimately spreads about 12ft/3.6m wide, and slow-growing *J. procumbens* "Nana" [zones 5–9], which eventually reaches 5–6ft/1.5–1.8m wide. These last two varieties need a sunny site. Well-drained and dry soils of most sorts are suitable for all three junipers, and they all thrive on shallow, chalky soils.
also for: ■ Shallow soils over chalk ■ Dry soils in hot, sunny sites

Prunus laurocerasus
e.g. "Otto Luyken"
[cherry laurel, laurel]

type of plant: hardy shrub [6–9]
flowering time: mid- to late spring and often autumn
flower color: white
height: 36in/90cm
Evergreen

The more or less prostrate branches of this shrub have upright tips. Together with the slender, shining, deep green leaves, each about 5in/12cm long, they create a dense mass some 5ft/1.5m wide. (Narrow-leaved *P. laurocerasus* "Zabeliana" spreads at least 8ft/2.4m wide.) Tiny, white flowers, arranged in "candles" up to 5in/12cm high, are followed by black berries. Apart from very alkaline or very dry soils, these plants can be grown almost anywhere. As long as light conditions are reasonably good, *P.l.* "Otto Luyken" makes a dense hedge, as does *P.l.* "Rotundifolia" (plants should be 24in/60cm apart.)
also for: ■ Dry shade ■ Dense shade ■ Atmospheric pollution ■ Hedging plants ■ Ornamental fruit

Euonymus fortunei
e.g. "Emerald Gaiety"

type of plant: hardy shrub/climber [5–9]
height: 24–36in/60–90cm as a shrub; 10ft/3m as a climber
Evergreen

There are numerous varieties of *E. fortunei* (see, for example, pp.151 and 174) and many of them are useful for ground cover. *E.f.* "Emerald Gaiety" is a slow-growing, dense and hummocky plant, usually spreading 4–5ft/1.2–1.5m wide. Its rounded, gray-green leaves, 1in/2.5cm or so long, have white edges. The foliage often becomes tinged with pink in winter, especially if the plant is grown in sun. In maturity, some specimens may produce longer, climbing, self-clinging shoots. *E.f.* "Harlequin" produces mottled, white-and-green leaves. Almost any soil is suitable for these very adaptable plants.
also for: ■ Atmospheric pollution ■ Climbing plants ■ Growing in containers ■ Variegated leaves

Euphorbia griffithii "Fireglow"
[spurge]

type of plant: hardy perennial [6–9]
flowering time: late spring to early summer
flower color: orange-red
height: 24–36in/60–90cm

Intensely colored bracts on this bushy, erect-stemmed perennial remain bright and conspicuous for several weeks. The branched flower heads, usually at least 3in/8cm across, appear at the end of stout shoots which are well clothed with slender, pink-ribbed leaves of deep rich green. Especially in a sunny site, the foliage turns orange and yellow in autumn. *E. griffithii* "Dixter" has dark orange flower heads and dark coppery green foliage. Both these plants are vigorous and easily grown in any moisture-retentive soil. In rich, damp soil they often spread much more widely than the usual 36in/90cm or so. Their cut stems exude a milky juice that can irritate skin.
also for: ■ Damp and wet soils ■ Colorful, autumn foliage

Lonicera pileata
[honeysuckle]

type of plant: hardy shrub [6–8]
height: 24–36in/60–90cm
Evergreen/Semi-evergreen

The densely foliated, more or less horizontal branches of this shrub create a distinctive, tiered pattern. Each neat, shining, pointed leaf, about 1¼in/3cm long, is dark green in maturity. *L. pileata* is a very adaptable plant that grows in almost any soil. It copes well with dry shade and with infertile conditions. Its rooting branches fairly quickly make a high, weed-excluding carpet 4–6ft/1.2–1.8m wide. Growth is usually good in full shade, but in really heavily shaded places the plant becomes too open to make effective cover. In very dry conditions it is not reliably evergreen. Inconspicuous, spring flowers are followed by violet berries, but only after a hot summer.
also for: ■ Dry shade ■ Atmospheric pollution

Stephanandra incisa "Crispa"
○◐

type of plant: hardy shrub [4–9]
flowering time: early summer
flower color: creamy white
height: 24–36in/60–90cm

This vigorous and wide-spreading plant makes excellent ground cover. It forms dense thickets of arching, interweaving, russet branches that are conspicuous and attractive after leaf-fall. Each leaf, 1½in/4cm long, is toothed, lobed and slightly curled. The foliage turns orange-red and yellow in autumn. Less remarkable perhaps are the clusters of starry flowers. Most soils are suitable for *S. incisa* "Crispa" as long as they are reasonably moisture-retentive and not excessively alkaline. Unless hard pruned, this shrub reaches 4–5ft/1.2–1.5m wide and it may ultimately be about 10ft/3m wide.
also for: ■ Atmospheric pollution ■ Decorative, green foliage ■ Colorful, autumn foliage ■ Ornamental bark or twigs

Heuchera
e.g. "Stormy Seas"
○◐

type of plant: hardy perennial [4–9]
flowering time: late spring to midsummer
flower color: white
height: 20in/50cm
Evergreen

The ruffled-edged, maroon-backed leaves of this heuchera are deep reddish purple heavily overlaid with gray. Each leaf is 3–4in/8–10cm wide. Heuchera leaf color ranges from pale greens (e.g. *H.* "Mint Frost") to rich purples (e.g. *H.* "Plum Pudding") and includes the unusual caramel-yellow of *H.* "Amber Waves." For a heuchera with red-purple leaves, see p.205. All these plants do especially well in moist, fertile soil with good drainage. They create dense clumps of growth and the more vigorous varieties are useful for ground cover (*H.* "Stormy Seas" spreads about 15in/38cm wide). The open, airy sprays of tiny flowers are carried, on clear, upright stems, well above the foliage.
also for: ■ Variegated leaves

Pleioblastus argenteostriatus
f. pumilus (syn. *P. humilis* var. pumilus, *Arundinaria pumila*)
○◐

type of plant: hardy perennial (bamboo) [7–11]
height: 18–30in/45–75cm
Evergreen

Spreading at least 6ft/1.8m wide, this vigorous and often invasive bamboo is useful for ground cover in large areas. Its thickets of upright, branched canes carry narrow, pointed, fresh green leaves, each about 6in/15cm long. The leaves become bleached at their tips and along their edges during winter. The canes are rich green when young. Any moisture-retentive soil is suitable for this bamboo, which needs a site sheltered from cold, drying winds. *P. argenteostriatus* f. *pumilus* is sometimes sold as *P. pygmaeus*, which is much smaller-leaved and rather less vigorous; its very slender canes grow densely and are 12–15in/30–38cm high.
also for: ■ Decorative, green foliage

Alchemilla mollis
[lady's mantle]
○◐

type of plant: hardy perennial [4–9]
flowering time: early to late summer
flower color: yellow-green
height: 18in/45cm

Lady's mantle has many admirable qualities: its copious, ground covering foliage is lime-green; the individual leaves, to 6in/15cm across, are rounded, scalloped and velvet textured; the airy sprays of tiny flowers are good for cutting; and the plant grows—and sows itself with abandon—almost anywhere. New and neater clumps of growth soon appear, if the whole plant is cut right back after midsummer. Even when quite young, plants are usually at least 24in/60cm wide. A smaller species is shown on p.326.
also for: ■ Heavy, clay soils ■ Damp and wet soils ■ Decorative, green foliage ■ Flowers suitable for cutting (and drying) ■ Green flowers ■ Long, continuous flowering period

Euphorbia polychroma
(syn. *E. epithymoides*)
[spurge]
○◐

type of plant: hardy perennial [4–9]
flowering time: mid- to late spring
flower color: bright yellow
height: 18in/45cm

The upright, clump-forming stems of *E. polychroma* support a neat dome of bright green, slender leaves. The plant is normally self-supporting and 18–24in/45–60cm wide. Its dome of foliage is topped with acid-yellow flower heads, each 2in/5cm or so across. In autumn, the leaves often become tinged with an unusual mixture of pink, yellow and apricot. This spurge can be grown in any fertile soil, as long as it is reasonably well drained. The flower heads last well when cut, but gardeners with sensitive skin must be especially careful when handling the cut stems as the milky juice which they exude can be a severe irritant.
also for: ■ Colorful, autumn foliage ■ Flowers suitable for cutting

Geranium "Johnson's Blue"
[cranesbill]
○◐

type of plant: hardy perennial [4–9]
flowering time: early to midsummer
flower color: clear blue
height: 18in/45cm

The flowers of *G.* "Johnson's Blue" are remarkably clear in color and delicate in shape. Up to 2in/5cm across, they are carried in open, branched heads above mid-green foliage that is deeply divided, lobed and toothed. The basal leaves form a dense, weed-proof mass of growth. The plant has slightly lax stems and usually spreads about 24in/60cm wide. It is easily grown in most soils, provided they are neither very dry nor likely to become waterlogged. Of similar size is *G.* "Brookside," another popular cranesbill, which has clear blue, white-eyed flowers.
also for: ■ Decorative, green foliage

Geranium x *oxonianum*
e.g. "Wargrave Pink"
(syn. *G. endressii*
"Wargrave Pink")
[cranesbill]
◯◑

type of plant: hardy perennial [5–8]
flowering time: early to late summer
flower color: salmon-pink
height: 18in/45cm
Evergreen

This vigorous, clump-forming perennial forms dense patches of fresh green foliage. It often spreads 36in/90cm wide. Its attractive leaves are toothed, lobed and conspicuously veined. The flowers, each about 1¼in/3cm across, are broadly funnel-shaped and carried in loose, branched clusters. They open in succession throughout summer. There are dozens of varieties of G. x oxonianum, most of them with flowers in some shade of pink but some of richer, reddish purple coloring (e.g. G. x o. f. *thurstonianum*) and a few with double or semi-double flowers (e.g. G. x o. f. *thurstonianum* "Southcombe Star"). Rich pink-flowered G. x o. "Claridge Druce" is very vigorous, and can cope with dry shade. These very easy plants thrive in most soils but they grow most densely in cool, moist conditions.
also for: ■ Decorative, green foliage ■ Long, continuous flowering period

Veronica gentianoides
[speedwell]
◯◑

type of plant: hardy perennial [5–8]
flowering time: late spring to early summer
flower color: pale gray-blue
height: 18in/45cm

The rich green, pointed leaves of this speedwell are arranged in rosettes that knit together into a weed-proof mat about 18in/45cm wide. Saucer-shaped flowers are held well above this low mass of glossy foliage in spikes about 7in/18cm long. The individual flowers tend to be rather short-lived. *V. gentianoides* "Tissington White" is white-flowered. *V.g.* "Variegata" has creamy white markings on its leaves and is less vigorous than the species. All these plants need fertile, well-drained soil that retains moisture easily. In dry conditions their mats of foliage become patchy.

Microbiota decussata
◯◑

type of plant: hardy conifer [3–8]
height: 12–18in/30–45cm
Evergreen

In autumn and winter the lacy, rather bright green foliage of this conifer turns purplish russet-bronze. (Some gardeners consider that this coloring makes M. decussata look as if it is dying.) The tiny, scale-like leaves are arranged in sprays, and these overlap to form dense masses of growth at least 5ft/1.5m wide. Any well-drained soil is suitable for this tough, very hardy plant.
also for: ■ Colorful, autumn foliage (winter color, too)

Bergenia
e.g. "Silberlicht"
(syn. *B.* Silverlight)
◯◑[◑]

type of plant: hardy perennial [3–8]
flowering time: early to mid-spring
flower color: white changing to pale pink
height: 12–15in/30–38cm
Evergreen

Most of the popular bergenias are good for ground cover. This hybrid is also notable for its freely produced, white flowers (typically, bergenias bear pink or purple flowers). Its dense heads of bell-shaped blooms are carried on stout, pink-tinged stems. The thick roots and broad, rounded, leathery leaves, 6–8in/15–20cm long, slowly form bold clumps of dark green growth up to 24in/60cm wide. Almost any soil is suitable for this plant but it is at its best in moisture-retentive soils with good drainage. Other bergenias with pale flowers include B. "Bressingham White" and B. "Beethoven," both of which are white-flowered and B. "Baby Doll" which is pale pink.
also for: ■ Heavy, clay soils ■ Decorative, green foliage

Geranium macrorrhizum
e.g. "Album"
[cranesbill]
◯◑●

type of plant: hardy perennial [4–8]
flowering time: late spring to early summer
flower color: pinkish white
height: 12–15in/30–38cm
Semi-evergreen

G. macrorrhizum and its varieties are highly efficient and very decorative excluders of weeds. G.m. "Album" has unusually pale flowers, about ¾in/2cm across, which have outer parts that are soft pink. The plant creates a dense, light green carpet of rounded, deeply lobed leaves, each of which is about 4in/10cm wide. The foliage is pungently and powerfully aromatic. Especially if this cranesbill is grown in sun, its upper layer of deciduous foliage becomes brightly colored in autumn. The lower, evergreen leaves persist and form a carpet of year-round cover. Although it revels in cool, moist soil, this reliable and adaptable plant can be grown in a wide range of soils and sites—it even tolerates dry shade. For details of G. macrorrhizum itself, see p.251. Other varieties include a variegated form.
also for: ■ Dry shade ■ Decorative, green foliage
■ Colorful, autumn foliage (see above) ■ Aromatic foliage

Primula denticulata
[drumstick primula]
○◑

type of plant: hardy perennial [6–9]
flowering time: early to late spring
flower color: usually lavender-blue
height: 12in/30cm

Drumstick primula is sturdy, reliable, long-lived and tolerant of a wide range of soil types. It is at its best in slightly acid to neutral loams that are humus-rich and that retain moisture easily. When several specimens are grown together, their rosettes of 10in/25cm-long, wrinkled leaves, which only develop fully after flowering time, merge into a weed-suppressing mass. The spherical flower heads, up to 3in/8cm in diameter, are borne on stout stems. There are varieties of this plant with purple, crimson and lilac flowers, and the white-flowered *P. denticulata* var. *alba* is popular.

Ajuga reptans
e.g. "Catlin's Giant"
[common bugleweed]
○◑

type of plant: hardy perennial [4–9]
flowering time: late spring to early summer
flower color: deep blue
height: 9–12in/23–30cm
Evergreen/Semi-evergreen

All the readily available varieties of *A. reptans* (for examples, see pp.176 and 205) make good ground cover, but this large-leaved, vigorous bugleweed is particularly useful. Its little, lipped flowers are arranged in spikes 6–8in/15–20cm long. Once the flowers have faded, then the new, rounded leaves lengthen into glossy ovals, up to 6in/15cm long. In summer and early autumn, the foliage is rich purplish chocolate-brown. Plants grown in sun have the best leaf color. *A.r.* "Catlin's Giant" does well in all reasonably moisture-retentive soils, but in moist, fertile conditions its carpet of rooting growth is at least 36in/90cm wide.
also for: ■ Heavy, clay soils ■ Purple, bronze, or red leaves

Astilbe chinensis var. pumila
○◑

type of plant: hardy perennial [5–9]
flowering time: late summer to early autumn
flower color: bright mauve-pink
height: 9–12in/23–30cm

With its neat, dense carpet of ferny leaves and its fairly vigorous habit of growth, *A. chinensis* var. *pumila* makes good ground cover. Tightly packed spikes of tiny flowers rise erectly above a mass of bright green, divided leaves. Each flower spike is about 6in/15cm long. The seedheads are rusty brown and long-lasting. Fertile soil that retains moisture throughout the summer is most suitable for this plant, but it tolerates rather drier conditions than most astilbes, especially if it is given a little shade. When well suited the plant grows to about 24in/60cm wide.
also for: ■ Damp and wet soils ■ Decorative, green foliage ■ Ornamental fruit (seedheads)

Campanula carpatica
[bellflower]
○◑

type of plant: hardy perennial [4–8]
flowering time: early to late summer
flower color: blue or mauve or purple or white
height: 8–12in/20–30cm

This very robust and floriferous, clump-forming plant creates flower-covered cushions of light green, usually heart-shaped, toothed leaves. These cushions spread slowly until they are 15in/38cm or more wide. Each of the flowers is an upturned, wide-open cup, about 1¼in/3cm across. Nurseries specializing in rock-garden plants usually list at least several of the numerous varieties of *C. carpatica*, including the popular, pure white *C.c.* f. *alba* "Weisse Clips" (syn. *C.c.* White Clips). Fertile, moisture-retentive but well-drained soil is most suitable for these plants.
also for: ■ Long, continuous flowering period

Geranium x cantabrigiense
e.g. "Cambridge"
[cranesbill]
○◑

type of plant: hardy perennial [5–8]
flowering time: late spring to midsummer
flower color: mauve-pink
height: 8–10in/20–25cm
Evergreen/Semi-evergreen

With its masses of ¾in/2cm-wide, open-faced blooms and its dense carpets of pretty leaves, *G. x cantabrigiense* "Cambridge" makes ground cover that is decorative as well as efficient. Each neat, glossy leaf is about 1½in/4cm across, attractively lobed and scalloped, and more or less circular in outline. The apple-scented foliage is light green for most of the year, but takes on bright tints of orange and red in autumn. Most soils are suitable for this plant, as long as they are at least fairly well drained. *G. x c.* "Biokovo" is another popular variety; its flowers are pink-tinged white.
also for: ■ Decorative, green foliage ■ Colorful, autumn foliage ■ Aromatic foliage

Viola cornuta
e.g. Alba Group
[horned violet, viola]
○◑

type of plant: hardy perennial [5–8]
flowering time: mainly late spring to midsummer
flower color: white
height: 6–9in/15–23cm
Evergreen

These horned violets are vigorous and their tufts of rich green, pointed, oval leaves spread into dense carpets of growth about 24in/60cm wide. Each of their numerous, slightly fragrant flowers is roughly 1in/2.5cm across. Other closely related violas that are suitable for ground cover include *V. cornuta* itself (usually lilac or violet flowered), *V.* "Belmont Blue" (pale blue) and *V.* "Victoria Cawthorne" (deep purplish pink). These plants grow best in a cool position where the soil is fertile, well drained and moisture-retentive. If they are trimmed after flowering, a second crop of blooms usually appears.
also for: ■ Long, continuous flowering period (particularly Alba Group and *V.* "Victoria Cawthorne")

Persicaria affinis
(syn. *Polygonum affine*)
e.g. "Superba" (syn. "Dimity")
[Himalayan knotweed]
○◑

type of plant: hardy perennial [3–9]
flowering time: midsummer to mid-autumn
flower color: pink changing to red
height: 6–8in/15–20cm

A long flowering season, leaves that are attractively colored in winter and a weed-proof, carpet-like habit of growth are all points in this plant's favor. However, in really fertile, moisture-retentive soil, it can be too vigorous, quickly exceeding its normal spread of 24in/60cm. Pale pink *P. affinis* "Donald Lowndes" is less vigorous. *P.a.* "Superba" has numerous, 3½in/9cm-long spikes of tiny, closely-packed flowers above dense masses of bright green, slender leaves. The foliage turns russet in autumn and persists during winter. The flower spikes too turn red-brown. *P. affinis* and its varieties are easily grown in any moist soil, as long as it is not waterlogged.
also for: ■ Colorful, autumn foliage (winter color, too) ■ Long, continuous flowering period

Persicaria vacciniifolia
(syn. *Polygonum vaciniifolium*)
○◑

type of plant: hardy perennial [6–9]
flowering time: late summer to mid-autumn
flower color: pale rose-pink
height: 6in/15cm
Semi-evergreen

Daintier than its relation in the previous illustration, but just as vigorous when well suited, this dense, creeping plant looks especially attractive if it is allowed to trail over a low wall. It produces large numbers of its slim, red-stemmed flower spikes, each of which is about 3in/8cm long. The shining, rich green leaves emerge quite late in spring and form a mat of neat growth, which turns rust-red in autumn and persists throughout the winter months. *P. vacciniifolia* is easily grown but it is most at home in moist, acid conditions. In mild areas with high rainfall it can be over 36in/90cm wide.
also for: ■ Acid soils ■ Colorful, autumn foliage (winter color, too)

Prunella grandiflora
(syn. *P.* x *webbiana*)
e.g. "Loveliness"
[selfheal]
○◑

type of plant: hardy perennial [5–8]
flowering time: early to midsummer
flower color: pale violet-blue
height: 6in/15cm
Semi-evergreen

The dense flower spikes of this vigorous plant are carried on erect stems. Each spike, clothed in whorls of two-lipped flowers, is up to 2½in/6cm long. As well as *P. grandiflora* "Loveliness," there are pink- and reddish-flowered varieties, and *P.g.* "Alba" is a readily available, white-flowered variety. All these easily pleased plants grow especially well in soil that remains moist during summer, making good, thick, rooting carpets of dark green, fairly slender leaves and seeding themselves—often liberally. When well suited, *P.g.* "Loveliness" spreads about 24in/60cm wide. The flowers of these plants are attractive to bees.
also for: ■ Heavy, clay soils

Campanula poscharskyana
[bellflower]
○◑

type of plant: hardy perennial [4–9]
flowering time: early summer to early autumn
flower color: bluish mauve
height: 4–6in/10–15cm
Evergreen

This vigorous plant should be reserved for areas where no other, weaker plants could be enveloped in its spreading mass of underground shoots and leafy stems. Its exuberance can be controlled to some extent by planting it in crevices in a wall or in paving. In places where it can be allowed to grow freely—on a rough bank or less formal parts of gardens, for instance—it makes useful ground cover. It normally spreads at least 24in/60cm wide. Its star-shaped flowers, each about ¾in/2cm across, are carried in sprays above the light green, rounded leaves. *C. poscharskyana* is easily grown, although it does have a preference for good drainage and a reasonable supply of moisture. *C.p.* "E.H. Frost" has very pale blue flowers.
also for: ■ Crevices in paving ■ Long, continuous flowering period

Fragaria Pink Panda = "Frel"
[strawberry]
○◑

type of plant: hardy perennial [4–9]
flowering time: late spring to early autumn
flower color: bright pink
height: 4–6in/10–15cm
Semi-evergreen

Even though a garden strawberry is one of its parents, *F.* Pink Panda seldom bears fruit. However, its rich green, three-lobed leaves and its spreading, rooting stems form a carpet of weed-suppressing growth almost all year round. In addition, the pretty, 1in/2.5cm-wide flowers appear in a series of flushes over an exceptionally long period. The plant grows well in most soils, as long as they are not hot and dry. It can become invasive in fertile, moisture-retentive soil with good drainage and, in any case, it spreads widely. *F.* x *ananassa* "Variegata" is also vigorous and it too is suitable for ground cover; its leaves are generously splashed with white and it has white flowers.
also for: ■ Decorative, green foliage ■ Long, continuous flowering period

Gunnera magellanica
○◐

type of plant: hardy/slightly tender perennial [7–9]
height: 4–6in/10–15cm

In contrast to its enormous relation, *G. manicata* (see p.226), this neat, little plant has leaves not much more than 2½–3in/6–8cm wide. These shining, rich green leaves are crinkled and almost circular, and they form a dense, rooting carpet of growth which is often at least 18in/45cm wide. Spikes of inconspicuous, little green flowers appear in summer. *G. magellanica* thrives in deep, fertile soil that is permanently damp but it also does well in ordinary, moisture-retentive soil.

also for: ■ Damp and wet soils ■ Decorative, green foliage

Primula "Wanda"
○◐

type of plant: hardy perennial [6–8]
flowering time: early to late spring
(but see description)
flower color: crimson-purple + yellow
height: 4–6in/10–15cm
Semi-evergreen/Deciduous

The flowers and the leaves of *P.* "Wanda" develop more or less simultaneously. Flowers are produced over a period of many weeks, and some blooms may appear before the onset of spring. The clusters of 1½in/4cm-wide, yellow-eyed flowers are very short-stalked at first but, as spring progresses, the whole plant lengthens and expands. Slightly bronze-tinged, crinkled, oval leaves are arranged in rosettes that often increase quickly, especially in fertile, moisture-retentive soil. Individual specimens of this vigorous, easily grown plant spread to 12–18in/30–45cm wide.

also for: ■ Long, continuous flowering period

Vinca minor
e.g. "Argenteovariegata"
(syn. *V.m.* "Variegata")
[lesser periwinkle]
○◐

type of plant: hardy shrub [5–9]
flowering time: mid-spring to early summer
(some later flowers)
flower color: pale violet-blue
height: 4–6in/10–15cm
Evergreen

In any well-drained soil, this little subshrub creates a tightly knit carpet of white-edged, grayish green leaves on long, rooting stems. Although it is not as vigorous as the green-leaved species (see p.83), *V. minor* "Argenteovariegata" still spreads about 24in/60cm wide. It is tolerant of dry shade, but leaf color and flowering are better in sunnier sites and reasonably moisture-retentive soil. The numerous varieties of *V. minor* also include *V.m.* "Aureovariegata," which has yellow-marked leaves and blue flowers, and *V.m.* "Alba Variegata" which has white flowers and yellow-variegated foliage. The neat, pointed leaves of all these plants are 1–1½in/2.5–4cm long; the starry flowers are 1in/2.5cm or so across. Lesser periwinkles are sometimes listed as perennials in catalogs.

also for: ■ Dry shade ■ Atmospheric pollution
■ Growing in containers ■ Variegated leaves

Cotoneaster dammeri
○◐

type of plant: hardy shrub [6–8]
flowering time: early summer
flower color: white
height: 4in/10cm
Evergreen

This is one of the very best cotoneasters for ground cover. Its long, rooting shoots and glossy leaves form a really close-knit carpet that can increase by up to 18–24in/45–60cm a year. The rounded leaves, each about 1¼in/3cm long, provide a rich green background for the little, flat-faced flowers. The more or less spherical berries are not much more than ¼in/0.5cm in diameter, but they are bright red and long-lasting. *C. dammeri* grows in almost any soil, as long as it is not waterlogged. Other evergreen cotoneasters that make good ground cover include the arching, mound-forming *C. conspicuus* "Decorus" and *C.* x *suecicus* "Coral Beauty." All these plants spread at least 6ft/1.8m wide.

also for: ■ Atmospheric pollution ■ Ornamental fruit

ADDITIONAL PLANTS, featured elsewhere in this book, that are suitable for ground-**cover**

Tellima grandiflora
[fringe cups]
◐[○]
type of plant: hardy perennial [4–9]
flowering time: late spring to early summer
flower color: pale green
height: 18–24in/45–60cm
Semi-evergreen

Ideally, T. grandiflora should be given well-drained but moisture-retentive soil and a lightly shaded position. However, it is a tolerant plant that can adapt to dry shade, heavy clay and sunny sites (although positions that are hot and dry are not suitable). Its upright stems carry a good covering of scalloped, light green leaves, each about 3in/8cm wide. In winter the foliage often becomes mottled with brown (plants in T. grandiflora Rubra Group—see p.243—have purplish red leaves that are particularly colorful in winter). The slender wands of tiny, bell-shaped flowers rise above the leaves. When well suited, the plant self-sows. It usually spreads about 18in/45cm wide.
also for: ■ Heavy, clay soils ■ Dry shade ■ Decorative, green foliage ■ Colorful autumn foliage (winter color, too) ■ Green flowers

Eomecon chionantha
◐[○]
[snow poppy]
type of plant: slightly tender/hardy perennial [7–9]
flowering time: late spring to early summer
flower color: white
height: 12–15in/30–38cm

In cool, humus-rich soil this vigorous plant spreads into substantial patches, at least 24in/60cm wide. Although it can become invasive, snow poppy is useful for suppressing weeds in large, informal areas of gardens. Its long-stalked leaves, up to 4in/10cm wide, have scalloped edges and are heart-shaped or rounded. The foliage color is an unusual, soft, rather pale green. Nodding, 1½in/4cm-wide flowers are sparsely produced. They are not long-lived. Open-textured, moisture-retentive soil is needed for this plant to grow well, and moisture is particularly important if a sunny site is chosen.
also for: ■ Decorative, green foliage

Epimedium perralderianum
[barrenwort]
◗[○]

type of plant: hardy perennial [7–9]
flowering time: mid- to late spring
flower color: yellow
height: 12in/30cm
Evergreen/Semi-evergreen

This robust plant's 18in/45cm-wide carpet of shiny, deep green foliage creates very efficient ground cover. The leaves of *E. perralderianum* are marbled with bronze when young, and they may become coppery in winter. Each toothed, heart-shaped leaflet is 2–3in/5–8cm long. The airy sprays of little flowers are carried on wiry stems. Other epimediums for ground cover include deciduous *E.* x *versicolor*, evergreen *E. pinnatum* subsp. *colchicum* and *E* x *perralchicum* "Fröhnleiten," and see also p.83. All these plants tolerate dry shade but they thrive in moist, humus-rich, fertile soil with good drainage. They appreciate shelter from cold, drying winds.
also for: ■ Dry shade ■ Purple, bronze, or red leaves (young leaves only) ■ Decorative, green foliage

Galium odoratum
(syn. *Asperula odorata*)
[sweet woodruff]
◗[○]

type of plant: hardy perennial [5–8]
flowering time: late spring to early summer
flower color: white
height: 6–9in/15–23cm

With its multitude of starry flowers and its carpet of pretty, whorled leaves, sweet woodruff is one of the most attractive ground covering perennials for informal places. The leaves are light green, against which the clusters of ¼in/0.5cm-wide flowers look particularly fresh. As the leaves begin to die back, they give off a sweet, hay-like scent. This vigorous plant grows in a wide range of soils. In cool soils that are both well-drained and moisture-retentive it may spread rapidly—to 36in/90cm or more. It grows satisfactorily, but less lustily, in dry, shady places.
also for: ■ Dry shade ■ Decorative, green foliage ■ Aromatic foliage (see above)

Omphalodes cappadocica
[navelwort]
◗[○]

type of plant: hardy perennial [6–9]
flowering time: mid- to late spring
flower color: bright clear blue
height: 6–9in/15–23cm
Semi-evergreen

In the cool, moist shade that this plant prefers, its foliage forms dense, spreading clumps of weed-proof growth. Individual specimens are usually about 15in/38cm wide. The neat, veined leaves also provide a good background for the wonderful, concentrated blue of the flowers. These little blooms, each less than ½in/1cm across, are arranged in loose sprays and *O. cappadocica* is in flower over many weeks—sometimes even into early summer. *O.c.* "Cherry Ingram" has flowers that are slightly larger and a deeper blue than those of the species. The flowers of *O.c.* "Starry Eyes" have white-striped petals. For a white-flowered navelwort, see p.124.
also for: ■ Long, continuous flowering period

Chiastophyllum oppositifolium
(syn. *C. simplicifolium,*
Cotyledon oppositifolia,
C. simplicifolia)
◗[○]

type of plant: hardy perennial [5–9]
flowering time: late spring to early summer
flower color: yellow
height: 6in/15cm
Evergreen

The light green, squeakily succulent leaves of *C. oppositifolium* are packed together into a close, rooting mat of growth. This slowly increases to 12in/30cm or more wide. Clusters of flowers, each about 1½in/4cm long and resembling catkins, are carried in sprays on reddish stems. As they age, the rounded, 2in/5cm-long leaves often turn a vivid red, especially if the plant has been grown in sun. General growth is best in moisture-retentive soil and a shaded place. However, as long as they are not dry, most well-drained soils give satisfactory results. A variegated form of this plant is shown on p.178.
also for: ■ Colorful, autumn foliage (see above)

ADDITIONAL PLANTS, featured elsewhere in this book, that are suitable for ground cover

◗[○] partial shade (or sun)

minimum height 36in/90cm or more
x *Fatshedera lizei,* see p.86
Mahonia aquifolium, see p.122
Skimmia japonica "Rubella," see p.34

minimum height between 12in/30cm and 36in/90cm
Dryopteris filix-mas, see p.81
Helleborus foetidus, see p.82
Hosta fortunei var. *albopicta,* see p.177
Hosta sieboldiana var. *elegans,* see p.196

Hosta undulata var. *undulata,* see p.178
Iris foetidissima, see p.261
Primula florindae, see p.78
Sarcococca hookeriana var. *humilis,* see p.314
Tellima grandiflora Rubra Group, see p.243

minimum height 12in/30cm or less
Ajuga reptans "Variegata," see p.178
Asarina procumbens, see p.348
Epilobium glabellum, see p.348
Epimedium x *rubrum,* see p.83
Gaultheria procumbens, see p.123
Hedera canariensis "Gloire de Marengo," see p.136

Hedera helix "Glacier," see p.124
Hedera helix "Green Ripple," see p.81
Hedera hibernica, see p.86
x *Heucherella alba* "Rosalie," see p.295
Phlox x *procumbens* "Variegata," see p.159
Polypodium vulgare, see p.83
Primula "Guinevere," see p.208
Primula vulgaris, see p.49
Rubus tricolor, see p.87
Saxifraga "Aureopunctata," see p.178
Saxifraga x *urbium,* see p.230
Symphytum ibericum, see p.123
Trachystemon orientalis, see p.83

Hosta lancifolia
[plantain lily]
◗

type of plant: hardy perennial [3–9]
flowering time: late summer to early autumn
flower color: lilac
height: 18in/45cm

H. lancifolia quite quickly creates weed-proof mounds of foliage about 12in/30cm high and up to 24in/60cm wide; it eventually forms sizable patches. The shiny, deep green leaves, each about 6in/15cm long, are narrow and pointed and have several pairs of prominent veins. The flowers are funnel-shaped and carried on slender stems well above the foliage. Nearly all the popular hostas are useful for ground cover (for the selection of hostas illustrated in this book, see the index of botanical names). H. "Ground Master," like H. lancifolia, is especially good; it has cream-edged, green leaves and spreads vigorously by means of creeping roots. All these plants appreciate fertile, moisture-retentive soil which is, preferably, well drained. Many of them luxuriate in damp soil.
also for: ■ Damp and wet soils ■ Decorative, green foliage

Luzula sylvatica (syn. L. maxima) "Marginata" (syn. "Aureomarginata") [woodrush]
◗

type of plant: hardy perennial [5–9]
flowering time: late spring to early summer
flower color: purple-brown + cream
height: 15–18in/38–45cm
Evergreen

Rooting as it spreads, this narrowly white-margined variety of the greater woodrush is useful for ground cover in cool, woodland conditions. Its loose, 3in/8cm-long heads of tiny flowers form a haze over the narrow, bright green leaves. L. sylvatica "Marginata" is vigorous (although not invasive like the species) and it can cope with dry shade. It is at its best in moist, well-drained, preferably acid soil, where it forms dense tufts of growth approximately 24in/60cm wide. L.s. "Aurea" has yellow leaves that are brightest in winter; it is about 12in/30cm high.
also for: ■ Acid soils ■ Dry shade ■ Variegated leaves

Reineckea carnea
◗

type of plant: hardy perennial [7–9]
height: 6–9in/15–23cm
Evergreen

R. carnea's slender, arching leaves are each about 12in/30cm long. Particularly in moist but well-drained, acid to neutral soil and lightly shaded places, its tufts of light green foliage grow densely and make good ground cover. The plant usually spreads up to 15in/38cm wide. Neither the spikes of little, pink, bell-shaped flowers nor the subsequent red berries appear very often in regions with cool summers. When they are produced, the flowers are lightly fragrant and they appear mainly in late spring and early summer.
also for: ■ Acid soils

Blechnum penna-marina
◗

type of plant: hardy fern [7–9]
height: 6in/15cm
Evergreen

This dainty, little fern produces tufts of leathery, dark green fronds above slowly spreading roots. The fertile fronds are erect and more sparsely foliated than the sterile fronds, which are shorter, evergreen and more nearly horizontal. B. penna-marina is at home in damp, acid to neutral soil. It is a most attractive plant for places such as the edges of woodland, or paving crevices in lightly shaded areas. It is not invasive but will, in time, cover sizable patches of ground.
also for: ■ Acid soils ■ Damp and wet soils ■ Crevices in paving ■ Decorative, green foliage

Arisarum proboscideum
[mouse plant]
◗

type of plant: hardy perennial [6–9]
flowering time: mid- to late spring
flower color: maroon + white
height: 4in/10cm

The hooded flowers of this strange, little plant have thin "tails," up to 6in/15cm long, so that they look like mice disappearing into the rich green, arrow-shaped leaves. These leaves, each 3–4in/8–10cm long, are much taller than the flowers, which are therefore more or less obscured. As well as having entertainment value, this plant also makes efficient ground cover. Individual specimens spread about 12in/30cm wide, but even just a few plants can eventually create quite wide areas of closely packed, glossy foliage. Mouse plant thrives in moist, fertile, humus-rich soil and cool, shady places.
also for: ■ Decorative, green foliage

Mahonia aquifolium
[Oregon grape]
◑●[○]

type of plant: hardy shrub [5–9]
flowering time: early to late spring
flower color: yellow
height: 3–4ft/0.9–1.2m
Evergreen

Oregon grape produces thickets of upright stems with glossy, deep green, spiny leaflets and dense, 3in/8cm-long clusters of flowers. The plant grows almost anywhere, including dry and heavily shaded places, although it is at its best in moist, well-drained soil and light shade. Its suckering roots spread slowly, usually covering an area about 5ft/1.5m wide. In fairly open sites, the foliage becomes richly red- or bronze-tinged during winter (*M. aquifolium* "Apollo" and *M.a.* "Atropurpurea" have especially good winter leaf color). Generous bunches of blue-black berries ripen from midsummer and are attractive to birds.

also for: ■ Shallow soils over chalk ■ Heavy, clay soils ■ Dry shade ■ Dense shade ■ Atmospheric pollution ■ Decorative, green foliage ■ Colorful, autumn foliage (winter color, too) ● Ornamental fruit

Aegopodium podagraria "Variegatum"
[variegated bishop's weed, variegated goutweed]
◑●

type of plant: hardy perennial [4–9]
flowering time: early summer
flower color: white
height: 18–24in/45–60cm

Although it is not rampantly invasive like the green-leaved species, variegated goutweed still grows strongly and is difficult to eradicate. It is, however, useful for lightening the gloom in shady sites since the creamy white and soft green of its 3in/ 8cm-long leaflets give a pale impression overall. Tiny, white flowers are carried in flattish heads on branching stems that rise well above the foliage. Almost any soil is suitable, and poor soil helps to restrain the vigor of the plant. However, in dry conditions growth becomes patchy, rather than dense and weed-excluding. Shoots or seedlings with entirely green leaves need to be dug up and removed immediately.

also for: ■ Heavy, clay soils ■ Dense shade ■ Variegated leaves

Brunnera macrophylla
◑●

type of plant: hardy perennial [4–8]
flowering time: mid- to late spring
flower color: bright blue
height: 18in/45cm

They may be very small—about ¼in/0.5cm across—but these flowers are glorious, bright blue. They are carried in branched heads above 24in/60cm-wide clumps of rough, heart-shaped, rich green leaves. The foliage becomes more coarse and rather shabby as the year progresses, but it remains good ground cover throughout the growing season. This is a tough and adaptable plant, but it grows most luxuriantly and sows itself most generously in shaded places where the soil is cool and moist. *B. macrophylla* is not suitable for hot, dry sites. For a variegated brunnera, see p.179.

also for: ■ Heavy, clay soils

Pachyphragma macrophyllum
◑●

type of plant: hardy perennial [5–8]
flowering time: early to mid-spring
flower color: pure white
height: 12in/30cm
Semi-evergreen

In a shady site and moist, humus-rich soil, the veined, almost circular leaves of this slow-growing plant form a carpet of dark, glossy greenery up to 36in/90cm wide. Individual leaves are approximately 4in/10cm in diameter. Dense heads of little, four-petaled flowers are followed by flattened seed pods. Provided conditions are not too dry, *P. macrophyllum* grows well under a deciduous tree or shrub. Its foliage does not fully expand until late spring. *Cardamine trifolia* is closely related; it is smaller but otherwise very similar.

also for: ■ Heavy, clay soils ■ Ornamental fruit (seed pods)

Epimedium grandiflorum
(syn. *E. macranthum*)
e.g. "Rose Queen"
[barrenwort]
◑●

type of plant: hardy perennial [4–9]
flowering time: mid-spring to early summer
flower color: deep pink + white
height: 9–12in/23–30cm

The unusually large (1½in/4cm wide), deeply colored flowers of this plant are held on thin, wiry stems. They look particularly attractive with the pinkish brown-purple of the new foliage. Shaped like elongated hearts, the numerous pretty leaflets are up to 4in/10cm when mature. *E. grandiflorum* "Rose Queen" forms a dense clump of growth, about 12in/30cm wide, and increases slowly. It tolerates dry shade but grows best in well-drained, fertile soil that is moist and humus-rich. (For a more vigorous epimedium, see p.120.)

also for: ■ Dry shade ■ Purple, bronze, or red leaves (young leaves only) ■ Decorative, green foliage

Symphytum ibericum
[comfrey]
◐●[○]

type of plant: hardy perennial [5–9]
flowering time: late spring to early summer
flower color: cream
height: 9–12in/23–30cm
Evergreen/Semi-evergreen

Hardly an exquisite embellishment to a garden, *S. ibericum* is useful in certain places, including the ground beneath shrubs or trees. The plant tolerates dry shade and, as long as the soil is not very dry, it will creep densely and rapidly, soon forming a carpet of coarse, veined leaves, each leaf up to 10in/25cm long. It spreads at least 24in/60cm wide and is potentially invasive, especially in rich, moist soil. Its ½in/1cm-long flowers are carried in branched heads. *S.* "Hidcote Blue" bears pale blue flowers; *S.* "Goldsmith" has handsome, yellow-edged leaves and is much less vigorous than *S. ibericum* (for an example of another variegated comfrey, see p.173).
also for: ■ Heavy, clay soils ■ Dry shade

Tiarella cordifolia
[foam flower]
◐●

type of plant: hardy perennial [3–8]
flowering time: late spring to early summer
flower color: pale cream
height: 9–12in/23–30cm
Evergreen

Handsomely lobed and interestingly colored, the 4in/10cm-long leaves of this foam flower make efficient and decorative ground cover in shady places. When fully expanded, the flower spikes, with their numerous, fluffy, little flowers, form a soft froth of pale cream. The veins of the lime-green leaves are stained bronze, and in late autumn and winter the whole leaf surface turns reddish bronze. *T. cordifolia* makes a weed-proof carpet of rooting growth in moisture-retentive soil and cool, shaded sites. It is often 24in/60cm wide and may be much more in ideal conditions. *T. wherryi* (see p.233) is more compact.
also for: ■ Decorative, green foliage ■ Colorful, autumn foliage (winter color, too)

Pulmonaria
e.g. "Sissinghurst White"
[lungwort]
◐●

type of plant: hardy perennial [4–8]
flowering time: early to mid-spring
flower color: white
height: 8–12in/20–30cm
Evergreen/Semi-evergreen

With its splashes of pale silvery green, the light green foliage of this lungwort looks particularly pretty with white flowers. Funnel-shaped blooms, each about ½in/1cm across and arranged in sprays, begin to open right at the beginning of spring. After flowering time, the leaves lengthen to about 8in/20cm or so. Especially when it is grown in the cool, moist conditions it likes best, *P.* "Sissinghurst White" forms good, ground covering clumps of growth 12–18in/30–45cm wide. This is an easily pleased plant, as long as it is not hot and dry.
also for: ■ Heavy, clay soils ■ Variegated leaves

Tolmiea menziesii "Taff's Gold"
[piggyback plant, thousand mothers, youth-on-age]
◐●

type of plant: hardy perennial [7–9]
flowering time: late spring to early summer
flower color: coppery brown
height: 8–12in/20–30cm foliage
Semi-evergreen

Although this plant's wispy, 18in/45cm-tall wands of little flowers are not very conspicuous, its light green, primrose-and cream-mottled foliage certainly is. The yellow coloration is most pronounced in lightly shaded sites. In sun the leaves are paler and less variegated and their edges tend to scorch; in very dark positions the foliage is a uniform light green. Individual leaves are lobed and about 4in/10cm long. *T. menziesii* "Taff's Gold" soon forms a spreading clump about 18in/45cm wide, and it makes good ground cover in moist, humus-rich soil. The common name arises from the way young plants form on the surface of the old leaves.
also for: ■ Variegated leaves

Pachysandra terminalis
[Japanese spurge]
◐●

type of plant: hardy perennial/shrub [5–9]
height: 8in/20cm
Evergreen

P. terminalis makes a neat, ground covering carpet of glossy, rich green leaves. These are attractively arranged in whorls, about 6in/15cm wide, on sprawling stems. Apart from its dislike of very limy soil, this tough and adaptable plant does well even underneath a tree or large shrub. It is most vigorous in moist, humus-rich soil. In time, it spreads over 36in/90cm wide. There is a variegated form of this plant (see p.181), and *P.t.* "Green Carpet" is a lower-growing variety with smaller leaves. These subshrubs produce short spikes of little, off-white flowers in spring but they are not particularly conspicuous, although they do have a slight, sweet scent.
also for: ■ Acid soils ■ Dry shade ■ Dense shade ■ Decorative, green foliage

Gaultheria procumbens
[checkerberry, wintergreen]
◐●[○] ✳

type of plant: hardy shrub [4–9]
flowering time: mid- to late summer
flower color: white or pinkish
height: 6in/15cm
Evergreen

This really dense and effective excluder of weeds spreads slowly, by underground shoots, until it is eventually very wide (well over 36in/90cm). The glossy leaves are broad ovals, about 1½in/4cm long, which are dark green when mature and sometimes tinged—as in this illustration—with maroon-purple in winter. Pendent, urn-shaped flowers are followed, in autumn, by long-lasting, spherical, red berries that are edible. All parts of *G. procumbens* are aromatic, having the penetrating, clean scent of wintergreen. Humus-rich, acid soil that is light and moist is most suitable for this plant.
also for: ■ Acid soils ■ Aromatic foliage ■ Ornamental fruit

Hedera helix
e.g. "Glacier"
[ivy]
◑●[○]

type of plant: hardy climber [6–10]
height: 6in/15cm as ground cover;
7–10ft/2.1–3m as a climber
Evergreen

Probably the best variegated ivy for ground cover, *H. helix* "Glacier" also performs well as a neat, dense, self-clinging climber. It can be grown on walls of any aspect. Its 1½in/4cm-long leaves have elegantly elongated central lobes, and the coloring is a particularly pretty combination of grays and greens with an edging of white. The foliage makes a close carpet of rooting, weed-excluding growth. This moderately vigorous ivy grows in almost any soil that is not either waterlogged or very hot and dry. It tolerates dry shade. Among the immense range of ivies, there are many others that are good for ground cover (see for instance, pp.86, 136 and 150).
also for: ■ Dry shade ■ Atmospheric pollution ■ Climbing plants ■ Growing in containers ■ Variegated leaves

Lamium maculatum
e.g. "Roseum"
[spotted deadnettle]
◑●

type of plant: hardy perennial [4–9]
flowering time: mid-spring to midsummer
flower color: pale pink
height: 6in/15cm
Semi-evergreen

There are various pink-flowered forms of *L. maculatum*, including *L.m.* "Roseum," which combines a clear flower color with white-striped leaves. Each leaf is heart-shaped, about 1½in/4cm long and basically deep soft green. The foliage and rooting stems form a close carpet of growth, 18in/45cm or more wide, above which rise the erect spikes of little, hooded flowers. *L.m.* "Roseum" grows in a wide range of soils but it is most vigorous and dense in moist but well-drained conditions. *L.m.* "Album" has white flowers, as does the popular variety shown on p.181.
also for: ■ Heavy, clay soils ■ Dense shade ■ Variegated leaves

Maianthemum bifolium
[false lily-of-the-valley]
◑●

type of plant: hardy perennial [3–9]
flowering time: late spring to early summer
flower color: creamy white
height: 6in/15cm

Looking like a miniature hosta in some respects, this creeping plant produces 36in/90cm-wide carpets of deep green foliage. Cool, moisture-retentive soil and shady places are most suitable. It may spread widely, and it is sometimes invasive in light, humus-rich soil. The leaves, two to a stem, are veined, roughly heart-shaped and each about 3in/8cm wide. There is usually some yellow autumn color. Numerous small, starry flowers are arranged in dense spikes. Red berries may follow. Well-established plants build up into thick, completely weed-proof layers of foliage, 12in/30cm or so high. False lily-of-the-valley grows well in, but does not require, acid to neutral soil.
also for: ■ Dense shade ■ Decorative, green foliage

Omphalodes verna "Alba"
[navelwort]
◑●

type of plant: hardy perennial [6–9]
flowering time: early to mid-spring
flower color: white
height: 6in/15cm
Semi-evergreen

The creeping stems and long-stalked, rich green, pointed leaves of this easily grown perennial make good ground cover (though *O. verna* "Alba" tends to grow rather less densely than *O. cappadocica*, see p.120). A tendency to invasiveness—especially in moist, well-drained soil—can be checked by giving the plant some short grass to compete with in an informal part of the garden. In some years the ½in/1cm-wide flowers may open before the beginning of spring. *O. verna* itself, commonly known as blue-eyed Mary, is also readily available; it has bright blue flowers with white "eyes." Both these plants usually spread quite quickly, to at least 24in/60cm wide.

Cornus canadensis
[creeping dogwood, bunchberry, dwarf cornel]

◐● ✳

type of plant: hardy perennial [2–8]
flowering time: late spring to early summer
flower color: white + greenish purple
height: 4–6in/10–15cm

In fairly moist, acid soil and the cool shade of light woodland this plant spreads quickly into a dense cover of creeping roots and erect stems. It often forms patches several yards wide. It can cope with less favorable conditions, including dry shade, but then it is less vigorous. Every stem is topped with a whorl of rounded, bright green, deeply veined leaves, in the center of which sits a little flower surrounded by conspicuous, white bracts, each up to ¾in/2cm long. Provided creeping dogwood has not been grown in too shady a position, its leaves become tinged with wine-red in autumn. There may also be dense clusters of fleshy, red berries, though the plant does not fruit regularly in cooler climates.

also for: ■ Acid soils ■ Dry shade ■ Dense shade ■ Colorful, autumn foliage ■ Ornamental fruit (see above)

Phlox stolonifera
e.g. "Blue Ridge"
[creeping phlox]

◐●

type of plant: hardy perennial [3–8]
flowering time: mid- to late spring
flower color: pale blue
height: 4–6in/10–15cm

The elegant, long-tubed flowers of this woodland plant are carried in loose, rather flat clusters, on upright stems. Each flower is about 1¼in/3cm across. Non-flowering shoots are covered with little, rounded leaves and they creep along the ground, rooting as they spread, forming mats of deep green growth about 18in/45cm wide. Ideally, *P. stolonifera* "Blue Ridge" should be grown in soil that is moist, well-drained and humus-rich. It has a preference for acid conditions; very alkaline conditions are not suitable. Varieties of *P. stolonifera* are available with white, pink, violet and purple flowers.

also for: ■ Acid soils

Viola riviniana Purpurea Group
(syn. *V. labradorica*, *V.l.* var. *purpurea*)
[dog violet, wood violet]

◐●

type of plant: hardy perennial [2–8]
flowering time: mainly mid- to late spring
flower color: purple-violet
height: 3–4in/8–10cm
Semi-evergreen

They may lack fragrance but, even in dry, shady places, these violets make purple-tinted carpets of foliage and then cover them with pretty flowers. Ideally, dog violets should be given cool, moist conditions, but they are sufficiently tough and vigorous to spread—often rapidly—in most soils and sites. They usually produce numerous, self-sown seedlings but these are easily uprooted if necessary. The leaf color of individual plants varies somewhat, from dark purple to purplish green, but it is best in positions that are not too dark. The flowers are small, each about ½in/1cm across, but they show up well against the dark, heart-shaped leaves.

also for: ■ Dry shade ■ Crevices in paving ■ Purple, bronze, or red leaves

---

ADDITIONAL PLANTS, featured elsewhere in this book, that are suitable for ground cover

◐◧/◐● partial (or full shade)/partial or full shade

minimum height 36in/90cm or more
Astilboides tabularis, see p.232
Euonymus fortunei "Silver Queen," see p.151
x *Fatshedera lizei,* see p.86
Prunus laurocerasus "Otto Luyken," see p.113
Sasa veitchii, see p.113
Skimmia x *confusa* "Kew Green," see p.310

minimum height between 12in/30cm and 36in/90cm
Bergenia cordifolia, see p.228
Dryopteris filix-mas, see p.81
Euonymus fortunei "Emerald Gaiety," see p.113
Euphorbia amygdaloides var. *robbiae,* see p.86
Geranium phaeum, see p.86
Geranium phaeum var. *phaeum* "Samobor," see p.180
Helleborus foetidus, see p.82
Helleborus x *hybridus,* see p.321

Helleborus x *hybridus* black-flowered, see p.332
Hosta "Halcyon," see p.196
Hosta sieboldiana var. *elegans,* see p.196
Iris foetidissima, see p.261
Jasminum nudiflorum, see p.318
Leucothoe Scarletta, see p.38
Lonicera pileata, see p.113
Polystichum aculeatum, see p.233
Polystichum setiferum Divisilobum Group, see p.233
Sarcococca hookeriana var. *humilis,* see p.314
Symphoricarpos x *chenaultii* "Hancock," see p.82

minimum height 12in/30cm or less
Asarum europaeum, see p.87
Bergenia "Silberlicht," see p.115
Convallaria majalis, see p.314
Geranium macrorrhizum, see p.251
Geranium macrorrhizum "Album," see p.115
Geranium nodosum, see p.82
Hedera canariensis "Gloire de Marengo," see p.136
Hedera helix "Green Ripple," see p.81

Hedera helix "Ivalace," see p.150
Hedera hibernica, see p.86
Hypericum calycinum, see p.82
Lamium galeobdolon "Hermann's Pride," see p.83
Lamium maculatum "Beacon Silver," see p.84
Lamium maculatum "White Nancy," see p.181
Liriope muscari, see p.83
Pachysandra terminalis "Variegata," see p.181
Parthenocissus quinquefolia, see p.240
Parthenocissus tricuspidata, see p.240
Pratia pedunculata, see p.159
Pulmonaria angustifolia, see p.50
Pulmonaria rubra "David Ward," see p.181
Pulmonaria rubra "Redstart," see p.321
Pulmonaria saccharata Argentea Group, see p.181
Rubus tricolor, see p.87
Tiarella wherryi, see p.233
Trachystemon orientalis, see p.83
Vinca major "Variegata," see p.175
Vinca minor, see p.83
Waldsteinia ternata, see p.84

Climbing plants

including shrubs needing support in order to grow upright

SOME VERY BEAUTIFUL and popular plants are climbers. For example, there is a clematis for every season of the year, as well as a climbing or rambling rose to suit nearly every site. The wide range of leaf shapes and colors produced by ivies (*Hedera*) makes these evergreen climbing plants especially versatile.

Considering the overall size that many climbers achieve, they take up surprisingly little space on the ground. For this reason, they are especially useful for providing both height and sizable blocks of color in restricted spaces.

When choosing a climber, an important consideration is the aspect of the site. In the northern hemisphere, structures that face south or west are the sunniest, warmest and most sheltered places. In these sites many plants flower especially freely and less hardy climbers will flourish. South-facing walls are particularly warm, but the soil beneath them can dry out very quickly; west-facing walls are slightly cooler, and dry soil is less likely to be a problem.

However, some climbers actually prefer a cool, shady place and these plants should be given either a north- or an east-facing site. Many shade-loving climbers thrive in a north-facing site, since the soil there tends to be consistently moist. East-facing sites are the coldest places, although walls of this aspect still provide some protection. Climbers suitable for an easterly as well as a northerly aspect are marked "✔✔" in the following list, but there are also certain shrubs—various firethorns (*Pyracantha*) and flowering quinces (*Chaenomeles*), for example—that flower earlier or display their fruits better if they are wall-trained.

Before making a final choice of climber, some thought should be given to the background against which the plant will be seen. Some reds and pinks, in particular, do not look good against brick, even when the brick is old and well weathered. It is worth bearing in mind that it is not only flowers but also fruits and autumn leaves that can clash with supporting structures.

Apart from covering walls, fences and so on, climbers are used to mask unsightly objects, including sheds and garages. Plants for this job include really vigorous climbers, such as mile-a-minute plant or silver flea vine (*Fallopia baldschuanica*), *Clematis montana* and many of its forms, and Boston ivy (*Parthenocissus tricuspidata*).

Climbers are also used to cover freestanding structures such as arches and pergolas, and they are often trained to cover tripods and similar supports within beds and borders, thereby lending height to mixed plantings. They are less frequently seen growing over and through other plants. Yet this can be a method of achieving particularly attractive and interesting combinations of color, texture and form, and it is also a way of enlivening plants that, in themselves, have very limited seasons of interest. (For some tried-and-tested combinations that include climbing plants, see my book *Take Two Plants*, David & Charles 1998).

Some climbers make good ground cover. Suitable plants in the following list include *Hydrangea anomala* subsp. *petiolaris* and *Hedera canariensis* "Gloire de Marengo"; for additional plants, see the *Ground Cover* list.

So many of the popular climbing plants are long-lived that annual climbers often get overlooked. However, sweet peas (*Lathyrus odoratus*) can make as pretty and fragrant a screen as most scented climbing roses, and the dark flowers of *Rhodochiton atrosanguineus* are as intriguing and sophisticated as any in this book. The short life-span and rapid growth of annual plants are obvious advantages in those circumstances where a covering or screen is wanted quickly but not permanently.

The growth of many climbers can be easily restricted, and most of these plants will adapt themselves to low walls, for example, by building up mounds of growth.

Wisteria sinensis
[Chinese wisteria]
○

type of plant: hardy climber [5–9]
flowering time: late spring to early summer
flower color: mauve-lilac
height: 30–50ft/9–15m; 5ft/1.5m grown
as a standard in a container

Chinese wisteria becomes laden with sumptuous, sweetly scented blossoms that cascades in clusters, up to 12in/30cm long, from stout, twining stems. As the numerous pea-flowers open, the elegant, divided foliage starts to expand. The pointed leaflets are, briefly, copper-tinged when young; they are mid-green in maturity. Chinese wisteria twines its way up a tree and, with strong support, it can be used to clothe a large wall. It needs rich, moist soil, a sunny position and some shelter in order to protect its flower buds from frost damage. It is sometimes trained, to about 5ft/1.5m, as a standard. In this form it makes an attractive, small tree that is especially suitable for containers. *W. sinensis* "Alba" is a good, white-flowered variety. Like the species, it is often several years old before it starts to flower.
also for: ■ Growing in containers (see above) ■ Decorative, green foliage ■ Fragrant flowers

Campsis x tagliabuana
"Madame Galen"
[trumpet creeper, trumpet vine]
○

type of plant: slightly tender climber [6–9]
flowering time: late summer to early autumn
flower color: deep salmon-red
height: 20–30ft/6–9m

Although it is freer-flowering in cool climates and also slightly hardier than either of its parents, this hybrid still needs a sheltered, sunny wall to become established fairly quickly and to flower really well. The richly colored "trumpets," about 3in/8cm long, are carried in clusters. They contrast strikingly with the deep green, divided leaves. *C. x tagliabuana* "Madame Galen" is a vigorous plant that clings to supports by means of aerial roots. It can be used for ground cover on a sunny bank or similar place, where it forms a shrubby mass of tough stems and tapering, toothed leaflets, about 36in/90cm high. It needs deep, moisture-retentive soil with good drainage.
also for: ■ Ground cover

Passiflora caerulea
[blue passionflower]
○

type of plant: slightly tender climber [8–11]
flowering time: early summer to early autumn
flower color: white + purple + blue
height: 20–30ft/6–9m
Semi-evergreen/Deciduous/Evergreen

The distinctive and exotic-looking, saucer-shaped flowers of this climber, with their intricately patterned and colored central areas, are each about 3in/8cm wide. They are produced over a long period but, except in hot summers, relatively few blooms are open at any one time. Blue passionflower grows quickly. It clings to a support, such as wire netting, by means of tendrils. There are always large quantities of the slender-lobed leaves and, in mild areas, these are evergreen. *P. caerulea* "Constance Elliott" has fragrant flowers that are more or less entirely white. Both the species and the variety need a warm, sheltered position and fertile, well-drained soil. The orange-yellow, egg-shaped fruits rarely ripen in cooler regions.
also for: ■ Ornamental fruit ■ Long, continuous flowering period (see above)

Solanum crispum "Glasnevin"
(syn. *S.c.* "Autumnale")
[Chilean potato vine]
○

type of plant: slightly tender shrub [7–9]
flowering time: early summer to mid-autumn
flower color: lilac-blue
height: 15–20ft/4.5–6m
Semi-evergreen

The long and rather unruly stems of this vigorous, scrambling shrub need to be tied to some sort of strong support to keep them upright. Provided it is given a warm, sheltered site and well-drained soil, the plant survives all but the most severe winters in cooler areas. *S. crispum* "Glasnevin" has an exceptionally long flowering season. It is very floriferous and produces its 6in/15cm-wide clusters of sweetly scented blossom especially freely in early summer and again in early autumn. At these times much of its pointed, veined foliage may be obscured by starry, yellow-anthered flowers.
also for: ■ Fragrant flowers ■ Long, continuous flowering period

Rosa e.g. "Albertine"
(Rambler)
[rose]
○

type of plant: hardy climber [5–9]
flowering time: midsummer
flower color: pale pink
height: 15ft/4.5m

This rambler's wonderfully fragrant, double flowers (about 3½in/9cm wide) have a rich, sweet scent. Their overall color combines two shades of pink: pale pink and apricot-pink. *R.* "Albertine" is vigorous and generally healthy, although mildew can be a problem if it is grown on a wall rather than on a pergola or arch or as a freestanding shrub. (As a shrub it is about 7ft/2.1m high and it sprawls widely.) Its stout, prickly stems carry dark-stalked leaves that are glossy, rich green. Any well-drained, fertile soil with reasonably good drainage is suitable.
also for: ■ Atmospheric pollution ■ Flowers suitable for cutting ■ Fragrant flowers

Cobaea scandens
[cathedral bells, cup and saucer vine]
○

type of plant: grown as half-hardy annual climber [9–11]
flowering time: midsummer to mid-autumn
flower color: greenish white changing to purple
height: 10–15ft/3–4.5m

The remarkable speed with which this plant grows makes it useful for covering even quite large areas for a short time. As well as its shapely flowers, C. scandens produces generous quantities of paired, pointed, oval leaves. Tubular, bell-shaped flowers, about 2in/5cm long, are carried on thick, reddish stalks. At first the flowers are pale green; as they age they turn purple and become slightly fragrant (the scent is honey-like). The saucer-like outer parts of each flower remain green. C. scandens f. alba has very pale green blooms that develop creamier tones as they mature. These plants need well-drained soil and a warm, sheltered site. They attach themselves to a support, such as wire netting, by means of tendrils.
also for: ■ Flowers suitable for cutting

Eccremocarpus scaber
[Chilean glory flower]
○

type of plant: half-hardy annual/perennial climber [9–10]
flowering time: early summer to mid-autumn
flower color: reddish orange
height: 10–15ft/3–4.5m
Semi-evergreen/Deciduous

Only in mild regions will this fast-growing climber produce persistent, woody stems. Elsewhere its top growth usually dies in winter and is renewed each spring. Chilean glory flower is quite often treated as an annual. There are normally large numbers of the brightly colored, tubular flowers, and each of these slender blooms is only about 1in/2.5cm long. The mass of much-divided, rich green foliage is made up of numerous little leaves, each not much more than 2–3in/5–8cm long. This tendrilled climber needs light but moisture-retentive soil. There are forms of the species with red and with yellow flowers.
also for: ■ Long, continuous flowering period

Ipomoea tricolor
(syn. I. rubrocaerulea)
"Heavenly Blue"
[morning glory]
○

type of plant: half-hardy annual climber [9–11]
flowering time: midsummer to early autumn
flower color: deep azure blue
height: 8–10ft/2.4–3m

The beautiful sky-blue of the flowers on I. tricolor "Heavenly Blue" is the color most often associated with morning glory, but there are also some varieties with pink and red flowers, and I.t. "Flying Saucers" has flowers that are striped in white and lilac-blue. Unless the plants are in a warm, sheltered, sunny site they do not perform well, but under suitable conditions they climb rapidly and bloom profusely. They need light, well-drained soil. Each trumpet-shaped flower is about 2½in/6cm wide and very short-lived (it will have faded by mid-afternoon). The light green leaves of these twining climbers are smooth and heart-shaped.

Rhodochiton atrosanguineus
(syn. R. volubile)
○

type of plant: grown as half-hardy annual climber [9–11]
flowering time: midsummer to mid-autumn
flower color: rose-maroon + deep purple
height: 6–10ft/1.8–3m

Although rich, moist soils are ideal for this climber, it performs well in most garden soils with good drainage. Each deeply colored flower has a very dark tube, 1½–2in/4–5cm long, that protrudes from its cup-shaped outer parts. These bizarre but stylish bells dangle among the rich green foliage. The leaves are heart-shaped and equipped with twining stalks that enable R. atrosanguineus to cling to various sorts of support.

Rosa e.g. Warm Welcome = "Chewizz" (Climbing Miniature)
[rose]
○

type of plant: hardy climber [6–9]
flowering time: early summer to mid-autumn
flower color: reddish orange
height: 6–8ft/1.8–2.4m

These semi-double blooms, 1½in/4cm across, are produced continuously over a long period. The sweetly but not very strongly scented flowers appear, in clusters, along the whole length of the plant's fairly erect stems, and this characteristic—as well as a modest stature—makes R. Warm Welcome a good choice for a large container. There are plenty of healthy, fairly broad, rather leathery leaves, which are reddish bronze when young and glossy, dark green in maturity. Most soils that retain moisture easily are suitable for this floriferous rose, although conditions do need to be reasonably fertile for it to perform really well. R. Laura Ford is another, popular Climbing Miniature rose; its semi-double flowers are yellow.
also for: ■ Fragrant flowers ■ Growing in containers ■ Long, continuous flowering period

Tropaeolum majus Tall Mixed
[nasturtium, Indian cress]
○

type of plant: grown as hardy annual
climber [10–11]
flowering time: early summer to mid-autumn
flower color: mixed—red, orange, yellow
height: 5–7ft/1.5–2.1m

Many of the most popular varieties of nasturtium are low-growing, trailing plants, but climbing varieties such as T. majus Tall Mixed are also available. Nasturtiums that climb do so by means of twining leaf-stalks. They all grow very rapidly. Their flowers, each about 2in/5cm wide, are broadly funnel-shaped, and the leaves are light green and almost circular. Both the flowers and leaves are edible; they have a tangy, peppery taste. Nasturtiums are very easily grown plants that flower especially well in poor, dry soils. The climbing and the trailing varieties make useful, temporary ground cover on hot, dry slopes. T.m. "Out of Africa" is a climbing nasturtium that not only has the usual, cheerful flowers but also bears leaves variegated with creamy white markings.
also for: ■ Dry soils in hot, sunny sites ■ Ground cover

Thunbergia alata
e.g. Suzie Hybrids
[black-eyed Susan vine]
○

type of plant: grown as half-hardy annual
climber [9–11]
flowering time: early summer to mid-autumn
flower color: mixed—orange, creamy white,
buff + dark purple-brown
height: 4–6ft/1.2–1.8m

Most fertile, well-drained soils are suitable for this twining climber but, if it is to be grown outdoors, it needs a sheltered position in full sun. Although T. alata Suzie Hybrids are usually trained up canes and similar supports, they can also be planted in hanging baskets. The rich green leaves are veined and pointed, and roughly triangular in shape. Each of the numerous, open-faced flowers is about 1½in/4cm wide.

ADDITIONAL CLIMBING PLANTS featured elsewhere in this book

○ sun

minimum height 10ft/3m or more
Actinidia kolomikta, see p.161
Clematis armandii, see p.297
Clematis rehderiana,
   see p.297

Solanum laxum "Album," see p.334.
Wisteria floribunda "Multijuga," see p.146

minimum height between 3ft/90cm and 10ft/3m
Abutilon megapotamicum, see p.145
Abutilon megapotamicum "Variegatum,"
   see p.163

Clematis cirrhosa var. balearica, see p.316
Clematis "Etoile Rose," see p.334
Hedera helix "Buttercup," see p.211
Lathyrus odoratus Galaxy Group, see p.269
Lathyrus odoratus "Noel Sutton," see p.299
Rosa Gertrude Jeykll, see p.300
Rosa Graham Thomas, see p.270

Celastrus orbiculatus
[oriental bittersweet, staff vine]
○ [◐]

type of plant: hardy climber [5–8]
height: 30–50ft/9–15m

In late autumn, this climber's numerous yellow capsules split to reveal shiny, orange-red, pea-sized seeds. The capsules and their seeds often remain decorative through much of winter. As the fruits are ripening, the broad, sometimes almost circular leaves, each 4in/10cm or more long, change from mid-green to yellow. All fertile, well-drained, moisture-retentive soils are suitable. This exceptionally vigorous, twining plant can be used to cover a wall of any aspect, and it looks good growing through a large tree. Fruiting is most prolific in sunny positions. Plants of C. orbiculatus offered for sale are usually self-fertile. However, male and female forms are available too, and both need to be grown together for fruit to develop.
also for: ■ Colorful, autumn foliage ■ Ornamental fruit

Rosa e.g. "Wedding Day"
(Rambler)
[rose]
○ [◐]

type of plant: hardy climber [5–9]
flowering time: early to midsummer
flower color: creamy white turning to pale pink
height: 20–25ft/6–7.5m

R. "Wedding Day" grows extremely strongly and is suitable for training into a mature and established tree and for covering a very large wall. Its yellow-budded, single flowers, each about 1in/2.5cm wide, are carried in big clusters. They have the rich, sweet fragrance of orange-blossom. They are followed by rounded, pinkish red hips. The plant's leaves are mid-green, glossy and quite slender. An even more vigorous rose, R. filipes "Kiftsgate," produces fragrant, creamy white, single flowers and it can grow more than 30ft/9m high. Both these plants are rampant and far too large for a small garden (R. "Wedding Day" is usually about 15ft/4.5m wide). Since they are so very vigorous, they can be grown successfully even in quite poor soils.
also for: ■ Atmospheric pollution
■ Ornamental fruit ■ Fragrant flowers

Rosa e.g. "New Dawn"
(syn. *R.* "The New Dawn")
(Climber)
[rose]
○[◐]

type of plant: hardy climber [5–9]
flowering time: early summer to early autumn
flower color: silvery pink
height: 10–15ft/3–4.5m
✔

This vigorous rose blooms continuously during the summer months with two main flushes early and late in the season. Its semi-double flowers, gently and prettily colored, open fully to about 3½in/9cm wide. They have a light, sweet fragrance and are carried in numerous clusters at the ends of long shoots. The foliage is healthy and consists of glossy, rounded leaflets. *R.* "New Dawn" is especially suitable for training over a pergola, arch or similar support, but it can also be trained on a wall (including a cool, lightly shaded wall). Well-drained, moisture-retentive and fertile soil suits this plant best, but it prospers in a wide range of conditions. *R.* "Compassion" is another popular climbing rose that is long-flowering and fragrant; its double flowers are salmon-pink and about 4in/10cm wide.
also for: ■ Flowers suitable for cutting ■ Fragrant flowers ■ Long, continuous flowering period

Tropaeolum peregrinum
(syn. *T. canariense*)
[Canary creeper]
○[◐]

type of plant: grown as hardy annual climber [10–11]
flowering time: early summer to mid-autumn
flower color: yellow
height: 6–10ft/1.8–3m

The pale, lobed leaves of this fast-growing climber make a pretty background for the numerous flowers. As long as the site is fairly sheltered, canary creeper can be grown in light shade, but there will be even more blooms in sunnier positions. Each graceful, fringed flower is about 1in/2.5cm long. Well-drained, fertile soil that does not dry out too readily is most suitable for this plant, but it is easily pleased. Its thin, twining stems need some sort of support around which to coil themselves and this can be other plants as well as, for instance, canes or wire netting.
also for: ■ Decorative, green foliage

Tropaeolum tuberosum
var. *lineamaculatum* "Ken Aslet"
○[◐]

type of plant: half-hardy perennial climber [8–10]
flowering time: midsummer to mid-autumn
flower color: red + orange
height: 6–10ft/1.8–3m

The flowers of *T. tuberosum* var. *lineamaculatum* "Ken Aslet" are small, about 1¼in/3cm long, but poised elegantly on arching, maroon stems and held conspicuously clear of the accompanying foliage. Each flower is a flared tube, the opulent coloring of which is enhanced by the paleness of the pretty, lobed leaves. This climber should have a moisture-retentive, fertile soil, and the planting position needs to be warm and sheltered. The twining leaf-stalks cling to any support—including other plants. In most regions, tubers of this plant should be lifted and stored during winter in a cool place. The flowers appear over a long, late season.
also for: ■ Decorative, green foliage ■ Long, continuous flowering period

Lathyrus latifolius
e.g. "White Pearl"
[perennial pea, everlasting pea]
○[◐]

type of plant: hardy perennial climber [5–9]
flowering time: early summer to early autumn
flower color: white
height: 6–8ft/1.8–2.4m

Although it lacks the fragrance of sweet peas, the perennial pea is a vigorous plant with a long flowering season. *L. latifolius* itself has brightly colored, usually magenta-pink pea-flowers, about 1½in/4cm wide, that are carried in loose spikes of at least half a dozen blooms. *L.l.* "White Pearl" is a popular, pure white variety. Well-drained soils of all types are suitable for these plants, and they are quite happy in poor soil. They climb by means of tendrils and look attractive scrambling through other plants. They can also be allowed to sprawl along the ground, when their broad, winged stems and bluish green leaflets create an entwined mass of growth about 24in/60cm high and 5ft/1.5m wide.
also for: ■ Ground cover ■ Flowers suitable for cutting ■ Long, continuous flowering period

Codonopsis clematidea
○[◐] (see description)

type of plant: hardy perennial climber [6–9]
flowering time: early to midsummer
flower color: pale blue-gray
height: 24in/60cm

Hidden away inside these nodding, bell-shaped flowers are strikingly colored markings of orange, black and dark purple-maroon. Each flower is about 1in/2.5cm long and has a stylish topknot of reflexed lobes. The leaves are grayish, pointed and have an unpleasant, musky smell. Cool, moist, humus-rich soil is suitable for this plant, and in warm, dry districts it benefits from some shade. Its slender, sprawling stems are easily broken and need shelter to prevent them from becoming damaged. *C. clematidea* looks good twining and scrambling through other plants (when it may reach up to 4–5ft/1.2–1.5m high). *C. ovata* has flowers of similar coloring but its stems are upright and non-twining, and it is more difficult to grow.

Fallopia baldschuanica (syn. *Polygonum baldschuanicum*) [mile-a-minute plant, silver flea vine]
○◐
type of plant: hardy climber [5–9]
flowering time: midsummer to early autumn
flower color: white
height: 40–50ft/12–15m
✔✔

F. baldschuanica can grow more than 15ft/4.5m in a single season, and this makes it useful for covering a large area quickly. The rampant, twining growths withstand very hard pruning, but the plant sometimes proves uncontrollable once established. F. baldschuanica can be planted in any soil, as long as it is not dry. North-, east- and west-facing positions are all suitable for this climber, but it tends to grow poorly when facing south. Dangling over and among the dark green, heart-shaped leaves, there are numerous, loose sprays of tiny flowers that are carried on upright stalks about 8in/20cm long.

Hydrangea anomala subsp. *petiolaris* (syn. *H. petiolaris*) [climbing hydrangea]
○◐
type of plant: hardy climber [5–9]
flowering time: early summer
flower color: white + creamy white
height: 30–50ft/9–15m
✔

Although vigorous, climbing hydrangea grows slowly in its first few years. However, once established, the aerial roots on its russet, peeling branches attach themselves to flat surfaces and the plant becomes self-supporting. A mature specimen is a magnificent sight, with masses of lacy flower heads, each about 9in/23cm wide. In autumn, the broad, deep green, pointed leaves turn clear yellow before falling. The ideal position is, perhaps, west-facing, but a north wall is also suitable and the coolness there helps to make the flowers last longer. Fertile, moisture-retentive soil is most suitable for this plant. When used as ground cover, climbing hydrangea slowly thickens into a 24in/60cm high, rooting carpet of greenery.
also for: ■ Atmospheric pollution ■ Ground cover ■ Colorful, autumn foliage

Schizophragma hydrangeoides
○◐
type of plant: hardy climber [5–8]
flowering time: mid- to late summer
flower color: cream + creamy white
height: 25–35ft/7.5–10.5m
✔✔

Until the aerial roots on its stems have attached themselves firmly to whatever support is provided, this climber grows slowly. Indeed it never grows very quickly but it is, eventually, large (it can sometimes reach more than 40ft/12m tall). S. hydrangeoides looks especially effective growing into a tree. The tiny flowers, carried in heads 8–10in/20–25cm across, are surrounded by much showier, diamond-shaped, petal-like sepals, each 1–2in/2.5–5cm long. The broad, rich green leaves turn yellow in autumn. Flowering is most profuse in sunny sites, but this very hardy climber grows well in shade. Ideally, there should be shade at the roots and sun on the top growth. Moist, humus-rich, well-drained soil gives good results. S.h. "Roseum" is less vigorous than the species, and its petal-like sepals are flushed rose-pink.
also for: ■ Colorful, autumn foliage

Clematis montana var. grandiflora
○◐

type of plant: hardy climber [5–9]
flowering time: late spring to early summer
flower color: white
height: 25–30ft/7.5–9m
✔

C. montana and many of its varieties—
including the variety shown here as an
example—are exceptionally vigorous and
ideal for growing into a tree or covering a
large structure. They climb
by means of twining leaf-stalks and
produce dense masses of tangled growth.
C.m. var. grandiflora is a very hardy form
with numerous, large flowers against dark
green, tripartite leaves. Each bloom is
3–4in/8–10cm wide with broad "petals."
The white flowers of C. montana itself
are about 2in/5cm wide and sometimes
vanilla-scented. Certain varieties are
consistently fragrant—including, for
instance, C.m. var. wilsonii, which has
white flowers that smell of chocolate,
and pale pink C. "Elizabeth" (see below).
All these plants are easily grown.
However, they do appreciate moisture-
retentive soil, and ideally they should
have shade at their roots and a lighter
position for their top growth.

Clematis e.g. "Elizabeth"
○◐

type of plant: hardy climber [6–9]
flowering time: late spring to early summer
flower color: soft pale pink; usually white
in shade
height: 20ft/6m
✔

This example of a pink-flowered
Montana Group clematis has sweetly
scented blooms, up to 3in/8cm across.
Its deep green leaflets are toothed and
pointed, and especially when they are
young they are bronze-tinted. Other
popular pinks in this Group include
C. montana var. rubens (the young foliage
of which is purple-tinged), doubles such
as C.m. var. r. "Broughton Star" and C.m.
var. r. "Marjorie," and the large-flowered,
mauve-pink C.m. var. r. "Tetrarose" (which
has dark purplish leaves). All these plants
climb by means of twining leaf-stalks.
Very vigorous varieties, such as C.m. var.
rubens, look good climbing into trees.
These easily pleased plants thrive in
moisture-retentive soil and in a site
where their roots are shaded and their
top growth is in sun. They are suitable
for a north wall.
also for: ■ Purple, bronze, or red leaves
(mainly young leaves) ■ Fragrant flowers

Pileostegia viburnoides
○◐

type of plant: slightly tender climber [7–10]
flowering time: late summer to early autumn
flower color: creamy white
height: 20ft/6m
Evergreen
✔ (see description)

P. viburnoides climbs by means of aerial roots. It grows slowly at first but
more rapidly once it is established. Its long, fairly slender, leathery leaves
provide a flattering background of rich, lustrous green for the heads of tiny
flowers. These branched flower heads are usually about 6in/15cm wide, and
the combination of generously sized flowers of restrained coloring and
good-looking foliage makes for a handsome and elegant plant. To grow
really well, P. viburnoides needs fertile, moisture-retentive soil with good
drainage. It is suitable for a fairly sheltered, north wall, as well as for a wall
of southern or western aspect.
also for: ■ Decorative, green foliage

Humulus lupulus "Aureus"
[hops]
◐◑
type of plant: hardy perennial climber [5–9]
height: 15ft/4.5m

Golden hop produces bold, shapely leaves, each about 6in/15cm long and deeply lobed. In the main growing season, the foliage color is a beautiful lime-yellow; by late summer the leaves are light yellowish green. This vigorous, often suckering plant grows quickly and produces long, twining trails of growth each season. It thrives in fertile soil, and some shelter from cold and drying winds is beneficial. In really sunny sites, the foliage colors well but there may be problems with scorching of the leaf edges. H. lupulus "Aureus" produces only a few pendent clusters of hop "flowers."
also for: ■ Yellow or yellow-green leaves

Rosa e.g. "Madame Alfred Carrière" (Noisette)
[rose]
○◐
type of plant: hardy climber [5–9]
flowering time: early summer to mid-autumn
flower color: white tinged with pink
height: 15ft/4.5m
✔

The main flowering season of this very hardy rose is summer, but its richly fragrant blooms will continue to appear in smaller numbers until well into autumn. Each fully double flower is about 2½in/6cm across. In sun and fertile, well-cultivated soil, growth is very vigorous and there will be plenty of flowers. Performance is also good in some shade, and this is a good climber for a north-facing wall. Its numerous leaves are light gray-tinged green. Other delicately colored roses for shaded walls include R. "New Dawn" (see p.130) and the creamy white rambler R. "Albéric Barbier."
also for: ■ Atmospheric pollution ■ Fragrant flowers ■ Long, continuous flowering period

Clematis e.g. "Alba Luxurians"
○◐
type of plant: hardy climber [4–9]
flowering time: midsummer to early autumn
flower color: white + green
height: 10–12ft/3–3.6m
✔

This vigorous Viticella Group clematis produces masses of green-tipped flowers among its light green leaflets. The cluster of dark anthers in the centre of each 2–3in/5–8cm bloom heightens the very attractive, pale and restrained coloring of the flowers. C. "Alba Luxurians" is easily grown and trouble-free as long as it has fertile, moisture-retentive soil with reasonable drainage. Ideally, it should have its top growth in sun and its roots in shade. There are numerous varieties in the Viticella Group with flowers in shades of blue, purple, red and pink, as well as in white. For another long-flowering clematis in this Group, see the double-flowered C. "Purpurea Plena Elegans" on p.134. All these plants climb using twining leaf-stalks.
also for: ■ Long, continuous flowering period

Clematis e.g. "Jackmanii"
○◐
type of plant: hardy climber [5–9]
flowering time: mid- to late summer
flower color: violet-purple fading to violet
height: 10ft/3m
✔

The abundant, 3–4in/8–10cm flowers of this very popular clematis look especially good against a light background, since this shows their velvety darkness to advantage. For those gardeners who prefer a fuller-looking flower, there is C. "Jackmanii Superba" (although plants sold under this name may, in fact, be the similarly colored, dark-centered C. "Gipsy Queen"). Another richly colored clematis with large flowers is shown on p.345. To perform really well, these and other large-flowered clematis need humus-rich, moisture-retentive soil with reasonably good drainage. Generally, they should have their roots in shade and their top growth in a lighter, sunnier position. In order to grow upright, their twining leaf-stalks need support of some sort to clasp. The mid- to deep green leaves of C. "Jackmanii" are oval and pointed and not usually produced in very large quantities.

Hedera helix
e.g. "Oro di Bogliasco"
(syn. H.h. "Goldheart")
[ivy]
○◐
type of plant: hardy climber [6–10]
height: 9–12ft/2.7–3.6m
Evergreen
✔✔

Although it is at first slow growing, this strikingly variegated ivy soon develops quickly. Its reddish, self-clinging stems and its small- to medium-sized leaves make a dense, close covering on walls of all aspects. The lobed and pointed leaves vary considerably in size, but on average they are about 2in/5cm long. The basic leaf color is very dark green; the central markings are clear yellow. (H. helix "Oro di Bogliasco" is not suitable for ground cover, since it tends to lose its variegation if grown horizontally.) Among the hundreds of varieties of H. helix, there are other popular, yellow-variegated ivies. These include H.h. "Goldchild," which has yellow margins to its gray-green leaves. All these plants grow in almost any soil, as long as it is not either hot and dry or waterlogged. Variegated types do not thrive in cold, very exposed positions.
also for: ■ Dry shade ■ Atmospheric pollution ■ Variegated leaves

Clematis e.g. "Markham's Pink"
○◐

type of plant: hardy climber [5–9]
flowering time: late spring to early summer
flower color: soft pink
height: 8–10ft/2.4–3m
✔

Compared with their close relation *C. alpina* (see p.135), *C. macropetala* and its associated varieties tend to be more vigorous, slightly later-flowering plants with flowers that are "fuller." *C.* "Markham's Pink" is a particularly popular variety (which is seen here scrambling through a variegated weigela), but *C. macropetala* itself is a very pretty violet-blue and *C.* "White Swan" is an attractive, white variety. The nodding flowers of these plants are about 3in/8cm wide. They are followed by fluffy seedheads. Given a cool root-run in reasonably fertile and well-drained soil, these clematis are easily grown. They flower best when their top growth is in a fairly sunny position. Their divided, slender-lobed leaves have twining stalks, by means of which the plants climb.
also for: ■ Ornamental fruit (seedheads)

Clematis e.g. "Purpurea Plena Elegans"
○◐

type of plant: hardy climber [6–9]
flowering time: midsummer to early autumn
flower color: soft rosy purple
height: 8–10ft/2.4–3m
✔

C. viticella is the parent of many attractive hybrids (see also, for instance, *C.* "Alba Luxurians" on p.133; in addition there are purples, such as *C.* "Polish Spirit," and reds, such as *C.* "Madame Julia Correvon"). *C.* "Purpurea Plena Elegans" has charming, double, rosette-like flowers, each about 2½in/6cm across and produced in large numbers over a long period. Like many Viticella Group clematis, this variety has slender stems and divided leaves, and it looks good twining over and through other plants. It is easily grown in most soils that are reasonably well-drained and moisture-retentive. It likes its roots to be cool and shaded, with its top growth in a lighter position.
also for: ■ Long, continuous flowering period

Rosa e.g. "Danse du Feu" (Climber)
[rose]
○◐

type of plant: hardy climber [4–9]
flowering time: early summer to early autumn
flower color: red-scarlet
height: 8–10ft/2.4–3m
✔✔

R. "Danse du Feu" has long been one of the best, readily available climbing roses for a north- or east-facing wall. Although flowering is freest in a sunny position, there will still be plenty of the brilliantly colored blooms in more shaded positions. The double flowers are about 3in/8cm wide. They are most shapely soon after opening from their dark red buds; later they flatten and their petals curl somewhat. The main flowering season is early summer, but sizable quantities of blooms are borne over several months. The plant has dark green, glossy leaves and rather stiff stems. *R.* "Paul's Scarlet Climber" [zones 6–10] is another brightly colored, floriferous rose for a shady wall. Both these roses can be grown in quite a wide range of soils but they are most successful in well-prepared, fertile ones.
also for: ■ Flowers suitable for cutting ■ Long, continuous flowering period

Ampelopsis brevipedunculata var. maximowiczii "Elegans" (syn. A. glandulosa var. brevipedunculata "Tricolor")
○◐

type of plant: hardy climber [6–9]
height: 7–10ft/2.1–3m

At about 3in/8cm long, these precisely lobed leaves are rather like miniaturized versions of hop leaves. In coloring, however, they are much more intricate. The basic foliage color is dark green but this is heavily splashed with white or a mixture of white and pink. The newest leaves—and the slender stems, too—are entirely pinkish red. After hot summers small bunches of berries are produced, and these ripen from violet to blue. Moist, though well-drained, soil is most suitable for *A. brevipedunculata* var. *maximowiczii* "Elegans," and it needs a site that is sheltered and warm. It climbs by means of tendrils that cling to rough surfaces.
also for: ■ Variegated leaves ■ Ornamental fruit (see above)

Aconitum volubile
[monkshood, aconite]
○◐

type of plant: hardy perennial climber [6–9]
flowering time: late summer to early autumn
flower color: lilac, often green-tinged
height: 6–8ft/1.8–2.4m

Although this vigorous, twining plant dies back each winter, *A. volubile* grows 6ft/1.8m or more each year. The lobed leaves are deep green with pale veins. Among them appear loose heads of hooded flowers, each flower about 1in/2.5cm long. *A. hemsleyanum* is a similar, climbing monkshood with darker violet blooms. The two plants are often confused. Any fertile soil that remains cool and moist is suitable. The stems do not readily lend themselves to being trained on to artificial supports, and both these climbers look much more attractive scrambling through shrubs. All parts of these plants are poisonous.
also for: ■ Heavy, clay soils

Clematis alpina
○●

type of plant: hardy climber [5–9]
flowering time: mid- to late spring
flower color: violet-blue + white
height: 5–8ft/1.5–2.4m

The graceful, little flowers of this clematis are poised on long stalks well clear of the ferny, slender-lobed leaves. Each flower is about 2in/5cm wide. It consists of four tapering "petals" around a conspicuous cluster of pale stamens. Long-lasting, fluffy seedheads develop later. As well as C. alpina itself and blue-flowered varieties such as C. "Frances Rivis," there are varieties with pink flowers (e.g. C. "Willy"), purple-pink flowers (e.g. C. "Ruby") and white flowers (e.g. C. "White Moth"). Moderately fertile, moisture-retentive soil with reasonable drainage suits these plants best. They look attractive scrambling over shrubs but are equally good on a wall or other artificial support. They climb by means of twining leaf-stalks.
also for: ■ Ornamental fruit (seedheads)

ADDITIONAL CLIMBING PLANTS featured elsewhere in this book

○● sun or partial shade

minimum height 10ft/3m or more
Akebia quinata, see p.307
Clematis "Perle d"Azur," see p.345
Euonymus fortunei "Emerald Gaiety," see p.113
Euonymus fortunei "Silver Queen," see p.151
Hedera colchica "Dentata Variegata," see p.171
Lonicera japonica "Aureoreticulata," see p.171
Lonicera japonica "Halliana," see p.307

Lonicera periclymenum "Graham Thomas," see p.344
Parthenocissus quinquefolia, see p.240
Parthenocissus tricuspidata, see p.240
Rosa "Zéphirine Drouhin," see p.307
Vitis coignetiae, see p.240

minimum height between 3ft/90cm and 10ft/3m
Clematis "Lasurstern," see p.149
Clematis "Niobe," see p.345

Clematis "Vyvyan Pennell," see p.288
Cotoneaster atropurpureus "Variegatus," see p.174
Cotoneaster horizontalis, see p.267
Euonymus fortunei "Emerald 'n' Gold," see p.174
Jasminum nudiflorum, see p.318
Tropaeolum speciosum, see p.30

minimum height 3ft/90cm or less
Hedera helix "Ivalace," see p.150

Lonicera x tellmanniana
[honeysuckle]
●[○]

type of plant: hardy climber [6–9]
flowering time: late spring to midsummer
flower color: bright apricot-yellow
height: 15ft/4.5m

The 2in/5cm-long, tubular flowers of this vigorous honeysuckle are arranged in bold whorls and are of a remarkable, rich amber coloring, but they do lack a sweet scent. They are red-tinged in bud. The leaves are rounded, mid-green ovals and quite large (up to 4in/10cm long). The plant has strong, twining stems, and it is suitable for growing into a tree as well as for covering a wall. It is healthiest, and flowers best, if positioned in some shade and given fertile, humus-rich, moisture-retentive soil. Its roots at least should be cool and shaded. L. tragophylla is a similar, even more impressive honeysuckle, with flowers nearly 4in/10cm long, but it is more difficult to grow than L. x tellmanniana.

Lonicera x brownii "Dropmore Scarlet"
[scarlet trumpet honeysuckle]
●[○]

type of plant: hardy climber [4–9]
flowering time: early summer to early autumn
flower color: scarlet
height: 12–15ft/3.6–4.5m
Semi-evergreen/Deciduous

Like the honeysuckle in the previous illustration, L. x brownii "Dropmore Scarlet" lacks fragrance. but its flowers, up to 1½in/4cm long and carried in eye-catching whorls, are brilliantly colored. They appear over an exceptionally long flowering season and contrast well with the cool, rather bluish green of the rounded leaves. This honeysuckle is vigorous and very hardy. However, it seems to flower best on a wall that is sheltered and warm and also, preferably, shaded. The roots, at least, should be positioned out of direct sunlight. The plant thrives in moisture-retentive soil that is rich and of a rather spongy texture. It climbs by twining its stems around supports. (For a honeysuckle with flowers that are both richly colored and sweetly scented, see the following plant and also p.312.)
also for: ■ Long, continuous flowering period

Lonicera x heckrottii "Gold Flame"
[honeysuckle]
●[○]

type of plant: hardy climber [6–9]
flowering time: early to late summer
flower color: deep pink + yellow
height: 10–15ft/3–4.5m
Semi-evergreen/Deciduous

The richly colored, fragrant flowers of L. x heckrottii "Gold Flame" are carried, in quite dense whorls, at the ends of twining shoots. Each flower is 1½–2in/4–5cm long and generally exudes a sweet, spicy scent. The leaves of the plant are oval; they are, at first, red-purple, maturing soon to blue-tinged dark green. Giving this climber moisture-retentive soil and some shade promotes good growth, and it also discourages aphids, which can be a problem in drier, sunnier conditions. The roots of the plant, at least, should be shaded. In cooler climates, the flowers are sometimes followed by red berries. These ripen from early autumn onward.
also for: ■ Ornamental fruit (see above) ■ Long, continuous flowering period

Clematis e.g. "Nelly Moser"
◑[○]

type of plant: hardy climber [5–9]
flowering time: late spring to early summer
and late summer to early autumn
flower color: palest mauve + deep carmine-pink
height: 8–12ft/2.4–3.6m
✔

In really sunny positions the flower color of this very popular clematis quickly "bleach." At least some shade is therefore advisable. The flowers are usually 5–6in/12–15cm wide, and even on individual specimens of C. "Nelly Moser" their exact color tends to vary from season to season. The tripartite leaves are composed of broad, pointed ovals of mid-green (it is the twining stalks of these leaves that enable the plant to climb). There are a number of large-flowered clematis hybrids with flowers of this sort of coloring, including, for example, the slightly brighter C. "Bees" Jubilee" [zones 5–9], which is also prone to fading in sunshine. They all produce the most impressive displays of flowers in moist, fertile, humus-rich soil.
also for: ■ Growing in containers

Clematis e.g. "Hagley Hybrid"
◑[○]

type of plant: hardy climber [5–9]
flowering time: early to late summer
flower color: pinkish mauve
height: 6–8ft/1.8–2.4m
✔

C. "Hagley Hybrid" is a very floriferous and healthy clematis with an exceptionally long flowering season. Its flowers are largest—about 6in/15cm wide—early in the season; later blooms are smaller. The plant climbs by means of twining leaf-stalks, and often looks especially attractive when it mingles with other climbers. This clematis blooms most freely in sun. However, its flowers tend to lose their color quite quickly in a sunny position and some shade is advisable. In any case, the roots of the plant should be shaded and cool. C. "Comtesse de Bouchaud" is another popular, large-flowered, pink clematis. Its flower color is brighter than that of C. "Hagley Hybrid." Moist, fertile, well-drained soil is most suitable.
also for: ■ Growing in containers ■ Long, continuous flowering period

---

ADDITIONAL CLIMBING PLANTS featured elsewhere in this book

◑[○] **partial shade (or sun)**

minimum height 10ft/3m or more
x *Fatshedera lizei*, see p.86

Hedera hibernica, see p.86
Lonicera periclymenum "Serotina,"
    see p.312
Parthenocissus henryana, see p.180

minimum height between 3ft/90cm and 10ft/3m
Hedera helix "Glacier," see p.124
Hedera helix "Green Ripple,"
    see p.81

Hedera canariensis "Gloire de Marengo" (syn. H.c. "Variegata")
[ivy]
◑●[○]

type of plant: slightly tender climber [8–11]
height: 10–15ft/3–4.5m; 9in/23cm as ground cover
Evergreen
✔ (see description)

This fast-growing ivy has large, more or less unlobed leaves. Each leaf, about 4in/10cm long, has a central area of mottled gray-green surrounded by an irregular, creamy white margin. In cold weather, the edges of the leaves may turn pink. The stems are maroon. Any soil—unless it is either hot and dry or waterlogged—is suitable. H. canariensis "Gloire de Marengo" attaches itself, not particularly tightly or closely, to a wall or similar surface by means of aerial roots. In warm climates it can be grown on a north-facing wall. Elsewhere, it is best in a fairly sheltered site since cold, dry winds tend to scorch its foliage. It makes a good, rooting carpet of ground cover, about 9in/23cm high and 5–6ft/1.5–1.8m wide.
also for: ■ Dry shade ■ Atmospheric pollution ■ Ground cover ■ Growing in containers ■ Variegated leaves

Berberidopsis corallina
[coral plant]
◑✳

type of plant: slightly tender climber [8–9]
flowering time: midsummer to early autumn
flower color: rich red
height: 10–12ft/3–3.6m
Evergreen
✔ (see description)

With shade and shelter and in moist, open soil that is acid to neutral this climber can produce plenty of its distinctive, red-stalked flowers. It is most at home in mild, humid climates (where it can be grown on a north-facing wall); it is not so easily pleased elsewhere. The globular, waxy blooms are each only about ½in/1cm in diameter, but the way they dangle elegantly beneath the fresh green, holly-like leaves makes them conspicuous. Coral plant is a lax twiner that needs plenty of support in order to grow upright. In climates with cool summers, a sunnier position may be needed to encourage it to flower well.
also for: ■ Acid soils

ADDITIONAL CLIMBING PLANTS featured elsewhere in this book

◑● **partial or full shade**

minimum height 10ft/3m or more
Euonymus fortunei "Emerald Gaiety,"
    see p.113
Euonymus fortunei "Silver Queen,"
    see p.151

x *Fatshedera lizei*, see p.86
Hedera hibernica, see p.86
Parthenocissus henryana, see p.180
Parthenocissus quinquefolia,
    see p.240
Parthenocissus tricuspidata,
    see p.240

minimum height between 3ft/90cm and 10ft/3m
Hedera helix "Glacier," see p.124
Hedera helix "Green Ripple," see p.81
Jasminum nudiflorum, see p.318

minimum height 3ft/90cm or less
Hedera helix "Ivalace," see p.150

Hedging plants

A HEDGE CAN PERFORM several functions, often simultaneously. Very commonly, hedges define boundaries, but they can also act as backdrops against which groups of plants are displayed, and they can be features in their own right—when used to create a maze or parterre, for example. They can carry out these almost architectural functions and, at the same time, provide shelter and privacy, screen unsightly objects and views, and, if sufficiently dense and thorny, they can discourage intruders. Informal hedges and screens in particular can provide food and shelter for wildlife.

A flowering hedge can be an impressive sight, and many of the hedging plants in this book have conspicuous flowers. Hedges can also be created by using fruiting plants. However, the production of flowers and fruits is usually reduced, at least to some extent, by regular, close clipping. Where plenty of flowers and fruits are wanted, plants should ideally be grown as informal hedges or screens.

Although flowering and fruiting hedges are certainly attractive, sometimes an altogether quieter, more restrained effect is required. Some of the most widely used hedging plants have insignificant or rather modest flowers but, with regular trimming, these plants produce close-textured blocks of uniform color. Evergreens of this sort include English holly (*Ilex aquifolium*), yew (*Taxus baccata*), and boxwood (*Buxus sempervirens*). European beech (*Fagus sylvatica*) and hornbeam (*Carpinus betulus*), which are also illustrated in this list, are the deciduous counterparts of these classic, evergreen hedging plants.

Some hedging plants have distinctly decorative foliage: the first plant described in this list (x *Cupressocyparis leylandii* "Castlewellan") produces rich yellow leaves, and there are various purple-leaved and variegated plants that are popular for hedging. Aromatic hedges can be made from plants such as rosemary (*Rosmarinus*) and lavender (*Lavandula*).

Another function of hedging is to provide shelter from wind. Plants make much more satisfactory windbreaks than solid barriers, such as walls, which often produce areas of harmful turbulence. Tough and hardy plants suitable for lessening the effects of cold winds include English holly and singleseed hawthorn (*Crataegus monogyna*), which are illustrated in this list, and sea buckthorn (*Hippophae rhamnoides*). For plants to provide shelter from salt- and sand-laden winds, see "Shrubs and trees suitable for windswept, seaside gardens," pp.88–92.

Evergreen and deciduous plants are dealt with separately in the following list. If a hedge is being grown to provide privacy or to block an unsightly view, then evergreens are usually the best choice. However, the dense twigginess of a well-maintained deciduous hedge can create an effective screen, even in winter.

Hedges that are used to enclose and conceal often need to be fast-growing, but they require frequent trimming if they are used for formal hedging. An indication of the rate of growth of larger plants in this list is shown as "height after six years."

Finally, two important points need to be borne in mind before planting a hedge: first of all, hedges take up considerable space; secondly, they draw nutrients and moisture from the soil around them, so that few plants can be grown really close to them.

In the list below two sets of heights are given for each plant with an average minimum height of more than 10ft/3m:
• the height that the plant may be expected to reach after six years if it is trained as part of a more or less formal hedge;
• the eventual height if the plant is grown as part of an informal hedge or screen, with minimal clipping or pruning.

x *Cupressocyparis leylandii*
(syn. x *Cuprocyparis leylandii*)
"Castlewellan"
(syn. "Galway Gold")
[Leyland cypress]
○

type of plant: hardy conifer [6–10]
height: 8–12ft/2.4–3.6m after six years;
80ft/24m as a screen

Young plants of this fast-growing, columnar plant have the brightest foliage color; mature plants tend to be an olive-tinged "old gold." In any case, the open sprays of tiny, scale-like leaves are less bright in winter. Though not so vigorous as x *C. leylandii* itself, which grows notoriously quickly, this variety still needs to be clipped two or three times a year if it is used for formal hedging. To make a formal hedge, plants need to be about 24in/60cm apart. Virtually any soil is suitable for x *C.l.* "Castlewellan," as long as it is of reasonable depth.
also for: ■ Yellow or yellow-green leaves

Berberis x *stenophylla*
[barberry]
○

type of plant: hardy shrub [6–9]
flowering time: mid- to late spring
flower color: yellow
height: 8–10ft/2.4–3m

When planted about 30in/75cm apart, specimens of this dense, prickly, sometimes suckering shrub form an impenetrable barrier. Long, curving branches arch above thickets of stems and are covered in masses of double, cup-shaped flowers, each ½in/1cm across. The thin, little leaves are deep green and spiny. *B.* x *stenophylla* is more successful in dry conditions than some other evergreen barberries. It is sufficiently vigorous and adaptable to cope with most soils, including heavy clays. When used for hedging it can be clipped hard but it is more commonly trimmed lightly after flowering.
also for: ■ Heavy, clay soils ■ Dry soils in hot, sunny sites ■ Atmospheric pollution

---

Erica erigena
(syn. *E. mediterranea*)
e.g. "Brightness"
[Irish heath, Mediterranean heath,
spring heath]
○

type of plant: slightly tender shrub [8–9]
flowering time: early to late spring
flower color: lilac-pink
height: 30–36in/75–90cm

In gardens with moisture-retentive, acid soil, the taller-growing, fairly erect varieties of some heaths and heathers can be used for hedging. The example illustrated here is attractive both when it is in deep red bud and during the many weeks when its ¼in/0.5cm-long, urn-shaped flowers are fully open. In winter, its tiny, thin, dark green leaves become bronzed. When used for informal hedging, plants should be about 12in/30cm apart. Varieties of *E. erigena* tolerate slightly alkaline conditions (and salt spray, too, but their brittle stems make them unsuitable for very windy positions in seaside gardens).
also for: Acid soils ■ Colorful, autumn foliage (winter color, too) ■ Long, continuous flowering period

---

Lavandula angustifolia
e.g. "Hidcote"
[lavender]
○

type of plant: hardy shrub [6–9]
flowering time: mid- to late summer
flower color: deep blue-violet
height: 18in/45cm

Hedges of lavender look neatest and flower most freely if they are grown on poor, really well-drained soil in full sun and if they are clipped at least once a year. *L. angustifolia* "Hidcote" is a dense, bushy plant with exceptionally dark flower spikes, each 1½–2in/4–5cm long, on top of clear stems. The flowers are attractive to bees. The narrow, gray-green leaves have a silvery cast to them and they, like the flowers, are richly and cleanly scented. When used to make a hedge, individual plants need to be 12–18in/30–45cm apart. For another *angustifolia* variety, see p.247.
also for: ■ Dry soils in hot, sunny sites ■ Growing in containers ■ Gray, blue-gray, or silver leaves ■ Aromatic foliage ■ Fragrant flowers

---

Santolina chamaecyparissus
(syn. *S. incana*)
[lavender cotton]
○

type of plant: hardy shrub [7–9]
flowering time: midsummer
flower color: bright yellow
height: 18in/45cm

Hard pruning each spring is essential if this silvery gray shrub is to form a neat, dense mound of ground cover or if it is to be used for low hedging. Pruned in this way, lavender cotton produces few, if any, of its long-stalked, button-like flowers, ½in/1cm wide. The plant must have good drainage. It thrives in hot, dry places. Its dense, much divided foliage, which consists of numerous, woolly leaflets, has a pleasant, pungent scent. Young plants for hedging or edging should be 12–18in/30–45cm apart. *S. chamaecyparissus* "Lemon Queen" has pretty, lemon-yellow flowers.
also for: ■ Dry soils in hot, sunny sites ■ Ground cover ■ Growing in containers ■ Gray, blue-gray, or silver leaves ■ Aromatic foliage

---

Teucrium chamaedrys)
[wall germander]
○

type of plant: hardy shrub [6–9]
flowering time: mid- to late summer
flower color: mauve-pink to rosy purple
height: 12–24in/30–60cm

The foliage of this erect-stemmed subshrub is glossy, wrinkled and dark green. It emits a sharp, almost metallic scent when bruised. Each toothed, oval leaf is only ¾in/2cm long, and the whole plant is neat and dense. Wall germander can be used to produce low, formal hedges. Its sprays of little, lipped flowers are carried close to its stems. Wall germander thrives in light, well-drained, preferably alkaline soil and looks attractive in dry stone walls and sunny rock gardens. When used for hedging, young plants should be approximately 18in/45cm apart. Hedges need an annual trimming, in spring.
also for: ■ Shallow soils over chalk ■ Dry soils in hot, sunny sites ■ Aromatic foliage

Thuja plicata
[arborvitae, western red cedar]
○[◐]

type of plant: hardy conifer [5–8]
height: 8–10ft/2.4–3m after six years;
70–100ft/21–30m as a screen

Western red cedar grows quickly. Fastest growth is on deep, moisture-retentive soil, but the plant is also successful on rather shallow, chalky soils. It responds well to clipping and makes a dense hedge, clothed to the ground in fruitily scented foliage. Young plants for hedging need to be about 24in/60cm apart. Trimming should be carried out once a year. The leaves are glossy, rich green and scale-like; they are arranged in large, flattened sprays. Untrimmed, the plant forms a narrowly conical tree. *T. occidentalis* "Smaragd" [zones 3–8] is a hardier plant of similar outline; it has bright green foliage and grows slowly to about 10ft/3m (eventually 20ft/6m or so). It, too, is good for hedging.
also for: ■ Shallow soils over chalk ■ Aromatic foliage

x *Cupressocyparis leylandii*
(syn. x *Cuprocyparis leylandii*)
[Leyland cypress]
○◐

type of plant: hardy conifer [6–10]
height: 12–18ft/3.6–5.4m after six years;
80–100ft/24–30m as a screen

Leyland cypress is infamously fast-growing and its extremely rapid rate of growth is often underestimated. With spacing of 30–36in/75–90cm, it can be used for formal hedging, but then its open sprays of dark, sometimes grayish green foliage need clipping at least two or three times a year. It is more suitable for making a large-scale screen. Grown as a free-standing specimen it forms a dense, broad column of growth with a tapering top. The leaves are tiny and scale-like. For a slower-growing, but still vigorous, yellow-leaved variety of this plant, see p.138. Virtually any soil is suitable, as long as it is of reasonable depth.

Ilex aquifolium
[English holly]
○◐

type of plant: hardy shrub/tree [6–9]
height: 3–5ft/0.9–1.5m after six years;
55–70ft/16.5–21m as a screen

English holly makes an excellent, impenetrable, formal hedge (young plants should be about 24in/60cm apart). It is also useful as a windbreak in cold areas and is a good topiary plant. Its wavy-edged, dark green, glossy leaves, to about 3in/8cm long, are armed with very sharp spines. The foliage is tough, hard and tolerant of salty winds and atmospheric pollution. Few of the red, ¼in/0.5cm-diameter berries are produced on fertilized female plants if they are part of a formal hedge that is pruned hard each year. Left unpruned, this holly forms a rather erect, pyramidal shape. It grows well in almost any soil and tolerates dry shade.
also for: ■ Dry shade ■ Windswept, seaside gardens ■ Atmospheric pollution ■ Growing in containers (clipped specimens) ■ Ornamental fruit (see above)

Taxus baccata
[English yew]
○◐

type of plant: hardy conifer [6–8]
height: 4–6ft/1.2–1.8m after six years;
40–60ft/12–18m as a screen

This very long-lived conifer is not as slow-growing as sometimes supposed, but it is supreme for creating dark, formal hedges and close-textured topiary. Its linear leaves, about 1in/2.5cm long, are arranged in comb-like sprays. All well-drained soils are suitable, and the plant tolerates deep shade and dry shade (although, to become established and grow successfully as a hedge, it should not be heavily shaded nor too dry and shaded). Grown as an unclipped specimen, English yew usually makes a round-headed to conical tree. Hedges need trimming once a year, in summer or early autumn. Young plants for hedging should be about 24in/60cm apart. The seeds in the small, red, berry-like fruits, like most other parts of the plant, are toxic.
also for: ■ Shallow soils over chalk ■ Acid soils ■ Dry soils in hot, sunny sites ■ Dry shade (see above) ■ Dense shade (see above) ■ Ornamental fruit (female plants)

Prunus lusitanica
[Portugal laurel]
○◐

type of plant: hardy/slightly tender shrub/tree [7–10]
flowering time: early summer
flower color: white
height: 3–4ft/0.9–1.2m after six years;
15–20ft/4.5–6m as a screen

In mild areas, freestanding specimens of this plant form bushy trees with layers of spreading branches. More usually, however, Portugal laurel is a wide, dense shrub. Because its glossy, dark green leaves are quite large (up to 5in/12cm long), it needs to be pruned, rather than clipped, if a neat, formal shape is wanted. The same is true of the less lime-tolerant, but even more shade-tolerant cherry laurel (*P. laurocerasus*), which also makes a good hedge. Almost any soil is suitable for Portugal laurel. Small, purple-black berries sometimes follow the long, slender spikes of heavily scented flowers. Plants used for hedging or screening need to be about 36in/90cm apart.
also for: ■ Shallow soils over chalk

Buxus sempervirens
[common boxwood]
○◐

type of plant: hardy shrub [6–8]
flowering time: spring
flower color: yellow
height: 24in/60cm after six years; 12–15ft/3.6–4.5m as a screen

This slow-growing, bushy plant is excellent for creating dense, fine-textured, formal hedges; it is also suitable for topiary. The dark green, oblong leaves, up to 1¼in/3cm long, are lustrous and leathery. Mature hedges are usually trimmed once a year, in summer. Left untrimmed, plenty of inconspicuous but sweetly scented, yellow flowers are produced in spring, and the plant forms an irregularly mounded, often somewhat sprawling shrub; after many decades, it becomes a round-headed tree. Used for hedging, young plants need to be about 18in/45cm apart. Almost any soil is suitable, but boxwood likes good drainage and thrives on chalk. It tolerates dense shade and dry shade but these conditions are not conducive to well-grown hedging.
also for: ■ Shallow soils over chalk ■ Dry shade (see above) ■ Dense shade (see above) ■ Atmospheric pollution ■ Growing in containers (clipped specimens) ■ Fragrant flowers (see above)

Ligustrum ovalifolium
[California privet]
○◐

type of plant: hardy shrub [6–11]
flowering time: midsummer
flower color: white
height: 6ft/1.8m after six years;
12–15ft/3.6–4.5m as a screen
Evergreen/Semi-evergreen

Since it grows quickly, privet needs trimming several times a year if it is to make a really neat hedge. It is a tough and tolerant plant that grows in most soils and that tolerates dense shade and dry shade. However, it has greedy roots and requires fertile, well-drained, moisture-retentive soil to flourish; it does not make a good hedge in dense or dry shade. Its leaves, up to 2½in/6cm long, are pointed, oval and mid- to dark green. Untrimmed specimens of privet are upright and openly branched; they produce 3in/8cm-long sprays of heavily scented flowers which are attractive to butterflies. For the yellow-variegated, golden privet (*L. ovalifolium* "Aureum"), see p.171. These privets should be 12–18in/30–45cm apart for hedging.
also for: ■ Dry shade (see above) ■ Dense shade (see above) ■ Atmospheric pollution

Elaeagnus x ebbingei
○◐

type of plant: hardy shrub [6–10]
flowering time: mid-autumn
flower color: creamy white
height: 10–15ft/3–4.5m

E. x ebbingei quickly forms a dense, bushy mass of leathery foliage; it is normally as wide as it is tall. Its broad, pointed leaves, each 3–4in/8–10cm long, are glossy dark olive-green above, silvery beneath. The young foliage is covered with silvery scales. From mid-autumn, mature plants produce tiny, very sweetly scented, creamy white flowers. Most well-drained soils are suitable for this vigorous plant. It tolerates quite dry conditions but does not prosper on shallow, chalky soils. It is outstandingly tolerant of salt-laden winds. Young plants for hedging need to be about 30in/75cm apart, and hedges should be pruned—rather than clipped—in late summer. *E. x e.* "Gilt Edge" and *E. x e.* "Limelight" are popular, yellow-variegated varieties.
also for: ■ Windswept, seaside gardens ■ Atmospheric pollution ■ Fragrant flowers

Osmanthus heterophyllus
(syn. *O. ilicifolius*)
○◐

type of plant: slightly tender shrub [7–9]
flowering time: early to mid-autumn
flower color: white
height: 10–15ft/3–4.5m

This prickly, slow-growing shrub is good for making a dense hedge (young plants for hedging should be 18–24in/45–60cm apart). The short-tubed, ¼in/0.5cm-wide flowers are arranged in clusters; they tend not to appear in large numbers, except on mature plants after hot summers, but they are sweetly and strongly fragrant. The shiny, dark green leaves are holly-like and up to 2½in/6cm long. Used for hedging, *O. heterophyllus* needs to be trimmed annually, in spring; allowed to grow freely, it is rounded and as wide as it is tall. Most soils are suitable, as long as they are reasonably well drained, and the plant appreciates a site sheltered from cold winds. For a variegated form of this shrub, see p.169.
also for: ■ Atmospheric pollution ■ Fragrant flowers (see above)

Buxus sempervirens
"Suffruticosa"
[boxwood]
○◐

type of plant: hardy shrub [6–8]
flowering time: spring
flower color: yellow
height: 24–30in/60–75cm

This very slow-growing variety of boxwood is often used wherever a low, formal edging is required. It is also useful for small-scale topiary. Grown as an untrimmed specimen, the plant makes a dense, rounded mass of bright, rich green, shining foliage; the newest growth is lime-green. Each oblong leaf is only about ½in/1cm long. Most soils are suitable, although the plant prefers well-drained, alkaline conditions. It tolerates dense shade and dry shade but, under these conditions, it does not make satisfactory edging. Young plants for edging should be 6–9in/15–23cm apart. Trimming is usually done once a year, normally in summer (closely clipped specimens bear only a few of the yellow, spring flowers; these are small but sweetly scented).
also for: ■ Shallow soils over chalk ■ Dry shade (see above) ■ Dense shade (see above) ■ Atmospheric pollution ■ Growing in containers (clipped specimens) ■ Fragrant flowers (see above)

ADDITIONAL EVERGREEN AND SEMI-EVERGREEN HEDGING PLANTS that are featured elsewhere in this book

○◐ **sun or partial shade**

minimum height 10ft/3m or more
Ilex aquifolium "Bacciflava," see p.258
Pyracantha "Orange Glow," see p.258

minimum height between 3ft/90cm and 10ft/3m
Cotoneaster franchetii, see p.259
Hypericum "Hidcote," see p.345
Ilex x meserveae Blue Angel, see p.242

Ligustrum ovalifolium "Aureum," see p.171
Lonicera nitida "Baggesen's Gold," see p.215
Photinia x fraseri "Red Robin," see p.206
Rhododendron "Praecox," see p.319
Taxus cuspidata, see p.63
Viburnum tinus, see p.318

minimum height 3ft/90cm or less
Lonicera nitida "Silver Beauty," see p.172
Prunus laurocerasus "Otto Luyken," see p.113

A few of the plants listed in this unillustrated section also grow in full shade but, in conditions of limited light, they do not make satisfactory hedging.

◐[○] **partial shade (or sun)**

minimum height 10ft/3m or more
Chamaecyparis pisifera "Boulevard," see p.195

Spiraea japonica
e.g. "Anthony Waterer"
○

type of plant: hardy shrub [4–8]
flowering time: mainly mid- to late summer
flower color: crimson-pink
height: 3–4ft/0.9–1.2m

Sometimes the slender, dark green leaves of *S. japonica* "Anthony Waterer" are marked with cream and pink, but the broad, flat flower heads, each 4–6in/10–15cm wide, are a more conspicuous and reliable attraction. The shrub's upright, densely twiggy branches make it suitable for informal hedging (individual specimens need to be about 15in/38cm apart), and its compact habit of growth means that it is also useful for ground cover. Almost any soil is suitable, but moisture-retentive ones produce particularly good results; shallow, chalky soils and dry soils are best avoided. Established hedging plants need clipping annually, after flowering. *S.j.* var. *albiflora* (syn. "Shirobana") is another popular variety; it has pink and white flowers on the same plant.
also for: ■ Heavy, clay soils ■ Atmospheric pollution ■ Ground cover ■ Variegated leaves (see above)

ADDITIONAL DECIDUOUS HEDGING PLANTS that are featured elsewhere in this book

○ **sun**

minimum height 10ft/3m or more
Fagus sylvatica Atropurpurea Group, see p.198
Hippophae rhamnoides, see p.89
Prunus cerasifera "Pissardii," see p.198
Tamarix tetrandra, see p.89

minimum height between 3ft/90cm and 10ft/3m
Berberis thunbergii f. *atropurpurea*, see p.200
Berberis thunbergii f. *atropurpurea* "Rose Glow," see p.163
Rosa "Ballerina," see p.146
Syringa pubescens subsp. *microphylla* "Superba," see p.299

Ulmus x hollandica "Jacqueline Hillier," see p.220

minimum height 3ft/90cm or less
Berberis thunbergii f. *atropurpurea* "Atropurpurea Nana," see p.202
Rosa gallica "Versicolor," see p.272

Crataegus monogyna
[singleseed hawthorn]
○[◐]

type of plant: hardy tree [4–9]
flowering time: late spring
flower color: white
height: 5–7ft/1.5–2.1m after six years;
25–30ft/7.5–9m as a screen

Singleseed hawthorn is outstandingly tough. It makes an excellent windbreak beside the sea and in exposed sites inland. Any soil is suitable, provided it is not waterlogged, and the plant tolerates very alkaline and very acid conditions. Unpruned specimens form round-headed trees that are covered, briefly, in flattish heads of ½in/1cm-wide, saucer-shaped flowers. The blossom is heavily scented. In early autumn, little bunches of dark red berries ripen. Spaced about 12in/30cm apart and clipped once or twice a year, plants make a dense, thorny hedge (with limited amounts of flowers and fruits). The dark green, glossy leaves have jagged lobes; each leaf is about 2in/5cm long.

also for: ■ Shallow soils over chalk ■ Acid soils ■ Heavy, clay soils ■ Windswept, seaside gardens ■ Atmospheric pollution ■ Ornamental fruit

Rosa e.g. "Blanche Double de Coubert" (Rugosa)
[rose]
○[◐]

type of plant: hardy shrub [4–9]
flowering time: early to late summer
(almost continuously)
flower color: white
height: 5ft/1.5m

Even when used for hedging, Rugosa roses need little attention. If necessary, these vigorous and healthy shrubs can be trimmed lightly in spring. Set about 36in/90cm apart, young plants knit into a sturdy, salt- and wind-resistant barrier. R. "Blanche Double de Coubert" is upright, bushy and prickly, with crinkled leaves of a gleaming rich green. Its semi-double blooms, each 3–4in/8–10cm across, have an excellent, clove-like fragrance. They make attractive cut flowers, although they are apt to become damaged by rain and, in wet summers, there may be limited supplies of blemish-free blooms. The flowers are only occasionally followed by red hips. Rugosa roses thrive in a wide variety of soils, including light and infertile soils.

also for: ■ Windswept, seaside gardens ■ Atmospheric pollution ■ Flowers suitable for cutting ■ Fragrant flowers

Potentilla fruticosa e.g. "Vilmoriniana"
[shrubby cinquefoil]
○[◐]

type of plant: hardy shrub [3–7]
flowering time: early summer to mid-autumn
flower color: pale cream
height: 4–5ft/1.2–1.5m

Many of the shrubby cinquefoils are spreading plants that create good, hummocky ground-cover. But the more upright varieties can be used to make informal hedges that flower freely over long periods and that need little or no pruning. Individual plants should be 24–30in/60–75cm apart. P. fruticosa "Vilmoriniana" is an erect and dense mass of little twigs and silky soft, silvery gray leaves. Each leaf is divided into several neat leaflets, ½in/1cm long. Numerous saucer-shaped flowers, about 1½in/4cm across, complete the gentle color scheme. Other upright potentillas include P.f. "Goldfinger," which has rich yellow flowers. As long as conditions are not wet or very dry, most soils are suitable for these adaptable plants. These wind-resistant shrubs thrive in seaside gardens.

also for: ■ Heavy, clay soils ■ Windswept, seaside gardens ■ Gray, blue-gray, or silver leaves ■ Long, continuous flowering period

---

ADDITIONAL DECIDUOUS HEDGING PLANTS that are featured elsewhere in this book

○[◐] **sun (or partial shade)**

---

minimum height between 3ft/90cm and 10ft/3m
Rosa "Fru Dagmar Hastrup," see p.92

minimum height 3ft/90cm or less

Fagus sylvatica
[European beech]
◦◑

type of plant: hardy tree [4–9]
height: 5–8ft/1.5–2.4m after six years;
80–100ft/24–30m as a screen

A mature hedge of beech can look very handsome and impressive. The leaves, wavy-edged, pointed ovals 3–4in/8–10cm long, emerge a fresh, bright green which turns dark and shiny. In autumn, the foliage becomes orange-russet and plants that have been clipped and are under 10ft/3m retain their withered leaves through winter. When used for formal hedging, young plants of beech—and purple beech (see p.198), or a mixture of the two—should be about 18in/45cm apart. Clipping needs to be carried out once or twice a year in summer. Grown naturally, European beech makes a magnificent, broad-headed tree and mature specimens have attractive, silvery gray bark. All well-drained soils are suitable for this tree and it thrives on chalk.
also for: ■ Shallow soils over chalk ■ Atmospheric pollution ■ Colorful, autumn foliage ■ Ornamental bark or twigs (see above)

Carpinus betulus
[hornbeam]
◦◑

type of plant: hardy tree [5–9]
height: 5–8ft/1.5–2.4m after six years;
60–80ft/18–24m as a screen

Hornbeam is often used as a substitute for beech in gardens with heavy soil, although any soil is suitable. It can be clipped very hard (trimming is usually carried out once or twice in late summer). The mid-green, pointed, oval leaves, each around 3in/8cm long, are toothed and deeply veined. They turn rich yellow in autumn. Plants that have been clipped and are under 10ft/3m retain their tawny, withered foliage through winter. Young plants for hedging should be 18–24in/45–60cm apart. When grown as a specimen tree, hornbeam has a broad, domed head with a gray-barked, fluted trunk, and it produces tassel-like clusters of yellow-brown, winged seeds in autumn.
also for: ■ Shallow soils over chalk ■ Heavy, clay soils ■ Atmospheric pollution ■ Colorful, autumn foliage ■ Ornamental fruit (see above) ■ Ornamental bark or twigs (see above)

Cotoneaster simonsii
◦◑

type of plant: hardy shrub [6–9]
flowering time: early summer
flower color: pink-tinged white
height: 6–8ft/1.8–2.4m
Semi-evergreen/Deciduous

C. simonsii is usually only semi-evergreen but, before they fall in autumn, the older leaves turn red and orange. The numerous clusters of oval, bright orange-red berries are particularly long-lasting. The fruits, up to ½in/1cm long, are preceded by little, cup-shaped flowers. This plant is erect with long, stiff branches. It can be used for semi-formal and informal hedging. Individual plants should be 18–30in/45–75cm apart and trimmed in late summer or early winter. Among the fully evergreen cotoneasters, red-berried *C. lacteus* is popular for hedging. Almost any soil is suitable for these shrubs but extremes of wetness and dryness should be avoided.
also for: ■ Atmospheric pollution ■ Colorful, autumn foliage ■ Ornamental fruit

Fuchsia "Riccartonii"
(syn. *F. magellanica* "Riccartonii")
◦◑

type of plant: hardy/slightly tender shrub [7–10]
flowering time: midsummer to mid-autumn
flower color: red + violet
height: 4–6ft/1.2–1.8m (see description)

In warmer, maritime regions, this vigorous, very nearly hardy fuchsia may be used for informal hedging. In really mild districts it is dense, arching and often more than 8ft/2.4m high; elsewhere it is smaller, more upright and not quite so floriferous. For screening and informal hedging, individual plants are about 24in/60cm apart; they usually need no trimming. Slender, bell-like flowers, up to 1½in/4cm across, dangle from the branches. The little leaves are neat, pointed and dark green; sometimes they are bronze tinged. Ideally, *F.* "Riccartonii" should have moist, well-drained soil, but it is an adaptable plant and easily grown. It is wind-resistant and suitable for planting in a seaside garden.
also for: ■ Windswept, seaside gardens ■ Long, continuous flowering period

---

ADDITIONAL DECIDUOUS HEDGING PLANTS that are featured elsewhere in this book

◦◑ sun or partial shade

minimum height 10ft/3m or more
Acer campestre, see p.21

Growing in containers

PUTTING A PLANT in a container is rather like putting a photograph in a frame: it draws attention to weak points as well as good points. What seemed like an attractive plant when it was growing in a well-filled border can look rather uninteresting when it is given a smartly painted tub all of its own.

Choosing short-lived plants for containers usually presents few problems and any mistakes are easily rectified; selecting longer-lived plants needs more careful consideration. Fortunately, most trees, shrubs, and woody climbers are suitable for growing in containers, the main exceptions being large plants with fleshy roots and those that require a very moist growing medium. In the latter case, the need for continual watering usually makes these plants impractical choices.

Growing plants in containers does tend to slow down growth rates, and in some cases it limits ultimate heights. If necessary, the growth of certain plants can be further restricted by frequent clipping or pruning. Another approach is to choose plants that are very slow-growing, such as *Salix* "Boydii" and *Acer palmatum* var. *dissectum* Dissectum Atropurpureum Group, both of which are illustrated in this list.

Many of the plants in the present list have unusually colored or interestingly shaped leaves, and most of these foliage plants are evergreen. Some foliage plants have large, bold leaves (see, for example, *Chamaerops humilis* and *Fatsia japonica*), which make them look especially jungly and exotic. Even attractive foliage that is deciduous looks good for a substantial part of the year, and there are a few shrubs that look interesting when they are leafless because their twigs are intriguingly shaped (see, for example, the Fuji cherry *Prunus incisa* "Kojo-no-mai," in this list).

Some plants are grown in containers because they can be clipped or pruned into "lollipops" or spirals or, indeed, bird or animal shapes, which can be every bit as striking as a mass of colorful leaves. Particularly suitable plants include *Myrtus communis* subsp. *tarentina* and *M. communis* itself, boxwood (*Buxus sempervirens*) and its varieties, as well as bay laurel (*Laurus nobilis*) and its yellow-leaved variety "Aurea." Some plants are naturally of a rather formal shape (see, for example, the slender, columnar *Juniperus*—one large, one small—illustrated in this list).

If the sole decorative feature of a plant is its blossom, then this should be really outstanding for the plant to look well in a container. Plants with large and flamboyant flowers are obvious choices (see, for example, *Hibiscus syriacus* "Woodbridge" and *Clematis* "Lasurstern" in this list). Long-flowering, very free-flowering and, especially in some settings, fragrant-flowered plants all make good choices, too.

There are advantages to growing plants in containers: restricting the roots of plants often results in the production of unusually large quantities of flowers and fruits; in areas with alkaline soil, lime-hating plants can be grown in containers filled with lime-free compost; in cold regions, half-hardy and tender plants can be grown outdoors and then lifted into a light, frost-free place during winter. (In very cold regions, few plants can be left outdoors in containers in winter, unless the containers are heavily insulated.)

The drawbacks to growing plants in containers are mainly to do with feeding, drainage and watering. In their artificial environment, plants in containers have to rely on gardeners for efficient drainage, and regular feeding and watering. In sunny positions, containers can rapidly become hot and dry; in shady sites the soil in containers can become stagnant unless properly drained, and there can be problems in winter with very cold or frozen roots.

Unless otherwise stated, the heights given in this list are for plants grown in open ground. Large plants grown in containers tend not to reach these heights; the heights of small and medium-sized plants are not greatly altered.

Juniperus scopulorum
"Skyrocket"
[Rocky Mountain juniper]
○

type of plant: hardy conifer [4–7]
height: 18–24ft/5.4–7.2m
Evergreen

Few conifers are quite as narrow as this juniper and, although it grows quite quickly, it makes a very striking plant for a large pot or tub, even if ultimately it outgrows the container. *J. scopulorum* "Skyrocket" looks especially impressive in rather formal surroundings. Its sprays of tiny, pointed, scale-like leaves are bluish gray-green. All well-drained soils, including those that are quite dry, are suitable for this plant. For a very slow-growing, columnar juniper, see p.149.
also for: ■ Dry soils in hot, sunny sites ■ Gray, blue-gray, or silver leaves

Chamaecyparis lawsoniana
e.g. "Ellwood's Gold"
[Lawson false cypress]
○

type of plant: hardy conifer [6–8]
height: 12–15ft/3.6–4.5m
Evergreen

After ten years, this very slow-growing conifer reaches only 4–5ft/1.2–1.5m high. Its tiny, scale-like leaves are held in erect sprays, the tips of which are golden yellow, giving a rich gold-green effect overall. By late summer, the foliage has faded to lime-green but the plant forms such a neat, dense pillar of growth that it always looks striking. A position in full sun is needed to produce and maintain good, golden-yellow leaf color. Well-drained, moisture-retentive soil is suitable. Rounded rather than columnar Lawson cypresses that are slow-growing and suitable for pots include the variety shown on p.164 and green-leaved *C. lawsoniana* "Gnome."
also for: ■ Yellow or yellow-green leaves

Hibiscus syriacus
e.g. "Woodbridge"
[rose of Sharon]
○

type of plant: hardy shrub [6–9]
flowering time: late summer to mid-autumn
flower color: pinkish red
height: 6–8ft/1.8–2.4m

The late, lengthy flowering season and the showiness of the flowers make *H. syriacus* "Woodbridge" and other varieties of *H. syriacus* good plants for containers. (For a blue-flowered variety, see p.334.) Although each 4in/10cm-wide flower is short-lived, numerous blooms are produced over a long period. Rose of Sharon performs particularly well in sheltered sites and in rich, well-drained, slightly alkaline to acid soil. All varieties of these upright plants are very late into leaf. Young specimens may bear few if any of the deep green, lobed and toothed leaves. Flowers are prone to rain damage.
also for: ■ Dry soils in hot, sunny sites ■ Atmospheric pollution ■ Long, continuous flowering period

Abutilon megapotamicum
○

type of plant: half-hardy/slightly tender shrub [8–11]
flowering time: early summer to mid-autumn
flower color: red + yellow
height: 6ft/1.8m
Evergreen/Semi-evergreen

If grown in a container, this rather tender shrub can easily be moved into a protected place – a cool greenhouse, for instance – during the coldest months. In really mild areas it can be planted permanently outdoors. In either case, it needs a warm, sheltered site and well-drained soil that remains moist during summer. Since the stems of *A. megapotamicum* are lax and spreading, some support is needed to enable them to grow upright. The pendant, lantern-like flowers, up to 1½in/4cm long, open in succession over several months. On *A.m.* "Variegatum" (see p.163) the slender, rich green leaves are mottled with yellow.
also for: ■ Climbing plants ■ Long, continuous flowering period

Prunus incisa "Kojo-no-mai"
[Fuji cherry]
○

type of plant: hardy shrub [6–8]
flowering time: early spring
flower color: pale pink changing to white
height: 5–8ft/1.5–2.4m

Since it grows slowly and has several decorative features, the Fuji cherry is a good choice for tubs and large pots. Its red-budded flowers, each ½in/1cm across, are bell-shaped and more or less pendent; they open before the foliage emerges. They are very numerous but fairly short-lived. However, in autumn, the slim, fresh green leaves, sharply toothed and only 1in/2.5cm or so long, turn shades of crimson and orange, and throughout the year the rounded mass of slender, zigzagging branches looks interesting. Most well-drained soils are suitable for this plant.
also for: ■ Colorful, autumn foliage ■ Ornamental bark or twigs

Taxus baccata "Standishii"
[yew]
○

type of plant: hardy conifer [6–8]
height: 5ft/1.5m
Evergreen

The deep yellow foliage of this very narrow, slow-growing conifer retains its color almost year long; it is an especially rich "old gold" in winter (the illustration shows a specimen in midwinter). Each thin, little leaf is about ¾in/2cm long. The small, red, berry-like fruits contain seeds that, like most of the other parts of the plant, are poisonous. Other yellow-leaved yews are larger, faster-growing plants. They include *T. baccata* "Semperaurea" (up to 10ft/3m), which is shrubby, with orange-gold leaves maturing to gold-yellow. These plants can be grown in a very wide range of well-drained soils.
also for: ■ Shallow soils over chalk ■ Acid soils ■ Dry soils in hot, sunny sites ■ Yellow or yellow-green leaves ■ Ornamental fruit

Wisteria floribunda
e.g. "Multijuga"
(syn. *W.f.* "Macrobotrys")
[Japanese wisteria]
○

type of plant: hardy climber [5–9]
flowering time: late spring to early summer
flower color: lilac + violet
height: 4–6ft/1.2–1.8m grown as a standard
in a container; 20–30ft/6–9m in open ground

This vigorous, twining climber is usually grown on a house wall, or over a pergola or arch or, occasionally, through a tree. It can also be trained as a standard in a very large container. The pea-flowers have a light, sweet scent. They are arranged in pendent clusters which, on this variety, are usually 24–36in/60–90cm long. The flowers develop at about the same time as the pale green, pointed leaflets. For the best results, *W. floribunda* "Multijuga" needs a sheltered site and fertile soil that retains moisture easily. Individual specimens are often several years old before they start to flower. *W.f.* "Alba" and *W.f.* "Rosea" are good varieties with white and pinkish flowers respectively.
also for: ■ Climbing plants ■ Fragrant flowers

Myrtus communis subsp. *tarentina*
(syn. *M.c.* "Jenny Reitenbach,"
M.c. "Microphylla," *M.c.* "Nana")
[dwarf myrtle]
○

type of plant: slightly tender/half-hardy shrub [8–9]
flowering time: midsummer to early autumn
flower color: pink-tinged creamy white
height: 4–5ft/1.2–1.5m
Evergreen

This compact subspecies of the common myrtle has leaves that are smaller and narrower than those of the species. It is also a slightly hardier plant. Each glossy, dark green, spicily aromatic leaf is about ¾in/2cm long. The plant is naturally dense, neat, and rounded. It can also be clipped closely, into hedging and shapes such as pyramids and "lollipops." (Hedging plants should be 12–18in/30–45cm apart.) Allowed to grow freely, dwarf myrtle has masses of sweetly scented, saucer-shaped flowers, followed by small, white berries. It needs a warm site and well-drained soil. It thrives by the sea.
also for: ■ Windswept, coastal gardens ■ Hedging plants ■ Aromatic foliage ■ Ornamental fruit ■ Fragrant flowers

Rosa e.g. "Ballerina"
(Hybrid Musk/Polyantha)
[rose]
○

type of plant: hardy shrub [5–10]
flowering time: mid- to late summer and early to mid-autumn
flower color: pink + white
height: 4ft/1.2m

In a large, deep container filled with fertile, moisture-retentive potting compost, this very free-flowering rose forms a rounded mass of glossy, bright green leaves and pretty flowers. The slightly fragrant, single flowers, each about 1¼in/3cm across, are arranged in big clusters. *R.* "Ballerina" grows densely, spreading about 36in/90cm or more wide, and is suitable for ground cover. It is also excellent when grown as a standard, and it can be used to create an informal hedge (young plants should be 30–36in/75–90cm apart).
also for: ■ Ground cover ■ Hedging plants

Mimulus aurantiacus
(syn. *Diplacus glutinosus,*
M. glutinosus)
[monkey flower]
○

type of plant: half-hardy/slightly tender shrub [9–10]
flowering time: late spring to early autumn
flower color: variable—shades of orange or yellow
height: 3–4ft/0.9–1.2m
Evergreen

Stylishly trumpet-shaped, 1½in/4cm-long flowers are produced by this erect, rather open shrub open throughout the summer months, and then a succession of blooms continues to appear well into autumn. Flower color is variable. Forms with red flowers are often sold as *M. aurantiacus* var. *puniceus*. The pale brown stems and the slim, glossy, rich green leaves are slightly sticky. Freely draining but moisture-retentive soil and a warm, sheltered site are needed for good growth. In areas with low winter temperatures, *M. aurantiacus* is best brought under cover during the colder months.
also for: ■ Long, continuous flowering period

Salvia microphylla var.
microphylla (syn. *S.m.*
var. *neurepia, S. grahamii*)
○

type of plant: half-hardy shrub [9–10]
flowering time: midsummer to mid-autumn (or first frosts)
flower color: bright red changing to crimson
height: 3–4ft/0.9–1.2m
Evergreen

The slender, upright stems of this subshrubby plant are topped with vividly colored, lipped flowers, each about 1in/2.5cm long. The lower parts of the stems are clothed in small, dull green leaves (which are blackcurrant-scented to some people). This fast-growing plant needs light, fertile soil and a site that is warm and sheltered. *S. microphylla* is a variable plant. *S.m.* var. *microphylla* "Newby Hall" produces larger, brighter flowers than the species, and the related hybrid *S x jamensis* "La Luna" has pale yellow flowers. Other subshrubby salvias with brilliantly colored blooms include scarlet-flowered *S. fulgens* and cerise-flowered *S. involucrata* "Bethellii."
also for: ■ Long, continuous flowering period

Pittosporum tenuifolium
"Tom Thumb"
○

type of plant: slightly tender/half-hardy shrub [9–10]
height: 36in/90cm
Evergreen

The new leaves of this dense, dome-shaped shrub are pale green and they contrast strongly with the glossy deep red-purple of the older foliage. Each leaf is a neat, 1½in/4cm-long oval with a shiny surface, and wavy edges that give the whole plant a lively appearance. Mature specimens of this slow-growing shrub produce very small but sweetly scented, dark red flowers in late spring and early summer. *P. tenuifolium* "Purpureum" also has dark purple foliage; it grows to about 10ft/3m tall. Both plants require well-drained but moisture-retentive soil and a warm, sheltered site. For an example of a variegated pittosporum, see p.161.
also for: ■ Purple, bronze, or red leaves ■ Fragrant flowers

Cryptomeria japonica "Vilmoriniana" [Japanese cedar]
○

type of plant: hardy conifer [6–9]
height: 24–36in/60–90cm
Evergreen

Its extremely slow growth rate, its tidy shape and its winter color all make this conifer a good choice for planting in containers. It normally grows about 4in/10cm per decade. Its foliage consists of tiny needles tightly packed on to very small branches. The leaves are rich green for most of the year, but in winter they turn purplish bronze. *C. japonica* "Vilmoriniana" forms a solid, mounded globe of growth. It needs moisture-retentive soil (moisture is particularly important for young specimens) and prefers slightly acid soil. A sunny site encourages neat growth and good winter foliage color.
also for: ■ Colorful, autumn foliage (winter color, too)

Abies balsamea Hudsonia Group [balsam fir]
○

type of plant: hardy conifer [4–8]
height: 24–30in/60–75cm
Evergreen

As long as this slow-growing conifer is kept well watered, it flourishes in a tub or pot. *A. balsamea* Hudsonia Group plants are neat, dense, and of a rounded, somewhat flat-topped shape. The winter leaf buds are pale and have a balsam-like scent, as do the thin, flattened, dark green leaves, which are up to ½in/1cm long. Moist soil, preferably well drained and slightly acid to neutral, is most suitable for this plant. *A.b.* "Nana" is similar.
also for: ■ Heavy, clay soils ■ Aromatic foliage

Hebe "Silver Queen" (syn. *H. elliptica* "Variegata," *H.* x *franciscana* "Variegata")
○

type of plant: slightly tender/half-hardy shrub [9–10]
flowering time: midsummer to mid-autumn
flower color: mauve
height: 24in/60cm
Evergreen

This dense, rounded shrub has just the sort of neat, closely set, almost unnaturally smart foliage that looks right in containers such as window boxes. The leathery leaves, about 2in/5cm long, are fairly slender and pointed. Their central portions are a mixture of light and dark green; their margins are broad and creamy white. The conspicuous variegation of the foliage is emphasized by the regular arrangement of the leaves, in a series of four-leaved crosses, up the plant's rather erect stems. There are squat spikes of wispy flowers, but these are not always very freely produced. This hebe prefers moist but well-drained soil. It grows well near the sea and in towns.
also for: ■ Atmospheric pollution ■ Variegated leaves

Rosa e.g. Sweet Dream = "Fryminicot" (Patio, Dwarf Floribunda or Dwarf Cluster-flowered) [rose]
○

type of plant: hardy shrub [6–10]
flowering time: early summer to mid-autumn
flower color: soft peach-pink
height: 18in/45cm

The thickly and luxuriantly petalled flowers of this bushy, little rose are of an attractive, old-fashioned shape. They are fully double, slightly fragrant, about 2½in/6cm across and they open in succession over many weeks. The stems are upright and clothed in plenty of glossy, deep green, toothed leaves. This is a very healthy rose. Other popular, small roses that are suitable for growing in containers include *R.* Sweet Magic, with its semi-double, pale orange and yellow flowers, and *R.* Anna Ford, which has orange flowers. Especially when they are grown in pots, these plants need regular feeding and watering and fertile, moisture-retentive soil.
also for: ■ Long, continuous flowering period

Helichrysum petiolare [licorice plant]
○

type of plant: half-hardy shrub/perennial [9–10]
height: 15–18in/38–45cm
Evergreen

Often treated as an annual and used for bedding or grown temporarily in containers, *H. petiolare* can remain outdoors all the year round in mild areas. Its pale, trailing stems and its silvery gray foliage usually form a mound of growth, but the plant can be trained vertically. The leaves, each about 1in/2.5cm across, are heart-shaped and woolly. The off-white flowers are long-stalked and arranged in dense, domed heads, up to 2in/5cm across. Many gardeners prefer to pinch out young flowering shoots. There is a cream-variegated variety of this plant, and *H.p.* "Limelight" has lime-green leaves. All these plants need good drainage and a warm position.
also for: ■ Gray, blue-gray, or silver leaves

Salix "Boydii"
○

type of plant: hardy shrub [4–7]
height: 12in/30cm

Catkins rarely appear on this thickset and extremely slow-growing willow. The stiff, upright branches carry rounded, little leaves, up to ¾in/2cm long, which are gray and downy when young and dark grayish green in maturity. Its very slow growth rate makes this shrub suitable for growing in various types of containers, including alpine troughs, as well as in a rock garden. *S.* "Boydii" needs moisture-retentive but well-drained soil. After about fifty years it may have reached 36in/90cm tall.

ADDITIONAL TREES, SHRUBS, AND WOODY CLIMBERS, featured elsewhere in this book, that are suitable for growing in containers

○ sun

minimum height 10ft/3m or more
Pittosporum "Garnettii," see p.161

minimum height between 3ft/90cm and 10ft/3m
Abutilon megapotamicum "Variegatum," see p.163
Aloysia triphylla, see p.245
Erica arborea "Albert's Gold," see p.211
Euonymus japonicus "Ovatus Aureus," see p.162
Hibiscus syriacus "Oiseau Bleu," see p.334
Laurus nobilis "Aurea," see p.211
Leptospermum scoparium "Red Damask,"
   see p.25
Luma apiculata "Glanleam Gold," see p.162
Myrtus communis, see p.298
Picea glauca var. albertiana "Conica," see p.25
Pittosporum tobira, see p.298

Rosa Warm Welcome, see p.128
Rosmarinus officinalis, see p.245
Wisteria sinensis, see p.127
Yucca filamentosa, see p.53

minimum height 3ft/90cm or less
Berberis thunbergii f. atropurpurea
   "Atropurpurea Nana," see p.202
Caragana arborescens "Walker," see p.54
Chamaecyparis lawsoniana "Minima Aurea,"
   see p.211
Chamaecyparis lawsoniana "Pygmaea Argentea,"
   see p.164
Convolvulus cneorum, see p.188
Coronilla valentina subsp. glauca "Citrina,"
   see p.335
Coronilla valentina subsp. glauca "Variegata,"
   see p.164

Cytisus x kewensis, see p.107
Halimium lasianthum, see p.55
Hebe ochracea "James Stirling," see p.212
Hebe rakaiensis, see p.106
Hebe "Youngii," see p.108
Ilex crenata "Golden Gem," see p.211
Juniperus squamata "Blue Star," see p.188
Lavandula angustifolia "Hidcote," see p.138
Melianthus major, see p.185
Phormium "Yellow Wave," see p.164
Platycladus orientalis "Aurea Nana,"
   see p.212
Pinus mugo "Mops," see p.15
Prostanthera cuneata, see p.246
Rosa "The Fairy," see p.275
Ruta graveolens "Jackman's Blue," see p.187
Santolina chamaecyparissus, see p.138
Yucca gloriosa "Variegata," see p.164

Chamaerops humilis
[dwarf fan palm]
○[◐]

type of plant: slightly tender/half-hardy
shrub [8–11]
height: 6–10ft/1.8–3m
Evergreen

In a large container or as part of an "exotic" planting scheme, these flamboyant fans of foliage look bold and stylish. Each beautifully symmetrical fan is approximately 24in/60cm wide. The slender, pointed leaflets are often rich olive-green, but they can be blue-green or yellow-green. In maturity, C. humilis may sucker, but it usually consists of a dense cluster of long, prickly stems. In ideal conditions and after many years, it develops a shaggy trunk. In cool climates, the plant grows slowly and even on older specimens the trunk is very short. The bunches of tiny, yellow flowers are regularly produced only in regions with hot summers and, in any case, they are mostly obscured by the foliage. For good growth this palm needs a warm, sheltered site and well-drained, moderately fertile soil. Established specimens are drought-tolerant.
also for: ■ Dry soils in hot, sunny sites (see above) ■ Decorative, green foliage

Cordyline australis
e.g. "Torbay Dazzler"
[giant dracaena, New Zealand
cabbage palm]
○[◐]

type of plant: half-hardy shrub [9–11]
flowering time: early summer
flower color: creamy white
height: 3–4ft/0.9–1.2m in a container;
up to 10ft/3m in open ground
Evergreen

There are numerous varieties of cabbage palm with colored and variegated leaves. Compared with the species (see p.223), many of these varieties tend to be slow-growing. C. australis "Torbay Dazzler" has the usual, narrow, leathery leaves, 24–36in/60–90cm long, but the soft green of its foliage is boldly striped and margined with white and cream. The midribs and bases of the leaves are often tinged with pink. In warm areas, mature specimens may produce plumes of wispy, sweetly scented flowers. Before flowering, the plant has a single trunk topped with one rosette of leaves; once it has flowered, it branches and additional rosettes form. Fertile, well-drained soil is most suitable for this plant. It grows well in a seaside garden but is not as salt- and wind-resistant as the species.
also for: ■ Windswept, coastal gardens
■ Variegated leaves

Juniperus communis
e.g. "Compressa"
[juniper]
○[◐]

type of plant: hardy conifer [3–8]
height: 30in/75cm
Evergreen

Where the common juniper (J. communis "Hibernica," see p.19) would be too large, this very similarly shaped but smaller and much slower-growing variety could be used. J.c. "Compressa" is suitable for planting in a sink, trough, window-box, or larger container, as well as in a rock garden and open ground. It forms a narrow, tapered column of tiny, needle-like leaves that are closely packed on the upright stems. The foliage is dark, slightly grayish green. Most well-drained soils—acid or alkaline—are suitable for this conifer and it is at home on thin, chalky soils. It grows well in dry, sunny places. It is not a vigorous plant and it needs shelter from cold winds if it is to prosper.
also for: ■ Shallow soils over chalk ■ Dry soils in hot, sunny sites

ADDITIONAL TREES, SHRUBS, AND WOODY CLIMBERS, featured elsewhere in this book, that are suitable for growing in containers

† = grown as clipped specimen

○[◐] sun (or partial shade)

minimum height 10ft/3m or more
Cordyline australis,
    see p.223

minimum height between 3ft/90cm and 10ft/3m
Choisya ternata Sundance, see p.214
Corokia cotoneaster, see p.265
Elaeagnus pungens "Maculata," see p.169
†Ilex x altaclerensis "Golden King," see p.168
†Ilex aquifolium "Argentea Marginata,"
    see p.168

†Ilex aquifolium "Ferox Argentea," see p.168
†Laurus nobilis, see p.249

minimum height 3ft/90cm or less
Erica carnea "King George," see p.317
Erica carnea "Vivellii," see p.344
Hebe pinguifolia "Pagei," see p.194

Fatsia japonica
(syn. Aralia sieboldii)
[Japanese aralia, Japanese fatsia]
○◐●

type of plant: slightly tender shrub [8–11]
flowering time: mid- to late autumn
flower color: cream
height: 6–10ft/1.8–3m
Evergreen

Big, handsome, deeply lobed leaves are the principal attraction of this shrub, which is often seen growing in large tubs, particularly in town gardens. Some of the lustrous, long-stalked leaves may be up to 15in/38cm wide. F. japonica creates a rounded, stout-stemmed mass of mid- to dark green foliage. It is usually as wide as it is tall. Although it tolerates dense shade, it needs a lighter position if there are to be more than just a few branched clusters of bobbly flower heads. The leathery foliage is excellent at withstanding the effects of salt and wind in seaside gardens. Most soils are suitable; those that are deep and moist encourage the growth of really large leaves. The flowers are followed by black, pea-sized berries.
also for: ■ Dense shade ■ Windswept, coastal gardens ■ Atmospheric pollution ■ Decorative, green foliage ■ Ornamental fruit

Clematis e.g. "Lasurstern"
○◐

type of plant: hardy climber [5–9]
flowering time: late spring to early summer and late summer to early autumn
flower color: deep violet-blue fading with age
height: 6–9ft/1.8–2.7m

When something really showy is wanted for a container, then a moderately vigorous clematis, either with large or with double flowers, makes a good choice. In its main, early flush of flowers, C. "Lasurstern" produces numerous broad-"petalled" blooms that are often at least 6in/15cm wide (the flowers that appear in the second flush are slightly smaller). C. "H.F. Young" is of similar coloring, and although its flowers, at 4in/10cm wide, are not as large, it is a very free-flowering and compact plant. Large-flowered clematis grown in containers need to be fed and watered regularly to insure that they perform really well. Their roots must remain cool and moist and, ideally, their top growth should be in a fairly sunny position. A double-flowered clematis is shown on p.288. These plants need support to which the twining stalks of their tripartite leaves can cling.
also for: ■ Climbing plants

Acer palmatum var. dissectum
Dissectum Atropurpureum
Group
[Japanese maple]
○◐

type of plant: hardy shrub [6–8]
height: 5–7ft/1.5–2.1m

Plants in this Group very slowly form spreading mounds of lacy foliage. Even when bare in winter, their conspicuously arching branches look interesting. Their deeply divided and finely cut leaves, each about 3in/8cm long, are a rich red-burgundy in spring. They become rather greener during summer and then turn crimson in autumn. To grow well, these plants need shelter from cold winds, and fertile soil that is moisture retentive and well drained. These conditions are often easier to achieve in a very lightly shaded site (too much shade results in a disappointing, rather "muddy" leaf color). Other cut-leaved Japanese maples with purple foliage include A. palmatum var. dissectum "Garnet," which has especially long-lasting, red-purple coloring. After many years these plants may be about 12ft/3.6m tall and tree-like.
also for: ■ Purple, bronze, or red leaves ■ Colorful, autumn foliage

Aucuba japonica
e.g. "Variegata" (syn. *A.j.* "Maculata")
[Japanese laurel]
○◑

type of plant: hardy shrub [7–10]
height: 5–7ft/1.5–2.1m
Evergreen

The Japanese laurels tolerate much and demand little. They are tough, rounded, bushy plants that grow in a very wide range of conditions, including dry shade and polluted atmosphere. They are excellent in containers, too. However, the variegated forms need reasonably good light for their glossy foliage to color well. *A. japonica* "Variegata" has pointed, oval, bright green leaves, to about 7in/18cm long, speckled with creamy yellow; the foliage of *A.j.* "Crotonifolia" is heavily splotched with pale yellow. Plain-leaved Japanese laurels grow in dense shade. Female plants, including *A.j.* "Variegata," bear red berries if fertilized by a male (the green-leaved variety *A.j.* "Rozannie" is self-fertile and very free-fruiting).
also for: ■ Heavy, clay soils ■ Dry shade ■ Atmospheric pollution ■ Variegated leaves ■ Ornamental fruit (see above)

Hydrangea macrophylla
(Hortensia)
e.g. "Madame Emile Mouillère"
○◑

type of plant: hardy/slightly tender shrub [6–9]
flowering time: midsummer to mid-autumn
flower color: white
height: 4–6ft/1.2–1.8m

The numerous Hortensia or mophead hydrangeas are classic tub plants and the variety shown here is often regarded as the classic, white hydrangea. Its bun-shaped blooms, each about 6in/15cm across, appear through midsummer to mid-autumn. New flowers are most numerous in summer. The plant flowers longest if grown in semi-shade, where the florets become green-tinged with age; in sun they take on pinkish tones. Blooms are best for dried rather than fresh arrangements. The tough, light green leaves are oval and pointed. This upright, rounded shrub thrives in rich, moisture-retentive soil. In colder climates it needs some shelter and, in any case, it may be easier to insure that the roots remain cool and moist if a lightly shaded position is chosen. It grows well in cities and by the sea. *H. arborescens* "Annabelle" has very large, white flowers.
also for: ■ Windswept, seaside gardens ■ Atmospheric pollution ■ Ornamental fruit ("seed" heads) ■ Flowers suitable for cutting (mainly drying) ■ Long, continuous flowering period

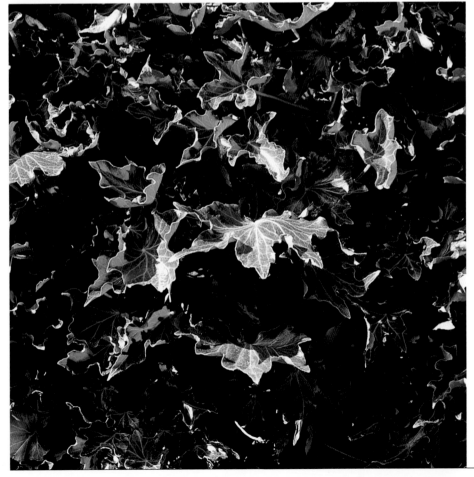

Hedera helix e.g. "Ivalace"
[ivy]
○◑●

type of plant: hardy climber [6–10]
height: 3–4ft/0.9–1.2m; 4–6in/10–15cm as ground cover

The numerous varieties of ivy include some that make especially good plants for pots and tubs. Among the interesting, green-leaved ivies of this sort is *H. helix* "Ivalace," with its curly-edged, glossy, deep olive-green leaves, each leaf prominently pale veined and up to 3in/8cm long. Another example is *H.h.* "Manda's Crested" (syn. "Curleylocks"), which has wavy-edged leaves that take on rusty tones in winter. Both these climbers make good ground cover, producing carpets of rooting growth 4–6in/10–15cm high. Among variegated forms, the green-and-white speckled *H.h.* "Kolibri," the slim-lobed, white-edged *H.h.* "Sagittifolia Variegata," and *H.h.* "Glacier" (see p.124) are all good for containers. Almost any soil that is not either waterlogged or very hot and dry is suitable for these plants. They tolerate dry shade, too. Green-leaved varieties can be grown in full and dense shade but variegated ones need more light to color well.
also for: ■ Dry shade ■ Dense shade ■ Atmospheric pollution ■ Ground cover ■ Climbing plants

Euonymus fortunei
e.g. "Silver Queen"
◯◐●

type of plant: hardy shrub/climber [5–9]
height: 36in/90cm as a shrub; 10ft/3m as a climber
Evergreen

Among the very many varieties of E. fortunei, E.f. "Silver Queen" is one of the more elegant. Its elongated, oval leaves, to 2½in/6cm long, are dark green with margins that are, at first, light yellow and then white. In cold weather the leathery foliage often becomes tinged with purplish pink. Initially, this bushy plant is very slow-growing. Well-established specimens often produce self-clinging, climbing shoots that may reach as much as 10ft/3m high. (Really mature plants—shrubby or climbing—may be up to twice the heights given here.) Although it is rather more upright and less spreading than some varieties of E. fortunei (see, for examples, pp.113 and 174), E.f. "Silver Queen" grows densely and is useful for ground cover. It is reputedly less hardy than some varieties, and a cold, windy site should therefore be avoided. Almost any soil that is not waterlogged gives good results.
also for: ■ Atmospheric pollution ■ Ground cover
■ Climbing plants ■ Variegated leaves

Fuchsia e.g. "Tom Thumb"
◯◐

type of plant: slightly tender shrub [8–11]
flowering time: midsummer to early autumn
flower color: red + mauve
height: 18in/45cm (see description)

Fuchsias grow best in well-drained but moisture-retentive soil in which their roots can remain cool. Since these plants need large pots or tubs to minimize the risk of drying out, the smaller hybrids are more practical choices for containers than the tall, vigorous varieties. F. "Tom Thumb" is both small and very free-flowering. Its fairly upright, arching growths are clothed in little, pointed, rich green leaves. The pendent, bell-like flowers are each about 1¼in/3cm wide. In really mild regions, where its top growth is not cut back by frost each winter, this plant may grow up to 36in/90cm tall. F. "Lady Thumb" is another small variety; its flowers are red and white.
also for: ■ Long, continuous flowering period

Rhododendron
e.g. "Wee Bee"
◯◐✱

type of plant: hardy shrub [6–9]
flowering time: mid- to late spring
flower color: rich rose-pink + light pink
height: 12–20in/30–50cm
Evergreen

This slow-growing rhododendron is dense and hummocky. Its tidy, little, mid-green leaves are often obscured by a mass of funnel-shaped blooms. These pretty, wavy-edged flowers, each 1½in/4cm across, are arranged in loose clusters. Other hybrids that are neat, small-leaved and suitable for growing in containers include yellow-flowered R. "Patty Bee" and pink-and-white R. "Ginny Gee." Although these plants are hardy, their flowers can be damaged by frost. They therefore benefit from some shelter, as well as moist, well-drained, humus-rich soil that is lime-free.
also for: ■ Acid soils

Rhododendron impeditum
◯◐✱

type of plant: hardy shrub [6–8]
flowering time: mid- to late spring
flower color: usually purplish blue
height: 12in/30cm
Evergreen

R. impeditum slowly forms a dense, spreading dome of very small, grayish leaves and stiff, little twigs. The plant is rather wider than it is tall. It is normally very floriferous and most specimens produce large numbers of the funnel-shaped, ¾in/2cm-long flowers. Like many rhododendrons with small leaves, R. impeditum does well in open, sunny positions—provided the soil is moisture-retentive and well drained. Although it tolerates neutral to very slightly alkaline conditions, it is best in lime-free soil. The foliage has a slight, fruity scent when bruised, and in winter the leaves may take on bronze tones.
also for: ■ Acid soils

ADDITIONAL TREES, SHRUBS, AND WOODY CLIMBERS, featured elsewhere in this book, that are suitable for growing in containers

† = grown as clipped specimen

◯◐ sun or partial shade

minimum height 10ft/3m or more
Euonymus fortunei "Emerald Gaiety," see p.113
Euonymus fortunei "Silver Queen," see p.151
Hedera colchica "Dentata Variegata," see p.171

minimum height between 3ft/90cm and 10ft/3m
Acer palmatum var. dissectum, see p.227
†Buxus sempervirens, see p.140

Clematis "Niobe," see p.345
Clematis "Vyvyan Pennell," see p.288
Corylus avellana "Contorta," see p.267
Euonymus fortunei "Emerald 'n' Gold," see p.174
Hydrangea macrophylla "Générale Vicomtesse de Vibraye," see p.30
†Ilex aquifolium, see p.139
†Ilex aquifolium "Bacciflava," see p.258
†Ilex x meserveae Blue Angel, see p.242
Lonicera nitida "Baggesen's Gold," see p.215
Rhododendron "Dopey," see p.30
Salix integra "Hakuro-nishiki," see p.172

minimum height 3ft/90cm or less
Buxus sempervirens "Suffruticosa," see p.141
Euonymus fortunei "Emerald Gaiety," see p.113
Euonymus fortunei "Emerald 'n' Gold," see p.174
Hedera helix "Congesta," see p.228
Hydrangea "Preziosa," see p.346
Hypericum x moserianum "Tricolor," see p.175
Rhododendron yakushimanum, see p.227
Skimmia x confusa "Kew Green," see p.310
Vinca minor "Argenteovariegata," see p.118

Camellia japonica
e.g. "Alba Simplex"
◐[◦] ✳

type of plant: hardy shrub [7–10]
flowering time: mid- to late spring
flower color: white
height: 6–8ft/1.8–2.4m
Evergreen

With their rather formal flowers and their glossy, leathery, evergreen leaves, many varieties of *C. japonica* make handsome tub plants. The most suitable varieties —and the example shown here is one—have a bushy, rather upright growth habit and tend to be relatively slow-growing. Although the single, flat flowers of *C.j.* "Alba Simplex" (each 3–4in/8–10cm wide) are not especially vulnerable, the petals of all white- and pale pink-flowered camellias are liable to damage in harsh weather and they benefit significantly from a sheltered position. Camellias in general flower very poorly if their roots are allowed to dry out and, particularly when these plants are grown in containers, attention must be paid to regular watering. The soil mixture should be well-drained, moisture-retentive and humus-rich, and it must be acid. In cooler regions, *japonica* varieties may need a sunny position to flower well and *williamsii* varieties (for examples of which, see p.29) are often more successful, although many of them are either too tall or too open to make really good tub plants.
also for: ■ Acid soils ■ Atmospheric pollution ■ Decorative, green foliage

Rhododendron
e.g. "Mother's Day"
[azalea]
◐[◦] ✳

type of plant: hardy shrub [6–10]
flowering time: late spring to early summer
flower color: bright cerise-red
height: 3–5ft/0.9–1.5m
Evergreen/Semi-evergreen

R. "Mother's Day" is a typically floriferous, evergreen azalea that grows densely, neatly, and slowly. Most of its rather frilly, funnel-shaped flowers are semi-double or double and, at 2in/5cm across, quite large. They are arranged in compact clusters of two to four blooms. The small, dark, roughly oval leaves sometimes become tinged with wine-red in winter. As this azalea matures, it becomes increasingly branched and wide-spreading. Other popular, evergreen azaleas with flowers that are bright red or strong pink include *R.* "Vuyk's Rosyred" and *R.* "Vuyk's Scarlet." All these plants need acid to neutral soil that is, ideally, moisture-retentive and well-drained. In cooler climates, these plants do well in sunny positions.
also for: ■ Acid soils

Rhododendron
e.g. "Rosebud"
[azalea]
◐[◦] ✳

type of plant: hardy shrub [6–10]
flowering time: late spring
flower color: rose-pink
height: 24–36in/60–90cm
Evergreen

There are a number of evergreen azaleas with double flowers: as well as *R.* "Rosebud" illustrated here, there is, for example, the popular *R.* "Blaauw's Pink," which has bright salmon-pink flowers, and a red-flowered variety is shown above. Like the numerous single-flowered azaleas, these are all slow-growing, very floriferous shrubs and, as such, good plants for growing in containers. They need a reasonably sheltered site and a cool, moist root-run in well-drained, lime-free soil. In cool districts they can be grown very successfully in sunny positions. *R.* "Rosebud" is a rather spreading plant with neat, little leaves which are dark green in maturity. Its flowers, which are 1–1½in/2.5–4cm wide, last well.
also for: ■ Acid soils

ADDITIONAL TREES, SHRUBS, AND WOODY CLIMBERS, featured elsewhere in this book, that are suitable for growing in containers

† = grown as clipped specimen

◐[◦] partial shade (or sun)

minimum height 10ft/3m or more
x *Fatshedera lizei*, see p.86
Hedera canariensis "Gloire de Marengo," see p.136

minimum height between 3ft/90cm and 10ft/3m
Camellia japonica "Adolphe Audusson," see p.32
Camellia japonica "Lavinia Maggi," see p.103
Clematis "Hagley Hybrid," see p.136
Clematis "Nelly Moser," see p.136
Hedera helix "Glacier," see p.124
Hedera helix "Green Ripple," see p.81
Hydrangea macrophylla "Ayesha," see p.103
Rhododendron "Palestrina," see p.33

minimum height 3ft/90cm or less
Berberis thunbergii "Aurea," see p.216
Rhododendron "Blue Danube," see p.33
Rhododendron Cilpinense Group, see p.34
Rhododendron "Curlew," see p.35
Skimmia japonica subsp. *reevesiana*,
   see p.260
Skimmia japonica "Rubella," see p.34

◐/◐● partial shade/partial or full shade

minimum height 10ft/3m or more
Euonymus fortunei "Emerald Gaiety," see p.113
Euonymus fortunei "Silver Queen," see p.151
x *Fatshedera lizei*, see p.86
Hedera canariensis "Gloire de Marengo,"
   see p.136

minimum height between 3ft/90cm and 10ft/3m
†*Buxus sempervirens*, see p.140
Dicksonia antarctica, see p.231
Fatsia japonica, see p.149
Hedera helix "Glacier," see p.124
Hedera helix "Green Ripple," see p.81

minimum height 3ft/90cm or less
Buxus sempervirens "Suffruticosa," s
   see p.141
Euonymus fortunei "Emerald Gaiety,"
   see p.113
Euonymus fortunei "Silver Queen,"
   see p.151
Hedera helix "Congesta," see p.228
Hedera helix "Ivalace," see p.150
Skimmia x confusa "Kew Green," see p.310

Crevices in paving

THERE IS SOMETHING very inviting about a sunny paved area. When a terrace or patio is dotted with small, floriferous plants, the effect is often particularly appealing. The solidity and inertia of paving contrasts interestingly with the softness and vitality of plants. For their part, plants soften the appearance of paved areas, and they link these areas with other, more intensively planted parts of the garden, such as beds and borders.

Many plants enjoy the warmth that paving both reflects and stores. They also appreciate the good drainage that is usually associated with the crevices between paving stones. Indeed, seedlings often find these crevices especially congenial, and plants that self-sow freely can sometimes be a nuisance in paving. (On the other hand, the job of controlling most seedlings can be easier in paving than it is in densely planted borders.) Finally, the soil beneath paving slabs is nearly always consistently cool and moist, and many plants respond well to these conditions.

Most terraces and paved areas are too small for large plants to be grown conveniently within them. Only in a really extensive area of paving are larger, upright plants needed to relieve the monotony of the flat surface, and it might be best to grow these more substantial specimens in large pots and tubs.

The plants selected for the following list are all fairly low-growing. The choice of plants for sunny areas of paving is large, but there are fewer suitable plants for shade. As well as the plants illustrated in the various shade sections of this list, there are elsewhere in the book, for example, decorative little plants such as dog violet (*Viola riviniana* Purpurea Group), small ferns such as *Blechnum penna-marina*, and London pride (*Saxifraga x urbium*) and its variegated form *Saxifraga* "Aureopunctata".

Many of the most popular plants for paving crevices are very free flowering. They include small *Campanula* (for example, *C. cochleariifolia*) and *Phlox*, some *Viola*

(for example, *Viola* "Maggie Mott" and *V. odorata* "Alba"), numerous fragrant *Dianthus* and plants such as fairy foxglove (*Erinus alpinus*). These plants are mainly perennial, but there are also a number of very floriferous annuals that thrive in the crevices between paving stones. Some are illustrated in this list; others include Livingstone daisy (*Dorotheanthus bellidiformis*) and varieties of sweet alyssum (*Lobularia maritima*).

Leaves as well as flowers can look good growing in crevices in paving. There are plants described below with variegated foliage and with leaves that are gray, yellow or dark bronze-brown. Some plants in this list have the bonus of aromatic foliage: Corsican mint (*Mentha requienii*) smells deliciously of peppermint, and *Thymus* Coccineus Group is one of several fragrant thymes that would make attractive additions to plantings on paved areas. The non-flowering form of chamomile (*Chamaemelum nobile* "Teneague") has fruitily scented foliage, and it can be walked on (as can, to a lesser extent, the mint and the thyme mentioned above). In general, however, the plants in this list are best grown on parts of paved areas where they will not be regularly and frequently trodden on.

No bulbous plants have been included in this list of plants suitable for growing in crevices in paving. The leaves of bulbs need to die down naturally, to nourish the plant for next year's flowering, and unsightly, withering foliage is not easy to conceal or disguise on areas of paving. However, small bulbs such as *Crocus*, *Scilla* and some daffodils (*Narcissus*) can certainly look attractive between paving stones, and particularly so in less formal parts of the garden.

**Erigeron karvinskianus
(syn. E. mucronatus)**
[fleabane]
○

type of plant: hardy/slightly tender
perennial [7–10]
flowering time: early summer to mid-autumn
flower color: white changing to soft pink
height: 9–12in/23–30cm
Evergreen

The numerous little daisies produced by this plant are carried on thin,
curving stems. The flowers, about ¾in/2cm across, create a cloud of pink
and white over a period of several months and, in mild climates, the plant
may be in bloom for most of the year. E. karvinskianus is easily grown in
most well-drained soils that do not become too dry. It is especially at home
in cracks and crevices and usually sows itself, often quite freely, in such
positions. The plant produces a spreading mass of rather lax stems and slim,
grayish green leaves.
also for: ■ Long, continuous flowering period

**Alyssum spinosum "Roseum"
(syn. Ptilotrichum spinosum
"Roseum")**
○

type of plant: slightly tender shrub [8–9]
flowering time: late spring to early summer
flower color: pale to deep pink
height: 9in/23cm
Evergreen/Semi-evergreen

This prickly subshrub produces a profusion of very small, four-petalled
flowers that are arranged in heads about 1¼in/3cm across. The plant forms
a dense, twiggy hummock of gray-leaved growth. Tiny, slender leaves
contribute to a particularly pretty, pink-and-gray color combination. In ideal
conditions A. spinosum "Roseum" spreads widely, to 2ft/60cm or more.
Good drainage is important. Gritty soils of most sorts are suitable.
also for: ■ Dry soils in hot, sunny sites ■ Ground-cover ■ Gray, blue-gray
or silver leaves

Crepis incana
[pink dandelion]
○

type of plant: slightly tender perennial [7–9]
flowering time: mid- to late summer
flower color: soft pale pink
height: 9in/23cm

C. incana needs a site that is really sunny and soil that has good drainage.
It looks especially attractive growing in paving cracks or rock gardens.
The dandelion-like flowers are about 1½in/4cm wide. They are carried
on branching stems above neat rosettes of grayish light green, hairy foliage.
Each leaf is prominently toothed and up 5in/12cm long. Individual plants
may be short-lived but there is usually some self-sowing, especially on the
rather poor soils which seem to suit this plant best.

Aster alpinus
○

type of plant: hardy perennial [3–7]
flowering time: late spring to early summer
flower color: violet + yellow
height: 8–10in/20–25cm

Nurseries with a large selection of rock-garden plants stock varieties of
A. alpinus with purple, pink and white flowers, as well as the species itself.
Like the species, these varieties produce slender leaves in tufts. The daisy-
like flowers, which are attractive to bees, are each up to 2in/5cm wide.
They are carried on erect stems and have conspicuous, central, yellow discs.
Provided that it drains well, any reasonably fertile soil is suitable for these
easily grown plants. Individual specimens may spread up to 18in/45cm wide.

Leontopodium alpinum
[edelweiss]
○

type of plant: hardy perennial [4–7]
flowering time: late spring to early summer
flower color: grayish white
height: 7in/18cm

Much of the edelweiss' subdued charm is due to the fact that its strange
flower heads, as well as its clumps of slender leaves and its erect stems, are
softly felted. In cultivation the plant is short-lived, but it is not difficult to
grow provided that it has plenty of sun and an alkaline to neutral soil that
is very well-drained and rather gritty. In some regions it may need shelter
from winter rains. It often looks its best on top of a dry stone wall, and it is
attractive in crevices between paving stones, too. Individual flower heads
can be as much as 4in/10cm across.
also for: ■ Shallow soils over chalk ■ Gray, blue-gray, or silver leaves

Dianthus deltoides
[maiden pink]
○

type of plant: hardy perennial [3–7]
flowering time: early to midsummer
flower color: carmine- or cerise-pink or white
height: 6–9in/15–23cm
Evergreen

Maiden pink's mat of narrow, densely packed, deep green leaves is almost
obscured at flowering time by an abundance of ½in/1cm-wide flowers.
Varieties with deeply colored blooms, such as the vivid cerise D. deltoides
"Leuchtfunk" (syn. Flashing Light), have coppery or dark green foliage. These
varieties tend to grow less strongly than the paler forms, which can spread
to about 15in/38cm wide. An alkaline soil that drains freely is ideal for all
these plants, and they thrive on dry stone walls as well as in crevices in
paving and at the front of borders. Their fringed flowers are scentless.
also for: ■ Shallow soils over chalk ■ Dry soils in hot, sunny sites
■ Ground cover

Hypericum olympicum
[St John's wort]
○

type of plant: hardy shrub [6–8]
flowering time: mid- to late summer
flower color: yellow
height: 6–9in/15–23cm

Although its dense mound of upright stems and blue-green, pointed leaves is rarely more than 9in/23cm high, H. olympicum produces flowers that are 1½–2in/4–5cm wide. Each bloom has a prominent tuft of stamens. The plant is easily grown in any really well-drained soil and looks pretty and colorful in sunny crevices in walls and paving, as well as in borders. It often self-sows. H.o. f. uniflorum "Citrinum" is similar but has pale lemon flowers.
also for: ■ Ground cover ■ Gray, blue-gray, or silver leaves

Limnanthes douglasii
[poached-egg plant]
○

type of plant: hardy/slightly tender annual [8–10]
flowering time: early summer to early autumn
flower color: yellow + white
height: 6–9in/15–23cm

Once it has been given the conditions it likes best—coolness and moisture at its roots and sunshine on its sprawling clump of bright green, feathery foliage—this quick-growing plant usually sows itself from year to year. However, poached-egg plant is very easy to grow in most garden soils and looks especially pretty in the crevices between paving stones and as an edging to a path. Its numerous saucer-shaped flowers, which are about 1in/2.5cm across, have a light, sweet fragrance and are very attractive to bees.
also for: ■ Fragrant flowers

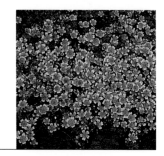

Arenaria montana
[sandwort]
○

type of plant: hardy perennial [3–7]
flowering time: late spring to early summer
flower color: white
height: 4–6in/10–15cm
Evergreen

Ideally, A. montana should have soil that is moist but, at the same time, very well-drained. Although this can be a difficult combination to maintain in beds and borders, it usually exists in the crevices in a wall or between paving stones. The narrow, grayish green leaves and prostrate stems of this vigorous plant mound up into a carpet of growth 12in/30cm or more wide. This becomes smothered in glistening white, cup-shaped flowers, about ¾in/2cm across, each of which has a small, lemon-yellow "eye".
also for: ■ Ground cover

Campanula garganica
e.g. "Dickson's Gold"
(syn. C.g. "Aurea")
[bellflower]
○

type of plant: hardy perennial [5–8]
flowering time: early to midsummer
flower color: lavender-blue
height: 4–6in/10–15cm
Semi-evergreen

Setting this plant in a wall or in paving draws attention to the attractive way in which the flower stems—seen here tipped with a profusion of buds—radiate from a neat mound of heart-shaped, gold-green leaves. C. garganica itself is also popular—and more vigorous. It can spread up to 12in/30cm wide, whereas C.g. "Dickson's Gold" may be only half that width. C. garganica produces quantities of starry, blue flowers, each about ¾in/2cm wide, above bright green leaves. Both these plants are easy to grow in well-drained soil that is also moisture-retentive.
also for: ■ Yellow or yellow-green leaves

Geranium subcaulescens
[cranesbill]
○

type of plant: hardy perennial [5–8]
flowering time: late spring to early summer
flower color: magenta-pink + black
height: 4–6in/10–15cm
Semi-evergreen/Evergreen

The very bright color of this plant's petals is intensified both by the almost black centers of the flowers and by the deep, soft green of the foliage. The cup-shaped flowers are about 1in/2.5cm wide. They are produced, in large numbers, on rather lax stems. G. subcaulescens forms rosettes of growth with tufts of deeply divided leaves. G. (Cinereum Group) "Ballerina" (see p.60) is somewhat similar, but its flowers are pale lilac-pink and they are produced over a longer flowering season. Both plants are drought-tolerant and thrive in light soils with good drainage.
also for: ■ Dry soils in hot, sunny sites ■ Decorative, green foliage

Phlox subulata
e.g. "Tamaongalei"
(syn. P.s. "Mikado")
[moss phlox, creeping phlox]
○

type of plant: hardy perennial [3–8]
flowering time: mid- to late spring
flower color: white + pink
height: 4–6in/10–15cm
Evergreen

The numerous varieties of moss phlox are very floriferous plants with dense mats or cushions of tiny, usually bright green leaves. They thrive in well-drained soil that is reasonably fertile. P. subulata "Tamaongalei" is slow-growing but eventually spreads about 18in/45cm wide. The flower clusters of other varieties are in various shades of red, purple, lilac and pink; P.s. "Maischnee" (syn. May Snow) is a popular white. The individual flowers of all these plants are approximately star-shaped and usually less than 1in/2.5cm across. A more vigorous variety, which is especially suitable for ground cover, is shown on p.109.
also for: ■ Ground cover

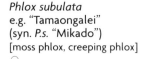

Veronica prostrata
(syn. V. rupestris)
[prostrate speedwell]
○

type of plant: hardy perennial [5–8]
flowering time: late spring to early summer
flower color: blue
height: 4–6in/10–15cm

V. prostrata's mat of toothed, bright green leaves often becomes almost completely obscured by its numerous, neat flower spikes. The plant spreads up to 18in/45cm wide. There are various forms of this easily grown and fairly vigorous plant: most of them have flowers in some shade of blue, but V.p. "Mrs Holt," for example, is a pink-flowered variety and V.p. "Trehane," which is less vigorous, has yellow leaves and blue flowers. All these plants thrive in light, well-drained soil. Their spikes of saucer-shaped flowers are usually 1½–2½in/4–6cm long.
also for: ■ Ground cover

Sedum spurium "Variegatum"
(syn. S.s. "Tricolor")
[stonecrop]
○

type of plant: hardy perennial [4–8]
flowering time: mid- to late summer
flower color: pink
height: 4in/10cm
Semi-evergreen

The trailing stems and fleshy leaf rosettes of S. spurium "Variegatum" form a rooting carpet some 15in/38cm wide. Each spoon-shaped, grayish green leaf is edged in pale cream and pink. The flowers are starry and borne in branching heads about 1½in/4cm across. Good drainage is important and the plant does well in hot, dry conditions. S. kamtschaticum var. kamtschaticum "Variegatum" is another readily available, small sedum with variegated foliage. It is yellow-flowered and its green, pink-tinged leaves have creamy white margins. Among the plain-leaved varieties of S. spurium, S.s. "Schorbuser Blut" (syn. Dragon's Blood) is popular; its flowers are a deep pinkish red.
also for: ■ Dry soils in hot, sunny sites ■ Variegated leaves

Sisyrinchium idahoense "Album"
(syn. S. "May Snow")
○

type of plant: hardy perennial [7–9]
flowering time: early to late summer
flower color: white
height: 4in/10cm
Semi-evergreen

There are a number of little sisyrinchiums that flourish and often sow themselves freely among paving stones. The individual flowers of these plants are usually short-lived, but they appear in succession over long periods. S. idahoense "Album" has starry blooms, 1in/2.5cm wide, which are carried on upright stems just above clumps of narrow, grayish leaves. Similar in size and habit of growth are plants in the S. californicum Brachypus Group; their flowers are yellow. Well-drained soils of most sorts are suitable. It is important that the plants do not become waterlogged during the winter months.
also for: ■ Long, continuous flowering period

Dianthus alpinus
[alpine pink]
○

type of plant: hardy perennial [3–7]
flowering time: early to late summer
flower color: pink or deep rose or crimson
height: 3–4in/8–10cm
Evergreen

D. alpinus has surprisingly large flowers for such a small plant: individual blooms are often 1½in/4cm wide. Their toothed petals are speckled with tiny, white spots. The flowers are carried on short stalks above hummocks of narrow, rich green leaves and they are usually so numerous that they obscure the foliage. D.a. "Joan's Blood" is a popular variety with vivid magenta-pink flowers. Both the species and its varieties are unscented. Ideally, these short-lived plants should be given a humus-rich, gritty soil that is, for preference, alkaline, but they prosper in almost any well-drained soil.
also for: ■ Shallow soils over chalk ■ Long, continuous flowering period

Geranium sessiliflorum subsp.
novae-zelandiae "Nigricans"
[cranesbill]
○

type of plant: hardy perennial [4–8]
flowering time: early to midsummer
flower color: white
height: 3in/8cm

The subtle, bronze-brown coloring and the diminutive size of this cranesbill's leaves mean that—intriguing and attractive though these leaves are—the plant is easily overlooked. Placing G. sessiliflorum subsp. novae-zelandiae "Nigricans" in some sort of container or in among paving stones isolates it and makes it more conspicuous. Each softly gleaming leaf is about 1in/2.5cm wide; the funnel-shaped flowers are even smaller. The foliage forms miniature tufts of growth. Although short-lived, this cranesbill self-sows liberally. It is happy in most soils with reasonable drainage.
also for: ■ Purple, bronze, or red leaves

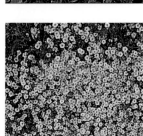

Phlox douglasii
e.g. "Boothman's Variety"
○

type of plant: hardy perennial [5–8]
flowering time: late spring to early summer
flower color: mauve + deep violet
height: 2–4in/5–10cm
Evergreen

Varieties of P. douglasii require very well-drained soil and plenty of warmth in summer (conditions which are usually present on dry stone walls and in the crevices between paving stones); they are able to withstand periods of drought. The dark, narrow leaves of these very free-flowering plants create ground-covering carpets of growth which are dense and hummocky and about 12in/30cm wide. The flat-faced flowers, each ½in/1cm across, are almost stemless. P.d. "Crackerjack" has bright magenta flowers and is another readily available variety.
also for: ■ Dry soils in hot, sunny sites ■ Ground cover

Thymus Coccineus Group
[thyme]
○

type of plant: hardy shrub/perennial [4–9]
flowering time: early to midsummer
flower color: bright crimson-purple
height: 2in/5cm
Evergreen/Semi-evergreen

Plants in *T.* Coccineus Group have little, rich green, tapering leaves which, with the trailing stems, create mats of variable width (up to 18in/45cm wide in the more vigorous forms). The foliage is aromatic—it smells like culinary thyme, but less strongly so. The tiny, lipped flowers are borne in clusters about ½in/1cm wide. They are attractive to bees and butterflies. Other trailing and prostrate thymes include varieties of *T. serpyllum* (for an example of which, see below). They all require really good drainage and they thrive in hot, dry situations. The more vigorous forms make attractive, small-scale ground-cover, but they do tend to develop bare patches after a few seasons. They can be trodden on but are not suitable for frequently used pathways.
also for: ■ Dry soils in hot, sunny sites ■ Ground cover (see above) ■ Aromatic foliage

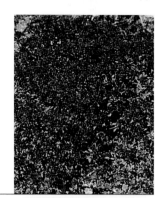

Thymus serpyllum var. *albus*
[creeping thyme]
○

type of plant: hardy shrub/perennial [4–9]
flowering time: early to midsummer
flower color: white
height: 1in/ 2.5cm
Evergreen/Semi-evergreen

The trailing stems of this subshrub root wherever they touch the ground and, with the light green foliage, they soon form a mat of growth about 15in/38cm wide. The tiny leaves are aromatic but only slightly so. Dense clusters of pure white flowers, about ½in/1cm across, are very freely borne. They are attractive to bees and butterflies. There are numerous varieties of *T. serpyllum*, including pink forms (such as *T.s.* "Pink Chintz" and *T.s.* "Annie Hall") and some red forms (see above, for a related Group of plants with reddish flowers). All these thymes need well-drained, rather dry soil in order to thrive. They make attractive ground cover, although they do have a tendency to become bare in patches after a few years. They can be walked on but should not be subjected to very hard wear and tear.
also for: ■ Dry soils in hot, sunny sites ■ Ground cover (see above)

ADDITIONAL PLANTS, featured elsewhere in this book, that are suitable for crevices in paving:

○ sun

minimum height between 6in/15cm and 12in/30cm
Aurinia saxatilis "Citrina," see p.108
Helianthemum "Mrs C.W. Earle," see p.58
Helianthemum "Rhodanthe Carneum," see p.189
Helianthemum "Wisley Primrose," see p.107
Iberis sempervirens, see p.107

minimum height 6in/15cm or less
Acaena saccaticupula "Blue Haze," see p.191
Aethionema "Warley Rose," see p.17
Antennaria microphylla, see p.108
Arabis alpina subsp. *caucasica* "Flore Pleno," see p.108

Arabis ferdinandi-coburgi "Old Gold," see p.167
Armeria maritima "Alba," see p.109
Aubrieta "Red Carpet," see p.109
Chamaemelum nobile "Treneague," see p.109
Convolvulus sabatius, see p.341
Cotula hispida, see p.191
Dianthus gratianopolitanus, see p.17
Dianthus "Pike's Pink," see p.60
Dorotheanthus bellidiformis Mixed, see p.61
Euphorbia myrsinites, see p.191
Geranium "Ballerina," see p.60
Gypsophila repens "Rosea," see p.60
Lithodora diffusa "Heavenly Blue," see p.109
Lobularia maritima "Oriental Night," see p.18

Lobularia maritima "Snow Crystals," see p.59
Phlox subulata "McDaniel's Cushion," see p.109
Saponaria ocymoides, see p.109
Sedum kamtschaticum var. *floriferum* "Weihenstephaner Gold," see p.342
Sedum spathulifolium "Cape Blanco," see p.61
Sedum spathulifolium "Purpureum," see p.203
Sempervivum arachnoideum, see p.191
Sempervivum tectorum, see p.61
Tanacetum haradjanii, see p.190
Thymus herba-barona, see p.248
Thymus pseudolanuginosus, see p.192
Thymus pulegioides "Bertram Anderson," see p.213
Thymus vulgaris "Silver Posie," see p.248

Malcolmia maritima Mixed
[Virginian stock]
○[◐]

type of plant: hardy/slightly tender annual [8–11]
flowering time: late spring to early autumn (see description)
flower color: mixed—lilac, pink, red, white
height: 6–9in/15–23cm

Virginian stock is a fast-growing plant that is very easy to grow. It should be sown where it is to flower—the spaces between paving stones on a sunny terrace being particularly congenial positions. The four-petalled flowers are about ¾in/2cm across and sweetly fragrant. They are borne in loose clusters on slender, branching stems, just above the narrow, grayish leaves. All well-drained soils are suitable, alkaline ones especially so. Seed can be sown at various points during the growing season, from late spring onward, to give a long flowering season. The plant often self-sows too.
also for: ■ Shallow soils over chalk ■ Fragrant flowers

Dryas octopetala
[mountain avens]
○[◐]

type of plant: hardy perennial [2–7]
flowering time: late spring to early summer
flower color: white
height: 3–4in/8–10cm
Evergreen

The lovely, anemone-like flowers of this subshrub are followed, in late summer, by fluffy seedheads. These are silvery or pinkish and 1in/2.5cm or so across. With its mass of trailing stems and glossy, scalloped leaves, the plant creates dense mats of ground-covering growth, which are eventually up to 36in/90cm wide. Each oak-like leaf is only about 1½in/4cm long. *D. octopetala* requires well-drained, humus-rich soil in order to thrive, but it is sufficiently vigorous to succeed in most soils with reasonable drainage.
also for: ■ Ground cover ■ Ornamental fruit (seedheads)

ADDITIONAL PLANTS, featured elsewhere in this book, that are suitable for crevices in paving

○[◐] sun (or partial shade)

minimum height 6in/15cm or less: *Acaena microphylla*, see p.111; *Geranium dalmaticum*, see p.111

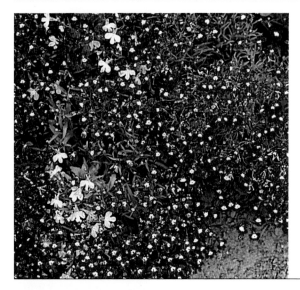

Lobelia erinus
e.g. "String of Pearls"
○◐

type of plant: grown as half-hardy annual [9–11]
flowering time: late spring to early autumn
flower color: mixed—white, light blue, dark blue, pink, red
height: 4–6in/10–15cm

Seed catalogs list numerous varieties of lobelia. The "bush" types, including *L. erinus* "String of Pearls," form neat, dense domes of growth that look attractive between paving stones. These plants are also useful for short-term ground cover. They produce masses of two-lipped flowers. Each flower is scarcely more than ¼in/0.5cm across and the slender leaves are almost equally small. Of the single-colored varieties, those with blue flowers—such as *L.e.* "Crystal Palace" (dark blue) and *L.e.* "Cambridge Blue" (light blue)—are particularly popular. Moisture-retentive, fertile soil is needed for good growth and a long flowering season.
also for: ■ Ground cover

Erinus alpinus
[fairy foxglove]
○◐

type of plant: hardy perennial [4–7]
flowering time: late spring to midsummer
flower color: mauve-pink
height: 3–4in/8–10cm
Evergreen

In full flower, *E. alpinus* is such a mass of bright bloom that it is not surprising that individual specimens are rather short-lived. However, the plant often perpetuates itself by self-seeding. It grows especially well in the crevices of walls, between paving stones and other places where the drainage is really good. The five-petalled flowers are arranged in small spikes, about 1½in/4cm long, above neat tufts of sticky, deep green foliage. There are varieties of *E. alpinus* with richly colored flowers, and *E.a.* var. *albus* has white flowers.
also for: ■ Dry soils in hot, sunny sites

Campanula cochlearifolia
(syn. C. pusilla)
[bellflower, fairies' thimbles]
○◐

type of plant: hardy perennial [6–8]
flowering time: mid- to late summer
flower color: mauve-blue, blue or gray-blue
height: 3in/8cm

C. cochlearifolia is an easily grown and vigorous plant, the creeping roots of which can sometimes be invasive. All well-drained soils are suitable, as long as they are also moisture-retentive. The bell-shaped flowers, each about ½in/1cm long, are carried on wiry stems. They are often so numerous that they completely conceal the tufts of little, rounded, bright green leaves. Readily available varieties of this plant include *C.c.* "Elizabeth Oliver," which has very pale blue, double flowers, and the white-flowered *C.c.* var. *alba*. All these plants are good in troughs and wall crevices as well as in paving.

ADDITIONAL PLANTS, featured elsewhere in this book, that are suitable for crevices in paving

○◐ sun or partial shade

minimum height 6in/15cm or less: | *Campanula poscharskyana*, see p.117 | *Viola* "Maggie Mott," see p.311
Asplenium trichomanes, see p.23 | *Saxifraga* "Gregor Mendel," see p.22 | *Viola* "Molly Sanderson," see p.332

Myosotis sylvatica
e.g. "Blue Ball"
[forget-me-not]
◐[○]

type of plant: hardy biennial/perennial [5–9]
flowering time: mid-spring to early summer
flower color: bright blue
height: 6in/15cm

In damp, lightly shaded areas of paving this short-lived plant covers its neat clump of mid-green, tongue-shaped leaves with a rounded cap of tiny, bright blue flowers. Each saucer-shaped bloom is scarcely more than ¼in/0.5cm wide. Forget-me-nots are, of course, also popular for spring bedding and a classic accompaniment to tulips. They grow in heavy soils for a limited period, but better drainage produces longer-lived specimens. Plenty of moisture is essential for good growth. As well as blue forget-me-nots, seed catalogs sometimes list pink- and white-flowered varieties and they often offer mixtures. The dwarf *M. sylvatica* Victoria Series plants, for example, are available both as separate colors and as a mixture.

Phlox x *procumbens* "Variegata" (syn. *P. amoena* "Variegata")
◑[◻]

type of plant: hardy perennial [7–8]
flowering time: late spring to early summer
flower color: purplish pink
height: 4–6in/10–15cm
Semi-evergreen/Evergreen

The leathery foliage of *P.* x *procumbens* "Variegata" forms cushions of growth 12in/30cm or more wide. Each slender, little leaf is edged in cream and there may be pink foliage color too, especially on the newer leaves. Some leaves are entirely cream-colored. The flat-faced flowers, about ¾in/2cm wide, are borne in clusters above the foliage. Unlike many variegated plants, this phlox is robust and vigorous. It thrives in humus-rich soil with good drainage and prefers acid conditions.
also for: ■ Ground cover ■ Variegated leaves

Mentha requienii (syn. *M. corsica*) [Corsican mint]
◑[◻]

type of plant: hardy/slightly tender perennial [7–9]
flowering time: late summer
flower color: lilac
height: ½in/1cm

The tiny, bright green leaves of the Corsican mint smell strongly of peppermint when crushed. The plant relishes the cool, moist root run and the good drainage that areas of paving usually provide. Its slender stems and rounded leaves spread indefinitely, in a close mat of growth, when it is well suited. In drier conditions it is less vigorous and it may be reduced to a mere film of greenery—but this too is attractive. Corsican mint can be walked on but it is not suitable for areas where it will be trodden on frequently. The tubular flowers, like the leaves, are tiny; they are carried in little spikes. The plant often self-sows.
also for: ■ Aromatic foliage

ADDITIONAL PLANTS, featured elsewhere in this book, that are suitable for crevices in paving

◑[◻] partial shade (or sun)

minimum height 12in/30cm or more	**minimum height between 6in/15cm and 12in/30cm**	**minimum height 6in/15cm or less**
Saxifraga x *urbium*, see p.230	*Saxifraga* "Aureopunctata," see p.178	*Asarina procumbens*, see p.348

Saxifraga e.g. "Pixie" [saxifrage]
◑

type of plant: hardy perennial [5–8]
flowering time: mid- to late spring
flower color: cream + pink
height: 2–3in/5–8cm
Evergreen

S. "Pixie" and related hybrids are much easier to grow than many plants in the genus. They thrive in most well-drained, moisture-retentive soils. The more vigorous hybrids make ground-covering cushions or mats of mossy growth, often 12in/30cm wide. Their flowers, which are borne on upright stems above the tiny, soft leaves, are usually cup-shaped and about ½–1in/1–2.5cm wide. Other hybrid saxifrages of this type include *S.* "Peter Pan," which has clear pink flowers, the crimson-flowered *S.* "Triumph" and the slow-growing *S.* "Cloth of Gold" (see p.217).
also for: ■ Ground cover

Pratia pedunculata
◑●

type of plant: hardy perennial [5–8]
flowering time: early to late summer
flower color: pale blue
height: ½–1in/1–2.5cm
Evergreen

Although this creeping, mat-forming plant is useful ground cover in cool, shady places, its prostrate stems and tiny, rounded leaves can spread rapidly over very large areas. Planting it between paving stones can contain its spread to some extent. *P. pedunculata* is especially at home in moisture-retentive soil, but it can tolerate drier conditions. The short-stalked, starry flowers, which are only ¼in/0.5cm wide, are produced over many weeks. In the variety *P.p.* "Country Park" the flowers are violet-blue.
also for: ■ Ground cover ■ Long, continuous flowering period

ADDITIONAL PLANTS, featured elsewhere in this book, that are suitable for crevices in paving

◑/◑● partial shade/partial or full shade

minimum height 6in/15cm or less: *Blechnum penna-marina*, see p.121; *Viola odorata* "Alba," see p.314; *Viola riviniana* Purpurea Group, see p.125

Variegated leaves

SOME GARDENERS LOVE every variegated leaf they set eyes on; others consider all variegated foliage an abhorrent perversion of nature. Yet, since there are very large differences in types of variegation, it is surprising that the subject of variegated leaves should be quite such a divisive one. As well as some shrill, multicolored, and very distinctly zoned leaves, there are also softly colored marblings and mottlings and subtle color combinations, such as gray-green and palest cream. Whatever the form and color of the variegation, patterned foliage can be very versatile. It can blend, enhance and enliven, and it can certainly extend the season of interest of many flowering plants.

The most familiar sort of variegation consists of a margin of either white or yellow around a central green area. The width and the regularity of this edge can vary considerably: the big, bold leaves of *Hedera colchica* "Dentata Variegata" have broad and very irregular margins of cream-yellow, while *Daphne odora* "Aureomarginata" has tapering leaves that are very narrowly and precisely edged in cream. On some plants the margin of the leaf is green and the central area contains the contrasting color. This "reversed" kind of variegation tends to be rather unstable, and sometimes the plants also produce all-green growths (which need to be removed promptly, before the entire plant becomes overwhelmed by more vigorous, plain green foliage).

There are, in addition, plants that are striped in contrasting colors. Normally, the stripes are longitudinal. More unusually, they form bands across the leaves: both zebra grass (*Miscanthus sinensis* "Zebrinus") and *Thuja plicata* "Zebrina" have this type of variegation.

Some plants produce leaves with a network of white or yellow veining across a green background (see, for example, *Arum italicum* subsp. *italicum* "Marmoratum" and *Lonicera japonica* "Aureoreticulata" in this list). And there are many plants with leaves that are marbled, spotted or mottled with two or more colors. These more diffuse kinds of markings often create quite a soft, "smudged" appearance, and they can be surprisingly successful components of quite informal plantings.

Just how conspicuous any variegated leaf appears to be and therefore how easy it is to place in the garden depends on several factors. There is the pattern of variegation itself, and the relationship of the colors in a variegated leaf is also important. Then there is the effect of sun and shade: in shaded sites particularly, white gleams so strikingly that it can outshine everything around it. Sun and shade also have a direct influence on the intensity of the colors in variegated leaves: as a broad generalization, most white-variegated plants appreciate shade. Where plants do well in either sun or shade, the brightness of the variegation tends to be greatest in sunshine.

The intensity of the leaf colors changes with the seasons in some plants. The variegation of several, popular perennials is brightest in spring (see, for example, *Hosta fortunei* var. *albopicta* and *Iris pseudacorus* "Variegata"). Certain plants, such as *Elaeagnus pungens* "Maculata," are most brightly variegated in winter. Another point to bear in mind is that many variegated varieties of plants produce fewer or smaller flowers than their green-leaved counterparts. This paucity of flowers will be seen as advantage by those gardeners who abhor the multitude of recently introduced plants that have very conspicuous flowers as well as variegated foliage.

Finally, the appearance of any sort of variegation is affected by the distance from which it is viewed. The colors and markings of large, variegated leaves can seem overwhelmingly bold and busy at close quarters, yet, at a distance, they give an overall impression of liveliness and lightness. On the other hand, very small leaves with delicate markings are best viewed close up.

For a beautifully illustrated survey of numerous variegated plants, see *Variegated Plants* by Susan Conder and Andrew Lawson (Cassell, 1994).

Liriodendron tulipifera "Aureomarginata"
[tulip tree]
○
type of plant: hardy tree [5–8]
flowering time: early to midsummer
flower color: yellowish green
height: 60ft/18m

The variegated form of the tulip tree is slower growing than the species (see p.219). Its curiously shaped, lobed, all-yellow leaves, each 4–5in/10–12cm long, soon mature to deep green with a broad and irregular edging of yellow. As summer progresses, the yellow markings become greener. Finally, in autumn, the foliage reverts to all-yellow. The tree is usually a neat cone of growth, which often broadens with age. Specimens are generally at least several years old before they begin to produce their cup-shaped blooms. Deep, fertile, moisture-retentive soil is most suitable for this tree.
also for: ■ Atmospheric pollution ■ Colorful, autumn foliage ■ Green flowers

Populus x jackii (syn. P. x candicans) "Aurora"
[poplar, aspen, cottonwood]
○
type of plant: hardy tree [4–8]
height: 40–50ft/12–15m

The expanding leaf buds of this fast-growing tree exude a balsam-like fragrance in spring. Heart-shaped leaves. about 5in/12cm long, may be all-white, or uniform deep green, or generously edged and marked with creamy white and tinged with pink. P. x jackii grows quickly, but bacterial canker often shortens its life. It naturally forms a broad column. All moisture-retentive soils are suitable for this tree and it may also be grown in damp ground. Its wide-spreading roots may damage building foundations.
also for: ■ Heavy, clay soils ■ Damp and wet soils ■ Atmospheric pollution

Thuja plicata "Zebrina"
[arborvitae, western red cedar]
○
type of plant: hardy conifer [6–8]
height: 40–50ft/12–15m
Evergreen

The fruitily scented foliage of this conifer is basically a glossy, rich green but it is conspicuously banded in creamy yellow. The variegation is most pronounced in late spring and early summer. The leaves are tiny and scale-like and arranged in flattened sprays of variable length and width. Clothed to the ground in foliage, the plant makes a broad, dense cone of growth. T. plicata "Zebrina" grows much more slowly than T. plicata itself (see p.139) but, like it, it tolerates alkaline and dry soils, although it performs best in deep, moist loam. It needs a site sheltered from the desiccating effects of cold winds.
also for: ■ Shallow soils over chalk ■ Aromatic foliage

Actinidia kolomikta
○
type of plant: hardy climber [5–9]
height: 12–15ft/3.6–4.5m

The extraordinary, ice-cream colors of this twining climber develop best on specimens planted against a warm wall. The broad, pointed leaves are about 6in/15cm long and basically mid-green. They emerge purplish, and some mature leaves remain flushed with this color, but others become liberally splashed with white and pink. The variegation fades before the leaves fall. The sweetly scented, cupped flowers are inconspicuous. Any well-drained, moderately fertile soil is suitable. The spectacular variegation is not present on the leaves of very young plants. Yellowish fruits, which are small and unobtrusive, are borne if male and female plants are grown together.
also for: ■ Climbers ■ Fragrant flowers

Pittosporum e.g. "Garnettii" (syn. P. tenuifolium "Garnettii")
○
type of plant: slightly tender/half-hardy shrub [9–10]
height: 10ft/3m
Evergreen ✄

As it matures, this dark-stemmed shrub's cone of bushy growth becomes rather more spreading. Each leaf is roughly oval and about 2in/5cm long, with a creamy white edge to the central area of pale gray-green. In winter the leaves often become flushed and spotted with pink and red. Other popular pittosporums with variegated foliage include the slightly less hardy P. tenuifolium "Silver Queen," which has pointed leaves, and P.t. "Irene Paterson," which has mottled gray, green, and white foliage. They usually need shelter, and soil that is well-drained but not dry. When mature, P. "Garnettii" may bear tiny, purple, honey-scented flowers in late spring.
also for: ■ Growing in containers ■ Fragrant flowers (see above)

Cornus alternifolia "Argentea" (syn. C.a. "Variegata")
[pagoda dogwood, green osier]
○
type of plant: hardy shrub/tree [4–8]
height: 8–10ft/2.4–3m

The pagoda dogwood is an airy edifice of horizontal branches and white-edged, gray-green foliage. The leaves are fairly slender and 2–3in/5–8cm long; they are often slightly misshapen. There are clusters of white flowers in spring, but these are inconspicuous among the white-variegated leaves. In some years there is reddish autumn foliage color. Although this exceptionally pretty plant survives low winter temperatures, it needs both shelter and sun to grow really well. Most well-drained soils are suitable. C. controversa "Variegata" [zones 6–9] is another readily available dogwood with tiered branches and variegated foliage. It eventually grows about 25ft/7.5m high. Its leaves have cream edges.

Luma apiculata
(syn. *Myrtus apiculata*, *M. luma*)
"Glanleam Gold"
○

type of plant: slightly tender/half-hardy
shrub [9–10]
flowering time: late summer to early autumn
flower color: white
height: 8–10ft/2.4–3m
Evergreen

Among its neatly and densely arranged, glossy leaves, this bushy shrub bears little, tufted flowers. These have a slight, sweet scent. The glossy, pointed leaves, ¾in/2cm long, are mottled in various shades of green and edged with creamy yellow. When crushed, the foliage emits a faint scent of lemon and spices. Flowering is especially good in hot summers, after which there are small, black edible berries. *L. apiculata* "Glanleam Gold" appreciates good drainage and performs especially well in humus-rich soil. It thrives in mild, moist regions and by the sea. It is a slow-growing plant.
also for: ■ Windswept, seaside gardens ■ Growing in containers
■ Ornamental fruit (see above)

Rhamnus alaternus
"Argenteovariegata"
[Italian buckthorn]
○

type of plant: slightly tender shrub [8–10]
height: 8–10ft
Evergreen ♀✂

The green-and-gray-marbled leaves of this shrub are edged in creamy white. Each glossy, leathery leaf is about 1¼in/3cm long. This upright, dark-stemmed plant quite quickly forms a dense pyramid and, since it responds well to hard pruning, it can be used for hedging (individual plants should be 18–24in/45–60cm apart). Only after hot summers or in really warm districts are the little, yellowish green flowers followed by large crops of black berries. Sheltered sites and most well-drained soils are suitable for this shrub and it thrives in alkaline conditions. It dislikes damp soil and a windy position.
also for: ■ Shallow soils over chalk ■ Atmospheric pollution ■ Hedging plants ■ Ornamental fruit (see above)

Buddleja davidii "Harlequin"
[butterfly bush, summer lilac]
○

type of plant: hardy shrub [6–9]
flowering time: mid- to late summer
flower color: deep purplish red
height: 6–8ft/1.8–2.4m

When young, the slender, pointed leaves of *B. davidii* "Harlequin" are splashed and irregularly edged with creamy yellow. As the foliage matures, the markings become whiter. The basic leaf color is a deep, slightly gray-green. Richly scented flowers spikes, about 9in/23cm long, are carried at the end of the plant's arching branches. The flowers are very attractive to butterflies. Though good drainage is important, this fast-growing shrub does well on a wide range of soil types. It tolerates quite dry conditions.
also for: ■ Shallow soils over chalk ■ Atmospheric pollution ■ Fragrant flowers

Griselinia littoralis "Variegata"
[broadleaf]
○

type of plant: slightly tender shrub [9–10]
height: 6–8ft/1.8–2.4m
Evergreen ♀✂

Although *G. littoralis* itself (see p.92) can withstand salt-laden gales, this variegated variety deserves a less exposed site and it should certainly be sheltered from cold, dry winds. It also requires soil with good drainage, since damage is most likely to occur if the roots are cold *and* wet in winter. The gleaming leaves of this dense, leafy and rather upright shrub are, at first, bright green and yellow; later the leaf margins soften to creamy white and the main leaf color is grayish green. Each leaf is a broadly oval and 2½–3in/6–8cm long. *G.l.* "Bantry Bay" is a smaller plant with foliage generously splashed with creamy yellow.
also for: ■ Windswept, seaside gardens

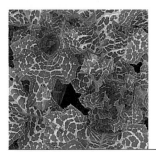

Euonymus japonicus
e.g. "Ovatus Aureus"
(syn. *E.j.* "Aureovariegatus")
○

type of plant: slightly tender shrub [8–10]
height: 5–7ft/1.5–2.1m
Evergreen ♀✂

The many variegated varieties of *E. japonicus* are dense, bushy shrubs with fairly upright branches and—if planted in full sun—brightly marked foliage. *E.j.* "Ovatus Aureus" has glossy, leathery, oval leaves, about 2in/5cm long; many leaves have broad, irregular margins of creamy yellow around deep green, but some are all-yellow. The larger varieties are often used for hedging, particularly by the sea, where they grow well (young plants should be about 18in/45cm apart). None of these shrubs is particular about soil provided it is well drained. These are useful evergreens for shallow, chalky soil.
also for: ■ Shallow soils over chalk ■ Windswept, seaside gardens
■ Atmospheric pollution ■ Hedging plants ■ Growing in containers

Silybum marianum
[Mary's thistle]
○

type of plant: hardy biennial [7–11]
flowering time: early to midsummer
flower color: purple
height: 4–5ft/1.2–1.5m

Veined in white and arranged in rosettes, the rich green, spiny leaves of *S. marianum* are very striking. The flowers are thistle-like, about 2in/5cm across and they too are prickly. They are carried, on erect stems, well above the leaves. Rather poor soil with good drainage is most suitable for this plant. Unless the fading flowers are removed promptly, there will be numerous self-sown seedlings. The flowers are attractive to bees and butterflies but some gardeners like to pinch out the flowering stems as they begin to form to insure that the plant produces plenty of leaves that stay in good condition over a long period. Each broad, lobed leaf is about 10in/25cm long.

Abutilon megapotamicum "Variegatum"

○

type of plant: half-hardy/slightly tender shrub [8–11]
flowering time: early summer to mid-autumn
flower color: red + yellow
height: 4ft/1.2m
Evergreen/Semi-evergreen

In cold regions this abutilon is usually grown in a conservatory or used as a dot plant in summer bedding; in mild areas it can be grown outdoors against a warm, sunny wall. The slightly arching stems carry gracefully pointed, bright green leaves, 2–3in/5–8cm long, which are heavily mottled with yellow. Very decorative, lantern-like, pendent flowers are produced over a period of several months. *A. megapotamicum* "Variegatum" needs fertile, well-drained soil and plenty of moisture in the growing season. The plain-leaved species is shown on p.145. Both plants need support in order to grow upright.
also for: ■ Climbing plants ■ Growing in containers ■ Long, continuous flowering period

Berberis thunbergii f. atropurpurea "Rose Glow" [barberry]

○

type of plant: hardy shrub [5–8]
flowering time: mid- to late spring
flower color: pale yellow + red
height: 4ft/1.2m

The rounded, 1in/2.5cm-long leaves of this shrub are, briefly, plain red-purple, but they soon become mottled with pink and gray. The clusters of little, cup-shaped flowers are followed, from late summer, by shining, rich red, droplet-shaped berries. In autumn, the foliage turns crimson and orange-red. *B. thunbergii* f. *atropurpurea* "Rose Glow" is a dense, rounded, prickly plant with arching stems. Apart from a dislike of wet and of very alkaline soils, it is easy to grow. *B.t. f. a.* "Harlequin" is taller and has creamier variegation. Both shrubs can be used for hedging (plants should be 18–24in/45–60cm apart).
also for: ■ Atmospheric pollution ■ Hedging plants ■ Colorful, autumn foliage ■ Ornamental fruit

Daphne odora "Aureomarginata"

○

type of plant: slightly tender shrub [8–9]
flowering time: midwinter to early spring
flower color: purple + palest pink
height: 4ft/1.2m
Evergreen

The elegantly tapered leaves of this plant are predominantly a soft mid-green, but each leathery leaf has a very thin, creamy yellow margin. Individual leaves are about 3in/8cm long. The trumpet-shaped flowers, almost white within, are carried in dense clusters at the ends of rather stout shoots. They are richly and sweetly fragrant. *D. odora* "Aureomarginata" slowly forms a spreading mound of foliage, which is almost always wider than it is high. The plant needs a sheltered, sunny site and fertile soil, to which, ideally, leaf mold has been added. Its roots should be kept cool in summer.
also for: ■ Fragrant flowers ■ Winter-flowering plants

Symphoricarpos orbiculatus "Foliis Variegatis" (syn. S.o. "Variegatus") [coral berry, Indian currant]

○

type of plant: hardy shrub [3–8]
height: 4ft/1.2m
✂

The numerous little leaves and slender, arching twigs of this shrub create a dense, billowy mass of growth. Each rounded leaf, about ¾in/2cm long, is bright green with an irregular margin of yellow. *S. orbiculatus* "Foliis Variegatis" is a very tolerant and easily grown shrub. However, if it is planted in shade, its leaf color is rather subdued and the foliage may revert to plain, unvariegated green. Almost any soil with reasonable drainage is suitable and, although this plant looks better if it is not parched, it can cope well with fairly dry conditions.
also for: ■ Atmospheric pollution

Canna "Striata" (syn. C. "Malawiensis Variegata," C. "Pretoria") [Indian shot]

○

type of plant: half-hardy perennial [9–11]
flowering time: midsummer to early autumn
flower color: light orange
height: 3–5ft/0.9–1.5m

The light, bright coloring of this canna's foliage is the result of conspicuous yellow stripes curvaceously applied to a basic leaf color of clear green. In shape and size, too, the foliage is striking: each leaf is broad and pointed, and often about 18in/45cm long. And then there are showy flowers as well —looking like big, exotic irises on purple-flushed, upright stems—although these blooms are not very freely produced in cool climates. *C.* "Striata" needs rich soil that retains moisture well, and it benefits from being grown in a sheltered site. For another canna with decorative foliage, see the purple-leaved variety shown on p.200.

Fuchsia magellanica e.g. "Versicolor" (syn. F. "Versicolor")

○

type of plant: hardy/slightly tender shrub [7–10]
flowering time: midsummer to early autumn
flower color: red + purple
height: 3–5ft/0.9–1.5m

Mature leaves of this bushy, rather erect fuchsia are a subtle combination of gray-green with thin margins of palest cream and, often, a reddish purple tinge overall. *F. magellanica* "Versicolor" is quite late into leaf. Its young foliage is smoky crimson-purple, and each leaf is a pointed oval, about 1¼in/3cm long. In cold areas, the plant may well be cut to the ground each year, but it quickly recovers in spring. In mild areas, this fuchsia is much taller and the little, dangling, bell-shaped flowers begin to open earlier. Moist, well-drained soil is ideal, but this is an adaptable plant. *F.m.* var. *molinae* "Sharpitor" has white-edged, gray-green leaves and very pale pink flowers.
also for: ■ Long, continuous flowering period

Yucca gloriosa "Variegata"
[Spanish dagger]
○

type of plant: slightly tender shrub [7–9]
height: 3–5ft/0.9–1.5m foliage height;
6–10ft/1.8–3m flower height (see description)
Evergreen

These rigid, very sharply pointed leaves, up to 24in/60cm long and glaucous green, form rosettes of salt-resistant foliage. Each leaf has a distinct edge of creamy yellow. In maturity, this slow-growing plant has a short, sometimes branching trunk. Spanish dagger flowers only spasmodically, except in hot, rather dry climates. The spikes of creamy white, bell-shaped flowers are often more than 5ft/1.5m long. They appear from late summer. Y. gloriosa "Variegata" thrives in really well-drained soil. Yellow-variegated Y. filamentosa "Bright Edge" and Y. flaccida "Golden Sword" are also popular.
also for: ■ Dry soils in hot, sunny sites ■ Windswept, seaside gardens ■ Growing in containers

Pleioblastus viridistriatus
(syn. Arundinaria auricoma,
P. auricomus)
○

type of plant: slightly tender/hardy perennial (bamboo) [7–10]
height: 3–4ft/0.9–1.2m
Evergreen

This especially colorful bamboo is suitable for a small garden, since its clumps of thin, purplish canes spread only slowly. Its slender, pointed leaves are about 7in/18cm long and they are brightly and boldly striped in yellow and pale green. Though the foliage quite often becomes damaged in winter, P. viridistriatus rejuvenates quickly if it is cut right back in spring. P. variegatus has white, boldly striped leaves on slender, green stems and is 24–30in/60–75cm high. Both plants need moisture-retentive, fertile soil with good drainage and a site that is sheltered from cold, drying winds.
also for: ■ Damp and wet soils

Chamaecyparis lawsoniana
"Pygmaea Argentea"
[Lawson false cypress]
○

type of plant: hardy conifer [6–8]
height: 36in/90cm
Evergreen

Very slow-growing, this neat, rounded conifer may well be only about 15in/38cm tall after ten years. It produces flattened fans of tiny, scale-like leaves. These are basically dark bluish green, but the whole plant is heavily "dusted" with cream. Though this pretty paleness is present in summer and winter, it is most pronounced in spring. The plant needs moist, well-drained soil. It requires sun for its distinctive coloring to develop properly, but if it is exposed to cold winds, frost—or, indeed, too much sun—then the foliage may scorch. C. lawsoniana "Summer Snow" has foliage of similar coloring; it is cone-shaped and about twice the size of C.l. "Pygmaea Argentea."
also for: ■ Growing in containers

Coronilla valentina subsp. glauca
(syn. C. glauca) "Variegata"
○

type of plant: slightly tender/half-hardy shrub [9]
flowering time: mainly midwinter to late spring (see description)
flower color: yellow
height: 36in/90cm
Evergreen

The numerous little leaflets of this dense, bushy plant are pale blue-green with a creamy white edging. Individual leaves are about 2in/5cm long and composed of up to thirteen leaflets. C. valentina subsp. glauca produces its sweetly scented little pea-flowers intermittently through summer and into autumn, as well as earlier in the year. A warm, sunny, sheltered site should be chosen for this shrub. It needs good drainage and does well in light, alkaline soil. C.v. subsp. g. "Citrina" (see p.335) has plain, bluish gray-green leaves. Both these plants may be short-lived.
also for: ■ Shallow soils over chalk ■ Growing in containers ■ Fragrant flowers ■ Winter-flowering plants ■ Long, continuous flowering period

Spiraea x vanhouttei Pink Ice
= "Catpan"
○

type of plant: hardy shrub [4–9]
flowering time: early summer
flower color: white
height: 36in/90cm

The foliage of this slow-growing shrub is pale pink, then creamy white, before it matures to several shades of green heavily mottled with white. Each leaf is toothed, diamond-shaped, and about 1in/2.5cm long. S. x vanhouttei itself has plain, green foliage and is about twice the height of S. x v. Pink Ice. It is an exceptionally free-flowering plant, although the display does not last long. Both the species and the variety produce thickets of reddish, wiry shoots and arching branches, along which are borne dense, rather flat clusters of little, bowl-shaped flowers. Fertile, moisture-retentive soil is most suitable, but these shrubs are tolerant, easily grown plants.
also for: ■ Heavy, clay soils

Phormium
e.g. "Yellow Wave"
○

type of plant: slightly tender perennial/shrub [9–11]
flowering time: mid- to late summer
flower color: soft red
height: 30–36in/75–90cm foliage height;
6–10ft/1.8–3m flower height (see description)
Evergreen ☀✂

Many hybrid phormiums are grown principally for their spectacular clumps of long, sword-shaped leaves. Only on mature specimens in regions with hot summers are the tall, upright heads of tubular flowers produced regularly. P. "Yellow Wave" has arching leaves, to 36in/90cm long, which are striped in yellow and yellowish green. Other popular variegated hybrids include P. cookianum subsp. hookeri "Tricolor," P. "Sundowner" and P. "Maori Maiden." They all like well-drained but moist soil. Their foliage is very long-lasting when cut. They are wind-resistant plants but P. tenax (see p.221) and its varieties are more suitable for exposed, seaside gardens.
also for: ■ Atmospheric pollution ■ Growing in containers

Glyceria maxima var. variegata (syn. *G. aquatica* "Variegata")
○

type of plant: hardy perennial (aquatic, grass) [5–9]
height: 24–30in/60–75cm

The lushest and leafiest specimens of this aquatic grass grow in damp or wet soil or in an inch or two of water. However, such is its vigor, the plant grows quite satisfactorily in ordinary, moisture-retentive garden soil. Its creeping, weed-proof roots are usually invasive and, except in large areas, should be confined. The long, arching, strap-shaped leaves, ¾in/2cm wide, are held on erect stems and each leaf is distinctly striped in deep green, cream and white. When young, the foliage is fairly upright and tinged purplish pink. There are open heads of greenish flowers in summer, but the main attraction of *G. maxima* var. *variegata* is its foliage.
also for: ■ Damp and wet soils ■ Ground cover

Eryngium bourgatii
[sea holly, eryngo]
○

type of plant: hardy perennial [5–9]
flowering time: mid- to late summer
flower color: violet-blue or blue-green
height: 24in/60cm

The dark, jagged, basal leaves of this clump-forming plant are pale-ribbed and heavily veined in silver. Each intricate, spiny leaf is about 3in/8cm long. Above this striking foliage rise blue, branching stems with numerous, small, teasel-like flower heads that are surrounded by slim, silvery blue bracts. Well-drained, rather dry soil is most suitable for *E. bourgatii*. *E. variifolium* also has white-veined leaves which, in its case, are rounded and evergreen. Flower heads of sea hollies look attractive from before they are fully colored until they fade—still retaining their shape—in autumn.
also for: ■ Dry soils in hot, sunny sites ■ Flowers suitable for cutting (and drying)

Iris pallida "Argentea Variegata"
○

type of plant: hardy perennial [4–9]
flowering time: late spring to early summer
flower color: lavender-blue
height: 24in/60cm

The bold stripes of white on the blue-green leaves of this iris are striking enough in themselves, but the arrangement of the foliage in stiff, slightly arching fans accentuates these markings. The leaves remain in good condition throughout the summer and into autumn. They, rather than the flowers, are the principal decorative feature of *I. pallida* "Argentea Variegata." However, the yellow-variegated counterpart of this iris—sold under various names, but correctly *I.p.* "Variegata"—is a more vigorous plant and it produces plenty of sweetly fragrant, 4in/10cm-wide flowers. Both varieties need plenty of sun, and fertile soil with good drainage.

Kalimeris yomena "Shogun"
○

type of plant: hardy perennial [4–9]
flowering time: late summer to early autumn
flower color: lilac
height: 18in/45cm

This aster-like plant is easily grown in most garden soils that are reasonably fertile and well drained, as long as they do not dry out readily. The foliage is more decorative than the sprays of small, yellow-centred daisies. Each neatly shaped, pointed, oval leaf, 1–1½in/2.5–4cm long, is light green with an irregular margin. This margin is, at first, white with some pink tinges, but it becomes creamier and then yellower through the summer months. *K. yomena* "Shogun" is upright and bushy with dark stems.

Pelargonium
e.g. "Caroline Schmidt"
○

type of plant: tender perennial [10–11]
flowering time: early summer to early autumn
flower color: bright red
height: 18in/45cm
Evergreen

Among the bedding pelargoniums commonly known as "geraniums" there are numerous cultivars with variegated leaves. Some of these plants are very boldly marked and brightly colored (see, for example, *P.* "Mr Henry Cox" on p.166). More subtly colored variegation is found on cultivars like *P.* "Caroline Schmidt," illustrated here. The rounded, scalloped leaves of this bushy plant, each about 3in/8cm across, are a gentle, pale gray-green with white margins. The large, hemispherical heads of double flowers are carried well clear of the foliage. This pelargonium needs a warm, sunny position and well-drained soil.

Sisyrinchium striatum
(syn. *Phaiophleps nigricans*)
"Aunt May" (syn. "Variegatum")
○

type of plant: hardy/slightly tender perennial [8–9]
flowering time: early to midsummer
flower color: pale yellow
height: 18in/45cm
Evergreen/Semi-evergreen

The iris-like leaves of this plant are broadly striped in creamy yellow and gray-green. Above the neat clumps of foliage rise spikes of pretty, clustered flowers, each flower ½in/1cm wide and stalkless. The flower color coordinates perfectly with the color scheme of the foliage. *S. striatum* "Aunt May" grows most satisfactorily in a sheltered position and in well-drained, rather poor soil. In exposed sites and cold gardens the tips of its leaves tend to become blackened, and if the roots are wet in winter the plant is not likely to survive long. This is, in any case, a rather short-lived plant.

Erysimum linifolium
"Variegatum"
[wallflower]
○

type of plant: slightly tender/hardy
perennial [8–9]
flowering time: late spring to midsummer
flower color: mauve
height: 12–18in/30–45cm
Semi-evergreen/Evergreen

The narrow, grayish green leaves of this wallflower are neatly and conspicuously edged in pale cream; they create a fairly loose mound of pretty foliage. Combined with the little flowers—each ½in/1cm wide—the overall effect is bright and lively. E. linifolium "Variegatum" is a short-lived plant that survives longest and flowers most prolifically in poor, sharply drained, preferably alkaline soil. It grows well in dry stone walls. In these sorts of conditions and in a fairly sheltered site, it is less prone to frost damage.
also for: ■ Shallow soils over chalk ■ Dry soils in hot, sunny sites

Pelargonium
e.g. "Mr Henry Cox"
(syn. P. "Mrs Henry Cox")
○

type of plant: tender perennial [10–11]
flowering time: early summer to early autumn
flower color: pale pink
height: 12–15in/30–38cm
Evergreen

Some of the bedding pelargoniums (often referred to as "geraniums") have very boldly variegated foliage, none more so than those known as fancy-leaved zonals—of which P. "Mr Henry Cox," illustrated here, is one of many possible examples. Its rounded, scalloped leaves are about 3in/8cm wide and banded in creamy yellow, bronze, red, and green. (P. "Dolly Varden" is of similar coloring; its clusters of flowers are scarlet.) P. Horizon Series and P. Orbit Series are examples of annual, seed-raised strains that have variegated foliage. All these plants have upright flower stalks above bushy foliage. They need well-drained soil and a warm, sunny site. For a zonal pelargonium with more subdued variegation, see p.165.

Salvia officinalis
e.g. "Tricolor"
[sage]
○

type of plant: slightly tender shrub/perennial
(herb) [8–9]
flowering time: midsummer
flower color: lilac-blue
height: 12–15in/30–38cm
Evergreen/Semi-evergreen

This little sage can look exceptionally decorative in the right setting. Its velvety, pointed leaves, 1½–2in/4–5cm long, are basically grayish green with irregular margins of very pale cream, but the newer growth is flushed with pink and pale red. The tubular, lipped flowers are arranged in short spikes. When bruised, the foliage emits the sharp scent characteristic of culinary sage. Although S. officinalis "Tricolor" makes a neat, rounded hummock of rather upright growth, especially if it is lightly trimmed each spring, it is really too small to be useful for ground cover. It thrives in really well-drained, light soil and full sun. For a more gently colored, variegated sage, see p.247.
also for: ■ Dry soils in hot, sunny sites ■ Aromatic foliage

Brassica oleracea cultivars
[ornamental cabbage]
○

type of plant: grown as hardy annual/
biennial [7–10]
height: 12in/30cm

Most ornamental cabbages have an interesting texture as well as unusual coloring. The various mixtures on offer generally include at least some plants with frilled and fluted leaves, in addition to the plants that are variegated or unusually colored. The more or less rounded leaves of these cabbages are up to 12in/30cm long, and they may be white, pink, red, or green, with or without edgings and veinings in contrasting colors. Leaf color intensifies in autumn as nights become colder. The plants need rich, well-drained, neutral to alkaline soil. If the leaves are used in flower arrangements, they smell unpleasant unless charcoal is added to the water.

Osteospermum
e.g. "Silver Sparkler"
○

type of plant: slightly tender/half-hardy
perennial [9–10]
flowering time: early summer to mid-autumn
flower color: white
height: 10–12in/25–30cm
Evergreen

A warm, sheltered site and soil that is light and well-drained are most suitable for O. "Silver Sparkler." It tolerates hot, dry conditions. Its dazzling white, dark-centered daisies, each 2–3in/5–8cm wide, open in succession over a period of several months. Flowering is often especially good in coastal gardens. Cloudy weather causes the flowers to close and then the blue undersides of the petals become visible. The slender, light green leaves, which form tufts of fairly upright growth, are edged in pale cream.
also for: ■ Dry soils in hot, sunny sites ■ Long, continuous flowering period

Pelargonium
e.g. "Vancouver Centennial"
○

type of plant: tender perennial [10–11]
flowering time: early summer to early autumn
flower color: reddish orange
height: 10–12in/25–30cm
Evergreen

In contrast to the pelargoniums shown above and on p.165, this "stellar" variety of zonal pelargonium has relatively open flower heads, each 3in/8cm across, which are made up of pretty, airy flowers. The leaves of this bushy plant are also distinctive, with their neat, symmetrical lobes of bright green and their central areas of bronzed brown. P. "Bird Dancer" is another popular stellar pelargonium; it produces pink flowers and its leaves have dark brownish edges. Both these plants need well-drained soil and a warm, sheltered site. Zonal pelargoniums are often referred to as "geraniums."

Tropaeolum majus
e.g. Alaska Series
[nasturtium, Indian cress]
○

type of plant: grown as hardy annual [10–11]
flowering time: early summer to mid-autumn
flower color: mixed—red, orange, yellow, cream
height: 10in/25cm

The pale, almost circular leaves of this non-climbing nasturtium have irregular, creamy white splashes and mottlings. If T. majus Alaska Series plants are grown in rather infertile soil with good drainage, there will be plenty of flowers. Each funnel-shaped bloom is about 2in/5cm wide. The leaves and the flowers of this plant are edible and they are sometimes used in salads. They have a peppery taste. The plants are bushy and sprawling and rather wider than they are tall. They make useful short-term ground cover, particularly on hot, dry slopes. T.m. "Out of Africa" is a taller, climbing nasturtium with variegated foliage.
also for: ■ Dry soils in hot, sunny sites ■ Ground cover

Tulipa praestans "Unicum"
[tulip]
○

type of plant: hardy bulb [5–9]
flowering time: early to mid-spring
flower color: orange-scarlet
height: 10in/25cm

With flowers bright and spruce as these tulips, this crisp, clean variegation seems just right. Each broad, pointed leaf, about 8in/20cm long, is gray-green with a conspicuous edging of cream. There are often several blooms on each stem. When fully open, the flowers are bowl-shaped and about 2½in/6cm wide. T. "New Design" is a taller, Triumph Group tulip with pale pink flowers and the same pattern of leaf variegation as T. praestans "Unicum." The edges of its leaves are pink-tinged white. For a tulip with a different sort of variegation, see below. All these plants need fertile soil with good drainage.
also for: ■ Flowers suitable for cutting

Pelargonium
e.g. "L"Elégante"
○

type of plant: half-hardy/tender perennial [9–11]
flowering time: early summer to early autumn
flower color: white + purple
height: 9in/23cm
Evergreen

The trailing, often rather brittle stems of ivy-leaved pelargoniums are embellished with neatly lobed, succulent leaves. The variety illustrated here has an especially appealing combination of delicately marked, white flowers and gray-green leaves, 1–2in/2.5–5cm wide, which are edged with ivory-white. In dry conditions the foliage tends to become suffused with a pale pinkish-mauve color and this is most noticeable on the white part of each leaf. When grown outdoors, this plant needs full sun and well-drained soil. It is able to withstand periods of drought. There are ivy-leaved pelargoniums with red, pink, lilac and purple flowers. Some varieties have variegated foliage.
also for: ■ Dry soils in hot, sunny sites

Tulipa
e.g. "Red Riding Hood"
(Greigii Group)
[tulip]
○

type of plant: hardy bulb [5–9]
flowering time: early spring
flower color: bright scarlet
height: 8in/20cm

Greigii Group tulips have broad, usually undulating, grayish leaves, which are striped or mottled with brown, maroon or brownish purple. Their flowers are pink, yellow, red or bicolored. T. "Red Riding Hood" has especially conspicuous markings on its leaves, as well as goblet-shaped, 2in/5cm-wide flowers with attractive black markings inside. Variegated foliage is also a feature of the Kaufmanniana Group tulips. Varieties such as the red-and-white flowered T. "Heart's Delight" have leaves with purple markings. Tulips in both these Groups thrive in light, fertile, well-drained soil and full sun. Their bulbs do not need lifting and storing after flowering each year.
also for: ■ Dry soils in hot, sunny sites

Arabis ferdinandi-coburgi
e.g. "Old Gold"
[rock cress]
○

type of plant: hardy perennial [5–7]
flowering time: mid- to late spring
flower color: white
height: 6–8in/15–20cm
Evergreen/Semi-evergreen

This floriferous plant's tiny, closely packed rosettes of foliage form an almost flat mat of growth, which spreads 12in/30cm or more wide. Each slender little leaf, about ¾in/2cm long, is rich green and shiny, with a creamy yellow to yellow edging; some leaves are entirely yellow. The loose flower heads are held, on slim stems, well above the foliage. A. procurrens "Variegata" (syn. A. ferdinandi-coburgi "Variegata") is a similar, slightly smaller plant with pale cream margins to its leaves. Both plants enjoy soil that is very well drained and, preferably, alkaline. They thrive in poor soil.
also for: ■ Shallow soils over chalk ■ Dry soils in hot, sunny sites ■ Ground cover ■ Crevices in paving

Nymphaea
e.g. "Marliacea Chromatella"
[waterlily]
○

type of plant: hardy perennial (aquatic) [5–10]
flowering time: early to late summer
flower color: yellow
height: 4–6in/10–15cm

N. "Marliacea Chromatella" has shapely flowers of a beautiful, limpid yellow. Each flower is about 6in/15cm wide. The olive-green leaves are almost circular and mottled with dark bronze. When young, the foliage is coppery with purple markings. This moderately vigorous hybrid spreads about 4ft/1.2m wide. It is suitable for water up to 36in/90cm deep. N. "Pygmaea Helvola" [zones 7–10] is a much smaller waterlily with maroon-mottled leaves and soft yellow flowers, 2–3in/5–8cm wide; it can be planted in water only 4–9in/10–23cm deep.

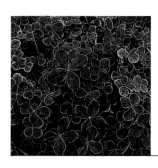

Trifolium repens "Purpurascens Quadrifolium"
[shamrock, white clover, Dutch clover]
○

type of plant: hardy perennial [5–9]
flowering time: early to late summer
flower color: white
height: 3–4in/8–10cm
Evergreen/Semi-evergreen

With their central portions of dusky purple and their bright green edges, these heart-shaped leaflets are striking and stylish. Each leaflet is about ¾in/2cm long. Spreading widely—usually to at least 24in/60cm—the creeping, rooting stems and the overlapping leaves form carpets of ground-covering growth. *T. repens* "Purpurascens Quadrifolium" is often invasive. It grows in most soils but it is especially at home in moist, well-drained conditions. Its dense, globular flower heads are very attractive to bees. The slimmer, bright green leaflets of *T. pratense* "Susan Smith" are veined in yellow. It too is a vigorous plant that is suitable for ground cover.
also for: ■ Ground cover ■ Long, continuous flowering period

ADDITIONAL PLANTS, featured elsewhere in this book, that have variegated leaves

○ **sun**

minimum height 3ft/90cm or less
Acorus gramineus "Ogon," see p.67
Carex elata "Aurea," see p.66

Hebe "Silver Queen," see p.147
Nymphaea "Odorata Sulphurea Grandiflora," see p.303
Origanum vulgare "Country Cream," see p.248

Salvia officinalis "Icterina," see p.247
Sedum spurium "Variegatum," see p.156
Thymus vulgaris "Silver Posie," see p.248

Ilex aquifolium
e.g. "Argentea Marginata"
[English holly]
○ [◐]

type of plant: hardy tree [7–9]
height: 40–50ft/12–15m
Evergreen ⚥✂

English holly has numerous varieties, many of which have variegated leaves. This example is, at first, bushy; after many years, it becomes a columnar tree. It is usually sold in its female form and bears large quantities of bright red berries if pollinated by a male plant. Its broad, spiny leaves, up to 3in/8cm long, are glossy and have creamy white edges. Other popular varieties of *I. aquifolium* with very pale cream edges to dark green leaves include *I.a.* "Handsworth New Silver" (female) and *I.a.* "Silver Queen" (in fact, male). These are all tough, adaptable plants that can be used to make hedges (plants should be about 24in/60cm apart); when clipped, they look decorative in large pots. Virtually any soil is suitable, as long as it is not wet or very dry. Leaf variegation is brightest in sunny sites.
also for: ■ Windswept, seaside gardens ■ Atmospheric pollution ■ Hedging plants ■ Growing in containers (clipped specimens) ■ Ornamental fruit

---

Ilex x *altaclerensis*
e.g. "Golden King"
[holly]
○ [◐]

type of plant: hardy shrub/tree [7–9]
height: 20–25ft/6–7.5m
Evergreen ⚥✂

Despite its masculine name, *I.* x *altaclerensis* "Golden King" is female and it produces red berries when pollinated by a male plant. Its broad leaves are about 4in/10cm long, glossy and almost devoid of prickles. Each rich green leaf has a wide, bright yellow margin. This slow-growing plant eventually makes a small, fairly broad-headed tree. It is good for hedging (plants should be 18–24in/45–60cm apart). The dark green leaves of *I.* x *a.* "Lawsoniana" (female) are yellow-centered. Almost any soil that is not very dry or wet is suitable for these plants. Their leaves are most brightly variegated in sun.
also for: ■ Windswept, seaside gardens ■ Atmospheric pollution ■ Hedging plants ■ Growing in containers (clipped specimens) ■ Ornamental fruit

---

Ilex aquifolium
e.g. "Ferox Argentea"
[English holly]
○ [◐]

type of plant: hardy shrub [7–9]
height: 15–20ft/4.5–6m
Evergreen ⚥✂

I. aquifolium "Ferox Argentea" very slowly forms a rounded, rather upright plant. Its fearsomely prickled leaves, 1–2in/2.5–5cm long, are dark green with cream margins. They are carried on dark purplish stems. Most soils and sites are suitable for this plant, but it is most conspicuously variegated in sunny sites. It dislikes only very dry or wet conditions and is otherwise easy to please. It grows well in seaside gardens and areas of atmospheric pollution, and it makes an interesting container plant. It is sometimes used for hedging. Since it is a male plant, there are no berries.
also for: ■ Windswept, seaside gardens ■ Atmospheric pollution ■ Growing in containers

---

Jasminum officinale
"Argenteovariegatum"
(syn. *J.o.* "Variegatum")
[jasmine]
○ [◐]

type of plant: slightly tender climber [7–10]
flowering time: midsummer to early autumn
flower color: white
height: 12–15ft/3.6–4.5m
Deciduous/Semi-evergreen

Like *J. officinale* itself, this cream-variegated variety has clusters of very richly fragrant, trumpet-shaped flowers that are most strongly scented in the evening and at night. However, in place of the plain, deep green foliage of the species, the variety has pale gray-green leaves with creamy white edges and occasional pink tinges. Each leaf has several slim, pointed leaflets, 1½–2in/4–5cm long. This twining climber benefits from shelter and warmth. It is happy in all reasonably fertile, well-drained soils. *J.o.* "Aureum" (syn. "Aureovariegatum") has foliage that is mottled and suffused with yellow. These plants produce plenty of good-quality foliage when hard pruned.
also for: ■ Climbing plants ■ Fragrant flowers

Elaeagnus pungens "Maculata" (syn. *E.p.* "Aureovariegata")
○ ◖◗

type of plant: hardy shrub [6–10]
height: 8–10ft/2.4–3m
Evergreen ♂✂

The foliage of this dense but spreading shrub is brightest in winter. Each dark green, glistening leaf, 2–3in/5–8cm long, has a broad, central area of yellow. After hot summers, tiny, very sweetly scented, cream flowers are borne during autumn. *E. pungens* "Maculata" is prone to producing plain green foliage, which must be removed. The plant thrives in most soils, although not on shallow, chalky soil, and it grows well in exposed, seaside gardens and in polluted air. It can be used for informal hedging (plants should be about 30in/75cm apart). *E. x ebbingei* "Limelight" [zones 6–9] is similar.
also for: ■ Windswept, seaside gardens ■ Atmospheric pollution ■ Hedging plants ■ Growing in containers ■ Fragrant flowers

Cornus alba
e.g. "Spaethii"
[redtwig dogwood]
○ ◖◗

type of plant: hardy shrub [3–8]
height: 6ft/1.8m
♂✂

The fresh green, tapered leaves of this dogwood are about 4in/10cm long and edged in bright yellow. Their coloring is gentler in shade. In autumn, the foliage turns soft orange, then falls, revealing the upright, deep red stems. The color of these shiny stems is richest if *C. alba* "Spaethii" is pruned really hard. A wide range of soils is suitable for this dense, rounded shrub, which grows especially fast in moist or wet conditions. Flat heads of inconspicuous, creamy white flowers appear from late spring. For another variegated variety, see p.68. *C.a.* "Aurea" has leaves that are entirely yellow.
also for: ■ Heavy, clay soils ■ Damp and wet soils ■ Atmospheric pollution ■ Colorful, autumn foliage ■ Ornamental bark or twigs

Osmanthus heterophyllus
e.g. "Goshiki"
(syn. *O.h.* Tricolor)
○ ◖◗

type of plant: slightly tender shrub [7–9]
height: 5–6ft/1.5–1.8m
Evergreen

The glossy, holly-like leaves of this dense, rounded shrub are rich green mottled with creamy yellow. Each leaf is sharply toothed and up to 2½in/6cm long. The very young foliage is pinkish bronze. *O. heterophyllus* "Variegatus" produces grayish leaves bordered in pale cream, and *O.h.* "Aureomarginatus" has very neat, yellow edges to its bright green leaves. All these osmanthus grow slowly and do best in sheltered sites. Most well-drained soils are suitable. After hot summers, mature specimens of *O.h.* "Goshiki" and *O.h.* "Aureomarginatus" bear tiny, tubular, white flowers in autumn; these are very sweetly scented. *O.h.* "Variegatus" rarely flowers.
also for: ■ Fragrant flowers

Miscanthus sinensis "Zebrinus"
[zebra grass]
○ ◖◗

type of plant: hardy perennial (grass) [6–9]
flowering time: mid-autumn
flower color: pinkish
height: 4–5ft/1.2–1.5 foliage height; to 8ft/2.4m
flower height (see description)

Horizontally banded foliage, like that of *M. sinensis* "Zebrinus," is fairly rare (although see the rush illustrated on p.69). The bands of creamy yellow on the deep green leaves are at their most conspicuous from midsummer. *M.s.* "Zebrinus" makes a dense, vase-shaped clump of foliage about as wide as it is high. Abundant quantities of the large, feathery flower heads tend to appear only after hot summers. Any soil is suitable for this grass, as long as it does not become too dry. The foliage is most colorful in sunny sites. *M.s.* "Morning Light" and *M.s.* "Variegatus" have leaves with longitudinal, white stripes.
also for: ■ Heavy, clay soils

Astrantia major "Sunningdale Variegated"
(syn. *A.m.* "Variegata")
[masterwort, Hattie's pincushion]
○ ◖◗

type of plant: hardy perennial [5–9]
flowering time: early to late summer
flower color: white or pinkish
height: 24–30in/60–75cm
♂✂

At their freshest and clearest in spring, the bold, white markings on these astrantia leaves turn yellower at about flowering time and then fade until the foliage is a uniform, soft green. The jagged-edged, deeply lobed leaves make weed-excluding clumps about 9in/23cm high. This variegated form of *A. major* is not as free-flowering as the species (for which see p.326), but it does produce the same charming and long-lasting, papery-textured flowers, each about 1in/2.5cm across. The plant thrives in fertile, moisture-retentive soil. Many gardeners feel that the leaf markings are brightest in sunny sites.
also for: ■ Damp and wet soils ■ Ground cover ■ Flowers suitable for cutting (and drying) ■ Long, continuous flowering period

Solidago flexicaulis "Variegata"
[goldenrod]
○ ◖◗

type of plant: hardy perennial [4–9]
flowering time: late summer to early autumn
flower color: yellow
height: 24–30in/60–75cm

This plant's strong, upright stems carry boldly yellow-splashed and yellow-mottled, pointed leaves. Each leaf is quite large (up to 6in/15cm long) and its variegation is brightest in spring and early summer. Individually, the daisy-like flowers are small but they are arranged, in loose, rounded clusters, around the top 6in/15cm or so of each stem. *S. flexicaulis* "Variegata" is robust and easily grown in most garden soils that do not dry out in summer. In rich loams the plant may well spread up to 36in/90cm wide.
also for: ■ Heavy, clay soils

Aquilegia vulgaris Vervaeneana Group (syn. A.v. "Woodside") [columbine, granny's bonnet]
○[◐]

type of plant: hardy perennial [5–9]
flowering time: late spring to early summer
flower color: pink or white or red or lilac
height: 24in/60cm (see description)

The height, the flower color and the leaf variegation of these columbines all vary from plant to plant. The numerous, lobed leaflets may be marbled, speckled, or streaked with yellow. Above this ferny foliage rise stiff, upright stems that carry the flowers, each of which is a cluster of spurred petals about ¾in/2cm long. The flower stems may be as little as 12in/30cm high or they may be more than 30in/75cm. A sunny position encourages bright variegation, and soil that is both well-drained and moist ensures that A. vulgaris Vervaeneana Group plants produce plenty of foliage.

Mentha suaveolens (syn. M. rotundifolia) "Variegata" [Apple mint]
○[◐]

type of plant: hardy perennial (herb) [6–9]
height: 12–18in/30–45cm

Brightly and crisply variegated, the neat, wrinkly leaves of this mint emit a rather dry, fruity smell when pressed. As the rounded, bright green leaves mature, their very pale cream markings become almost white. Each leaf is about 1in/2.5cm long; it may be edged in white, splashed with white, all-white or, indeed, all-green. M. suaveolens "Variegata" usually flowers sparsely, and the pink flowers are modest. Easily grown in any moisture-retentive soil, this mint can be invasive in rich, moist soil. If regularly divided, its spreading clumps of slightly curving stems make good ground cover. Ginger mint (M x gracilis "Variegata") has yellow-marked leaves.
also for: ■ Heavy, clay soils ■ Ground cover ■ Aromatic foliage

Teucrium scorodonia "Crispum Marginatum"
○[◐]

type of plant: hardy shrub/perennial [6–9]
flowering time: mid- to late summer
flower color: pale greenish yellow
height: 12in/30cm
Evergreen

The edges of these yellowish, light green leaves are crimped and puckered, and beaded with white. Each leaf is 1½–2in/4–5cm long. This teucrium and its varieties have a preference for light, poor, dryish soil, and in these conditions they grow densely and make useful ground cover. However, as long as there is reasonably good drainage, they grow well in quite a wide range of soils. When bruised, the foliage emits a slightly musty scent. Tiny flowers are carried in long, slender spikes above the spreading mass of foliage. T. scorodonia "Crispum" has plain green, puckered leaves.
also for: ■ Ground cover

Houttuynia cordata "Chameleon"
○[◐]

type of plant: hardy perennial [5–9]
flowering time: early to midsummer
flower color: white
height: 8–10in/20–25cm

The basic leaf color of this creeping plant is dark green but it is the bright pink-red and the acid yellow that catch the eye. This variegation is most marked when H. cordata "Chameleon" is grown in sun. However, general growth is good only in moist to wet conditions and, in some situations, a little shade may help conserve moisture. The plant can also be grown in very shallow water. In fertile conditions particularly, this creeping plant is vigorous and its red-stemmed, heart-shaped leaves create a dense mass of ground-covering growth at least 18in/45cm wide. Each leaf is orange scented and 2–3in/5–8cm long. The strange flower spikes "sit" on four white bracts.
also for: ■ Damp and wet soils ■ Ground cover ■ Aromatic foliage

ADDITIONAL PLANTS, featured elsewhere in this book, that have variegated leaves

○[◐] sun (or partial shade)

minimum height between 3ft/90cm and 10ft/3m
Cornus alba "Elegantissima," see p.68

minimum height 90cm/3ft or less
Acorus calamus "Argenteostriatus," see p.70
Cordyline australis "Torbay Dazzler," see p.148

Melissa officinalis "Aurea," see p.250
Oenanthe javanica "Flamingo," see p.70
Schoenoplectus lacustris subsp. tabernaemontani "Zebrinus," see p.69

Acer platanoides "Drummondii" [Norway maple]
○◑

type of plant: hardy tree [4–8]
flowering time: mid-spring
flower color: greenish yellow
height: 30–40ft/9–12m

The very finely pointed, five-lobed leaves of this tree are bright green with broad margins of greenish yellow. The variegation becomes whiter as the growing season progresses. Each leaf is 4–5in/10–12cm long. Before the leaves unfurl, the tree bears numerous, conspicuous clusters of flowers. A. platanoides "Drummondii" has a broad, sometimes almost globular head of densely foliated branches. It grows well on a very wide range of soils, including heavy clays and shallow soils over chalk. Unfortunately, it tends to revert and any green-leaved shoots need to be removed as soon as possible to prevent the more vigorous, plain green growth becoming predominant.
also for: ■ Shallow soils over chalk ■ Heavy, clay soils ■ Atmospheric pollution

Hedera colchica
e.g. "Dentata Variegata"
[ivy]
○ ◐

type of plant: hardy climber [6–10]
height: 12–15ft/3.6–4.5m; 9in/23cm as
ground cover
Evergreen ♀✂

H. colchica "Dentata Variegata" is one of the most dramatic of the variegated ivies. Its more or less heart-shaped leaves are up to 8in/20cm long and the foliage color is a striking mixture of green and gray-green, with broad, irregular, yellow-cream margins. This fast-growing plant makes a rather loosely adhering climber (it produces some aerial roots) and it is particularly successful used as ground cover, when it creates carpets of growth about 9in/23cm high. *H.c.* "Sulphur Heart" (syn. "Paddy's Pride") is another popular variety. It has central splashes of yellow on its bright green leaves. Both varieties grow in almost any soil that is not waterlogged. They need reasonably good light to color well, but they are not suitable for sunny places that are very hot and dry. See the unillustrated sections of this list for page numbers of other variegated ivies.
also for: ■ Dry shade ■ Atmospheric pollution ■ Ground cover ■ Climbing plants ■ Growing in containers

Lonicera japonica
"Aureoreticulata"
[Japanese honeysuckle]
○ ◐

type of plant: hardy climber [7–9]
height: 10–15ft/3–4.5m
Evergreen/Semi-evergreen ♀✂

The intricate yellow veining on the leaves of this honeysuckle manages to produce an effect that is pretty and precise, rather than fussy. The foliage is particularly bright in a sunny position but, unless the plant's roots, at least, can be cool and moist, there may be problems with aphids and mildew. A partially shaded site is therefore likely to be a more practical choice in many gardens. (North-facing walls that are very sheltered are acceptable.) In some shade and in soil that is not only moist but also fertile and humus-rich, there should be plenty of healthy foliage on this twining climber. Toward the end of each trail the leaves are pointed and oval, and about 1½in/4cm long. The basic leaf color is a light yellowish green. In most summers, there are only a few sweetly scented flowers. Since its stems root in contact with soil, *L. japonica* "Aureoreticulata" can be used for ground cover, when it makes a bushy mass about 9in/23cm high.
also for: ■ Ground cover ■ Climbing plants

Ligustrum ovalifolium "Aureum"
[California privet]
○ ◐

type of plant: hardy shrub [6–11]
flowering time: midsummer
flower color: white
height: 9–12ft/2.7–3.6m
Evergreen/Semi-evergreen ♀✂

Hedges of *L. ovalifolium* "Aureum" need clipping several times a year if they are to remain really neat and tidy. Unpruned, California privet makes an attractive, freestanding shrub with an open network of twigs on fairly upright branches. The pointed leaves, each about 2in/5cm long, are most distinctly variegated in sun. Markings vary, and some leaves may be entirely yellow, but there are usually broad, irregular margins of bright yellow around bright green central areas. *L.o.* "Argenteum" has creamy white edges to its soft green leaves. Both varieties produce clusters of flowers that are attractive to butterflies but that have a heavy, musty smell. Almost any soil is suitable for these tough, long-suffering plants, but growth is best in fertile, well-drained soil that is not too dry. When used for hedging, plants should be about 18in/45cm apart.
also for: ■ Dry shade ■ Atmospheric pollution ■ Hedging plants

Prunus lusitanica "Variegata"
[Portugal laurel]
○ ◐

type of plant: hardy/slightly tender shrub [8–10]
flowering time: early summer
flower color: white
height: 6–10ft/1.8–3m
Evergreen ♀✂

Subtly colored and discreetly marked, the variegated form of Portugal laurel slowly makes a broad cone of dense growth. Its elegant, pointed leaves—each 3–4in/8–10cm long and with a subdued sheen—are held on red stalks. They have central areas of soft green which are surrounded by narrow, creamy white margins. There may be some pink tinging of the foliage in winter. Wispy, saucer-shaped flowers are arranged in long, slender spikes. They have a not particularly pleasant, hawthorn-like scent, and may be followed by little berries, which ripen from red to black. Any well-drained soil is suitable for this shrub and it grows successfully in shallow, chalky soil.
also for: ■ Shallow soils over chalk

Acer negundo
e.g. "Flamingo"
[box elder, ash-leaved maple, Manitoba maple]
○ ◐

type of plant: hardy shrub/tree [4–9]
height: 6–8ft/1.8–2.4m as a shrub; 30ft/9m unpruned (see description)

This decorative variety of box elder is best when cut back hard in spring and then trimmed in summer. Treated like this, it forms a fairly upright, open shrub with plenty of shrimp-pink new growths as well as older, green-and-white variegated leaves. The rather pendulous, pink-stalked leaflets are 2–3in/5–8cm long. Each bright green leaflet is edged in white. *A. negundo* "Elegans" has yellow-margined foliage. Although box elder is particularly at home on moisture-retentive soil, it is adaptable and most soils are suitable. The species is wind-tolerant but these varieties grow best when sheltered.
also for: ■ Shallow soils over chalk ■ Heavy, clay soils ■ Atmospheric pollution

Buxus sempervirens
e.g. "Aureovariegata"
(syn. *B.s.* "Aurea Maculata")
[boxwood]
○◐●

type of plant: hardy shrub [6–8]
height: 6–8ft/1.8–2.4m
Evergreen ♀✂

B. sempervirens "Aureovariegata" slowly forms a spreading, bushy but rather open mass of leathery foliage. The leaves, each about 1in/2.5cm long, are rounded and softly gleaming. They are rich green with irregular streakings of creamy yellow. B.s. "Elegantissima" is dense, upright and very slow-growing, and has creamy white leaf edges. Boxwood is easily grown in any well-drained soil. It thrives in alkaline conditions and tolerates dry shade. The variegated forms retain their markings remarkably well in some shade. The yellow, spring flowers of these plants are small but they are sweetly scented.
also for: ■ Shallow soils over chalk ■ Dry shade ■ Atmospheric pollution ■ Fragrant flowers

Photinia davidiana
(syn. *Stranvaesia davidiana*)
"Palette"
○◐

type of plant: slightly tender shrub [7–9]
flowering time: early to midsummer
flower color: white
height: 6–8ft/1.8–2.4m
Semi-evergreen

On first emerging, these leaves are flushed a soft, pretty pink, but a mixture of foliage colors soon develops. In spring and summer the leaves are usually a combination of pink, pale cream, pale bronze, and bright rich green. When fully mature, each glossy, elegantly tapering leaf is a uniform, rich green and up to 5in/12cm long. In autumn, some of the older leaves turn red. Compared with the species, slow-growing P. davidiana "Palette" is bushier—although still erect and fairly open—and it does not always flower or fruit well. The pendent berries are pink-red. It needs shelter from cold winds. Most soils are suitable, but cool, moist, well-drained ones are ideal.
also for: ■ Atmospheric pollution

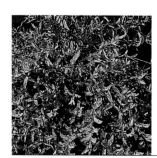

Viburnum tinus "Variegatum"
[laurustinus]
○◐

type of plant: slightly tender shrub [8–10]
flowering time: late autumn to early spring
flower color: white
height: 5–8ft/1.5–2.4m
Evergreen ♀✂

Like the familiar, green-leaved species (see p.318), this dense, bushy, usually cone-shaped plant produces clusters of pink-budded flowers. (As with the species, there are particularly large numbers of blooms during mild spells.) The cream-edged leaves are fairly slender, pointed and 2½–3in/6–8cm long. Their central areas are a mixture of soft greens and light greens. V. tinus "Variegatum" grows more slowly than the species and it is slightly more tender. Its fairly thin-textured leaves "burn" in cold, exposed sites. Most soils are suitable for this plant but it is at its best in moisture-retentive ground.
also for: ■ Heavy, clay soils ■ Atmospheric pollution ■ Winter-flowering plants ■ Long, continuous flowering period

Weigela "Florida Variegata"
○◐

type of plant: hardy shrub [5–8]
flowering time: late spring to early summer
flower color: pink
height: 4–5ft/1.2–1.5m
♀✂

The margins of this shrub's pointed, light green leaves are yellowish, then pale cream. Although deciduous, the foliage remains in remarkably good condition until late autumn or early winter. (As temperatures drop, some leaf edges may become tinged with pink.) The clusters of 1¼in/3cm-long, funnel-shaped flowers are borne fairly close to the main, upright stems on W. "Florida Variegata." They appear in particularly large numbers in sunny sites. This is an easy-going plant, but fertile, moisture-retentive soil encourages it to produce plenty of good-quality foliage. W. "Praecox Variegata" is very similar. The foliage of both varieties lasts well when cut.
also for: ■ Heavy, clay soils ■ Atmospheric pollution

Salix integra "Hakuro-nishiki"
(syn. *S.i.* "Albomaculata")
○◐

type of plant: hardy shrub [6–9]
height: 4–6ft/1.2–1.8m

Frequently offered for sale as a standard, of about 36in/90cm, the chief attraction of this open, slightly pendulous shrub is its very pale, mottled foliage. The slender, pointed leaves, up to 2in/5cm long, are a mixture of white and dark green. The youngest foliage is pink, and some pink tinging often remains on the older leaves. Shiny, red-brown or purplish branches are interesting punctuation marks in this mass of light color. When the plant is trained as a standard and clipped, the foliage looks almost like a pale, fluffy ball. S. integra "Hakuro-nishiki" is best on deep, moisture-retentive soil; in drier conditions it needs some shade and shelter.
also for: ■ Heavy, clay soils ■ Damp and wet soils ■ Growing in containers

Lonicera nitida
e.g. "Silver Beauty"
[boxleaf honeysuckle]
○◐

type of plant: hardy shrub [7–9]
height: 3–5ft/0.9–1.5m
Evergreen ♀✂

Giving an impression of grayness overall, the numerous, slender leaves of this shrub are dark green with white margins. The individual leaves are very small (about ½in/1cm long). They are neatly arranged in fan-like sprays on arching branches. Especially when young, L. nitida "Silver Beauty" is spreading and sometimes almost prostrate. It builds up into a fairly open mass of growth with an irregular outline, but it can be clipped to form a finely textured hedge and it can be used for topiary. It is not fussy about soil, provided conditions are not either wet or very dry. Plants used for hedging should be about 12in/30cm apart.
also for: ■ Atmospheric pollution ■ Hedging plants

Phalaris arundinacea var. picta "Picta" (syn. *P.a.* "Elegantissima") [gardeners' garters]

type of plant: hardy perennial (grass) [4–9]
flowering time: early to midsummer
flower color: cream
height: 36in/90cm

Before the slim flower heads of this grass mature, the arching leaves are crisply and cleanly striped in bands of rich green and white; later they become less distinctly variegated. However, cutting the plant right back some time in summer encourages fresh, new growth with clear markings. During autumn the foliage turns an attractive, pale buff color. In most garden soils, this is a vigorous, often invasive plant, and in rich, damp soil the running roots spread very widely indeed. *P. arundinacea* var. *picta* "Feesey" is a less vigorous variety with a higher proportion of white in each leaf. Both these dense, spreading grasses can be grown in very shallow water.
also for: ■ Damp and wet soils ■ Ground cover ■ Colorful, autumn foliage

Symphytum x uplandicum (syn. *S. peregrinum*) "Variegatum" [comfrey]

type of plant: hardy perennial [5–9]
flowering time: late spring to early summer
flower color: lilac-pink changing to blue
height: 36in/90cm; foliage height 12in/30cm
Evergreen/Semi-evergreen

The basal leaves of this plant are big, bold and hairy. Each gray-green leaf may be more than 12in/30cm long, and it has a generous, pale cream margin. Clusters of ¾in/2cm-long, tubular flowers are carried on erect stems. If, after flowering, the plant is cut right back, then a second crop of large, basal leaves is produced. However, some gardeners prefer to pinch out the flowering stems before they develop. Foliage quality and general growth are best in soil that remains moist throughout the growing season. *S.* "Goldsmith" is also available. Its leaves are edged in yellow. Unlike some of their green-leaved relations, these plants are vigorous but not invasive.
also for: ■ Heavy, clay soils ■ Ground cover

Physostegia virginiana subsp. speciosa "Variegata" [obedient plant]

type of plant: hardy perennial [4–8]
flowering time: early autumn
flower color: bright lilac-pink
height: 30–36in/75–90cm

The common name of this perennial refers to the fact that the individual flowers stay "put" when moved to a new position. These tubular blooms are borne in neat spikes on erect stems. At least as attractive as the flowers are the leaves of this variety. They are generally narrow, about 4in/10cm long, and grayish green with broad margins of pale cream. *P. virginiana* subsp. *speciosa* "Variegata" does not perform well in soil that becomes dry in summer, but in rich, moist conditions the spreading roots may become mildly invasive.
also for: ■ Flowers suitable for cutting

Hosta fortunei var. aureomarginata (syn. *H.* "Obscura Marginata," *H.* "Yellow Edge") [plantain lily]

type of plant: hardy perennial [3–9]
flowering time: midsummer
flower color: violet
height: 30in/75cm

Provided this popular and reliable hosta has moist soil, it can be grown with equal success in sun or light shade. Its bold, pointed leaves, up to 10in/25cm long, are more or less heart-shaped. They have margins of light greenish yellow around central areas of rich, soft green. The variegation is maintained well into autumn (although in very strong sunlight the yellow margins may fade). As well as handsome, ribbed foliage, there are good heads of trumpet-shaped flowers. The dense clump of foliage produced by this plant is biggest and thickest—about 18in/45cm high by 36in/90cm wide—in rich, damp soil and a cool position. This is one of the more slug-resistant hostas.
also for: ■ Damp and wet soils ■ Ground cover

Lysimachia punctata "Alexander" [loosestrife]

type of plant: hardy perennial [4–8]
flowering time: mid- to late summer
flower color: bright yellow
height: 30in/75cm

When they first emerge, the pointed leaves of this bushy, upright plant are, briefly, a soft reddish pink. Soon, they are gray-green with broad, irregular margins of palest cream, giving a crisp, clean effect overall. The numerous cup-shaped flowers, about ¾in/2cm across, are carried close to the plant's stems and they are attractively interspersed with the variegated foliage. Almost any reasonably moisture-retentive soil is suitable for *L. punctata* "Alexander," although it is at its best in damp conditions. It is also suitable for wet ground. It is not as vigorous as the species (for which, see p74).
also for: ■ Heavy, clay soils ■ Damp and wet soils

Phlox paniculata "Norah Leigh"

type of plant: hardy perennial [4–8]
flowering time: late summer to early autumn
flower color: pale lilac-pink
height: 30in/75cm

The flower heads of this border phlox are gently colored and quite small, but the erect stems of conspicuously variegated foliage are certainly eye-catching. Each tapering leaf has a very broad and irregular margin of ivory around a central area of fairly deep green. Individual leaves are 3–4in/8–10cm long. *P. paniculata* "Harlequin" is a newer variety, with violet-purple flowers and creamy yellow variegation. Since *P.p.* "Norah Leigh" is not very vigorous, it needs a moist, well-drained, really fertile soil to look its best. The flowers of both *P.p.* "Norah Leigh" and *P.p.* "Harlequin" have a sweet scent, but neither of them is a particularly fragrant variety.
also for: ■ Flowers suitable for cutting ■ Fragrant flowers (see above)

Iris pseudacorus "Variegata"
[yellow flag]
○◐

type of plant: hardy perennial [5–9]
flowering time: early summer
flower color: yellow + brown
height: 24–36in/60–90cm
✂

Even when the light yellow-and-green variegation of this iris has faded to a soft mid-green (as it does gradually from flowering time onward), the sword-like shape and upright stance of the leaves continue to look striking. The flowers, each 3–4in/8–10cm across, tend to mingle with—rather than rise above—the plant's foliage. *I. pseudacorus* "Variegata" is very adaptable: it grows well in damp or wet soil, in shallow water (up to 10in/25cm deep) and in ordinary, moisture-retentive soil. The wetter and richer the growing conditions, the taller the plant is. *I. laevigata* "Variegata" is another moisture-loving, variegated iris. Its flowers are blue and the stripes on its leaves are gray-green and white.
also for: ■ Damp and wet soils

Euonymus fortunei
e.g. "Emerald 'n' Gold"
○◐

type of plant: hardy shrub/climber [5–9]
height: 24in/60cm as a shrub; 6–8ft/1.8–2.4m
as a climber
Evergreen

Especially when this plant is grown in sun, the edges of its bright green leaves are a strong, clear yellow. In a sunny site there are also likely to be purplish pink tinges on the foliage in winter. Each leathery leaf is pointed, oval and 1–2in/2.5–5cm long. *E. fortunei* "Emerald 'n' Gold" is, at first, slow-growing. Its fairly erect shoots and dense foliage mound up into dense hummocks of growth 3–4ft/0.9–1.2m wide. In maturity, the plant may produce self-clinging, climbing shoots. *E.f.* Blondy is a newer cultivar with rich green leaves boldly splashed with creamy yellow, and there are many other varieties of *E. fortunei* (for examples, see pp.113 and 151). These shrubs grow in almost any soil and, although they do not require alkaline conditions, they are useful evergreens for shallow soils over chalk.
also for: ■ Atmospheric pollution ■ Ground cover ■ Climbing plants
■ Growing in containers

Molinia caerulea subsp. caerulea
"Variegata"
[purple moor grass]
○◐

type of plant: hardy perennial (grass) [5–9]
flowering time: late summer to early autumn
flower color: purplish
height: 24in/60cm

The slender, pointed leaves of this grass are, at first, erect. They then arch outward from the dense center of the plant and form tidy tussocks of growth 12in/30cm or so high. Each leaf is neatly and conspicuously striped in cream and mid-green. This decorative variegation remains fresh until well into autumn, when the foliage turns the color of parchment. There are sometimes purplish pink tinges on the leaves. Slender flower spikes, held well above the tussocks of foliage, ripen into straw-colored seedheads. Their pale stems turn yellow. Moist, preferably acid soil is most suitable for this grass, but it is easily grown anywhere that does not dry out in summer.
also for: ■ Colorful, autumn foliage ■ Ornamental fruit (seedheads)

Cotoneaster atropurpureus
"Variegatus"
(syn. *C. horizontalis* "Variegatus")
○◐

type of plant: hardy shrub [5–8]
flowering time: early summer
flower color: pink
height: 18–24in/45–60cm; 4–6ft/1.2–1.8m
against a wall

The gray-green, white-edged leaves of this cotoneaster are ¼in/0.5cm long; they turn deep pink and russety orange in autumn. Like the rather similar *C. horizontalis*, this plant has a fan-like arrangement of twigs and it too can be trained to spread up walls of any aspect, or its arching branches can be allowed to sprawl horizontally. It is, however, a much less vigorous, slower-growing plant. Its little, cup-shaped flowers are freely produced and very attractive to bees, but they are rarely followed by red berries. Any soil, as long as it is not waterlogged or very dry, suits this plant.
also for: ■ Climbing plants ■ Colorful, autumn foliage ■ Ornamental bark
or twigs

Persiciaria virginiana
(syn. *Polygonum virginianum*,
Tovara filiformis, T. virginiana)
Variegata Group "Painter's
Palette"
[knotweed, fleeceflower]
○◐

type of plant: hardy perennial [7–9]
height: 18–24in/45–60cm

It may be fairly late into growth in spring, but this bushy, clump-forming plant makes a mass of ground-covering leafiness that is colorful over a long period. The leaves are broad, pointed ovals, up to 6in/15cm long, with conspicuous, red-brown "V" marks on a background of cream and mainly mid-green marbling. The foliage is carried on upright, branching stems. Many gardeners like to remove the wispy, brown flowers that appear in late summer, since they feel they detract from the foliage. To prevent the leaves from wind damage, *P. virginiana* Variegata Group plants need a sheltered site and they require moist, fertile soil to grow well. *P. microcephala* "Red Dragon" has pale green and gray "V" marks on its red-purple leaves.
also for: ■ Ground cover

Arum italicum subsp. italicum "Marmoratum" (syn. A. italicum "Pictum")
○ ●

type of plant: hardy tuber [7–9]
flowering time: late spring
flower color: greenish cream
height: 15–24in/38–60cm
✄

This remarkable plant saves all its best efforts for late in the gardening year. From late summer, drumstick heads of poisonous, orange-red berries develop on thick, bare stems. Then, during autumn, exceptionally resilient, deep green, spear-shaped leaves emerge in succession and last until early the following summer. The leaves are largest and most luxuriant in shade (individual leaves can be well over 12in/30cm long), but the beautiful, pale veining is most prominent in sun. The cowl-shaped flowers are neither long-lived nor especially decorative. As long as the roots of the plant remain cool and moist, a sunny site is suitable. A. italicum subsp. italicum "Marmoratum" tolerates dry shade, but it is considerably smaller and less lush under such conditions.
also for: ■ Dry shade (see above) ■ Ornamental fruit

Hypericum x moserianum "Tricolor" (syn. H. x m. "Variegata") [St John's wort]
○ ●

type of plant: slightly tender/half-hardy shrub [9–10]
flowering time: midsummer to mid-autumn
flower color: yellow
height: 15–20in/38–50cm
Semi-evergreen

These leaves are variegated in a particularly pretty combination of cream, green, and pink, but some gardeners feel that the arrival of the cup-shaped, yellow flowers makes for an altogether too "busy" effect. H. x moserianum "Tricolor" needs a more sheltered site than other popular hypericums but it is not fussy about soil, as long as conditions are not very dry. Its slender, pointed leaves are about 2in/5cm long. They are carried on deep red, arching branches, at the tips of which the flowers appear. When growing well this rounded shrub can make good ground cover. It is normally a little wider than it is tall. In cold regions this plant may die back each winter.
also for: ■ Growing in containers ■ Long, continuous flowering period

Vinca major "Variegata" (syn. V.m. "Elegantissima") [greater periwinkle]
○ ◐ ●

type of plant: hardy shrub [7–9]
flowering time: mainly mid-spring to early summer
flower color: lavender-blue
height: 12–18in/30–45cm
Evergreen ✄

V. major "Variegata" puts up with many difficulties. However, leaf color and flowering are best in well-lit positions and not too dry soil. The plant forms a rather bumpy, ground-covering mass of broadly oval, pointed leaves on stems that are either erect and flowering or long and trailing. These longer, flowerless stems root as they spread and established plants can be more than 3–4ft/0.9–1.2m wide. The glossy green leaves, to 2½in/6cm long, have conspicuous margins which are, at first, creamy yellow and then white. V.m. "Maculata" has yellow marbling in the centres of its leaves.
also for: ■ Dry shade ■ Dense shade ■ Atmospheric pollution ■ Ground cover

Hakonechloa macra "Aureola"
○ ●

type of plant: hardy perennial (grass) [6–9]
height: 12–15in/30–38cm

The arching leaves of this slow-growing grass overlap densely to form mounds of weed-suppressing growth about 18in/45cm wide. Each tapered leaf is randomly striped and is approximately 10in/25cm long. In shade, the coloring is predominantly lime-green, with dark green stripes; in sunnier positions, it is dark green and strong yellow. Cool autumn weather produces a suffusion of pink or red in the foliage. From late summer there may be tiny, bronze-purple flowers (some are visible in this mid-autumn photograph), but they are rather eclipsed by the bright foliage. H. macra "Aureola" thrives and spreads slowly in moist, fertile soil with good drainage.
also for: ■ Ground cover

Carex oshimensis "Evergold" (syn. C. hachijoensis "Evergold," C. morrowii "Evergold") [sedge]
○ ●

type of plant: hardy perennial [7–9]
height: 12in/30cm
Evergreen

In sun, the 12in/30cm-long, elegantly arching leaves of C. oshimensis "Evergold" have pale yellow central stripes and deep green margins. In light shade, the central stripes are creamier and the variegation is less pronounced. The plant forms a mound of growth about 15in/38cm wide. It thrives in moist but well-drained soil that is moderately fertile. (Its brown, short-stalked flowers appear in spring and are of minimal interest.) Other popular, variegated sedges include the variety shown on p.66. C. morrowii "Variegata" and C. siderosticha "Variegata" are further examples. Both these plants have white-variegated leaves.
also for: ■ Ground cover

Liriope muscari
e.g. "Variegata"
[lilyturf]
○◐

type of plant: hardy perennial [6–10]
flowering time: late summer to late autumn
flower color: mauve
height: 9–12in/23–30cm
Evergreen

Each slender, arching leaf of this plant, 8in/20cm or so long, has distinct edges of pale cream either side of a central, rich green stripe. The overall impression is quite pale. The plant is less vigorous than the species (see p.83) but, even so, its dense tufts of foliage, each about 12in/30cm wide, make useful ground-cover. It prospers in most light, well-drained soils, as long as they are acid to neutral. It tolerates dry, shady conditions but, for the best foliage and the most numerous flower spikes, a reasonably sunny site and not too dry a soil should be provided. *L.m.* "Gold-banded" and *L.m.* "John Burch" are two varieties with yellow-striped leaves.
also for: ■ Acid soils ■ Dry shade ■ Ground cover ■ Long, continuous flowering period

Holcus mollis "Albovariegatus"
○◐

type of plant: hardy perennial (grass) [5–9]
height: 6–9in/15–23cm
Evergreen

The running roots of this grass can spread very widely. Each of the erect, velvety leaves has a thin, central stripe of soft green and broader margins of palest cream. From a distance, a patch of this creeping, mat-forming grass looks like a small, white lawn. The greenish, summer flowers are not very numerous or decorative. It is best to remove them by clipping the plant lightly. If allow to set seed, *H. mollis* "Albovariegatus" produces offspring that are uniformly green-leaved and extremely invasive. For good, dense, ground-covering growth, this plant needs moisture-retentive but well-drained soil.
also for: ■ Ground cover

Barbarea vulgaris "Variegata"
[variegated winter cress]
○◐

type of plant: hardy biennial/perennial [5–9]
height: 6in/15cm foliage height; 12–18in/30–45cm flower height

Variegated winter cress usually comes true from seed. However, if the flowers are pinched out (preferably before they start to develop and certainly before they set seed), then the plant is longer-lived and there are larger quantities of foliage. Each rich green, lobed leaf usually has numerous creamy yellow markings of various sorts. The basal leaves, about 5in/12cm long, form rosettes of growth. The foliage is edible and has a peppery taste. If the branched heads of little, yellow flowers are allowed to mature in summer, the plant is biennial and dies after flowering. Plants are lushest and leafiest in rich, moist soil.

Ajuga reptans
e.g. "Burgundy Glow"
[bugle]
○◐

type of plant: hardy perennial [4–9]
flowering time: late spring to early summer
flower color: rich blue
height: 4–6in/10–15cm
Evergreen/Semi-evergreen

The basic gray-green of this bugle's foliage is heavily overlaid with a mixture of pink and clear wine-red. The edges of the leaves are pale cream. Leaf color is richest in sunny sites and on the new growth produced just after flowering time; it is gentler and grayer in some shade. In soil that retains moisture easily, *A. reptans* "Burgundy Glow" makes excellent ground cover and spreads into dense carpets of growth more than 24in/60cm wide. *A.r.* "Multicolor" (syn. "Rainbow") also has richly colored, variegated leaves (the dark bronze foliage is splashed with yellow, pink, and red). The flowers of both these plants are arranged in erect spikes up to 6in/15cm long; the leaves are oval and 2–3in/5–8cm long. For a variegated bugle of less exuberant coloring, see p.178.
also for: ■ Heavy, clay soils ■ Ground cover

ADDITIONAL PLANTS, featured elsewhere in this book, that have variegated leaves

○◐ sun or partial shade

minimum height 10ft/3m or more
Euonymus fortunei "Emerald Gaiety," see p.113
Euonymus fortunei "Silver Queen," see p.151

minimum height between 3ft/90cm and 10ft/3m
Ampelopsis brevipedunculata var. *maximowiczii* "Elegans," see p.134
Aucuba japonica "Variegata," see p.150
Cotoneaster atropurpureus "Variegatus," see p.174
Euonymus fortunei "Emerald 'n' Gold," see p.174
Hedera helix "Oro di Bogliasco," see p.133

minimum height 3ft/90cm or less
Euonymus fortunei "Emerald Gaiety," see p.113
Euonymus fortunei "Silver Queen," see p.151
Hedera colchica "Dentata Variegata," see p.171
Heuchera "Stormy Seas," see p.114
Sasa veitchii, see p.113
Vinca minor "Argenteovariegata," see p.118

Pieris japonica
e.g. "Variegata"
◐[○] ✱

type of plant: hardy shrub [6–9]
flowering time: early to mid-spring
flower color: white
height: 6–8ft/1.8–2.4m
Evergreen ✂

Unlike some pieris, *P. japonica* "Variegata" does not have very colorful young foliage (the new leaves are only lightly tinged with pink). Nor are its drooping sprays of tiny flowers especially numerous. But its slender, gray-green leaves, up to 2½in/6cm long, are narrowly edged in pale cream, and this is an attractive combination of colors. It is important that this dense, rounded and slow-growing plant has a sheltered site, since the leaves and the flowers can be damaged by frost and wind. It must also have moist but well-drained, lime-free soil. A newer variety —*P.* "Flaming Silver"—produces colorful, red new growths as well as variegated foliage. It grows very slowly and is smaller than *P. japonica* "Variegata."
also for: ■ Acid soils

Kerria japonica "Picta"
(syn. *K.j.* "Variegata")
◐[○]

type of plant: hardy shrub [5–9]
flowering time: mid- to late spring
flower color: yellow
height: 3–4ft/0.9–1.2m

Smaller and less floriferous than the familiar, double-flowered variety of *K. japonica* (see p.289), *K.j.* "Picta" has very pretty, rather pale foliage. Each sharply toothed, tapering leaf is about 1½in/4cm long, with a narrow, creamy white margin surrounding a gray-green, central area. The slender, smooth, green twigs are conspicuous and attractive in winter. They form the basis of a dense, wispy mass of growth that is, in maturity, wider than it is tall. Easily grown in many types of soil, this variegated kerria produces foliage that looks fresh and dainty over a long period, especially when the plant is given a lightly shaded position in not too exposed a site. The flowers are single, buttercup-like and approximately 1in/2.5cm wide.
also for: ■ Heavy, clay soils ■ Ornamental bark or twigs

Hosta fortunei var. albopicta
[plantain lily]
◐[○]

type of plant: hardy perennial [3–9]
flowering time: midsummer
flower color: pale lilac
height: 30in/75cm
✂

As long as there is plenty of moisture, this very popular hosta can be grown in a sunny position. Before the long stalks of funnel-shaped flowers appear, each leaf is a beautiful, buttery yellow edged in dark and light green. Even when the variegation of the broad, ribbed leaves softens, after flowering time, to two tones of green, the foliage continues to look handsome. Individual leaves are up to 9in/23cm long. Grown in deep, fertile soil that is always moist, *H. fortunei* var. *albopicta* forms a substantial, ground-covering clump of leaves about 24in/60cm high and up to 36in/90cm wide. *H.* "Gold Standard" is a readily available variety of somewhat similar coloring. Its greenish yellow leaves are edged in rich green.
also for: ■ Damp and wet soils ■ Ground cover

Lunaria annua (syn. *L. biennis*)
var. *albiflora* "Alba Variegata"
[honesty]
◐[○]

type of plant: hardy biennial [6–9]
flowering time: late spring to midsummer
flower color: white
height: 30in/75cm

This variegated form of honesty produces the flat, translucent seed pods that are such familiar ingredients of dried arrangements. However, its broad, pointed, deep green leaves, edged and variably marked in white, are a good deal more striking than those of the plain-leaved species, particularly in spring and early summer when the variegation is boldest. Individual leaves are up to 6in/15cm long. *L. annua* var. *albiflora* "Variegata" also has foliage edged in white; its loose clusters of ½in/1cm-wide flowers are purplish crimson. Most well-drained soils are suitable for these upright, bushy plants, and they grow quite successfully in dry shade. They both self-sow.
also for: ■ Dry shade ■ Ornamental fruit (seed pods)

Scrophularia auriculata
(syn. *S. aquatica*) "Variegata"
[water betony, water figwort]
◐[○]

type of plant: hardy perennial (aquatic) [5–9]
height: 24–36in/60–90cm
Evergreen (basal leaves only)

If the tiny, brown flowers of this upright plant are removed just as they begin to develop, then the big, boldly marked leaves stay clearly variegated over a very long period and the whole plant remains tidy and relatively dense. As well as smaller leaves on the thick, stiff, square-sectioned stems, there are large basal leaves which are evergreen and up to 10in/25cm long. All the leaves are tapering ovals of light grayish green with broad and irregular edges of palest cream. *S. auriculata* "Variegata" grows especially well in dappled shade and thrives in rich, moist soil. It also flourishes in damp and boggy ground, and in water up to 6in/15cm deep.
also for: ■ Heavy, clay soils ■ Damp and wet soils

Hosta undulata var. undulata
[plantain lily]
◐[○]

type of plant: hardy perennial [3–9]
flowering time: early to midsummer
flower color: pale lilac
height: 24–30in/60–75cm
✂

The distinctively twisted or wavy leaves of *H. undulata* var. *undulata* are white-centered and irregularly margined in rich green. Each pointed leaf is approximately 6in/15cm long. As individual plants become older, the proportion of white in their leaves tends to lessen. This is not a vigorous hosta and its leaves are inclined to scorch in sun. It therefore needs moist, fertile soil for good growth and a reasonably sheltered site to insure that its leaves look their best. The funnel-shaped flowers are carried, on pale stalks, well above the tightly packed clump of foliage (which is 12–15in/30–38cm high and spreads about 18in/45cm wide).
also for: ■ Damp and wet soils ■ Ground cover

Saxifraga "Aureopunctata"
(syn. *S. umbrosa* "Variegata," *S.* x *urbium* "Aureopunctata")
[London pride]
◐[○]

type of plant: hardy perennial [6–9]
flowering time: late spring to early summer
flower color: pale pink
height: 9–12in/23–30cm
Evergreen

Although easily pleased by most soils and many sites, *S.* "Aureopunctata" is particularly at home in a cool place and well-drained but moisture-retentive soil. Its spoon-shaped, bright green, leathery leaves are flecked with yellow. They are arranged in rosettes about 3in/8cm wide. Variegation is most pronounced in sunny positions. The foliage forms dense carpets of neat growth and looks good between paving stones or as an edging to a path. Airy sprays of tiny, starry flowers are carried, on slender, reddish stems, well above the foliage.
also for: ■ Ground cover ■ Crevices in paving

Chiastophyllum oppositifolium
(syn. *C. simplicifolium, Cotyledon oppositifolia, C. simplicifolia*) "Jim's Pride" (syn. "Frosted Jade")
◐[○]

type of plant: hardy perennial [6–9]
flowering time: late spring to early summer
flower color: yellow
height: 4–6in/10–15cm
Evergreen

The neat, succulent foliage of this mat-forming plant is variegated in a most attractive color combination of cream and light grayish green. Older leaves are edged in cream, while the youngest growths are often entirely cream colored. Each rounded, undulating leaf is about 2in/5cm long, but leaf size varies considerably. Above the loose rosettes of foliage, reddish stems bear pendent, catkin-like flower sprays (for an illustration of which, see the green-leaved species on p.120). Cool, moist conditions are most suitable for *C. oppositifolium* "Jim's Pride" but it is easily grown in any soil that is reasonably well-drained and not too dry. Given adequate moisture, it tolerates sun.

Ajuga reptans
e.g. "Variegata"
[bugle]
◐[○]

type of plant: hardy perennial [4–9]
flowering time: late spring to early summer
flower color: light blue
height: 4in/10cm
Evergreen/Semi-evergreen

Less vigorous than most varieties of *A. reptans* (for further examples, see index of botanical names), this prettily variegated variety is still useful for ground-cover, as long as it has moist soil. It spreads slowly but surely and, when well suited, makes a close carpet of growth 12–18in/30–45cm wide; in drier, less favourable conditions it does not provide weed-proof cover. Its oval leaves, 1½–2in/4–5cm long, are gray-green with touches of creamy white. Some leaves are suffused with purplish pink. The leafy flower spikes, though not very freely produced, are a particularly attractive combination of light blue interspersed with gray and cream.
also for: ■ Heavy, clay soils ■ Ground cover

ADDITIONAL PLANTS, featured elsewhere in this book, that have variegated leaves

◐[○] partial shade (or sun)

minimum height 10ft/3m or more
Hedera canariensis "Gloire de Marengo," see p.136
Parthenocissus henryana, see p.180

minimum height between 3ft/90cm and 10ft/3m
Hedera helix "Glacier," see p.124

minimum height 3ft/90cm or less
Cyclamen hederifolium, see p.84
Hedera canariensis "Gloire de Marengo," see p.136

Hedera helix "Glacier," see p.124
x *Heucherella alba* "Rosalie," see p.295
Iris foetidissima "Variegata," see p.180
Phlox x *procumbens* "Variegata," see p.159
Pulmonaria longifolia, see p.180

Philadelphus coronarius
"Variegatus"
[mock orange]
◖
type of plant: hardy shrub [5–8]
flowering time: early summer
flower color: white
height: 6–8ft/1.8–2.4m
⚲✂

Reasonably moist soil and a sheltered, partially shaded position are needed to insure that the foliage of this mock orange does not become disfigured by drought or scorched by cold, dry winds or sun. Each tapering, 2in/5cm-long leaf is light green with a broad, creamy white margin. The white blossom, although not always produced in large quantities, adds to the pale and pretty appearance of this upright shrub. The flowers are cup-shaped, richly and sweetly scented, and each about 2.5cm/1in across. *P.* "Innocence" has dark green leaves variably marked with light yellow. Both these plants are fairly slow-growing.
also for: ■ Fragrant flowers

Hosta crispula
[plantain lily]
◖
type of plant: hardy perennial [3–9]
flowering time: early to midsummer
flower color: pale lavender
height: 30–36in/75–90cm
⚲✂

H. crispula is one of the most graceful variegated hostas. Its broad, wavy-edged leaves have elegantly tapering, slightly twisted tips. The basic leaf color is rich green; the irregular margins are white. Individual leaves can be 12in/30cm long. If it is not to end up looking rather battered, particularly after its trumpet-shaped flowers have faded, this hosta must have a position that is both shaded and sheltered. For really good growth it also needs a deep, rich soil that is always moist. It slowly makes a dense mass of leaves, about 24in/60cm high and 36in/90cm wide, above which rise the tall flower stems.
also for: ■ Damp and wet soils ■ Ground cover

Brunnera macrophylla
e.g. "Hadspen Cream"
◖
type of plant: hardy perennial [4–8]
flowering time: mid- to late spring
flower color: bright blue
height: 18in/45cm

There are a number of variegated forms of *B. macrophylla*, including this popular variety, which has leaves of light green edged in creamy yellow. All the varieties produce sprays of tiny, vivid blue flowers, each flower about ¼in/0.5cm across. Their individual leaves vary considerably in size, but they are usually about 6in/15cm long at flowering time. Other readily available brunneras with variegated foliage include *B.m.* "Dawson's White" (syn. "Variegata") with broad, white margins to its leaves, *B.m.* "Langtrees," which has leaf edges spotted with silvery gray, and *B.m.* "Jack Frost," the dark green leaves of which are conspicuously pale veined. The foliage of all these clump-forming plants, particularly of *B.m.* "Dawson's White," benefits from shelter, some shade and moist soil. These conditions minimize unsightly damage caused by the drying effects of sun, wind and dryness at the roots.
also for: ■ Heavy, clay soils

Erythronium californicum
"White Beauty"
(syn. *E. revolutum*
"White Beauty")
[dog's tooth violet, trout lily]
◖
type of plant: hardy bulb [5–9]
flowering time: mid- to late spring
flower color: palest cream
height: 9in/23cm

This much-admired plant usually increases into sizeable clumps if it is supplied with moist, humus-rich, well-drained soil and given a cool site. *E. californicum* "White Beauty" seems to be most at home in acid to neutral soil. Its 2–3in/5–8cm wide, lily-like flowers peer down above broad, light green leaves that are subtly marbled with pale green. *E.* "Pagoda" is another popular, vigorous dog's tooth violet; its flowers are pale yellow; its leaves are only faintly mottled.

Erythronium dens-canis
[dog's tooth violet, trout lily]
◖
type of plant: hardy bulb [3–8]
flowering time: mid-spring
flower color: purplish pink
height: 4–6in/10–15cm

Under the shade of tall, deciduous trees and in well-drained, humus-rich soil, dog's tooth violets may increase quite quickly. These charming plants are suitable for naturalizing in short, thin grass. Their 1¼in/3cm-long flowers, with their backswept petals, hang above pointed leaves, the markings and colors of which vary somewhat—although a combination of turquoise-green and purplish brown is common. There are several named forms of *E. dens-canis*, with flowers ranging in color from deep purple to pale pink and including white.

ADDITIONAL PLANTS, featured elsewhere in this book, that have variegated leaves

◖ partial shade

minimum height 3ft/90cm or less: *Hosta undulata* var. *albomarginata*, see p.79; *Luzula sylvatica* "Marginata," see p.121; *Trillium luteum*, see p.313

Parthenocissus henryana
(syn. *Vitis henryana*)
◐●[○]

type of plant: slightly tender/hardy climber [7–9]
height: 15–20ft/4.5–6m

Less overwhelmingly vigorous than some of its relations, *P. henryana* is decorative over a very long period. Not only do its shapely leaves turn rich red in autumn but they are also subtly variegated in spring and summer. Especially in shade, the veins of the leaves stand out in a beautiful silvery pattern. Each leaf is deeply divided into several lobes, which are 3–4in/ 8–10cm long. The young foliage is bronze. The basic color of the mature leaves varies somewhat from a rich soft green to a green suffused with reddish purple. Although this plant clings by means of adhesive tendrils, it is usually several years before it starts to climb strongly. It may be grown on a north wall, as long as this is not very cold and exposed. Well-drained but fairly moist, fertile soil is most suitable for this climber.
also for: ■ Atmospheric pollution ■ Climbing plants ■ Colorful, autumn foliage

Geranium phaeum var. phaeum
e.g. "Samobor"
[dusky cranesbill, mourning widow]
◐●

type of plant: hardy perennial [4–8]
flowering time: late spring
flower color: dark maroon
height: 24in/60cm
Semi-evergreen

Reminiscent of the foliage of some pelargoniums (or bedding "geraniums"), the lobed and veined leaves of this cranesbill have conspicuous, dark chocolate "horseshoes" that nearly match the color of the plant's nodding, ¾in/2cm-wide flowers. Each leaf is rounded, bright green and up to 6in/15cm across. The foliage forms clumps of growth. *G. phaeum* (see p.86) and its varieties are very tolerant plants; they do well in damp shade, but they grow in quite dry, shaded conditions too. Their flowers are very attractive to bees. Other variegated cranesbills include *G. phaeum* "Variegatum," which has pale cream markings and touches of crimson on its leaves, and *G. x monacense* var. *monacense* "Muldoon," which has chocolate-spotted leaves.
also for: ■ Damp and wet soils ■ Dry shade ■ Dense shade ■ Ground cover

Polygonatum x hybridum
"Striatum"
(syn. *P. x h.* "Variegatum")
[common Solomon's seal]
◐●

type of plant: hardy perennial [4–9]
flowering time: late spring
flower color: white + green
height: 24in/60cm

Each of this plant's gently curved stems has an almost horizontally held topping of wavy-edged, pointed leaves. The mid- to light green foliage is striped and edged in pale cream. From the undersides of the stems green-tipped, tubular flowers, ½in/1cm long, dangle prettily. For gardeners who find this stripy variegation slightly too "busy," there are the leaves of *P. odoratum* var. *pluriflorum* "Variegatum" (syn. *P. falcatum* "Variegatum") on which only the edges are cream colored. Both these plants need a cool, shaded site and moist, humus-rich soil for there to be plenty of good-quality foliage. Although they are both moderately vigorous, they do not tolerate dry and dense shade as successfully as *P. x hybridum* (see p.295).

Iris foetidissima "Variegata"
[stinking gladwyn, stinking iris]
◐●[○]

type of plant: hardy perennial [7–9]
height: 18in/45cm
Evergreen

Throughout the year these long, pointed leaves look clean and crisp. Each gray-green leaf has a very pale cream stripe down one side—the shadier the site, the paler the variegation. The foliage, which smells of roast beef when cut, is arranged in fans and, as the leaves lengthen, they arch. Moist soil and shade encourage the most luxuriant growth, but the plant is very easily pleased and copes well with, for instance, shallow, chalky soils and dry shade. It forms slowly increasing clumps of growth. *I. foetidissima* itself (see p.261) produces very striking berries, but *I.f.* "Variegata" rarely bears flowers or fruits.
also for: ■ Shallow soils over chalk ■ Dry shade

Pulmonaria longifolia
[lungwort]
◐●[○]

type of plant: hardy perennial [5–8]
flowering time: mid- to late spring
flower color: rich bright blue
height: 12in/30cm

The long, narrow leaves of *P. longifolia* are an excellent deep green, against which their white spotting and spattering is particularly eye-catching. Individual leaves may be as much as 18in/45cm long, especially when the plant is grown in moist, fertile soil and a shaded, sheltered site. As well as clumps of handsome foliage, there are dense bunches of small, funnel-shaped, intensely blue flowers. *P. longifolia* is more sun-tolerant than most lungworts, but its wonderful flower color is longer-lasting in shade. Among the varieties of this plant, *P.l.* "Bertram Anderson" is outstanding for its well-marked, strikingly shaped leaves and vivid flower color.
also for: ■ Heavy, clay soils

Pulmonaria saccharata
Argentea Group
[lungwort]
◖●

type of plant: hardy perennial [4–8]
flowering time: early to mid-spring
flower color: red changing to violet-blue
height: 9–12in/23–30cm
Evergreen/Semi-evergreen

Plants in *P. saccharata* Argentea Group vary in just how heavily marked their leaves are, but the foliage of most specimens is more or less entirely pale silvery green. The rough, pointed leaves are large—nearly 12in/30cm long—and, especially in a cool, shady place and moist, fertile soil, they make good, ground-covering clumps of growth. The funnel-shaped flowers are small and carried in little clusters. There are several varieties of *P. saccharata* which differ from one another in the color of their flowers and in how heavily spotted their leaves are.
also for: ■ Heavy, clay soils ■ Ground cover

Pulmonaria rubra "David Ward"
[lungwort]
◖●

type of plant: hardy perennial [5–8]
flowering time: late winter to early spring
flower color: coral-pink
height: 9in/23cm
Evergreen

For gardeners who find the splotchiness of some lungwort leaves unattractive, there is this neatly variegated foliage in an especially pretty combination of pale sage-green and white. At flowering time the velvety, tapering leaves are 3–4in/8–10cm long. They expand fully as the clusters of ½in/1cm-wide, funnel-shaped flowers fade. Unfortunately, this most attractive foliage is easily scorched if *P. rubra* "David Ward" is exposed to too much sun or wind. In a cool, sheltered place and moisture-retentive soil the plant thrives and produces plenty of fresh, pretty leaves.
also for: ■ Heavy, clay soils ■ Ground cover ■ Winter-flowering plants

Pachysandra terminalis
"Variegata"
[Japanese spurge]
◖●

type of plant: hardy perennial/shrub [6–9]
height: 6in/15cm
Evergreen

The slightly twisted, grayish green leaves of this plant are neatly margined in creamy white. They cover the ground as effectively as the green foliage of *P. terminalis* itself (see p.123), but the plant is less vigorous and spreads more slowly. The diamond-shaped leaves are arranged in whorls, about 4in/10cm wide, at the erect tips of sprawling stems. Provided it has some shade and a soil that is not very alkaline, *P.t.* "Variegata" grows satisfactorily in many sites, including dry places under trees. However, it really thrives in moisture-retentive, humus-rich soil. Its spikes of rather inconspicuous, off-white flowers appear in spring. They have a slight, sweet scent.
also for: ■ Acid soils ■ Dry shade ■ Ground cover

Lamium maculatum
e.g. "White Nancy"
[spotted deadnettle]
◖●

type of plant: hardy perennial [4–9]
flowering time: mid-spring to early summer
flower color: white
height: 5–8in/12–20cm
Semi-evergreen

Each of these 1½in/4cm-long, heart-shaped leaves is completely silvered except for a thin margin of green. Instead of the usual spikes of purplish or pink, lipped blooms, this variety of *L. maculatum* has white flowers. The overall effect is remarkably pale, and so this is a very useful small plant for enlivening the gloom of densely shaded places in particular. It makes excellent, carpeting ground cover in a cool place and moist, well-drained soil; in drier conditions it is inclined to become patchy and *L.m.* "Beacon Silver" (see p.84) is a better choice for dry shade. The leaves of *L.m.* "Pink Pewter" resemble those of *L.m.* "White Nancy"; the flowers are pink.
also for: ■ Heavy, clay soils ■ Dense shade ■ Ground cover

ADDITIONAL PLANTS, featured elsewhere in this book, that have variegated leaves

◖● partial or full shade

minimum height 10ft/3m or more
Euonymus fortunei "Emerald Gaiety," see p.113
Euonymus fortunei "Silver Queen," see p.151
Hedera canariensis "Gloire de Marengo," see p.136

minimum height between 3ft/90cm and 10ft/3m
Buxus sempervirens "Aureovariegata," see p.172
Hedera helix "Glacier," see p.124

minimum height 3ft/90cm or less
Aegopodium podagraria "Variegatum," see p.122
Euonymus fortunei "Emerald Gaiety," see p.113
Euonymus fortunei "Silver Queen," see p.151
Hedera canariensis "Gloire de Marengo," see p.136
Hedera helix "Glacier," see p.124

Lamium galeobdolon "Hermann's Pride," see p.83
Lamium maculatum "Beacon Silver," see p.84
Lamium maculatum "Roseum," see p.124
Podophyllum hexandrum, see p.261
Pulmonaria "Sissinghurst White," see p.123
Sasa veitchii, see p.113
Tolmiea menziesii "Taff's Gold," see p.123
Vinca major "Variegata," see p.175

Gray, blue-gray, or silver leaves

OF ALL THE PLANTS with foliage that is regarded as unusual, those with gray leaves enjoy the most widespread popularity. As well as a few slightly less common plants and some recent introductions, this book features many gray-leaved plants that, in one form or other, have been popular for generations. There are, for example, favorite cottage garden plants, such as lavenders (*Lavandula*) and carnations (*Dianthus*), dusty miller (*Lychnis coronaria*), catmint (*Nepeta* x *faassenii*), and lambs' ears (*Stachys byzantina*). On a larger scale, plants such as the blue Atlas cedar (*Cedrus atlantica* Glauca Group) and the willow-leaved pear (*Pyrus salicifolia* "Pendula") have long been admired.

A fairly wide range of foliage colors are included under the general heading of this list. Many gray leaves are, in fact, a grayish green of some sort, while foliage of a really pale, almost white-gray is usually described as silver. An element of gray is also present in plants described as "blue," such as the various "blue" conifers, blue fescue (*Festuca glauca*) and its varieties, and blue oat grass (*Helictotrichon sempervirens*). Some gray-leaved plants are a very subtle mixture of colors: *Rosa glauca*'s leaves, for example, are a smoky blend of gray and plum.

What all these different and sometimes elusive colors have in common is an ability to lighten and brighten. However, gray leaves need to be used carefully: since gray is an inert color, plantings with a preponderance of gray can end up looking flat and lifeless, and pale gray foliage in particular can be so eye-catching that it eclipses everything around it.

Nevertheless, when used with discretion, gray or grayish leaves are a useful source of contrast in planting schemes. Gray foliage also makes pale colors still more delicate and dark, rich colors richer and more glowing. It emphasizes the "heat" of radiant oranges and reds and it combines flatteringly with cool blues and icy whites.

It is not only the coloring of gray or grayish leaves that makes them attractive and useful but also the considerable variety in their size, texture, and shape. Size of leaf varies from about 36in/90cm long (see *Cynara cardunculus*) to the tiny, needle-like leaves of various conifers and the much-divided, wispy or feathery foliage of plants such as *Artemisia schmidtiana* "Nana" and *Santolina pinnata* subsp. *neapolitana*. The texture of many gray leaves is hairy (see, for example, *Stachys byzantina* and *Ballota pseudodictamnus*) or silky (see *Convolvulus cneorum*). In contrast, some gray foliage—that of the sedums, for example—is succulent and smooth, while most of the blue-gray conifers and grasses have leaves that feel hard and dry.

Among all these gray, blue, and silver leaves of different sizes and textures are many different leaf shapes. There are leaves that are sword-shaped (see *Astelia chathamica* and *Sisyrinchium striatum*), paddle-shaped (*Othonna cheirifolia*), feather-like (*Tanacetum haradjanii*), or almost circular (*Eucalyptus gunnii*).

There is, in addition, considerable variation in plant habit, from the strikingly slim and upright (see, for example, *Juniperus scopulorum* "Skyrocket") to the almost flat and mat-like (see *Thymus pseudolanuginosus* and *Raoulia australis*) with plenty of mounds, clumps, tufts, and sprawling masses in between.

Choosing gray-leaved plants for sunny sites and for hot, dry conditions is easy and anyone planning a gravel garden or some other planting scheme for an arid site will find that many of the most suitable plants have gray foliage. The choice for moister positions is more restricted, but it does include plants such as *Salix lanata*, *Anaphalis triplinervis*, and *Lysimachia ephemerum*. For moister, shadier places there are, for example, handsome hostas and ferny-leaved dicentras. Additional plants that give a grayish effect and that like cool, moist conditions include perennials such as *Pulmonaria saccharata* Argentea Group and *Lamium maculatum* "White Nancy," both of which produce leaves that are very heavily marked with white.

Cedrus atlantica
Glauca Group
[blue Atlas cedar]
○

type of plant: hardy conifer [6–9]
height: 80ft/24m
Evergreen

As young trees, these conifers are of a rather narrow pyramidal shape, but they broaden very considerably as they age. Their beautiful, silvery blue foliage consists of 1in/2.5cm-long needles arranged in dense whorls. The upright, barrel-shaped cones are blue-gray when immature and, on older trees especially, they are not immediately visible among the upper branches. *C. atlantica* "Glauca Pendula" also has silvery blue leaves; it slowly forms an exceptionally wide-spreading, weeping tree roughly 15–20ft/4.5–6m high. These cedars grow in well-drained soils of all types, including chalky and limy soils, but they live longest when the soil depth is good.
also for: ■ Ornamental fruit

Populus alba
[white poplar]
○

type of plant: hardy tree [3–9]
height: 60–70ft/18–21m

This fast-growing, suckering tree has a domed, open head. It often grows at an angle, and sometimes produces several main stems (when it is rather smaller than indicated here). The leaves, up to 4in/10cm long, are usually lobed. The all-white, young foliage matures to dark gray-green above and white below; in autumn, the leaves turn yellow. In hot climates the bark is pale, silvery gray. *P. alba* is very wind-tolerant, and it adapts to a wide range of soils. Its long, shallow roots can damage buildings and drains.
also for: ■ Shallow soils over chalk ■ Heavy, clay soils ■ Damp and wet soils ■ Windswept, seaside gardens ■ Atmospheric pollution ■ Colorful, autumn foliage ■ Ornamental bark or twigs (see above)

Picea pungens
e.g. "Koster"
[Colorado spruce]
○

type of plant: hardy conifer [3–9]
height: 30–40ft/9–12m

Overall, this conifer is narrowly conical to columnar, but it usually has an irregular outline, partly because some of the main branches grow horizontally, while others are more upright. Both the color and the arrangement of the foliage are striking. The palest, bluest foliage is produced on the youngest shoots; older leaves are darker and more nearly green. The leaves are stiff, sharp needles, each about 1in/2.5cm long, and they are arranged in stout whorls on the russet stems. *P. pungens* "Koster" and other silvery blue varieties of *Picea pungens* (such as *P.p.* "Hoopsii," which has denser and brighter blue foliage) need deep, moist, preferably acid to neutral soil and, ideally, shelter.
also for: ■ Acid soils

Pyrus salicifolia "Pendula"
[willow-leaved pear]
○

type of plant: hardy tree [5–9]
flowering time: mid-spring
flower color: white
height: 15–20ft/4.5–6m

The stiffly pendent branches of this dome-shaped tree are covered in slender, willow-like leaves, up to 3½in/9cm long. The foliage is very pale and silvery in spring; by midsummer the upper surface of each leaf has become gray-green. Clusters of saucer-shaped flowers appear alongside the silky-haired young leaves. This tough and vigorous tree does well in any reasonably well-drained, fertile soil.
also for: ■ Atmospheric pollution

Verbascum olympicum
[mullein]
○

type of plant: hardy perennial/biennial [6–9]
flowering time: midsummer to early autumn
flower color: yellow
height: 6ft/1.8m

Often dying after flowering, this impressive plant produces a great, branched flower stem above its huge rosette of woolly, silvery gray foliage. The leaves, which can be as much as 24in/60cm long, are broad and pointed. The flower stem is studded with clusters of saucer-shaped flowers and it too is pale and woolly. Rather poor, preferably alkaline soils with good drainage are most suitable for *V. olympicum*, which thrives in a dry spot. The biennial, yellow-flowered *V. bombyciferum* has similar, large, felted leaves which are gray-white. Both these plants self-sow.
also for: ■ Shallow soils over chalk ■ Dry soils in hot, sunny sites ■ Long, continuous flowering period

Cynara cardunculus
[cardoon]
○

type of plant: hardy/slightly tender perennial [7–9]
flowering time: early to midsummer
flower color: purple
height: 5–8ft/1.5–2.4m

Each of these huge, jagged, silvery leaves may be 36in/90cm or more long. Gardeners who grow cardoon for its foliage alone remove the emerging flower stalks. When prevented from flowering, the plant forms a clump of foliage 4–5ft/1.2–1.5m high and as much across. However, when this perennial is left to its own devices, it produces impressive, thistle-like flowers. These are attractive to bees, and make good if rather prickly material for dried arrangements. Fertile, well-drained soil that is also reasonably moisture-retentive gives the best results. Young specimens of cardoon may need protection, especially in their first winter.
also for: ■ Flowers suitable for cutting (mainly drying)

Onopordum acanthium
[cotton thistle, Scotch thistle]
○

type of plant: hardy biennial/perennial [6–10]
flowering time: mid- to summer
flower color: pinkish purple
height: 1.5–2.4m/5–8ft
✂

O. acanthium is popular with flower arrangers both for its very prickly flowers and for its pale gray leaves. The latter are large (usually at least 18in/45cm long, often much more), wavy-edged, pointed, and covered in cobwebby hairs. They form a rosette at the base of the plant, as well as clothing the stout, branching flower-stalks. Each flower head is up to 2in/5cm across and typically Scotch thistle in shape. Any well-drained soil is suitable, but fertile conditions produce the largest and most imposing plants. If prevented from flowering, this plant is perennial—although short-lived—and its leaves are particularly large.
also for: ■ Flowers suitable for cutting

Astelia chathamica
(syn. *A.c.* "Silver Spear")
○

type of plant: slightly tender/half-hardy perennial [9–10]
height: 4–5ft/1.2–1.5m
Evergreen

The young foliage of this clump-forming perennial is erect and of a dramatically bright and metallic silver. As they age, the eye-catching, sword-shaped leaves, each of which may be more than 5ft/1.5m long, become greener and more arching. There are clusters of tiny, greenish or reddish flowers, but these are more or less hidden at the base of the leaves. However, on female plants that have been fertilized by male plants, the flowers are followed by bright orange berries which ripen from late summer onward. *A. chathamica* needs open-textured, acid soil that does not dry out.
also for: ■ Acid soils ■ Ornamental fruit (see above)

Brachyglottis (Dunedin Group) "Sunshine"
(syn. *Senecio grayi, S. laxifolius*)
○

type of plant: hardy shrub/slightly tender [8–10]
flowering time: early to midsummer
flower color: yellow
height: 3–4ft/0.9–1.2m
Evergreen ✂

When pruned fairly hard, this rather lax shrub forms dense mounds of gray-green foliage. Each oval leaf is 2½–3in/6–8cm long, white-felted beneath, and with a very thin, white margin. The foliage is carried on pale green, slightly curving stems; it is very long-lasting when cut. The "daisies," which are also pale stemmed, are silvery in bud. *B.* "Sunshine" grows successfully in exposed maritime areas, where it can be used for informal hedging (plants should be about 24in/60cm apart). This fairly adaptable shrub is at its best in well-drained soil and full sun. It thrives in mild, moist climates.
also for: ■ Windswept, seaside gardens ■ Atmospheric pollution ■ Ground cover ■ Hedging plants

Eucalyptus gunnii
[cider gum]
○

type of plant: slightly tender shrub [7–9]
flowering time: mid- to late summer
flower color: white or cream
height: 3–4ft/0.9–1.2m grown as a shrub for its juvenile foliage (see description)
Evergreen ✂

If it is pruned very hard every year, cider gum develops a bushy mass of shoots and produces only juvenile leaves, which are almost circular, 1½–2in/4–5cm across, and usually bright silvery blue. They make really long-lasting material for cutting. Unpruned plants very quickly form slender, open-headed trees, 50–70ft/15–21m high, with lance-shaped, sage-green leaves and peeling, pale greenish cream and brownish gray bark. Mature trees bear clusters of prominently stamened flowers. Moist but well-drained soil that is acid to neutral is most suitable. The plants need shelter. *E. perriniana* [zones 8–9] also has silvery blue, rounded, juvenile leaves.
also for: ■ Acid soils ■ Atmospheric pollution ■ Ornamental bark or twigs

Euphorbia characias subsp. *wulfenii*
[spurge]
○

type of plant: slightly tender/hardy shrub/perennial [7–10]
flowering time: mid-spring to early summer
flower color: yellow-green
height: 3–4ft/0.9–1.2m
Evergreen ✂

This erect, clump-forming subshrub produces bold, blue-green "bottle-brushes" of foliage, and its broad, cylindrical heads of little, cup-shaped flowers may be up to 12in/30cm long. It needs good drainage, shelter from winds and some warmth. (In really mild areas it can be grown in light shade.) Both the foliage and the flowers are popular for cutting, but take care, since the milky juices from the cut stems can irritate eyes and skin. Varieties with particularly glaucous leaves include *E. characias* "Blue Wonder" and *E.c.* "Portuguese Velvet"; *E.c.* subsp. *characias* "Humpty Dumpty" is low growing.
also for: ■ Dry soils in hot, sunny sites ■ Flowers suitable for cutting ■ Green flowers ■ Long, continuous flowering period

Helictotrichon sempervirens
(syn. *Avena candida*)
[blue oat grass]
○

type of plant: hardy perennial [4–9]
flowering time: early to midsummer
flower color: blue-tinged pale yellow
height: 3–4ft/0.9–1.2m
Evergreen ✂

The numerous, very thin leaves of blue oat grass are vivid blue-gray. They arch slightly, forming a dense, interestingly textured clump of growth that is approximately 18in/45cm high. Above this rise stiff stems, topped with slender, plume-like flower heads. The leaf color is most intense on plants grown in really well-drained soils. For a smaller grass of similar coloring, see p.188.
also for: ■ Shallow soils over chalk ■ Dry soils in hot, sunny sites

Kniphofia caulescens
[red-hot poker, torch flower]
○

type of plant: hardy perennial [6–9]
flowering time: late summer to early autumn
flower color: soft red fading to yellow
height: 3–4ft/0.9–1.2m
Evergreen

Not only does this unusually hardy *Kniphofia* produce dramatic, thick-stalked flower spikes, but it also has long, arching, strap-shaped leaves of a striking blue-gray. These leaves are arranged in great tufts that arise from short, woody stems. The flower heads, typically about 6in/15cm long, are dense and conspicuously erect. To perform well, *K. caulescens* must have good drainage as well as plenty of moisture in summer. It thrives in seaside gardens.

Melianthus major
[honey bush]
○

type of plant: half-hardy/slightly tender shrub/perennial [9–10]
flowering time: late spring to midsummer
flower color: maroon
height: 3–4ft/0.9–1.2m
Evergreen

These highly decorative leaves are each 12–18in/30–45cm long. The gray- or blue-green leaflets, curved and conspicuously toothed, are elegantly poised on stout, rather spreading stems. Spikes of tubular flowers appear only on mature plants and in mild regions—where the plant may be 6–10ft/1.8–3m high. Indeed, in colder areas the plant may well die back in winter, but it sprouts again in late spring and grows quickly to 3–4ft/0.9–1.2m. For plenty of good foliage, deep, fertile, moisture-retentive soil is needed; a poor soil encourages flower production at the expense of foliage quality. *M. major* needs a warm, sheltered site.
also for: ■ Growing in containers

Phlomis fruticosa
[Jerusalem sage]
○

type of plant: slightly tender shrub [8–10]
flowering time: early to midsummer
flower color: bright yellow
height: 3–4ft/0.9–1.2m
Evergreen

Since it likes sandy soil and a mild climate, Jerusalem sage does well in maritime districts, but the brittleness of its pale, upright stems makes it unsuitable for very windy sites. Its bright flowers are carried in dense clusters at the end of the stems. Each felted leaf is up to 4in/10cm long, gray-green above and white beneath. Regular pruning produces plenty of good-quality foliage and also helps to keep this vigorous plant neat and dense. Older, unpruned specimens tend to become open and sprawling. *P. italica* [zones 9–10] is a similar but smaller plant; it has prettily colored, lilac-pink flowers and gray leaves.
also for: ■ Dry soils in hot, sunny sites

Salix lanata
[woolly willow]
○

type of plant: hardy shrub [3–7]
flowering time: mid- to late spring
flower color: yellow or yellow-gray
height: 36in/90cm

Woolly willow is an exception to the general rule that gray-leaved plants need well-drained, rather dry soils. This slow-growing shrub actually prefers cool, moist conditions and it thrives in damp and wet soil. Its rounded leaves, each about 2in/5cm long, are gray and woolly. Together with the stout, rather upright stems, they create a bushy, spreading mass of growth that is usually wider than it is tall. The flowers are dense, upright catkins. Female catkins are longer (3in/8cm) and more colorful than the male catkins. *S. helvetica* is bowl-shaped and has paler gray foliage, and *S. exigua* is a larger, often suckering plant with slim leaves.
also for: ■ Heavy, clay soils ■ Damp and wet soils ■ Ground cover

Artemisia absinthium
"Lambrook Silver"
[wormwood, absinth]
○

type of plant: hardy perennial [4–9]
flowering time: mid- to late summer
flower color: dull yellow
height: 30in/75cm
Evergreen/Semi-evergreen ✂

Although reasonably well-drained soil gives good results, dry soil and full sun insure that the deeply divided foliage of this subshrub are a really pale silvery gray. The leaves, up to 4in/10cm long, are silky in texture and have a pungent, rather dry scent. They are borne on upright stems that form clumps of growth. Although less attractive than the foliage, the bobbly flowers of *A. absinthium* "Lambrook Silver" have their own charm; they are interspersed with tiny, gray leaves and carried in long, slender spikes. Some gardeners like to remove the spent flower stems to prevent the plant from becoming shabby and untidy.
also for: ■ Dry soils in hot, sunny sites ■ Aromatic foliage

Artemisia ludoviciana
e.g. "Valerie Finnis"
[western mugwort]
○

type of plant: hardy perennial [6–9]
flowering time: midsummer to early autumn
flower color: yellowish buff-gray
height: 24–30in/60–75cm
Semi-evergreen

The emphatically jagged, silvery gray leaves of this artemisia are each about 5in/12cm long and palest gray when young. They have a fresh, sharp scent. The foliage is carried in rosette-like formations, on upright stems that spread, but not too quickly. The plumes of little, felted flowers are less attractive than the foliage and, in any case, this particular variety of white sage tends not to be free-flowering. *A. ludoviciana* itself is taller, patchier in growth and it flowers freely; it can spread invasively. *A.l.* "Silver Queen" has leaves that are less jagged than those of *A.l.* "Valerie Finnis." Freely draining soil and a sunny site are most suitable for these plants.
also for: ■ Dry soils in hot, sunny sites ■ Aromatic foliage

Crambe maritima
[sea kale]
○

type of plant: hardy perennial [6–9]
flowering time: late spring to early summer
flower color: white
height: 24–30in/60–75cm

As well as being good to eat, the long, lobed leaves of sea kale are strikingly glaucous and decorative. Each fleshy, crinkly-edged leaf can be as much as 24in/60cm long. The leaves are largest when the plant is grown in deep, well-drained soil but—as long as drainage is good—poor, light soil is quite suitable too. The large, dense heads of four-petaled flowers are borne, on thick stems, above the sprawling mounds of foliage. Most people find the sweet scent of sea kale flowers unattractive.

Lychnis coronaria
[dusty miller, rose campion]
○

type of plant: hardy perennial/biennial [4–8]
flowering time: mid- to late summer
flower color: magenta-pink
height: 24–30in/60–75cm

L. coronaria and its white-flowered variety (see the following illustration) have rather slender, softly felted leaves that are silvery gray. Leaves at the base of the plants are up to 7in/18cm long. The erect but widely branching flower stems are also gray. They rise above the basal clumps of foliage and end in flat-faced flowers, up to 1¼in/3cm in diameter. The flower color is sizzling in the species, cool in the variety. Plants in *L. coronaria* Oculata Group have pink-eyed, white flowers. *L. coronaria* and its varieties are usually short-lived. They live longest on poor, dry soils. They self-sow, often prolifically.
also for: ■ Dry soils in hot, sunny sites

Lychnis coronaria "Alba"
[dusty miller, rose campion]
○

type of plant: hardy perennial [4–8]
flowering time: mid- to late summer
flower color: white
height: 24–30in/60–75cm

See preceding plant.

Santolina pinnata subsp. neapolitana
○

type of plant: slightly tender shrub [7–9]
flowering time: midsummer
flower color: bright lemon-yellow
height: 24–30in/60–75cm
Evergreen

The wispy foliage on this shrub forms a rounded mass of gray-greenery that is neat and dense, provided the plant is clipped at least once a year. If the long-stalked, button-like flowers are allowed to develop, they should be removed promptly after fading to keep the plant from becoming lanky. Each sharply but pleasantly aromatic leaf is 1½–2in/4–5cm long. Light, well-drained soil is most suitable, and hot, dry conditions encourage dense growth. *S. pinnata* subsp. *neapolitana* "Edward Bowles" has pale cream flowers. Both plants can be used for informal hedging (plants should be 12in/30cm apart).
also for: ■ Dry soils in hot, sunny sites ■ Ground cover ■ Hedging plants ■ Aromatic foliage

Achillea "Moonshine"
[yarrow]
○

type of plant: hardy perennial [4–8]
flowering time: early summer to early autumn
flower color: bright lemon yellow
height: 24in/60cm
Evergreen/Semi-evergreen

Silvery green, filigree foliage is just one of the attractive features of *A.* "Moonshine." Another is its tiny flowers, arranged in flat, 4in/10cm-wide heads and carried on strong, branching stems. When cut, the blooms are very long-lasting, and they dry well too. The plant forms generous clumps of foliage in any well-drained soil, provided the soil is at least reasonably moisture-retentive. If it is to flower really well, this perennial needs frequent division. *A.* "Taygetea" also has grayish green foliage and pale yellow flowers; it is 18–24in/45–60cm tall.
also for: ■ Flowers suitable for cutting (and drying) ■ Long, continuous flowering period

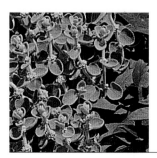

Ballota pseudodictamnus
○

type of plant: slightly tender perennial/shrub [8–9]
flowering time: early to midsummer
flower color: white + mauve
height: 18–24in/45–60cm
Evergreen/Semi-evergreen ⚬✂

Variously regarded as a perennial and as a shrub, *B. pseudodictamnus* forms a clump of upright, slightly sprawling stems. These stems are white and woolly and clothed in neat, rounded, gray-green leaves, up to 1¼in/3cm long, which are also woolly. Tiny flowers, with pale green, downy, funnel-shaped outer parts, are borne close to the stems. The plant must have good drainage, since it is liable to die in cold, wet winters. It is illustrated here with *Salvia officinalis* "Purpurascens."
also for: ■ Dry soils in hot, sunny sites ■ Ground cover

Cerinthe major "Purpurascens"
○

type of plant: grown as hardy annual [7–9]
flowering time: late spring to late summer
flower color: deep purple
height: 18–24in/45–60cm

C. major "Purpurascens" is easily grown in any soil with reasonable drainage. It does, however, have a tendency to flop, and poor, free-draining soil encourages denser, more upright growth. Pale stems end in several, deeply colored, tubular flowers, about 1¼in/3cm long. These are surrounded by conspicuous, purple-tinged, blue bracts. The deep, smoky coloring of these flowers and their bracts is enhanced by distinctly blue-green leaves, which are smooth and heart-shaped and which clasp the stems of the plant.

Lotus hirsutus (syn. Dorycnium hirsutum)
○

type of plant: hardy/slightly tender shrub [7–9]
flowering time: midsummer to early autumn
flower color: pink-tinged white
height: 18–24in/45–60cm
Deciduous/Semi-evergreen

Pale gray-green leaflets, each a pointed oval up to ¾in/2cm long, and their gray stems create a spreading mound of silky, soft growth. Young plants of this subshrub are more upright. The clusters of pea-flowers, which are produced over a period of many weeks, are followed, from late summer onward, by fat, little, shiny pea-pods, which ripen first to reddish brown, then black. This short-lived plant requires soil with really good drainage. *L. hirsutus* does well in poor, dry conditions. In regions with cold winters it is deciduous.
also for: ■ Dry soils in hot, sunny sites ■ Ground cover ■ Ornamental fruit (seed pods) ■ Long, continuous flowering period

Ruta graveolens "Jackman's Blue" [rue]
○

type of plant: hardy shrub [5–9]
flowering time: mid- to late summer
flower color: yellow
height: 18–24in/45–60cm
Evergreen ♂✂

Full sun is needed to encourage really "blue" leaf color on this rue, and hard pruning is required to maintain a neat, dense, rounded shape. Each many-lobed leaf is 3–4in/8–10cm long and has a strange, dry, pungent scent. Cup-shaped flowers are borne in clusters. Contact with the foliage and the cut stems can produce allergic blistering of the skin in sunny weather. The plant prefers light soils and thrives in dry conditions. It can be used to make a low, informal hedge (plants should be about 12in/30cm apart), and it looks good in containers, too. In cold, windy gardens some shelter is advisable.
also for: ■ Dry soils in hot, sunny sites ■ Hedging plants ■ Growing in containers ■ Aromatic foliage

Sisyrinchium striatum (syn. Phaiophleps nigricans)
○

type of plant: hardy/slightly tender perennial [8–9]
flowering time: early to midsummer
flower color: pale yellow
height: 18–24in/45–60cm
Evergreen/Semi-evergreen

Although grown primarily for its pretty, cup-shaped flowers, each about ½in/1cm wide, this plant also has attractive, rather pale, grayish green foliage. In quantity, the upright fans of narrowly sword-shaped leaves provide a good contrast to plants of a more rounded or spreading habit of growth. From these clumps of foliage emerge the strong flower stems with their stalkless flowers. *S. striatum* is easy to grow and sows itself readily in any soil with reasonable drainage. It is at its best on rather poor, well-drained soil; it is particularly short-lived on soil that is prone to waterlogging in winter. For the variegated form of this plant, see p.165.

Parahebe perfoliata (syn. Veronica perfoliata) [digger's speedwell]
○

type of plant: slightly tender perennial [8–10]
flowering time: mid- to late summer
flower color: blue-violet
height: 18in/45cm
Evergreen

Digger's speedwell has rounded leaves that look as if they have been pierced by the lax, spreading stems. Each pale-veined, gray- or blue-green leaf is up to 2in/5cm across. In many situations, this subshrubby plant looks untidy but, if it is positioned so that it can hang over a low wall, its sprawling habit of growth seems attractive. Loose spikes of little, starry flowers arch when in tassel-like bud; they are erect in bloom. A sheltered, sunny site and well-drained, preferably sandy soil are most suitable for this plant.

Stachys byzantina (syn. S. lanata, S. olympica) [lambs' ears]
○

type of plant: hardy perennial [5–9]
flowering time: midsummer
flower color: mauve-pink
height: 15–18in/40–45cm
Evergreen ♂✂

The furry foliage of this mat-forming plant is as nice to feel as it is to look at. Each slender, pointed, silvery gray leaf is velvety soft, and up to 4in/10cm long (although about 10in/25cm long on *S. byzantina* "Big Ears"). The flower spikes, in which little, lipped flowers are interspersed with small leaves, are woolly too. Gardeners who consider that they detract from the appearance of the foliage prefer the virtually non-flowering *S.b.* "Silver Carpet" (see p.191). All three plants—but *S.b.* "Silver Carpet" especially—make good ground cover. They are very easy to grow in any well-drained soil and they thrive in hot, dry conditions. They do not grow well in regions with wet winters.
also for: ■ Dry soils in hot, sunny sites ■ Ground cover

Calluna vulgaris
e.g. "Silver Knight"
[heather, ling]
○ ✱

type of plant: hardy shrub [5–8]
flowering time: late summer to early autumn
flower color: mauve-pink
height: 15in/38cm
Evergreen

The tiny, gray, downy leaves and the erect stems of this heather create a dense hummock of ground-covering growth. In winter, the foliage turns a darker purplish gray. (C. vulgaris "Silver Queen," is consistently pale and woolly; it is more difficult to grow.) C.v. "Silver Knight" is illustrated here in late spring, when some of its single, bell-shaped flowers, each about ¼in/0.5cm long, still remain, although pale and dried. C. vulgaris and its varieties need an open position and lime-free soil that has good drainage but retains moisture easily. These plants succeed in infertile conditions. Their flowers are attractive to bees. For a gray-leaved heath, see p.26.
also for: ■ Acid soils ■ Ground-cover

Convolvulus cneorum
○

type of plant: slightly tender/half-hardy shrub [8–10]
flowering time: late spring to late summer
flower color: white + yellow
height: 12–18in/30–45cm
Evergreen

There is a beautiful silky sheen to the silvery gray foliage of this hummocky plant and it is set off to perfection by the simplicity of the funnel-shaped flowers. These open, to about 1½in/4cm across, from slim, pink-tinged buds. The leaves are slender and around 1½in/4cm long. C. cneorum survives most winters in inland and moderately cold gardens if it is grown in dry soil and given a sheltered site in full sun. Even in ideal conditions, however, this is not a long-lived plant.
also for: ■ Dry soils in hot, sunny sites ■ Ground cover ■ Growing in containers ■ Long, continuous flowering period

Juniperus squamata
e.g. "Blue Star"
[juniper]
○

type of plant: hardy conifer [5–8]
height: 12–18in/30–45cm
Evergreen

In winter, this juniper's foliage turns from an intense blue-gray to a darker, steely gray (the illustration shows J. squamata "Blue Star" in midwinter). The needle-like, ¼in/0.5cm leaves are packed densely on stiff branches. The overall shape is neat and mounded. J.s. "Blue Carpet" (see p.107) has foliage of similar coloring; its habit of growth is almost prostrate. Any well-drained soil is suitable for these plants, which thrive in shallow, chalky soils, poor, dry soils and sandy soils.
also for: ■ Shallow soils over chalk ■ Dry soils in hot, sunny sites ■ Growing in containers

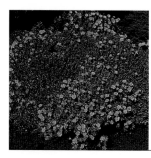

Euryops acraeus
(syn. E. evansii)
○

type of plant: slightly tender shrub [8–10]
flowering time: late spring to early summer
flower color: yellow
height: 12–15in/30–38cm
Evergreen

E. acraeus is densely branched and covered with a mass of narrow, 1¼in/3cm-long, silvery gray leaves that are arranged in whorl-like tufts. The plant forms a very neat dome of growth. Bobbly, little, silver flower buds open out into bright yellow daisies, each about 1in/2.5cm across. Really well-drained soil and a site in full sun are most suitable for this plant. It is not usually long-lived.

Festuca glauca
[blue fescue]
○

type of plant: hardy perennial (grass) [4–9]
flowering time: early to midsummer
flower color: blue-gray
height: 12in/30cm
Evergreen

Blue fescue's thin, rolled leaves are a remarkably bright blue-gray. They form dense, bristly-looking tufts of growth 6–8in/15–20cm high. The slender flower heads are less eye-catching than the foliage but, in late summer, they ripen to attractive, golden seedheads. There are varieties of F. glauca, such as F.g. "Elijah Blue" and F.g. "Blaufuchs" (syn. Blue Fox), that have foliage that is even more brightly colored than that of the species. All these plants grow slowly. They need light, dryish soil and full sun to look their best.
also for: ■ Dry soils in hot, sunny sites ■ Ground cover

Hebe pimeleoides "Quicksilver"
○

type of plant: slightly tender shrub [8–10]
flowering time: mid- to late summer
flower color: purplish mauve
height: 12in/30cm
Evergreen

H. pimeleoides "Quicksilver" has a more graceful, open habit of growth than most hebes. Its dark, arching stems and tiny, pointed leaves create an almost lacy effect. The foliage color is a conspicuous, light silvery blue and, even without the 1in/2.5cm-long spikes of starry flowers, this is a decorative plant. (The illustration shows the plant well after flowering time, in mid-autumn.) Established plants are always wider than they are tall. H.p. "Quicksilver" needs light soil and a position in full sun. It is at home in dry places.
also for: ■ Dry soils in hot, sunny sites

Tanacetum ptarmiciflorum
(syn. *Pyrethrum ptarmiciflorum*)
"Silver Feather"
○

type of plant: grown as half-hardy annual [9–10]
height: 12in/30cm

There are various plants that have pale gray foliage and that are suitable for use in summer bedding schemes. They include *T. ptarmiciflorum* "Silver Feather." This mounded, softly hairy plant has feathery leaves, 3–4in/ 8–10cm long. Many seed catalogs also list varieties of *Senecio cineraria* (syn. *Cineraria maritima*), such as "Silver Dust," which has lacy, very pale gray foliage. Flower buds on any of these plants should be removed so that plenty of good-quality foliage is produced. In really mild areas, these subshrubs may be perennial. They all need light, really well-drained soil and full sun.

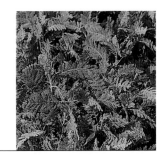

Veronica spicata subsp. *incana*
(syn. *V. incana*)
[speedwell]
○

type of plant: hardy perennial [4–8]
flowering time: early to midsummer
flower color: deep purple-blue
height: 12in/30cm

This speedwell soon forms a spreading clump of elegantly pointed, silvery gray leaves, each about 3in/8cm long. Above this clump of growth rise upright spikes of long-stamened, starry flowers. The whole plant is covered in silver hairs. Among the various, popular *V. spicata* hybrids, only the deep pink *V.s.* "Heidekind" is gray-leaved and readily available. Both plants are easy to grow in light soils.
also for: ■ Dry soils in hot, sunny sites ■ Ground cover

Lychnis flos-jovis "Hort's Variety"
[flower of Jove, flower of Jupiter]
○

type of plant: hardy perennial [5–9]
flowering time: early to late summer
flower color: mid-pink
height: 10–12in/25–30cm

Although easily pleased in any well-drained soil, *L. flos-jovis* "Hort's Variety" is at its very best in dry, rather poor soils. There its tufts of downy-soft, gray leaves are particularly pale and silvery, and the whole plant is especially neat and dense. Each slender, pointed leaf is 3–4in/8–10cm long. Clear pink flowers, 1in/2.5cm across, are arranged in clusters at the top of pale gray, upright stems. *L. flos-jovis* itself is variable: its flowers may be red, red-purple, pink or white; it is usually about 18in/45cm high.
also for: ■ Dry soils in hot, sunny sites ■ Long, continuous flowering period

Gazania e.g. Talent Series
○

type of plant: grown as half-hardy annual [9–11]
flowering time: midsummer to early autumn
flower color: mixed—yellow, pink, cream, orange, bronze + contrasting zones
height: 10in/25cm

All the popular gazanias produce large, short-stemmed, daisy-like flowers that often have central zones of contrasting color. As an added attraction, some varieties, including *G.* Talent Series, have foliage that is gray and felted. The individual leaves of these plants are up to 6in/15cm long; they consist of several pairs of blunted-ended leaflets. Gazanias are vigorous, spreading and fairly drought-tolerant. They thrive in light, well-drained soil and really sunny places. In cloudy weather the blooms close, but those of *G.* Daybreak Series tend to stay open longer. (*G.* Daybreak Series has green leaves.)

Anthemis punctata subsp. *cupaniana*

type of plant: hardy perennial [7–9]
flowering time: late spring to early summer (some later flowers too)
flower color: white + yellow
height: 9–12in/23–30cm
Evergreen/Semi-evergreen

When grown in well-drained soil and cut back hard after flowering, *A. punctata* subsp. *cupaniana* makes dense, spreading mats of pale silvery gray foliage, which darkens in winter. The leaves, up to 5in/12cm long, are very finely divided and they have a pleasant, pungent scent. Long-stalked, bright white flowers are produced in succession over several weeks. Each "daisy" is about 2½in/6cm across. This plant grows quickly and may spread as much as 36in/90cm wide.
also for: ■ Ground cover ■ Aromatic foliage

Helianthemum
e.g. "Rhodanthe Carneum"
(syn. *H.* "Wisley Pink")
[rock rose, sun rose]
○

type of plant: hardy shrub [6–9]
flowering time: late spring to midsummer
flower color: deep red
height: 9–12in/23–30cm
Evergreen

This variety of sun rose has narrow, silvery gray leaves, up to 1½in/4cm long; the foliage of some other forms (for examples, see pp.58 and 107) is green or gray-green. *H.* "Rhodanthe Carneum" is floriferous and vigorous. It quickly makes a hummock of growth, and this stays neat and dense if the plant is cut back after flowering. Each orange-centered, 1in/2.5cm-wide bloom sheds its petals during the afternoon, but numerous buds open in succession. Sun roses thrive in warm, sunny places and in fast-draining soil.
also for: ■ Dry soils in hot, sunny sites ■ Ground cover ■ Crevices in paving

Othonna cheirifolia
(syn. *Othonnopsis cheirifolia*)
○

type of plant: slightly tender shrub [8–10]
flowering time: early to midsummer
flower color: yellow
height: 9–12in/23–30cm
Evergreen

In light soil and a warm, sunny place, this little shrub creates a loose, spreading mass of sprawling stems with upright tips. The foliage color is a striking blue-gray. Each paddle-shaped leaf is about 3in/8cm long and rather fleshy in texture. The daisy-like flowers, 1½in/4cm across, may continue to appear intermittently into early autumn.
also for: ■ Dry soils in hot, sunny sites

Ranunculus gramineus
[buttercup, crowfoot]
○

type of plant: hardy perennial [7–9]
flowering time: late spring to early summer
flower color: yellow
height: 9–12in/23–30cm

Like the weedy common buttercup, *R. gramineus* has flowers with shiny petals; unlike the weed, however, it is compact and non-invasive. Its grassy, distinctly gray-green leaves, each 6–8in/15–20cm long, are slender. They form clumps of growth at the base of numerous, thin, branching stems. The flowers are cup-shaped and up to ¾in/2cm wide. All reasonably moisture-retentive, fertile soils with good drainage are suitable.

Centaurea bella
[knapweed, hardheads]
○

type of plant: hardy perennial [5–8]
flowering time: early to midsummer
flower color: pale pink to mauve-pink
height: 9in/23cm

This plant's bluish gray-green foliage forms low, ground-covering mounds. Each leaf is composed of several, pointed leaflets, the undersides of which are covered in white hairs. The cornflower-like blooms are held on pale stems and are about 1½in/4cm across. They are attractive to bees and butterflies, but they tend not to be produced in large numbers. *C. bella* thrives in free-draining soil and a sunny place.
also for: ■ Ground cover

Sedum "Ruby Glow"
[stonecrop]
○

type of plant: hardy perennial [4–9]
flowering time: late summer to early autumn
flower color: crimson-red
height: 9in/23cm

Purplish tints develop on the blue-green foliage of *S.* "Ruby Glow." The leaves are pointed, roughly oval, and succulent. They are carried on red, sprawling stems that terminate in loose, 2in/5cm-wide clusters of starry flowers. *S.* "Vera Jameson" and *S.* "Bertram Anderson" are similar, lax or prostrate, late-flowering stonecrops. The former has dusky purplish foliage and soft pink flowers; the latter bears purplish leaves and wine-colored flowers. All these plants tolerate short periods of drought and grow densely in drying soil, but they are not at their best if they become parched in summer. Most well-drained soils—either poor or moderately fertile—are suitable.
also for: ■ Ground cover

Erodium chrysanthum
[heron's bill, stork's bill]
○

type of plant: hardy perennial [7–9]
flowering time: early to midsummer and often intermittently until late summer/early autumn
flower color: pale yellow
height: 8–10in/20–25cm

The dainty, finely divided foliage of this plant provides a very flattering background for the sprays of pale yellow, five-petaled flowers. The leaves are slightly hairy, about 1½in/4cm long and have a bluish tinge to their silvery green coloring. They form mounds of tufted growth. For *E. chrysanthum* to thrive, really well-drained, gritty and preferably alkaline soil is needed.
also for: ■ Shallow soils over chalk

Tanacetum haradjanii
(syn. *Chrysanthemum haradjanii*)
○

type of plant: hardy perennial [7–10]
flowering time: midsummer
flower color: yellow
height: 6–8in/15–20cm
Evergreen

T. haradjanii benefits from being viewed at close quarters. It has exquisite, silvery gray leaves, 2–3in/5–8cm long, which are divided and subdivided and look like tiny, gray feathers. When bruised, the foliage emits an attractive, sharp scent. Loose heads of tiny, button-like flowers are carried on pale stems, but some gardeners remove the flowers before they develop fully, since they feel that these "buttons" detract from the foliage. Given a warm position and really well-drained, not too fertile soil, this plant soon forms a mounded carpet of growth up to 12in/30cm wide.
also for: ■ Dry soils in hot, sunny sites ■ Ground cover ■ Crevices in paving ■ Aromatic foliage

Euphorbia myrsinites
[spurge]
○

type of plant: hardy perennial [5–8]
flowering time: mid-spring to early summer
flower color: greenish yellow
height: 6in/15cm
Evergreen

More or less prostrate stems of this plant radiate from a central point, and this arrangement is emphasized by the way the fleshy, blue-gray leaves are packed all along each stem. The sprawling growth is often up to 24in/60cm wide. Little, cupped flowers are born in clusters—each about 2in/5cm across—at the ends of the stems. Growth is densest and the whole plant is at its best in rather poor, dry soils. *E. myrsinites* looks especially attractive where it can trail down over the edge of a wall or large pot; it also looks handsome in paving. There are usually some self-sown seedlings each year. The cut stems of this plant exude a milky juice which can irritate skin.
also for: ■ Dry soils in hot, sunny sites ■ Crevices in paving

Acaena saccaticupula
"Blue Haze" (syn. *A.* "Pewter")
[New Zealand burr, bidi-bidi]
○

type of plant: hardy perennial [6–8]
height: 4–6in/10–15cm
Semi-evergreen

The smoky blue-gray leaves of this vigorous plant are composed of numerous little leaflets that give a ferny effect overall. Russet stems root as they spread, forming a tangle of growth—up to 36in/90cm wide—which is especially dense in really well-drained, rather poor soil and full sun. Spherical flower heads, up to ¾in/2cm in diameter, are carried on long, reddish stems. From midsummer they ripen into dark red burrs. This creeping plant can be invasive; growing it in the cracks between paving stones, where it looks very attractive, can restrict its spread to some extent.
also for: ■ Dry soils in hot, sunny sites ■ Ground cover ■ Crevices in paving ■ Ornamental fruit

Cotula hispida
○

type of plant: slightly tender/half-hardy perennial [9–11]
flowering time: early summer
flower color: bright yellow
height: 4–6in/10–15cm
Evergreen

From a mat of unusually soft, silvery gray foliage rise thin, wiry stems, on top of which are perched bright yellow "buttons," each ½in/1cm wide. The leaves are very finely divided, and they create a dense, pale carpet of growth, up to 12in/30cm wide. *C. hispida* needs sharply drained, gritty soil and a position in full sun. In regions with cold, damp winters this plant is best grown in an alpine house. Where conditions are really dry and there are few prolonged frosts, it can be grown outdoors and it looks appealing in, for instance, the crevices between paving stones.
also for: ■ Crevices in paving (see above)

Stachys byzantina
(syn. *S. lanata, S. olympica*)
"Silver Carpet"
[lambs' ears]
○

type of plant: hardy perennial [5–9]
height: 4–6in/10–15cm
Evergreen ⚥

This virtually non-flowering variety of *S. byzantina* has leaves that are broader—and a little longer—than those of the species (for which, see p.187). Since they are also longer-stemmed, they make especially good material for cutting. The silvery gray foliage creates a dense, softly woolly carpet some 24in/60cm wide. Growth is particularly good in full sun and light, dry soil but any well-drained soil is suitable. In regions with wet winters, the foliage as well as the roots of *S.b.* "Silver Carpet" become waterlogged and then rotten.
also for: ■ Dry soils in hot, sunny sites ■ Ground cover

Artemisia schmidtiana "Nana"
[wormwood, absinth]
○

type of plant: hardy perennial [3–7]
height: 3–4in/8–10cm
Evergreen/Semi-evergreen

These very finely cut leaves create a mounded carpet of silky growth of a most attractive, pale silvery gray. The foliage, which is sharply aromatic, is arranged in little tufts. Each leaf is about 1in/2.5cm long. The spikes of small, yellowish flowers are not very numerous or conspicuous and, unless they are removed, the plant tends to become loose and open. *A. stelleriana* "Boughton Silver" is another popular, low-growing wormwood; its deeply divided, very pale gray leaves have rounded lobes, and it makes good ground cover. Both these plants grow best in dry, poor soil.
also for: ■ Dry soils in hot, sunny sites ■ Aromatic foliage

Sempervivum arachnoideum
[cobweb houseleek]
○

type of plant: hardy perennial [5–9]
flowering time: early to midsummer
flower color: rose-pink
height: 3–4in/8–10cm
Evergreen

Delicate cat's cradles of cobwebby hairs are strung across the leaf tips of this drought-resistant plant. The green or reddish rosettes of fleshy foliage appear silvery because of the hairs. These rosettes, each about ¾in/2cm across, form a tight, solid mound of growth, above which the starry flowers are held on leafy stalks. Cobweb houseleek needs light, well-drained soil. It suffers in regions where its hairy foliage often becomes wet in winter. *S. arachnoideum* subsp. *tomentosum* is especially cobwebby.
also for: ■ Dry soils in hot, sunny sites ■ Crevices in paving

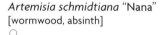

Oxalis adenophylla
○

type of plant: hardy perennial [4–9]
flowering time: late spring to early summer
flower color: purple-pink
height: 3in/8cm

O. adenophylla is a well-behaved relative of some troublesome weeds. Its fan-like, gray-green leaves are circular in outline and composed of numerous, slender, folded leaflets. They form a dense clump above the bulbous roots of the plant. The blushing, maroon-eyed flowers are 1in/2.5cm wide and funnel-shaped. With peat or leaf mold added, most well-drained soils are suitable for this plant, which grows most successfully in regions where its roots are either dry or frozen during the winter months.

Thymus pseudolanuginosus
(syn. *T. lanuginosus*)
[thyme]
○

type of plant: hardy shrub/perennial [5–9]
flowering time: midsummer
flower color: pale lilac-pink
height: 1in/2.5cm
Evergreen

Tiny, softly hairy, gray-green leaves on this subshrub emit a pleasantly astringent scent when bruised. There are small, lipped flowers, arranged in rounded heads, but they are not very freely produced. This thyme thrives in light, gritty soil and a dry situation, and it looks especially attractive growing between paving stones and in a wall crevice. It spreads fairly quickly into fleecy mats approximately 12–18in/30–45cm wide.

also for: ■ Dry soils in hot, sunny sites ■ Ground cover ■ Crevices in paving ■ Aromatic foliage

Raoulia australis
○

type of plant: hardy perennial [7–9]
height: ½in/1cm
Evergreen

A dense, silvery gray "film" of growth is created by these tongue-shaped leaves, each of which is less than ¼in/0.5cm long. In summer it bears a scattering of tiny, stemless flowers, which are pale yellow and generally considered insignificant. Despite needing very well-drained, gritty soil, R. australis must not be allowed to dry out completely. It grows slowly enough to be suitable for planting in a trough or sink. R. hookeri has leaves that are even more silvery. Both these plants rot if their foliage becomes very wet in winter.

ADDITIONAL PLANTS, featured elsewhere in this book, that have gray, blue-gray, or silver leaves

○ sun

minimum height 10ft/3m or more
Acacia dealbata, see p.297
Cytisus battandieri, see p.297
Elaeagnus "Quicksilver," see p.52
Eucalyptus pauciflora subsp. niphophila, see p.264
Hippophae rhamnoides, see p.89
Juniperus scopulorum "Skyrocket," see p.145

minimum height between 36in/90cm and 10ft/3m
Atriplex halimus, see p.91
Buddleja "Lochinch," see p.298
Leymus arenarius, see p.53
Perovskia "Blue Spire," see p.14
Romneya coulteri, see p.299

minimum height 36in/90cm or less
Aethionema "Warley Rose," see p.17
Alyssum spinosum "Roseum," see p.154
Antennaria microphylla, see p.108
Arabis alpina subsp. caucasica "Flore Pleno," see p.108

Artemisia arbrotanum, see p.245
Artemisia "Powis Castle," see p.56
Asphodeline lutea, see p.53
Aurinia saxatilis "Citrina," see p.108
Caryopteris x clandonensis "Heavenly Blue," see p.15
Catananche caerulea, see p.276
Centranthus ruber, see p.15
Coronilla valentina subsp. glauca "Citrina," see p.335
Dianthus "Doris," see p.283
Dianthus gratianopolitanus, see p.17
Dianthus "Haytor White," see p.283
Dianthus "Inchmery," see p.302
Dianthus "Mrs Sinkins," see p.302
Dianthus "Pike's Pink," see p.60
Erica tetralix "Alba Mollis," see p.26
Erysimum "Bowles" Mauve," see p.337
Eschscholzia californica Thai Silk Series, see p.58
Geranium "Ballerina," see p.60
x Halimiocistus wintonensis "Merrist Wood Cream," see p.56

Halimium lasianthum, see p.55
Helianthemum "Wisley Primrose," see p.107
Helichrysum italicum subsp. serotinum, see p.247
Helichrysum petiolare, see p.147
Helichrysum "Schwefellicht," see p.282
Hypericum olympicum, see p.155
Juniperus squamata "Blue Carpet," see p.107
Lavandula angustifolia "Hidcote," see p.138
Lavandula angustifolia "Loddon Pink," see p.56
Leontopodium alpinum, see p.154
Nepeta x faassenii, see p.107
Papaver somniferum "Black Paeony," see p.329
Papaver somniferum "Paeony Flowered," see p.253
Salvia argentea, see p.55
Santolina chamaecyparissus, see p.138
Sedum "Herbstfreude," see p.106
Sedum spathulifolium "Cape Blanco," see p.61
Silene uniflora "Robin Whitebreast," see p.59
Teucrium fruticans, see p.54
Verbascum "Gainsborough," see p.15
Verbascum "Helen Johnson," see p.336

Chamaecyparis lawsoniana
e.g. "Pembury Blue"
[Lawson false cypress]
○[◐]
type of plant: hardy conifer [6–8]
height: 35–45ft/10.5–13.5m
Evergreen

Generally regarded as the bluest of the Lawson false cypresses, *C. lawsoniana* "Pembury Blue" matures into a fairly slim cone of somewhat pendent, bright blue-gray foliage that is arranged in loose fans. Individual leaves are like tiny, overlapping scales. Most soils are suitable for this conifer, but it is best where moisture and good drainage are present. It makes a good screening plant and can be used for informal hedging (when plants should be about 24in/60cm apart). However, it does not thrive in an exposed position.
also for: ■ Hedging plants

Sorbus hupehensis
[Hubei mountain ash]
○[◐]
type of plant: hardy tree [5–8]
flowering time: late spring
flower color: white
height: 25–30ft/7.5–9m

Many mountain ashes have elegant, divided foliage that becomes richly colored in autumn but, as an added attraction, the numerous, lozenge-shaped leaflets of this particular species are a distinctive blue-green. Before the foliage turns red in autumn, loose, pendent bunches of red-stalked berries ripen to white or pale pink. These eye-catching fruits, each about ¼in/0.5cm wide, often remain on the tree well into winter (although the plant is inclined to crop heavily every other year, rather than every year). The berries are preceded by 4in/10cm-wide heads of clustered flowers. Most soils are suitable for this upright, broadly columnar tree, although it is short-lived on shallow, chalky soils. It grows most successfully in ground that is well-drained but moisture-retentive.
also for: ■ Colorful, autumn foliage
■ Ornamental fruit

Chamaecyparis lawsoniana
e.g. "Ellwoodii"
[Lawson false cypress]
○[◐]
type of plant: hardy conifer [6–8]
height: 10–15ft/3–4.5m
Evergreen

The upright branches of this slow-growing conifer are covered with neat, dense sprays of foliage. These sprays are composed of tiny, scale-like leaves that are basically gray-green but that become bluer in winter. Well-drained, moisture-retentive soils of various types are suitable for this plant. It most often has a rather bushy habit of growth but, by training a single leading shoot against a cane, a particulary well-shaped, narrowly conical specimen can be produced. For an even slower-growing, golden yellow "sport" of *C. lawsoniana* "Ellwoodii," see p.145.

Rosa glauca
(syn. *R. rubrifolia*)
[rose]
○[◐]
type of plant: hardy shrub [2–8]
flowering time: early summer
flower color: bright pink + white
height: 6–8ft/1.8–2.4m

R. glauca's foliage is a subtle mixture of gray and plummy red, with the gray tones predominating when the plant is grown in a lightly shaded position. The long, arching, almost prickle-free stems are also plum-colored. They carry single flowers, each about 1½in/4cm across, that are followed by shiny, round hips. These ripen from brown to orange-red in late summer, and the foliage turns briefly yellow in mid-autumn before falling. To produce plenty of new, strongly colored shoots and good-quality foliage, *R. glauca* needs to be pruned fairly hard and given fertile, moisture-retentive soil.
also for: ■ Ornamental fruit

Macleaya microcarpa
"Kelway's Coral Plume"
[plume poppy]
○[◐]
type of plant: hardy perennial [4–9]
flowering time: mid- to late summer
flower color: buff-pink
height: 5–7ft/1.5–2.1m

Large, deeply lobed leaves of this vigorous and sometimes invasive plant contrast beautifully with the loose plumes of tiny, apricot-budded flowers. The foliage color is usually gray-green (the undersides of the leaves are grayish white). Each rounded and conspicuously veined leaf may be up to 10in/25cm across. *M. microcarpa* "Kelway's Coral Plume" produces numerous, upright, rather pale stems. It is at its robust best in a sunny position, and in deep soil that is moist but well drained. *M. cordata* has pale beige flowers but is otherwise similar.

Juniperus virginiana "Gray Owl"
[juniper]
○[◐]

type of plant: hardy conifer [3–9]
height: 4–7ft/1.2–2.1m
Evergreen

Yellow branches on this broadly V-shaped conifer are clothed in soft, bluish gray foliage. The leaves are thin, and mainly adult and scale-like (rather than juvenile and needle-like). Growth is densest in the center of the plant, and is more open toward the branch tips. If necessary, it can be pruned and this encourages denser growth that is valuable if the plant is being used for ground cover. *J. virginiana* "Gray Owl" grows quickly, reaching 12ft/3.6m or more wide. It is an adaptable plant that does well in most soils and a wide range of sites, but it is particularly at home in a sunny position and well-drained soil. For details of other junipers with blue-gray foliage, see pp.107 and 188.
also for: ■ Dry soils in hot, sunny sites ■ Ground cover

Sequoia sempervirens "Adpressa"
[coast redwood]
○[◐]

type of plant: hardy conifer [7–9]
height: 3–6ft/0.9–1.8m if pruned (see description)
Evergreen

Although, initially, this conifer grows slowly for many years, its rate of growth eventually accelerates and its ultimate height is 20–30ft/6–9m. The plant can be trimmed regularly as it matures, and this treatment produces neat, dense growth and a rounded or conical shape. Trimming also enhances the production, from late spring, of numerous new shoots that are, at first, conspicuously cream-colored. As they age, the rows of blunt-ended, little leaves become grayer and, finally, they turn a deep rich green. Left untrimmed, this conifer is normally conical with a fairly open framework of sweeping, curving branches. *S. sempervirens* "Adpressa" grows best in moist but well-drained soil. It does not prosper in a cold, windy garden.

Paeonia mlokosewitschii
[peony]
○[◐]

type of plant: hardy perennial [5–8]
flowering time: mid- to late spring
flower color: lemon-yellow
height: 24in/60cm

Simple, elegant blooms, up to 5in/12cm wide, are produced by this peony, but the petals are shed quite quickly. However, as well as bowl-shaped flowers, *P. mlokosewitschii* bears very attractive foliage and interesting seed pods. The shapely, oval leaflets are pinkish bronze at first, maturing to a soft, subtle gray-green; in some autumns, they turn gentle shades of orange and yellow before dying. A more reliable autumn feature are the seed pods, which open to reveal eye-catching red and black seeds. This long-lived plant slowly forms a mound of growth. It thrives in deep, well-cultivated soil with good drainage. In regions with hot summers it benefits from some shade.
also for: ■ Ornamental fruit (seed pods)

Anaphalis triplinervis
[pearly everlasting]
○[◐]

type of plant: hardy perennial [4–9]
flowering time: midsummer to early autumn
flower color: white + yellow
height: 18in/45cm

This clump-forming perennial has numerous, gray-green, ribbed leaves on pale, more or less upright stems. Each slender, felted leaf has a white underside and is about 2½in/6cm long. Papery flowers, which are arranged in small clusters, are "everlasting" and suitable for drying. Even in bud they look attractive. The plant is easy to please: indeed, far from demanding perfectly drained soil—as so many gray-leaved plants do—*A. triplinervis* droops and loses some of its foliage if it is very dry. Given moisture-retentive soil with reasonable drainage, it thrives and is likely to spread quite quickly. *A.t.* "Sommerschnee" (syn. Summer Snow) is slightly smaller.
also for: ■ Ground cover ■ Flowers suitable for cutting (and drying) ■ Long, continuous flowering period

Hebe pinguifolia "Pagei"
○[◐]

type of plant: hardy/slightly tender shrub [8–10]
flowering time: late spring to early summer
flower color: white
height: 6–9in/15–23cm
Evergreen

The leathery, rounded leaves, each ½in/1cm long, on this almost prostrate shrub create a close-textured, blue-gray carpet of weed-suppressing growth. The plant roots as it spreads and is usually 24–36in/60–90cm wide. Starry flowers are arranged in small clusters that appear mainly at the end of the stems. Other popular hebes with grayish foliage include *H. albicans*, *H.* "Red Edge" and *H.* "Pewter Dome." All these rounded shrubs grow 18–24in/45–60cm high. Like *H. pinguifolia* "Pagei," they need soil that is well drained but not dry.
also for: ■ Atmospheric pollution ■ Ground cover ■ Growing in containers

Saxifraga paniculata
(syn. S. aizoon)
[saxifrage]

○[●]

type of plant: hardy perennial [2–7]
flowering time: early summer
flower color: creamy white
height: 6in/15cm
Evergreen

The toothed leaves of this long-lived saxifrage make a tight carpet of silvery green rosettes, each up to 1in/2.5cm across. The leaf edges are encrusted with tiny beads of lime. Cup-shaped, ½in/1cm-wide flowers—seen here in bud—are carried in loose sprays, on erect stems, well above the foliage. Various forms of S. paniculata are available from specialist nurseries. They include S.p. var. baldensis, which has very small rosettes of foliage, as well as varieties with yellow and with pink flowers. All these plants are easy to grow, provided they have sharply drained, alkaline conditions. Their roots should not become parched in summer. In warmer districts, they benefit from some shade in the middle of the day.
also for: ■ Shallow soils over chalk

ADDITIONAL PLANTS, featured elsewhere in this book, that have gray, blue-gray, or silver leaves

○[●] sun (or partial shade)

minimum height 10ft/3m or more
Sorbus aria "Lutescens," see p.19

minimum height between 36in/90cm and 10ft/3m
Potentilla fruticosa "Vilmoriniana," see p.142

Thalictrum aquilegiifolium
[meadow rue]

○●

type of plant: hardy perennial [5–9]
flowering time: early to midsummer
flower color: mauve or purplish lilac
height: 36–42in/90–105cm

The fluffy flower heads of this clump-forming perennial are popular for fresh flower arrangements, and the seedheads dry well. The flowers are borne, on slender, upright stems, well above the ferny foliage, which is also very attractive. Each leaf, up to 12in/30cm long, is divided into numerous, smooth, rounded leaflets that are a blue-tinged light gray-green. This species of meadow rue needs good, moisture-retentive soil. White-flowered T. aquilegiifolium var. album is also readily available. T. flavum subsp. glaucum has blue-gray foliage and pale yellow flowers.
also for: ■ Flowers suitable for cutting (and drying)

Lysimachia ephemerum
[loosestrife]

○●

type of plant: hardy/slightly tender perennial
[7–9]
flowering time: mid- to late summer
flower color: white
height: 36in/90cm

Each of these slim and slightly fleshy, gray-green leaves is about 6in/15cm long. The starry flowers, which are arranged in slender spikes, are followed by rounded seed pods. L. ephemerum forms clumps of upright stems. Any soil that does not dry out in summer is suitable, but the plant grows especially well in a damp place. It can also be planted in wet, boggy ground.
also for: ■ Damp and wet soils

ADDITIONAL PLANTS, featured elsewhere in this book, that have gray, blue-gray, or silver leaves

○● sun or partial shade

minimum height between 36in/90cm and 10ft/3m: Rubus thibetanus, see p.267

Chamaecyparis pisifera
"Boulevard"
[Sawara cypress]

●[○]

type of plant: hardy conifer [5–9]
height: 15–20ft/4.5–6m
Evergreen

The silvery blue of this conifer's feathery foliage is most intense in a partially shaded position and during the summer months. The tiny, pointed leaves are carried in tight clusters that are soft to the touch. C. pisifera "Boulevard" quickly forms a dense, rather bushy cone of growth. It can be lightly trimmed and is sometimes used for hedging (when individual plants should be about 24in/60cm apart). It needs soil that is reliably moist and thrives in a cool climate with high rainfall. Although it tolerates some alkalinity, it is much better in neutral to slightly acid soil.
also for: ■ Hedging plants

Hosta sieboldiana var. elegans
[plantain lily]
◑[○●]

type of plant: hardy perennial [3–9]
flowering time: early to midsummer
flower color: palest lilac
height: 30–36in/75–90cm
✄

In ideal conditions—some shade and deep, rich, moist soil—the individual leaves of this magnificent hosta can be well over 12in/30cm wide. Even in reasonably moisture-retentive conditions the plant forms a dense clump of growth, eventually 4–5ft/1.2–1.5m wide. It is slower to establish in heavy clays, but thrives there too. In cool climates this hosta can be grown in sun, provided it has plenty of moisture. Its broadly heart-shaped leaves, thick-textured, puckered and often cupped, are blue-gray with an attractive surface "bloom." This waxy coating and the really blue leaf color are retained longest in at least some shade. The thickset, trumpet-shaped flowers only just overtop the foliage. In autumn, the foliage is, briefly, rich yellow and the seedheads are quite attractive, too. H. "Krossa Regal" is another example of a readily available, big, bold hosta with blue-gray leaves.
also for: ■ Heavy, clay soils ■ Damp and wet soils ■ Ground cover

Hosta e.g. "Halcyon"
(Tardiana Group)
[plantain lily]
◑[●]

type of plant: hardy perennial [3–9]
flowering time: mid- to late summer
flower color: grayish lilac-mauve
height: 18in/45cm
✄

Where the hosta illustrated above is too large and wide-spreading, this popular, blue-gray variety would be a suitable substitute. Its long-stalked, elegantly tapering leaves, each about 8in/20cm long, soon create a mound of ground-covering growth 12–15in/30–38cm high. This mound is thickest and widest in rich, damp soil, but all fertile, moisture-retentive soils give satisfactory results. The intense blue of the foliage lasts longest in at least some shade (although in full shade there are fewer of the dense heads of trumpet-shaped flowers). Other small- to medium-sized hostas with blue-gray leaves include H. "Blue Moon" and H. "Hadspen Blue."
also for: ■ Damp and wet soils ■ Ground cover

Athyrium niponicum var. pictum
(syn. A.n. f. metallicum,
A. goeringianum "Pictum")
[Japanese painted fern]
◑

type of plant: hardy fern [4–8]
height: 15in/38cm

As each frond unfurls, the leaf color changes from maroon to silvery gray. This pale, almost metallic coloring enhances the delicate laciness of the foliage. An attractive maroon-purple is retained on the stems and the mid-ribs of the leaves. The almost horizontally held fronds, each about 12in/30cm long, form clumps of growth that are most luxuriant in a sheltered, lightly shaded site and spongy, moisture-retentive, rather acid soil.
also for: ■ Acid soils

Dicentra e.g. "Stuart Boothman"
(syn. D. "Boothman's Variety")
◑[○]

type of plant: hardy perennial [5–8]
flowering time: late spring to midsummer
flower color: dusty pink
height: 12–15in/30–38cm

The delicately ferny, bluish gray leaves of this spreading dicentra make an especially flattering setting for the "old rose" pink of its flowers. Each leaf is 4–6in/10–15cm long and divided into numerous, slender leaflets. The flowers, like little, elongated lockets, dangle from arching stems. D. "Langtrees" is another popular dicentra with grayish foliage; it is taller and has pink-tinged, cream flowers and blue-gray foliage. Both these plants like cool, moist, well-drained soil and a fairly sheltered site. Very alkaline conditions are best avoided. In full sun most of the flowers fade during early summer.

Sanguinaria canadensis
f. multiplex "Plena"
[bloodroot, red puccoon]
◑●[○]

type of plant: hardy perennial [3–9]
flowering time: mid-spring
flower color: white
height: 6in/15cm

Emerging upright and folded, the rounded, lobed leaves of this plant expand fully on their stiff stems only after the flowers have faded. Individual leaves may be as much as 12in/30cm wide, although 4–6in/10–15cm is more typical. The foliage is glaucous gray-green; it dies down in summer. The fully double, 2in/5cm-wide flowers of S. canadensis f. multiplex "Plena" are fairly short-lived, but they do last longer than the single blooms of S. canadensis itself. Cool, moist, humus-rich soil and a shady place provide the ideal growing conditions for both these plants. Their stout roots, which spread slowly, contain red sap—hence the common name.

ADDITIONAL PLANTS, featured elsewhere in this book, that have gray, blue-gray, or silver leaves

◑[○]/◑ partial shade (or sun)/partial shade

minimum height 36in/90cm or less: Dicentra "Bacchanal," see p.349; Mertensia virginica, see p.78

Purple, bronze, or red leaves

PURPLE, BRONZE, OR RED LEAVES have been popular for many years. The rich, deep shades of these leaves not only complement vibrant flower colors but also contrast effectively with paler foliage and flowers of "cool" colors.

Many widely grown plants have purple leaves. Shrubs such as *Cotinus coggygria* "Royal Purple" and *Berberis thunbergii* f. *atropurpurea*, and perennials such as *Heuchera micrantha* var. *diversifolia* "Palace Purple" and *Ajuga reptans* "Atropurpurea," are familiar ingredients of many gardens (all are illustrated in the present list).

Not surprisingly perhaps, the exact color of so-called purple foliage varies a good deal, and many purple leaves are in fact a reddish plum or crimson. Some purple-leaved plants are so dark that they appear black or, at least, nearly black (see *Ophiopogon planiscapus* "Nigrescens" and *Sambucus nigra* f. *porphyrophylla* "Gerda" among "black" plants listed on pp.328–32).

Plants that have foliage of a brownish purple include, for example, *Weigela florida* "Foliis Purpureis," *Actaea simplex* Atropurpurea Group, and *Lysimachia ciliata* "Firecracker," all of which are illustrated in the present list. These brownish purples are quite close to the various bronze or chocolate-brown tones seen in the foliage of plants such as *Ligularia dentata* "Desdemona" and *Ranunculus ficaria* "Brazen Hussy." However, they are quite distinct from the true reds that are a striking feature of a relatively small number of plants that includes, for example, *Imperata cylindrica* "Rubra."

Some plants have foliage that is purplish, bronze, or red but only when it is young. The color may be a bonus to leaves that are already attractively shaped, as in the case of various *Epimedium*, or it may enhance the appearance of early flowers. In certain cases, the immature foliage is considered the main decorative feature of the plant. *Pieris* "Forest Flame" and *Photinia* x *fraseri* "Red Robin," for example, are grown almost exclusively for their young, red leaves.

The placing of purple, bronze, or reddish foliage in the garden needs some thought. Large plants with very deeply colored foliage can produce a surprisingly heavy and drab effect; small, dark-leaved plants can "disappear" when viewed from even quite a short distance. Combining dark-leaved plants with foliage and flowers that are lighter in color can help to lessen these problems.

Purple-leaved plants with foliage that seems animated and airy include *Euphorbia dulcis* "Chameleon," with its willowy mass of little leaves, and *Foeniculum vulgare* "Purpureum," which has very finely divided foliage. Reddish or purple-leaved plants that are bold and striking—and yet neither oppressively dark nor likely to "disappear"—include *Phormium tenax* Purpureum Group and varieties of castor bean (*Ricinus communis*), examples of which are described below.

Most plants with purple, bronze, or red leaves need a sunny site in order to produce really colorful foliage (in shade, their foliage is often an unremarkable, dusky green). Among the exceptions are *Viola riviniana* Purpurea Group and *Saxifraga* "Wada."

The range of evergreen plants with purple foliage is also limited. However, this list does feature some widely grown evergreens, including purple sage (*Salvia officinalis* "Purpurascens"), the little succulent *Sedum spathulifolium* "Purpureum," and *Phormium tenax* Purpureum Group. (See also *Pittosporum tenuifolium* "Tom Thumb" on p.146). As some compensation for the relative lack of evergreens, quite a number of deciduous, purple-leaved plants produce good autumn color: for example, *Cotinus coggygria* "Royal Purple," *Berberis thunbergii* f. *atropurpurea* and the purpleleaf grape (*Vitis vinifera* "Purpurea") in this list all become richly or brightly colored during the autumn months.

For plants with leaves that take on purple, bronze, or red tints during autumn and winter, see "Plants with colorful autumn foliage," pp.234–43.

Fagus sylvatica
Atropurpurea Group
[European beech]
○
type of plant: hardy tree [4–9]
height: 80–100ft/24–30m
✂

The color of plants sold under this name varies but all forms have young leaves that are pink or pale red, mature foliage that is dark purple, and coppery autumn color. The leaves are wavy-edged, pointed ovals 3–4in/8–10cm long. These broad-headed, spreading trees thrive in alkaline conditions and are suitable for all well-drained soils. They can be used for hedging (plants should be about 18in/45cm apart). Purple-leaved beeches include pendulous-branched *F.s.* "Purpurea Pendula" (10–15ft/3–4.5m high). *F.s.* "Dawyk Purple" is slender, upright and reaches 60ft/18m or more.
also for: ■ Shallow soils over chalk ■ Atmospheric pollution ■ Hedging plants ■ Colorful, autumn foliage

Acer platanoides
e.g. "Crimson King"
[Norway maple]
○
type of plant: hardy tree [4–8]
flowering time: mid-spring
flower color: red-tinged yellow
height: 40–50ft/12–15m

Although the foliage of this vigorous tree shines and therefore reflects some light, it is of such a dark color that the plant needs careful placing so that it does not look too "heavy." The leaves, each about 5in/12cm long, have five pointed lobes. At first, the foliage is reddish purple; it is a deep brown-purple throughout summer; in autumn, it takes on red and orange tints. Numerous flower clusters appear before the leaves unfurl. *A. platanoides* "Crimson King" creates a dense, more or less rounded crown of growth. This tough and adaptable plant can be grown in almost any soil.
also for: ■ Shallow soils over chalk ■ Heavy, clay soils ■ Atmospheric pollution ■ Colorful, autumn foliage

Catalpa x erubescens "Purpurea"
○
type of plant: hardy tree [5–9]
flowering time: late summer
flower color: white + purple
height: 40–50ft/12–15m

This hybrid catalpa produces broad, lobed leaves each of which is up to 15in/38cm long. When the foliage emerges, in late spring or early summer, it is very dark purple; in maturity it is bright green. Bell-shaped flowers, each about 2in/5cm across, are arranged in large, open, upright clusters and are followed by thin, brown seed pods, up to 15in/38cm long. Most soils suit this wide, spreading tree, but growth is especially good in fertile, moisture-retentive soil. It needs a sheltered site and does best in areas with hot summers. The illustration shows the upright growths of a pollarded specimen.
also for: ■ Heavy, clay soils ■ Atmospheric pollution ■ Ornamental fruit (seed pods)

Gleditsia triacanthos "Rubylace"
[honeylocust]
○
type of plant: hardy tree [4–9]
height: 20–30ft/6–9m

On first emerging, late in spring, the feathery foliage of this tree is distinctly wine-red. The color then deepens and softens and becomes greener. There is some yellowish autumn color. Each leaf is about 6in/15cm long and composed of numerous, slender leaflets. The tree is spreading and broad-headed and, in maturity particularly, it is often thorny. It needs shelter from strong winds. Most well-drained soils that are reasonably fertile are suitable for this tree, which thrives in dry, sunny climates and copes well with dry soil. *G. triacanthos* "Rubylace" is tolerant of very polluted air. For details of the popular, yellow-leaved variety of honeylocust, see p.210.
also for: ■ Dry soils in hot, sunny sites ■ Atmospheric pollution

Malus "Royalty"
[crabapple]
○
type of plant: hardy tree [4–8]
flowering time: mid- to late spring
flower color: deep purple-pink
height: 18–22ft/5.4–6.6m

Unlike some purple-leaved varieties, this crabapple has foliage that remains glossy and richly red-purple throughout summer. It becomes redder in autumn. Each leaf is a tapering oval, up to 4in/10cm long. The clusters of cup-shaped flowers are freely produced. As the blossom ages, its deep, dusky coloring lightens. Flowers are followed by dark red, ½in/1cm-diameter fruits that ripen in autumn. The tree is upright when young, and in maturity usually becomes as wide as it is high. *M.* "Royalty" is easily grown, but moist, well-drained soil—including fairly heavy clay—is most suitable.
also for: ■ Heavy, clay soils (see above) ■ Atmospheric pollution ■ Ornamental fruit

Prunus cerasifera
e.g. "Pissardii" (syn. *P. pissardii*)
[cherry plum, myrobalan]
○
type of plant: hardy tree [3–8]
flowering time: early spring
flower color: pink fading to white
height: 15–20ft/4.5–6m
✂

P. cerasifera "Pissardii" and *P.c.* "Nigra" are popular plums. The foliage on *P.c.* "Pissardii" emerges a coppery color and becomes deep red-purple, while *P.c.* "Nigra" has dark purple foliage and pink flowers on dark purple stems. Both plants bear oval, pointed leaves that are about 2in/5cm long. Masses of little saucer-shaped flowers appear before the foliage. Both varieties are used for hedging and screening (plants should be about 18in/45cm apart). Left untrimmed, they form round-headed trees. They grow in any well-drained soil, as long as it is not wet or very dry. *P. x cistena* also has red-purple leaves; it is a shrub (about 5ft/1.5m tall) with very pale pink flowers.
also for: ■ Atmospheric pollution ■ Hedging plants

Cercis canadensis "Forest Pansy"
[Eastern redbud]
○

type of plant: hardy shrub/tree [5–9]
height: 12–15ft/3.6–4.5m

C. canadensis "Forest Pansy" produces heart-shaped, rich plum-purple leaves, up to 5in/12cm long, that hang gracefully on long stalks from spreading branches. As the foliage matures, attractive green veining develops, but the basic purple coloring lasts very well. In cooler climates, the plant grows quite slowly and the tight clusters of late spring, pink pea-flowers seldom appear. It usually develops as a broad shrub, but it can form a round-headed tree of 25–30ft/7.5–9m high. Loamy, moisture-retentive soil with good drainage gives the best results. A sheltered site should be chosen, since late frosts can damage the young leaves and any blossom.

Corylus maxima "Purpurea"
[purple-leaved filbert]
○

type of plant: hardy shrub [5–8]
flowering time: late winter to early spring
flower color: purplish
height: 10ft/3m (see description)

Purple-leaved filbert is normally pruned hard every other year or so, in order to produce plenty of new growth with large, deep purple leaves. Left unpruned, the plant forms a tree up to 20ft/6m tall, and produces edible nuts in purple-suffused husks. The rounded, conspicuously veined leaves, up to 5in/12cm long, are a particularly dark purple, and the foliage can seem rather heavy *en masse* in summer. Pendent catkins, 2–3in/5–8cm long, precede the leaves. Almost any soil is suitable for this vigorous plant. Growth is upright at first, more spreading with age.
also for: ■ Shallow soils over chalk ■ Heavy, clay soils ■ Ornamental fruit (see above) ■ Winter-flowering plants

Cotinus coggygria
e.g. "Royal Purple"
[smoke bush, Venetian sumac]
○

type of plant: hardy shrub [5–9]
flowering time: mid- to late summer
flower color: pink-purple
height: 8–10ft/2.4–3m
✂

Emerging rather late in spring, the deep red-purple leaves of *C. coggygria* "Royal Purple" are rounded, softly silk-textured and each about 3in/8cm long. In autumn, they turn red; the color is particularly bright on poor, well-drained soil and in a dry climate. Hard pruning increases the leaf size and keeps the plant rounded and shrubby (unpruned it can be tree-like and up to 15ft/4.5m high). Pruning also diminishes production of the smoky clouds of tiny flowers and the subsequent, hazy seedheads. Other purple-leaved cotinus include *C.* "Grace," which has reliably brilliant autumn color.
also for: ■ Colorful, autumn foliage ■ Ornamental fruit (seedheads)

Physocarpus opulifolius
"Diabolo"
[ninebark]
○

type of plant: hardy shrub [3–8]
flowering time: early summer
flower color: pale pink
height: 6–8ft/1.8–2.4m
✂

The chief attraction of *P. opulifolius* "Diabolo" is its dark purple-bronze, gleaming, neatly lobed foliage. Its flower clusters are small and much less decorative. Each toothed and veined leaf is up to 3in/8cm long. Foliage color is best in sun and, although this shrub appreciates moist soil that is neutral to acid, it is usually very easy to grow in most soils. However, it does not tolerate very alkaline conditions. Its growth habit is upright and the numerous stems are richly colored. Mature branches have bark that peels attractively.
also for: ■ Acid soils ■ Damp and wet soils ■ Ornamental bark or twigs

Phormium tenax Purpureum Group
[New Zealand flax]
○

type of plant: slightly tender perennial/shrub [8–11]
flowering time: mid- to late summer
flower color: very dark red
height: 5–6ft/1.5–1.8m foliage height;
8–10ft/2.4–3m flower height (see description)
Evergreen ✂

A huge bunch of sword shapes is created by the stiff, leathery leaves of these plants. Leaf color is variable but, in the best forms, it is a vibrant, coppery purple. In warm regions, mature specimens regularly produce towering, upright heads of fairly small, tubular flowers. Slender, brown seed pods ripen later. Rather open-textured soil that is consistently moist is most suitable for these plants. Shelter and some winter protection are needed in colder, inland regions, but growth is especially good in seaside gardens. There are numerous phormiums with red, purple, and bronze leaves (*P.* "Bronze Baby" is about 24in/60cm high); others are variegated.
also for: ■ Damp and wet soils ■ Atmospheric pollution

Ricinus communis
e.g. "Carmencita"
[castor bean]
○

type of plant: grown as half-hardy annual [9–11]
height: 5–6ft/1.5–1.8m

The young leaves of this very fast-growing plant are a shining and luxurious reddish brown; as they mature, they become progressively greener—and larger. Each bold, lobed leaf, on its thick, red-brown stem, may be 10in/25cm or more across. Spikes of rather inconspicuous flowers appear in summer; the bright red, prickly fruits that follow are much more decorative, but they contain highly poisonous seeds. *R. communis* "Impala" grows to 3–4ft/0.9–1.2m high; its younger leaves are red-purple and its fruits are maroon. Both plants perform best in fertile, humus-rich soil with good drainage.
also for: ■ Ornamental fruit

Foeniculum vulgare
e.g. "Purpureum"
(syn. *F.v.* "Bronze")
[fennel]
○

type of plant: hardy perennial (herb) [5–9]
flowering time: midsummer to early autumn
flower color: bright yellow
height: 5ft/1.5m

This plant's gossamer-fine foliage, which smells and tastes of aniseed, is punctuated by smooth, upright stems. The youngest leaves are bronze-purple; as they mature, they change to bronze and finally bluish green. In the light soils and sunny places that are most suitable for it, *F. vulgare* "Purpureum" sows itself freely. Some gardeners prefer to pinch out the flat clusters of flowers while they are still in bud, in order to prevent a mass of seedlings appearing. This treatment also tends to increase the amount of foliage produced.
also for: ■ Dry soils in hot, sunny sites ■ Aromatic foliage

Berberis thunbergii
f. *atropurpurea*
[barberry]
○

type of plant: hardy shrub [5–8]
flowering time: mid- to late spring
flower color: pale yellow + red
height: 4–6ft/1.2–1.8m

These broadly oval, 1¼in/3cm-long leaves are purple-mahogany in spring and summer, turning orange-red in autumn. *B. thunbergii* f. *atropurpurea* is dense, rounded, and very thorny, and it makes an excellent hedge (plants should be 18–24in/45–60cm apart). Small clusters of cup-shaped flowers are followed by scarlet, droplet-shaped berries. Other purple-leaved berberis include very upright *B.t.* f. *a.* "Helmond Pillar" and very dark *B.* x *ottawensis* f. *purpurea* "Superba" (6–8ft/1.8–2.4m tall); see also p.202. All these plants grow well in almost any soil, as long as it is not very alkaline or wet.
also for: ■ Atmospheric pollution ■ Hedging plants ■ Colorful, autumn foliage ■ Ornamental fruit

---

Canna e.g. "Wyoming"
[Indian shot]
○

type of plant: half-hardy perennial [9–11]
flowering time: midsummer to early autumn
flower color: tangerine
height: 4–6ft/1.2–1.8m

As well as bold, dusky foliage, this upright plant produces iris-like flowers that are large and showy. The very broad, pointed leaves are purplish brown with darker purple veining. Individual leaves are often about 18in/45cm long. Other cannas with interesting foliage include *C.* "Striata" (see p.163) and *C. indica* "Purpurea," which has deep red-orange flowers and dark purple leaves. All these plants are popular for inclusion in "tropical" plantings. They need moist, fertile soil and they should be given a warm, sheltered site. In colder regions, the plants need to be lifted in autumn and overwintered in a frost-free place. In these areas, cannas tend not to flower very freely.

Atriplex hortensis var. rubra
[red mountain spinach, red orache]
○

type of plant: hardy annual [6–9]
flowering time: mid- to late summer
flower color: reddish purple
height: 4–5ft/1.2–1.5m

The exact color of *A. hortensis* var. *rubra* tends to vary and some strains are more red than purple. In the deep plum-purple strain illustrated here, the leaves—tapering triangles up to 6in/15cm long—are borne on plum-colored stems. These stems are upright at first and they can be kept so by pinching out the flower buds. But if the plant is allowed to flower and to produce its spikes of attractive, rich purple, disc-shaped seeds, it may need staking. The plant is edible and is often available from stockists of herbs, as well as being listed in both the flower and the vegetable sections of seed catalogs. It needs deep, rich, moisture-retentive soil for really lush growth. It self-sows.
also for: ■ Ornamental fruit (seedheads)

Clematis recta "Purpurea"
○

type of plant: hardy perennial [3–9]
flowering time: mid- to late summer
flower color: white
height: 3–5ft/0.9–1.5m

The masses of little, starry flowers produced by this clematis exude a heavy scent that some people find attractive. The flowers, each about ¾in/2cm across, are followed by small, wispy seedheads. This herbaceous, non-climbing clematis is clump-forming and has rather untidy, branching growths that need support in order to grow upright. On *C. recta* itself the fairly slender, pointed leaflets are green or gray-green; on *C.r.* "Purpurea" the young foliage is rich purple—although just how dark this coloring is tends to vary from plant to plant. Most soils, as long as they are reasonably well drained, are suitable for this easily grown clematis.
also for: ■ Ornamental fruit (seedheads) ■ Fragrant flowers (see above)

Weigela florida "Foliis Purpureis"
○

type of plant: hardy shrub [5–8]
flowering time: late spring to early summer
flower color: purplish pink
height: 3–4ft/0.9–1.2m
✂

This slow-growing shrub needs a position in full sun. If it is planted in even quite light shade, the dark brown-purple flush on its leaves becomes an uninteresting brownish green. Each leaf is a broad, pointed oval up to 2in/5cm long. There are, normally, large numbers of the clustered, funnel-shaped flowers. The plant is fairly erect overall, with stiff, somewhat arching branches. Fertile soils of various types produce good specimens of *W. florida* "Foliis Purpureis," but it grows really well in soil that remains reasonably moist through the spring and summer months. *W.* "Victoria" has rather darker purple-flushed leaves and red flowers.
also for: ■ Heavy, clay soils ■ Atmospheric pollution

Dahlia "Bishop of Llandaff" (Miscellaneous)
○

type of plant: half-hardy tuber [9–10]
flowering time: late summer to mid-autumn
flower color: scarlet
height: 36–42in/90–105cm

Sizzling scarlet flowers combined with gleaming, blackish purple-green foliage make D. "Bishop of Llandaff" a dramatic plant for "hot" color schemes. The single to semi-double blooms, each about 3in/8cm across, are carried—on almost black stems—above the toothed and tapering leaflets. Except in really warm regions, the tubers need to be lifted and stored in a frost-free place each winter. To perform well, the plant needs rich, moist soil and good drainage. See pp. 202 and 270, for examples of other dahlias with dark foliage. The flowers of all these plants are excellent for cutting.
also for: ■ Flowers suitable for cutting

Hebe "Mrs Winder" (syn. H. "Waikiki")
○

type of plant: slightly tender shrub [8–10]
flowering time: late summer to mid-autumn
flower color: violet-blue
height: 30–36in/75–90cm
Evergreen

Densely clothed in narrow leaves, up to 1½in/4cm-long, this rounded shrub makes good ground cover, especially when several specimens are planted together. The foliage is rich red-purple from spring into summer; in winter it is purple. The youngest stems are chestnut-colored. Although they appear intermittently over a long period, the short flower spikes are not very freely produced. Other popular hebes with purple or red foliage include the lower-growing H. "Red Edge"; its gray-green leaves are flushed with red in winter and spring and margined with red at other times. Both these plants need plenty of sun and well-drained soil that is not too dry.
also for: ■ Ground cover

Aster lateriflorus e.g. "Prince"
○

type of plant: hardy perennial [4–8]
flowering time: early to mid-autumn
flower color: pale pink
height: 24in/60cm

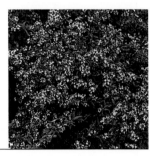

The stems and leaves of this twiggy, clump-forming plant are dark blackish purple. The coloring is especially rich before flowering time. There are masses of little daisies, each about ½in/1cm wide, as well as numerous, narrow leaves. A. lateriflorus "Lady in Black" is similar, but about twice as tall A.l. "Prince"; A.l. "Horizontalis" has wide-spreading stems with pink and white flowers, and dark green leaves that are tinged coppery purple in autumn. All these plants should be given soil that is moisture-retentive and well-drained. A sunny position ensures good leaf color and plenty of flowers.
also for: ■ Flowers suitable for cutting

Salvia officinalis "Purpurascens" [purple sage]
○

type of plant: slightly tender shrub/perennial (herb) [7–9]
flowering time: early to midsummer
flower color: violet-purple
height: 24in/60cm
Evergreen/Semi-evergreen ✄

If clipped lightly in spring and grown in well-drained, dryish soil, this erect and bushy plant forms a neat, dense hummock. Its felted leaves are slender, pointed ovals, up to 3in/8cm long. When young, the foliage is purple; with age, it acquires gray overtones. Small, two-lipped flowers are carried on branching stems above the foliage. Some forms of purple sage produce very few flowers, even if they are not clipped. Although not as strongly aromatic as green-leaved common sage (S. officinalis), the leaves of purple sage have the same pungent scent. For examples of other sages with colored foliage, see pp.166 and 247.
also for: ■ Dry soils in hot, sunny sites ■ Ground cover ■ Aromatic foliage

Euphorbia dulcis "Chameleon" [spurge]
○

type of plant: hardy perennial [4–9]
flowering time: late spring to early summer
flower color: lime-green
height: 18–24in/45–60cm

E. dulcis "Chameleon" makes a bushy, slim-stemmed mass of rich chocolate-purple. At first, the foliage is a rather redder color but, as it matures, it darkens. Each leaf is fairly slender, blunt-ended and up to 2½in/6cm long. Tiny, acid-green blooms are surrounded by purple, leaf-like bracts. Autumn foliage color is most often a mixture of pinks and apricots. This plant needs well-drained, reasonably moisture-retentive soil. The milky juice that oozes from the cut stems can irritate skin and eyes. Other purple-leaved spurges include E. amygdaloides "Purpurea" (syn. "Rubra") [zones 7–9], which has dusky red-purple leaves, and the smaller variety shown on p.203.
also for: ■ Colorful, autumn foliage

Penstemon digitalis "Husker Red"
○

type of plant: hardy perennial [3–9]
flowering time: early to midsummer
flower color: palest soft pink
height: 18–24in/45–60cm
Semi-evergreen

The fairly slender, pointed leaves, the stems, and the small, outer parts of the flowers of P. digitalis "Husker Red" are all rich maroon-purple. The coloring is especially good before the plant comes into full flower. Foxglove-like blooms, each about 1in/2.5cm long, are produced, rather sparsely, on upright stems that rise above semi-evergreen, basal rosettes of foliage. Well-drained, fertile soil and a position in full sun give the best results.

Perilla frutescens var. *crispa* (syn. *P.f.* var. *nankinensis*)
○

type of plant: half-hardy annual [8–10]
height: 18–24in/45–60cm

The glistening, deep purple or dark bronze leaves of this upright plant have crisply crinkled edges. When bruised, the foliage emits a warm, clean scent with undertones of both mint and sage. The decoratively frilly leaves, each about 3in/8cm long, are broadly oval, pointed and conspicuously veined. Fertile, moisture-retentive soil with good drainage gives the best results. Since the leaves can be used in cooking, *P. frutescens* var. *crispa* is often listed in the vegetable or herb sections of seed catalogs.
also for: ■ Aromatic foliage

Sedum telephium subsp. *maximum* "Atropurpureum" [stonecrop]
○

type of plant: hardy perennial [5–9]
flowering time: late summer to mid-autumn
flower color: buff-pink
height: 18–24in/45–60cm

Both the color and the texture of these leaves are attractive. Each oblong leaf, up to 3in/8cm long, is smooth, thick, and fleshy, and an opulent, dark maroon. Stout, purplish stems are topped with flattish heads of numerous, starry flowers, which last well in water. When dried, they are an attractive, rich brown. *S. telephium* subsp. *maximum* "Atropurpureum" is upright and forms fairly open clumps of growth. It needs soil with good drainage, but conditions must not be very dry. *S.* "Matrona" (see p.280) is a newer, increasingly popular variety with more substantial clumps of purple-flushed foliage and large heads of soft pink flowers.
also for: ■ Flowers suitable for cutting (and drying)

Imperata cylindrica "Rubra" (syn. *I.c.* "Red Baron") [Japanese blood grass]
○

type of plant: slightly tender perennial (grass) [7–10]
flowering time: late summer
flower color: silvery
height: 15–20in/38–50cm

At first, only the tips of these narrow, upright leaves are red but, as summer progresses, the rich coloring spreads almost to the base of each flat, ½in/1cm-wide leaf blade. The foliage is arranged in tufts, and the plant increases slowly. Rich, moisture-retentive soil is most suitable for this grass. Only in regions with hot summers are substantial quantities of the slim flower spikes regularly produced. In these areas *I. cylindrica* "Rubra" can be grown in light shade.

Dahlia e.g. "Redskin"
○

type of plant: half-hardy annual [9–10]
flowering time: midsummer to mid-autumn
flower color: mixed—red, orange, yellow, scarlet, lilac
height: 15in/38cm

Most of the mixtures of annual, bedding dahlias, which are raised from seed each year, are fairly short, bushy plants. Many of them, including the variety shown here, need no staking. *D.* "Redskin" has tapering, oval leaflets that are dark greenish bronze, and this enhances the rich, "hot" colors of the double and semi-double flowers (each of which are 2–3in/5–8cm wide). *D.* "Diabolo" is another example of a popular, annual, bedding dahlia with dark bronze foliage. Both these mixtures need rich, moisture-retentive soil with good drainage. Their flowers last well when cut.
also for: ■ Flowers suitable for cutting

Berberis thunbergii f. *atropurpurea* e.g. "Atropurpurea Nana" (syn. *B.* "Little Favourite," *B.t.* "Crimson Pygmy") [barberry]
○

type of plant: hardy shrub [5–8]
flowering time: mid- to late spring
flower color: pale yellow + red
height: 12–24in/30–60cm

So neatly and densely bun-shaped is this little shrub that, if several specimens are planted together, they will slowly grow into weed-proof cover. *B. thunbergii* f. *atropurpurea* "Atropurpurea Nana" is also suitable for low hedging (plants should be about 18in/45cm apart). In spring and summer, the rounded leaves, up to 1in/2.5cm long, are deep red-purple; in autumn, they turn dark russet-crimson. The small, cup-shaped flowers of this virtually thornless berberis are arranged in little clusters. They are followed by scarlet, droplet-shaped berries. *B.t.* f. *a.* "Bagatelle" is even more compact; it has reddish new growths. Both these plants are easily grown in almost any soil, provided it is not very alkaline or wet.
also for: ■ Atmospheric pollution
■ Ground cover ■ Hedging plants
■ Growing in containers ■ Colorful, autumn foliage ■ Ornamental fruit

Euphorbia cyparissias
"Fens Ruby"
(syn. *E.c.* "Clarice Howard")
[cypress spurge]
○

type of plant: hardy perennial [4–9]
flowering time: late spring to midsummer
flower color: yellow-green
height: 6–9in/15–23cm

This plant's upright stems and thin, blue-green leaves create a spreading mass of growth, which in poor soils is dense enough to make useful ground cover. Young leaves are red-purple, and this coloring is retained on the tips of the mature growths until autumn, when the foliage turns yellow. The flowers are arranged in branched heads, each about 3½in/9cm across. As they fade, the floral parts become tinged with orange. This variety is vigorous enough to spread to at least 24in/60cm wide, while *E. cyparissias* itself is green-leaved and invasive. Both plants like light soils. The cut stems of these spurges exude a milky juice that can irritate skin.
also for: ■ Dry soils in hot, sunny sites ■ Ground cover (see above) ■ Colorful, autumn foliage ■ Green flowers

Sedum spathulifolium
e.g. "Purpureum"
[stonecrop]
○

type of plant: hardy perennial [5–8]
flowering time: early to midsummer
flower color: golden yellow
height: 3–4in/8–10cm
Evergreen

As spring and summer progress, each of this plant's reddish purple rosettes of fleshy foliage becomes increasingly whitened, in its center at least, by a dusting of waxy powder. *S. spathulifolium* "Purpureum" is vigorous and soon makes a close mat of rooting growth, often 18in/45cm wide, in any soil that drains quickly. It thrives in hot, dry conditions. In poor soil particularly, it often becomes bright red in winter. Its starry flowers are arranged in clusters, each about 1in/2.5cm across, on top of short stems. A gray-leaved variety of *S. spathulifolium* is shown on p.61. Other low-growing stonecrops with purple foliage include forms of *S. spurium*, such as *S.s.* "Schorbuser Blut" (syn. Dragon's Blood).
also for: ■ Dry soils in hot, sunny sites ■ Ground cover ■ Crevices in paving

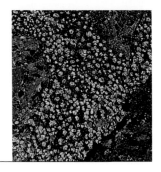

ADDITIONAL PLANTS, featured elsewhere in this book, that have purple, bronze, or red leaves

† = only young leaves are purple, bronze, or red

○ sun

minimum height 10ft/3m or more
†*Prunus* "Amanogawa," see p.13
†*Prunus* "Kanzan," see p.95
†*Prunus sargentii*, see p.236
†*Prunus* "Taihaku," see p.13

minimum height between 3ft/90cm and 10ft/3m
†*Callicarpa bodinieri* var. *giraldii* "Profusion," see p.253
Dahlia "David Howard," see p.270
†*Nandina domestica*, see p.236

minimum height 3ft/90cm or less
Dianthus barbatus Nigrescens Group, see p.330

Geranium sessiliflorum subsp. *novae-zelandiae* "Nigricans," see p.156
Lobelia "Queen Victoria," see p.66
†*Oenothera fruticosa* "Fyrverkeri," see p.339
†*Origanum laevigatum* "Herrenhausen," see p.17
Pittosporum tenuifolium "Tom Thumb," see p.146
Sedum telephium "Matrona," see p.280
Sempervivum tectorum, see p.61

Acer pseudoplatanus
"Brilliantissimum"
[sycamore maple, planetree maple]
○[◑]

type of plant: hardy tree [5–10]
height: 15–20ft/4.5–6m

Like the common sycamore maple (*Acer pseudoplatanus*), *A.p.* "Brilliantissimum" is an easily grown plant that thrives in a wide range of soil types. Its five-lobed leaves, up to 6in/15cm long, are a remarkable shrimp-pink when young. As they mature, they turn clear yellow, then almost white. They are finally soft green. This tree grows slowly, producing a dense, rounded crown of stout branches on a short trunk. *A.p.* "Prinz Handjéry" is similar, although not quite so densely branched.
also for: ■ Shallow soils over chalk ■ Heavy, clay soils ■ Atmospheric pollution

Vitis vinifera "Purpurea"
[purpleleaf grape]
○[◑]

type of plant: hardy climber [6–9]
height: 10–15ft/3–4.5m

Each of this tendrilled climber's decoratively lobed leaves is 4–6in/10–15cm long. Its young leaves are grayish, maturing to a rather somber purple that—on infertile soil particularly—turns to rich, crimson-claret in autumn. Against a warm, sheltered wall and in deep, fertile soil *V. vinifera* "Purpurea" may grow more than 20ft/6m high, and bunches of ornamental but very bitter-tasting, purple-black grapes are regularly produced. Green-leaved *V.* "Brandt" also colors well in autumn and, among its bronze-red autumn foliage, there are large bunches of edible, blue-black grapes.
also for: ■ Climbing plants ■ Colorful, autumn foliage ■ Ornamental fruit

Actaea simplex
Atropurpurea Group
(syn. *C. racemosa* "Purpurea,"
Cimicifuga simplex var. *simplex*
Atropurpurea Group)
[baneberry]
○[◐]

type of plant: hardy perennial [4–8]
flowering time: early to mid-autumn
flower color: pink-tinged white
height: 4–6ft/1.2–1.8m

Plants in this Group vary but they all have leaves that are some sort of dark brownish purple. The foliage is divided into numerous jagged and pointed leaflets, each 3–4in/8–10cm long. Leaves are particularly deeply colored in positions of full sun. These clump-forming plants thrive in damp, rich soils, although they also do well in any soil that is reasonably fertile and moisture-retentive. The dark-stemmed flowers, up to 12in/30cm long, are shaped like very slender bottle-brushes (see p.79 for an indication of the flower shape). Not everyone finds their scent attractive, although the flowers are visited by butterflies. *A. simplex* Atropurpurea Group "Brunette" has particularly well-colored, dark brown-purple leaves.
also for: ■ Damp and wet soils

Eupatorium rugosum "Chocolate"
[white snakeroot]
○[◐]

type of plant: hardy perennial [5–9]
flowering time: early to mid-autumn
flower color: white
height: 4ft/1.2m
✂✕

Younger growths on this bushy perennial are deep maroon-brown and even the more mature foliage has a dusky cast to it. The nettle-like leaves, up to 5in/12cm long, are conspicuously toothed and veined. They are carried on very upright, dark maroon stems that form clumps of growth. The heads of little, fluffy flowers are attractive to butterflies, but in cool climates these late-season blooms are often rather scarce. Leaf color is darkest and richest in sun; in light shade the foliage is dark but greener tones predominate. Moist but well-drained soil is needed for good growth.

Ligularia dentata
(syn. *L. clivorum*)
e.g. "Desdemona"
○[◐]

type of plant: hardy perennial [4–8]
flowering time: midsummer to early autumn
flower color: yellow-orange
height: 3–4ft/0.9–1.2m

Dark chocolate-purple suffuses the flower stems as well as leaves of this plant. As summer progresses, the coloring becomes greener, although the undersides and veins of the leathery, kidney-shaped leaves remain purplish maroon. Vivid daisies, each about 3in/8cm across, are carried in clusters well clear of the foliage clumps. Damp and boggy conditions produce the most impressive specimens of *L. dentata* "Desdemona" (with leaves more than 12in/30cm wide), but growth is vigorous in all fertile, moisture-retentive soils. *L.d.* "Othello" is a very similar variety.
also for: ■ Heavy, clay soils ■ Damp and wet soils

Crocosmia x crocosmiiflora
e.g. "Solfatare"
(syn. *C. x c.* "Solfaterre")
○[◐]

type of plant: slightly tender perennial [7–9]
flowering time: late summer
flower color: apricot-yellow
height: 24in/60cm

In addition to its sprays of pretty, 1¼in/3cm-long flowers (which last well in water), *C. x crocosmiiflora* "Solfatare" has interestingly colored foliage, which forms clumps of upright growth. The slender, pointed leaves are a smoky, bronzed green that intensifies from midsummer onward. A similar sort of leaf color is found in varieties such as red-flowered *C. x c.* "Dusky Maiden" and yellow-flowered *C. x c.* "Gerbe d'Or." All these plants are best grown in fertile soil that is well drained and that remains moist in summer. They thrive in mild areas with high rainfall and benefit from shelter and some winter protection in frost-prone regions.
also for: ■ Flowers suitable for cutting

Cryptotaenia japonica
f. *atropurpurea*
○[◐]

type of plant: hardy perennial/biennial [7–10]
height: 18–24in/45–60cm

Tiny, pink-tinged flowers appear on *C. japonica* f. *atropurpurea* in midsummer, but they are insignificant compared to the dark purple foliage. Each leaf consists of three, broad lobes, 2½–3in/6–8cm long, and the stems, as well as the leaves, are dark purple. The plant forms clumps of upright growth. Most soils are suitable but rich ones produce the lushest foliage. The leaves and stems are used in Japanese cooking; they have a fresh, angelica-like flavour.

Heuchera micrantha var. diversifolia "Palace Purple"
○【●】

type of plant: hardy perennial [4–8]
flowering time: mid- to late summer
flower color: pale pink
height: 18–24in/45–60cm
Evergreen ♂✂

This popular plant's crinkled, lobed leaves form ground-covering clumps of growth. Individual leaves may be 6in/15cm long and need sun to achieve a good depth of really rich, bronzish red-purple. However, plants sold under this name vary somewhat, and some may have brown rather than purple leaves no matter how much sun they receive. Airy sprays of tiny flowers, which are carried well above the 12in/30cm-high mound of gleaming foliage, ripen into pinkish seedheads. Fertile, well-drained soil that retains moisture gives the best results. H. "Rachel" is another popular variety with red-purple leaves, and there are numerous new cultivars.
also for: ■ Ground cover

Uncinia rubra
[hook sedge]
○【●】

type of plant: slightly tender perennial [8–10]
height: 12in/30cm
Evergreen

The stiff, grass-like foliage of U. rubra is shiny, rich red-brown with some brighter red striping. It forms a tussock of slightly arching growth. The narrow, pointed leaves are up to 15in/38cm long. Dark brown flower spikes are produced in late summer but these are inconspicuous. A sheltered site is usually needed and moist, rather spongy soil produces the best growth. In colder gardens, the foliage may become damaged during winter and the plant may look rather scruffy until well into summer. The autumn foliage of Panicum virgatum "Rubrum" [zones 5–9] is a somewhat similar, brownish red color; this grass, which likes a sunny site, grows up to 4ft/1.2m high.

Plantago major "Rubrifolia" (syn. P.m. "Atropurpurea")
[plantain]
○【●】

type of plant: hardy perennial [4–9]
flowering time: mid- to late summer
flower color: greenish purple
height: 9–12in/23–30cm

The soft, greenish maroon-purple of these deeply veined leaves is most pronounced in a sunny site. Long, slender flower spikes (seen here in bud) are of similar color, and make interesting material for dried flower arrangements. There is a most satisfactory contrast between these slim flower spikes and the broad, approximately oval leaves, each of which can be more than 6in/15cm long. P. major "Rubrifolia" is an adaptable, easily grown plant, but the rosettes of foliage are particularly large and bold in moisture-retentive, fertile soil. There are usually numerous self-sown seedlings; they too are maroon-purple.
also for: ■ Flowers suitable for cutting (mainly drying)

Ajuga reptans
e.g. "Atropurpurea"
[bugle]
○【●】

type of plant: hardy perennial [4–9]
flowering time: late spring to early summer
flower color: deep blue
height: 6in/15cm
Evergreen/Semi-evergreen

Full sun brings out the richest leaf color on this creeping plant but, if the foliage is to form a dense, ground-covering carpet, then the roots must be fairly moist. Leafy spikes of little, lipped flowers rise erectly above the dark bronze-purple foliage. Each gleaming, oval leaf is about 3½in/9cm long. Other varieties of A. reptans with purple or bronzed leaves include A.r. "Braunherz," which has deep brownish purple foliage, A.r. "Catlin's Giant" (see p.116) and A.r. "Pink Surprise," which has pink flowers and purplish leaves.
also for: ■ Heavy, clay soils ■ Ground cover

Nymphaea
e.g. "James Brydon"
[waterlily]
○【●】

type of plant: hardy perennial (aquatic) [5–10]
flowering time: mid- to late summer
flower color: pink changing to rosy red
height: 4–6in/10–15cm
≈

This very free-flowering waterlily is best grown in water 18–36in/45–90cm deep. Its roots should be planted in rich, loamy mud. The young leaves are purplish maroon; the more mature foliage is only slightly mottled, although a purple-bronze color is often retained on the leaf edges. Fully mature, the almost circular leaves are basically dark green and up to 10in/25cm across. Cup-shaped flowers, each about 5in/12cm wide, smell slightly of apples. N. "James Brydon" spreads about 36in/90cm wide. Other popular waterlilies with bronzed foliage include N. "Marliacea Chromatella" (see p.167) and white-flowered N. "Gonnère."

ADDITIONAL PLANTS, featured elsewhere in this book, that have purple, bronze, or red leaves:

† = only young leaves are purple, bronze, or red

○● sun or partial shade

minimum height between 3ft/90cm and 10ft/3m
†Rheum palmatum, see p.223

minimum height 3ft/90cm or less
Acaena microphylla, see p.111
Mentha aquatica, see p.70
†Spiraea japonica "Goldflame," see p.214

Acer palmatum f. atropurpureum
[Japanese maple]
○◐

type of plant: hardy tree/shrub [6–8]
height: 12–18ft/3.6–5.4m

Plants sold under this name vary, but they all produce graceful, rather open networks of branches and their elegant, lobed leaves, each about 3in/8cm long, create a layered effect. The foliage is deep red-purple for much of spring and summer, becoming greenish purple in late summer. In autumn it often turns rich red and scarlet, although individual specimens differ in the brilliance of their coloring. In time, these maples become tree-like and really mature plants can be more than 25ft/7.5m tall. They dislike dry soil and exposed positions and thrive in sheltered sites and moist, fertile, well-drained soil. In anything other than very light shade, leaf color tends to be greenish rather than purple. Other popular, purple-leaved Japanese maples include the cut-leaved plant shown on p.149, and *A.p.* "Bloodgood," which has foliage of a long-lasting, deep red-purple.
also for: ■ Colorful, autumn foliage

Photinia x fraseri "Red Robin"
○◐

type of plant: slightly tender/hardy [7–9]
flowering time: late spring to early summer
flower color: white
height: 6–10ft/1.8–3m
Evergreen ✄

As illustrated here, the new foliage of this upright shrub is rich red in mid-spring; by the end of summer it is bronze; fully mature, the glossy, pointed leaves, up to 8in/20cm long, are deep green. Although this plant does become denser with age, its habit of growth is always fairly open. Its clusters of little, saucer-shaped flowers are less striking than the young foliage. They tend to be sparsely produced, except in hot climates. *P. x fraseri* "Red Robin" can be used for hedging (young plants should be about 36in/90cm apart). The trimming involved in maintaining a hedge encourages plenty of new, colorful growth. This lime-tolerant plant requires well-drained but moisture-retentive soil, so shallow, chalky conditions are not suitable. Some shelter is usually advisable.
also for: ■ Hedging plants

Viburnum sargentii "Onondaga"
○◐

type of plant: hardy shrub [4–9]
flowering time: late spring to early summer
flower color: white + pale pink
height: 5–7ft/1.5–2.1m

This upright, rather gaunt shrub has lobed, maple-like leaves, 3–4in/8–10cm long, which are rich coppery red-brown when young. By midsummer the foliage is deep green. The "lacecap" flowers are soft pinkish red in bud. In full bloom, the outer flowers are white, saucer-shaped and about ¾in/2cm across; the closely packed, inner flowers are pale pink. In autumn the foliage turns a bronzed purple-red. Mature plants bear bunches of shiny, bright red berries from late summer. *V. sargentii* "Onondaga" grows well in all moisture-retentive soils.
also for: ■ Heavy, clay soils ■ Colorful, autumn foliage ■ Ornamental fruit

Rodgersia podophylla
○◐

type of plant: hardy perennial [5–8]
flowering time: early to midsummer
flower color: cream
height: 3–4ft/0.9–1.2m

The leaves of this clump-forming plant are divided into several leaflets, each of which resembles a duck's foot in outline. Especially in damp or boggy soil that is also fertile, these bold leaves can be well over 12in/30cm long. When young, the foliage is wrinkled and rich maroon bronze; as it matures, it turns mid-green. Particularly in a sunny site, it may become bronze again in midsummer and it often reddens in autumn. When grown in sun, the plant must have reliably moist soil; it can tolerate drier conditions in some shade. Its leaves benefit from being sheltered from cold winds. Branched heads of star-shaped flowers may be rather sparsely borne.
also for: ■ Heavy, clay soils ■ Damp and wet soils ■ Ground cover ■ Decorative, green foliage ■ Colorful, autumn foliage

Anthriscus sylvestris "Ravenswing"
[cow parsley, Queen Anne's lace]
◯◐

type of plant: hardy biennial/perennial [4–9]
flowering time: late spring to early summer
flower color: pink-tinged white
height: 30–36in/75–90cm

Pale, airy flower heads and deeply colored, lacy foliage make this a striking and decorative plant. Its much-divided leaves, up to 12in/30cm long, are very dark brown-purple, with an attractive sheen. They form clumps of growth, above which rise the delicate flowers on their dark stems. At best, *A. sylvestris* "Ravenswing" is a short-lived perennial. However, it tends to self-sow freely and some of the seedlings will have dark foliage. As long as it is not too dry, any well-drained soil is suitable for this plant.

Lysimachia ciliata "Firecracker"
[loosestrife]
◯◐

type of plant: hardy perennial [3–9]
flowering time: mid- to late summer
flower color: yellow
height: 30–36in/75–90cm

Both *L. ciliata* itself and *L.c.* "Firecracker" are vigorous, upright plants that thrive and spread widely—sometimes invasively—in all moisture-retentive soils. They also do well in damp and wet soils. Their leaves are pointed ovals up to 6in/15cm long. In the species, only the young foliage is chocolate colored; the mature foliage is soft green. In the variety, the foliage retains a deep rich brownish purple coloring throughout the growing season. The flowers of both plants are star-shaped, 1in/2.5cm wide and arranged in loose sprays.
also for: ■ Damp and wet soils

Carex comans bronze
[sedge]
◯◐

type of plant: hardy perennial [6–9]
height: 12–15in/30–38cm
Evergreen

Various species and varieties of *Carex* produce leaves in some shade of bronze. The form shown here creates a dense, arching, often swirling mound of pale chocolate-brown foliage. *C. buchananii* is more upright and of a reddish brown color; *C. flagellifera* consists of a tuft of red-ginger foliage. Both these last two plants are taller than *C. comans*. All three sedges have very fine leaves. They are all easily grown in most soils and thrive as long as they are not dry. The flowers of *C. comans* are inconspicuous, brown spikes that are produced in summer.
also for: ■ Ground cover (*C. comans* bronze only)

Begonia e.g. Cocktail Series
◯◐

type of plant: grown as half-hardy annual [9–11]
flowering time: early summer to early autumn
flower color: mixed—red, pink, white + bicolors
height: 6–8in/15–20cm

Many of the Semperflorens begonias, so widely used for bedding, have foliage that is bronze or purple. The rounded, fleshy leaves of all *B.* Cocktail Series plants, for example, are rich, shiny bronze. These neat, bushy plants produce numerous sprays of single, ¾in/2cm-wide flowers. Compared with the flowers of some other Semperflorens begonias, the blooms of *B.* Cocktail Series plants are less likely to become scorched or bleached in strong sun. However, these plants do still need well-drained, preferably acid to neutral soil that remains moist; they do not prosper in hot, dry conditions.
also for: ■ Acid soils

Ranunculus ficaria "Brazen Hussy"
[lesser celandine, pilewort]
◯◐

type of plant: hardy tuber [5–8]
flowering time: early to mid-spring
flower color: rich yellow
height: 4in/10cm

Once the shiny, saucer-shaped flowers of *R. ficaria* "Brazen Hussey" have faded, the foliage starts to die back. The tufts of glossy, dark chocolate-brown leaves may be short-lived, but they provide a very flattering background for the flowers (each of which is about ¾in/2cm wide). *R. ficaria* is a exceptionally variable plant and there are dozens of cultivars, including white-, orange-, and double-flowered forms. The heart-shaped leaves of these plants are basically green with some dark bronze markings. Fertile, moisture-retentive soils of all sorts are suitable.
also for: ■ Heavy, clay soils

ADDITIONAL PLANTS, featured elsewhere in this book, that have purple, bronze, or red leaves

† = only young leaves are purple, bronze, or red

◯◐ sun or partial shade

minimum height 10ft/3m or more
†*Amelanchier canadensis,* see p.28
†*Cercidiphyllum japonicum,*
   see p.240

†*Clematis* "Elizabeth," see p.132

minimum height between 3ft/90cm and 10ft/3m
Acer palmatum var. *dissectum* Dissectum
   Atropurpureum Group, see p.149
†*Aesculus parviflora,* see p.242
†*Drimys lanceolata,* see p.250
†*Rhododendron* "Berryrose," see p.30

minimum height 3ft/90cm or less
Ajuga reptans "Catlin's Giant,"
   see p.116
Astilbe "Fanal," see p.228
†*Rhododendron williamsianum,*
   see p.112
†*Rodgersia pinnata* "Superba,"
   see p.73

Primula "Guinevere"
(syn. *P.* "Garryard Guinevere")
●◗[○]

type of plant: hardy perennial [5–8]
flowering time: early to late spring
flower color: lilac-pink + yellow
height: 4–6in/10–15cm
Semi-evergreen

Sometimes *P.* "Guinevere" flowers so freely that its dark purplish bronze leaves are more or less obscured. The 1¼in/3cm-wide, primrose-like blooms are arranged in generous clusters on red stems. Particularly large numbers of these clusters are produced if the plant is divided frequently. After flowering time, the spoon-shaped, wrinkled leaves lengthen, up to 5in/12cm. In cool, rich, moist soil the plant quickly makes dense clumps of ground-covering growth. In cold climates, it may need a sunny position to flower well.
also for: ■ Ground cover

ADDITIONAL PLANTS, featured elsewhere in this book, that have purple, bronze, or red leaves

●◗[○] **partial shade (or sun),** † = only young leaves are purple, bronze, or red

minimum height 3ft/90cm or less: †*Epimedium perralderianum,* see p.120; †*Epimedium* x *rubrum,* see p.83

Pieris e.g. "Forest Flame"
◐ ✱

type of plant: hardy shrub [6–9]
flowering time: mid- to late spring
flower color: creamy white
height: 6–10ft/1.8–3m
Evergreen ⚬✄

In spring, the young foliage of this dense, upright, slow-growing shrub is a startlingly bright pinkish red. It later fades to pink and then cream. In maturity, the slender, pointed leaves, up to 5in/12cm long, are dark green and glossy. Drooping clusters of slightly fragrant, bell-shaped flowers are often 6in/15cm long. Although *P.* "Forest Flame" itself is hardy, its young growths need shelter from icy winds and frosts. Moist, humus-rich, well-drained soil is ideal. Conditions must be lime-free. For gardeners who do not have lime-free soil, *Photinia* x *fraseri* "Red Robin" (see p.206) is a possible pieris substitute.
also for: ■ Acid soils ■ Flowers suitable for cutting

Dryopteris erythrosora
[buckler fern]
◐

type of plant: hardy fern [5–9]
height: 18–24in/45–60cm
Semi-evergreen

The fronds of this fern emerge pink and then turn a yellowish coppery color; the fully mature foliage is shiny and rich green. Provided that the plant has been given a shady, sheltered site and humus-rich soil that remains moist, the foliage can stay fresh-looking well into winter. Each much-divided frond may be up to 24in/60cm long. *D. erythrosora* forms small clumps of growth and increases slowly.
also for: ■ Decorative, green foliage

Saxifraga "Wada"
(syn. *S. fortunei* "Wada")
[saxifrage]
◐●

type of plant: hardy perennial [6–8]
flowering time: mid- to late autumn
flower color: white
height: 12in/30cm
Deciduous/Semi-evergreen

Since they appear so late in the year, this plant's constellations of lopsided "stars" need shelter from rough autumn weather. Shelter—with some shade and moist, open-textured, humus-rich soil—also encourages the production of good quantities of the softly gleaming, red-backed leaves. The upper surface of each rounded, scalloped leaf is a rich, bronzed purple-red. Individual leaves are up to 4in/10cm across and the foliage forms clumps of growth. Other *S. fortunei* selections include *S.* "Blackberry and Apple Pie," which has dark green leaves with red edges and red undersides. *S.* "Mount Nachi" is smaller with red-marked, coppery leaves.

ADDITIONAL PLANTS, featured elsewhere in this book, that have purple, bronze, or red leaves

† = only young leaves are purple, bronze, or red

◐/◐● **partial shade/partial or full shade**

minimum height 3ft/90cm or less
†*Epimedium grandiflorum* "Rose Queen," see p.122
†*Epimedium* x *youngianum* "Niveum," see p.232

†*Leucothoe* Scarletta, see p.38
Viola riviniana Purpurea Group,
see p.125

Yellow or yellow-green leaves

FOR GARDENERS WHO LIKE FOLIAGE in general and unusually colored foliage in particular, plants with yellow leaves are an especially attractive source of one of the warmer and more vitalizing colors. Although the range of readily available plants that have yellow leaves is not very large, it does include plants of many different types. The following list features trees, shrubs, climbers, and perennials, among which are distinctive plants such as herbs, grasses, and conifers.

Yellow foliage varies considerably in color. *Thuja occidentalis* "Rheingold" and *Libertia peregrinans*, for example, have leaves that are almost orange, at least at some time in the year. Other plants, such as the popular yellow-leaved form of marjoram (*Origanum vulgare* "Aureum") and the lovely *Acer shirasawanum* "Aureum," have foliage that is of a more straightforward, sunny yellow. There are also some plants, mainly conifers, that produce foliage of a particularly rich golden yellow; others are of a sharp acid-yellow (*Geranium* "Ann Folkard" and *Berberis thunbergii* "Aurea," for example); a few plants—*Hebe ochracea* "James Stirling" is one—have leaves that are, unusually, ocher-toned.

The coloring of some yellow-leaved plants changes with the seasons. Certain conifers and heathers, for example, become more richly or brightly colored during the colder months, and quite a few deciduous, yellow-leaved plants tend to become greener as the growing season progresses. Only a small number of deciduous, yellow-leaved plants have colorful autumn foliage.

In addition to the influence of seasons, leaf color is affected by how much sun or shade individual plants receive in particular positions. Some deciduous, yellow foliage is of a rather delicate texture and, in strong sunlight or in dry growing conditions, there may well be unsightly browning of the leaf edges. While shade may mean that leaf color is not as bright as it would be in full sun, it does usually insure that any yellowness is longer-lasting and that foliage remains in good condition.

Tough, thick leaves, such as those of conifers and heathers and some deciduous plants too, can withstand full exposure to light, and there are many plants that color really well only in a sunny position.

Even among just the most widely available yellow-leaved plants there is a remarkable variety of leaf size, shape, and texture. This list contains several plants with large, broad leaves (see, for example, *Catalpa bignonioides* "Aurea" and *Hosta fortunei* var. *albopicta* f. *aurea*), as well as many plants with narrow, needle-like leaves (*Erica arborea* "Albert's Gold" and *Cedrus deodara* "Aurea," for example). There are also plants with deeply lobed leaves (*Tanacetum parthenium* "Aureum") and with stringy foliage (*Chamaecyparis pisifera* "Filifera Aurea" and *Hebe ochracea* "James Stirling"). The foliage texture of these plants ranges from the smooth to the conspicuously veined and from the stiff, dense and dry to the thin-textured and moist.

Nurseries specializing in foliage plants stock a wider range of yellow-leaved plants than is shown in this book. Additional trees with yellow foliage include maples such as *Acer cappadocicum* "Aureum," the English oak *Quercus robur* "Concordia," and *Alnus incana* "Aurea," which is a yellow-leaved form of the gray alder. Some nurseries offer yellow-leaved shrubs such as varieties of flowering currant (*Ribes sanguineum* "Brocklebankii"), guelder rose (*Viburnum opulus* "Aureum"), and ornamental, white-stemmed bramble (*Rubus cockburnianus* "Goldenvale"). Specialist stockists of herbs and of grasses are particularly good sources of smaller plants with yellow leaves, but many nurseries offering a good selection of perennials include plants like the yellow-suffused *Stachys byzantina* "Primrose Heron," *Luzula sylvatica* "Aurea" (which has foliage that is yellow in winter), and *Veronica prostrata* "Trehane" (a speedwell that has yellow leaves and deep blue flowers).

For foliage variegated with yellow see "Plants with variegated leaves," pp.160–81.

Robinia pseudoacacia "Frisia"
[black locust]
○
type of plant: hardy tree [4–8]
flowering time: early summer
flower color: creamy white
height: 40–50ft/12–15m

Although the lacy foliage of this upright, round-headed tree emerges very late in spring, it remains bright throughout summer. Contrasting effectively with the dark branches, the oval leaflets are vivid yellow to lime-yellow, until they turn deeper orange-yellow in late summer. Each leaf is about 8in/20cm long. Young stems bear red thorns. The blossoms are very attractive to bees. In cooler climates, only older plants may flower. This tree is easily grown in most soils. It is suitable for poor and for light, dry soils, but its foliage is of better quality in reasonably moist conditions.
also for: ■ Dry soils in hot, sunny sites ■ Atmospheric pollution ■ Colorful, autumn foliage ■ Fragrant flowers

Gleditsia triacanthos "Sunburst"
[honeylocust]
○
type of plant: hardy tree [4–9]
height: 30–40ft/9–12m

Unlike many yellow-leaved plants, this thornless variety of honeylocust grows quite quickly. Its grayish branches spread widely into airy layers of shiny, golden-yellow foliage. The leaves, each 6–8in/15–20cm long, have numerous, slender leaflets that do not unfurl until late in spring. They remain yellow during most of the summer, becoming greener as they mature. For a brief period, they are yellow again in autumn. Any fertile, well-drained soil is suitable and G. triacanthos "Sunburst" copes well with dry conditions. It is tolerant of very polluted air. In an exposed site, it is liable to wind damage. For a purple-leaved variety of honeylocust, see p.198.
also for: ■ Dry soils in hot, sunny sites ■ Atmospheric pollution

Cupressus macrocarpa
e.g. "Goldcrest"
[Monterey cypress]
○
type of plant: hardy/slightly tender conifer [7–10]
height: 30ft/9m
Evergreen

Although it broadens with age, this conifer remains a dense and fairly narrow cone of growth throughout its life. For much of the year the leaf color is a striking, yellowish lime-green but, provided the plant has been positioned in full sun, the foliage turns bright golden-yellow in winter. Its fruitily aromatic leaves are tiny and scale-like, and they are arranged in attractive, feathery plumes. Almost any well-drained soil is suitable for C. macrocarpa "Goldcrest," but it needs a site sheltered from cold, drying winds. It grows especially well in mild, maritime regions. It is one of the fastest-growing yellow-leaved conifers.
also for: ■ Aromatic foliage

Catalpa bignonioides "Aurea"
[Indian bean tree, southern catalpa]
○
type of plant: hardy tree [5–10]
flowering time: mid- to late summer
flower color: white + purple
height: 25–30ft/7.5–9m

C. bignonioides "Aurea" is late into leaf. Its broadly heart-shaped leaves (up to 9in/23cm long) are coppery when very young, then bright yellow into late summer. Mature specimens produce bell-shaped flowers, 2in/5cm wide, in large, erect, open clusters. These are often followed by very long, thin seed pods, which are brown when ripe. If the plant is cut right back early each year, it forms a big shrub with extra-large leaves; unpruned, it slowly makes a tree with a wide, rounded head of growth. It needs a sheltered site and prefers moist, fertile soil. This tree thrives in regions with hot summers.
also for: ■ Heavy, clay soils ■ Atmospheric pollution ■ Ornamental fruit (seed pods)

Chamaecyparis pisifera
"Filifera Aurea"
[Sawara cypress]
○
type of plant: hardy conifer [5–9]
height: 15–20ft/4.5–6m
Evergreen

Especially when young, this cypress grows slowly—after ten years it may be expected to have reached a height of 3–4ft/0.9–1.2m. As it ages, it becomes broader, until it is eventually a large, wide-spreading cone of weeping growth. The "strings" of golden-yellow foliage—each about 4in/10cm long—give a lacy effect overall. Dry conditions are not suitable for this plant, which is at its best in cool climates with fairly high rainfall and in deep, moist, well-drained soil. It has a preference for slightly acid to neutral conditions. C. pisifera "Filifera Aurea" requires sun for its foliage to color well.

Thuja occidentalis
e.g. "Rheingold"
[American arborvitae, eastern arborvitae]
○
type of plant: hardy conifer [3–8]
height: 6–10ft/1.8–3m
Evergreen

In autumn and winter, the orange tones in this conifer's rich gold foliage become particularly pronounced. T. occidentalis "Rheingold" varies in habit of growth but, whether it is globular or conical when young, it eventually has a broadly conical outline. It grows densely and slowly. Most soils, including heavy clays, give satisfactory results but deep, moist loam is ideal. When crushed, the sprays of tiny leaves emit a pineapple-like scent. Other popular arborvitaes with orange- or bronze-gold tints in their foliage include T. plicata "Rogersii" and T.p. "Stoneham Gold" [zones 5–8].
also for: ■ Heavy, clay soils ■ Aromatic foliage ■ Colorful, autumn foliage (winter color, too)

Laurus nobilis "Aurea"
[bay laurel, sweet bay]
○
type of plant: slightly tender shrub (herb) [8–10]
height: 5–8ft/1.5–2.4m
Evergreen ✂

L. nobilis itself (see p.249) has rich green, tapered leaves that are widely used in cookery. This yellow-leaved variety also has sweetly aromatic foliage and, like the species, it too can be used for topiary. However, it is slower-growing, and it requires full sun and a sheltered site to produce foliage of a good golden yellow color. A;though the leaves, each 3–4in/8–10cm long, look their brightest in late winter and early spring, the broad cone of foliage is attractive throughout the year. (The illustration shows the plant in mid-autumn.) This shrub needs well-drained soil. It grows well near the sea.
also for: ■ Windswept, seaside gardens ■ Growing in containers ■ Aromatic foliage

Hedera helix "Buttercup"
[ivy]
○
type of plant: hardy climber [6–10]
height: 5–7ft/1.5–2.1m
Evergreen

This self-clinging climber needs good light to color well. In shade, the neatly lobed leaves are pale green; in sun, they are yellow almost all year long, becoming only a little less bright during the colder months. Growth tends to be slow, particularly in the initial stages, and it is worth giving this ivy moisture-retentive and reasonably fertile soil. In very sunny, rather dry positions the foliage is inclined to scorch. Each leaf is quite small—1½–2in/4–5cm wide. The leaves of *H. helix* "Angularis Aurea," with which *H.h.* "Buttercup" is sometimes confused, are about 4in/10cm wide and mottled green-and-yellow.
also for: ■ Atmospheric pollution ■ Climbing plants

Erica arborea
e.g. "Albert's Gold"
[tree heath]
○
type of plant: hardy/slightly tender shrub [7–10]
height: 5–6ft/1.5–1.8m
Evergreen

Only a few flowers are produced by this tree heath, but its upright plumes of foliage make a very striking, finely textured mass of bright golden-yellow. The tiny, needle-like leaves are most richly colored in winter. (*E. arborea* "Estrella Gold" does produce plenty of white, bell-shaped flowers, but its foliage is basically lime-green rather than yellow.) *E.a.* "Albert's Gold" tolerates a limited amount of alkalinity but is best in well-drained, acid to neutral soil. *E.a.* var. *alpina* is a really free-flowering tree heath that produces profuse quantities of sweet-scented, white flower clusters among its green leaves.
also for: ■ Acid soils ■ Growing in containers

Juniperus x *pfitzeriana*
(syn. *J.* x *media*)
e.g. "Pfitzeriana Aurea"
[juniper]
○
type of plant: hardy conifer [4–9]
height: 3–5ft/0.9–1.5m
Evergreen

The leaves of *J.* x *pfitzeriana* "Pfitzeriana Aurea" are tiny, pointed and scale-like. When young they are bright yellow; they mature to yellowish green. This vigorous conifer can spread more than 10ft/3m wide; it makes good, large-scale ground-cover. Its main branches slant upward, and have arching tips and hanging branchlets. *J.* x *p.* "Old Gold" is another semi-prostrate variety, but it is much slower-growing and more compact; it retains its gold coloring year-round. *J.* x *p.* "Sulphur Spray" has pale yellow foliage. All these plants grow well in a range of soils, although good drainage is advisable.
also for: ■ Shallow soils over chalk ■ Dry soils in hot, sunny sites ■ Ground cover

Chamaecyparis lawsoniana
e.g. "Minima Aurea"
[Lawson false cypress]
○
type of plant: hardy conifer [6–8]
height: 3–4ft/0.9–1.2m
Evergreen

This little conifer's stiff, upright branches carry slightly twisted sprays of tiny, scale-like leaves. These are golden-yellow—yellow-green beneath—almost all year long. The plant is dense and cone-shaped. *C. lawsoniana* "Minima Aurea" grows very slowly and is especially useful for long-term planting in containers. Moisture-retentive soil with good drainage is most suitable. For a slow-growing, medium-sized Lawson false cypress with yellow leaves, see p.145.
also for: ■ Growing in containers

Ilex crenata "Golden Gem"
[Japanese holly]
○
type of plant: hardy shrub [6–8]
height: 3–4ft/0.9–1.2m
Evergreen

New growth on this holly is golden-yellow; by summer the foliage is yellow-green. Each neat, shining, pointed leaf is normally little more than ½in/1cm long. The plant grows slowly, its stiff, densely foliated branches spreading into a gently undulating mass. Such a slow growth rate, combined with its attractive coloring and lack of prickles, make this Japanese holly particularly suitable for planting in containers. Most moisture-retentive soils, including clay, are suitable for this plant, although it does have a preference for acid to neutral conditions. This particular variety of Japanese holly rarely flowers or fruits.
also for: ■ Heavy, clay soils ■ Growing in containers

Valeriana phu "Aurea"
[valerian]
○

type of plant: hardy perennial [5–8]
flowering time: early to midsummer
flower color: white
height: 30–36in/75–90cm
Semi-evergreen ♀✄

In spring, this clump-forming plant produces loose, 9in/25cm-high tufts of clear yellow leaves, which turn light green during summer. The basal leaves, each 6–8in/15–20cm long, are divided and lobed. They are retained through the winter months. Less decorative than the foliage are the little, domed flower heads, carried on openly branched stems. Some gardeners like to remove these flowers before they develop fully. Moisture-retentive but well-drained soil and a sunny position are needed to encourage good growth and the production of plenty of colorful foliage.

Platycladus orientalis
(syn. Thuja orientalis)
e.g. "Aurea Nana"
○

type of plant: hardy conifer [6–9]
height: 24–36in/60–90cm
Evergreen

Since this conifer's sprays of tiny, scale-like leaves are held more or less vertically, the plant has a distinctive texture and pattern. In summer the foliage is bright gold-green; it assumes a deeper, bronze-tinged color in winter. P. orientalis "Aurea Nana" retains its neat, dense, oval shape throughout its life. Moist, loamy soil produces the best specimens of this plant. Especially when young, it needs shelter from cold winds.
also for: ■ Growing in containers

Caryopteris x clandonensis "Worcester Gold"
○

type of plant: hardy/slightly tender shrub [7–9]
flowering time: late summer to early autumn
flower color: violet-blue
height: 24–30in/60–75cm

The spreading stems of this aromatic shrub are clothed in slender, toothed leaves, each about 2in/5cm long. The foliage is yellow-green and most colorful before the clusters of long-stamened, tubular flowers have opened fully. Overall C. x clandonensis "Worcester Gold" makes a fairly dense mound of growth, with the flowers appearing towards the ends of the rather curving stems. Light, well-drained soil is most suitable for this shrub, which thrives on chalk and in a dry, sunny site. The foliage smells of varnish when bruised.
also for: ■ Shallow soils over chalk ■ Dry soils in hot, sunny sites ■ Aromatic foliage

Calluna vulgaris
e.g. "Gold Haze"
[heather, ling]
○ ✳

type of plant: hardy shrub [5–8]
flowering time: late summer to early autumn
flower color: white
height: 18in/45cm
Evergreen

The tiny, narrow, overlapping leaves of C. vulgaris "Gold Haze" are light greenish yellow, deepening in late summer and autumn. Single flowers, each less than ¼in/0.5cm long, are clustered around the ends of the more or less erect stems; they are very attractive to bees. When clipped lightly each spring and grown in moisture-retentive but well-drained, acid soil in an open position, this bushy plant makes good ground-cover. Other yellow-leaved varieties include C.v. "Beoley Gold (bright yellow foliage all year round) and C.v. "Golden Carpet" (4in/10cm high). The foliage of some yellow-leaved varieties becomes red or orange in winter (see the example on p. 237).
also for: ■ Acid soils ■ Ground cover

Hebe ochracea "James Stirling"
○

type of plant: hardy/slightly tender shrub [7–10]
height: 18in/45cm
Evergreen

This slow-growing shrub has interestingly textured and intriguingly colored foliage. The leaves are tiny scales that clasp the shoots, and the sprays of stringy foliage look conifer-like. Their coloring is an unusual, ocher-green that becomes slightly more bronze in winter. Particularly in cool climates, few if any of the starry, white flowers appear in late spring and early summer. The branches are erect with arching tips, and the plant forms a rather flat-topped mass of growth, usually about 24in/60cm wide. Good drainage is needed and, although the shrub can withstand periods of drought, it is best in reasonably moist soil. It grows well in chalky and in poor soils.
also for: ■ Shallow soils over chalk ■ Growing in containers

Tanacetum parthenium (syn. Chrysanthemum parthenium, Pyrethrum parthenium) "Aureum"
[golden feverfew]
○

type of plant: hardy perennial/half-hardy annual [4–9]
flowering time: midsummer to early autumn
flower color: yellow-tinged white + yellow
height: 18in/45cm
Semi-evergreen ♀✄

The little, daisy-like flowers of this short-lived, self-sowing plant are often removed at an early stage, particularly when the bright lime-yellow leaves are to be used in summer bedding schemes. Each deeply lobed, sharply aromatic leaf is about 3in/8cm long and, when prevented from flowering, T. parthenium "Aureum" forms bushy tufts of foliage about 6in/15cm high. Seed catalogs often list the dwarf variety T.p. "Golden Moss," which has especially small leaves. These plants are easy to grow in light, well-drained soil.
also for: ■ Aromatic foliage

Geranium "Ann Folkard"
[cranesbill]
○

type of plant: hardy perennial [5–8]
flowering time: early summer to mid-autumn
flower color: bright magenta + black
height: 15–18in/38–45cm

The long, wandering stems of this wide-spreading cranesbill carry deeply lobed leaves which, when young, are bright greenish yellow; older leaves are a fairly sharp, light green. Each leaf consists of five toothed and pointed leaflets. Intensely colored, black-eyed flowers, each about 1½in/4cm across, appear in profusion over a very long period. Spreading in a tangle of lax stems up to 4ft/1.2m wide, G. "Ann Folkard" sometimes "climbs" into nearby, tall plants. It is happy in a wide range of soils, as long as there is reasonable drainage.
also for: ■ Long, continuous flowering period

Libertia peregrinans
○

type of plant: slightly tender/hardy perennial [8–10]
flowering time: early to midsummer
flower color: white
height: 12–18in/30–45cm
Evergreen

The extraordinary leaf color of this little plant is strongest in winter and spring. Then the stiff, veined foliage—which is basically olive-green—is most conspicuously striped with orange and suffused with ocher. The individual leaves are narrow and pointed. Sprays of iris-like flowers, each bloom less than 1in/2.5cm across, nestle among the fans of foliage. Orange seed pods ripen from late summer. Slightly acidic soil that is well-drained but moisture-retentive produces good growth (very alkaline conditions are not suitable). Leaf color is most intense in full sun and in not too fertile soil. *L. peregrinans* spreads by means of creeping roots.
also for: ■ Ornamental fruit (seed pods)

Festuca glauca "Golden Toupee"
[blue fescue]
○

type of plant: hardy/slightly tender perennial (grass) [8–9]
flowering time: early to midsummer
flower color: pale soft yellow
height: 12in/30cm
Evergreen

During spring, the slim and spiky leaves of this tidy, tussock-forming grass are distinctly yellow; from summer onward, they mature to glaucous yellow. The slender flower heads tend not to be very freely produced. They are carried well clear of the leaf mound, which is 6–8in/15–20cm high. Like the fescues with gray-blue foliage (for an example of which, see p.188), *F. glauca* "Golden Toupee" appreciates light soil and a site in full sun. However, compared with the blue fescues it has leaves that are more prone to frost damage and, in colder regions, it can look bedraggled until quite late in spring.
also for: ■ Dry soils in hot, sunny sites ■ Ground cover

Origanum vulgare "Aureum"
[golden oregano]
○

type of plant: hardy perennial (herb) [4–8]
height: 9in/23cm
Evergreen/Semi-evergreen

As the summer months progress, the leaves of golden oregano become less yellow and more khaki in color, but the plant remains an attractive, close-knit clump of erect growths set with neatly arranged ovals of aromatic foliage. When bruised, the leaves, each about ¼in/2cm long, emit the usual sweet, peppery, marjoram scent. They can be used in cooking. This plant has a preference for alkaline soil, and sun and good drainage are important. However, in very dry conditions the foliage is apt to become scorched. *O.v.* "Aureum" seldom produces many of the little, pink, summer flowers, which are borne more profusely by the species. Other yellow-leaved marjorams include *O.v.* "Gold Tip," which has gold-tipped, green leaves.
also for: ■ Shallow soils over chalk ■ Ground cover ■ Aromatic foliage

Thymus pulegioides
e.g. "Bertram Anderson"
(syn. *T.* "Anderson's Gold,"
T. x *citriodorus* "Bertram
Anderson," *T.* "E.B. Anderson")
[thyme]
○

type of plant: hardy shrub/perennial [6–9]
height: 3–4in/8–10cm
Evergreen

Given really well-drained soil and plenty of sun, this subshrub forms a dense carpet of ½in/1cm-long, slenderly oval leaves. It spreads 8–12in/20–30cm wide. The foliage is pungently scented and heavily suffused with yellow (although reversion to plain green is sometimes a problem). There are usually only a very few clusters of pale mauvish flowers. *T.* "Doone Valley" is another low-growing thyme of yellowish coloring; its dark leaves are splashed and spotted with deep yellow, and its flowers are mauve-pink. Among the slightly taller thymes with yellow leaves, there is, for example, *T. pulegioides* "Aureus" (syn. *T.* x *citriodorus* "Aureus"), which has lemon-scented foliage that is mottled with gold; the plant grows about 9in/23cm tall.
also for: ■ Dry soils in hot, sunny sites ■ Ground cover ■ Crevices in paving ■ Aromatic foliage

ADDITIONAL PLANTS, featured elsewhere in this book, that have yellow or yellow-green leaves

○ **sun**

minimum height 10ft/3m or more
Chamaecyparis lawsoniana "Ellwood's Gold,"
 see p.145

x *Cupressocyparis leylandii* "Castlewellan,"
 see p.138

minimum height between 3ft/90cm and 10ft/3m
Taxus baccata "Standishii," see p.145

minimum height 3ft/90cm or less
Calluna vulgaris "Robert Chapman,"
 see p.237
Campanula garganica "Dickson's Gold,"
 see p.155

Cedrus deodara "Aurea"
[golden deodar cedar]
○[◑]

type of plant: hardy conifer [7–9]

height: 15–20ft/4.5–6m

Evergreen

The 2in/5cm-long needles of this elegant conifer are suffused with golden yellow when young; the mature foliage is a greener yellow. Leaf color is richest in sun; it is gentler but still attractive in light shade. The plant forms a cone of distinctively arching and pendulous branches. Golden deodar cedar is initially slow growing, and needs shelter when young. It should be given deep, fertile, well-drained soil. *C. deodara* "Golden Horizon" also has leaves that are yellow; it is a variable but usually wide-spreading and semi-prostrate plant.

Physocarpus opulifolius "Dart's Gold"
[ninebark]
○[◑]

type of plant: hardy shrub [3–8]

flowering time: early summer

flower color: greenish white

height: 5–6ft/1.5–1.8m

✄

Even quite late in autumn—when they are lime-green—the neatly shaped, three-lobed leaves of *P. opulifolius* "Dart's Gold" look good. In spring and early summer they are bright golden yellow. Each toothed and conspicuously veined leaf is usually 1½–2in/4–5cm wide. The clusters of flowers are a good deal less conspicuous than the foliage. In general, this is a tough and very easily grown shrub, but it does not grow well in very alkaline conditions and there may be some sun scorch on the leaves of plants grown in full sun on dryish soils. Moist soil that is neutral to acid is ideal. The thicket-forming stems of this shrub are basically erect with some arching, upper growth. Mature specimens have attractive, peeling bark.

also for: ■ Acid soils ■ Damp and wet soils ■ Ornamental bark or twigs

Choisya ternata Sundance = "Lich"
[Mexican orange blossom]
○[◑]

type of plant: slightly tender shrub [8–10]

height: 4–5ft/1.2–1.5m

Evergreen ✄

The youngest leaves of this dense, rounded plant are bright yellow; during summer, the coloring becomes rather softer. In partial shade the foliage is yellow-green but, in hot climates particularly, some shade may be needed to prevent sun scorch of the leaves. Compared with the species (see p.289), *C. ternata* Sundance is slower growing and usually lacks all but a few of the fragrant, white flowers; its tripartite leaves are arranged in the same way and the smooth, shapely leaflets have the same sharp scent. Each leaf is about 3in/8cm long. The foliage lasts very well when cut. *C.* Goldfingers is a more recent introduction; its bright yellow leaflets are much narrower than those of *C. ternata* Sundance. These plants are best in a sheltered position. Most well-drained soils are suitable.

also for: ■ Growing in containers ■ Aromatic foliage

Spiraea japonica e.g. "Goldflame"
○[◑]

type of plant: hardy shrub [4–8]

flowering time: midsummer

flower color: crimson-pink

height: 30–36in/75–90cm

Before its flattish heads of densely clustered flowers appear, this shrub's young foliage is a bright coppery red-orange. As the small flower heads develop, the neatly toothed and pointed leaves, up to 3in/8cm long, become yellow; after flowering time, the foliage is green. Not everyone likes the combination of deep pink flowers and yellow foliage. Hard pruning in early spring prevents flowering and also encourages lots of new leaf growth. This bushy, rounded shrub has a preference for moisture-retentive soil, but it is a very adaptable plant. Particularly if soil conditions are rather dry, its leaves may scorch and a slightly shaded site may be needed.

also for: ■ Heavy, clay soils ■ Atmospheric pollution ■ Ground cover ■ Purple, bronze or red leaves (young leaves only)

Fuchsia magellanica var. gracilis "Aurea"
○[◑]

type of plant: hardy/slightly tender shrub [7–10]

flowering time: midsummer to mid-autumn

flower color: scarlet + violet

height: 24–36in/60–90cm

The slender, pointed leaves of this arching shrub are generally greenish gold—although the sunnier the site, the more gold and less green the leaf color. Against this brightly colored background, the graceful, pendent flowers are conspicuous, despite the fact that—at around ¾in/2cm across—they are quite small. In areas with low winter temperatures, *F. magellanica* var. *gracilis* "Aurea" is more or less herbaceous; in mild regions, it grows taller, shrubbier and is earlier flowering. *F.* "Genii" is also popular; it is up to 36in/90cm tall and has red-stemmed, greenish yellow leaves, and flowers that are cerise and violet. Both these fuchsias grow best in moisture-retentive, well-drained soil in which their roots can remain cool.

also for: ■ Long, continuous flowering period

Tradescantia Andersoniana Group e.g. "Blue and Gold"
[spiderwort]
○ [◐]

type of plant: hardy perennial [5–9]
flowering time: early summer to early autumn
flower color: royal blue
height: 12–18in/30–45cm

This striking, yellow-leaved variety of spiderwort has the usual long flowering period, during which its individually short-lived, three-petalled flowers open in succession. Each bloom is about 1½in/4cm across. Flowers are carried just above the rather tangled clump of stiff, fleshy stems and narrow, curving leaves. The rich, bright coloring of the flowers is highlighted by their yellow stamens as well as by the green-yellow foliage. Foliage color is brightest in sun but in climates with hot summers some shade may be necessary to prevent leaf scorch. Any reasonably well-drained soil is suitable, provided it does not dry out in summer. This variety of spiderwort is sometimes sold as *T.* Andersoniana Group "Sweet Kate."
also for: ■ Long, continuous flowering period

ADDITIONAL PLANTS, featured elsewhere in this book, that have yellow or yellow-green leaves

○ [◐] sun (or partial shade)

minimum height 3ft/90cm or less: *Lysimachia nummularia* "Aurea," see p.112

Ptelea trifoliata "Aurea"
[golden hop tree, stinking ash]
○ ◐

type of plant: hardy tree/shrub [4–9]
height: 10–15ft/3–4.5m

Golden hop tree produces a spreading, rounded head of growth and is most often seen as a low-branching tree or a bushy shrub. Its new foliage is soft yellow; it emerges quite late in spring. The leaves are divided into three pointed leaflets, each about 3in/8cm long. Stems and leaf-stalks of the youngest growths are also yellow. Leaves mature to yellow-green, then green and, finally, in autumn, they turn butter-yellow. Mature foliage is strongly and sharply aromatic, as are the bark and unripe fruit. Inconspicuous, greenish white flowers—seen here in bud—appear from early summer. Not everyone agrees that their sweet smell is pleasant. The flowers are followed by bunches of soft yellow, flat, rounded fruits. Any fertile soil with good drainage is suitable for this plant. A moderately sheltered site is advisable.
also for: ■ Colorful, autumn foliage
■ Aromatic foliage ■ Ornamental fruit
■ Fragrant flowers (see above)

Sambucus racemosa e.g. "Plumosa Aurea"
[European red elder]
○ ◐

type of plant: hardy shrub [4–7]
flowering time: mid-spring
flower color: pale yellow
height: 7–9ft/2.1–2.7m

In strong sun, these deeply cut leaves are a particularly bright yellow but they may also become sun-scorched. This damage is less likely to occur if growing conditions are moist or if a lightly shaded position has been chosen. The slender, fringed leaflets, up to 6in/15cm long, are copper-colored when very young. Pruned hard to produce plenty of large leaves, *S. racemosa* "Plumosa Aurea" is bushy and irregularly dome-shaped with few, if any, cone-shaped clusters of little flowers or subsequent red berries. This adaptable plant can be grow in a very wide range of soils, including soils that are shallow and chalky and those that are damp. *S.r.* "Sutherland Gold" has slightly less bright foliage and is not so prone to scorching in full sun.
also for: ■ Shallow soils over chalk ■ Heavy, clay soils ■ Damp and wet soils

Lonicera nitida "Baggesen's Gold"
[boxleaf honeysuckle]
○ ◐

type of plant: hardy shrub [7–9]
height: 4–6ft/1.2–1.8m
Evergreen ♀✂

This shrub's ½in/1cm-long leaves, on their fan-like, branching shoots, can vary from soft gold to a brighter "old" gold. This stronger coloring is most evident in spring and is especially marked on plants grown in full sun. In a shaded site the leaves tend to be yellow-green. In winter the foliage can become bronzed. Left unpruned, *L. nitida* "Baggesen's Gold" grows densely but with some longer shoots creating an irregular outline. It can be clipped, either for topiary (when it looks good in containers) or for hedging (young plants should be about 12in/30cm apart). Although this is an easily grown shrub that is suitable for a wide range of soils, its leaves may become scorched in dry conditions.
also for: ■ Atmospheric pollution ■ Hedging plants ■ Growing in containers

Deschampsia flexuosa "Tatra Gold"
[crinkled hair grass]
○◐

type of plant: hardy perennial (grass) [4–9]
flowering time: early to midsummer
flower color: purplish bronze
height: 18in/45cm
Evergreen

In spring, the new leaves of this grass are a vivid yellow; as they mature, they become bright yellow-green. Each arching leaf is very thin, and the foliage forms tufts of growth about 6in/15cm high. Flowers are arranged in glinting, bronzed sprays, each about 4in/10cm long. When fully developed, these are held well above the foliage. Although the flower heads are good for cutting and drying, larger deschampsias (for an example of which, see p.289) provide more useful material for indoor arrangements. *D. flexuosa* "Tatra Gold" grows best in moisture-retentive soil that is acid to neutral.
also for: ■ Acid soils

ADDITIONAL PLANTS, featured elsewhere in this book, that have yellow or yellow-green leaves

○◐ sun or partial shade

minimum height 10ft/3m or more: *Humulus lupulus* "Aureus," see p.133

Weigela Briant Rubidor = "Olympiade"
◐[○]

type of plant: hardy shrub [5–8]
flowering time: late spring to early summer
flower color: rich crimson
height: 5–6ft/1.5–1.8m
✂

The slender-tipped, oval leaves of this spreading shrub vary in color from soft yellow to yellow-green, and make long-lasting material for cutting. Sometimes the foliage is yellow-green with gold edges. Each leaf is about 3in/8cm long. There are usually numerous clusters of funnel-shaped flowers. *W.* "Looymansii Aurea" also has yellow leaves; its flowers are pink. Most soils are suitable for these shrubs, but those that remain moist in summer produce plants with good-quality foliage and plenty of flowers. Some shade prevents leaf scorch in regions with hot summers.
also for: ■ Heavy, clay soils ■ Atmospheric pollution

Berberis thunbergii "Aurea"
[barberry]
◐[○]

type of plant: hardy shrub [5–8]
flowering time: mid- to late spring
flower color: yellow + pink
height: 30–36in/75–90cm

By the end of summer these rounded leaves, each about ¾in/2cm long, have become pale green but, until then, they are a vivid acidic yellow—a color that is enhanced by the reddish twigs. Good light is needed for bright leaf color but, except in areas with cool summers, the plant is best grown in a sheltered, lightly shaded position to protect the young foliage from frost and wind damage and to ensure that the mature leaves do not become sun-scorched. The little, cup-shaped flowers are less interesting than the foliage. There may be scarlet, droplet-shaped berries and also some rusty-orange autumn color, particularly if the plant is in a sunny position. This dense, rounded, thorny shrub grows slowly. It is not fussy about soil, but very alkaline conditions should be avoided. The foliage suffers if the plant is too dry.
also for: ■ Atmospheric pollution ■ Growing in containers

Filipendula ulmaria "Aurea"
[meadowsweet, queen of the meadow]
◐[○]

type of plant: hardy perennial [3–8]
flowering time: mid- to late summer
flower color: white
height: 24–30in/60–75cm

The divided leaves of this clump-forming plant are bright greenish gold when they expand in spring, and become progressively greener and rather paler during summer. Each leaflet is veined, pointed and about 1½in/4cm long. Reddish stems rise erectly through the leafy mass, and are topped with foamy clusters of numerous, tiny flowers. These emit a very sweet scent. (Since the plant self-sows and produces very vigorous, green-leaved seedlings, as well as seedlings with yellow leaves, many gardeners take the precaution of removing the flowers.) *F. ulmaria* "Variegata" has yellow stripes and splashes on its leaves. Both these plants are best in really moist or boggy soil. In drier places, and in full sun, their foliage often scorches.
also for: ■ Damp and wet soils ■ Fragrant flowers

Acer shirasawanum "Aureum" (syn. *A. japonicum* "Aureum") [maple]
◖

type of plant: hardy tree/shrub [6–8]
height: 15–20ft/4.5–6m

For many years, this maple will be a small, rounded shrub. Eventually it forms an elegant tree with layers of foliage borne on more or less horizontal branches. As well as some shade (to prevent leaf scorch), this plant must have moist, well-drained soil and shelter from cold winds. The leaves, with their rather shallow, pointed lobes, are like miniature fans, each 3–4in/8–10cm long. They emerge a sharp, greenish yellow and remain a sunny mid-yellow all summer. In late summer and autumn, the leaf edges may turn red. Taller and faster-growing maples with yellow leaves include *A. cappadocicum* "Aureum," which has yellow foliage in spring and early summer and again in autumn; it grows to 50ft/15m tall.

Philadelphus coronarius "Aureus" [mock orange]
◖

type of plant: hardy shrub [4–8]
flowering time: early summer
flower color: creamy white
height: 6–8ft/1.8–2.4m
✂

P. coronarius, with its plain green foliage, flourishes in dry soils and sunny sites but this yellow-leaved variety needs reasonably moist soil and some shade to look its best. In full sun, its pointed leaves, up to 3½in/9cm long, are a clear gold-yellow, but they become yellow-green quite quickly and they are inclined to scorch. In full shade, the foliage is an unremarkable green. Partial shade, however, insures that the leaves are a decorative, slightly greenish yellow almost all summer long. The flowers of this upright, rather twiggy shrub are small (about 1in/2.5cm across) and arranged in clusters. They have a powerful, sweetly aromatic fragrance.
also for: ■ Atmospheric pollution ■ Fragrant flowers

Milium effusum "Aureum" [Bowles' golden grass, golden wood millet]
◖

type of plant: hardy perennial (grass) [5–8]
flowering time: late spring to midsummer
flower color: yellow
height: 24–30in/60–75cm
Semi-evergreen ✂

In spring, all parts of this tufted grass are suffused with a beautiful, bright golden yellow. Later in the year, the flat, strap-shaped leaves, up to 12in/30cm long, are a softer, paler yellow. By late summer they are lime-green. Loose, wispy flower heads are carried well clear of the slowly spreading mass of arching foliage. Bowles' golden grass thrives—and self-sows mildly—in cool, lightly shaded places and in rich, moisture-retentive soil with good drainage.

Hosta fortunei var. *albopicta* f. *aurea* [plantain lily]
◖

type of plant: hardy perennial [3–9]
flowering time: midsummer
flower color: pale purplish lilac
height: 18–24in/45–60cm

Cool, moist conditions are essential for *H. fortunei* var. *albopicta* f. *aurea*, which grows best in deep, rich soil. Its elegantly pointed and conspicuously veined leaves, about 7in/18cm long, are thin-textured and therefore liable to scorch in sun or if the roots of the plant are dry. Foliage is a clear bright yellow in spring; it gradually becomes greener during summer. It forms clumps of growth about 14in/35cm high and up to 24in/60cm wide, above which rise clear stems with funnel-shaped flowers. Other popular hostas with yellow foliage include small-leaved *H.* "Hydon Sunset" and the very large-leaved *H.* "Sum and Substance" (the latter plant is best grown in sun).
also for: ■ Damp and wet soils ■ Ground cover

Saxifraga "Cloth of Gold" (syn. *S. exarata* subsp. *moschata* "Cloth of Gold") [saxifrage]
◖

type of plant: hardy perennial [5–7]
flowering time: late spring to early summer
flower color: white
height: 3–4in/8–10cm
Evergreen

Neat, little rosettes of divided, golden-yellow leaves are the main attraction of *S.* "Cloth of Gold." Each leaf rosette is 1in/2.5cm or less across. The flat-topped clusters of tiny, starry flowers, carried on slim stems above the cushion of soft, mossy foliage, are often rather sparsely produced. This saxifrage needs moist but sharply draining soil in order to thrive. It also requires some shade to prevent leaf scorch.

Lamium maculatum e.g. "Aureum" (syn. *L.m.* "Gold Leaf," *L.m.* "Golden Nuggets") [spotted deadnettle]
◖●

type of plant: hardy perennial [4–9]
flowering time: mid-spring to early summer
flower color: dusty mauve-pink
height: 3–4in/8–10cm
Semi-evergreen

From even quite a short distance, the white stripes on these leaves are not very visible and the overall effect is one of rather sharp, greenish yellow. Each leaf is heart-shaped, toothed and about 1¼in/3cm long. Foliage color is brightest in spring and early summer. In dryish soils, and particularly in sun, the leaf edges are liable to become desiccated and brown. In any case, general growth is best in moist soil and a cool, shady site. Compared with most varieties of *L. maculatum*, *L.m.* "Aureum" is not very vigorous. Its little carpet of growth is usually only about 12in/30cm wide. For examples of more vigorous varieties, see the index of botanical names.
also for: ■ Heavy, clay soils

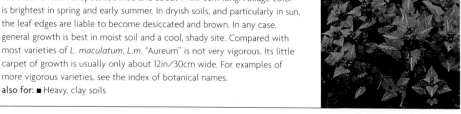

Decorative, green foliage

IT MIGHT SEEM AS IF ONLY the shape of a green leaf would make it decorative, but there are, in fact, green leaves that are interestingly textured, impressively sized and—perhaps surprisingly to some gardeners—of rather unusual coloring. In addition, exactly how the leaves of a particular plant are arranged on the stems or branches of that plant can create a distinctive pattern of foliage, and that too can be attractive. All these extra decorative qualities can, of course, enhance an already beautiful leaf shape.

Plants in this list that have interestingly textured leaves range from *Geranium renardii* and *Potentilla megalantha*, with their felted or velvety foliage, to *Bergenia cordifolia* and New Zealand flax (*Phormium tenax*), which are leathery leaved. Different again are leaves such as those of *Viburnum rhytidophyllum*, which have a conspicuously wrinkled surface, and those of *Beta vulgaris* subsp. *cicla* var. *flavescens* "Rhubarb Chard," which are splendidly puckered and glossy.

Two plants that combine a notably smooth leaf surface with an unusually light, apple-green leaf color are the neat and tidy *Hebe rakaiensis* and, on an altogether larger scale, the salt- and wind-resistant broadleaf (*Griselinia littoralis*)—see p.106 and p.92, respectively. Other plants that produce attractive, light green foliage include the lacy leaved maple *Acer palmatum* var. *dissectum* and the so-called sensitive fern (*Onoclea sensibilis*).

Dark-leaved plants in this list include distinctive conifers, such as the Chilean pine or monkey puzzle (*Araucaria araucana*), bold perennials such as *Acanthus spinosus*, and ferns such as hard shield fern (*Polystichum aculeatum*). Many of the plants that are suitable for heavily shaded positions have foliage that is an especially deep rich green (see "Plants tolerant of dense shade," pp.85–7, for examples).

Although the summer foliage of all the plants in the list below is a shade of green, some of them have leaves that are differently colored for a limited period, mainly during spring or autumn. For example, the mature foliage of the ornamental rhubarb *Rheum palmatum* is rich green, yet on first emerging, the leaves are red; in autumn, the light green leaves of the tulip tree (*Liriodendron tulipifera*) turn yellow, and the dark leaflets of *Sorbus reducta* change to deep maroon, bronze, and red.

An interesting texture or an unusual shade of green can make a leaf more decorative, but so too can exceptional size. In rich soil and with a constant supply of moisture *Gunnera manicata* often produces leaves more than 6ft/1.8m wide. Other large-leaved plants in this list that can bring an exotic or jungly look to gardens in temperate regions include the Japanese angelica tree (*Aralia elata*), a number of bamboos, and perennials such as *Astilboides tabularis*.

In contrast to big, bold leaves, there are plenty of green-leaved plants that have small-scale foliage or leaves that are intricately divided. Many of the ferns in this list produce beautifully light and lacy fronds that create a fine-textured, airy effect. Larger plants with small-scale foliage include the black elder (*Sambucus nigra* f. *laciniata*) and *Sophora microphylla*.

The leaves of some plants in this list are not especially decorative in themselves, but the way in which they are arranged on the plant produces an interesting and attractive pattern. The individual leaves of Brewer spruce (*Picea breweriana*), for example, are not remarkable. Yet, as this conifer matures, it produces long, hanging branchlets, which create elegant curtains of foliage.

Some plants are very densely foliated (*Ulmus* x *hollandica* "Jacqueline Hillier" and *Hedera helix* "Congesta" in this list, for example), and this produces a quite different kind of effect. London pride (*Saxifraga* x *urbium*) may be ordinary and obliging, but the way in which the leaves of this familiar, little plant are arranged in rosettes creates a very satisfyingly patterned carpet of growth all year long.

Liriodendron tulipifera
[tulip tree]
○

type of plant: hardy tree [5–8]
flowering time: early to midsummer
flower color: yellowish green
height: 70–100ft/21–30m

The strangely shaped leaves of this tree—each one looking as if it were lacking a central lobe—are light green, until autumn when they turn buttery yellow. Each leaf is up to 6in/15cm long. On deep, moist, fertile soil in warm regions *L. tulipifera* grows quickly. It is most often seen as a neat cone of growth, either narrow or broad, with thick main branches (although *L.t.* "Fastigiatum" is narrow and upright, particularly when it is young). Specimens are usually at least ten years old before they produce many of their cup-shaped flowers. A variegated tulip tree is shown on p.161.
also for: ■ Atmospheric pollution ■ Colorful, autumn foliage ■ Green flowers

Araucaria araucana
[Chilean pine, monkey puzzle]
○

type of plant: hardy conifer [7–10]
height: 60–80ft/18–24m
Evergreen

This conifer's distinctive shape and its whorls of strange foliage make it instantly recognizable to many gardeners. Mature specimens of *A. araucana* tend to lose their lower branches and to have broad, domed "mop-heads" of dark growth on very straight trunks. The bark is wrinkled and the branches curve and sweep boldly. The leaves, each up to 2in/5cm long, are stiff, leathery, and sharp-pointed. Most soils are suitable for this fairly slow-growing tree but it is best in moisture-retentive, well-drained conditions. It needs an open site.
also for: ■ Ornamental bark or twigs

Juglans regia
[English walnut]
○

type of plant: hardy tree [5–9]
height: 60–80ft/18–24m

Each of this tree's glossy, mid-green leaves is about 12in/30cm long, with up to nine shapely, pointed leaflets. When young, *J. regia* grows quickly and it soon forms a spreading crown of often slightly twisted branches. The trunk, which may also curve somewhat, is pale and smooth when the tree is young; it is darker and ridged on older specimens. The resinous foliage emerges late in spring and is, briefly, deep coppery purple. Mature trees produce edible walnuts, but fruiting is not always reliable. Deep, fertile, well-drained soil and a warm, sheltered site give the best results. Black walnut (*Juglans nigra*; see p.263) also has bold foliage.

Picea breweriana
[Brewer spruce]
○

type of plant: hardy conifer [6–9]
height: 40–60ft/12–18m
Evergreen

The weeping habit of this conifer takes several years to develop, but established specimens bear hanging branchlets that are often more than 24in/60cm long. The foliage is slightly blue-tinged deep green. Individual leaves are narrow and flattened and up to 1½in/4cm long. Young plants grow slowly and are broadly pyramidal in shape. The outline of older specimens may be more columnar. A site sheltered from cold winds, and deep, preferably neutral to acid soil that retains moisture, provide the ideal growing conditions for Brewer spruce. It thrives in mild areas with high rainfall. Other conifers with pendulous growths include *Chamaecyparis nootkatensis* "Pendula" (up to 100ft/30m tall). See also pp.210 and 214.

Koelreuteria paniculata
[golden-rain tree, pride of India, varnish tree]
○

type of plant: hardy tree [5–9]
flowering time: mid- to late summer
flower color: yellow
height: 30–40ft/9–12m

In cool and wet climates, the outstanding feature of *K. paniculata* is usually its foliage, since the tall, branched heads of slim-petaled flowers tend to be rather sparsely borne, except in warmer, drier areas. The numerous, pendent, toothed leaflets are each 12–18in/30–45cm long. Foliage emerges light red, becomes mid-green and then turns warm yellow in autumn (when inflated, pink-tinged seed pods, each up to 2in/5cm long, may develop). Mature trees are broadly round-headed and often as wide as they are tall. Well-drained soil and a sheltered site are preferable. The plant is suitable for dry soil.
also for: ■ Dry soils in hot, sunny sites ■ Colorful, autumn foliage ■ Ornamental fruit (seed pods; see above)

Paulownia tomentosa
[foxglove tree, empress tree]
○

type of plant: hardy/slightly tender tree [7–9]
flowering time: late spring
flower color: pinkish lilac
height: 30–40ft/9–12m

Left to its own devices, foxglove tree quickly makes a rounded, openly branched tree with broad, softly hairy leaves, each 8–10in/20–25cm wide. Before the bright green foliage unfurls, large, upright clusters of sweetly scented, tubular blooms begin to open. Only older plants flower and, in any case, the winter flower buds are easily damaged during frosty and wet weather. In cool, wet areas, foxglove tree may be treated as a foliage plant and cut back hard each year. Grown this way, it is 6–10ft/1.8–3m high and equipped with leaves more than 24in/60cm across. Whether or not it is cut back, it needs a sheltered site and deep, fertile soil.
also for: ■ Atmospheric pollution ■ Fragrant flowers

Sophora microphylla
○

type of plant: slightly tender shrub [8–10]
flowering time: late spring
flower color: rich yellow
height: 8–10ft/2.4–3m
Evergreen/Semi-evergreen

The elegant wispiness of this shrub's foliage is created by numerous, tiny, rounded leaflets that are arranged in two neat rows on each leaf. Individual leaves are 4–6in/10–15cm long. The richly colored flowers are altogether bolder: they are greenish in bud, opening to about 2in/5cm long, and they hang in dense clusters, close to the plant's branches. Flowers are followed by long, thin, brown seed pods, which resemble strings of beads. Only well-established specimens of this vase-shaped shrub flower freely and, in any case, a warm, sheltered site is needed. In colder districts this plant should be given the protection of a wall. Light, well-drained loam is ideal for *S. microphylla*.
also for: ■ Ornamental fruit (seed pods)

Abutilon vitifolium
○

type of plant: slightly tender shrub [8–9]
flowering time: late spring to midsummer
flower color: usually lavender-blue
height: 6–10ft/1.8–3m; 20ft/6m or more in ideal conditions in mild areas
Semi-evergreen/Deciduous

In mild, moist climates this rather short-lived shrub may become almost tree-like. Elsewhere, even when it is given appropriately well-drained soil and a sheltered site, it will be much smaller. In any case, *A. vitifolium* quickly makes an open, rather sparsely branched plant with conspicuously pale gray shoots. Its attractive, vine-like leaves, 4–6in/10–15cm long, are light green and covered in tiny, white hairs. The open-faced flowers are up to 3in/8cm wide and slightly pendent. *A.v.* var. *album* has white flowers.

Salix fargesii
[willow]
○

type of plant: hardy shrub [6–8]
height: 6–8ft/1.8–2.4m

The rather upright stems of this very slow-growing shrub ripen to a glossy brown-red, and look especially handsome beside the gleaming rich green of the foliage. In winter, the stems and slender, rich red buds are conspicuous and decorative. Green catkins, which appear with the leaves in spring, are less remarkable. Most moisture-retentive soils are suitable for this openly branched, eventually substantial shrub, but damp, fertile conditions give the most satisfactory results. Some shelter is advisable to protect the leaves, which may be more than 6in/15cm long, and also the winter buds.
also for: ■ Heavy, clay soils ■ Damp and wet soils ■ Ornamental bark or twigs

Ulmus x hollandica
"Jacqueline Hillier"
[elm]
○

type of plant: hardy shrub/tree [5–8]
height: 6–8ft/1.8–2.4m

The veined, rather rough-textured leaves on this slow-growing plant are only about 1½in/4cm long. They are crowded along the numerous, straight, stiff-looking branches, so that the overall effect is one of finely patterned denseness. The rich green foliage is retained on the plant until early winter. Before they fall, the leaves may turn soft yellow. Normally, *U. x hollandica* "Jacqueline Hillier" grows as a more or less rounded, suckering shrub, but it can be trained to form a small tree, or a number of specimens can be about 18in/45cm apart to create a hedge. It is only partially resistant to Dutch elm disease. Any reasonably well-drained soil is suitable.
also for: ■ Hedging plants

Crambe cordifolia
○

type of plant: hardy perennial [6–9]
flowering time: early to midsummer
flower color: white
height: 6ft/1.8m

Each dark green, lobed and crinkled leaf produced by this deep-rooted perennial is usually at least 12in/30cm across. Although they may not be things of very great beauty, these heart-shaped leaves are certainly bold and they provide an interesting contrast to the floral froth of the plant. They create a great mound of growth, 3–4ft/0.9–1.2m high, which dies down toward the end of summer. Above this, huge clouds of tiny, four-petalled flowers are carried on strong, widely branching stems. The flowers have an oily scent, which is perceptible on warm days. This imposing plant needs plenty of space. *C. cordifolia* tolerates poor soil but reasonably fertile, well-drained soil gives better results.

Phormium tenax
[New Zealand flax]
○

type of plant: slightly tender/hardy perennial/
shrub [7–11]
flowering time: mid- to late summer
flower color: deep soft red
height: 5–7ft/1.5–2.1m foliage height;
10–12ft/3–3.6m flower height (see description)
Evergreen ⚇✂

Although it lacks the spectacular coloring of some phormiums, New Zealand flax is a very striking plant. Its tough, leathery leaves form a huge clump of olive-green sword shapes, above which tower branching heads of fairly small, tubular flowers, followed by slender, brown seed pods. In warm districts, established plants flower regularly. The plant grows well in mild regions with high rainfall (where leaves may be 8ft/2.4m or more long). It thrives by the sea. In colder, inland gardens it requires a sheltered position and may need winter protection. Open-textured soil that is consistently moist, but not wet is especially suitable. The foliage is very long-lasting when cut.
also for: ■ Damp and wet soils ■ Atmospheric pollution

Musa basjoo
[Japanese banana]
○

type of plant: half-hardy/slightly tender
perennial [9–10]
height: 4–6ft/1.2–1.8m; 15ft/4.5m outdoors in
frost-free regions

If they are not to become torn and tattered, the huge, arching, bright green leaves of this plant must have a sheltered site. In any case, warmth, shelter, and winter protection are needed, even in areas with quite mild winters. Where hard frosts are likely, Japanese banana is best treated as a conservatory or greenhouse plant, or used as summer bedding. Individual leaves are often about 4ft/1.2m long. The leaf bases form a slender "trunk." In warm climates, mature plants produce spikes of brown and cream flowers, which are followed by small, greenish bananas that are unpalatable. Rich, well-drained soil is most suitable for this plant.

Brachyglottis monroi
(syn. *Senecio monroi*)
○

type of plant: slightly tender/hardy shrub [8–10]
flowering time: early to midsummer
flower color: yellow
height: 24–36in/60–90cm
Evergreen

The olive-green, leathery leaves of this shrub have attractive, crimped edges and white-felted undersides. Each leaf is up to 1½in/4cm long. The plant produces numerous, little branches and, when young, these too are white-felted. With their close covering of foliage they create a neat, dense dome of growth, which is effective as ground cover. The sprays of small, daisy-shaped flowers are freely produced. Like its popular, larger relation (see p.184), *B. monroi* thrives beside the sea and in all soils with good drainage.
also for: ■ Ground cover

Libertia formosa
○

type of plant: slightly tender/hardy
perennial [8–11]
flowering time: late spring to early summer
flower color: white
height: 24–36in/60–90cm
Evergreen

Even when there are none of the charming sprays of white flowers present, this plant's generous clump of arching, leathery leaves looks handsome. The 1½in/4cm-wide flowers are saucer-shaped and held on stiff, upright stems. They are succeed by little clusters of orange-brown seed pods. The basal leaves, up to 24in/60cm long, are narrow, pointed, and rich green. *L. formosa* thrives in mild areas with high rainfall and in moist but well-drained soil. It has a preference for—but does not require—neutral to acid conditions. The flower clusters of *L. grandiflora* are more open than those of *L. formosa*, but otherwise it is a very similar plant.
also for: ■ Ornamental fruit (seed pods)

Incarvillea delavayi
○

type of plant: hardy perennial [6–8]
flowering time: early to midsummer
flower color: rich rose-pink
height: 18–24in/45–60cm

The rich green, divided foliage of this perennial is of a sufficiently strong shape not to be completely outshone by the 3in/8cm-wide, flaring, trumpet-shaped flowers. The leaves, each as much as 12in/30cm long, are arranged in a rosette; the numerous leaflets are slender and toothed. After dying down in autumn, *I. delavayi* does not reappear until late spring. Its fleshy roots should be planted in a sunny site and in soil that is well drained and fertile. *I.d.* "Snowtop" (syn. "Alba") has white flowers. As a minor attraction, these plants produce long seed pods that ripen to brown as the summer months pass.

Potentilla megalantha
(syn. *P. fragiformis*)
[cinquefoil]
○

type of plant: hardy perennial [5–7]
flowering time: late spring to early summer
flower color: bright yellow
height: 9in/23cm

The toothed and scalloped leaves of this perennial form clumps of velvety, softly gleaming greenery. Each tripartite leaf is about 3in/8cm long. Saucer-shaped flowers are held on erect stalks above the foliage. At up to 1½in/4cm across, they are large for the size of plant. They appear in large numbers over several weeks and, as flowering progresses, the plant becomes rather looser in growth. It is easily grown in most soils with good drainage.

Castanea sativa
[Spanish chestnut, sweet chestnut]
○ [●]

type of plant: hardy tree [6–9]
flowering time: early to midsummer
flower color: yellow
height: 80–100ft/24–30m

Only large spaces can accommodate this imposing tree, which quickly makes a very broad column of growth, spreading as it matures. Its bold, rich green, glossy leaves, 8in/20cm or more long, are conspicuously toothed. They turn yellow in autumn. Catkins are produced at the branch tips. Male catkins are showy; female ones develop into bristly fruits containing edible nuts. (Fruiting is best in regions with hot summers.) On really mature specimens the grooved bark spirals up the trunk. This vigorous tree is best on deep, slightly acid soil with good drainage. *C. sativa* is a good choice for light soils.
also for: ■ Colorful, autumn foliage ■ Ornamental fruit ■ Ornamental bark or twigs (see above)

Pittosporum tenuifolium
○ [●]

type of plant: slightly tender/half-hardy shrub/tree [9–10]
height: 15–25ft/4.5–7.5m
Evergreen ♀✂

The glossy, light olive-green leaves of *P. tenuifolium* are borne on rather upright stems, which are dark when young. Each wavy-edged leaf is 1½–2in/4–5cm long and very long-lasting when cut. Young specimens grow quickly and are columnar; older plants have more spreading, oval heads of growth. In mild areas this dense plant is often used for hedging (plants should be about 18in/45cm apart). It grows well near the sea, although not in positions fully exposed to salt-laden gales. Inland, it needs a site that is warm and sheltered. Mature specimens produce flowers in late spring, and although the bell-shaped blooms are inconspicuous— they are only ½in/1cm wide and dark red— they are very sweetly scented, particularly in the evening. Well-drained but moisture-retentive soil is most suitable for this plant. See pp.161 and 146 for pittosporums with variegated and purple leaves.
also for: ■ Windswept, seaside gardens ■ Hedging plants ■ Fragrant flowers

Trachycarpus fortunei
(syn. *Chamaerops excelsa*)
[Chusan palm, windmill palm]
○ [●]

type of plant: slightly tender/hardy palm [8–11]
flowering time: early summer
flower color: yellow fading to cream
height: 12–18ft/3.6–5.4m; to about 35ft/10.5m in very mild regions
Evergreen

Big fans of pleated foliage and a stocky, hairy bark give this palm its distinctive appearance. The long-stalked leaves are made up of numerous, narrow, deep green lobes, each of which can be more than 36in/90cm long. Although it is slightly hardier than cabbage palm (*Cordyline australis*, see following page), it is much less wind-resistant and needs a sheltered site to grow well. Mature specimens produce large, branched clusters of tiny flowers. In warm regions, female plants may bear dark blue berries. Chusan palm requires well-drained soil.
also for: ■ Ornamental bark or twigs

Cordyline australis
[cabbage palm, cabbage tree]
○◐

type of plant: half-hardy/slightly tender shrub/tree [9–11]

flowering time: early summer

flower color: creamy white

height: 12–15ft/3.6–4.5m; to about 30ft/9m in very mild regions

Evergreen

These spiky-looking rosettes of narrow, leathery, mid- to light green leaves give a subtropical look to many gardens in very mild areas. Individual leaves are 24–36in/60–90cm long. Mature specimens are tree-like, with rough-barked trunks. These older plants may produce large plumes of tiny, sweetly scented, wispy flowers that can ripen into white berries. *C. australis* does not grow well where it is exposed to very cold winds, but it is tolerant of strong winds that carry warm air and it is very salt-resistant. In inland gardens it is often grown in a container and brought under cover in winter. It needs fertile, well-drained soil. A variegated cabbage palm is shown on p.148.

also for: ■ Windswept, seaside gardens ■ Growing in containers ■ Fragrant flowers (see above)

Pseudosasa japonica
(syn. *Arundinaria japonica*)
○◐

type of plant: hardy perennial (bamboo) [7–11]

height: 10–15ft/3–4.5m

Evergreen

Particularly in fertile soil that is moist or damp and in regions with mild winters, the dense thickets formed by this bamboo can sometimes spread extensively. It is probably best used for screening or for covering large, informally planted areas of ground. Its lance-shaped leaves are bright green, glossy and often 12in/30cm or more long. Since the foliage is liable to become damaged by cold winds, a site with some shelter is advisable. The canes are erect, deep olive-green when young and beige when mature. As well as liking damp conditions, this bamboo grows in most soils that are reasonably moisture-retentive.

also for: ■ Damp and wet soils ■ Ground cover ■ Ornamental bark or twigs

Rheum palmatum
[Chinese rhubarb]
○◐

type of plant: hardy perennial [6–9]

flowering time: early summer

flower color: greenish cream to rich pink

height: 5–7ft/1.5–2.1m

Even when mature and no longer reddish purple, the rich green, jagged foliage of *R. palmatum* is most impressive. Individual leaves 3ft/90cm across are not uncommon and the foliage makes huge, weed-smothering clumps of growth 3–4ft/0.9–1.2m high and about 6ft/1.8m wide. Young leaves emerge from red buds and are, at first, a crumpled mass of red, acquiring more purplish tones as they expand. Until the branching heads of starry flowers appear, this redness is retained on the undersides of the leaves. Rich, really moist soil is needed to produce good specimens of this plant. The foliage starts to die back from midsummer.

also for: ■ Heavy, clay soils ■ Damp and wet soils ■ Ground cover ■ Purple, bronze, or red leaves (young leaves only)

Paeonia delavayi
[peony]
○◐

type of plant: hardy shrub [6–8]

flowering time: late spring to early summer

flower color: deep maroon-crimson + yellow

height: 5–6ft/1.5–1.8m

The luxuriously colored, slightly nodding flowers of this peony are generously filled with yellow stamens and may be up to 5in/12cm wide. The flowering season is only about two to three weeks long but the strikingly elegant, deeply cut leaves are decorative for much longer. Each slender, bright green leaflet, itself deeply cut, is about 4in/10cm in length. (Unfortunately, the dead leaves are retained on *P. delavayi* in winter.) The plant has a very open, rather upright habit of growth. *P.d.* var. *ludlowii* (syn. *P. lutea* var. *ludlowii*) bears yellow flowers and is more vigorous. Both these long-lived shrubs thrive in deep, moist, well-drained soil. However, they are tolerant of quite a wide range of soils (including chalky soils, as long as they are not too dry and shallow). Their young growths are susceptible to frost damage and the plants should therefore be given a sheltered position.

Acanthus spinosus
[bear's breeches]
○◐

type of plant: hardy/slightly tender perennial [7–10]

flowering time: midsummer to early autumn

flower color: purple + white

height: 4ft/1.2m

The dark foliage of this clump-forming plant arches upward and outward, emphasizing the length and the jagged outline of individual leaves, some of which may be 36in/90cm long. The spires of spiny, hooded flowers and the subsequent seedheads are good for large indoor arrangements (a developing flower head is shown here). Almost any soil is suitable for this ground-covering plant, but it establishes most quickly in deep, fertile, well-drained soil. It self-sows, sometimes freely. Plants in *A. spinosus* Spinosissimus Group have fewer flowers, but their leaves are even more finely cut.

also for: ■ Heavy, clay soils ■ Ground cover ■ Flowers suitable for cutting ■ Long, continuous flowering period

Crocosmia masoniorum
○[◐]

type of plant: slightly tender/hardy perennial [7–9]
flowering time: mid- to late summer
flower color: orange
height: 3–4ft/0.9–1.2m

The pleated, sword-shaped leaves of this particular crocosmia are especially broad and bold. They make a clump of fairly upright growth which, together with the arching sprays of intensely colored blooms, produces a strikingly handsome effect. The flowers, each about 2in/5cm long, are upward-facing funnels with prominent stamens; they last well in water. *C. masoniorum* likes slightly drier conditions than the majority of crocosmias and it prospers in quite light soils with good drainage. It may need some protection in colder regions. *C. paniculata* (orange-red flowers) is another species with particularly handsome foliage. Other popular orange-flowered crocosmias include *C. x crocosmiiflora* "Star of the East" (soft, clear orange blooms) and *C. x c.* "Emily MacKenzie" (rich orange flowers). For additional crocosmias in this book, see the index of botanical names.
also for: ■ Flowers suitable for cutting

Rheum "Ace of Hearts"
(syn. *R.* "Ace of Spades")
[ornamental rhubarb]
○[◐]

type of plant: hardy perennial [5–9]
flowering time: early to midsummer
flower color: very pale pink or cream
height: 3–4ft/0.9–1.2m

The heart-shaped leaves of *R.* "Ace of Hearts" are basically soft mid-green, but their veins and their long stalks are purplish crimson and there are tinges of this color on the undersides of the leaves, too. Individual leaves are about 15in/38cm long. Deep, rich soils that are moist—or even permanently damp—produce particularly lush, leafy, weed-smothering clumps of growth. Wispy sprays of little, starry flowers are carried, on erect stems, above the foliage. For an ornamental rhubarb that is even bigger and bolder, see the previous page.
also for: ■ Heavy, clay soils ■ Damp and wet soils ■ Ground cover

Hemerocallis
e.g. "Golden Chimes"
[daylily]
○[◐]

type of plant: hardy perennial [5–9]
flowering time: mainly early to midsummer
flower color: deep yellow + red-brown
height: 30in/75cm
Semi-evergreen

Some of the new daylily hybrids have rather broad, not particularly attractive foliage, but the leaves of this excellent, older plant—and of many other daylilies, too—are slender and grass-like. They create a clump of bright green, arching, ground-covering growth. Brown-backed flowers, each about 2in/5cm wide, are shaped like flared trumpets. Individually these flowers are very short-lived but numerous brown buds open in succession. *H.* "Stella de Oro" is another popular, very floriferous hybrid with yellow flowers and attractive foliage. Daylilies are easily grown in moisture-retentive soils, including heavy clays and damp soils. They are at their best when conditions are fertile, and they are especially free-flowering in sun.
also for: ■ Heavy, clay soils ■ Damp and wet soils ■ Ground cover

Geranium pratense
e.g. "Mrs Kendall Clark"
[meadow cranesbill]
○[◐]

type of plant: hardy perennial [4–8]
flowering time: early to midsummer
flower color: pale gray-blue
height: 24–30in/60–75cm

The handsome, deep green leaves of this clump-forming plant are divided into several lobes, which themselves are further divided. Individual leaves are up to 7in/18cm long. In autumn, the foliage turns yellow, orange, and red (the coloring is brightest on light soils). Subtly colored, saucer-shaped flowers, about 1½in/4cm wide, are held well above the foliage, on branching stems that usually need support. *G. pratense* and its varieties like drier conditions than many of the taller cranesbills. They thrive in soils with good drainage, including shallow, chalky ones. Other popular varieties include *G.p.* "Striatum" (which has blue-and-white streaked flowers), *G.p.* "Plenum Violaceum" and *G.p.* "Plenum Caeruleum" (which have long-lasting, double flowers in rich violet and lavender-blue respectively) and *G. pratense* var. *pratense* f. *albiflorum* (which has white, single flowers). When growing well, the single-flowered varieties self-sow freely.
also for: ■ Shallow soils over chalk ■ Colorful, autumn foliage

Sorbus reducta
○[◐]

type of plant: hardy shrub [5–7]
flowering time: late spring to early summer
flower color: white or palest pink
height: 18–30in/45–75cm

Upright stems on this thicket-forming, often suckering shrub carry ferny, little leaves, up to 4in/10cm long. The numerous, neatly pointed leaflets are a lustrous, slightly blue-tinged dark green; in mid-autumn they take on rich tones of maroon, bronze and red. From late summer, long-lasting berries begin to ripen. These bright pink, spherical fruits are preceded by small clusters of saucer-shaped flowers. *S. reducta* is not difficult to grow but is most at home in moist, humus-rich soil with good drainage. It is particularly successful in cooler regions. It eventually spreads about 6ft/1.8m wide.
also for: ■ Atmospheric pollution ■ Colorful, autumn foliage
■ Ornamental fruit

Beta vulgaris subsp. *cicla*
var. *flavescens*
e.g. "Rhubarb Chard"
[Swiss chard]
○[◐]

type of plant: grown as hardy annual [6–9]
height: 18–24in/45–60cm

The puckering and the rich green glossiness of these leaves are emphasized by contrastingly smooth stalks and midribs that are a spectacular, vibrant red. This dramatic color extends into the veins of each broad, oblong leaf. Although easily grown in most soils, this edible, spinach-like plant is best in fertile, moisture-retentive soil with good drainage. A reliable supply of moisture prevents premature flowering and subsequent deterioration of the foliage. Swiss chard forms tight clumps of fairly upright stalks. The leaves are usually about 12in/30cm long.

Geranium clarkei
e.g. "Kashmir White"
[cranesbill]
○[◐]

type of plant: hardy perennial [6–8]
flowering time: early to midsummer
flower color: white + lilac-gray
height: 15in/38cm

The leaves of this cranesbill are deeply divided into seven lobes, which are themselves deeply cut, so that the plant's low mound of foliage is a loose mass of intricate shapes. Each veined, mid-green leaf is up to 6in/15cm across. Branched stems carry beautifully simple, delicately veined flowers, 1–1½in/2.5–4cm wide. This fairly vigorous plant spreads—often widely—by underground shoots. It likes well-drained soil but is not difficult to grow in most soils. *G. clarkei* "Kashmir Pink" is pink-flowered; *G.c.* "Kashmir Purple" is very vigorous and has rich purple flowers.

Geranium renardii
[cranesbill]
○[◐]

type of plant: hardy perennial [6–8]
flowering time: early summer
flower color: pale gray + mauve
height: 9–12in/23–30cm

Sometimes there are only a few branched clusters of subtly veined, little flowers on this clump-forming cranesbill but, in any case, its foliage is very attractive. Sage-green leaves have well-defined, rounded lobes and a most satisfactory, felted, wrinkled texture. They are about 2½in/6cm wide. Although the mound of growth created by these leaves is usually not much more than 12in/30cm wide, it is dense and makes effective ground cover. *G. renardii* grows best in poor, well-drained soils, including shallow, chalky ones.

also for: ■ Shallow soils over chalk ■ Ground cover

ADDITIONAL PLANTS, featured elsewhere in this book, that have decorative, green foliage

○[◐] sun (or partial shade)

minimum height 10ft/3m or more
Griselinia littoralis, see p.92
Liquidambar styraciflua, see p.237
Phyllostachys aurea, see p.265
Phyllostachys nigra, see p.330
Sorbus cashmiriana, see p.256
Sorbus vilmorinii, see p.256

minimum height between 3ft/90cm and 10ft/3m
Acanthus mollis, see p.110
Chamaerops humilis,
    see p.148
Crocosmia "Lucifer," see p.285
Tropaeolum peregrinum,
    see p.130
Tropaeolum tuberosum var. *lineamaculatum*
    "Ken Aslet," see p.130

minimum height 3ft/90cm or less
Aponogeton distachyos, see p.307
Crocosmia x *crocosmiiflora* "Jackanapes,"
    see p.287
Geranium dalmaticum, see p.111
Geranium x *magnificum*, see p.239
Geranium sanguineum, see p.111
Hemerocallis "Pink Damask," see p.110
Plantago major "Rosularis," see p.325

Aralia elata
[Japanese angelica tree]
○◐

type of plant: hardy shrub/tree [4–9]
flowering time: late summer to early autumn
flower color: creamy white fading to pinkish beige
height: 10–15ft/3–4.5m; up to 30ft/9m
(see description)

Except in mild districts, where it may develop into a small tree, this sparsely and openly branched plant usually forms a suckering shrub. It is easily grown in most soils. Growth is fast when Japanese angelica tree is young and when it is given a sheltered site and rich, moist soil with good drainage. The bold, horizontally held foliage appears late in spring. When fully expanded, some of the leaves—with their dozens of dark green, pointed, rather pendent leaflets—may be up to 4ft/1.2m long. There is some yellow autumn color. Tiny flowers are carried in very large, branching heads. *A. elata* "Variegata" has leaves edged and marked in creamy white. Both these plants have prickly stems.

also for: ■ Atmospheric pollution

Viburnum rhytidophyllum
[leatherleaf viburnum]
○◑

type of plant: hardy shrub [6–8]
flowering time: late spring to early summer
flower color: creamy white
height: 10–15ft/3–4.5m
Evergreen

This vigorous, upright shrub is considered by some to be rather gloomy-looking. It has dark green, glossy, wrinkled leaves, each about 8in/20cm long and gray-beige beneath. Against the rounded mass of dark, rather pendent foliage, the buff-felted flower buds are conspicuous all through winter and into spring. They open into 6in/15cm-wide, domed heads of tiny flowers that are followed by large bunches of shiny, red berries. These are black when fully ripe. Crops of fruit are heavy when several specimens of this shrub are grown together. A sheltered site and moist, fertile soil produces particularly good growth, but this is an adaptable plant and most soils are suitable.
also for: ■ Shallow soils over chalk ■ Heavy, clay soils ■ Ornamental fruit

Fargesia murielae
(syn. *Arundinaria murielae,*
Sinarundinaria murielae)
[umbrella bamboo]
○◑

type of plant: hardy perennial (bamboo) [6–11]
height: 8–12ft/2.4–3.6m
Evergreen

This clump-forming bamboo produces large quantities of narrow, pointed, bright green leaves that shift and rustle in the breeze. Each leaf is about 4in/10cm long. As the canes age and turn yellow, they tend to arch outward and this emphasizes the impression of leafiness. Umbrella bamboo is wind-resistant and it can be grown in sunny places, but it is at its very best in sites that are not too open or hot. It thrives in moist, fertile soils, including those that are permanently damp. *F. murielae* "Simba" is only about 6ft/1.8m tall. *F. nitida* [zones 5–11] is also elegant and leafy; its canes are upright and purplish.
also for: ■ Damp and wet soils ■ Ornamental bark or twigs

Hydrangea aspera Villosa Group
(syn. *H. villosa*)
○◑

type of plant: slightly tender/hardy shrub [7–9]
flowering time: late summer to early autumn
flower color: variable—often rich violet + pale rose-lilac
height: 6–10ft/1.8–3m

Hydrangeas in this Group have imposing leaves as well as impressive flowers. Each rather open flower head can be 8in/20cm or more across; the slender, pointed leaves, softly hairy and deep green with golden undersides, are often 9in/23cm long. The foliage does not unfurl until late spring. These rounded, wide-spreading shrubs produce numerous, rather upright branches. Villosa Group hydrangeas are lime-tolerant but do not thrive in shallow soils over chalk, since conditions there are too dry. Deep, moist, humus-rich soil with good drainage gives the best results. The plants also need some shelter in order to grow really well. In a warm, protected garden, they may exceed 12ft/3.6m in height. *H. aspera* subsp. *sargentiana* also has large, hairy leaves and these are particularly impressive because they are so broad.

Gunnera manicata
○◑

type of plant: slightly tender perennial [7–10]
flowering time: late spring to early summer
flower color: khaki-green
height: 6–8ft/1.8–2.4m

The thick, cone-like flowers of this clump-forming plant are 24–36in/60–90cm high, but even they are inconspicuous beneath the vast, lobed and veined, deep green leaves on their thick, prickled stalks. *G. manicata* is usually grown in damp or boggy ground near water and, in these circumstances, leaves more than 6ft/1.8m wide are not uncommon. Slightly drier conditions are also suitable, as long as the soil is deep and fertile. The crowns and leaf buds are liable to frost damage.
also for: ■ Damp and wet soils ■ Ground cover

Sambucus nigra f. laciniata
[black elder]
○◑

type of plant: hardy shrub [4–8]
flowering time: early summer
flower color: white
height: 6–8ft/1.8–2.4m

It may not be quite such an elegant plant as the cut-leaved Japanese maple in the next illustration, butblack elder is less fussy about growing conditions and it is a good deal faster-growing. Its very finely divided foliage is composed of numerous, slender, mid-green leaflets. Musk-scented flowers are carried in heads 8in/20cm or more across. Bunches of black berries ripen in late summer. A wide range of soils is suitable. To insure plenty of large, ferny leaves, conditions need to be reasonably fertile and moist, and the plant should be pruned hard every few years. *S. racemosa* "Tenuifolia" is much slower-growing, and has almost thread-like foliage.
also for: ■ Shallow soils over chalk ■ Heavy, clay soils ■ Damp and wet soils ■ Ornamental fruit

Acer palmatum var. *dissectum*
[Japanese maple]
○◑

type of plant: hardy shrub [6–8]
height: 5–7ft/1.5–2.1m

With its spreading mound of conspicuously arching branches, this shrub looks interesting even in winter. Its beautiful, filigree foliage is light green. In autumn, it turns rich yellow or orange. The leaves, each around 3in/8cm long, are deeply divided into slender leaflets, which themselves are dissected. The plant dislikes dryness and cold winds. It needs a sheltered site and fertile soil that is moist as well as free-draining. In some circumstances, the ideal conditions are most easily achieved in a lightly shaded site. For a purple-leaved form of this plant, see p.149. Both these maples are very slow growing plants that are suitable for a large container. After many decades, *A. palmatum* var. *dissectum* may be about 12ft tall/3.6m and tree-like.
also for: ■ Growing in containers
■ Colorful, autumn foliage

Choisya "Aztec Pearl"
○◑

type of plant: slightly tender shrub [8–10]
flowering time: mainly late spring to early summer; some flowers late summer to early autumn
flower color: white
height: 4–6ft/1.2–1.8m
Evergreen

The sweetly fragrant, pink-budded flowers of C. "Aztec Pearl" do not have such a rich, strong fragrance as those of *C. ternata* (for which, see p.289). However, its rich green foliage is especially pretty, and the numerous, slim, shiny leaflets, to 3½in/9cm long, look most attractive with the clusters of starry, 1in/2.5cm-wide flowers. The foliage is sharply and pleasantly aromatic when bruised or cut. This rounded, sometimes slightly loose and open shrub is at its best in a warm, sheltered site. Any reasonably well-drained soil is suitable.
also for: ■ Aromatic foliage ■ Fragrant flowers

Rhododendron yakushimanum
○◑ ✱

type of plant: hardy shrub [5–9]
flowering time: late spring to early summer
flower color: light pink fading to white
height: 3–5ft/0.9–1.5m
Evergreen

At first, the slender, recurved leaves of this very slow-growing rhododendron are covered in cream-colored hairs; in maturity, they are glossy, dark green above and brown-felted below. The foliage is arranged in striking, almost whorl-like groups. Each leathery leaf is about 4in/10cm long. Funnel-shaped, 1½in/4cm-long flowers are held in rounded trusses. *R. yakushimanum* needs an open-textured, acid soil that is humus-rich and moisture-retentive. It forms a dense dome of growth that is eventually 7–8ft/2.1–2.4m wide.
also for: ■ Acid soils ■ Growing in containers

Shibataea kumasaca
○◑

type of plant: hardy perennial (bamboo) [6–9]
height: 3–5ft/0.9–1.5m
Evergreen

In cool climates, this bamboo forms clumps of growth, rather than spreading widely at the roots, and it increases slowly. In many areas it is therefore suitable for planting in small spaces. Its broad, tapered, 3in/8cm-long leaves are rich bright green. The leaf tips become attractively bleached in winter. The foliage is borne, in almost whorl-like clusters, on erect, greenish yellow canes. *S. kumasaca* forms a dense mass of growth, which can be clipped and used to create a "hedge." A moist soil is necessary for good growth and moisture is particularly important if the bamboo is planted in a sunny site.
also for: ■ Damp and wet soils ■ Ground cover

Geranium psilostemon
(syn. *G. armenum*)
[cranesbill]
○◑

type of plant: hardy perennial [5–8]
flowering time: early to late summer
flower color: magenta-pink + black
height: 3–4ft/0.9–1.2m

When it is covered in masses of sizzlingly vibrant, 1½in/4cm-wide flowers, the foliage of this vigorous cranesbill is rather overshadowed. However, the broad, deeply lobed and deeply cut basal leaves, to 8in/20cm long, are handsome and even the little, stem leaves make an attractive background for the floral fireworks. In autumn the foliage turns from a fairly bright mid-green to red. *G. psilostemon* makes clumps of growth that are often lax enough to require some support. It is easily pleased but performs particularly well—flowering for weeks on end—in fertile soil with good drainage.
also for: ■ Colorful, autumn foliage ■ Long, continuous flowering period

Tsuga canadensis
e.g. "Jeddeloh"
[Canada hemlock]
○◐

type of plant: hardy conifer [4–8]
height: 3–4ft/0.9–1.2m
Evergreen

These flat, ¾in/2cm-long and slightly curved leaves are a fresh, light green and neatly arranged. They create a lively, almost feathery pattern. The plant grows slowly and the layered, semi-pendulous branches form a dense dome that often has a slight hollow in the center. Moist, well-drained soil is needed, and growth is best in cool, humus-rich, neutral soil. *T. canadensis* "Jeddeloh" must have shelter from cold, drying winds.

Astilbe e.g. "Fanal"
○◐

type of plant: hardy perennial [4–8]
flowering time: early to late summer
flower color: deep red
height: 24in/60cm

Astilbes with deeply colored flowers—such as the variety shown here—tend to have dark rich green foliage that, in its immature state, is maroon or bronze. Numerous, toothed leaflets form thick clumps of ferny growth, above which the dense spires of tiny flowers rise erectly. *A.* "Fanal" is in bloom for many weeks, starting earlier than many astilbes and continuing into late summer. Its flower heads are each about 8in/20cm long. In autumn, they ripen into handsome, red-brown seedheads. Astilbe hybrids, of which there are many, are long-lived plants that grow best in moist or damp soil that is fertile and humus-rich. In drier conditions, some shade is advisable.
also for: ■ Damp and wet soils ■ Ground cover ■ Purple, bronze, or red leaves (young leaves only) ■ Ornamental fruit (seedheads) ■ Long, continuous flowering period

Hedera helix
e.g. "Congesta"
[ivy]
○◐●

type of plant: hardy shrub [5–9]
height: 24in/60cm
Evergreen

The numerous, upright stems of this non-climbing ivy are closely set with arrow-shaped leaves, to 1in/2.5cm long, which are dark and shining. *H. helix* "Erecta" is a similarly shrubby variety, although it produces more rounded leaves and may reach 4ft/1.2m in height. Both these ivies are slow-growing plants and so are suitable for planting in a container or on a rock garden. They can be grown in most soils but are best in reasonably moisture-retentive conditions.
also for: ■ Heavy, clay soils ■ Growing in containers ■ Atmospheric pollution

Bergenia cordifolia
○◐[●]

type of plant: hardy perennial [3–8]
flowering time: mainly mid-spring
flower color: mauve-pink
height: 18in/45cm

Evergreen ✂

Both in the garden and in arrangements indoors, these bold, wavy-edged leaves, about 8in/20cm wide, are useful for providing a contrast to more intricately patterned plants. The leathery foliage lasts very well in water. It is rich mid-green for most of the year but in cold weather may acquire reddish purple tinges. Clusters of 1in/2.5cm-long, bell-shaped flowers are produced intermittently through spring. The first blooms often open in early spring and are liable to frost damage. The flower-stalks are thick, reddish and rhubarb-like. Leaves of *B. cordifolia* "Purpurea" become rich red-purple in winter; its flowers are magenta-pink. Both plants form ground-covering clumps of foliage in almost any soil, as long as it is not waterlogged or very hot and dry.
also for: ■ Heavy, clay soils ■ Dry shade ■ Ground cover

Carex comans "Frosted Curls"
[sedge]
○◐

type of plant: hardy/slightly tender perennial [7–9]
height: 12in/30cm
Evergreen

The thin, arching leaves of *C. comans* "Frosted Curls" are curled at their tips and of a very pale silvery green. They form dense clumps of growth. Loamy soil and a sheltered site seem to produce the best specimens of this plant, but it is easily pleased in most soils, as long as they are not dry. The green flower spikes, produced in summer, are inconspicuous. For an example of a bronze-colored sedge with very fine leaves, see p.207.
also for: ■ Ground cover

Corydalis cheilanthifolia
○◐

type of plant: hardy perennial [5–8]
flowering time: mid-spring to early summer
flower color: yellow
height: 12in/30cm
Evergreen

Especially in a cool, shady place and in light but moisture-retentive soil, this is a plant with a long flowering season. However, it is adaptable and most sites and soils are suitable—provided either the soil is quite moist or the site is sufficiently shaded to conserve moisture. C. cheilanthifolia usually self-sows freely and often ends up growing in a shady wall. Its rosettes of long, bright green leaves form clumps of much divided, ferny foliage. Particularly in cold weather, the leaves may become bronze-tinted. The tubular flowers, each about ½in/1cm long, are arranged in spikes.

also for: ■ Ground cover ■ Long, continuous flowering period

Astilbe e.g. "Sprite"
○◐

type of plant: hardy perennial [6–9]
flowering time: midsummer to early autumn
flower color: pale pink
height: 10–12in/25–30cm

Even before its pretty, wide-branching flower heads develop, this astilbe's neat clumps of deeply cut leaves are very attractive. The young foliage is, briefly, bronzed; the mature leaves are shining, rich green and sometimes tinged with bronze. Flower sprays are up to 6in/15cm long. When they fade, they ripen into long-lasting seed heads of bright tan. A. "Willie Buchanan" and A. "Bronce Elegans" are two further examples of *simplicifolia* hybrids. They are similar to A. "Sprite" but have rather denser flower heads of richer pink coloring. All these plants appreciate cool growing conditions and they thrive in moist, fertile soil. In slightly drier conditions they need some shade.

also for: ■ Damp and wet soils ■ Ground cover ■ Ornamental fruit (seedheads)

ADDITIONAL PLANTS, featured elsewhere in this book, that have decorative, green foliage

○◐ **sun or partial shade**

minimum height 10ft/3m or more
Acer griseum, see p.266
Acer palmatum "Ōsakazuki," see p.241
Acer palmatum "Sango-kaku," see p.266
Acer pensylvanicum, see p.266
Akebia quinata, see p.307
Azara microphylla, see p.317
Camellia x williamsii "Donation," see p.29
Chamaecyparis obtusa "Nana Gracilis," see p.29
Decaisnea fargesii, see p.258
Ligustrum lucidum, see p.100
Parthenocissus quinquefolia, see p.240
Parthenocissus tricuspidata, see p.240
Pileostegia viburnoides, see p.132
Sciadopitys verticillata, see p.28
Trochodendron aralioides, see p.325
Vitis coignetiae, see p.240

minimum height between 3ft/90cm and 10ft/3m
Aesculus parviflora, see p.242
Aruncus dioicus, see p.72
Astilbe chinensis var. *taquetii* "Superba," see p.112
Camellia x williamsii "J.C. Williams," see p.29
Choisya ternata, see p.289
Cotoneaster horizontalis, see p.267
Darmera peltata, see p.73

Drimys lanceolata, see p.250
Fatsia japonica, see p.149
Filipendula rubra, see p.71
Itea ilicifolia, see p.325
Ligularia "The Rocket," see p.72
Mahonia x media "Charity," see p.318
Osmunda regalis, see p.72
Thalictrum delavayi "Hewitt's Double," see p.289
Tropaeolum speciosum, see p.30

minimum height 3ft/90cm or less
Alchemilla conjuncta, see p.326
Alchemilla mollis, see p.114
Asplenium trichomanes, see p.23
Astilbe chinensis var. *pumila*, see p.116
Astilbe "Deutschland," see p.76
Bergenia "Bressingham Ruby," see p.242
Bergenia "Silberlicht," see p.115
Chaerophyllum hirsutum "Roseum," see p.75
Corydalis lutea, see p.347
Cotoneaster horizontalis, see p.267
Cyperus longus, see p.75
Euphorbia amygdaloides var. *robbiae*, see p.86
Fragaria Pink Panda, see p.117
Geranium x cantabrigiense "Cambridge," see p.116
Geranium endressii, see p.347
Geranium "Johnson's Blue," see p.114

Geranium macrorrhizum, see p.251
Geranium macrorrhizum "Album," see p.115
Geranium x oxonianum "Wargrave Pink," see p.115
Geranium wallichianum "Buxton's Variety," see p.347
Gunnera magellanica, see p.118
Hemerocallis lilioasphodelus, see p.310
Heuchera cylindrica "Greenfinch," see p.326
Hosta "Royal Standard," see p.309
Houttuynia cordata "Flore Pleno," see p.77
Hydrangea quercifolia, see p.242
Lysichiton americanus, see p.77
Myrrhis odorata, see p.250
Paeonia lactiflora "Festiva Maxima," see p.309
Paeonia lactiflora "Sarah Bernhardt," see p.309
Paeonia officinalis "Rubra Plena," see p.291
Parthenocissus quinquefolia, see p.240
Parthenocissus tricuspidata, see p.240
Pleioblastus argenteostriatus f. *pumilis*, see p.114
Rodgersia pinnata "Superba," see p.73
Rodgersia podophylla, see p.206
Sanguisorba obtusa, see p.75
Sinacalia tangutica, see p.73
Stephanandra incisa "Crispa," see p.114
Tanacetum vulgare var. *crispum*, see p.251
Viburnum davidii, see p.259
Vitis coignetiae, see p.240

Dryopteris affinis "Cristata"
(syn. *D.a.* "Cristata The King,"
D. pseudomas "Cristata")
[golden male fern]
◑[◎]

type of plant: hardy fern [4–8]

height: 36in/90cm

Semi-evergreen

The fronds of *D. affinis* "Cristata" are symmetrically ornamented with little, tassel-like elaborations on their tips. Well into winter, the foliage is still rich green and decorative. The plant is vigorous and forms bold, arching clumps of growth in most soils, including those that are not especially moist and cool. However, it is at its most luxuriant in humus-rich, moisture-retentive conditions and in a sheltered, shady place. Individual fronds can be about 4ft/1.2m long.

Gentiana asclepiadea
[willow gentian]
◑[◎]

type of plant: hardy perennial [6–9]

flowering time: late summer to early autumn

flower color: mid- to deep blue

height: 24–30in/60–75cm

The stems of this clump-forming plant emerge upright but, as they lengthen, they arch conspicuously and this habit of growth emphasizes the attractive, paired arrangement of the leaves and the elegance of the 2in/5cm-long, trumpet-shaped flowers. In autumn, the glossy, pointed leaves turn from bright mid-green to yellow. A cool position and moist, humus-rich soil are suitable for this plant, but it is easily grown and can be given a sunnier site, as long as the soil remains moist in summer. Forms and varieties of the willow gentian are available in various shades of blue, and there is also a white-flowered variety.

also for: ■ Colorful, autumn foliage

Begonia grandis subsp. *evansiana*
◑[◎]

type of plant: slightly tender tuber [7–9]

flowering time: late summer to mid-autumn

flower color: pale pink

height: 12–18in/30–45cm

This begonia produces its shiny, wrinkled, lopsidedly heart-shaped leaves late in spring. They are often a pinkish copper color when new. The older foliage, which is pea- to olive-green, may be tinted red-brown on its undersurfaces. Each leaf is about 4in/10cm long. Pendent sprays of 1¼in/3cm-wide, single flowers are carried on pale pink-tinged, fleshy stems. This rounded, bushy plant needs a position that is warm and sheltered. It can be grown in most well-drained, moisture-retentive soils, provided they are not very alkaline. There is an attractive, white-flowered variety of *B. grandis* subsp. *evansiana*.

Saxifraga x *urbium*
[London pride]
◑[◎]

type of plant: hardy perennial [6–9]

flowering time: late spring to early summer

flower color: pale pink

height: 12in/30cm

Evergreen

London pride is easy to grow in most soils, but its rosettes of leathery, spoon-shaped leaves are largest—as much as 6in/15cm wide—in a cool, moist, shady place. (In drier, sunnier conditions the plant is considerably smaller and more compact.) The foliage makes carpets of weed-suppressing growth about 4in/10cm high; single plants can, when well suited, spread well over 15in/38cm wide. The cloud-like masses of tiny flowers, on their slender stalks, are in marked contrast to the thickset appearance of the foliage. A variegated form of London pride is shown on p.178.

also for: ■ Heavy, clay soils ■ Ground cover ■ Crevices in paving

Aruncus aethusifolius
◑[◎]

type of plant: hardy perennial [4–8]

flowering time: early to mid-summer

flower color: off-white

height: 9–12in/23–30cm

The mounds of finely dissected, ferny foliage produced by *A. aethusifolius* associate well with the fluffy plumes of tiny flowers. Each erect-stemmed plume is about 5in/12cm long. In autumn, the bright green foliage takes on pink and crimson tints, particularly if the plant has been grown in some sun. As long as it has soil that is fertile and retains moisture easily, this is an easily grown perennial. It thrives in cool, woodland soils. The pink-buff seedheads are an additional, if minor attraction.

also for: ■ Colorful, autumn foliage

ADDITIONAL PLANTS, featured elsewhere in this book, that have decorative, green foliage

◐[○] partial shade (or sun)

minimum height 10ft/3m or more
x *Fatshedera lizei*, see p.86

minimum height between 3ft/90cm and 10ft/3m
Angelica archangelica, see p.327
Camellia japonica "Adolphe Audusson," see p.32
Camellia japonica "Alba Simplex," see p.152
Camellia japonica "Lavinia Maggi," see p.103
Hedera helix "Green Ripple," see p.81
Mahonia japonica, see p.312

minimum height 3ft/90cm or less
Arisaema candidissimum, see p.312
Cyclamen coum, see p.320
Dicentra eximia, see p.82
Dicentra spectabilis, see p.294
Dicentra spectabilis "Alba," see p.294
Dryopteris filix-mas, see p.81
Eomecon chionantha, see p.119
Epimedium perralderianum,
   see p.120
Epimedium x rubrum, see p.83
x *Fatshedera lizei*, see p.86

Galium odoratum, see p.120
Hedera helix "Green Ripple,"
   see p.81
Helleborus argutifolius, see p.327
Helleborus foetidus, see p.82
Iris foetidissima, see p.261
Mahonia aquifolium, see p.122
Polypodium vulgare, see p.83
Rubus tricolor, see p.87
Tellima grandiflora, see p.119
Tellima grandiflora Rubra Group,
   see p.243

Dicksonia antarctica
[Tasmanian tree fern, man fern]
◐

type of plant: half-hardy/slightly tender
fern [9–10]
height: 6–10ft/1.8–3m
Evergreen/Semi-evergreen

This fashionably exotic- and jungly-looking tree fern thrives outdoors in really mild, moist areas and in warm, sheltered town gardens. Its huge, much divided, leathery fronds are sometimes more than 6ft/1.8m long. They form an enormous, lacy rosette which sits on top of a shaggy "trunk." The foliage is dark green in maturity. *D. antarctica* needs a site protected from cold and dry air, and acid soil that remains constantly moist. It looks good in a large container.
also for: ■ Acid soils ■ Growing in containers

Athyrium filix-femina
[lady fern]
◐

type of plant: hardy fern [4–9]
height: 24–36in/60–90cm

If this fern is grown in a cool place and in moist, humus-rich soil, then its exquisitely lacy fronds keep their fresh, yellowish green color for many months. The plant does not do well in dry places. As they mature, the elegant, much divided fronds arch gracefully, having been more erect when they are young. Individual fronds may be about 36in/90cm long. There are numerous varieties of lady fern. They include *A. filix-femina* "Minutissimum," which is much smaller than the species, and *A. f.-f.* "Frizelliae," which has narrow, almost bobbly-looking fronds. There are also various tasselled, curled and feathered forms.
also for: ■ Damp and wet soils

Smilacina racemosa
[false Solomon's seal]
◐

type of plant: hardy perennial [4–9]
flowering time: late spring to early summer
flower color: creamy white
height: 24–36in/60–90cm

The more or less erect stems of *S. racemosa* arch at their tips and form small thickets of growth. The broad, veined leaves, each 4–6in/10–15cm long and wavy-edged, create striking masses of light green foliage. Dense, fluffy-looking heads of tiny flowers, which elongate to 4–5in/10–12cm, are borne at the ends of the stems. They are yellowish in bud, often turning pinkish beige as they age. They have a deliciously sweet and fresh fragrance. Humus-rich soil, preferably acid to neutral, and a cool site provide the ideal growing conditions for this bold and stylish perennial.
also for: ■ Ground cover ■ Fragrant flowers

Onoclea sensibilis
[sensitive fern]
◐

type of plant: hardy fern [4–8]
height: 24in/60cm

At the first touch of frost, this fern's arching, boldly incised, sterile fronds turn brown—hence the common name. Up until then, they are a most attractive, pale green. The more finely divided, fertile fronds are erect and bear bead-like lobes from midsummer onward. They turn very dark brown and persist through winter. Sensitive fern is a vigorous plant that can spread extensively. Individual plants are usually at least 36in/90cm wide. They make good ground cover in soils that are wet or permanently moist and, preferably, neutral to acid.
also for: ■ Damp and wet soils ■ Ground cover

**Asplenium scolopendrium
(syn. *Phyllitis scolopendrium*)
[hart's tongue fern]**
◐

type of plant: hardy fern [5–8]
height: 18–24in/45–60cm
Evergreen

Hart's tongue fern forms clumps of distinctive, strap-shaped, undivided fronds. It thrives in alkaline soil that is well-drained and also moist and humus-rich. When growing well, it spreads up to 24in/60cm wide and makes good ground cover. In drier conditions, it is smaller and its typically bright green coloring is less rich. When the fronds first unfurl in spring they are an attractive, fresh, yellowish green. For an example of one of the many varieties of this fern, see below.
also for: ■ Shallow soils over chalk ■ Ground cover

**Asplenium scolopendrium
(syn. *Phyllitis scolopendrium*)
e.g. Undulatum Group
[hart's tongue fern]**
◐

type of plant: hardy fern [5–8]
height: 12in/30cm
Evergreen

The numerous varieties of hart's tongue fern include plants in the Undulatum Group, shown here, on which the more or less smooth leaf edges of the species (see above) are replaced by wavy margins. Other readily available variants include *A. scolopendrium* Crispum Group plants, which have tightly crimped leaf margins, and *A. scolopendrium* Cristatum Group plants, which have fronds with frilly crests at their tips. All these clump-forming plants are at their best in light, well-drained, preferably alkaline soil that is also humus-rich and moisture-retentive. They can cope with some dryness, but drier conditions produce less luxuriant growth and a leaf color that is less rich and bright.
also for: ■ Shallow soils over chalk

**Epimedium x youngianum
e.g. "Niveum"
[barrenwort]**
◐

type of plant: hardy perennial [5–9]
flowering time: mid- to late spring
flower color: pure white
height: 6–9in/15–23cm
Semi-evergreen/Deciduous

All barrenworts have their sprays of little flowers complemented by cleanly shaped, pointed leaflets. Although many larger barrenworts are very useful for ground cover, *E. x youngianum* "Niveum" is almost too small, even though it does form dense clumps of growth. Its elegantly heart-shaped leaves, to about 3in/8cm long, are suffused with brown-bronze when young; later they are bright green; in autumn they take on reddish tints, and they persist into winter. Sprays of nodding, spurred flowers are carried on reddish stems. *E. x y.* "Roseum" (syn. "Lilacinum") has mauve-pink to purplish flowers. Both plants thrive in well-drained, fertile, moisture-retentive soil. They also tolerate quite dry, shady conditions.
also for: ■ Dry shade ■ Purple, bronze, or red leaves (young leaves only) ■ Colorful, autumn foliage (winter color, too)

ADDITIONAL PLANTS, featured elsewhere in this book, that have decorative, green foliage

◐ partial shade

---

minimum height 3ft/90cm or less
Actaea matsumurae "White Pearl," see p.79
Actaea rubra, see p.261

Arisarum proboscideum, see p.121
Blechnum penna-marina, see p.121
Blechnum spicant, see p.37
Corydalis flexuosa "China Blue," see p.349
Dryopteris erythrosora, see p.208

Hacquetia epipactis, see p.349
Hosta lancifolia, see p.121
Matteuccia struthiopteris, see p.79
Thalictrum kiusianum, see p.37

**Astilboides tabularis
(syn. *Rodgersia tabularis*)**
◐●

type of plant: hardy perennial [5–8]
flowering time: midsummer
flower color: ivory
height: 4–5ft/1.2–1.5m

Especially when young, the shallowly dished, almost circular leaves of this moisture-loving plant are a conspicuously pale green. Each great foliar "saucer" is poised on a long, clear stalk. The drooping plumes of small flowers, carried 18–24in/45–60cm above the foliage, are less impressive than the leaves. In rich, damp soil and a sheltered site, some specimens of *A. tabularis* produce leaves more than 36in/90cm wide; in slightly drier conditions, a fully shaded position may help to conserve moisture and maintain coolness.
also for: ■ Heavy, clay soils ■ Damp and wet soils ■ Ground cover

Polystichum setiferum
e.g. Divisilobum Group
[hedge fern]
◖●

type of plant: hardy fern [5–8]
height: 24–30in/60–75cm
Evergreen/Semi-evergreen

Their densely filigreed foliage makes plants in the Divisilobum Group some of the most beautiful forms of fern. The fronds spread—each frond with a slight twist—from a dense, central crown. On young growth, the midribs have shaggy, orange-brown scales. The rich soft green leaf coloring is retained into winter, even in cold climates. Well-drained, moisture-retentive soil is suitable for these slow-growing ferns and, although they tolerate drier conditions too, they do not prosper in parched soils. There are numerous forms of soft shield fern, including some with dense, overlapping foliage.
also for: ■ Shallow soils over chalk
■ Ground cover

Polystichum aculeatum
[hard shield fern, prickly shield fern]
◖●

type of plant: hardy fern [4–8]
height: 24in/60cm
Evergreen

As its common name suggests, the foliage of hard shield fern is tough and leathery. The plant makes clumps of finely divided, shining, dark greenery. When young, the slender fronds are yellow-green and the "leaf"-stalks are shaggy and russet-colored. Each frond is upright but with a slight curve that produces a lively effect in each clump of fronds. Hard shield fern grows particularly well in moist soil that has good drainage, but it is adaptable and prospers in a range of soils and in moderately dry conditions.
also for: ■ Shallow soils over chalk ■ Ground cover

Adiantum pedatum
[maidenhair fern]
◖●

type of plant: hardy fern [3–8]
height: 12–15in/30–38cm

The fresh green fronds of this exceptionally pretty fern are arranged in circular fans that are poised, more or less horizontally, on top of dark stems. Cool, leafy, preferably acid soil that retains moisture easily is most suitable for this plant, and a sheltered site ensures that the foliage looks its best. The clumps of thin, wiry stems increase slowly. A. venustum also has pretty, rather more feathery foliage; it is about half the height of A. pedatum but its carpets of growth spread much more quickly.

Tiarella wherryi
(syn. T. collina)
◖●

type of plant: hardy perennial [6–8]
flowering time: late spring to early summer
flower color: white or pink-tinged white
height: 9in/23cm
Evergreen

Compared with T. cordifolia (see p.123), T. wherryi is a much less vigorous plant. It slowly forms neat clumps of lobed, maple-like leaves, with each leaf up to about 5in/12cm long. The foliage is pale soft green that is often overlaid with bronze or red, particularly in colder weather. The leaves of T.w. "Bronze Beauty" are pale green and deep red-bronze. Both these plants grow well in light woodland, or wherever their top growth remains shaded and their roots stay cool and moist—ideally in humus-rich, well-drained soil. Their small, starry flowers are carried in erect, dark-stemmed spikes.
also for: ■ Ground cover

ADDITIONAL PLANTS, featured elsewhere in this book, that have decorative, green foliage

◖[●] / ◖● partial shade (or full shade)/partial or full shade

minimum height 10ft/3m or more
x Fatshedera lizei, see p.86
Parthenocissus quinquefolia, see p.240
Parthenocissus tricuspidata, see p.240

minimum height between 3ft/90cm and 10ft/3m
Fatsia japonica, see p.149
Hedera helix "Green Ripple," see p.81

minimum height 3ft/90cm or less
Asarum europaeum, see p.87

Bergenia cordifolia, see p.228
Bergenia "Silberlicht," see p.115
Convallaria majalis, see p.314
Dryopteris filix-mas, see p.81
Epimedium grandiflorum "Rose Queen," see p.122
Euphorbia amygdaloides var. robbiae, see p.86
x Fatshedera lizei, see p.86
Geranium macrorrhizum, see p.251
Geranium macrorrhizum "Album," see p.115
Geranium phaeum, see p.86
Hedera helix "Congesta," see p.228
Hedera helix "Green Ripple," see p.81

Helleborus foetidus, see p.82
Iris foetidissima, see p.261
Kirengeshoma palmata, see p.38
Leucothoe Scarletta, see p.38
Mahonia aquifolium, see p.122
Maianthemum bifolium, see p.124
Pachysandra terminalis, see p.123
Parthenocissus quinquefolia, see p.240
Parthenocissus tricuspidata, see p.240
Polygonatum x hybridum, see p.295
Ramonda myconi, see p.87
Rubus tricolor, see p.87
Tiarella cordifolia, see p.123
Waldsteinia ternata, see p.84

Colorful, autumn foliage

including plants with evergreen leaves that
change color in late autumn and winter

MENTION AUTUMN FOLIAGE and right away many gardeners will think of great, glowing swathes of Virginia creeper (*Parthenocissus quinquefolia*) or masses of blistering red maples (*Acer*). Yet there are numerous small- and medium-sized plants with good autumn foliage, and it is quite wrong to think that all plants with spectacular foliage in autumn are rather dull during the rest of the year.

Many magnificent tall trees develop excellent autumn leaf color but so too do numerous medium-sized shrubs and small trees. This list includes, for example, staghorn sumach (*Rhus typhina*), burning bush (*Euonymus alatus*), and the small, slow-growing Japanese maple *Acer palmatum* "Ôsakazuki," all of which are reliable sources of striking autumn color. In addition, there are small, evergreen conifers that assume bronze or purplish hues in the colder months (see, for example, *Platycladus orientalis* "Rosedalis," *Cryptomeria japonica* "Vilmoriniana," and *Microbiota decussata*).

Herbaceous plants, the overwhelming majority of which are medium-sized or small, are a source of colorful autumn foliage that is often overlooked. Yet, the cranesbill (*Geranium*) and the bergenia in this list, for example, have leaves that are just as attractively colored in autumn as the foliage of many better known shrubs and trees. There are also grasses—see, for instance, *Miscanthus sinensis* "Gracillimus" in this list—that turn beautiful shades of parchment and ivory in autumn.

Small plants are obviously useful in a small garden, but they are also invaluable in larger spaces where there is room to create groups of plants with colorful autumn foliage. The full range of autumn foliage colors is quite impressive, and all sorts of mixtures and combinations can be concocted (for some examples, see the "Autumn Foliage" section in my book *Take Two Plants*, David & Charles 1998). However, it is worth remembering that bright red or orange leaves often look particularly dramatic when planted beside plain, green foliage, including expanses of lawn.

No matter how spectacular its autumn leaves are, any plant grown for autumn color should, ideally, have at least one other feature that makes it attractive at other times of the year, too. Autumn foliage plants that earn their keep at other seasons include elegantly shaped maples, such as *Acer palmatum* and its varieties, and handsome foliage plants such as crimson glory vine (*Vitis coignetiae*) and oakleaf hydrangea (*H. quercifolia*). Some autumn foliage plants have fragrant flowers—possible examples include common yellow azalea (*Rhododendron luteum*) and *Fothergilla major*—and a considerable number of the plants illustrated in "Plants with ornamental bark or twigs," pp.262–7, produce excellent autumn color.

All autumn foliage plants, large and small, benefit greatly from being positioned so that they can be lit, for a part of the day at least, by the low, soft sun of autumn. As a broad generalization, some sunshine is needed to produce—as well as to show to advantage—really good autumn color (although, of course, not all plants are suitable for a very sunny position).

Soil also affects autumn color. Quite a few of the plants in this list require or, at least, prefer acid soil, and poor rather than rich soil tends to encourage the production of intense colors.

Shelter is another important consideration when choosing a site for autumn foliage plants. The brilliant, dying leaves of many deciduous plants will blow away all too quickly in a windy position.

Finally, climate influences autumn color. The ideal climate has long, hot summers followed promptly by cold weather. Not all the plants of a New England fall perform quite so spectacularly when grown in a region in which summers are tepid and autumns are mild and wet. If a plant colors disappointingly in a particular climate, this is noted in the description.

Larix decidua
[European larch]
○
type of plant: hardy conifer [3–8]
height: 80–120ft/24–36m

Before the foliage falls from this deciduous conifer in late autumn, it turns rich yellow—having emerged a particularly bright, fresh green early in spring. The leaves are needle-like and arranged in little tufts up to 2in/5cm wide. European larch grows quickly and, although it is tall, it is a light and airy tree. Its conical head of widely spaced main branches broadens considerably with age. Most soils are suitable for this vigorous plant, but it does not flourish if its roots are either very dry or wet, or if conditions are very alkaline. It makes a good windbreak inland.

Quercus rubra
(syn. Q. borealis)
[Northern red oak]
○✱
type of plant: hardy tree [3–9]
height: 80ft/24m

Northern red oak grows very quickly and soon forms a rounded, spreading head of growth. Its foliage is mid- to dark green until autumn, when the bold, sharply lobed leaves, up to 9in/23cm long, turn soft red-brown or yellowish tan. Young trees tend to have especially large and sharply lobed leaves that usually color particularly well, often turning a good, deep red. Scarlet oak (Q. coccinea) is about the same size as Northern red oak but it has brighter red autumn foliage on a narrower and more open head of branches. Both trees grow on most soils, provided they are lime-free; they are good on rather light soils.
also for: ■ Acid soils ■ Atmospheric pollution

Quercus palustris
[pin oak]
○✱
type of plant: hardy tree [4–9]
height: 70–80ft/21–24m

The lower branches of this conical tree are slightly pendulous and they give a graceful air to the whole plant. In regions with hot summers, the glossy, mid-green foliage turns deep brown-red. The newest growths change first, to scarlet, and there is, temporarily, a two-toned effect. Where summers are cool, autumn color is less reliable. The leaves, each 4–5in/10–12cm long, are deeply and sharply cut into seven lobes. Pin oak is much used as a street tree in some towns and cities. It grows in a wide range of acid to neutral soils but it thrives in damp and wet conditions. It grows quickly when young.
also for: ■ Acid soils ■ Heavy, clay soils ■ Damp and wet soils ■ Atmospheric pollution

Acer saccharum
[sugar maple, hard maple, rock maple]
○
type of plant: hardy tree [4–9]
height: 60–80ft/18–24m

Sugar maple provides the backbone of autumn color in New England; in mild, wet areas, the display is briefer and less brilliant. When coloring well, the attractive, five-lobed leaves, 4–6in/10–15cm long, turn from mid-green to bright orange-red and gold. Sugar maple is a handsome tree with a dense, broadly oval crown. A number of distinctive varieties have been named, including columnar forms such as A. saccharum subsp. nigrum "Temple's Upright." Any reasonable soil is suitable for A. saccharum and its varieties, but their shallow roots mean that they are liable to salt damage if planted near roads where salt is used to melt ice.
also for: ■ Decorative, green foliage

Ginkgo biloba
[maidenhair tree]
○
type of plant: hardy conifer [4–9]
height: 60–80ft/18–24m

When young, this upright tree is rather narrow and slow growing. It broadens with age. Its leathery leaves, each about 3in/8cm across, are shaped like little fans; they are pale green in spring, mid-green or yellow-green in summer and butter-yellow in autumn. Maidenhair tree grows in most soils. The best results are obtained by planting it in deep, fertile soil and giving it a position in full sun. After hot summers, mature female trees produce fleshy fruits which, as they decay, smell very unpleasant. There are several narrow, upright varieties of this tree.
also for: ■ Heavy, clay soils ■ Atmospheric pollution ■ Decorative, green foliage

Acer rubrum
[red maple, scarlet maple, swamp maple]
○
type of plant: hardy tree [3–9]
flowering time: early spring
flower color: red
height: 70ft/20m

Most young specimens of red maple produce excellent autumn color, their dark green, lobed leaves—each 4in/10cm long—turning first scarlet and orange and then deep red. The autumn color of older trees is usually more subdued. With age, red maple becomes less upright and more spreading and rounded (although columnar varieties are available). Dense clusters of red flowers appear on the naked branches early in spring. A. rubrum October Glory is a smaller tree with shiny foliage that reliably turns glowing crimson-red in autumn. A. rubrum and its varieties tend to color especially well on acid to neutral soil that is moist.
also for: ■ Acid soils ■ Decorative, green foliage

Fraxinus angustifolia "Raywood"
[narrow-leaved ash]
○

type of plant: hardy tree [6–10]
height: 50–70ft/15–21m

In autumn the foliage of this vigorous, wind-resistant tree changes from glossy, dark green to burnished and bronzed wine-purple. Each 9in/23cm-long leaf is divided into as many as thirteen very slim, pointed leaflets. The fairly upright branches create a dense, oval head of growth that becomes more spreading and rounded with age. Almost all soils are suitable, including those that are alkaline, as long as they are reasonably moisture-retentive. Narrow-leaved ash can be grown on heavy soils but then its autumn color is less likely to be good.
also for: ■ Atmospheric pollution

Prunus sargentii
[Sargent cherry]
○

type of plant: hardy tree [4–9]
flowering time: mid-spring
flower color: pink
height: 25–30ft/7.5–9m

Early each autumn, brilliant scarlets and reds suffuse the foliage of this cherry, giving a regular and reliable display of vivid color. The spring blossom, although less dramatic, is certainly pretty. Numerous, saucer-shaped flowers, each about 1½in/4cm wide, appear in small clusters on the bare branches. The flowers are soon joined by pointed leaves that are bronze-red when young, dark green and 3–4in/8–10cm long when mature. Sargent cherry grows quickly and soon spreads widely, often making a rather flat-topped tree. Any well-drained, reasonably fertile soil is suitable.
also for: ■ Purple, bronze, or red leaves (young leaves only)

Cryptomeria japonica
Elegans Group
[Japanese cedar]
○

type of plant: hardy conifer [7–8]
height: 20–25ft/6–7.5m
Evergreen

This almost fluffy-looking, bluish green foliage is attractive all year, but especially so when it turns purplish or coppery in late autumn and winter. The needle-shaped leaves are soft and up to 1in/2.5cm long and the foliage is arranged in slightly weeping tiers of growth. At their tidiest, plants in *C. japonica* Elegans Group are bushily pyramidal. However, by the time they are about 20ft/6m high, they are often rather unstable, and some old specimens grow with their trunks lying on the ground and their branches standing erect. Moist but well-drained, slightly acid soil is most suitable for these plants. They need shelter from cold winds.

Rhus typhina
[staghorn sumach]
○

type of plant: hardy shrub [3–9]
height: 10–15ft/3–4.5m

Early in autumn, the slender, hanging, deep green leaflets of the staghorn sumach change to glowing reds and oranges. The leaflets appear late in spring and are usually 8–10in/20–25cm long. From late summer, female plants carry erect, furry spikes of long-lasting, crimson fruits, up to 8in/20cm long. After leaf-fall, the wide heads of antler-like branches are fully visible. Plants sucker, often freely. Specimens that form trees fork near the ground. Almost any soil is suitable but autumn color is best on light soils and in full sun. *R. typhina* "Dissecta" (syn. "Laciniata") has ferny, very deeply cut foliage.
also for: ■ Atmospheric pollution ■ Decorative, green foliage ■ Ornamental fruit (see above)

Nandina domestica
[heavenly bamboo]
○

type of plant: slightly tender shrub [7–9]
flowering time: mid- to late summer
flower color: white
height: 5–6ft/1.5–1.8m
Evergreen/Semi-evergreen

This upright shrub produces a mass of divided leaves on arching stems. New growth is dusky purple, while mature foliage is bright green. From late summer onward the shapely, pointed leaflets take on rich red or purple tones. The plumes of starry flowers (seen here in bud) can be up to 15in/38cm long. These are most likely to be followed by sprays of bright red berries in areas with hot summers. *N. domestica* "Fire Power" is a dwarf variety with excellent, red, autumn foliage color. Moist, well-drained soil and a sheltered site is most suitable for these plants.
also for: ■ Decorative, green foliage ■ Ornamental fruit (see above) ■ Purple, bronze, or red leaves (young leaves only)

Platycladus orientalis
(syn. *Thuja orientalis*) "Rosedalis"
○

type of plant: slightly tender/hardy conifer [7–9]
height: 24–42in/60–105cm
Evergreen

In spring, this slow-growing, neatly rounded conifer produces young leaves that are creamy yellow and soft to the touch. In summer the foliage is sea-green, and in winter it turns brownish purple. The tiny, needle-shaped leaves stand out from the leaf stems and give a rather feathery appearance to the plant. *Chamaecyparis thyoides* "Ericoides" also turns purple in winter; it is conical in outline, about twice the height of *Platycladus orientalis* "Rosedalis" and has dense, soft foliage. Both these plants are best in moisture-retentive soil that is reasonably well drained. They need a sheltered site. *Chamaecyparis thyoides* "Ericoides" prefers neutral to slightly acid conditions.

Bassia scoparia f. *trichophylla*
(syn. *Kochia trichophylla*)
[burning bush, summer cypress]
○

type of plant: half-hardy annual [9–11]
height: 24–36in/60–90cm

Even before late summer, when its feathery foliage begins to change from fresh, light green to rich, bronzed crimson, this is a striking plant. Its neat, almost prim, egg-like shape may account for the frequency with which it is grown with other short-lived or tender plants in formal bedding schemes. However, its very thin, pointed leaves (each about 2in/5cm long) create a dense, finely textured mass which can look interesting with perennial plants, too. Light, open, fertile soil is most suitable for this plant, which needs a reasonably sheltered position.
also for: ■ Decorative, green foliage

Ceratostigma plumbaginoides
(syn. *Plumbago larpentiae*)
○

type of plant: hardy/slightly tender perennial [6–8]
flowering time: late summer to mid-autumn
flower color: bright blue
height: 12–15in/30–38cm

At its best in regions with hot summers, this subshrubby perennial can be rather shy-flowering in cooler areas. It needs a warm, sheltered site in full sun to encourage plenty of flower clusters to develop. Each five-lobed, open-faced flower is up to ¾in/2cm across. The diamond-shaped leaves are bright green until autumn, when they take on rich crimson and purplish tones. *C. plumbaginoides* has spreading roots and it is often twice as wide as it is high. In the well-drained, fertile soil it prefers, it can form quite large patches of growth. It makes good ground cover. In colder regions, the numerous, erect stems die back each winter.
also for: ■ Ground cover ■ Long, continuous flowering period

Calluna vulgaris
e.g. "Robert Chapman"
[heather, ling]
○★

type of plant: hardy shrub [5–8]
flowering time: late summer to early autumn
flower color: light purple
height: 12in/30cm
Semi-evergreen

The tiny, narrow, overlapping leaves of *C. vulgaris* "Robert Chapman" are gold in summer and orange in autumn. During winter they deepen to vivid red (the colder the weather, the more intense the color). Bell-shaped flowers, each less than ¼in/0.5cm long, are clustered densely around the ends of upright stems. The flowers are very attractive to bees. This ground-covering heather is about twice as wide as it is high. Similar foliage varieties include *C.v.* "Sir John Charrington" (mauve-pink flowers) and *C.v.* "Wickwar Flame" (crimson). All these plants need an open position and soil that is moisture-retentive, well drained and acid. They thrive in infertile conditions.
also for: ■ Acid soils ■ Ground cover ■ Yellow or yellow-green leaves

ADDITIONAL PLANTS, featured elsewhere in this book, that have colorful, autumn foliage

○ sun

minimum height 10ft/3m or more
Acer platanoides "Crimson King," see p.198
Betula utilis var. *jacquemontii*, see p.263
Fagus sylvatica Atropurpurea Group, see p.198
Koelreuteria paniculata, see p.219
Larix kaempferi, see p.25
Liriodendron tulipifera, see p.219
Liriodendron tulipifera "Aureomarginata," see p.161
Metasequoia glyptostroboides, see p.65
Morus nigra, see p.95
Platanus x *hispanica*, see p.94
Populus alba, see p.183
Populus nigra "Italica," see p.94

Prunus "Amanogawa," see p.13
Prunus avium "Plena," see p.95
Prunus x *subhirtella* "Autumnalis," see p.316
Prunus "Taihaku," see p.13
Pyrus calleryana "Chanticleer," see p.95
Robinia pseudoacacia "Frisia," see p.210
Sorbus "Joseph Rock," see p.253

minimum height between 3ft/90cm and 10ft/3m
Berberis thunbergii f. *atropurpurea*, see p.200
Berberis thunbergii f. *atropurpurea* "Rose Glow," see p.163
Callicarpa bodinieri var. *giraldii* "Profusion," see p.253

Cotinus coggygria "Royal Purple," see p.199
Prunus incisa "Kojo-no-mai," see p.145
Thuja occidentalis "Rheingold," see p.210

minimum height 3ft/90cm or less
Berberis thunbergii f. *atropurpurea* "Atropurpurea Nana," see p.202
Ceratostigma willmottianum, see p.337
Cryptomeria japonica "Vilmoriniana," see p.147
Erica erigena "Brightness," see p.138
Euphorbia cyparissias "Fens Ruby," see p.203
Euphorbia dulcis "Chameleon," see p.201
Pennisetum alopecuroides "Hameln," see p.277
Stipa tenuissima, see p.278

Liquidambar styraciflua
[sweetgum]
○[◐]

type of plant: hardy tree [5–8]
height: 50–70ft/15–21m

At its best, the autumn foliage of this tree is a spectacular mixture of red, orange, and purple but not all specimens are equally colorful. In any case, the deep green summer foliage is very handsome. Each glossy leaf, which may be as much as 6in/15cm across, is elegant and maple-like with shapely, pointed lobes. The foliage appears late in spring. When young, sweetgum is a broad-based pyramid of growth; it forms a wide dome in maturity. Deep, moist soil that is, preferably, acid to neutral, produces the best growth and the best autumn color, but most soils are suitable. Full sun also encourages good color, and shelter ensures that it lasts well.
also for: ■ Damp and wet soils ■ Decorative, green foliage

Malus tschonoskii
[crabapple]
○【●】

type of plant: hardy tree [4–8]
flowering time: late spring
flower color: white, tinged pink at first
height: 40ft/12m

This crabapple does produce fruits but these are small and not especially prolific or decorative. They are yellowish green, with a red tinge, and are preceded by cupped, 1½in/4cm-wide flowers that are arranged in small clusters. The plant's outstanding feature is its autumn foliage. Before they fall, the broad, pointed leaves, up to 5in/12cm long, turn from glossy mid-green to rich shades of red, orange, and purplish bronze. *M. tschonoskii* is a tough and adaptable plant that grows well in a wide range of soils. Although it tolerates some shade, its autumn colors create most impact in a sunny position. With age, its conspicuously upright branches become more spreading.
also for: ■ Heavy, clay soils ■ Atmospheric pollution

Nyssa sylvatica
[black gum, sour gum, tupelo]
○【●】✳

type of plant: hardy tree [4–9]
height: 35–70ft/10.5–21m

In cooler climates, this tree does not often exceed the lesser of the two heights given here and its growth rate is only moderate. Young specimens are quite narrowly pyramidal in shape; older trees are broader and either conical, often with very wide-spreading lower branches, or columnar. The leaves are pointed ovals, up to 6in/15cm long, and usually glossy. In mid-autumn they turn from deep green to shades of orange, yellow and red, with the reds predominating just before leaf-fall. *N. sylvatica* thrives in deep, fertile, lime-free soil. Its roots need consistent moisture and it is suitable for planting in damp ground near water.
also for: ■ Acid soils ■ Damp and wet soils

Cercis canadensis
[eastern redbud]
○【●】

type of plant: hardy tree [5–9]
flowering time: late spring to early summer
flower color: purple-pink
height: 25ft/7.5m

This round-headed tree is native to the eastern and central US, where its 4in/10cm-long, heart-shaped leaves turn yellow in autumn and where its clusters of red-budded, ½in/1cm flowers are produced in large quantities. In cooler, wetter climates, neither its flowering nor the coloring of its foliage in autumn is reliable and a purple-leaved variety (see p.199) is a better choice. The leaves of *C. canadensis* are bronze when young; they mostly appear after the flowers. Well-drained, loamy soil that remains moist, at least in winter and spring, seems to be most suitable for this tree and it appreciates a site with some shelter.

Fothergilla major
○【●】✳

type of plant: hardy shrub [5–9]
flowering time: late spring
flower color: greenish white
height: 8ft/2.4m

As well as spectacular, long-lasting foliage color from about mid-autumn, *F. major* produces sweetly scented, "bottle-brush" flowers, each around 1½in/4cm long. The shiny, veined leaves are broad and rounded. They appear late in spring and are up to 4in/10cm long. Their autumn coloring is a glowing mixture of red, crimson, orange, and gold. Sunshine encourages good autumn color—and profuse flowering—but this upright shrub does also need cool, moist, humus-rich soil that is well drained and lime-free. Generally, this plant is only 3–4ft/0.9–1.2m high after ten years. Plants in the *F.m.* Monticola Group often have outstandingly bright autumn foliage.
also for: ■ Acid soils ■ Fragrant flowers

Rhododendron luteum
[pontic azalea]
○【◑】✳

type of plant: hardy shrub [5–8]
flowering time: late spring to early summer
flower color: yellow
height: 6–10ft/1.8–3m

In full bloom, pontic azalea is a mass of 1½in/4cm-long, funnel-shaped flowers. These exude a penetratingly sweet scent. The summer foliage is a good, rich green, and in autumn the slim, pointed leaves, up to 4in/10cm long, turn glowing orange-red (in this illustration, the color is in the process of developing fully). The shrub is upright and has an open habit of growth. Ideally, it should be given moist, spongy soil but, provided conditions are lime-free, it tolerates slightly drier conditions than most plants in its genus. The plant often suckers, and it can be a prolific self-sower.
also for: ■ Acid soils ■ Atmospheric pollution ■ Fragrant flowers

Euonymus alatus
[burning bush, winged spindle tree]
○【●】

type of plant: hardy shrub [5–9]
height: 6–8ft/1.8–2.4m

Except when several specimens of this shrub are grown together, the hanging, scarlet-seeded fruits develop only erratically. However, the intense pinkish red of the autumn foliage can always be relied on. This long-lasting color is particularly good on plants grown in full sun. *E. alatus* slowly makes a wide, rather flat-topped mass of stiff, spreading branches and dark green, pointed leaves (each up to 3in/8cm long). The branches have flat, corky "wings" that are conspicuous in winter. The plant grows well on most soils with reasonable drainage and it thrives on chalk. For a smaller variety, see right.
also for: ■ Shallow soils over chalk ■ Ornamental fruit (see above)
■ Ornamental bark or twigs

Miscanthus sinensis e.g. "Gracillimus"
○◖◗

type of plant: hardy perennial (grass) [5–9]
height: 4–5ft/1.2–1.5m

Although it rarely flowers in climates with cool summers, this vase-shaped grass is decorative over many months. It forms dense clumps of upright stems and very narrow, curved leaves. The foliage color is spft green; the midribs are pale. In autumn, the leaves and stems turn ripe yellow-buff. (The illustration shows *M. sinensis* "Gracillimus" in midwinter.) Most soils are suitable but moist conditions are ideal. When the plumes of tiny, reddish flowers appear, they are carried on stems to 8ft/2.4m high. *M.s.* "Silberfeder" (syn. Silver Feather) flowers freely even in cooler climates; its leaves turn yellow before falling in autumn, but its seedheads last almost all winter.
also for: ■ Heavy, clay soils

Aronia melanocarpa [black chokeberry]
○◖◗

type of plant: hardy shrub [3–8]
flowering time: late spring to early summer
flower color: white
height: 3–5ft/0.9–1.5m

In the later part of autumn, the foliage of this upright, suckering shrub turns rich orange, red, and wine-red. Earlier in the year, the glossy, pointed leaves, each 2–3in/5–8cm long, are dark green. Branched heads of round-petaled flowers are followed by pendent, pea-sized berries that ripen to black in early autumn. Although these fruits are not long-lasting, they can contrast well with the autumn foliage, and they are certainly attractive to many birds. Most soils are suitable for this tough and very adaptable plant. It is particularly at home in moist or damp soil that is neutral to slightly acid.
also for: ■ Damp and wet soils ■ Atmospheric pollution ■ Ornamental fruit (see above)

Euonymus alatus "Compactus" [burning bush, winged spindle tree]
○◖◗

type of plant: hardy shrub [5–9]
height: 3–4ft/0.9–1.2m

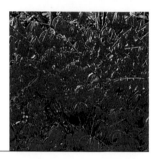

Like the species (see left), *E. alatus* "Compactus" has dark green, pointed leaves that reliably turn a spectacular, pink-crimson in autumn, and the color is similarly long-lasting. It too has corky "wings" that are attached to its spreading branches and that make the shrub look interesting in winter. However, this variety grows much more densely and slowly than the species. In North America, it is often used for low hedging. Although it appreciates good drainage, *E. alatus* "Compactus" is not fussy about soil; it grows well on chalk. It tends not to produce many of its scarlet-seeded fruits in Britain.
also for: ■ Shallow soils over chalk ■ Hedging plants ■ Ornamental fruit (see above) ■ Ornamental bark or twigs

Geranium x *magnificum* [cranesbill]
○◖◗

type of plant: hardy perennial [4–8]
flowering time: early summer
flower color: violet-blue
height: 18–24in/45–60cm

The vividly colored flowers of this vigorous cranesbill are up to 2in/5cm wide. They appear in large numbers, although for a fairly short period. However, *G.* x *magnificum* is interesting in autumn as well as summer. Its basal leaves, each 4–5in/10–12cm across, are rich green and almost circular in outline. They are divided into rounded, toothed lobes. The foliage forms spreading clumps of weed-proof growth that turn orange and red in autumn. A wide range of at least reasonably well-drained soils is suitable for this adaptable plant. Other cranesbills with good autumn color include *G. psilostemon* (see p.227) and *G. macrorrhizum* and its varieties (see pp.115 and 251). With all these plants, autumn color is best in a sunny site.
also for: ■ Ground cover ■ Decorative, green foliage

ADDITIONAL PLANTS, featured elsewhere in this book, that have colorful, autumn foliage

○◖◗ sun (or partial shade)

minimum height 10ft/3m or more
Betula pendula, see p.264
Betula pendula "Youngii," see p.99
Castanea sativa, see p.222
Celastrus orbiculatus, see p.129
Crataegus phaenopyrum, see p.98
Nothofagus antarctica, see p.27
Sorbus aria "Lutescens," see p.19
Sorbus cashmiriana, see p.256
Sorbus hupehensis, see p.193
Sorbus vilmorinii, see p.256

Tilia "Petiolaris," see p.98
Trachelospermum jasminoides, see p.304
Viburnum opulus "Xanthocarpum," see p.68
Vitis vinifera "Purpurea," see p.203

minimum height between 3ft/90cm and 10ft/3m
Cornus alba "Elegantissima," see p.68
Cornus alba "Kesselringii," see p.331
Cornus alba "Sibirica," see p.265
Cornus alba "Spaethii," see p.169
Cornus sericea "Flaviramea," see p.265
Euonymus europaeus "Red Cascade," see p.257

Ribes odoratum, see p.305
Rosa "Fru Dagmar Hastrup," see p.92
Rosa "Roseraie de l"Haÿ," see p.343
Viburnum opulus "Compactum," see p.257

minimum height 3ft/90cm or less
Calamagrostis arundinacea, see p.111
Euphorbia palustris, see p.68
Geranium dalmaticum, see p.111
Geranium pratense "Mrs Kendall Clark," see p.224
Geranium sanguineum, see p.111
Sorbus reducta, see p.224

Parthenocissus tricuspidata
(syn. *Vitis inconstans*)
[Boston ivy]
○◐●

type of plant: hardy climber [5–8]
height: 70ft/21m; also suitable for ground-cover
(see description)

Both this climber (often incorrectly called Virginia creeper) and the one in the following illustration are famous for the brilliance of their autumn foliage color. Their leaves start to redden quite early in autumn. Before they fall, Boston ivy's strong green, maple-like leaves, up to 8in/20cm across, turn rich crimson and scarlet; Virginia creeper's pointed leaflets, to 4in/10cm long, change from mid-green to blood-red. These climbers are extremely vigorous and quite unsuitable for small spaces. They can be used to cover a wall of any aspect, although in regions of hot summers, a position in full sun is best avoided. Virginia creeper looks particularly attractive when grown through a tall tree; it is not such a close-clinging plant as Boston ivy. When used for ground cover, Virginia creeper forms a looser and slightly higher mass of growth (about 12in/30cm high as against 9in/23cm high for Boston ivy; both plants spread about 10ft/3m wide). To become established quickly, these climbers need a good depth of fertile soil. Once established, they attach themselves to surfaces by means of tendrils with adhesive discs. For a less vigorous parthenocissus, see p.180.
also for: ■ Atmospheric pollution ■ Ground cover ■ Climbing plants ■ Decorative, green foliage (*P. quinquefolia* in particular)

Parthenocissus quinquefolia
(syn. *Vitis quinquefolia*)
[Virginia creeper]
○◐●

type of plant: hardy climber [4–9]
height: 50ft/15m

See preceding plant.

Vitis coignetiae
[crimson glory vine]
○◐○

type of plant: hardy climber [5–9]
height: 50ft/15m; 24in/60cm as ground cover

The shield-shaped, deeply veined leaves of this magnificent, tendrilled climber can be as much as 12in/30cm wide. With the first cold weather of autumn, the foliage turns from rich green to tawny shades of yellow, orange, and purple-crimson. The autumn colors are long-lasting. They are brightest on plants facing south or west, but other aspects are almost equally suitable. Crimson glory vine is very fast-growing and extremely vigorous. It looks especially attractive climbing into a tall tree (where it may reach up to 80ft/24m high). If its shoots are pegged down, it can make good ground cover (up to 24in/60cm high and 15ft/4.5m or more wide). The plant grows well in deep, fertile, moisture-retentive soil but autumn colors are often best on rather infertile soil. The inedible, black grapes are more or less obscured by the foliage.
also for: ■ Ground cover ■ Climbing plants ■ Decorative, green foliage

Cercidiphyllum japonicum
[katsura tree]
○◐

type of plant: hardy tree [6–9]
height: 40ft/12m (see description)

In autumn, katsura tree not only looks good, since its rounded leaves turn yellow, pink, and red, but it also smells good, because the dying foliage emits a pervasive smell of caramelized sugar. The plant grows quickly in deep, fertile, humus-rich soil, and autumn color is best in neutral to acid conditions. This tree may be multistemmed, or, if grown as a single stem, more than 70ft/21m high with a slender, oval crown. In either case, the plant has elegant, airy layers of slightly pendulous branches. The emerging leaves are reddish bronze and, unless the tree has a sheltered position, these may become damaged by frost and cold winds. The summer leaves are bluish green and 2–3in/5–8cm wide.
also for: ■ Acid soils ■ Purple, bronze, or red leaves (young leaves only) ■ Aromatic foliage (see above)

Cornus florida
[flowering dogwood]
◯◐

type of plant: hardy tree/shrub [6–9]
flowering time: late spring to early summer
flower color: white
height: 20ft/6m

C. florida produces a mass of striking, flower-like bracts along its wide-spreading branches. These bracts, to 2in/5cm long, surround the tiny heads of true flowers. (The subsequent red berries are less eye-catching than the bracts and are, in any case, soon eaten by birds.) In autumn, the oval, often twisted leaves, each 3–4in/8–10cm long, turn from dark green to rich shades of red and purple. This plant needs moist, fertile, and preferably acid soil. Flowering is best after hot summers; in cool-summer climates, pink-bracted C.f. f. rubra tends to be the freest flowering form. Other varieties are numerous. They include the free-flowering C.f. "White Cloud," C.f. "Cherokee Chief," which has bright red-pink bracts, and the variegated foliage variety C.f. "Welchii" (syn. "Tricolor").

Parrotia persica
[Persian ironwood]
◯◐

type of plant: hardy tree/shrub [5–8]
flowering time: late winter to early spring
flower color: red
height: 18–25ft/5.4–7.5m

Persian ironwood often forms a very wide-spreading shrub with almost horizontal, somewhat drooping branches. However, it can make a broad-headed, short-trunked tree (sometimes up to 40ft/12m tall), and then the brown-and-green mottled bark becomes a conspicuous feature. In autumn, the wavy-edged, glossy, deep green leaves, up to 5in/12cm long, turn amber, orange, and dark red. All fertile, well-drained soils produce satisfactory results but moisture and acidity ensure really spectacular autumn colors. On mature specimens, the bare branches are studded with dense clusters of tiny, tufted flowers, which create a crimson haze in winter sunshine.
also for: ■ Acid soils (see above) ■ Ornamental bark or twigs ■ Winter-flowering

Eucryphia glutinosa
◯◐✱

type of plant: slightly tender shrub/tree [7–9]
flowering time: mid- to late summer
flower color: white
height: 12–18ft/3.6–5.4m
Semi-evergreen/Deciduous

In mild areas and in rich, moist, acid soil with good drainage, E. glutinosa often becomes crowded with white blossom. However, this is a slow-growing plant and its beautiful, simple, saucer-shaped flowers, to 2½in/6cm across, seldom appear in large quantities on specimens less than five years old. Toward the end of autumn, the numerous, glossy, pointed leaflets, each about 1in/2.5cm long, turn from dark green to orange and red. They often hang on the branches for weeks. If this upright, bushy plant is given a position in sun, it is particularly important to ensure that the roots remain cool and moist. It needs shelter from cold winds and hot sun.
also for: ■ Acid soils

Acer palmatum "Ôsakazuki"
[Japanese maple]
◯◐

type of plant: hardy shrub/tree [6–8]
height: 12–15ft/3.6–4.5m

The autumn color of some Japanese maples—including A. palmatum itself—is variable, and it can be very disappointing. But the airy layers of rich green foliage produced by the variety shown here always turn a brilliant flame-crimson in mid-autumn. Each deeply and delicately lobed leaf is up to 5in/12cm long. A.p. "Ôsakzuki" is upright at first but, as it slowly matures, it forms a low-forking tree with a rounded head of growth. After many years it may exceed 20ft/6m. It needs well-drained soil that retains moisture easily, and it dislikes dryness and cold winds. A. japonicum "Aconitifolium" is another small maple that reliably produces brilliant autumn leaf color; it is about 10ft/3m tall and its deeply cut leaves turn scarlet, gold, and orange before falling.
also for: ■ Decorative, green foliage

Ilex x meserveae
e.g. Blue Angel
[blue holly]
○◐

type of plant: hardy shrub [5–9]
height: 8–10ft/2.4–3m
Evergreen

Seen here in mid-autumn when they have acquired their cold-weather tinge of purple, these leaves are dark bluish green for most of the year. Each leaf is less than 2in/5cm long. Its spines look sharp but they are, in fact, soft. The plant slowly forms a wide, bushy mass of very glossy growth, with strong, upright shoots of dark purple. It is suitable for hedging and topiary. When pollinated by a male plant—such as *I. x meserveae* Blue Prince—this holly bears clusters of deep red berries. (In cooler climates, *I. x m.* Blue Angel is sometimes not very free-fruiting; *I. x m.* Blue Princess is more reliable.) Blue hollies are not difficult to grow, but they appreciate moisture and good drainage. *I. x m.* Blue Angel is the least hardy of the varieties.
also for: ■ Hedging plants ■ Growing in containers (clipped specimens) ■ Ornamental fruit (see above)

Aesculus parviflora
[bottlebrush buckeye]
○◐

type of plant: hardy shrub [5–9]
flowering time: mid- to late summer
flower color: white
height: 7–10ft/2.1–3m

A. parviflora forms a thicket of numerous, slender stems; it spreads by suckers, but not invasively so. Its broad, rounded mass of growth is usually wider than it is tall. Each of its big, bold leaves is deeply divided into several pointed leaflets, the largest of which may be more than 9in/23cm long. The foliage emerges pinkish bronze, matures to deep green and turns a clear, bright yellow in autumn. Little, wispy flowers are arranged in erect spikes, up to 12in/30cm long; in cooler climates, they are rarely followed by small, pear-shaped fruits. Most soils are suitable for this shrub, although very dry and very alkaline conditions are best avoided.
also for: ■ Heavy, clay soils ■ Atmospheric pollution ■ Decorative, green foliage ■ Purple, bronze, or red leaves (young leaves only)

Hydrangea quercifolia
[oak-leaved hydrangea]
○◐

type of plant: hardy shrub [5–9]
flowering time: midsummer to mid-autumn
flower color: white, becoming purple- or rust-tinged
height: 3–5ft/0.9–1.5m

In autumn, these large and interestingly shaped, oak-like leaves turn from mid-green to plush shades of bronze, purple, and crimson. Each leaf is up to 8in/20cm long. Pyramidal flowers heads are freely produced in hot-summer climates, but in regions with cool summers this brittle-stemmed, spreading plant flowers rather sparsely and the foliage is a more reliable decorative feature. In warm regions the plant usually requires some shade and it is taller as well as more floriferous. Moist, fertile soil with good drainage is ideal for this hydrangea, but it is not a demanding plant. Popular varieties of *H. quercifolia* include double-flowered *H.q.* "Snow Flake."
also for: ■ Decorative, green foliage ■ Long, continuous flowering period

Bergenia
e.g. "Bressingham Ruby"
○◐

type of plant: hardy perennial [3–8]
flowering time: mid- to late spring
flower color: bright deep pink
height: 12–15in/30–38cm
Evergreen

The 7in/18cm-long, rounded leaves of *B.* "Bressingham Ruby" form ground-covering clumps of leathery foliage. If the plant has been grown in rather light, poor soil and given a sunny position, the foliage turns from rich green to a deep beetroot color in cold weather; otherwise, the winter foliage is usually a more subdued purplish maroon. Clusters of bell-shaped flowers are borne on thick maroon stems. Other bergenias with leaves that color well in winter include red-flowered *B.* "Abendglut" (syn. Evening Glow) and *B.* "Wintermärchen" and pink-flowered *B.* "Sunningdale." All these plants are tolerant of a wide variety of soil types, as long as conditions are not hot and very dry. In exposed positions, their flowers may sometimes be damaged by frosts.
also for: ■ Heavy, clay soils ■ Ground cover ■ Decorative, green foliage

ADDITIONAL PLANTS, featured elsewhere in this book, that have colorful, autumn foliage

○◐ sun or partial shade

minimum height 10ft/3m or more
Acer campestre, see p.21
Acer griseum, see p.266
Acer palmatum f. atropurpureum, see p.206
Acer palmatum "Sango-kaku," see p.266
Acer pensylvanicum, see p.266
Amelanchier canadensis, see p.28
Carpinus betulus, see p.143
Carpinus betulus "Fastigiata," see p.44
Cornus kousa var. chinensis, see p.28
Decaisnea fargesii, see p.258
Fagus sylvatica, see p.143
Fagus sylvatica "Pendula," see p.21
Halesia carolina, see p.29
Hydrangea anomala subsp. petiolaris, see p.131
Ptelea trifoliata "Aurea," see p.215
Schizophragma hydrangeoides, see p.131
Sorbus aucuparia, see p.28
Stewartia pseudocamellia Koreana Group,
    see p.266
Taxodium distichum, see p.71

minimum height between 3ft/90cm and 10ft/3m
Acer palmatum var. dissectum, see p.227
Acer palmatum var. dissectum Dissectum
    Atropurpureum Group, see p.149
Clethra alnifolia, see p.308
Corylus avellana "Contorta," see p.267
Cotoneaster atropurpureus "Variegatus," see p.174
Cotoneaster horizontalis, see p.267
Cotoneaster simonsii, see p.143
Hamamelis x intermedia "Pallida," see p.318
Osmunda regalis, see p.72
Phytolacca polyandra, see p.331
Rhododendron "Daviesii," see p.309
Rhododendron "Gibraltar," see p.102
Viburnum x burkwoodii, see p.308
Viburnum x carlcephalum, see p.308
Viburnum plicatum f. tomentosum "Mariesii,"
    see p.45
Viburnum sargentii "Onondaga," see p.206

minimum height 3ft/90cm or less
Cotoneaster atropurpureus "Variegatus," see p.174
Cotoneaster horizontalis, see p.267

Euphorbia griffithii "Fireglow," see p.113
Euphorbia polychroma, see p.114
Geranium x cantabrigiense "Cambridge,"
    see p.116
Geranium macrorrhizum, see p.251
Geranium macrorrhizum "Album," see p.115
Geranium psilostemon, see p.227
Geranium wallichianum "Buxton's Variety,"
    see p.347
Hydrangea "Preziosa," see p.346
Lysimachia clethroides, see p.73
Microbiota decussata, see p.115
Molinia caerulea subsp. caerulea "Variegata,"
    see p.174
Parthenocissus quinquefolia, see p.240
Parthenocissus tricuspidata, see p.240
Persicaria affinis "Superba," see p.117
Persicaria vacciniifolia, see p.117
Phalaris arundinacea var. picta "Picta,"
    see p.173
Rodgersia podophylla, see p.206
Stephanandra incisa "Crispa," see p.114
Vitis coignetiae, see p.240

Enkianthus campanulatus
◐○ ✱

type of plant: hardy shrub [5–8]
flowering time: late spring to early summer
flower color: cream + pink
height: 8–12ft/2.4–3.6m

Although they are very prettily colored, the clusters of hanging, ½in/1cm-long bells borne by this shrub are perhaps best appreciated in arrangements indoors. However, the autumn foliage glows brilliantly and is a conspicuous feature even at some distance outdoors. The neat, pointed, light green leaves, each about 1½in/4cm long, turn red and yellowish orange in autumn. When young, E. campanulatus is erect; in maturity, it becomes more spreading, open and twiggy. Deep, moist soil that is humus-rich and lime-free is ideal. The plant needs shelter from cold winds. E.c. "Red Bells" bears red flowers on red stalks.
also for: ■ Acid soils ■ Flowers suitable for cutting

Tellima grandiflora Rubra Group
(syn. T.g. "Purpurea")
[fringe cups]
◐○

type of plant: hardy perennial [4–9]
flowering time: late spring to early summer
flower color: green + purple-pink
height: 18–24in/45–60cm
Semi-evergreen

The light green, conspicuously veined leaves of T. grandiflora Rubra Group plants take on pinkish bronze tones during summer. Each prettily lobed and scalloped leaf is about 3in/8cm wide. In winter, the foliage is burnished purple-maroon (although the exact color is variable). Slender wands of tiny, bell-shaped flowers are held well above the 10in/25cm-high mounds of foliage. In well-drained, moisture-retentive soil, these perennials usually spread quickly, forming good ground cover, and they often self-sow. However, they adapt successfully to conditions ranging from dry shade to heavy clay.
also for: ■ Heavy, clay soils ■ Dry shade ■ Ground cover ■ Decorative, green foliage ■ Green flowers

ADDITIONAL PLANTS, featured elsewhere in this book, that have colorful, autumn foliage

◐○ partial shade (or sun)

minimum height 10ft/3m or more
Parthenocissus henryana, see p.180
Styrax japonicus, see p.32

minimum height 3ft/90cm or less
Aruncus aethusifolius, see p.230
Epimedium x rubrum, see p.83
Gentiana asclepiadea, see p.230
x Heucherella alba "Rosalie," see p.295

Mahonia aquifolium, see p.122
Tellima grandiflora, see p.119

◐ partial shade

minimum height 3ft/90cm or less
Epimedium x youngianum "Niveum," see p.232

◐● partial or full shade

minimum height 10ft/3m or more

Parthenocissus henryana, see p.180
Parthenocissus quinquefolia, see p.240
Parthenocissus tricuspidata, see p.240

minimum height 3ft/90cm or less
Cornus canadensis, see p.125
Leucothoe Scarletta, see p.38
Parthenocissus quinquefolia, see p.240
Parthenocissus tricuspidata, see p.240
Polygonatum x hybridum, see p.295
Tiarella cordifolia, see p.123

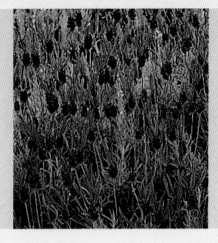

PLANTS WITH

Aromatic foliage

AROMATIC LEAVES are associated with herb-scented cooking, medieval gardens, ancient folk-medicine, and vacations in the sun. No wonder we find plants with aromatic foliage so appealing.

When we think of aromatic leaves, plants such as rosemary (*Rosmarinus*) and lavender (*Lavandula*) spring quickly to mind, but there are plenty of other sources of fragrant foliage, and the scents of these leaves vary considerably. The foliage of some aromatic plants smells very much like other flowers or fruits: the leaves of lemon verbena (*Aloysia triphylla*), for example, are indeed strongly lemon scented, and caraway thyme (*Thymus herba-barona*) does have the fragrance of caraway; plenty of plants, besides the true mints (*Mentha*), also smell like mint; and there are quite a few aniseed-scented plants, too. Some leaves have a very distinctive aroma: lad's love or southernwood (*Artemisia arbrotanum*) and *Tanacetum* both have foliage that smells strongly and strangely sweet—and not everyone likes these scents.

Perhaps the easiest way to enjoy aromatic foliage is to grow a few of the plants in this list beside a garden seat. Some aromatic leaves, notably those of *Helichrysum italicum* subsp. *serotinum*, exude their fragrance freely, especially on hot days. However, the foliage of most aromatic plants must be bruised before the scent is perceptible, and a garden seat is a comfortable place to carry out this pleasant task. Some gardeners like to plant low, aromatic plants in the gaps between paving stones, and there are even a few of these plants that do not object to being trodden on (see, for example, the non-flowering form of chamomile, *Chamaemelum nobile* "Treneague").

As well as smelling good, the plants in this list look good, too. Some of them, including the *Monarda* and *Dictamnus*, have flowers that are at least as attractive as their leaves. Others, such as the variegated thyme (*Thymus vulgaris* "Silver Posie"), the variegated oregano (*Origanum vulgare* "Country Cream," and golden sage (*Salvia officinalis* "Icterina"), are grown as much for their appearance as for the fragrance of their leaves. There are also numerous, good-looking, gray-leaved plants that are aromatic (for which see also "Plants with gray, blue-gray, or silver leaves," pp.182–96).

One of the functions of the fragrant oils in many aromatic plants is to provide protection against desiccating hot winds and scorching sun, so it is not surprising that many of these plants grow well in full sun and really well-drained soil. However, there are aromatic plants that grow well in some shade: a number of the mints adapt to or even enjoy partial shade, while larger, shade-tolerant, aromatic plants include *Choisya*.

As in the other lists of this book, plants with culinary uses are marked "(herb)" after "type of plant." Nurseries specializing in herbs offer numerous aromatic plants with variegated or unusually colored leaves, or with distinctively scented leaves. Thymes and mints, in particular, are rich sources of decorative foliage and unusual fragrances. When planting evergreen culinary herbs, such as thyme and rosemary, it is worth remembering that they are much more likely to be used during the colder months if they are within easy reach of the kitchen, rather than planted far away, down a dark and slippery path.

The dried leaves of some aromatic plants, such as lemon verbena (*Aloysia triphylla*), various lavenders, and certain species of *Pelargonium*, are not often used in cookery but are popular ingredients of potpourri and scented sachets.

For the keen collector of the less usual perfumes, there are, for example, roses with fragrant foliage (they include the pink-flowered Rubiginosa hybrid *Rosa* "Lady Penzance," which has apple-scented leaves). However, for many, it is the familiar lavenders, rosemaries, and thymes that will always be the quintessential—and the most desirable—aromatic plants.

Aloysia triphylla
(syn. *A. citriodora*, *Lippia citriodora*)
[lemon verbena]
○

type of plant: half-hardy shrub [9–10]
height: 5–6ft/1.5–1.8m

Lemon verbena can be forgiven for its rather loose habit of growth and its wispy, ineffective spikes of tiny flowers because its foliage has such an intense and deliciously fresh, lemon fragrance. (The leaves retain this fragrance well when dried.) The plant is bushier—and flowerless—if it is pruned hard each spring or if its growing tips, at least, are pinched out. Each slender, pointed leaf, about 4in/10cm long, is light bright green. Only in really mild areas does lemon verbena develop a framework of permanent branches outdoors; elsewhere, frost cuts it to ground level. In colder areas it is often best grown in a container and brought under cover in winter. It needs well-drained, rather dry and infertile soil.
also for: ■ Growing in containers

Rosmarinus officinalis
[rosemary]
○

type of plant: slightly tender shrub (herb) [8–10]
flowering time: late spring to early summer
flower color: pale lavender-blue
height: 4–5ft/1.2–1.5m
Evergreen

These very narrow, leathery leaves, up to 1¼in/3cm long, emit a rich, warm scent; they are dark green above and almost white below, giving a slightly gray effect overall. In time, the upright branches of this fast-growing shrub tend to become more curved. The little, lipped flowers are borne in profusion. Varieties of *R. officinalis* include *R.o.* "Sissinghurst Blue" with bright blue flowers; there are pink- and white-flowered forms, too. For a prostrate rosemary, see p.59. For hedging, *R.o.* "Miss Jessopp's Upright" is especially suitable, but the species is also useful. (Hedging plants should be 18–24in/45–60cm apart.) All these plants thrive in full sun and light, well-drained soil. They grow well in hot, dry sites and tolerate salt spray.
also for: ■ Dry soils in hot, sunny sites ■ Windswept, seaside gardens ■ Hedging plants ■ Growing in containers

Agastache foeniculum
(syn. *A. anethiodora*, *A. anisata*)
[anise hyssop]
○

type of plant: slightly tender perennial (herb) [7–10]
flowering time: late summer to early autumn
flower color: blue-violet + violet
height: 36in/90cm

The conspicuously upright stems of this bushy plant are clothed in downy, grayish foliage that smells and tastes of aniseed. The veined and pointed leaves can be used in cooking, and they make a refreshing herbal tea. Solid flower spikes, each 2–3in/5–8cm long, appear at the ends of the stems and consist of richly colored, violet bracts and bluish flowers. In autumn, the flower heads become buff-colored and the stems turn yellow. *A. rugosa* bears pinker flower heads. Both plants like a warm site and well-drained, fertile soil. Their flowers are very attractive to bees.

Artemisia arbrotanum
[lad's love, southernwood]
○

type of plant: hardy shrub [5–8]
flowering time: late summer
flower color: yellowish
height: 30–36in/75–90cm
Deciduous/Semi-evergreen

The leaves of this erect, brittle-stemmed shrub are beautifully lacy and of a lovely, gray-green color. The newest foliage is delicate, pale green. Each much-divided leaf is about 2in/5cm long and very aromatic, with a strangely sweet, almost fruity scent that not everyone thinks is attractive. (However, there are some forms of this plant that have a scent that is more lemon-like.) The flowers, which are a good deal less decorative than the foliage, are arranged in long clusters. *A. arbrotanum* is easily grown in any soil with good drainage. It is best in light, rather dry soil and a sunny position.
also for: ■ Dry soils in hot, sunny sites ■ Gray, blue-gray, or silver leaves

Pelargonium
e.g. "Graveolens"
[geranium]
○

type of plant: tender perennial [9–11]
flowering time: mainly early to mid-summer
flower color: pink
height: 24–36in/60–90cm
Evergreen

Widely grown as a house plant in cooler regions, this popular, scented-leaved pelargonium can also be grown outside in the summer months and brought under cover when there is danger of frost. It is a vigorous plant with an erect and bushy habit of growth. Its long-stemmed, rather bright green, crinkled leaves are divided and lobed; they give off a delicious, rose-and-lemon scent when pinched. Starry flowers, each about ½in/1cm across, are arranged in little clusters. Other rose-scented pelargoniums include *P.* "Lady Plymouth," which is a cream-variegated sport of *P.* "Graveolens," and *P.* "Attar of Roses." All these plants need well-drained soil.
also for: ■ Decorative, green foliage

Prostanthera cuneata
[alpine mint bush]
○

type of plant: slightly tender/half-hardy shrub [8–10]
flowering time: early summer
flower color: blue-tinged white
height: 24–36in/60–90cm
Evergreen

The upright, branching stems of this dense and rounded shrub are thickly covered with dark, glossy leaves that are only ¼in/0.5cm long. When bruised, the foliage emits a strong, rather sweet, mint-like scent. Little, lipped flowers are produced in large quantities. Given a warm, sheltered site and well-drained, humus-rich soil, alpine mint bush survives most relatively mild winters. It has a preference for but does not require acid to neutral soil. *P. rotundifolia* is a larger, even less hardy plant with sweetly aromatic foliage and purplish lilac flowers.
also for: ■ Growing in containers

Pelargonium quercifolium
[oak-leaved geranium]
○

type of plant: tender perennial [9–11]
flowering time: mainly mid-spring to early summer
flower color: pink + purple
height: 24in/60cm
Evergreen

When its foliage is bruised, *P. quercifolium* releases a strong, balsam-like scent. The leaves, which are dark and sticky, are shaped like those of English oak. Young leaves in particular show dark purple staining along the veins. This is a variable plant but, most commonly, it is shrubby and fairly erect. Its open-faced flowers are arranged in clusters, each about 1¼in/3cm wide. Other aromatic species include *P. tomentosum* (which has large, downy, peppermint-scented leaves), *P. crispum* (which is lemon-scented—as is its cream-variegated variety) and *P. odoratissimum* (which smells of apples). For a rose-scented variety, see the previous page. All these plants need well-drained soil.
also for: ■ Decorative, green foliage

Hyssopus officinalis
[hyssop]
○

type of plant: hardy shrub/perennial (herb) [6–9]
flowering time: midsummer to early autumn
flower color: deep blue
height: 18–24in/45–60cm
Semi-evergreen

Since it is dense and bushy, hyssop makes good ground cover, especially if it is cut back hard each spring. Its upright stems are clothed in narrow, pointed, dark green leaves, up to 2in/5cm long. The foliage smells and tastes mint-like and slightly bitter. Hyssop can be used to form a low, aromatic hedge (young plants should be about 12in/30cm apart). It grows best in well-drained, alkaline soil and full sun. Bees and butterflies are attracted to the spikes of little, tubular flowers. There are variants of hyssop which have white and pink flowers.
also for: ■ Shallow soils over chalk ■ Dry soils in hot, sunny sites ■ Ground cover ■ Hedging plants

Lavandula stoechas subsp. pedunculata
[French lavender]
○

type of plant: slightly tender shrub [7–10]
flowering time: late spring to early summer and often late summer to early autumn
flower color: dark maroon-purple + bright purplish violet
height: 18–24in/45–60cm
Evergreen

In really well-drained soil and a warm, sheltered site this powerfully aromatic plant freely exudes its refreshing, pine-like scent. The fragrance comes from the erect, 1¼in/3cm-long flowers as well as the slender, light green leaves. In this subspecies, the jauntily top-knotted flowers are carried above the neat, bushy mass of foliage. Other French lavenders include cerise-flowered *L. stoechas* "Kew Red," white-flowered *L.s.* f. *leucantha*, and *L.s.* "Willow Vale," which has numerous, purple flowers. Bees find the flowers of these plants very attractive.
also for: ■ Dry soils in hot, sunny sites ■ Fragrant flowers

Allium tuberosum
[Chinese chives, garlic chives]
○

type of plant: slightly tender/hardy bulb (herb) [7–10]
flowering time: late summer to mid-autumn
flower color: white
height: 18in/45cm

Chinese chives produce their clusters of star-shaped flowers in time to accompany other late summer blooms. The flowers are very attractive to butterflies and bees. Each flower head is about 2in/5cm across. The flat, narrow, mid-green leaves are mildly garlic-flavoured, and they can be used as a vegetable and as flavoring. This clump-forming plant is best grown in light, rich soil that retains moisture, although most well-drained soils give satisfactory results.
also for: ■ Flowers suitable for cutting

Lavandula angustifolia
e.g. "Munstead"
[lavender]
○

type of plant: hardy shrub [6–9]
flowering time: midsummer
flower color: lavender-blue
height: 18in/45cm
Evergreen

L. angustifolia and its varieties, including *L.a.* "Munstead," have flowers and foliage that are warmly and cleanly fragrant. The scent tends to be strongest on light, dry, rather infertile soil and in full sun. These conditions—along with at least one trim a year—also encourage neat, bushy growth. *L.a.* "Munstead" produces flower spikes that are fairly short (each spike is about 1½in/4cm long). They are attractive to bees and butterflies and are carried on clear stalks above the erect-stemmed mass of narrow, light green leaves. This lavender can be used to make a fragrant hedge (young plants should be about 15in/38cm apart). For another lavender suitable for hedging, see p.138.

also for: ■ Dry soils in hot, sunny sites ■ Hedging plants ■ Fragrant flowers

Salvia officinalis e.g. "Icterina"
(syn. *S.o.* "Variegata")
[golden sage]
○

type of plant: slightly tender shrub/perennial (herb) [7–9]
height: 18in/45cm
Semi-evergreen

These soft, grayish green leaves are marbled with yellow and their subtle coloring blends harmoniously with many other plants. Each felted leaf is about 2in/5cm long, and it has the warm, astringent scent of plain, green-leaved common sage (*S. officinalis*). Golden sage rarely flowers. Its erect stems and slender, pointed, oval leaves create a dense mound of growth that is neatest if the plant is clipped lightly each spring. For examples of other sages with colored foliage, see pp.166 and 201. All these bushy subshrubs thrive in light, dryish soil.

also for: ■ Dry soils in hot, sunny sites ■ Variegated leaves

Calamintha nepeta subsp.
nepeta (syn. *C. nepetoides*)
[lesser calamint]
○

type of plant: hardy perennial [5–9]
flowering time: late summer to mid-autumn
flower color: pale blue
height: 12–15in/30–38cm

This bushy plant, with its numerous upright stems, is a haze of palest blue for many weeks. The flowers are lipped and rather less than ½in/1cm long; they are very attractive to bees. When pinched, the little, oval, deep green leaves emit a spearmint-like scent. In the wild *C. nepeta* subsp. *nepeta* grows in dry places; in cultivation it seems to appreciate some moisture as well as good drainage. *C.n.* subsp. *glandulosa* "White Cloud" is a similar plant but its flowers are white.

also for: ■ Long, continuous flowering period

Satureja montana
[winter savory]
○

type of plant: hardy shrub/perennial (herb) [7–10]
flowering time: midsummer to mid-autumn
flower color: lilac-blue to purple
height: 12–15in/30–38cm
Semi-evergreen

Winter savory is a highly aromatic plant with dark green, little leaves that smell and taste like a hotter, more peppery version of thyme. Its twiggy, upright growths are clothed in narrow, pointed leaves, up to 1¼in/3cm long. Especially if clipped each spring, this subshrub forms a neat, ground-covering hummock of growth. Its dense spikes of tubular, lipped flowers are attractive to bees. White-flowered creeping savory (*S. spicigera*) is also readily available and it too can be used in cooking. Both these plants need well-drained soil and full sun. They thrive in hot, dry positions.

also for: ■ Dry soils in hot, sunny sites ■ Ground cover ■ Long, continuous flowering period

Helichrysum italicum
subsp. *serotinum*
(syn. *H. angustifolium* subsp.
serotinum, H. serotinum)
○

type of plant: slightly tender shrub/perennial [8–10]
flowering time: mid- to late summer
flower color: deep yellow
height: 9–15in/23–38cm
Evergreen/Semi-evergreen

On warm days, the needle-fine, pale gray foliage of this subshrub gives off a strong smell of spices. In cooler weather, the 1½in/4cm-long leaves need to be pinched to release their unmistakable aroma. Erect, pale gray stems carry flattish clusters of bobbly, "everlasting" flowers but, if the plant is trimmed in spring, to discourage lankiness, then no flowers form. Really well-drained or dry soil and a site in full sun also promote neat, bushy growth. This plant has a preference for alkaline conditions. *H. splendidum* is similar though not spice-scented; it is about 36in/90cm tall, silvery leaved and its flowers dry well.

also for: ■ Shallow soils over chalk ■ Dry soils in hot, sunny sites ■ Gray, blue-gray, or silver leaves

Tagetes Gem Series
e.g. "Tangerine Gem"
[marigold]
○

type of plant: half-hardy annual [9–11]
flowering time: early summer to early autumn
flower color: yellow-orange
height: 9in/23cm

Some marigolds have leaves that emit a distinctly unpleasant scent when they are bruised, but the slender, little, deep green leaflets of many Signet marigolds—of which *T.* Gem Series "Tangerine Gem" is an example—are sweetly citrus-scented. Signet marigolds are bushy, upright plants that produce large numbers of charming, single blooms, each about 1in/2.5cm across. These annuals thrive in well-drained soil and a warm, sunny site. They are often especially free-flowering on rather poor soils. Gem Series marigolds are available as mixtures, and in shades of yellow as well as orange.

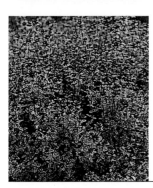

Thymus vulgaris "Silver Posie"
[thyme]
○

type of plant: hardy shrub/perennial (herb) [7–9]
flowering time: late spring to early summer
flower color: pale mauve-pink
height: 6–9in/15–23cm
Evergreen

From a distance, the overall effect of this upright, bushy subshrub is pale and grayish. In fact, the light green leaves, each ¼–½in/0.5–1cm long, have white margins. The foliage is pungently aromatic, with a slightly lemony fragrance. Numerous dark red-purple buds, arranged in short, branched spikes, open into tiny, lipped flowers. Any soil that drains well is suitable for *T. vulgaris* "Silver Posie," but light, dryish ones give excellent results. Other pale, variegated thymes include *T.* x *citriodorus* "Silver Queen" and the mat-forming *T.* "Hartington Silver" (syn. "Highland Cream"). For a caraway-scented thyme, see below. A lemon-scented thyme is shown on p.213. The flowers of all these plants are attractive to bees.
also for: ■ Dry soils in hot, sunny sites ■ Crevices in paving ■ Variegated leaves

Origanum vulgare
e.g. "Country Cream"
[oregano]
○

type of plant: hardy perennial (herb) [4–8]
height: 6–8in/15–20cm
Evergreen/Semi-evergreen

The leaves of this decorative variety of oregano have the usual peppery smell and taste. They can be used in cookery, just like the foliage of the plain green-leaved species. In this case, however, each ¾in/2cm-long, soft green, oval leaf is irregularly edged with a broad band of pale cream. *O. vulgare* "Country Cream" forms a bushy mass of closely packed, more or less upright stems. Although *O. vulgare* and its varieties are particularly at home in light, well-drained, preferably alkaline soil, they succeed in most soils with reasonable drainage. This variegated variety seldom flowers. For details of a golden oregano, see p.213.
also for: ■ Shallow soils over chalk ■ Variegated leaves

Thymus herba-barona
[caraway thyme]
○

type of plant: slightly tender shrub/perennial (herb) [8–11]
flowering time: early to midsummer
flower color: pink or lilac
height: 2–4in/5–10cm
Evergreen

When bruised, the tiny (¼in/0.5cm-long), rich green leaves of this mat-forming subshrub release a strong scent of caraway. They are arranged on wiry stems that root where they touch the soil. The plant usually spreads 8–12in/20–30cm wide. Numerous, little clusters of lipped flowers are carried just above the foliage. Light, gritty soil is necessary for good growth, and the plant thrives in dry, sunny sites—including the cracks between paving stones. As well as caraway thyme and the various lemon-scented thymes (for an example of which, see p.213), there are thymes with leaves that smell of, for instance, camphor (*T. camphoratus*) and oranges (*T.* "Fragrantissimus").
also for: ■ Dry soils in hot, sunny sites ■ Crevices in paving

Laurus nobilis
[bay laurel, sweet bay]
○[◐]

type of plant: slightly tender shrub (herb) [8–10]
height: 5–6ft/1.5–1.8m as a standard;
10–15ft/3–4.5m or more as a freestanding
shrub/tree (see description)
Evergreen

This warmly aromatic shrub is often planted in a large container and clipped into a topiary shape, such as a mophead, pyramid, or cone. It can be used for hedging in mild areas (young plants should be 18–24in/45–60cm apart). When allowed to grow freely, bay forms an upright, pyramidal shrub. In regions with really mild climates, it may be tree-like and more than 30ft/9m high. The leaves, up to 4in/10cm long, are tapered and a gleaming, rich green. They are prone to "burning" in cold winds, although they withstand the milder, salt-laden breezes of the seaside remarkably well. For the yellow-leaved variety of L. nobilis, see p.211. Both plants need well-drained soil and, in cold areas, the species as well as the variety should be given a warm, sunny site.
also for: ■ Windswept, seaside gardens ■ Hedging plants ■ Growing in containers

Monarda
e.g. "Cambridge Scarlet"
[bee balm]
○[◐]

type of plant: hardy perennial [4–9]
flowering time: midsummer to early autumn
flower color: rich red
height: 30–36in/75–90cm

The dark green, veined and pointed leaves of M. "Cambridge Scarlet" are sometimes used to make an herbal tea. They have a strong, fresh, orange-like scent. The tubular flowers, up to 2in/5cm long, are arranged in spidery-looking heads on upright stems. The blooms are attractive to bees. To grow vigorously and to flower well, the roots of this clump-forming perennial need to be moist throughout the growing season. (However, the plant does not do well if its roots are wet in winter.) In dry summers, mildew can be a problem. Other monardas with deeply colored flowers include M. "Mahogany" (claret-red flowers) and the mildew-resistant M. "Scorpion" (violet-purple). For a paler-flowered variety, see p.69. In damp, fertile conditions these plants may become invasive.
also for: ■ Damp and wet soils ■ Flowers suitable for cutting ■ Long, continuous flowering period

Dictamnus albus var. purpureus
[burning bush, dittany, gas plant]
○[◐]

type of plant: hardy perennial [3–8]
flowering time: early summer
flower color: usually purplish pink
height: 24–36in/60–90cm

D. albus var. purpureus is so powerfully aromatic that, on hot, still days in summer, its enveloping haze of vaporized oils can sometimes be ignited. Both the long-stamened, star-shaped flowers and the deep green, divided leaves have a fresh, lemon-like scent. The flowers are arranged in spikes, about 6in/15cm long, which rise erectly above the clumps of foliage. D. albus itself is white-flowered (see p.20). Both these long-lived plants thrive in fertile, preferably alkaline soil with good drainage. They grow well in dry, sunny positions.
also for: ■ Shallow soils over chalk ■ Dry soils in hot, sunny sites ■ Fragrant flowers

Melissa officinalis "Aurea" (syn. M.o. "Variegata") [lemon balm]
○◖

type of plant: hardy perennial (herb) [4–9]
height: 24in/60cm

In spring the foliage of this herb is basically yellow, with a suffusion of rich green along the main veins of each 3in/8cm-long leaf. If M. officinalis "Aurea" is allowed to produce its little, whitish flowers—and these are very attractive to bees—the leaves soon become entirely green. If the stems are cut back in early to midsummer, a fresh set of shoots with well-colored leaves develops. The foliage is deliciously and sharply lemon-scented. This vigorous and easily grown plant creates a dense, billowing mass of upright growth in most soils, but it is happiest in rather dry soils in a sunny place. It even tolerates dryness in a little shade. M.o. "All Gold" has plain yellow leaves; it needs a partially shaded site to protect its foliage from sun scorch.
also for: ■ Dry soils in hot, sunny sites ■ Dry shade (see above) ■ Ground cover ■ Variegated leaves

Allium schoenoprasum [chives]
○◖

type of plant: hardy bulb (herb) [4–9]
flowering time: early summer
flower color: mauve-pink
height: 10in/25cm

The narrow, cylindrical, edible leaves of this plant are bright green. They smell and taste mildly of onions. The foliage forms neat clumps of growth and the plants, with their dense, 1in/2.5cm-wide flower heads held on erect stems, make an attractive edging to paths and borders. When grown for their leaves, chives should be given rich, moist soil. However, the flowers are more freely produced in lighter and drier soils. In most circumstances, the plants increase readily. A. schoenoprasum "Forescate" is vigorous and has brighter, pinker flowers than the species.

ADDITIONAL PLANTS with aromatic foliage that are featured elsewhere in this book

○◖ sun (or partial shade)

minimum height 10ft/3m or more
Laurus nobilis,
    see p.249
Thuja plicata, see p.139

minimum height between 3ft/90cm and 10ft/3m
Artemisia lactiflora, see p.284
Choisya ternata Sundance, see p.214

minimum height 3ft/90cm or less
Acorus calamus "Argenteostriatus," see p.70

Dictamnus albus, see p.20
Houttuynia cordata "Chameleon,"
    see p.170
Mentha aquatica, see p.70
Mentha suaveolens "Variegata," see p.170
Monarda "Croftway Pink," see p.69

Drimys lanceolata (syn. D. aromatica, Tasmannia aromatica) [pepper tree]
○◑

type of plant: slightly tender shrub [8–10]
flowering time: mid- to late spring
flower color: white or cream
height: 8–10ft/2.4–3m
Evergreen

When crushed, the leaves of D. lanceolata release a clean, spicy scent. The immature, copper-colored foliage is more aromatic than the older, bright mid-green leaves. Each leaf is slender and gleaming, and 2–3in/5–8cm long. The bark is also aromatic. Little, loose clusters of starry, ½in/1cm-wide flowers are followed, on fertilized female plants, by small, black berries. Overall, the plant is very neat and dense, with upright branches. The younger stems are an attractive, soft crimson. In all but the mildest regions, this shrub needs a warm, sheltered site. It grows best in soil that is well-drained but also moisture-retentive.
also for: ■ Purple, bronze, or red leaves (young leaves only) ■ Decorative, green foliage

Myrrhis odorata [sweet Cicely, garden myrrh]
○◑

type of plant: hardy perennial (herb) [5–8]
flowering time: early summer
flower color: white
height: 3–4ft/0.9–1.2m

Although the lacy, bright green foliage of sweet Cicely smells like varnish or polish when bruised, it imparts a sweet, aniseed flavour to food when used in cooking. The flower heads, each about 2in/5cm across, are borne on upright, hollow stems. Each head consists of numerous, crowded, star-shaped blooms. These ripen into shiny, brown, nutty-flavored seeds. Some gardeners like to pinch out the flower buds to prevent the usual masses of self-sown seedlings from appearing. This treatment also improves the taste of the leaves. Sweet Cicely grows best in moist soils, including areas near streams and ponds, but it does not do well in very heavy or waterlogged conditions. The plant emerges early in spring and does not die down until early winter.
also for: ■ Damp and wet soils ■ Decorative, green foliage

Mentha spicata
[spearmint]
○◐

type of plant: hardy perennial (herb) [5–9]
flowering time: late summer to early autumn
flower color: pale mauve
height: 24in/60cm

Nurseries specializing in herbs list many different mints, including mints that smell of lemon, Eau de Cologne, and peppermint. *M. spicata* is the species most commonly grown for use in cooking. Its rich green leaves, each about 2½in/6cm long, are crinkled, toothed, and pointed; they have a clean, minty taste and smell. Apple mint (*M. suaveolens*) is regarded by some cooks as having a more subtle, less pungent flavour. Both these upright plants are very vigorous. They spread—indefinitely and invasively—by underground stems. Their flowers, which are attractive to bees, are arranged in dense spikes, up to 4in/10cm long. Both plants need moisture-retentive soil. *M. spicata* var. *crispa* has curly-edged leaves. For other *Mentha* in this book, see the index of botanical names.
also for: ■ Heavy, clay soils

Tanacetum vulgare var. crispum
○◐

type of plant: hardy perennial [4–9]
height: 24in/60cm

Less invasive than the species, this cut-leaved variety of tanacetum is still vigorous, and it can spread widely—up to 36in/90cm or more—by means of underground stems. Its intricately divided, deeply toothed leaves, each about 5in/12cm long, are borne on upright stems. The foliage is bright rich green. When bruised, it emits a strong, rather sweet scent. This variety of tanacetum usually produces only a few clusters of bright yellow, button-shaped flowers from late summer onward. Almost any reasonably well-drained soil is suitable. *T. vulgare* "Isla Gold" has yellow leaves.
also for: ■ Decorative, green foliage

Geranium macrorrhizum
[cranesbill]
○◐●

type of plant: hardy perennial [4–8]
flowering time: late spring to early summer
flower color: magenta-pink
height: 12–15in/30–38cm
Semi-evergreen

The rounded, deeply lobed, light green leaves of this weed-proof plant release a strong and pungent fragrance when bruised. Each leaf is about 4in/10cm across. Upper leaves often assume bright colors in autumn, especially if the plant has been grown in sun. The carpet of growth is usually about 24in/60cm wide. Cool, moist soil and dappled shade provide the ideal conditions for *G. macrorrhizum*, but it is robust and adaptable and does well in full shade, in sun and in most soils; it even copes with dry shade. For a very pale pink variety of this species, see p.115; other varieties include plants with mid-pink and with reddish flowers, and there is a variety with cream-streaked foliage.
also for: ■ Dry shade ■ Ground cover ■ Decorative, green foliage ■ Colorful, autumn foliage (see above)

ADDITIONAL PLANTS with aromatic foliage that are featured elsewhere in this book

○◐ **sun or partial shade**

minimum height 10ft/3m or more
Cercidiphyllum japonicum, see p.240
Chamaecyparis obtusa "Nana Gracilis," see p.29
Ptelea trifoliata "Aurea," see p.215

minimum height between 3ft/90cm and 10ft/3m
Choisya "Aztec Pearl," see p.227
Choisya ternata, see p.289
Hypericum "Hidcote," see p.345

Rhododendron "Praecox," see p.319

minimum height 3ft/90cm or less
Geranium x cantabrigiense "Cambridge," see p.116
Geranium macrorrhizum "Album," see p.115
Houttuynia cordata "Flore Pleno," see p.77
Skimmia x confusa "Kew Green," see p.310

◐▣ **partial shade (or sun)**

minimum height 3ft/90cm or less
Galium odoratum, see p.120

Gaultheria procumbens, see p.123
Mentha requienii, see p.159

◐● **partial or full shade**

minimum height 3ft/90cm or less
Gaultheria procumbens, see p.123
Geranium macrorrhizum, see p.251
Geranium macrorrhizum "Album," see p.115
Skimmia x confusa "Kew Green," see p.310

Ornamental fruit

including plants with ornamental seedheads or seed pods

FRUITS ARE DISTINCTIVE and welcome features of both gardens and indoor arrangements since their shapes usually differ quite markedly from those of flowers and foliage, and most of them ripen at a time when the main season for flowers has passed. Gardeners may miss the blossom of spring and summer, but the fruits of autumn have their own special attraction.

The following list contains plants that bear fruits of many kinds. There are berries and cones, of course, but "pepper-pot" seed pods, translucent and inflated pods, fluffy seedheads, and crisp, spherical seedheads are all here, too. Some of the fruits are edible as well as ornamental: for example, excellent jellies can be made from some crabapples (*Malus*) and from the apple-like fruits of flowering and Japanese quinces (*Chaenomeles*).

Although many ornamental fruits are red, the range of colors is not limited to this end of the color spectrum. A number of the plants illustrated here produce blue or purple fruits, and this strange coloring can be very striking (see, for example, the berries and pods of *Callicarpa bodinieri* var. *giraldii* "Profusion," *Decaisnea fargesii* and *Viburnum davidii*). Other plants, such as hollies (*Ilex*), firethorns (*Pyracantha*), and cotoneasters, which are normally associated with red or orange-red berries, have varieties that bear yellow fruits. These fruits seem to be less attractive to birds; they therefore last longer each season than some red fruits.

In general, seedheads and seed pods are less brilliantly colored than berries, but many gardeners now recognize that the bare stems and fruiting heads of certain plants are excellent enliveners of the autumn and winter scene—especially when these plant "skeletons" become dusted with frost. In the following list, the seedheads of teasels (*Dipsacus*) are particularly long-lasting in the garden, but in other lists there are, for example, *Sedum*, *Astilbe*, and grasses, many of which have long-lasting seedheads. (For plants with ornamental seedheads that dry well for arrangements indoors, see entries marked "Dr" in "Decorative plants with flowers suitable for cutting," pp.268–95.)

For maximum effect, fruits of all sizes, shapes, and colors need a background that is at least consistent, so that all parts of the fruiting plant or group of plants are equally conspicuous. Just how well the fruit stands out against its background is, of course, affected by the color of the background and the degree to which this contrasts with the color of the fruit. Some plants—mainly evergreens or semi-evergreens, such as hollies and some cotoneasters—provide their own contrasting background of foliage.

Many popular plants with ornamental fruit are self-fertile, but there are some that have male and female flowers on separate plants and, in these cases, both sexes must be grown for fertilization and subsequent fruit production to take place. In a small garden particularly, there may not be room to grow more than a single specimen of a plant and whether a plant is self-fertile or not is an important piece of information. Hollies and skimmias, for example, tend to have male and female flowers on separate plants (although *Ilex aquifolium* "J.C. van Tol" is unusual in being a self-fertile holly and *Skimmia japonica* subsp. *reevesiana* is a self-fertile skimmia).

The majority of plants in this list are certainly not one-season wonders. *Clematis* "Bill MacKenzie," *Berberis darwinii*, and *Rosa* "Geranium," for example, produce flowers that are, arguably, even more decorative than their very attractive fruits. Other plants produce fragrant flowers or good-looking, evergreen foliage or glowing autumn foliage as well as decorative berries or seed pods.

In general, plants will usually produce the most abundant crops of fruit when they are grown in the least shady suitable position.

Sorbus "Joseph Rock"
[mountain ash]
○

type of plant: hardy tree [4–8]
flowering time: late spring
flower color: creamy white
height: 25–30ft/7.5–9m

Long after they have ripened—from cream to orange-tinted yellow—the berries of S. "Joseph Rock" are still hanging, uneaten by birds. These fruits, in their generous bunches, contrast strikingly with the foliage, both when the numerous, toothed, 1¼in/3cm-long leaflets are bright green and when they change, in autumn, to orange, red, caramel, and coppery purple. The berries, each nearly ½in/1cm wide, are preceded by little, five-petalled flowers that are arranged in clusters about 4in/10cm across. This slender-headed tree has upright branches. It can be grown in most soils but it is best in fertile, well-drained, moisture-retentive soil. It is prone to the disease of fireblight.
also for: ■ Colorful, autumn foliage ■ Decorative, green foliage

Clerodendrum trichotomum
○

type of plant: slightly tender shrub [7–9]
flowering time: late summer to mid-autumn
flower color: white
height: 8–12ft/2.4–3.6m; up to 18ft/5.4m
as a tree

The large, loose clusters of sweetly fragrant, jasmine-like flowers produced by C. trichotomum are followed by vivid turquoise-blue berries. Each berry is backed by a bright crimson "star," and the contrast is striking. The plant forms either a bushy, rounded clump of upright stems or a wide-canopied, small tree. It tends to sucker. Its bold, heart-shaped leaves, up to 8in/20cm long and deep green, have a nutty, oily scent that most people find unpleasant. The top growth may die back in cold winters. A warm, sheltered site and well-drained, humus-rich soil produce the best specimens. C. bungei is a smaller, suckering shrub with pungently scented, deep pink flowers; it is often invasive.
also for: ■ Fragrant flowers ■ Long, continuous flowering period

Ilex cornuta
[Chinese holly]
○

type of plant: hardy shrub [7–9]
height: 8–12ft/2.4–3.6m
Evergreen

Chinese holly is better adapted to climates with hot summers and mild winters than most other hollies. Its distinctive, almost rectangular leaves, up to 3½in/9cm long, are thick, glossy and dark green. They are armed with a few, very sharp spines that give them their "horned" appearance. The bright red berries, up to ½in/1cm in diameter, last through winter. The plant is self-fertile. It is dense and rounded, and usually wider than it is tall. Among the numerous cultivars of Chinese holly, I. cornuta "Burfordii" fruits very freely and is much used for hedging; it lacks the three-pointed leaf tip of the species.
also for: ■ Decorative, green foliage

Colutea arborescens
[bladder senna]
○

type of plant: hardy shrub [6–9]
flowering time: midsummer to early autumn
flower color: yellow
height: 8–10ft/2.4–3m

This vigorous, loosely and openly branched shrub grows in a very wide range of soils. C. arborescens tolerates atmospheric pollution and coastal conditions, too. Its pea-flowers, each about ¾in/2cm long, are arranged in clusters. Toward the end of the long flowering season, inflated, pale green seed pods begin to develop. These are large—up to 3in/8cm long—and almost translucent. The foliage is composed of little, light green, oval leaflets. This fast-growing plant tends to become rather twiggy and leggy with age.
also for: ■ Shallow soils over chalk ■ Heavy, clay soils ■ Dry soils in hot, sunny sites ■ Windswept, seaside gardens ■ Atmospheric pollution ■ Long, continuous flowering period

Callicarpa bodinieri var. giraldii
"Profusion"
○

type of plant: hardy shrub [6–9]
height: 6ft/1.8m

From early in autumn until early winter, thick conglomerations of violet-mauve, ⅛in/0.3cm-diameter berries encircle the erect shoots of this shrub. In autumn, too, the otherwise unremarkable, diamond-shaped leaves turn from dark green to shades of purple. The young leaves are bronzed purple. C. bodinieri var. giraldii "Profusion" should be given fertile, well-drained soil. A sunny position not only encourages good fruiting but also shows the glistening, very unusually colored berries to advantage. When several specimens are grown in a group, especially heavy crops of fruit are produced.
also for: ■ Purple, bronze, or red leaves (young leaves only) ■ Colorful, autumn foliage

Papaver somniferum
e.g. "Paeony Flowered"
[opium poppy]
○

type of plant: hardy annual [7–9]
flowering time: early to midsummer
flower color: mixed—red, white, pink, purple, lilac
height: 30–36in/75–90cm

The spectacularly frilled, fully double flowers of these easily grown poppies are followed by smooth, blue-green, "pepper-pot" seed pods, each usually about 1¼in/3cm long. Both the flowers and seed pods are popular for cutting, and the seed pods can also be dried. (For a "black"-flowered variety of opium poppy, see p.329.) The lobed and jagged leaves of these erect plants are about 5in/12cm long and of a striking, pale blue-green. Deep soil that is fertile and well drained is ideal but most soils with reasonable drainage give satisfactory results.
also for: ■ Gray, blue-gray, or silver leaves ■ Flowers suitable for cutting (and drying)

Scabiosa stellata
e.g. "Drumstick"
[pincushion flower, scabious]
○

type of plant: hardy/slightly tender annual [7–9]
flowering time: mid- to late summer
flower color: pale lilac-blue
height: 12–18in/30–45cm

Light soils are most suitable for *S. stellata* "Drumstick," but it is easily grown in any soil with reasonable drainage. Its flat flowers, with their pincushion-like centers, are carried, on strong, more or less upright stems, well above the pale grayish, toothed and pointed leaves. The flowers are followed by crisp-textured, spherical seedheads, 1¼in/3cm across, that dry on the plant. When ripe, the seedheads are beige with delicate brown markings. They are long-lasting and excellent for dried flower arrangements. The flowers are attractive to bees and butterflies.
also for: ■ Flowers suitable for cutting (mainly drying)

Geum montanum
[avens]
○

type of plant: hardy perennial [6–9]
flowering time: late spring to early summer
flower color: rich yellow
height: 6in/15cm
Semi-evergreen

The chief glory of *G. montanum* is its mass of 1½in/4cm-wide, cup-shaped flowers, but the fluffy, red-tinged seedheads that follow are charming and decorative. Rich green, wrinkled leaves are divided into rounded leaflets, and the foliage forms dense, slowly creeping tufts of glossy greenery. Any good soil with reasonable drainage is suitable, but cool, humus-rich soils give particularly good results. Other small plants with attractive, fluffy seedheads include *Dryas octopetala* and *Pulsatilla vulgaris* (see pp.157 and 17 respectively).

ADDITIONAL PLANTS, featured elsewhere in this book, that have ornamental fruit

† = ornamental seedheads/seed pods

○ **sun**

minimum height 10ft/3m or more
†*Catalpa bignonioides*, see p.95
†*Catalpa bignonioides* "Aurea," see p.210
†*Catalpa x erubescens* "Purpurea," see p.198
Cedrus atlantica Glauca Group, see p.183
†*Cercis siliquastrum*, see p.13
Corylus maxima "Purpurea," see p.199
Hippophae rhamnoides, see p.89
†*Koelreuteria paniculata*, see p.219
†*Kolkwitzia amabilis* "Pink Cloud," see p.14
Malus "Royalty," see p.198
Passiflora caerulea, see p.127
Picea omorika, see p.94
Platanus x hispanica, see p.94
Rhus typhina, see p.236
†*Sophora japonica*, see p.94

minimum height between 3ft/90cm and 10ft/3m
†*Achillea filipendulina* "Gold Plate," see p.270
Astelia chathamica, see p.184

†*Atriplex hortensis* var. *rubra*, see p.200
†*Baptisia australis*, see p.25
Berberis thunbergii f. *atropurpurea*, see p.200
Berberis thunbergii f. *atropurpurea* "Rose Glow," see p.163
†*Cortaderia selloana* "Pumila," see p.269
Cotinus coggygria "Royal Purple," see p.199
Luma apiculata "Glanleam Gold," see p.162
Myrtus communis, see p.298
Myrtus communis subsp. *tarentina*, see p.146
Nandina domestica, see p.236
Rhamnus alaternus "Argenteovariegata," see p.162
Ricinus communis "Carmencita," see p.199
Rosa "Fritz Nobis," see p.299
†*Sophora microphylla*, see p.220
†*Stipa gigantea*, see p.52
Taxus baccata "Standishii," see p.145

minimum height 3ft/90cm or less
Acaena saccaticupula "Blue Haze," see p.191
†*Agapanthus* Ardernei Hybrid, see p.273

†*Agapanthus* "Bressingham Blue," see p.273
†*Allium hollandicum*, see p.271
†*Asphodeline lutea*, see p.53
Berberis thunbergii f. *atropurpurea* "Atropurpurea Nana," see p.202
†*Clematis recta* "Purpurea," see p.200
†*Erica vagans* "Mrs D.F. Maxwell," see p.26
†*Eucomis bicolor*, see p.323
†*Libertia formosa*, see p.221
†*Libertia peregrinans*, see p.213
†*Lotus hirsutus*, see p.187
†*Morina longifolia*, see p.275
†*Nigella damascena* "Miss Jekyll," see p.282
†*Papaver orientale* Goliath Group "Beauty of Livermere," see p.271
†*Papaver orientale* "Patty's Plum," see p.274
†*Papaver somniferum* "Black Paeony," see p.329
†*Phlomis russeliana*, see p.105
†*Pulsatilla vulgaris*, see p.17
Rosa gallica "Versicolor," see p.272
†*Sedum* "Herbstfreude," see p.106
†*Sedum telephium* "Matrona," see p.280
†*Stipa calamagrostis*, see p.54

Ilex opaca
[American holly]
○◖◗

type of plant: hardy tree [5–9]
height: 30ft/9m
Evergreen

American holly's matt, rather light green leaves, up to 3½in/9cm long, are usually spiny. Female plants that have been pollinated bear clusters of bright red, long-lasting berries from about mid-autumn onward. Each berry is approximately ¼in/0.5cm in diameter. This slow-growing plant forms a dense pyramid of growth with branches to the ground. Older specimens are slightly more open. American holly grows in a wide range of soils, although very alkaline conditions should be avoided. Its preference is for moist, well-drained, humus-rich soil. It benefits from a sheltered position in colder regions. The varieties of this species include yellow-berried, variegated, and especially free-fruiting forms.
also for: ■ Atmospheric pollution ■ Hedging plants

Malus e.g. "John Downie"
[crabapple]
○【◐】

type of plant: hardy tree [4–8]
flowering time: late spring
flower color: white
height: 25ft/7.5m

Of all the popular varieties of ornamental crabapple, M. "John Downie" produces the best-flavoured fruit for making crabapple jelly. It usually crops heavily, bearing quantities of its egg-shaped, red-flushed orange fruits, each of which is about 1¼in/3cm long. Clusters of cup-shaped, spring flowers emerge from pink buds. The leaves of this crabapple are broad, pointed, and rich green. Although this is basically an upright tree, it spreads with age and, on mature specimens, the branches arch slightly. Other readily available crabapples with red fruit include M. x scheideckeri "Red Jade," which is a small weeping tree, and "Royalty" (see p.198). All these plants are easily grown in most soils, including moderately heavy clays, but they are not satisfactory either on wet or on very dry soils.
also for: ■ Heavy, clay soils (see above)
■ Atmospheric pollution

Abies koreana
[Korean fir]
○【◐】

type of plant: hardy conifer [6–8]
height: 20–30ft/6–9m
Evergreen

Even very young specimens of this conifer produce numerous cones among their stout "sausages" of dark green, silver-backed foliage. The violet-blue cones, up to 3in/8cm long, are erect and cylindrical. They become colorful from late spring onward. Korean fir slowly forms a bushy pyramid of growth. It needs deep, moist soil that is, ideally, well-drained and neutral to slightly acid. A. koreana "Silberlocke" has twisted leaves that give it a silvery appearance.
also for: ■ Heavy, clay soils

Celastrus scandens
[American bittersweet,
climbing bittersweet, staff vine]
○【◐】

type of plant: hardy climber [4–8]
height: 20–30ft/6–9m

This is an attractive plant in autumn when a profusion of pea-sized, yellowish orange capsules split open to reveal scarlet seeds. Male and female plants need to be grown together for fruiting to occur. American bittersweet is a very vigorous, twining climber and is suitable for growing into a large tree. It fruits best in a sunny position and well-drained, fertile soil. The broad, often rounded leaves are mid-green and up to 4in/10cm long.
also for: ■ Climbing plants

Malus x zumi "Golden Hornet"
(syn. M. "Golden Hornet")
[crabapple]
○【◐】

type of plant: hardy tree [4–8]
flowering time: late spring
flower color: white
height: 20–25ft/6–7.5m

The branches of this crabapple usually stay thickly clustered with bright yellow, 1in/2.5cm-diameter fruits until well into winter. These fruits are preceded by cupped flowers that open, from pink buds, among bright green, toothed, oval leaves. When young, this tree is erect but, as it matures, it assumes a rounded, more open, and slightly weeping habit of growth. Most soils, including moderately heavy clays, are suitable, although this plant does not thrive either in wet or in very dry conditions. Due to their especially good flavor, the fruits of M. "John Downie" (see above) are preferable to those of M. x zumi "Golden Hornet" for making crabapple jelly.
also for: ■ Heavy, clay soils (see above)
■ Atmospheric pollution

Crataegus x _lavallei_ "Carrierei"
[hawthorn]
○[◐]
type of plant: hardy tree [6–9]
flowering time: early summer
flower color: white
height: 20ft/6m
Semi-evergreen in milder regions only

This tough and usually trouble-free hawthorn has a dense, spreading head of almost thornless, twisting branches. Its leaves are broad, pointed ovals of glossy dark green. They turn dark bronzy red late in autumn (although autumn color is not reliable and the display is sometimes very short-lived). Numerous clusters of red-stamened, unpleasantly scented flowers are followed by round, ¾in/2cm-diameter berries. These fruits ripen, in late autumn, to orange-red and often persist until spring. Almost any soil is suitable for these trees, as long as it is not too dry.
also for: ■ Shallow soils over chalk ■ Heavy, clay soils ■ Atmospheric pollution ■ Colorful, autumn foliage (see above)

Clematis
e.g. "Bill MacKenzie"
(syn. _C. orientalis_ "Bill MacKenzie," _C. tangutica_ "Bill MacKenzie")
○[◐]
type of plant: hardy climber [6–9]
flowering time: midsummer to mid-autumn
flower color: yellow + dark red
height: 15–20ft/4.5–6m

Numerous, thick-"petaled," 3in/8cm-wide flowers are produced by this very vigorous clematis. Slender stems also carry finely divided leaves, the twining stalks of which clasp any suitable support. This clematis looks good climbing into a tree. Its bell-shaped flowers open, in succession, over a long period and, as they fade, they turn into silky, silvery seedheads. _C. tangutica_ is another yellow-flowered clematis, possibly a parent of _C._ "Bill MacKenzie," and it too has decorative seedheads. Both plants are happy in most well-drained soils of reasonable fertility. Their top growth should, ideally, be in sun and their roots should be shaded.
also for: ■ Climbing plants ■ Long, continuous flowering period

Sorbus cashmiriana
[mountain ash]
○[◐]
type of plant: hardy tree/shrub [5–8]
flowering time: late spring
flower color: pinkish white
height: 15–20ft/4.5–6m

The ½in/1cm-wide berries of this sorbus ripen from late summer onward and are long lasting. They look like large pearls. Leaves, up to 8in/20cm long, are composed of numerous, rich green, pointed leaflets that turn russet or deep yellow in autumn. The foliage falls quite early and the bunches of berries look particularly striking hanging from dark, leafless branches. The fruits are preceded by clusters of little, cup-shaped flowers, each cluster about 5in/12cm across. This slow-growing mountain ash has an open, rounded, spreading head of growth; it is more upright when young. It is sometimes grown as a shrub. Well-drained but moisture-retentive soil produces the best specimens. Since the berries are soft, they are liable to bruising. A windy site is, therefore, inadvisable.
also for: ■ Decorative, green foliage ■ Colorful, autumn foliage

Sorbus vilmorinii
[mountain ash]
○[◐]
type of plant: hardy shrub/tree [6–7]
flowering time: late spring to early summer
flower color: white
height: 15ft/4.5m

Whether it forms a shrub or small tree, _S. vilmorinii_ is at first upright and then much more wide-spreading, with a dense, rounded head of growth. The numerous dark green leaflets, about ¾in/2cm long, create a light and delicate effect. In autumn, the foliage turns a bronzy mixture of purple and red. Berries, each about ¼in/0.5cm across, are preceded by 4in/10cm-wide heads of little, five-petalled flowers. At first the ripe fruit is rosy red; it then changes to pink and is finally almost white. It usually lasts until late autumn. This fairly slow-growing mountain ash thrives in mild, moist regions. It needs deep, moisture-retentive soil.
also for: ■ Decorative, green foliage ■ Colorful, autumn foliage

Arbutus unedo
[strawberry tree, manzanita]
○●●

type of plant: slightly tender shrub/tree [7–9]
flowering time: mid- to late autumn
flower color: white or pink-tinged white
height: 10–15ft/3–4.5m; up to 30ft/9m in very mild regions
Evergreen

This handsome plant produces a profusion of little, pendent, urn-shaped flowers at roughly the same time as globular, warty fruits are ripening from the previous year's flowers. Each scarlet, strawberry-like fruit is about ¾in/2cm across. In mild areas with high rainfall, *A. unedo* forms a bushy, broad-headed tree; elsewhere it is a rounded shrub. When young, it grows slowly. Its leathery, rich green leaves, up to 4in/10cm long, are neat and glossy. Older stems have peeling bark that may be a good red-brown but is often grayish. The plant is tolerant of salt-laden winds; inland, it often needs a sheltered site. Well-drained soils of all sorts are suitable, but extreme alkalinity should be avoided. *A. unedo* f. *rubra* has dark pink flowers.
also for: ■ Windswept, seaside gardens ■ Atmospheric pollution ■ Ornamental bark or twigs (see above)

Euonymus europaeus
"Red Cascade"
[spindle tree]
○●●

type of plant: hardy shrub/tree [5–8]
height: 8–10ft/2.4–3m

Even a single specimen of this notably free-fruiting form of spindle tree produces numerous, hanging clusters of red fruits. However, if it is grown alongside two or three other specimens, so that the maximum amount of cross-pollination can take place, then fruiting will be particularly good. The four-lobed fruits, each about ¾in/2cm across, contain orange seeds. They ripen in early autumn, when the slender, undulating, 3in/8cm-long leaves turn from deep green to dark purplish crimson or red. All soils with reasonable drainage are suitable. This plant is particularly at home on chalk. Its branches and greenish stems form a slightly untidy cone of growth.
also for: ■ Shallow soils over chalk ■ Colorful, autumn foliage

Berberis darwinii
[barberry]
○●●

type of plant: hardy/slightly tender shrub [7–9]
flowering time: mid-spring
flower color: orange
height: 6–10ft/1.8–3m
Evergreen

Cup-shaped flowers and spherical berries are produced in large quantities on this rather erect, dome-shaped shrub. The flowers are double, about ¼in/0.5cm across and arranged in hanging clusters. They are followed, from the end of summer, by black berries that have an attractive, blue bloom. Both the flowers and the fruit are shown to advantage against the gleaming, rich green, holly-like leaves, each of which is about 1in/2.5cm long. This dense and prickly plant is good as an informal hedge or screen (plants for hedging should be about 30in/75cm apart). Any soil that does not become very dry is suitable. Shallow, chalky soils should be avoided. *B. darwinii* copes well with atmospheric pollution and salty winds.
also for: ■ Heavy, clay soils ■ Windswept, seaside gardens ■ Atmospheric pollution ■ Hedging plants

Viburnum opulus
e.g. "Compactum"
[guelder rose, European cranberry bush]
○●●

type of plant: hardy shrub [4–8]
flowering time: early summer
flower color: white
height: 4–6ft/1.2–1.8m

This small and very free-fruiting variety of guelder rose grows densely and is usually as wide as it is tall. It is an adaptable and undemanding plant that thrives in permanently damp soil, in ordinary, moisture-retentive soil and even in shallow, chalky soil. Its pretty, 3in/8cm-wide lacecap flowers are followed, in autumn, by numerous bunches of glowing, translucent berries. These ½in/1cm-wide berries are very attractive to birds and therefore not very long-lasting (unlike the yellow berries of *V. opulus* "Xanthocarpum," see p.68). As the fruits ripen fully, the lobed leaves often turn rosy red.
also for: ■ Shallow soils over chalk ■ Heavy, clay soils ■ Damp and wet soils ■ Colorful, autumn foliage

ADDITIONAL PLANTS, featured elsewhere in this book, that have ornamental fruit

† = ornamental seedheads/seed pods

○●● sun (or partial shade)

minimum height 10ft/3m or more
Castanea sativa, see p.222
Celastrus orbiculatus, see p.129
Crataegus monogyna, see p.142
Crataegus phaenopyrum, see p.98
Ilex x altaclerensis "Golden King," see p.168
Ilex aquifolium "Argentea Marginata," see p.168
Malus floribunda, see p.99

Rosa "Wedding Day," see p.129
Sorbus aria "Lutescens," see p.19
Sorbus hupehensis, see p.193
Viburnum opulus "Xanthocarpum," see p.68
Vitis vinifera "Purpurea," see p.203

minimum height between 3ft/90cm and 10ft/3m
†Calamagrostis x acutiflora "Karl Foerster," see p.284
Cornus alba "Kesselringii," see p.331
Cornus alba "Sibirica," see p.265

Euonymus alatus, see p.238
Rosa "Fru Dagmar Hastrup," see p.92
Rosa glauca, see p.193
Rosa "Penelope," see p.304

minimum height 3ft/90cm or less
Acaena microphylla, see p.111
Aronia melanocarpa, see p.239
†Dryas octopetala, see p.157
Euonymus alatus "Compactus," see p.239
†Paeonia mlokosewitschii, see p.194
Sorbus reducta, see p.224

Ilex aquifolium
e.g. "Bacciflava"
(syn. *I.a.* "Fructu Luteo")
[English holly]
○◑

type of plant: hardy shrub/tree [7–9]
height: 40–50ft/12–15m
Evergreen

Since they are not very attractive to birds, these lemon-yellow berries are long-lasting. They ripen in autumn and usually persist through winter. *I. aquifolium* "Bacciflava" is female and produces berries only if pollinated by a male holly. It is erect and forms a deep green pyramid of glossy, sharply spined foliage. Individual leaves are up to 3in/8cm long. It can be used for hedging (plants should be about 24in/60cm apart) and, when clipped into simple shapes, it looks decorative in a large container, although pruning does reduce fruit production. This is quite a slow-growing plant. It is tough and can be planted near the sea and in areas of atmospheric pollution. Any soil is suitable, unless it is very dry or wet.
also for: ■ Windswept, seaside gardens ■ Atmospheric pollution ■ Hedging plants ■ Growing in containers (clipped specimens)

Cotoneaster frigidus "Cornubia"
(syn. *C.* "Cornubia")
○◑

type of plant: hardy shrub/tree [6–8]
flowering time: early summer
flower color: white
height: 15–20ft/4.5–6m
Semi-evergreen/Deciduous

Long, arching branches on *C. frigidus* "Cornubia" spread over a considerable area, and the plant is usually as wide as it is tall. In time, it forms a small tree. It bears numerous, usually very persistent, red berries, some nearly ½in/1cm long, in generous bunches. A flattering accompaniment to the berries are the dark green, veined and pointed leaves. The fruits are preceded by flattish clusters of saucer-shaped flowers. This impressive plant grows and fruits well in any reasonably fertile soil, as long as it is not waterlogged or very dry.
also for: ■ Atmospheric pollution

Ilex aquifolium
e.g. "J.C. van Tol"
[common holly, English holly]
○◑

type of plant: hardy shrub/tree [7–9]
height: 15–20ft/4.5–6m
Evergreen

Most hollies bear male and female flowers on separate plants and therefore both sexes must be grown if regular crops of berries are wanted. *I. aquifolium* "J.C. van Tol" is a self-fertile variety that bears abundant, bright red berries each year, even if no other holly is nearby (although it crops particularly well if grown alongside a male plant). Its glossy, dark green leaves, up to 3in/8cm long, are pointed and oval and have almost no prickles. The plant fairly slowly makes a broad, rather open pyramid of dark-stemmed growth with subsidiary branches that are horizontal or drooping. *I.a.* "J.C. van Tol" can be used for hedging and topiary, but denser and more upright hollies are usually preferable. Almost any soil is suitable, provided it is not either wet or very dry. The plant tolerates salty winds and atmospheric pollution. *I.a.* "Pyramidalis" is also self-fertile. *I.a.* "Golden van Tol" has yellow-edged leaves; it fruits sparsely.
also for: ■ Windswept, seaside gardens ■ Atmospheric pollution ■ Hedging plants (see above)

Decaisnea fargesii
○◑

type of plant: hardy shrub [7–9]
flowering time: early summer
flower color: yellowish green
height: 10–15ft/3–4.5m

The bean-like, violet-blue pods of this shrub are fat and fleshy, and can be up to 6in/15cm long. They ripen in mid-autumn. In cooler areas, they tend to appear in sizable quantities only after hot summers. Fruit production is improved if several plants are grown together in a group and if a sheltered site is provided. This striking plant has bold, divided leaves, each 24–36in/60–90cm long, with numerous, often broad, pointed leaflets that turn yellow in autumn. Its bell-shaped flowers hang in drooping, tassel-like spikes, 12in/30cm or so long. *D. fargesii*'s thick stems are upright, especially when the plant is young. Moisture-retentive soil with good drainage is most suitable for this slow-growing, rather sparsely branched shrub.
also for: ■ Decorative, green foliage ■ Colorful, autumn foliage ■ Green flowers

Pyracantha
e.g. "Orange Glow"
[firethorn]
○◑

type of plant: hardy shrub [6–9]
flowering time: late spring to early summer
flower color: white
height: 10–15ft/3–4.5m
Evergreen

This vigorous, bushy, rather upright plant usually produces heavy crops of bright orange or reddish orange berries, even in a shaded position. It is often trained against a wall—all aspects are suitable. It can also be used to make a dense and very thorny hedge (young plants should be about 24in/60cm apart). Its fairy slender, blunt-nosed leaves, up to 1½in/4cm long, are glossy and dark green. The fruits, about ¼in/0.5cm across, are preceded by flattish heads of rather unpleasantly scented, little flowers. Most soils, including heavy clays, are suitable for *P.* "Orange Glow," although it does not do well in very alkaline conditions. For a yellow-berried pyracantha, see p.45.
also for: ■ Heavy, clay soils ■ Atmospheric pollution ■ Hedging plants

Cotoneaster salicifolius
e.g. "Exburyensis"
○◑

type of plant: hardy shrub [6–8]
flowering time: early summer
flower color: white
height: 8–10ft/2.4–3m
Semi-evergreen/Evergreen

This vigorous, arching cotoneaster produces heads of numerous, saucer-shaped flowers that develop into pendent clusters of yellow, sometimes apricot-tinged berries. These globular, ¼in/0.5cm-diameter fruits are long-lasting. They are complemented by the bright rich green of the plant's long, pointed, deeply veined leaves. C. salicifolius "Rothschildianus" is similar but its fruits are a richer yellow. Both these shrubs are easily grown in most soils and only object to waterlogged or very dry conditions.
also for: ■ Atmospheric pollution

Rosa "Geranium"
(syn. R. moyesii "Geranium")
[rose]
○◑

type of plant: hardy shrub [5–9]
flowering time: early summer
flower color: scarlet
height: 7–8ft/2.1–2.4m

The flagon-shaped, orange-red hips of this moyesii hybrid rose ripen in late summer. Each fruit is about 1½in/4cm long. The hips follow numerous, simple, single flowers, each 2in/5cm across. R. "Geranium" is a vigorous plant and its arching branches usually spread at least 5ft/1.5m wide. The foliage is composed of small, slightly grayish green, rounded leaflets. R. moyesii itself is a larger plant (10–12ft/3–3.6m high) with red hips. Both the species and R. "Geranium" thrive in fertile, loamy soil but they are sufficiently vigorous to tolerate less favorable conditions.

Cotoneaster franchetii
○◑

type of plant: hardy shrub [7–9]
flowering time: early to midsummer
flower color: pink-tinged white
height: 6–9ft/1.8–2.7m
Evergreen/Semi-evergreen

In early autumn, the pale orange-red berries of this graceful cotoneaster begin to ripen. They are egg-shaped, about ¼in/0.5cm long and arranged in small clusters on a mass of slender, arching growths. The younger shoots are pale grayish; mature growths are darker. Neat, pointed, lustrous leaves, 1¼in/3cm long, are grayish sage-green. In colder climates, the more mature foliage may turn yellow, orange, and dark red in autumn before falling. The little, clustered, cup-shaped flowers are less decorative than the berries. C. franchetii grows in a wide range of soils but prefers good drainage; it is not tolerant of waterlogging. It can be used for informal hedging or screening. Although very exposed positions are unsuitable, this shrub grows well in a seaside garden.
also for: ■ Windswept, seaside gardens
■ Atmospheric pollution ■ Hedging plants

Dipsacus fullonum
(syn. D. sylvestris)
[teasel]
○◑

type of plant: hardy biennial [4–9]
flowering time: mid- to late summer
flower color: rosy purple
height: 4–6ft/1.2–1.8m

In an informal setting, a big group of teasels can look most attractive. The plant is visited by bees when it is in thistle-like flower. When its seeds are ripe, it attracts various birds. Its bristly, tan-colored seedheads, each up to 3in/8cm long, are held on strong, prickly, upright stems. They persist into winter, and they dry well for indoor arrangements. The dark green, basal leaves are 12–15in/30–38cm long and pointed, with pale midribs. They have usually withered by flowering time. All moisture-retentive soils are suitable for this plant. It usually self-sows.
also for: ■ Heavy, clay soils ■ Flowers suitable for cutting (mainly drying)

Viburnum davidii
○◑

type of plant: hardy/slightly tender shrub [8–9]
flowering time: early summer
flower color: white
height: 3–4ft/0.9–1.2m
Evergreen

Even if there is room for only a solitary specimen of V. davidii, it is still very much worth growing for its handsome foliage. For berries to develop, however, at least two plants—one male, one female—must be present. The red-stalked, clustered fruits, each just over ¼in/0.5cm long, are turquoise-blue. The heads of tiny, tubular flowers are less remarkable. This neat, slow-growing plant makes a ground-covering dome of deeply veined, pointed leaves, 4–6in/10–15cm long. It needs fertile, moisture-retentive soil for its dark green, gleaming foliage to look its best.
also for: ■ Heavy, clay soils ■ Ground cover
■ Decorative, green foliage

Physalis alkekengi var. *franchetii*
[Chinese lantern, Japanese lantern]
○◐

type of plant: hardy perennial [5–8]
height: 24–30in/60–75cm

These red-orange, papery "lanterns," up to 2in/5cm across, keep their color well when dried for indoor arrangements. They are ripe from late summer or early autumn, but they look attractive even when they are still green. The "lanterns" enclose bright red, berry-like fruits. Summer flowers are tiny, white and inconspicuous among the fairly large, mid-green, pointed leaves. *P. alkekengi* var. *franchetii* forms patches of rather weak, upright stems. It is often invasive, its roots spreading widely in almost any soil.

also for: ■ Flowers suitable for cutting (mainly drying)

ADDITIONAL PLANTS, featured elsewhere in this book, that have ornamental fruit

† = ornamental seedheads/seed pods

○◐ **sun or partial shade**

A few of the plants listed in this unillustrated section will grow in full shade but not all of them fruit freely in conditions of very limited light. See the ◐● "partial or full shade" list (right) for plants that will fruit satisfactorily in full shade.

minimum height 10ft/3m or more

minimum height between 3ft/90cm and 10ft/3m

minimum height 3ft/90cm or less

Skimmia japonica subsp. *reevesiana* (syn. *S. reevesiana*)
◐[○] *

type of plant: hardy shrub [7–9]
flowering time: mid- to late spring
flower color: creamy
height: 24in/60cm
Evergreen

The hard, deep red berries of this spreading, rather open shrub ripen in autumn and they usually last through winter and into spring (the illustration shows the plant in mid-spring, with the sweetly fragrant, starry flowers in bud). Each oval fruit is just under ½in/1cm long. Leaves are rich green, leathery, and rather slender. *S. japonica* subsp. *reevesiana* is self-fertile. Other berrying skimmias, such as *S.j.* "Nymans" and *S.j.* "Veitchii," which fruit even more freely, are female and need to be planted near a male plant so that fertilization can take place. (Male plants have showy, fragrant flowers; female flowers are smaller and scentless.) Cool, moist, well-drained soil is most suitable for these plants. They are not good in alkaline soil, and *S.j.* subsp. *reevesiana* requires acid soil.

also for: ■ Acid soils ■ Atmospheric pollution ■ Growing in containers ■ Fragrant flowers

---

ADDITIONAL PLANTS, featured elsewhere in this book, that have ornamental fruit

† = ornamental seedheads/seed pods

◐[○] **partial shade (or sun)**

A few of the plants listed in this unillustrated section will grow in full shade but not all of them fruit freely in conditions of very limited light. See the ●● "partial or full shade" list (right) for plants that will fruit satisfactorily in full shade.

minimum height 10ft/3m or more

minimum height between 3ft/90cm and 10ft/3m

minimum height 3ft/90cm or less

Lunaria rediviva
[perennial honesty]
◗

type of plant: hardy perennial [6–9]
flowering time: late spring to early summer
flower color: pale lilac
height: 30–36in/75–90cm

The elliptical, tapering pods of this perennial honesty are rather more elegant than the rounded, translucent seed pods of biennial honesty. Each pendent pod, up to 3in/8cm long, ripens to an almost transparent, silvery beige. As a bonus, the four-petalled flowers, each about 1in/2.5cm across, are sweetly fragrant. They are carried in loose heads above large, approximately heart-shaped leaves. The plant forms substantial clumps of upright stems and dark green foliage, particularly in the moist, well-drained soils it likes best. It is, however, tolerant of dry shade. It usually self-sows. There is sometimes good, yellow, autumn leaf color.

also for: ■ Dry shade ■ Fragrant flowers ■ Flowers suitable for cutting (mainly drying)

Actaea rubra
[red baneberry, snakeberry]
◗

type of plant: hardy perennial [4–8]
flowering time: mid-spring to early summer
flower color: white
height: 18in/45cm

These luscious-looking, highly poisonous berries begin to ripen from midsummer onward. They last until well into autumn. The fruits, each up to ½in/1cm in diameter, are arranged in dense heads that may be so heavy that the slender stems bend under their weight. Before this, the long-stamened flowers are held, just above the clumps of foliage, in fluffy-looking clusters, each up to 2in/5cm long. The leaves are divided into numerous, toothed and pointed leaflets. *A. pachypoda* (syn. *A. alba*) produces white berries and is about twice the height of *A. rubra*. Both plants thrive in cool, moist, humus-rich soil that is fertile.

also for: ■ Decorative, green foliage

ADDITIONAL PLANTS, featured elsewhere in this book, that have ornamental fruit

† = ornamental seedheads/seed pods

◗ partial shade

minimum height between 3ft/90cm and 10ft:/3m
†*Cardiocrinum giganteum*, see p.313

Iris foetidissima
[stinking iris, stinking gladwyn]
◗●[○]

type of plant: hardy perennial [6–9]
flowering time: early summer
flower color: lilac + yellowish green
height: 18–24in/45–60cm
Evergreen

During autumn, the seed pods of *I. foetidissima* open to reveal rows of red or orange-red berries, each berry ½in/1cm across. These fruits remain decorative right through winter. The early summer flowers are very modestly colored and much less impressive. Handsome, arching, sword-shaped leaves form ground-covering clumps of rich, lustrous green growth in almost any soil, including shallow, chalky soil. *I. foetidissima* tolerates dry and dense shade. Ideally, however, it should be given moisture-retentive soil and at least some shade. *I.f.* var. *citrina* has yellowish flowers, broad leaves and large, orange berries. The variegated form (see p.180) is also attractive. The leaves of all these plants smell of roast beef when cut or bruised.

also for: ■ Shallow soils over chalk ■ Dry shade ■ Dense shade ■ Ground cover ■ Decorative, green foliage

Podophyllum hexandrum
(syn. P. emodi)
◗●

type of plant: hardy perennial [5–8]
flowering time: mainly late spring to early summer
flower color: white or pale pink
height: 12–18in/30–45cm

As well as surprisingly large, bright red fruit, *P. hexandrum* also produces lovely, simple flowers and interesting foliage. The cup-shaped blooms, about 2in/5cm across, "sit" on top of deeply lobed leaves that, at first, are folded close to the long leaf-stalks. When newly expanded, the leaves are heavily mottled with purplish brown but this mottling gradually disappears; the mature leaves are plain, light green. Shiny, plum-like fruits, up to 2in/5cm long, begin to ripen in late summer. Moist, humus-rich soil is most suitable for this plant. *P. peltatum* [zones 4–9] is much more vigorous; its fruits are pale yellow and its leaves are plain green.

also for: ■ Variegated leaves (younger leaves only)

ADDITIONAL PLANTS, featured elsewhere in this book, that have ornamental fruit

† = ornamental seedheads/seed pods

◗● partial or full shade

minimum height between 3ft/90cm and 10ft/3m
Sarcococca confusa, see p.321

minimum height 3ft/90cm or less
Cornus canadensis, see p.125
†*Pachyphragma macrophyllum*, see p.122
Sarcococca hookeriana var. *humilis*, see p.314

PLANTS WITH

Ornamental bark or twigs

including plants with ornamental canes

NOT LONG AGO, growing plants with decorative bark or twigs was considered a rather rarefied pastime, but now many gardeners appreciate plants of this sort. The ornamental qualities of bark and twigs are especially valuable in winter and, although winter flowers are welcome, the following list includes some of the more substantial and reliable components of an interesting winter garden.

A plant described as having ornamental bark generally produces a trunk and main branches with a decorative, outer covering, while the term "twigs" refers to smaller, subsidiary growths and younger shoots. Specimens of trees with interesting bark are often most impressive when they are fairly mature, mainly because of their considerable size but sometimes because their bark becomes strikingly craggy with age (see, for example, *Pinus sylvestris, Juglans nigra,* and *Betula pendula*).

By contrast, it is usually the youngest growths that are most colorful or interestingly shaped on plants grown for their twigs. Varieties of *Cornus alba* and *C. sericea,* for example, are normally cut back very hard at least every other year, in order to encourage new, really well-colored stems. Some willows such as *Salix alba* subsp. *vitellina* "Britzensis" behave in the same way. As well as looking good in the garden, colored or interestingly shaped twigs are attractive in indoor arrangements.

Plants with green twigs may not be quite as dramatic as their more brightly or exotically colored counterparts, but they too are attractive. Many of the plants commonly known as "broom," such as *Cytisus* and *Genista,* have green shoots, which give an evergreen appearance to these deciduous shrubs.

A few plants bear unusually shaped twigs. Corkscrew hazel (*Corylus avellana* "Contorta") produces a mass of wiggly, twisted twigs, and dragon's claw willow (*Salix babylonica* var. *pekinensis* "Tortuosa") puts on a similar performance on a larger scale. Some gardeners would regard *Corokia cotoneaster*'s wire netting tangle of

twigs—from which it gets its common name of "wire-netting bush"—as a mere curiosity. The canes of various bamboos in this book are altogether more elegant, as is, for example, the delicate tracery of zigzagging growths on the Fuji cherry *Prunus incisa* "Kojo-no-mai."

For maximum impact, plants with ornamental bark or twigs must be carefully positioned. The very pale bark of *Betula utilis* var. *jacquemontii* looks spectacular when seen against a mass of dark, evergreen leaves, but is much less impressive against a whitewashed wall. *Prunus serrula* has a richly colored, polished trunk that always looks attractive, but when winter sun shines orange-red through the peeling bark of its older branches, the plant seems almost to be on fire. The varieties of *Cornus* mentioned above also look their best when planted where sun illuminates them in winter.

Particularly where space is limited, it is worth choosing plants that have decorative features in addition to their ornamental bark and twigs. There are, for example, varieties of *C. alba* (such as *C.a.* "Elegantissima" and *C.a.* "Spaethii") that produce variegated foliage as well as red stems, and all the maples (*Acer*) in this list bear attractive green leaves that turn shades of yellow, red, or orange in autumn. The widely grown *C. horizontalis* has intriguingly shaped twigs, good green foliage, and attractive autumn color as well as bright berries.

Specialist trees and shrub nurseries stock some less common plants with ornamental bark and twigs. Gardeners in fairly mild areas may like to grow *Arbutus menziesii*, which, although less readily available than *A. unedo*, has peeling, orange-red bark that is very striking. Other less usual plants have branches or stems with curious thorns: cockspur hawthorn (*Crataegus crus-galli*), for example, is equipped with ferocious, curved thorns, each up to 3in/8cm long, and the numerous, translucent thorns of *Rosa sericea* subsp. *omeiensis* f. *pteracantha* glow rich red when the sun shines through them.

Pinus sylvestris
[Scots pine]
○

type of plant: hardy conifer [3–8]
height: 70–100ft/21–30m
Evergreen

In large gardens and informal settings this variable, adaptable, and very hardy plant looks ruggedly handsome. Its needle-like leaves, 2–3in/5–8cm long, are dark and often a bluish or grayish green, especially in summer. Young plants are fast-growing and conical; mature specimens are dome-headed with long, clear trunks, which are russet-brown and gray, and deeply fissured on their lower parts. The bark on the branches is flaking and orange-tan. Most soils are suitable, although growth is best on well-drained, moist, acid soil. Scots pine makes a good windbreak inland. Corsican pine (*P. nigra* subsp. *laricio*, syn. *P.n.* subsp. *maritima*; zones 5–9) also has attractive, fissured bark; it is lime-tolerant and makes an excellent, maritime windbreak.
also for: ■ Acid soils

Juglans nigra
[black walnut]
○

type of plant: hardy tree [4–9]
height: 75ft/22.5m

On older specimens of this magnificent, round-headed tree, the very dark and deeply ridged bark is often diamond-patterned. The main branches are dark too. Black walnut grows quickly when young, especially on deep, fertile soil, and it is at its best in hot-summer climates. Its bold, resinous leaves can be up to 24in/60cm long, with as many as twenty-three slender, glossy, dark green leaflets. In autumn, the foliage turns bright yellow, although sometimes only briefly. The nuts have a musky taste and their outer husks decay messily once the fruits have fallen.
also for: ■ Decorative, green foliage ■ Colorful, autumn foliage (see above)

Betula utilis var. jacquemontii
(syn. *B. jacquemontii*)
[Himalayan birch]
○

type of plant: hardy tree [6–9]
height: 40–60ft/12–18m

The horizontally banded, peeling bark of *B. utilis* var. *jacquemontii* is pale creamy white and especially dazzling when lit by low, winter sun. The upright branches are pale, too, and they form the basis of a cone-shaped head of airy growth. In autumn, the broad, pointed, 3in/8cm-long leaves turn from dark green to deep yellow. *B.u.* var. *j.* "Jermyns" has pure white, unbanded bark, and its yellowish, spring catkins, at about 6in/15cm long, are conspicuous and decorative. Ideally, these trees should be grown in acid to neutral loam, but most soils with reasonable drainage are suitable. Other popular, white-barked birches include *B. pendula* (see following page), *B. papyrifera* (which has bark that peels in large strips) and *B. ermanii* (which has creamy white and pinkish bark).
also for: ■ Colorful, autumn foliage

Salix babylonica var. pekinensis
"Tortuosa"
(syn. *S. matsudana* "Tortuosa")
[dragon-claw willow]
○

type of plant: hardy tree [5–9]
height: 30–40ft/9–12m

Not only the twigs but also the leaves of this fast-growing tree are contorted, and there is some twisting evident on the oldest branches, too. The foliage, which often remains on the plant until early winter, is bright light green, but it may take on some yellowish tones in autumn. Each slender leaf is about 4in/10cm long. ALthough growth is best on deep, moisture-retentive soil, almost any soil is suitable for *S. babylonica* var. *pekinensis* "Tortuosa" and it can be planted in damp and wet ground. Its roots can be invasive. With age, it becomes less markedly upright. *S.* "Erythroflexuosa" is a smaller, spreading tree with twisted twigs which are orange-yellow when young.
also for: ■ Heavy, clay soils ■ Damp and wet soils

Eucalyptus pauciflora subsp. *niphophila*
(syn. *E. niphophila*)
[cabbage gum, weeping gum]
○

type of plant: hardy tree [6–9]
flowering time: usually late summer
flower color: white or cream
height: 20–30ft/6–9m
Evergreen

The often leaning trunk or trunks of this slender, openly branched, domed tree are mottled in creamy white, gray, and green. Most of the leaves are narrow, curved, and pointed, up to 6in/15cm long and deep gray-green. They are carried on red twigs that later develop a silvery white bloom. Clusters of tufted flowers are carried close to the stems. Most well-drained soils are suitable for this tree, but it appreciates moist, slightly acid soil. Cabbage gum is tolerant of salty winds by the sea but needs shelter from cold winds inland. *E. dalrympleana* [zones 8–9] also has pale bark and gray foliage.
also for: ■ Windswept, seaside gardens ■ Atmospheric pollution ■ Gray, blue-gray, or silver leaves

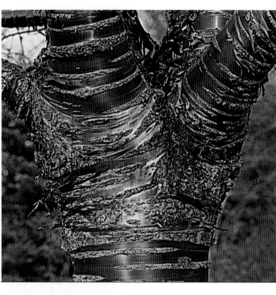

Prunus serrula
[cherry]
○

type of plant: hardy tree [5–9]
flowering time: mid- to late spring
flower color: white
height: 20–25ft/6–7.5m

The remarkable bark of this cherry is richly red-brown and is sleekly polished between the horizontal banding. With age, it peels. Older trees, like the specimen shown here, have larger areas of craggy, horizontal banding. The clustered, open-faced flowers are small—¾in/2cm across—and partly obscured by the emerging foliage of the tree. However, the foliage is decoratively slim and willowy and, together with the wide-spreading branches, it gives the tree a shapely, rounded head. In late summer, there are very small, red fruits, and in some autumns the dark green foliage turns yellow. Most well-drained soils are suitable for this cherry.

Salix alba subsp. *vitellina*
"Britzensis"
(syn. *S.a.* "Chermesina")
[white willow]
○

type of plant: hardy shrub/tree [3–8]
height: 10ft/3m when cut back hard

When pruned hard, either every year or every other year, *S. alba* subsp. *vitellina* "Britzensis" produces a bowl-shaped mass of upright, very bright orange-red winter shoots. Unpruned specimens quickly form erect, wind-resistant trees, up to 80ft/24m high, but their winter shoots are less brightly colored. The narrow, pointed, dark green leaves, up to 4in/10cm long, have pale undersides, and these give the foliage a rather gray appearance overall. Most soils are suitable for this willow, as long as they are reasonably deep, and the plant thrives in damp and wet ground. Even specimens that are regularly pruned hard have very wide-spreading roots, which can damage foundations and drains.
also for: ■ Heavy, clay soils ■ Damp and wet soils ■ Atmospheric pollution

---

ADDITIONAL PLANTS, featured elsewhere in this book, that have ornamental bark or twigs

○ **sun**

minimum height 10ft/3m or more
Araucaria araucana, see p.219
Eucalyptus gunnii, see p.184
Kolkwitzia amabilis "Pink Cloud,"
    see p.14
Larix kaempferi, see p.25

Platanus x *hispanica,* see p.94
Populus alba, see p.183

minimum height between 3ft/90cm and 10ft/3m
Cytisus x *praecox* "Allgold," see p.97
Cytisus x *praecox* "Warminster," see p.53
Perovskia "Blue Spire," see p.14
Physocarpus opulifolius "Diabolo," see p.199

Prunus incisa "Kojo-no-mai," see p.145
Salix fargesii, see p.220
Salix hastata "Wehrhahnii," see p.41
Spartium junceum, see p.52

minimum height 3ft/90cm or less
Genista hispanica, see p.105
Genista lydia, see p.97

Betula pendula
[European white birch]
○ [◑]

type of plant: hardy tree [2–8]
height: 40–60ft/12–18m

European white birch is a rather narrow-headed tree with a delicate tracery of dark, pendulous branchlets and a shimmering. airy mass of triangular, toothed leaves, each about 2in/5cm long. It grows quickly but is fairly short-lived. Younger trees develop trunks and main branches that have peeling, white bark; on older trees, the bark becomes craggy, with black fissures. In autumn, the foliage turns greenish gold. This birch can be grown in a wide range of soils, including poor soils and dry soils, although slightly acid to neutral loam is ideal. It dislikes waterlogged conditions. For a birch with bright white bark, see p.263; in contrast, *B. nigra* has shaggy, dark russet-brown bark.
also for: ■ Atmospheric pollution ■ Colorful, autumn foliage

Phyllostachys aurea
[fishpole bamboo, golden bamboo]
○【●】

type of plant: hardy perennial (bamboo) [6–11]
height: 12–16ft/3.6–4.8m
Evergreen

The knobbly, upright canes of *P. aurea* are green when young; they mature to a beautiful, soft yellow. The plant is clump-forming in cool climates, but in warmer regions it may grow much taller and spread more widely. Its numerous, elegant, pointed leaves, up to 6in/15cm long, are usually yellowish green. *P. aureosulcata* f. *spectabilis* produces canes, which are yellow with green grooves, and their lower parts often zigzag; the foliage is deep green. Both these bamboos appreciate fertile, moisture-retentive soil and shelter from cold winds.
also for: ■ Decorative, green foliage

Cornus sericea "Flaviramea"
(syn. *C. stolonifera* "Flaviramea")
[yellow-stemmed dogwood]
○【●】

type of plant: hardy shrub [2–8]
height: 6–8ft/1.8–2.4m

These vivid green-yellow stems look very striking beside the red or black shoots produced by varieties of *C. alba* (see, for instance, the following plant, and also the index of botanical names). Stem color is best on young growths and on specimens planted in sun. To encourage plenty of new growth this vigorous, suckering shrub needs to be pruned really hard every year or two. In autumn, the oval, pointed leaves, up to 5in/12cm long, turn from light green to buttery yellow. Most moisture-retentive soils are suitable, but this dogwood is particularly at home in damp and wet sites. In ideal conditions, the upright stems form thickets more than 10ft/3m wide.
also for: ■ Heavy, clay soils ■ Damp and wet soils ■ Atmospheric pollution ■ Colorful, autumn foliage

Cornus alba e.g. "Sibirica"
(syn. *C.a.* "Westonbirt")
[redtwig dogwood]
○【●】

type of plant: hardy shrub [3–7]
flowering time: late spring to early summer
flower color: creamy white
height: 5–6ft/1.5–1.8m

Although it is grown principally for the glowing red of its erect and shiny, winter stems, *C. alba* "Sibirica" has other good features, too. It is a tough, adaptable shrub that can be grown in almost any soil; it thrives in damp and wet positions. Its 2in/5cm-wide clusters of bluish white berries are conspicuous—more so than its flower heads—against its deep green, oval, pointed leaves, each about 4in/10cm long. The foliage turns red and orange in autumn. Stem color is brightest on the youngest growths and when plants are grown in sun. Really hard pruning, at least every other year, produces plenty of new stems but at the expense of flowers and berries. For other varieties of *C. alba*, see the index of botanical names. See also the plant in the preceding illustration.
also for: ■ Heavy, clay soils ■ Damp and wet soils ■ Atmospheric pollution ■ Colorful, autumn foliage ■ Ornamental fruit (see above)

Corokia cotoneaster
[wire-netting bush]
○【●】

type of plant: slightly tender shrub [9–10]
flowering time: late spring
flower color: yellow
height: 5ft/1.5m
Evergreen

Very slowly, this intriguing plant creates a dense, rounded mass of dark twigs that, with its twistings and interlacings, produces a general effect of a stiff, contorted tangle. Shoots are rather sparsely clothed in tiny (½in/1cm-long), dark green, rounded leaves. The flowers are tiny, too; they are star-shaped and have a warm, coconut-like scent. After hot summers they may be followed by little, red or yellow berries. Well-drained soil is needed and the plant benefits from being sheltered from cold winds. In mild areas it can be grown in a lightly shaded position. It is drought-tolerant.
also for: ■ Hot, dry soils ■ Growing in containers ■ Fragrant flowers

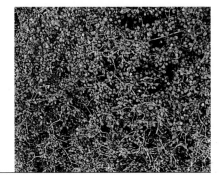

ADDITIONAL PLANTS, featured elsewhere in this book, that have ornamental bark or twigs

○【●】 sun (or partial shade)

minimum height 10ft/3m or more
Betula pendula "Youngii," see p.99
Castanea sativa, see p.222
Phyllostachys nigra, see p.330

Pseudosasa japonica, see p.223
Trachycarpus fortunei, see p.222

minimum height between 3ft/90cm and 10ft/3m
Cornus alba "Elegantissima," see p.68
Cornus alba "Kesselringii," see p.331

Cornus alba "Spaethii," see p.169
Euonymus alatus, see p.238
Physocarpus opulifolius "Dart's Gold," see p.214

minimum height 3ft/90cm or less
Euonymus alatus "Compactus," see p.239

Stewartia (syn. *Stuartia*) *pseudocamellia* Koreana Group
○◐✻

type of plant: hardy tree/shrub [5–8]
flowering time: mid- to late summer
flower color: white
height: 40ft/12m

At first pyramidal and shrubby, *S. pseudocamellia* develops into a broadly columnar tree with an attractive, mottled trunk. In ideal conditions it may eventually reach more than 50ft/15m high. Its light red-brown bark often peels to reveal shades of orange, ocher, and greenish gray beneath. The bark is most brightly colored in spring. In autumn, the foliage turns from deep green to orange-red or to yellow and red (the coloring is often especially good on *S.p.* Korean Group plants, a specimen of which is shown here). The leaves, up to 4in/10cm long, are broad and pointed. When plants are several years old they begin to produce camellia-like, yellow-stamened flowers, 2in/5cm across. Ideal conditions are a site sheltered from cold winds, and deep, moist, humus-rich soil that is acid and well drained.
also for: ■ Acid soils ■ Colorful, autumn foliage

Acer griseum
[paperbark maple]
○◐

type of plant: hardy tree [4–8]
height: 20–30ft/6–9m

Paperbark maple is decorative throughout the year. Its prettily lobed, tripartite leaves, about 3in/8cm long, are briefly chocolate-colored when they emerge, late in spring. The foliage is deep green through summer, until late autumn when it turns red and orange. However, the chief glory of the plant is the glowing orange-cinnamon bark that peels from its branches and trunk in papery strips. Paperbark maple is upright when young; it grows quite slowly into a oval- to round-headed tree. Most soils are suitable, although well-drained, moisture-retentive soil produces the best specimens.
also for: ■ Atmospheric pollution ■ Decorative, green foliage ■ Colorful, autumn foliage

Acer palmatum "Sango-kaku"
(syn. *A.p.* "Senkaki")
[Japanese maple]
○◐

type of plant: hardy tree [6–8]
height: 20ft/6m

The new, winter shoots of this upright tree are a vivid and very striking orange-pink. The illustration shows a specimen in mid-autumn; even though the twigs are now mature and more quietly colored (and also partially obscured by foliage), they are still conspicuous. The elegant, deeply lobed leaves, about 2½in/6cm long, are just as decorative as the plant's bark. When it emerges from pink buds, the foliage is orange-tinged; it matures to light green and then turns yellow or apricot-gold before falling. This Japanese maple likes well-drained soil that retains moisture, and a sheltered site; it dislikes dryness and cold winds.
also for: ■ Decorative, green foliage ■ Colorful, autumn foliage

Acer pensylvanicum
[moosewood, striped maple]
○◐

type of plant: hardy tree [3–7]
flowering time: late spring
flower color: greenish yellow
height: 15–25ft/4.5–7.5m

The bark of *A. pensylvanicum* is deep olive- to jade-green with subtle but conspicuous, longitudinal, white stripes. The newest shoots are pink and white. Additional attractions include little, bell-shaped flowers in dangling strings up to 6in/15cm long, and clear butter-yellow autumn color. The bright green, shallowly lobed leaves are large—up to 8in/20cm long. Mature specimens of this maple are upright with broad heads of growth (the illustration shows a fairly young plant). Most soils are suitable, but this tree does not thrive if conditions are either very alkaline or dry. In hot-summer climates it should be given a partially shaded position. When ideally suited, it may reach 30–40ft/9–12m high. Other similar maples include *A. davidii* and *A. rufinerve*.
also for: ■ Heavy, clay soils ■ Decorative, green foliage ■ Colorful, autumn foliage

Corylus avellana "Contorta"
[corkscrew hazel]

○◑

type of plant: hardy shrub [5–9]
flowering time: late winter
flower color: yellow
height: 8–10ft/2.4–3m

The extraordinary, contorted twigs of this slow-growing shrub are hung with slightly twisted catkins, each about 2in/5cm long. The mid-green, coarse-textured leaves that follow are also coiled and twisted, and 3in/8cm or more long; they turn yellow in autumn. Overall, the curled twigs and upright main branches create a fairly rounded shape. Almost any soil is suitable for C. avellana "Contorta." Other plants with twisted branches include the dragon's claw willow (see p.263).
also for: ■ Shallow soils over chalk ■ Heavy, clay soils ■ Growing in containers ■ Colorful, autumn foliage ■ Winter-flowering plants

Leycesteria formosa
[Himalayan honeysuckle]

○◑

type of plant: hardy/slightly tender shrub [7–9]
flowering time: mainly mid- to late summer
flower color: claret + white
height: 6–8ft/1.8–2.4m

The youngest of this plant's upright, bamboo-like stems are bright, fresh green. From each stem's arching tip dangle tassels of flowers (each tassel is about 4in/10cm long). The tiny flowers are surrounded by conspicuous, wine-colored bracts. These persist while the dark purple berries develop. When ripe, in late autumn, the fruits smell of butterscotch, and birds find them very attractive. L. formosa produces an abundance of tapering, bright to rich green leaves, each up to 7in/18cm long. It grows quickly and self-sows in all reasonably well-drained, fertile soils. In cold regions, the stems die back in winter, but the plant makes new growth from the base in spring.
also for: ■ Ornamental fruit

Rubus thibetanus
(syn. R.t. "Silver Fern")
[ornamental bramble]

○◑

type of plant: hardy shrub [6–9]
flowering time: early to midsummer
flower color: purple
height: 6–8ft/1.8–2.4m

When the leaves of R. thibetanus fall, thickets of pale, thorny stems become fully visible. Particularly if the plant has been given a position where it can be illuminated by the low, winter sun, these stems are very striking. The basic stem coloring is rich brownish purple but this is heavily overlaid with a thick, white bloom. The foliage is decorative, too, with its numerous, hairy, silvery gray leaflets. Saucer-shaped flowers, ½in/1cm across, may be followed by round, black fruits. This suckering plant grow in most soils. R. cockburnianus is more vigorous and spreading; R.c. "Goldenvale" produces yellow leaves.
also for: ■ Gray, blue-gray, or silver leaves

Cotoneaster horizontalis

○◑

type of plant: hardy shrub [5–8]
flowering time: early summer
flower color: pinkish white
height: 2ft/60cm; up to 8ft/2.4m against a wall

The distinctive, "herringbone" twigs produced by this long-lived shrub are not only attractive in themselves, but they also help to set off all the other good features of the plant. The "herringbones" can either be allowed to build up into a ground-covering heap or they can be given a wall or similar support, of any aspect, up which to spread. Neat, rich green, glossy leaves, each about ½in/1cm long, turn a mixture of burnt orange and crimson late in autumn. Little, cup-shaped flowers, which are attractive to bees and wasps, are followed in early autumn by rows of long-lasting, ¼in/0.5cm-wide, red berries. Almost all soils, provided they are not waterlogged, are suitable for this cotoneaster.
also for: ■ Atmospheric pollution ■ Ground cover ■ Climbing plants ■ Decorative, green foliage ■ Colorful, autumn foliage ■ Ornamental fruit

ADDITIONAL PLANTS, featured elsewhere in this book, that have ornamental bark or twigs

○◑ sun or partial shade

minimum height 10ft/3m or more
Carpinus betulus, see p.143
Carpinus betulus "Fastigiata," see p.44
Fagus sylvatica, see p.143
Parrotia persica, see p.241
Taxodium distichum, see p.71

minimum height between 3ft/90cm and 10ft/3m
Cotoneaster atropurpureus "Variegatus," see p.174
Cotoneaster horizontalis, see p.267
Fargesia murielae, see p.226
Kerria japonica "Pleniflora," see p.289

minimum height 3ft/90cm or less
Cotoneaster atropurpureus "Variegatus," see p.174
Stephanandra incisa "Crispa," see p.114

◑◙ partial shade (or sun)

minimum height 3ft/90cm or less
Kerria japonica "Picta," see p.177

DECORATIVE PLANTS WITH
Flowers suitable for cutting

including plants with flowers or seedheads suitable for drying

IT IS NOT ALWAYS EASY to decide whether flowers can be cut to bring indoors or whether they should be left to adorn the garden. Of course, the ideal is to have sufficient space for a separate cutting garden, so that the appearance of beds and borders is not spoiled by being depleted of flowers. However, most gardens these days are too small to have a special area for growing flowers solely for cutting.

One solution to the conundrum is to grow plenty of interesting foliage for cutting (see the various lists in this book that deal with decorative or unusually colored leaves, and see particularly plants marked "✂" in those lists). Many leaves last very well as cut material, and some remain fresh for an exceptionally long time. Attractive foliage can be used either to augment necessarily limited amounts of flowers from the garden or to make bought flowers look interestingly different.

The numerous shrubs, perennials, bulbs, and annuals described below are decorative garden plants that also happen to have flowers that last well when cut. Certain plants are not included in this list, even though they are useful for cutting, because, for one reason or another, they look rather out of place when grown alongside other plants in beds and borders. For example, very large-flowered hybrid gladioli and many early-flowering, spray chrysanthemums have been excluded. Plants of this sort perform better and are more easily cultivated when they are securely staked and grown in rows. A few other plants have been excluded because their small size limits their versatility as cut flowers.

Some gardeners are very wary of cutting woody plants for flower arrangements: certain plants of this sort respond badly to being cut, and some very slow-growing shrubs are impractical sources of cut material. However, many woody plants, especially shrubs, make beautiful cut flowers, at no detriment to the general health of the plants. Indeed, shrubs such as the popular varieties of *Forsythia*, *Philadelphus* and common lilac (*Syringa*

vulgaris), as well as most roses, actually benefit from moderate cutting. For descriptions of a wide range of woody plants and their suitability for cutting, see the still very useful *Shrub Gardening for Flower Arrangement* by Sybil Emberton (Faber and Faber, 1973).

Plants in this list with flowers or seedheads that are suitable for drying are marked "Dr" after the summaries of details. Some so-called everlasting flowers, such as straw flowers (*Xerochrysum bracteatum* "Summer Solstice," for example) and various sea lavenders (*Limonium platyphyllum*), retain their shape and color particularly well. Other plants, such as poppies (*Papaver*) and love-in-a-mist (*Nigella damascena*), produce seedheads that do not bear a very close resemblance to the flowers that preceded them.

In planning dried arrangements for the winter months, it is sometimes easy to forget that many seedheads look just as decorative in the garden as in the house. The larger *Sedum* and *Astilbe*, for example, are two groups of plants with seedheads that make striking winter decoration both outdoors and indoors. The seedheads of some grasses such as *Calamagrostis* x *acutiflora* "Karl Foerster" also last well.

One of the features that makes some flowers especially suitable as cutting material is their lovely scent, and there are numerous fragrant plants in this list. They include favorites such as lilacs, sweet peas (*Lathyrus*), roses, and sweet Williams (*Dianthus barbatus*). "Plants with fragrant flowers," pp.296–314, contains many more suggestions of beautifully scented flowers that last well when cut.

For plants that do not make good cut flowers but which do have ornamental seedheads and seed pods, see "Plants with ornamental fruit," pp.252–61.

Syringa vulgaris
e.g. "Madame Lemoine"
[common lilac, French lilac]
○

type of plant: hardy shrub [4–8]
flowering time: late spring
flower color: white
height: 10–12ft/3–3.6m

Most lilacs with white flowers are popular for cutting, but *S. vulgaris* "Madame Lemoine" is a favorite because of its particularly dense and heavy flower heads. Each 6in/15cm-long head is composed of masses of very sweetly scented, double flowers. This tough, rather broad but upright shrub grows well in most fertile soils and appreciates good drainage. It thrives on shallow soils over chalk and, once established, on chalky clays too. *S.v.* "Maud Notcutt" bears white, single flowers. The leaves of these plants are smooth, broad, pointed ovals of fresh green, up to 4in/10cm long.
also for: ■ Shallow soils over chalk ■ Heavy, clay soils (see above)
■ Atmospheric pollution ■ Fragrant flowers

Lathyrus odoratus
e.g. Galaxy Group
[sweet pea]
○

type of plant: hardy annual climber [7–9]
flowering time: early summer to early autumn
flower color: mixed—pink, salmon, red, blue, white
height: 6–8ft/1.8–2.4m

Where plenty of cut flowers of various colors are wanted, sweet peas such as *L. odoratus* Galaxy Group are ideal. Indeed, cutting the clustered blooms of these vigorous, free-flowering plants encourages them to produce yet more of their 1½in/4cm-wide, long-stemmed flowers. Mixtures of *L.o.* Galaxy Group cultivars always include at least some scented flowers. These tendrilled climbers need a support to cling to and, to flower well, they require rich, well-drained soil. Their mid-green foliage consists of pairs of oval, pointed leaflets.
also for: ■ Climbing plants ■ Fragrant flowers (see above)

Helianthus
e.g. "Lemon Queen"
[sunflower]
○

type of plant: hardy perennial [5–8]
flowering time: late summer to mid-autumn
flower color: pale yellow
height: 5–6ft/1.5–1.8m

The numerous, pale blooms of this perennial sunflower are borne on leafy, branching stems, with the dark green of the veined and pointed, oval leaves complementing the clear color of the flowers. Compared with some of the annual sunflowers, these flowers are softly colored and quite small (3–4in/8–10cm across). This makes them easier to mix with other plants, both in the garden and when cut and used in arrangements indoors. *H.* "Loddon Gold" is a popular, perennial sunflower with double flowers; its densely petalled blooms are golden yellow. Both of these plants are easily grown but they are at their best in full sun and moderately heavy, well-drained soil.

Cortaderia selloana
e.g. "Pumila"
[pampas grass, tussock grass]
○

type of plant: hardy perennial (grass) [6–10]
flowering time: late summer to mid-autumn
flower color: creamy white
height: 5ft/1.5m
Evergreen/Semi-evergreen, mainly Dr

C. selloana "Pumila" produces numerous, dense, thick-stemmed plumes, each about 24in/60cm long, which make impressive additions to flower arrangements—both fresh and dried. In the garden, the seedheads last into winter. *C.s.* "Aureolineata" (syn. "Gold Band") has yellow-edged foliage. Taller pampas grasses include the pale-plumed, 8ft/2.4m-high *C.s.* "Sunningdale Silver." The narrow, sharp-edged leaves of all these plants form dense tussocks of arching growth at least 4ft/1.2m wide. Deep, fertile, well-drained soil is suitable for these grasses, which also grow well in damp—but not wet—soil.
also for: ■ Damp and wet soils ■ Ornamental fruit (seedheads) ■ Long, continuous flowering period

Rosa e.g. "Buff Beauty"
(Hybrid Musk)
[rose]
○

type of plant: hardy shrub [6–9]
flowering time: early summer to early autumn (see description)
flower color: apricot-yellow fading to palest yellow
height: 5ft/1.5m

R. "Buff Beauty" forms a loose mass of dark, large-leaved growth that is as wide as it is tall. New leaves are copper colored. Its fully double, 3½in/9cm-wide flowers have a light, sweet scent. They are at their very best in midsummer; the sprays of later flowers are a good deal less numerous. Other popular roses of approximately this coloring include the climber *R.* "Gloire de Dijon" and the floribunda or cluster-flowered *R.* Amber Queen—both of which have fragrant flowers. For a pink-flowered, hybrid musk rose, see p.304. All these roses thrive in fertile, moisture-retentive soil.
also for: ■ Fragrant flowers

Centaurea macrocephala
[knapweed, hardheads]
○

type of plant: hardy perennial [4–9]
flowering time: mid- to late summer
flower color: rich yellow
height: 4–5ft/1.2–1.5m
Dr

Whether in shiny, brown bud or in thistle-like flower, or when its knobbly seedheads have formed, this sturdy plant is interesting both in the garden and in arrangements indoors. Each flower head is about 2in/5cm across and consists of a mass of thin petals set in a "cup" of shiny bracts. The stout flower stems rise erectly out of clumps of long, mid-green, jagged leaves. *C. macrocephala* needs well-drained, fertile soil that remains moist during summer. Its flowers are attractive to bees and butterflies.

Achillea filipendulina "Gold Plate"
[yarrow]
○

type of plant: hardy perennial [4–8]
flowering time: mid- to late summer
flower color: bright yellow
height: 4ft/1.2m
Evergreen, Dr

The tiny flowers on this strong-stemmed plant are arranged in dense, rather flat heads up to 6in/15cm wide. They are very long-lasting when cut, and they keep almost all their strong, bright color when dried. The flowers rise well clear of the plant's clumps of mid-green, ferny leaves. A. "Moonshine" (see p.186) is a similar but substantially smaller variety with paler yellow flowers. For an example of one of the newer yarrows, see p.274. All these plants require well-drained soil. A. filipendulina "Gold Plate" thrives in both moisture-retentive and dry soils.
also for: ■ Dry soils in hot, sunny sites ■ Ornamental fruit (seedheads)

Aster novae-angliae "Harrington's Pink"
[New England aster]
○

type of plant: hardy perennial [4–9]
flowering time: early to mid-autumn
flower color: light pink
height: 4ft/1.2m

The stems of this clump-forming plant are very strong and upright, but the large, loose sprays of yellow-centered flowers may be heavy enough to make staking advisable, especially if the plant is being grown for cut flowers. Among asters of this type, the 1½in/4cm-wide flowers of A. novae-angliae "Harrington's Pink" last much better than most when cut. A.n.-a. "Andenken an Alma Pötschke" is a widely available cultivar with vivid cerise flowers. Other varieties have violet, red-purple, mauve, or white blooms. Their stems are clothed with long, slender, pointed leaves. All these plants grow well in fertile, moisture-retentive soil. They tend to be much less prone to mildew than A. novi-belgii varieties.
also for: ■ Heavy, clay soils

Rosa e.g. Graham Thomas = "Ausmas" (Shrub)
[rose]
○

type of plant: hardy shrub [5–9]
flowering time: early summer to mid-autumn (see description)
flower color: rich yellow
height: 4ft/1.2m

One of the most popular of the recently introduced, so-called English roses, R. Graham Thomas is a vigorous, healthy plant. Each of its warmly colored blooms is about 4½in/11cm across, fully double and well scented, with a slight fruitiness to the fragrance. The flowers are freely produced, in a series of separate flushes, over a long period. They are excellent for cutting. Even though basically quite erect, the plant has upper growths that are long and arching and these enable it to be trained as a short climber. The leaves are shiny and rich, bright green. Although it can cope with poor soils, R. Graham Thomas is best in well-cultivated, fertile soil that retains moisture easily. For a pink rose of this type, see p.300.
also for: ■ Climbing plants (see above) ■ Fragrant flowers

Dahlia e.g. "David Howard" (Decorative, Miniature)
○

type of plant: half-hardy tuber [9–10]
flowering time: late summer to mid-autumn
flower color: orange-yellow
height: 3½ft/1.05m

Dahlias are a very useful source of flamboyant and exotic color late in the gardening year. They also make long-lasting cut flowers. Really large-flowered dahlias look out of place in mixed plantings, but there are numerous varieties, including the two shown here and below, that have quite small blooms that fit in well with other plants. The flowers of D. "David Howard" are about 3in/8cm wide and of an interesting, caramelized color, and the toothed, pointed leaflets are a very dark bronze-green (for another dark-leaved dahlia, see p.201). The dense, very dark flower heads of D. "Moor Park" are only 2in/5cm or so in diameter. Specialist nurseries stock dozens of varieties of dahlia in a wide range of colors, including reds, pinks, yellows, and white. In general, the plants are upright and bushy. They all require rich, well-drained, moisture-retentive soil to perform well. In all but the warmest regions, tuberous dahlias need storing in frost-free conditions during winter.
also for: ■ Purple, bronze, or red leaves (D. "David Howard" only)

Dahlia e.g. "Moor Place" (Pompon)
○

type of plant: half-hardy tuber [9–10]
flowering time: late summer to mid-autumn
flower color: deep maroon-purple
height: 3½ft/1.05m

See preceding plant.

Eremurus stenophyllus subsp. *stenophyllus* (syn. *E. bungei*) [foxtail lily, desert candle]
○
type of plant: hardy perennial [5–9]
flowering time: early to midsummer
flower color: sharp yellow fading to rich orange-gold
height: 3–5ft/0.9–1.5m

Most foxtail lilies are magnificent, tall plants carrying their dense spikes of flowers on long, clear, wiry stems. They can make spectacular additions to large-scale arrangements indoors. *E. stenophyllus* subsp. *stenophyllus* produces tapering flower spikes, 12in/30cm or so long, above low tufts of thin, grayish green leaves. (The foliage often dies back by midsummer.) The plant needs moisture in late spring and early summer and then, ideally, a period of dryness for the remaining summer months. Flowering is best in climates with cold winters, and ideal growing conditions are rich, sandy loam and full sun. *E.* x *isabellinus* "Cleopatra" (tangerine flowers) and *E. robustus* (pale pink; up to 10ft/3m high) are other popular foxtail lilies.

Echinacea purpurea (syn. *Rudbeckia purpurea*) [coneflower]
○
type of plant: hardy perennial [4–9]
flowering time: midsummer to early autumn
flower color: purplish pink to magenta + orange-brown
height: 3–4ft/0.9–1.2m

This rather variable plant produces numerous, strong, upright stems above a dark mass of large, pointed leaves. Each stem carries a single, daisy-like flower, 4–5in/10–12cm across, with a prominent, central cone and slightly reflexed petals. The flowers of *E. purpurea* "Magnus" can be as much as 7in/18cm wide. For a white-flowered variety, see p.277. Coneflowers are attractive to bees, and they are long-lasting when cut. Ideally, these plants should have fertile, humus-rich soil that is moisture-retentive and well drained.
also for: ■ Long, continuous flowering period

Papaver orientale e.g. Goliath Group "Beauty of Livermere" [oriental poppy]
○
type of plant: hardy perennial [4–9]
flowering time: early summer
flower color: blood-red + black
height: 3–4ft/0.9–1.2m
Dr

The sheer extravagance of oriental poppies makes them desirable as cut flowers, even if they do need careful preparation. As well as the luxuriantly colored variety illustrated here, which has blooms as much as 8in/20cm wide, there are richly colored varieties such as *P. orientale* "Allegro" and *P.o.* "Türkenlouis"; for softer colored blooms, see p.274. Flowers are followed by large, smooth, "pepper-pot" seed pods. All these robust, bristly perennials form rather upright clumps of growth with the flowers held well above mid-green foliage. They need well-drained soil that is deep and fairly fertile. Their long, divided leaves tend to die back from midsummer.
also for: ■ Ornamental fruit (seed pods)

Allium hollandicum (syn. *A. aflatunense*)
○
type of plant: hardy bulb [7–9]
flowering time: late spring to early summer
flower color: purplish pink
height: 36in/90cm
Dr

Whether fresh or dried, the 4in/10cm-wide, hemispherical flower heads of *A. hollandicum* look striking on their long, clear stems. Each hemisphere is made up of numerous, starry flowers on individual stalks. The strap-shaped leaves soon die back. *A.h.* "Purple Sensation" is a popular variety with rich violet flowers. These plants are easily grown in any well-drained soil but they flower especially well in fertile conditions. Their flowers are attractive to bees. Other *Allium* with dense flower heads of this type include the much taller *A. giganteum*. *A.* "Globemaster" has spherical flower heads 6–8in/15–20cm in diameter.
also for: ■ Ornamental fruit (seedheads)

Aster novi-belgii e.g. "Marie Ballard" [New York aster]
○
type of plant: hardy perennial [4–8]
flowering time: early to mid-autumn
flower color: light blue
height: 36in/90cm

A. novi-belgii "Marie Ballard" is only one of many possible examples of blue-flowered New York asters. Its fully double flowers, each 2in/5cm or more across, last very well when cut. They are carried on branching stems that are clothed with numerous, slender, little, mid-green leaves. The stems form clumps of growth. Other popular asters of this type include the large-flowered, deep pink *A. n.-b.* "Fellowship." Whites, violets, and reds are also available. Mildew affects many of the varieties (the reds seem especially prone to this disease), but it is less likely to be a problem if plants are grown in fertile soil that remains moist during summer and early autumn.
also for: ■ Heavy, clay soils

Cosmos bipinnatus e.g. Sensation Series
○
type of plant: half-hardy/slightly tender annual [8–11]
flowering time: midsummer to early autumn
flower color: mixed—crimson, pink, white
height: 36in/90cm

Although the sizzling flower colors and very finely cut, ferny foliage of cosmos look good in the garden, it is perhaps as cut flowers that these bushy annuals are most popular. They thrive in light, poor soils and sheltered positions. The long-stemmed, saucer-shaped blooms of *C. bipinnatus* Sensation Series cultivars are each 3–4in/8–10cm wide. Other popular mixtures of annual cosmos include *C.b.* "Sea Shells," which has flowers with intriguing, tubular petals, and the shorter-growing, bushier *C.b.* Sonata Series plants. (*C.b.* Sonata Series "Sonata White" is also offered as a separate color). The foliage of these various cosmos is usually a bright green.
also for: ■ Decorative, green foliage

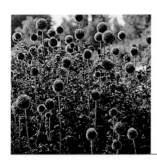

Echinops ritro
[globe thistle]
○

type of plant: hardy perennial [3–9]
flowering time: mid- to late summer
flower color: blue
height: 36in/90cm
Dr

The rich, steely blue of these flower heads is particularly striking combined with the near-white of their stout stems. Even before they color fully, the dense, 1½in/4cm, spherical heads are eye-catching. Once they open completely, the flowers are attractive to bees and butterflies. The fresh flowers last well in water and the seedheads can be dried. Jagged, thistle-like leaves, dark green above and grayish beneath, form a clump of growth. Any well-drained soil is suitable and this vigorous plant is often at its best in rather infertile conditions. *E. ritro* "Veitch's Blue" has flowers of a deeper blue, while *E. sphaerocephalus* "Arctic Glow" produces white flower heads on dark stems.

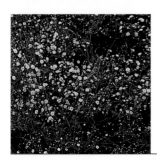

Gypsophila paniculata
e.g. "Bristol Fairy"
[baby's breath]
○

type of plant: hardy perennial [4–9]
flowering time: mid- to late summer
flower color: white
height: 36in/90cm
Dr

These "clouds" of ½in/1cm-wide, double flowers provide the classic accompaniment to sweet peas, but they look attractive with many other blooms, too. They can also be dried. Most of the slim, dark leaves of *G. paniculata* "Bristol Fairy" are obscured by its mass of wiry, much-branched flower stems. Even in the light, well-drained soils and sunny sites it likes best, this is a fairly short-lived plant. It has a preference for alkaline conditions but its deep roots are not content in shallow, chalky soils. For an example of an annual gypsophila, see p.281.
also for: ■ Dry soils in hot, sunny sites

Iris e.g. "Jane Phillips"
(Tall Bearded)
○

type of plant: hardy perennial [4–9]
flowering time: early summer
flower color: soft pale blue
height: 36in/90cm

Tall bearded irises are available in colors ranging from white, through pinks (see p.274), blues, oranges, yellows, purples, bronzes, and browns, to near-blacks (see p.329) and bicolors. They make attractive cut flowers as well as decorative garden plants. These irises are tough and easily pleased but, to produce large numbers of blooms for cutting, they need a really sunny position and freely draining, preferably neutral soil. *I.* "Jane Phillips" has sweetly scented flowers, 5in/12cm-wide. Several flowers are produced on each of its stems, and they are carried well clear of the grayish green, sword-shaped leaves. *I.* "Blue Rhythm" bears blue, lemon-scented flowers.
also for: ■ Fragrant flowers

Lilium e.g. "Star Gazer"
[lily]
○ ✱

type of plant: hardy bulb [6–9]
flowering time: mid- to late summer
flower color: rich carmine + white
height: 36in/90cm

The opulent fragrance of this Oriental hybrid lily fills the air whether the flowers are cut and brought indoors or the plant is grown outdoors. Even though *L.* "Star Gazer" has strong stems, it often needs staking because its flowers can be up to 6in/15cm wide and there may be as many as eight, upward-facing blooms to a stem. Its leaves are glossy, deep green and pointed. The plant needs acid, preferably humus-rich soil. Good drainage is also important. The ideal planting position is one where the flowers are in sun and the roots are shaded. Lilies are available in a wide range of colors—and scents—and many are long-lasting as cut flowers.
also for: ■ Acid soils ■ Fragrant flowers

Rosa gallica "Versicolor"
(syn. *R. mundi*, *R. mundi* "Versicolor")
[rosa mundi rose]
○

type of plant: hardy shrub [4–9]
flowering time: early to midsummer
flower color: crimson + palest pink + white
height: 36in/90cm

This ancient rose produces large quantities of its charming, semi-double flowers, each about 3½in/9cm wide. Orange hips follow the slightly scented flowers. The plant has a bushy, suckering habit of growth, with plenty of veined and pointed, dark green leaves on its bristly stems. It makes a good hedge (young plants should be 30–36in/75–90cm apart). *R. gallica* "Versicolor" is easily grown and most soils are suitable but, ideally, it should be given a rich, medium loam. Other decoratively striped roses include *R.* "Ferdinand Pichard," which has fragrant, crimson-and-white flowers and is about 5ft/1.5m tall.
also for: ■ Hedging plants ■ Ornamental fruit

Xerochrysum bracteatum
(syn. *Bracteantha bracteata*, *Helichrysum bracteatum*)
e.g. "Summer Solstice"
[straw flower] ○

type of plant: half-hardy annual [9–11]
flowering time: midsummer to early autumn
flower color: mixed—red, orange, yellow, white, pink
height: 36in/90cm
height: 90cm/36in   mainly Dr

Even when fresh, the petal-like bracts of these flowers feel dry and, when dried, the brightness of their colors is such that they look fresh. These erect-stemmed plants are easy to grow in all well-drained soils; they appreciate alkaline conditions. If they are to be used in dried arrangements, the flowers should be picked before the central yellow disks are visible. Seed catalogs usually list smaller varieties—of 12–15in/30–38cm high—and varieties with pastel-colored flowers, as well as long-stemmed plants like those shown here. The rich green leaves of these plants are slender and pointed.
also for: ■ Shallow soils over chalk

Rosa e.g. Blue Moon = "Tannacht" (Hybrid Tea or Large-flowered)
[rose]
○

type of plant: hardy shrub [6–9]
flowering time: early summer to mid-autumn
flower color: lilac-pink
height: 30–42in/75–105cm

R. Blue Moon and roses of similar coloring are not really blue. They are, however, an unusual color for roses. The 4in/10cm-wide, double blooms of R. Blue Moon are freely produced and freshly and sweetly fragrant. They make good, long-stemmed cut flowers (but they are susceptible to damage in wet summers). The plant is vigorous and has erect stems which are rather sparsely clothed in broad, dark green leaves. For plenty of large, well-formed flowers, this rose needs fertile, moisture-retentive soil with good drainage. R. Rhapsody in Blue bears fragrant, blue-purple flowers; two fragrant, bluish ramblers are R. "Bleu Magenta" and R. "Veilchenblau."
also for: ■ Fragrant flowers ■ Long, continuous flowering period

Agapanthus e.g. Ardernei Hybrid
[African lily]
○

type of plant: hardy/slightly tender perennial [7–10]
flowering time: mid- to late summer
flower color: white
height: 30–36in/75–90cm
Dr

Like the blue-flowered hybrid illustrated in the following entry, this lovely, white variety is excellent for cutting. Its trumpet-shaped flowers are arranged in hemispherical heads, each 6–7in/15–18cm across. Smooth, strong stems rise from clumps of arching, rich green, strap-shaped leaves. The flowers are followed by attractive, papery seed pods. Given rich, moisture-retentive soil and a position in full sun, A. Ardernei Hybrid plants are reliably free-flowering. Other good, white-flowered African lilies include A. campanulatus var. albidus, which grows to about 24in/60cm high.
also for: ■ Ornamental fruit (seed pods)

Agapanthus e.g. "Bressingham Blue"
[African lily]
○

type of plant: hardy/slightly tender perennial [7–10]
flowering time: mid- to late summer
flower color: rich violet-blue
height: 30–36in/75–90cm
Dr

Among the numerous varieties of African lily, A. "Bressingham Blue" is one of the hardiest and most free-flowering. Its long, thick stems support heads of nodding, tubular flowers which last well when cut. Each head is 4–5in/10–12cm across. The papery seed pods can be dried. The foliage forms clumps of upright to arching, strap-shaped, bright green leaves. Other blue varieties include A. "Lilliput" (12–18in/30–45cm high) and the virtually hardy, variable A. Headbourne hybrids; a white-flowered hybrid is shown above. All these plants need plenty of sun and rich, well-drained soil that remains moist during summer. They are exceptionally tolerant of atmospheric pollution.
also for: ■ Ornamental fruit (seed pods)

Alstroemeria ligtu hybrids
[Peruvian lily]
○

type of plant: slightly tender perennial [7–11]
flowering time: early to midsummer
flower color: mixed—pale pink, deep pink, apricot, yellow, cream
height: 30–36in/75–90cm

Both individually and en masse these beautifully marked and prettily colored flowers are most attractive. They are very long-lasting when cut. Each shapely, open trumpet is about 2in/5cm long, and the flowers are carried in large heads on strong, upright stems. Toward the end of summer, the slender, slightly twisted, mid-green leaves start withering and the plants begin to die back. Fertile, moisture-retentive soil with good drainage and a sheltered position are the most suitable conditions for A. ligtu hybrids. Once established, they resent disturbance.

Consolida ajacis (syn. C. ambigua, Delphinium consolida) e.g. Hyacinth Series
[larkspur]
○

type of plant: hardy annual [7–9]
flowering time: early to late summer
flower color: mixed—blue, violet, pink, white
height: 30–36in/75–90cm
Dr

The taller varieties of larkspur are useful, long-lasting cut flowers. They can also be dried. Plants in C. ajacis Hyacinth Series produce conspicuously erect flower spikes, up to 18in/45cm tall, which are densely packed with double blooms. The cut flowers respond especially well to being given a long soak in deep water immediately after they have been picked. The bright green leaves are deeply cut and almost feathery looking. These classic cottage garden plants are easy to grow in a sunny, sheltered site and in most soils with good drainage but, for plenty of good-quality flowers, conditions need to be fertile.

Gladiolus murielae (syn. G. "Murieliae," Acidanthera bicolor var. murieliae, A. murieliae)
○

type of plant: half-hardy corm [9–11]
flowering time: late summer to early autumn
flower color: white + purplish red
height: 30–36in/75–90cm

Especially if they have been picked in bud, the very sweetly scented flowers of G. murielae last well in water. Each bloom has spreading petals and a very long, thin tube. Typically, the flowers are 2–3in/5–8cm wide. The rather bright green leaves are narrow and arranged in fans. Only in the very mildest climates can the corms be left in the ground in winter; in most areas it is necessary to store them in a frost-free place. Full sun, a sheltered site and good drainage encourage this plant to flower freely. G. tristis is a slightly hardier [zones 8–11] gladiolus with creamy white flowers that are spicily fragrant in the evening, at night and during dull weather.
also for: ■ Fragrant flowers

Iris e.g. "Party Dress" (Tall Bearded)
○

type of plant: hardy perennial [4–9]
flowering time: early summer
flower color: pink + tangerine
height: 30–36in/75–90cm

Part of the attraction of tall bearded irises—both for cutting and for growing in the garden—is the considerable variation in the color of their flowers. The shape of their flowers varies, too, and *I.* "Party Dress," for example, has full, frilled blooms. The sword-shaped leaves of these irises are arranged in fan-like sheaves; they are usually grayish green. All these plants need full sun and really well-drained, preferably neutral soil to succeed. Specialist nurseries offer hundreds of varieties of tall bearded irises in white and in shades of yellow, orange, bronze, brown, and purple. For a fragrant, blue-flowered bearded iris, see p.272. A variety with nearly black flowers is illustrated on p.329.

Papaver orientale e.g. "Patty's Plum" [oriental poppy]
○

type of plant: hardy perennial [4–9]
flowering time: early summer
flower color: dusky plum-mauve
height: 30–36in/75–90cm
Dr

Although oriental poppies need some preparation to insure that they last as cut flowers, their large (up to 6in/15cm-wide), flamboyant blooms, in a good range of interesting colors, make them attractive to flower arrangers. *P. orientale* "Patty's Plum" has blooms of an unusual, smoky color; most oriental poppies are either red (for an example of which, see p.271), white (e.g. *P.o.* "Perry's White"), or pink (e.g. *P.o.* "Mrs Perry"). Large, "pepper-pot" seed pods are also attractive, both fresh and dried. The clumps of long, divided, mid-green leaves usually begin to die back in midsummer. To grow well, these poppies need deep, reasonably fertile soil with good drainage.
also for: ■ Ornamental fruit (seed pods)

Achillea "Lachsschönheit" (syn. A. "Salmon Beauty") [yarrow]
○

type of plant: hardy perennial [4–8]
flowering time: midsummer to early autumn
flower color: light salmon-pink fading to cream
height: 30in/75cm

Galaxy Hybrids, of which this softly colored variety is an example, are available in a wide range of attractive colors—from bright red (A. "Fanal"), through pretty pinks like A. "Lachsschönheit," to soft creams and yellows (A. "Hoffnung," syn. "Great Expectations"). They all make good cut flowers, and the blooms are attractive to bees and butterflies. They grow and flower best in well-drained but moisture-retentive soil. A. "Lachsschönheit" produces its numerous, flattish, 5in/12cm-wide heads of flowers above slightly untidy clumps of much divided, fairly dark green leaves. Other popular, pale-flowered *Achillea* include A. *millefolium* "Lilac Beauty"; the Summer Pastels Group is a mixture of mainly pale colors.

Chrysanthemum e.g. "Mary Stoker" (Early-flowering Outdoor Spray: Rubellum)
○

type of plant: hardy perennial [5–9]
flowering time: early to mid-autumn
flower color: pale apricot + yellow
height: 30in/75cm

Plants derived from *C. rubellum* provide cut flowers that are just as useful and long-lasting as those of the early-flowering, florists' chrysanthemums. Moreover, their bushy habit and free-flowering nature make them much better choices for mixing with other plants in a bed or border. The slender-rayed flowers produced by C. "Mary Stoker" are each about 2in/5cm across. They are carried on branched stems above clumps of soft green, lobed leaves. Other Rubellum Group chrysanthemums include the fragrant, clear pink C. "Clara Curtis" and bronze-red C. "Duchess of Edinburgh." They all do well in fertile soil with good drainage.

Eryngium alpinum [sea holly]
○

type of plant: hardy perennial [5–8]
flowering time: early to late summer (see description)
flower color: mauve-blue
height: 30in/75cm
Dr

Even before their color is fully developed, these flower heads are strikingly shaped and the plant is, in effect, long-flowering. As each ruffled, mock-prickly head matures, the ruff and the central cone become suffused with a steely mauve-blue color. The flower heads, which are 3in/8cm or more wide, last well both in the garden and in indoor arrangements. They dry successfully, too. Erect and branching, blue stems carry jagged, mid-green leaves. Although *E. alpinum* tolerates some dryness, it is at its best in deep, well-drained soil that does not become parched. *E. x oliverianum* is a related hybrid with flowers that are surrounded by less intricate, blue ruffs.
also for: ■ Long, continuous flowering period (see above)

x Solidaster luteus "Lemore" (syn. Solidago "Lemore")
○

type of plant: hardy perennial [5–9]
flowering time: midsummer to early autumn
flower color: primrose-yellow
height: 30in/75cm

Most well-drained soils are suitable for this upright perennial with its rather flat, branched heads of numerous, tiny (½in/1cm) daisies. x S. luteus "Lemore" flowers particularly well if lifted and divided frequently—every two to three years ideally. The sturdy stems, which are clothed in slender, mid-green leaves, create clumps of growth. The flowers last extremely well when cut.

Alstroemeria psittacina
(syn. A. pulchella)
[Peruvian lily]
○

type of plant: slightly tender perennial [8–10]
flowering time: late summer to early autumn
flower color: maroon-crimson + green
height: 24–36in/60–90cm

In contrast to the pastel colors of the popular *A. ligtu* hybrids (see p.273), there are the richly colored flowers of *A. psittacina*. Each of its fluted funnels is about 2in/5cm long and the loose flower heads are carried on stiff, upright stems. The slender leaves are bright green. In cold districts, this plant needs a deep winter mulch to protect its tuberous roots. In warm regions with fairly high rainfall it can become invasive. It needs soil that is rich, moisture-retentive and well drained. In cooler climates, it should be given a sheltered site. The flowers are long-lasting when cut.

Morina longifolia
[whorlflower]
○

type of plant: hardy perennial [5–8]
flowering time: mid- to late summer
flower color: white changing to crimson
height: 24–36in/60–90cm
Evergreen, mainly Dr

Some gardeners find the spicily fragrant, thistle-like leaves of whorlflower more attractive than its smallish flowers but, when the latter have faded, the upright stems are set—at decreasing intervals—with whorls of soft green "cups." These look interesting both in the garden and in dried arrangements indoors. The leaves, which are glossy dark green and up to 10in/25cm long, form dense rosettes of growth. Deep, very well-drained soil and a sheltered site produces the best specimens of this stylish but often rather short-lived perennial.
also for: ■ Decorative, green foliage ■ Aromatic foliage ■ Ornamental fruit (seedheads)

Rosa e.g. "The Fairy"
(Polyantha)
[rose]
○

type of plant: hardy shrub [5–9]
flowering time: midsummer to mid-autumn
(see description)
flower color: soft pink
height: 24–36in/60–90cm

As well as providing sprays of pretty, double flowers for cutting, this rose is useful for ground cover. The flowers, each about 1½in/4cm across, start opening relatively late in summer and continue, very nearly continuously, until well into autumn. *R.* "The Fairy" forms a hummock of growth, spreading 3–4ft/0.9–1.2m wide, with numerous, shiny, rich green leaves on prickly, basically upright branches. Apart from a susceptibility to black spot, this is a healthy rose and easily grown in a wide range of soils.
also for: ■ Ground cover ■ Growing in containers

Achillea ptarmica
The Pearl Group
[sneezewort]
○

type of plant: hardy perennial [4–9]
flowering time: midsummer to early autumn
flower color: white
height: 24–30in/60–75cm
Dr

These bright, bobbly flowers appear in loose, branched clusters, each around 4in/10cm across, at the top of stiff stems. They last well when cut for an indoor arrangement, and they can also be dried. The plant sometimes spreads into sizable patches, especially in rich soils, and it may be invasive. Although it enjoys moist, even quite damp—but not wet—conditions, it does well in ordinary, moisture-retentive soil, too. Seed-raised specimens of *A. ptarmica* The Pearl Group plants are variable: some are more double and of a cleaner white than others. They all have leaves that are dark, slender and undivided.
also for: ■ Damp and wet soils

Antirrhinum majus
e.g. "Madame Butterfly"
[snapdragon]
○

type of plant: grown as half-hardy annual [8–10]
flowering time: midsummer to mid-autumn
flower color: mixed—white, yellow, orange, pink, red
height: 24–30in/60–75cm

Although snapdragons have a decided preference for dry and stony soil, when grown for cutting they are best given light soil that is also fertile and not too dry. *A. majus* "Madame Butterfly" is a double-flowered, tall variety with sturdy, upright, branching stems, and slim, glossy, deep green leaves at the base of the plant. Many of the intermediate varieties are 18–24in/45–60cm high, and they too make good cut flowers: *A. majus* Sonnet Series plants are particularly floriferous and wind-tolerant. Dwarf varieties (for an example, see p.57) are useful for bedding in dry soils.

Centaurea cyanus
e.g. "Blue Diadem"
[bachelor's buttons, cornflower]
○

type of plant: hardy annual [7–9]
flowering time: midsummer to early autumn
flower color: rich blue
height: 24–30in/60–75cm
Dr

C. cyanus "Blue Diadem" is a particularly large-flowered and deeply colored variety of annual cornflower. The loose sprays of blooms are good for cutting, and they also dry well, too. Each of the flowers, with its generous ruff of outer florets, is about 3in/8cm across. This erect plant has narrow, grayish leaves. Annual cornflowers are often offered as mixtures, and these normally include plants with pink, mauve, white, and rose-colored blooms as well as blue-flowered plants. Smaller varieties, such as the mixed *C.c.* Florence Series that are about 15in/38cm tall, are available, too. All these plants are easily grown in reasonably fertile, well-drained soil. The species itself looks very attractive naturalized in grass, and its flowers are attractive to bees and butterflies.

Gladiolus communis subsp. byzantinus (syn. G. byzantinus)
○

type of plant: hardy/slightly tender corm [6–10]
flowering time: late spring to early summer
flower color: magenta
height: 24–30in/60–75cm

This daintily shaped but potently colored species of gladiolus is hardier and much easier to grow than the large-flowered, florists' hybrids. Indeed, in a warm place and light soil it sometimes increases rapidly and it can become mildly invasive; it is less vigorous in heavier soil (though it does not do well in ill-drained conditions). The plant can be naturalized in grass. Its slender, purplish buds open to reveal funnel-shaped flowers, which last well when cut. There are normally 15–20 flowers, each 2in/5cm wide, on each strong stem. Narrow, pointed, mid-green leaves are arranged in upright fans.
also for: ■ Dry soils in hot, sunny sites

Helianthus annuus
e.g. "Music Box"
[sunflower]
○

type of plant: hardy annual [7–10]
flowering time: midsummer to mid-autumn
flower color: mixed—cream, yellow, red, bicolors + black
height: 24–30in/60–75cm

As well as the varieties with huge, yellow blooms on very tall stems, there are also shorter-growing annual sunflowers with smaller flowers in less usual colors. These smaller plants are often more versatile as cut flowers. *H. annuus* "Music Box" produces numerous, daisy-like flowers on branching stems above large, dark green, heart-shaped leaves. Each flower is 4–5in/10–12cm wide. Other single-color, annual sunflowers include *H.a.* "Italian White" (4in/10cm-wide cream-colored flowers with black centers) and *H.a.* "Velvet Queen" (deep red, brown-centered flowers, about 7in/18cm wide). *H.a.* "Italian White" lasts particularly well when cut. All these plants are easy to grow in most well-drained, reasonably moisture-retentive soils.

Liatris spicata (syn. L. callilepis)
[blazing star, gayfeather]
○

type of plant: hardy perennial [4–9]
flowering time: late summer to early autumn
flower color: bright mauve-pink
height: 24–30in/60–75cm

These fluffy flowers and long, narrow, rather bright green leaves are especially eye-catching on stiff, very upright stems. The flower spikes, each 12in/30cm or so long, last very well when cut. Unusually, the individual flowers open from the top of each spike downward, rather than from the bottom up. They are attractive to bees. *L. spicata* is a robust plant that grows both in fertile, well-drained soil and in damp, marshy conditions. There are a number of varieties of this plant, including white-flowered *L.s.* "Floristan Weiss" and *L.s.* "Kobold" (syn. Goblin), which is only 15–18/38–45cm in high and has mauve-pink flowers.
also for: ■ Damp and wet soils

Briza media
[common quaking grass]
○

type of plant: hardy perennial (grass) [5–9]
flowering time: late spring to midsummer
flower color: green tinged with purple-brown, ripening to soft yellow
height: 24in/60cm
mainly Dr

This sparsely leaved, tufted grass has heart-shaped spikelets that quiver in the slightest breeze. They dangle in open sprays from erect stems and look pretty both in dried and in fresh arrangements. Each little spikelet is just over ¼in/0.5cm long. The leaves are mid-green and thin. Almost all soils with reasonable drainage are suitable. For an annual species of quaking grass, see p.281. It, too, is excellent for drying.

Callistephus chinensis
e.g. Duchesse Series
[China aster]
○

type of plant: half-hardy annual [9–10]
flowering time: late summer to mid-autumn
flower color: mixed—white, yellow, mauve, red, blue, pink
height: 24in/60cm

The dense, chrysanthemum-like flowers on this bushy, upright plant are very long-lasting when cut. Each flower is about 3in/8cm wide. Other varieties have flowers with, for instance, very slim petals, quilled petals, or feathery petals; there are also single-flowered and shorter-growing varieties. The stems of all these plants are clothed in dark green, pointed, oval leaves. All varieties need a sheltered site and well-drained, fertile soil. The soil-borne disease wilt can be a problem with China aster varieties, although *C. chinensis* Duchesse Series plants are fairly resistant. In some seed catalogues, China asters are indexed under "aster."

Catananche caerulea
[Cupid's dart]
○

type of plant: hardy perennial [4–9]
flowering time: early to late summer
flower color: variable—blue to lilac-blue + dark purple
height: 24in/60cm
Dr

Even when it is given the light, well-drained, rather dry soil it likes best, this is not a very long-lived plant. However, its dark-centered flowers, each 1–2in/2.5–5cm across, are excellent for cutting and drying. The flowers sit in "cups" composed of pale, papery bracts that have a silky, silvery sheen. Thin, wiry stems rise well clear of the low, rather sparse clumps of slender, gray-green leaves. There are attractive, white-flowered varieties of *C. caerulea*.
also for: ■ Gray, blue-gray, or silver leaves ■ Long, continuous flowering period

Echinacea purpurea
(syn. *Rudbeckia purpurea*)
e.g. "White Swan"
[coneflower]
○

type of plant: hardy perennial [4–9]
flowering time: midsummer to early autumn
flower color: greenish white + orange-brown
height: 24in/60cm

White-flowered forms of *Echinacea*, including *E. purpurea* "White Swan," are cool-colored alternatives to the rich purplish pinks of the species (see p.271) and some of its varieties. These strong-stemmed, upright plants, with their rich green, pointed leaves, bloom over a long period and make excellent cut flowers. The prominent, central cone in each flower becomes gingery as the flower matures. Each flower is 4–5in/10–12cm across. Fertile, humus-rich soil is most suitable for these plants.
also for: ■ Long, continuous flowering period

Erigeron e.g. "Dunkelste Aller"
(syn. *E.* Darkest of All)
[fleabane]
○

type of plant: hardy perennial [5–8]
flowering time: early to late summer
flower color: violet-blue + yellow
height: 24in/60cm

The fleabanes shown here and in the following entry flower very freely over many weeks. They are easy to grow, provided they are given fertile, well-drained soil that does not dry out in the warmer months of the year. These plants form neat clumps of growth with slender, pointed leaves of a slightly grayish green. The daisy-like flowers are 1½–2in/4–5cm across: those of *E.* "Dunkelste Aller" are semi-double, while *E.* "Quakeress" has single flowers that are attractive to butterflies. Other popular hybrids include *E.* "Schneewittchen" (syn. Snow White) and *E.* "Rosa Juwel" (syn. Pink Jewel). The flowers of all these varieties last well when cut and placed in water.
also for: ■ Long, continuous flowering period

Erigeron e.g. "Quakeress"
[fleabane]
○

type of plant: hardy perennial [5–8]
flowering time: early to late summer
flower color: pale lilac-pink + yellow
height: 24in/60cm

See preceding plant.

Gaillardia e.g. "Burgunder"
[blanket flower]
○

type of plant: hardy perennial [4–9]
flowering time: early to mid-autumn
flower color: dark red + yellow
height: 24in/60cm

For months on end the long, straight stems of this plant are topped with richly colored daisies, each 3–4in/8–10cm across. These flowers are excellent for cutting. Since *G.* "Burgunder" is a seed-raised variety, it varies a little and some of its flowers are yellow-tipped, while others are plain red. The plant is bushy with long, slender, mid-green leaves. It is short-lived, especially in damp climates, and needs good drainage. The plant thrives in light, rather gritty soil and an open, sunny place. *G.* "Kobold" (syn. Goblin) is a popular dwarf variety of blanket flower, growing only 10in/25cm tall; it has yellow-edged, red flowers.
also for: ■ Dry soils in hot, sunny sites ■ Long, continuous flowering period

Pennisetum alopecuroides (syn. *P. compressum*) e.g. "Hameln"
[fountain grass]   ○

type of plant: hardy/slightly tender perennial (grass) [7–10]
flowering time: late summer to mid-autumn
flower color: greenish white ripening to purplish brown
height: 24in/60cm
Dr

P. alopecuroides itself often does not flower very freely but this slightly shorter variety produces plenty of bristly flower heads, up to 5in/12cm long. They are an interesting addition to flower arrangements, both fresh and dried. *P.a.* "Hameln," with its dense tuft of slim, arching leaves, also looks good in the garden. In autumn, the deep green foliage turns rich yellow. Neither the species nor its variety is a plant for a cold, wet garden. Both plants need a sheltered, sunny position and rather light, well-drained soil. *Hystrix patula* [zones 4–9], which is a slightly taller grass, also has flowers like bottle-brushes, and these, too, are good for drying.
also for: ■ Ground cover ■ Colorful, autumn foliage

Rudbeckia hirta
e.g. "Goldilocks"
[black-eyed Susan]
○

type of plant: grown as half-hardy annual/ hardy biennial [4–9]
flowering time: midsummer to mid-autumn
flower color: golden yellow + deep ginger-brown
height: 24in/60cm

The strong-stemmed flowers of this plant can last as long as two weeks in water. Some of the flowers are fully double, others are semi-double. They all have central, gingery brown cones that are most clearly visible in the blooms that are semi-double. Erect stems are clothed in plenty of rather bright green, bristly leaves, which are mainly oval and pointed. There are single-flowered varieties of *R. hirta*, too, including *R.h.* "Marmalade," which has golden-orange daisies up 5in/12cm across. The flowers of *R.h.* "Goldilocks" are about 3in/8cm across. Most moisture-retentive soils are suitable for these plants and reasonable drainage is an advantage.

Stipa tenuissima
○

type of plant: hardy perennial (grass) [7–10]
flowering time: early summer
flower color: pale green ripening to buff
height: 24in/60cm

Although some gardeners prefer to prolong the life of this short-lived grass by cutting it down at the end of autumn, it can continue to look very attractive in its dried, yellow-buff state, as this midwinter illustration shows. Everything about this grass is slender and delicate: the bright green, summer leaves, up to 12in/30cm long, are thin and almost thread-like, and the profusion of slim flower panicles creates a shimmering mass that moves in the gentlest of breezes. The foliage forms a neat, dense, rather upright tuft of growth. Good drainage and a warm position encourage the formation of plenty of flower heads. In a hot, dry site, *S. tenuissima* sows itself freely.
also for: ■ Dry soils in hot, sunny sites ■ Colorful, autumn foliage

Tulipa e.g. "Fantasy" (Parrot Group) [tulip]
○

type of plant: hardy bulb [5–9]
flowering time: late spring
flower color: pale pink + rose pink + green
height: 24in/60cm

The extravagantly fringed and feathered Parrot Group tulips are popular with flower arrangers. In common with many other tulips of this type, *T.* "Fantasy" has very large blooms (about 5in/12cm wide); the green markings on the outer petals are also characteristic. These tulips require a site sheltered from wind. Good drainage is also important, and the plants last longest if they are lifted each year and replanted in late autumn. Other Parrot Group tulips that look interesting in flower arrangements include *T.* "Black Parrot" (with dark purple blooms), *T.* "Blue Parrot" (which is, in fact, bright violet), and *T.* "Estella Rijnveld" (red and white petals). The leaves of these plants are gray-green, broad and pointed.

Tulipa e.g. "Gudoshnik" (Darwinhybrid Group) [tulip]
○

type of plant: hardy bulb [5–9]
flowering time: mid-spring
flower color: apricot-pink + orange-scarlet
height: 24in/60cm

Often brightly colored and with long, strong stems, Darwinhybrid Group tulips make good cut flowers. Many of the varieties, including the example shown here, have blooms streaked, flushed or spotted with a second color. The leaves of these tulips are grayish, broad, and upright. Like almost all tulips, Darwinhybrids grow best in fertile, well-drained soil and in a site that receives plenty of sun. They also need shelter from strong winds, since their flowers are often more than 3in/8cm across. Even in ideal conditions, the bulbs tend to dwindle in size from season to season and they usually require replacing every few years.

Zinnia elegans e.g. Dahlia-flowered Mixed
○

type of plant: half-hardy/tender annual [9–11]
flowering time: midsummer to early autumn
flower color: mixed—red, pink, orange, white, yellow
height: 24in/60cm

Most zinnias are bushy, upright plants with fairly thick stems, but in the case of tall varieties with large, fully double flowers—and the blooms of this and similar varieties may be nearly 5in/12cm across—the stems can break in windy conditions. However, in a sheltered site, plenty of flowers appear and remain undamaged, especially if the weather is dry during the flowering season. In regions with wetter summers, varieties such as *Z. haageana* "Persian Carpet" (15in/38cm high) are more satisfactory; this mixture has mainly bicolored flowers, each about 1½in/4cm across. Both these varieties of zinnia perform best in a warm position and light, rich, well-drained soil. Their pointed leaves are a fairly light green.

Aster amellus e.g. "King George"
○

type of plant: hardy perennial [4–9]
flowering time: early to mid-autumn
flower color: violet-blue + yellow
height: 20–24in/50–60cm

Varieties of *A. amellus* are generally long-lived, healthy plants with large, attractively simple flowers. *A.a.* "King George" is a notably free-flowering variety, which produces numerous slim-petalled flowers, each 2in/5cm or more across, which last well when cut. Although the plant is somewhat lax, the branching flower stems are strong. They form clumps of mid-green, narrow-leaved growth. *A.a.* "Veilchenkönigin" (syn. Violet Queen) has violet-purple flowers. Most soils are suitable, especially if they retain moisture during summer and early autumn. These plants have a preference for alkaline conditions.

Tulipa e.g. "Hamilton" (Fringed Group) [tulip]
○

type of plant: hardy bulb [5–9]
flowering time: late spring
flower color: yellow
height: 20in/50cm

The smooth petals of Fringed Group tulips have contrasting crisp edges and this gives the flowers a certain zany charm. These tulips are available in reds, pinks, violets, and white, as well as yellow. Their cup-shaped flowers are usually 2½–3in/6–8cm wide. Some varieties, such as the red and yellow *T.* "Fringed Beauty," have fringes that differ in color from the main body of the flower. Other exotically shaped tulips include those in the Parrot Group (for an example of which, see above). All these plants require soil with good drainage and a site with plenty of sun. Their flowers tend to decrease in size from year to year, even when the bulbs are lifted (after the broad, pointed, blue-gray leaves have died down), and then replanted in autumn.

Dianthus barbatus e.g. "Auricula-Eyed Mixed" [sweet William]
○

type of plant: grown as hardy biennial [6–9]
flowering time: late spring to early summer
flower color: mixed—crimson, red, pink, white + contrasting zones
height: 18–24in/45–60cm

These conspicuously pale-eyed flowers are a familiar sight in florists' shops. Little, fringed blooms are arranged in dense, flattish heads, each about 4in/10cm across. The flowers emit a sweet, clove-like scent, although it is not always very pronounced in all mixtures. The stems are strong and well clothed in rich green, slender, pointed leaves. Shorter forms of sweet William are available (for an example, see p.303) and a particularly dark-flowered variety is shown on p.330. All these plants like well-drained, slightly alkaline soil and plenty of sun.
also for: ■ Fragrant flowers (see above)

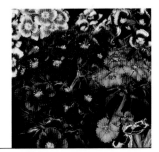

Gladiolus "The Bride"
○

type of plant: slightly tender/half-hardy corm [8–10]
flowering time: early summer
flower color: white
height: 18–24in/45–60cm

This charming and elegant x *colvillei* hybrid gladiolus produces several, shapely trumpets on each of its stiff stems. The flowers are about 2in/5cm wide and there are delicate, yellow-green markings on the lower petals. The flowers last very well when cut. G. "The Bride" needs a warm, sheltered spot, and good drainage is important, too. When well suited, the plant forms substantial patches; it is easily grown in warmer regions. Its long, thin, grayish leaves sometimes emerge so early that, in colder regions, they liable to frost damage.

Gomphrena globosa Mixed [globe amaranth]
○

type of plant: half-hardy annual [9–11]
flowering time: midsummer to early autumn
flower color: mixed—purple, red, pink, orange, white
height: 18–24in/45–60cm
mainly Dr

These dense, rounded flower heads are carried on strong stems. Each clover-like flower head is about 1½in/4cm long and made up of numerous flowers with papery bracts that are long-lasting when dried. The plant itself is upright and bushy with slender, slightly hairy, mid-green leaves. It needs soil that is really well-drained but also moisture-retentive, and the planting position must be warm and sheltered. Given these conditions, G. *globosa* Mixed plants grow quickly.

Iris Dutch Hybrids Mixed
○

type of plant: hardy/slightly tender bulb [7–10]
flowering time: early summer
flower color: mixed—blue, yellow, purple, white + bicolors
height: 18–24in/45–60cm

In light soils, these bulbous irises are easy to grow; in heavier soils, particularly in colder regions, they flower better if the bulbs are lifted in late summer, dried, and then replanted in autumn. Their flowers are carried on stiff, strong stems; there is usually one bloom, about 3in/8cm across, per stem. They are excellent for cutting—the dark blue variety, *I.* "Professor Blaauw," is a popular florists' flower. Some specialist growers may list a few varieties in separate colors, as well as mixtures. The rather light green leaves of these irises are long, thin, and channelled.

Lagurus ovatus [hare's tail]
○

type of plant: hardy annual (grass) [7–9]
flowering time: early to late summer
flower color: pale green ripening to cream
height: 18–24in/45–60cm
mainly Dr

Among the commonly available annual grasses, hare's tail grass has ripened flower heads that are distinctively dense and fluffy. They look just as decorative in the garden as in dried arrangements. Each flower head is about 2in/5cm long, and the stems are thin and upright. Slender, light green leaves are produced in tufts but they tend to be rather sparse. Most well-drained soils are suitable for this grass, although it is especially at home in light, sandy soils.

Lavatera trimestris e.g. "Mont Blanc" [mallow]
○

type of plant: slightly tender/hardy annual [8–10]
flowering time: midsummer to early autumn
flower color: white
height: 18–24in/45–60cm

Annual mallows make good cut flowers. *L. trimestris* "Mont Blanc" is a popular variety that produces a mass of bright white blooms, each 3–4in/8–10cm wide, on sturdy, upright stems. Flowering is particularly good in a sheltered site. The leaves of the plant are deep green and lobed. *L.t.* "Silver Cup" is another commonly grown variety; it is slightly taller and has large, rose-pink flowers. Most garden soils with reasonable drainage are suitable for these plants. Some seed catalogs also list varieties of *Malope trifida*. These are similar to *L. trimestris* cultivars, although their funnel-shaped flowers are often slightly smaller; they, too, make good cut flowers.

Limonium (syn. *Statice*) *platyphyllum* (syn. *L. latifolium*) [sea lavender]
○

type of plant: hardy perennial [4–9]
flowering time: late summer to early autumn
flower color: lavender-blue
height: 18–24in/45–60cm
Evergreen/Semi-evergreen, mainly Dr

All the popular sea lavenders have persistent parts to their tiny flowers and these create a decorative effect when dried. As well as clouds of flowers on branching stems, this perennial species produces a ground-covering rosette of broad, dark green, leathery leaves, each of which may be more than 12in/30cm long. Any well-drained soil is suitable for *L. platyphyllum*, but it is especially at home in deep, sandy loam and in a coastal setting. *L.p.* "Violetta" has flowers of rich purple. For annual sea lavender, see the following plant.

also for: ■ Dry soils in hot, sunny sites ■ Ground cover

Limonium sinuatum (syn. *Statice sinuata*) Mixed [sea lavender, statice]
○

type of plant: grown as half-hardy annual [8–10]
flowering time: midsummer to early autumn
flower color: mixed—blue, pink, yellow, apricot, white
height: 18–24in/45–60cm
mainly Dr

The upright, branched stems of *L. sinuatum* Mixed plants are stiff and strong. They carry clusters of crisp flowers that are good for cutting but that are especially popular for drying, since they retain their colors well. Each cluster is about 4in/10cm long. Large, lobed leaves form basal rosettes of dark greenery. Most well-drained soils are suitable but these "everlastings" have a preference for light, sandy soil. For perennial sea lavender, see the preceding plant.

Nerine bowdenii
○

type of plant: slightly tender bulb [8–10]
flowering time: early to mid-autumn
flower color: pink
height: 18–24in/45–60cm

The distinctively curled and brightly colored petals of *N. bowdenii* stay fresh for a long time when the flowers have been picked, and they are remarkably weatherproof in the garden. The funnel-shaped blooms, each about 3in/8cm wide. are arranged in clusters on top of clear, sturdy stems. The largest number of blooms are produced when the plant is grown in well-drained soil at the base of a sunny wall. Just before the flowers open, the bright green, strap-shaped leaves start to die back, rather untidily. New leaves appear as the flowers fade.

Pennisetum orientale
○

type of plant: slightly tender perennial/half-hardy annual (grass) [7–9]
flowering time: midsummer to early autumn
flower color: pale mauve-pink changing to mauve-gray
height: 18–24in/45–60cm
Dr

This densely tufted grass produces attractive, fluffy flower spikes that are often likened to hairy caterpillars. Each spike is about 5in/12cm long, and it arches above the mass of neatly radiating, very slim, dark bluish green leaves. Flowering is particularly good during hot, dry summers, and the plant tolerates periods of drought. *P. orientale* is longest-lived in warm areas; in colder districts it is best raised each year from seed. Well-drained, light soil and, if necessary, a dry mulch in winter increase the chances of this grass surviving as a perennial.

also for: ■ Dry soils in hot, sunny sites

Sedum telephium "Matrona" (syn. *S.* "Matrona") [stonecrop]
○

type of plant: hardy perennial [5–9]
flowering time: late summer to mid-autumn
flower color: soft pink
height: 18–24in/45–60cm
Dr

This sturdy and vigorous stonecrop carries its matt, fleshy leaves and wide heads of flowers on a closely packed mass of strong, dark, upright stems. The flower heads can be up to 6in/15cm wide. In winter they persist as handsome, red-brown seedheads and look good both in the garden and in dried arrangements indoors. The foliage is grayish in spring but, as the summer months progress, it becomes suffused with purple—sometimes richly so, though the color is not as dark as that of *S. telephium* subsp. *maximum* "Atropurpureum" (see p.202). Most well-drained soils are suitable but very fertile conditions tend to result in lush, floppy growth and disappointing leaf color.

also for: ■ Ground cover ■ Purple, bronze or red leaves ■ Ornamental fruit (seedheads)

Allium cernuum
[nodding onion, wild onion]
○

type of plant: hardy bulb [3–8]
flowering time: early to midsummer
flower color: variable—pink-magenta
to rose-purple
height: 18in/45cm
Dr

As a change from *Allium* with more or less rounded, drumstick-like flower heads, there is *A. cernuum* with its graceful, pendent flowers hanging from stems that are, themselves, elegant and arching. The flowers turn into attractive seedheads in which the seed pods face more nearly outward. *A. carinatum* subsp. *pulchellum* [zones 6–9] also has loose heads of nodding flowers; in this case the flower color is lilac-purple. The deep green leaves of these plants are long and thin. (Unusually for an *Allium*, the foliage of *A. cernuum* lacks an oniony smell.) Both plants are vigorous and can form sizable patches. They are easily grown in well-drained, fertile soil.

Briza maxima
[big quaking grass, puffed wheat]
○

type of plant: hardy annual (grass) [6–9]
flowering time: late spring to late summer
flower color: green-tinged russet or purple,
ripening to pale straw
height: 18in/45cm
mainly Dr

Glossy, heart-shaped spikelets on this vigorous grass dangle from hair-fine stalks and tremble whenever they are moved. The spikelets are up to ½in/1cm long and they are carried in open, airy clusters. They are very easy to dry successfully. The leaves of this upright, tufted plant are long, thin, and light green. Any well-drained soil is suitable for greater quaking grass. *B. media* (see p.276) is a perennial species of quaking grass and it, too, is excellent for drying.

Coreopsis grandiflora
e.g. "Early Sunrise"
[tickseed]
○

type of plant: hardy annual/half-hardy
annual/hardy perennial [6–9]
flowering time: early summer to early autumn
flower color: deep yellow
height: 18in/45cm

Often grown as an annual, this short-lived perennial produces masses of bright, semi-double flowers on thin, strong stems. Each flower is 2in/5cm or so across. The attractively ragged-edged blooms rise clear of a low clump of bright green, mostly strap-shaped leaves. *C.* "Sunray" is a fully double variety that is also popular; it, too, is often treated as an annual. These plants are easy to grow in light, moderately fertile soil. They make very good cut flowers.

Gypsophila elegans
e.g. "Covent Garden"
○

type of plant: hardy/slightly tender annual [7–9]
flowering time: early summer to early autumn
flower color: white
height: 18in/45cm

Although there are pink-flowered varieties of *G. elegans*, the white varieties, such as the one illustrated here, are more popular. Well-drained, preferably alkaline soil is most suitable for these plants but, provided drainage is good, they grow quickly in most soils. Their tiny flowers—each only about ½in/1cm across—are clustered, on much-branched stems, and form pale, cloud-like masses. The leaves are grayish and narrow. For a taller-growing, perennial gypsophila, see p.272.
also for: ■ Shallow soils over chalk ■ Dry soils in hot, sunny sites

Hordeum jubatum
[squirrel-tail grass]
○

type of plant: grown as hardy annual (grass) [5–9]
flowering time: early to midsummer
flower color: silvery green ripening to beige
height: 18in/45cm
mainly Dr

The bristles that fan out so conspicuously and elegantly from the inflorescences of this grass may be as much as 3in/8cm long. The arching flower heads are perched on top of erect stems, above dense tufts of thin, light green leaves. They make interesting, if rather brittle and fragile, material for dried arrangements. *H. jubatum* prospers in most well-drained soils and it tolerates quite long periods of drought. It is sometimes an invasive self-sower.
also for: ■ Dry soils in hot, sunny sites

Nigella damascena
e.g. "Miss Jekyll"
[love-in-a-mist]
○

type of plant: hardy annual [6–10]
flowering time: early to midsummer
flower color: blue
height: 18in/45cm
Dr

After its lovely, blue blooms have faded, this upright plant produces inflated seed pods that are attractive in dried arrangements. The 1½in/4cm-wide flowers, with their wispy appendages, are good for cutting and the whole plant looks good because of its mass of very finely cut, bright green foliage. *N. damascena* Persian Jewel Series cultivars have white, blue, pink, rose-red, and violet flowers. Any soil that is reasonably well-drained is suitable for these plants.

also for: ■ Decorative, green foliage ■ Ornamental fruit (seed pods)

Phlox drummondii
e.g. Tapestry Mixed
○

type of plant: half-hardy annual [9–10]
flowering time: early to late summer
flower color: mixed—pink, red, white, lavender, yellow + bicolors
height: 18in/45cm

This mixture of annual phlox has an unusually high proportion of pale and softly colored flowers, and it is useful for bedding and containers as well as good for cutting. Even when the stems are cut and placed in water, the numerous, little buds continue to open, in succession, so that there is a long-lasting display. Each rounded, densely packed flower head is about 5in/12cm wide. Not all of the differently colored flowers in *P. drummondii* Tapestry Mixed are sweetly scented, but many are. The plants themselves are bushy, and their branched stems are clothed with slender, pointed, light green leaves. Rich soil with good drainage is most suitable for these plants.

also for: ■ Fragrant flowers (see above)

Salvia viridis (syn. *S. horminum*)
e.g. "Bouquet"
(syn. "Monarch Bouquet")
[annual clary sage]
○

type of plant: hardy/slightly tender annual [7–10]
flowering time: early to late summer
flower color: mixed—pink, blue, white, purple
height: 18in/45cm
Dr

The true flowers of *S. viridis* "Bouquet" are tiny and inconspicuous but they are surrounded by colorful, dark-veined bracts, each of which is up to 1½in/4cm-long. The bracts retain their color very well when dried and they are also long-lasting when treated as fresh flowers. Some seed catalogs list single-color varieties as well as mixtures. The erect stems of these bushy plants bear hairy, approximately oval leaves. Light soils that are poor to moderately fertile are ideal for growing varieties of *S. viridis*.

Schizostylis coccinea
e.g. "Mrs Hegarty"
[Kaffir lily]
○

type of plant: hardy perennial [6–9]
flowering time: mid- to late autumn
flower color: pale pink
height: 18in/45cm

Kaffir lilies, including this prettily colored, late-flowering variety, are excellent, long-lasting cut flowers. Each bloom is shallowly cup-shaped and up to 1½in/4cm across. Slender buds open in succession on strong, upright, wiry stems. Other Kaffir lilies include the earlier-flowering, soft pink *S. coccinea* "Sunrise" and white-flowered *S.c.* f. *alba*. *S.c.* "Major" (see p.66) has rich red flowers. All these plants like fertile soil that is moderately moist to damp, and a warm position. Under these conditions many of them increase quite quickly. Their ribbed leaves are slim and sword-shaped, and they form tufted clumps of bright greenery that usually persist through winter.

also for: ■ Damp and wet soils

Helichrysum "Schwefellicht"
(syn. *H. Sulphur Light*)
○

type of plant: hardy perennial [5–9]
flowering time: mid- to late summer
flower color: pale yellow changing to mustard then tawny yellow
height: 15–18in/38–45cm
Dr

The slender, pointed leaves of this more or less erect plant are held in upright tufts near the base of the stems. They appear at intervals on the upper growths, too. They are silvery gray, felted, and emit a warm, pungent smell when bruised. Papery, "everlasting" flower heads, up to ½in/1cm wide, look attractive even after their official flowering period is over, and they dry well, too. They are carried in dense clusters on pale, branched stems. *H.* "Schwefellicht" thrives in really well-drained, rather light soils, including shallow, chalky soils, and it creates slowly spreading clumps of growth.

also for: ■ Shallow soils over chalk ■ Dry soils in hot, sunny sites ■ Gray, blue-gray, or silver leaves ■ Aromatic foliage

Stokesia laevis (syn. *S. cyanea*)
[Stokes' aster]
○

type of plant: hardy perennial [6–9]
flowering time: midsummer to early autumn
flower color: blue or lilac
height: 15–18in/38–45cm
Evergreen/Semi-evergreen

S. laevis flowers continuously over many weeks, especially if the pretty, cornflower-like blooms are picked regularly. The flower heads, each 3–4in/8–10cm across, stay fresh in water for a considerable time. They are borne on upright stems above rosettes of long, pointed, mid-green leaves that have pale midribs. The plant is easily grown in most well-drained soils, although it has a preference for acid conditions and light, moist soil. Examples of popular varieties of Stokes' aster include white-flowered *S.l.* "Alba," *S.l.* "Blue Star" (which has large, clear blue flowers) and yellow-flowered *S.l.* "Mary Gregory."

also for: ■ Acid soils ■ Long, continuous flowering period

Dianthus e.g. "Haytor White"
(syn. D. "Haytor")
[carnation, pink]
○

type of plant: hardy perennial [4–8]
flowering time: early to midsummer; some flowers later, mainly early autumn
flower color: white
height: 12–15in/30–38cm
Evergreen

D. "Haytor White" is a vigorous and floriferous modern pink that produces double flowers with an excellent, sweet, and spicy fragrance. These flowers make most attractive material for cutting and they last well in water. Each strong-stemmed bloom is about 2in/5cm wide. Narrow, pointed leaves in bluish gray-green form low tussocks of growth, above which the erect flower stems rise clearly. Pinks of all sorts grow well in alkaline conditions. To flower well they must have good drainage and a sunny site. The numerous varieties of modern pink have single to fully double flowers in red, pink, and white. There are plenty of very pretty bicolors as well: D. "Gran's Favorite," for example, has sweetly scented, maroon-centered, white flowers with each petal edged in maroon. Not all modern pinks are fragrant.
also for: ■ Shallow soils over chalk ■ Dry soils in hot, sunny sites ■ Gray, blue-gray, or silver leaves ■ Fragrant flowers

Lychnis viscaria
(syn. Viscaria vulgaris)
"Splendens Plena"
[German catchfly]
○

type of plant: hardy perennial [4–8]
flowering time: early to midsummer
flower color: bright magenta-pink
height: 12–15in/30–38cm

The dark, sticky stems of this plant may not be pleasant to handle, but they are straight and strong and topped with open clusters of vividly colored, double flowers that last well when cut. Each flower is about 1in/2.5cm across. The leaves of L. viscaria "Splendens Plena" are long and narrow; they form a low clump of tidy, dark green growth. As long as drainage is good, most garden soils are suitable.

Sedum spectabile
e.g. "Iceberg"
[stonecrop]
○

type of plant: hardy perennial [5–9]
flowering time: late summer to early autumn
flower color: white
height: 12–15in/30–38cm
Dr

In the well-drained, moderately fertile, and reasonably moisture-retentive soil that suits it best, S. spectabile "Iceberg" produces plenty of long-lasting flowers. After the flowers have faded there are rich brown seedheads, and these are suitable for drying (although the mixture of white flowers and brown seedheads during the fading process is not very attractive). Each dense, flat flower head, 4–5in/10–12cm across, is composed of numerous starry flowers, which are greenish in bud. Since the clumps of upright stems are clothed in pale green, fleshy, oval leaves, the overall impression is pale and cool. In contrast, the flowers of S.s. "Brilliant" are vivid hot pink. The flowers of both plants are very attractive to bees and butterflies.
also for: ■ Ground cover ■ Decorative, green foliage

Tagetes "Vanilla"
[marigold]
○

type of plant: half-hardy annual [9–11]
flowering time: early summer to early autumn
flower color: creamy white
height: 12–15in/30–38cm

Many marigolds are too low-growing to be useful for cutting, although they are popular for bedding and for containers. Among the rather taller varieties, T. "Vanilla" is attractive because of its unusually pale coloring; taller marigolds in the typical, bright yellows, oranges, and golds include those in T. Crackerjack Series (to 30in/75cm high). All these African marigolds have fully double flowers—each about 4in/10cm wide—that last well in water but that may become damaged in wet weather. They are stout, upright plants with deeply cut, rich green foliage that is rather unpleasantly scented. Although they grow in poor, dry soil, flowering is especially profuse in reasonably fertile, well-drained soil that does not dry out too readily. They need a warm, sheltered site.

Dianthus e.g. "Doris"
[carnation, pink]
○

type of plant: hardy perennial [4–8]
flowering time: early to midsummer and early autumn
flower color: pale pink + deep pink
height: 12in/30cm
Evergreen

Although there are numerous varieties of modern hybrid pink to choose from (for an example of a pure white modern pink, see above), D. "Doris" is perhaps the best-known of these plants. Its strong-stemmed, double flowers, each about 2in/5cm across, are spicily fragrant and good for cutting. They are borne above narrow, pointed leaves that form a pale gray mound of growth. To perform well, modern pinks must have good drainage and full sun. They have a preference for alkaline conditions. As well as single-colored flowers and blooms that have a deeper-colored "eye," like D. "Doris," there are many very attractive "laced" and "fancy" modern pinks. Laced pinks produce petals edged in a contrasting color and an "eye" of that color too; fancies have stripes or flecks of contrasting color on their petals.
also for: ■ Shallow soils over chalk ■ Dry soils in hot, sunny sites ■ Gray, blue-gray, or silver leaves ■ Fragrant flowers

Muscari comosum "Plumosum"
(syn. *M.c.* "Monstrosum")
[tassel grape hyacinth]
○

type of plant: hardy bulb [4–9]
flowering time: late spring to early summer
flower color: mauve-blue to mauve-purple
height: 9–12in/23–30cm

Since these frizzy, tangled-headed flowers are sterile, they are long-lasting and particularly suitable for cutting. The so-called tassel grape hyacinth (which is not, in fact, a hyacinth) is easy to grow in any well-drained soil. To encourage it to produce plenty of its feathery, 4in/10cm-long flower heads, it needs a warm site in full sun. The flowers often bend slightly on their slender stems, and the narrowly strap-shaped, mid-green leaves are apt to be rather untidy.

ADDITIONAL DECORATIVE PLANTS, featured elsewhere in this book, that have flowers suitable for cutting

† = mainly suitable for drying

○ sun

minimum height 10ft/3m or more
Acacia dealbata, see p.297
Cobaea scandens, see p.128
Magnolia grandiflora "Exmouth," see p.297
Prunus x subhirtella "Autumnalis," see p.316
Rosa "Albertine," see p.127
Syringa x josiflexa "Bellicent," see p.40
Syringa vulgaris "Charles Joly," see p.96
Syringa vulgaris "Katherine Havemeyer,"
    see p.297

minimum height between 3ft/90cm and 10ft/3m
†Cynara cardunculus, see p.183
Escallonia "Apple Blossom," see p.90
Escallonia "Iveyi," see p.298
Lathyrus odoratus "Noel Sutton,"
    see p.299
Leymus arenarius, see p.53
Onopordum acanthium, see p.184
Rosa Gertrude Jekyll, see p.300
Rosa Peace, see p.97
Stipa gigantea, see p.52
Syringa pubescens subsp. microphylla "Superba,"
    see p.299

minimum height 3ft/90cm or less
Achillea millefolium "Cerise Queen," see p.105
Achillea "Moonshine," see p.186
Allium cristophii, see p.57
Allium tuberosum, see p.246
Amaranthus caudatus var. viridis, see p.323
Anthemis tinctoria "Wargrave Variety," see p.336
Asphodeline lutea, see p.53
Aster x frikartii "Mönch," see p.336
Aster lateriflorus "Prince," see p.201
Aster novi-belgii "Jenny," see p.42
Buphthalmum salicifolium, see p.340
Calluna vulgaris "H.E. Beale," see p.106
Centaurea hypoleuca "John Coutts," see p.106
Chrysanthemum carinatum "Court Jesters,"
    see p.16
Clematis tubulosa "Wyevale," see p.300
Coreopsis verticillata, see p.338
Dahlia "Bishop of Llandaff," see p.201
Dahlia "Redskin," see p.202
Delphinium x ruysii "Pink Sensation," see p.335
Dianthus barbatus Nigrescens Group, see p.330
Dianthus "Inchmery," see p.302
Dianthus "Mrs Sinkins," see p.302
Erica vagans "Mrs D.F. Maxwell," see p.26
Eriophorum angustifolium, see p.67
Eryngium bourgatii, see p.165
Eryngium giganteum, see p.54

Eryngium x tripartitum, see p.55
Euphorbia characias subsp. wulfenii, see p.184
Filipendula vulgaris "Multiplex," see p.16
Hedysarum coronarium, see p.300
Helenium "Butterpat," see p.41
Helenium "Moerheim Beauty," see p.41
Iris "Sable," see p.329
Iris unguicularis, see p.316
Moluccella laevis, see p.323
Narcissus "Pipit," see p.302
Papaver somniferum "Black Paeony," see p.329
Papaver somniferum "Paeony Flowered," see p.253
Rosa Fragrant Cloud, see p.300
Rosa Whisky Mac, see p.301
Scabiosa atropurpurea "Chile Black," see p.330
Scabiosa caucasica "Clive Greaves," see p.15
†Scabiosa stellata "Drumstick," see p.254
Schizostylis coccinea "Major," see p.66
Sedum "Herbstfreude," see p.106
Sedum telephium subsp. maximum
    "Atropurpureum," see p.202
Stipa calamagrostis, see p.54
Tulipa praestans "Unicum," see p.167
Tulipa "Queen of Night," see p.330
Tulipa "Spring Green," see p.324
Zantedeschia aethiopica "Crowborough," see p.66
Zantedeschia aethiopica "Green Goddess,"
    see p.323

Artemisia lactiflora
[white mugwort]
○ [◐]

type of plant: hardy perennial [4–9]
flowering time: late summer to mid-autumn
flower color: creamy white
height: 4–5ft/1.2–1.5m
Dr

This sturdy, clump-forming plant requires rich, moist soil; when its roots are dry the dark green, deeply cut leaves soon wilt. Its tiny, slightly scented flowers are arranged in plumes, up to 24in/60cm long, on stiff, upright stems. The flowers become creamier as they age and, when fully developed, they make good cut flowers. They dry well too. The foliage emits a resinous scent when bruised. Plants in *A. lactiflora* Guizhou Group have stems and young leaves that are flushed with brownish purple.

also for: ■ Aromatic foliage ■ Long, continuous flowering period

Calamagrostis x acutiflora
"Karl Foerster"
[feather reed grass]
○ [◐]

type of plant: hardy perennial (grass) [5–9]
flowering time: mid- to late summer
flower color: reddish bronze
height: 4ft/1.2m
mainly Dr

The strikingly straight and erect stems of this grass bear slender plumes of flowers, about 8in/20cm long, which fade to beige-yellow in autumn. The seedheads (seen here in late autumn) remain decorative in the garden throughout winter and they are good for cutting and drying, too. They are held well clear of the dense clumps of narrow, mid-green leaves. The plant spreads only slowly, even in the moist, humus-rich soil that suits it best. *C.* x *acutiflora* "Overdam" is also readily available; its white-striped leaves are arranged in a rather loose clump. Other grasses with good winter seedheads include free-flowering varieties of *Miscanthus sinensis*, such as *M.s.* "Silberfeder" (syn. "Silver Feather"), and *Stipa calamagrostis* (see p.54).

also for: ■ Ornamental fruit (seedheads)

Crocosmia e.g. "Lucifer"
○【◑

type of plant: hardy perennial [5–9]
flowering time: mid- to late summer
flower color: flame-red
height: 4ft/1.2m

The brilliantly colored, elegantly disposed flowers of this popular crocosmia appear earlier than those of many other varieties. Each spray of flowers is about 6in/15cm long. C. "Lucifer" is vigorous and particularly at home in well-drained, fertile soil in regions with fairly high summer rainfall. It may need a sheltered position and some winter protection in especially frost-prone areas. It makes an excellent cut flower. The flowers are held just above the mid-green, broadly sword-shaped leaves, which are pleated and form substantial clumps of growth. C. "Emberglow" is another example of a crocosmia with richly colored, red flowers; it grows up to 30in/75cm high.
also for: ■ Decorative, green foliage

Gladiolus papilio
○【◑

type of plant: slightly tender/half-hardy corm [8–10]
flowering time: late summer to early autumn
flower color: variable—often gray-mauve + yellow + purple
height: 36in/90cm

For all the subtle charms of its delicate, muted coloring and its graceful demeanor, this plant is vigorous and it can increase at considerable speed, spreading rapidly by underground stems. Slim, pointed buds develop on arching stems and open to bell-shaped flowers, each about 1½in/4cm across. The flower colors and markings are variable, but they often have an intriguingly blurred and clouded appearance. In order to flower well, G. papilio needs fertile soil which does not dry out in summer. Its upright, narrowly sword-shaped leaves are light grayish green.

Lychnis chalcedonica
[Jerusalem cross, Maltese cross]
○【◑

type of plant: hardy perennial [4–8]
flowering time: early to midsummer
flower color: scarlet
height: 36in/90cm

A brilliant flower color is characteristic of many plants in the genus *Lychnis*, but few of them have quite such eye-catchingly large, dense flower heads as *L. chalcedonica*. Its flat-topped heads are carried on stiff, upright, hairy stems. They are usually 3–4in/8–10cm across but they can be as much as 5in/12cm wide. The blooms may not last especially long when cut, but their color and shape make them striking and distinctive additions to arrangements. The flower heads are largest and the plant grows most strongly in moist to slightly damp soil that is fertile. There are often self-sown seedlings. The stems, which are clasped by pairs of rather bright green, pointed leaves, usually need staking and a sheltered site is advisable. The flowers of *L.c.* var. *albiflora* are palest pink. *L.c.* "Flore Pleno" has double, red flowers.

Phlox carolina
e.g. "Miss Lingard"
○【◑

type of plant: hardy perennial [5–8]
flowering time: late spring to early summer
flower color: white
height: 36in/90cm

P. carolina "Miss Lingard" flowers some weeks earlier than the more commonly seen varieties of P. paniculata, and it is very much less prone to mildew than them. It produces its long-tubed, flat-faced blooms, up to 1in/2.5cm wide, in rounded clusters. The flowers are sweetly fragrant. P. carolina "Bill Baker" is a popular variety; it grows 12–18in/30–45cm tall and its white-"eyed," pink flowers appear from late spring to midsummer. For the best results, both these upright plants need moist but well-drained soil that is rich in organic material. Their bright green leaves are thick, glossy and pointed.
also for: ■ Fragrant flowers

Sidalcea e.g. "Elsie Heugh"
[false mallow, prairie mallow]
○【◑

type of plant: hardy perennial [6–9]
flowering time: mid- to late summer
flower color: pale pink
height: 36in/90cm

These branched spires of decorative blooms make attractive cut flowers that last well in water. They rise above clumps of rounded, mid-green, basal leaves. The individual flowers, each about 2in/5cm across, have prettily fringed petals. As well as pale pink varieties such as S. "Elsie Heugh," there are darker pink varieties, such as S. "William Smith," and S. candida produces white flowers. All these plants are at their very best in regions with mild winters and cool, rather damp summers. They flower longest when grown in fertile, moisture-retentive soil and a sunny position. Especially if they are cut back after their first flush of flowers, they often bloom again in autumn.

Aster pilosus var. pringlei "Monte Cassino" (syn. A. pringlei "Monte Cassino")
○[◖]

type of plant: hardy perennial [4–8]
flowering time: early to late autumn
flower color: white + yellow
height: 30–36in/75–90cm

This popular florists' flower is easy to grow and attractive in the garden too. The plant forms clumps of growth and produces a mass of tiny, yellow-centered daisies (each flower is about ½in/1cm across). There are numerous, thin, little, mid-green leaves on the rather upright stems, and the overall effect is light, airy, and finely patterned. To perform well, A. pilosus var. pringlei "Monte Cassino" needs moisture-retentive, fairly fertile soil. Other readily available, small-flowered asters include A. ericoides "Pink Cloud," A. lateriflorus "Horizontalis" and A.l. "Prince" (see p.201 for the last plant, which has dark leaves and stems).
also for: ■ Heavy, clay soils

Leucanthemum x superbum (syn. Chrysanthemum maximum) e.g. "Wirral Supreme" [Shasta daisy]
○[◖]

type of plant: hardy perennial [4–9]
flowering time: mid- to late summer (see description)
flower color: white + yellow
height: 30–36in/75–90cm

Shasta daisies are excellent for cutting. Double-flowered L. x superbum "Wirral Supreme" has a thickly petaled, central area in each of its 3in/8cm-wide blooms. Its flowers are carried on clear, upright stems, high above the clump of slim, dark green, basal leaves. Semi-double and single-flowered varieties are available, too, while L. x s. "Phyllis Smith" has wispy-looking flowers with finely cut petals. Single-flowered L. x s. "Snowcap" is only 18in/45cm tall. All these plants have white flowers. For a creamy yellow variety with blooms about 4in/10cm wide, see L. x s. "Sonnenschein" (below). Shasta daisies are easily grown in most well-drained soils but they flower particularly profusely in moderately fertile, moisture-retentive conditions. Frequently divided plants often flower almost all summer.

Leucanthemum x superbum (syn. Chrysanthemum maximum) e.g. "Sonnenschein" [Shasta daisy]
○[◖]

type of plant: hardy perennial [4–9]
flowering time: mid- to late summer (see above)
flower color: pale creamy yellow + yellow
height: 24–30in/60–75cm

See preceding plant.

Anthericum liliago [St Bernard's lily]
○[◖]

type of plant: hardy perennial [5–9]
flowering time: early summer
flower color: white
height: 24in/60cm

Some gardeners prefer to grow St Bernard's lily in informal parts of their garden—at the edge of light woodland or naturalized in grass, for instance—since its thin, grayish leaves create a rather untidy, though weed-proof clump of growth. However, the flowers are charming and elegant. They are yellow-anthered stars, each about 1in/2.5cm across, arranged in loose spikes on long, clear stems. They are excellent for cutting. Most well-drained, fertile soils are suitable for this plant. A. ramosum produces airy sprays of smaller flowers.
also for: ■ Ground cover

Campanula persicifolia e.g. "Chettle Charm" [peach-leaved bellflower]
○[◖]

type of plant: hardy perennial [4–8]
flowering time: early to midsummer
flower color: white + blue
height: 24in/60cm
Evergreen

Among all the lovely bellflowers, the peach-leaved varieties are outstanding. If they are regularly dead-headed, they are in bloom for many weeks. The flowers, which are each about 2in/5cm across, last well when cut. They are carried, in slender sprays, on thin, wiry stems, well above rosettes of narrow, evergreen leaves. The foliage is often deep green. There are many varieties of C. persicifolia to choose from, but all have flowers in white or some shade of lilac-blue. A few—like the delicately colored variety shown here—are white with a suffusion of blue. Varieties vary considerably in the size and shape of their flowers. C.p. "Telham Beauty," for instance, has single flowers up to 3in/8cm wide, and there are single-, semi-double, and double-flowered forms. For the best results, all these plants should be given fertile, moisture-retentive soil with good drainage.

Crocosmia x crocosmiiflora
e.g. "Jackanapes"
○【◐】

type of plant: hardy perennial [6–9]
flowering time: late summer to early autumn
flower color: orange-red + yellow
height: 24in/60cm

Crocosmias are increasingly popular, late-flowering, cormous perennials with blooms in various shades of yellow (see p.204), orange (see p.224), and red (see p.285). Most of them make good cut flowers. The variety shown here produces clumps of slender, pointed, upright leaves that are mid-green. Some varieties, including the one shown on p.204, produce bronze-green foliage. The wiry, branching stems of C. x crocosmiiflora "Jackanapes" carry sprays of fairly small but conspicuously colored flowers. Each funnel-shaped bloom is 1in/2.5cm or so long. Well-drained soil that does not dry out in summer is most suitable for this plant. It thrives in mild, rather moist climates. In cold regions, winter protection is advisable.
also for: ■ Decorative, green foliage

Platycodon grandiflorus
[balloon flower]
○【◐】

type of plant: hardy perennial [4–9]
flowering time: late summer
flower color: blue to violet-blue
height: 24in/60cm

Pointed, slightly glaucous leaves on this plant emerge quite late in spring and form a clump of growth, above which rise stiff, upright stems carrying curious, balloon-like buds. The buds open out into 2in/5cm-wide, bell-shaped flowers. There are varieties of P. grandiflorus with flowers in white, pale pink, and various shades of blue, violet, and purple. Rich blue P.g. "Mariesii" is readily available; it is earlier-flowering and rather smaller than the species. All these plants like well-drained, fertile soil that does not dry out readily and that is, ideally, slightly acid. They may take some time to become established. They make good cut flowers.

Matthiola
e.g. "Brompton Stocks Mixed"
[stock]
○【◐】

type of plant: slightly tender/hardy biennial [7–10]
flowering time: late spring to early summer
flower color: mixed—red, pink, lavender, mauve, white
height: 18in/45cm

The flowers of these upright, bushy plants exude a full, aromatic fragrance. They are densely clustered above slender, gray-green leaves. In most mixtures, a high proportion of the flowers—each of which is 1–1½in/2.5–4cm wide—are double. They last well when cut. M. Legacy Series stocks are also popular; they, too, are grown as biennials (although they are sometimes treated as half-hardy annuals, in which case the flowering season is midsummer to early autumn). They are fragrant and, compared to Brompton stocks, slightly smaller-flowered and shorter. Both types are best in a warm, sheltered site and rich, light but moist soil.
also for: ■ Fragrant flowers

Narcissus
e.g. "Cheerfulness" (Double)
[daffodil]
○【◐】

type of plant: hardy bulb [6–9]
flowering time: mid-spring
flower color: white + cream
height: 15–18in/38–45cm

There are several, very sweetly scented flowers on each of this daffodil's strong stems. Individual flowers are 1½–2in/4–5cm across; they have fully double centers. N. "Yellow Cheerfulness" is a soft yellow version of this daffodil. Both plants make excellent cut flowers. They perform best if given rich, well-drained soil that remains moist during spring and a sheltered, sunny site where the bulbs ripen well during the summer months. For an earlier-flowering, Double daffodil, see p.293. Some flower arrangers also enjoy using the strangely shaped flowers of Split-corona daffodils: N. "Cassata," for example, has white petals and a yellow, split, and flattened cup with frilled edges. N. "Cheerfulness" and N. "Yellow Cheerfulness" are sometimes listed as Tazetta varieties in bulb catalogues. Both plants have strap-shaped, grayish green, basal leaves.
also for: ■ Fragrant flowers

Clarkia amoena
(syn. Godetia amoena, G. grandiflora)
e.g. "Azalea-flowered Mixed"
[satin flower]
○【◐】

type of plant: hardy/slightly tender annual [7–10]
flowering time: early to late summer
flower color: mixed—pink, red, salmon, white
height: 15in/38cm

All the medium or tall varieties of satin flower make cut good flowers, but those with semi-double blooms, like the mixture shown here, last the longest in water. C. amoena varieties are erect and bushy plants with plenty of slender, pointed, rich green leaves. Their generous clusters of fluted, funnel-shaped flowers are borne at the tips of the stems. (The individual flowers of C.a. "Azalea-flowered Mixed" are up to 2in/5cm across.) Varieties of C. unguicularis (syn. C. elegans) have flowers that are more evenly spaced along their stems; they, too, make good cut flowers. All these easily grown annuals prefer slightly acid, light but moist soil. Rich soil and too much moisture result in unsatisfactory growth with few flowers.

Narcissus e.g. "Geranium"
(Tazetta)
[daffodil]
○[◐]

type of plant: hardy bulb [5–9]
flowering time: mid- to late spring
flower color: white + reddish orange
height: 15in/38cm

Some Tazetta daffodils are only half-hardy and they are grown mainly for display in pots indoors or, under glass, for cut flowers. However, others, such as *N.* "Geranium," are hardy and make good garden plants. This vigorous cultivar produces richly and sweetly scented, 2½in/6cm-wide flowers. These are borne in clusters of about three to five blooms on each, sturdy stem. *N.* "Minnow" is another popular Tazetta daffodil that is a good garden plant; it produces several, fragrant, pale yellow flowers, with deeper yellow cups, on each of its 6–8in/15–20cm stems. It is suitable for naturalizing in short grass. Both these daffodils like rich, well-drained, moisture-retentive soil and they flower best in a sunny position. They have fairly broad, strap-shaped, grayish green, basal leaves.
also for: ■ Fragrant flowers

Calendula officinalis
e.g. Fiesta Gitana Group
[pot marigold, English marigold]
○[◐]

type of plant: hardy annual [6–10]
flowering time: early summer to early autumn
flower color: mixed—creamy yellow, gold, orange
height: 12in/30cm

Although *C. officinalis* Fiesta Gitana Group marigolds are not tall, their firm flower-stalks are long enough to make them useful for cutting. They are also popular for bedding displays. The upright stems are well covered with mid-green, fairly slender leaves. The double flowers, up to 4in/10cm across, are freely produced, and they last well in water. Taller varieties include *C.o.* Kablouna Series and *C.o.* Pacific Beauty Series; these double-flowered plants are about 24in/60cm high. They are sometimes available in separate colors. Pot marigolds are very easy to grow. They perform well in poor soils and are happy in almost any soil with good drainage.

ADDITIONAL DECORATIVE PLANTS, featured elsewhere in this book, that have flowers suitable for cutting

† = mainly suitable for drying

○[◐] sun (or partial shade)

minimum height 10ft/3m or more
Rosa "New Dawn," see p.130
Rosa "Roseraie de l'Haÿ," see p.343

minimum height between 3ft/90cm and 10ft/3m
Acanthus spinosus, see p.223
Lathyrus latifolius "White Pearl," see p.130

Philadelphus "Silberregen," see p.305
Philadelphus "Virginal," see p.99
Rosa "Blanche Double de Coubert," see p.142

minimum height 3ft/90cm or less
Anaphalis triplinervis, see p.194
Astrantia major "Sunningdale Variegated,"
  see p.169
Camassia leichtlinii subsp. *leichtlinii,* see p.43
Crocosmia x crocosmiiflora "Solfatare," see p.204
Crocosmia masoniorum, see p.224

Iris chrysographes black-flowered, see p.331
Iris x robusta "Gerald Darby," see p.69
Iris sibirica "Perry's Blue," see p.69
Iris sibirica "White Swirl," see p.69
Monarda "Cambridge Scarlet," see p.249
Monarda "Croftway Pink," see p.69
†*Plantago major* "Rubrifolia," see p.205
Reseda odorata, see p.305
Rudbeckia fulgida var. *sullivantii* "Goldsturm,"
  see p.343
Solidago "Goldenmosa," see p.44

Hydrangea paniculata
e.g. "Grandiflora"
[hydrangea]
○◐

type of plant: hardy shrub [4–9]
flowering time: late summer to mid-autumn
flower color: white changing to soft, pale pink
height: 8–10ft/2.4–3m
mainly Dr

When hard pruned each spring and grown in rich, loamy soil, this hydrangea can produce flower heads more than 12in/30cm long. These maintain their conical shape well when dried and, with careful conditioning, they can be used as fresh cut flowers, too. *H. paniculata* "Grandiflora" is vigorous. It quickly forms a substantial shrub with erect branches, which arch at their tips under the weight of the flowers, and broad, pointed, mid-green leaves. *H.p.* "Kyushu" is another popular cultivar; its flower heads are narrower and less dense than those of *H.p.* "Grandiflora," and it has glossy foliage. In a windy site, the flower heads of both these shrubs can become damaged.
also for: ■ Ornamental fruit ("seed" heads)

Clematis e.g. "Vyvyan Pennell"
○◐

type of plant: hardy climber [5–9]
flowering time: late spring to early summer
and late summer
flower color: lilac-blue
height: 7–10ft/2.1–3m

Since their flowers last so well, double-flowered clematis, such as the example shown here, are popular with flower arrangers. Their strikingly conspicuous blooms also make them interesting ingredients for growing in containers. *C.* "Vyvyan Pennell" produces fluffy, frilly flowers that are 4–6in/10–15cm wide early in the season; the later flowers (and some flowers on young plants) are single and of more violet coloring. The three-part leaves are rich green. To produce plenty of good-quality blooms, these double-flowered clematis need rich, moisture-retentive soil that is well drained. Their roots should be cool and shaded, while their top growth should be able to twine into a lighter position. Other popular, clematis with double flowers include white-flowered *C.* "Duchess of Edinburgh." For a clematis with small, double blooms, see p.134.
also for: ■ Climbing plants ■ Growing in containers

Kerria japonica "Pleniflora"
○◐

type of plant: hardy shrub [5–9]
flowering time: mid- to late spring
flower color: bright golden yellow
height: 6–10ft/1.8–3m

In almost any soil—fertile or poor, acid or alkaline—and in almost any site, this erect and suckering shrub produces an abundance of yellow "pompoms" on its numerous, bright green stems. Each of these double flowers is about 1¼in/3cm across. If the plant is pruned regularly after flowering, it makes plenty of new, green, twiggy growth that is conspicuous and attractive in winter. The leaves of K. japonica "Pleniflora" are veined, pointed, sharply toothed, and bright green. For a variegated form of K. japonica, see p.177.
also for: ■ Heavy, clay soils ■ Atmospheric pollution ■ Ornamental bark or twigs

Choisya ternata
[Mexican orange blossom]
○◐

type of plant: slightly tender/hardy shrub [7–9]
flowering time: mainly late spring to early summer; some flowers early to mid-autumn
flower color: white
height: 6–8ft/1.8–2.4m
Evergreen

The very sweetly fragrant flowers and the shiny, sharply aromatic foliage of this shrub look good in arrangements. Rich green, three-part leaves last exceptionally long in water and provide an excellent background for the clusters of pale, open-faced flowers, each of which is about 1in/2.5cm across. In a warm, sheltered site, C. ternata thrives in partial shade; in a cold garden, it needs a sunny position. Most reasonably moisture-retentive soils are suitable, although there is some yellowing of the leaves in very alkaline conditions. In warmer regions the plant grows well on heavy clays, but drainage needs to be good in colder places. In most gardens, this dense, rounded shrub grows quickly.
also for: ■ Heavy, clay soils (see above) ■ Decorative, green foliage ■ Aromatic foliage ■ Fragrant flowers

Thalictrum delavayi
(syn. T. dipterocarpum)
"Hewitt's Double"
[meadow rue]
○◐

type of plant: hardy perennial [5–9]
flowering time: midsummer to early autumn
flower color: rich mauve
height: 4–5ft/1.2–1.5m

This graceful plant produces little, double "pompoms" that are long-lasting and good for cutting. The flowers are each only ½in/1cm long, but they are carried in impressively large, airy, branched masses above clumps of ferny, mid-green foliage. The flower heads are largest when T. delavayi "Hewitt's Double" is grown in fertile soil that is both moist and well-drained. Unless a sheltered position has been chosen, the flowering stems usually need support.
also for: ■ Decorative, green foliage ■ Long, continuous flowering period

Deschampsia cespitosa
e.g. "Bronzeschleier"
(syn. D.c. Bronze Veil)
[tufted hair grass, tussock grass]
○◐

type of plant: hardy perennial (grass) [4–9]
flowering time: early to midsummer
flower color: pale silvery green ripening to bronze
height: 3–4ft/0.9–1.2m
Evergreen

Whether fresh or dried, these loose, curving flower heads, each 12in/30cm or more long, make lovely material for cutting. (When dried, the flowers are parchment-colored.) The flower stems are erect, rising above thin, dark green, arching leaves which form dense tussocks 18–24in/45–60cm high. D. cespitosa "Goldtau" (syn. Golden Dew) is a rather smaller plant with flower heads that ripen to a bright golden yellow. These grasses thrive in moisture-retentive soils that are acid to neutral.
also for: ■ Acid soils ■ Ground cover

Melica altissima "Atropurpurea"
[Siberian melick]
○◐

type of plant: hardy perennial (grass) [6–9]
flowering time: early to late summer
flower color: purple changing to rosy pink
height: 36in/90cm
mainly Dr

The erect then arching flower stems of M. altissima "Atropurpurea" are hung with numerous spikelets of rich purple. The one-sided flower heads, each 6–8in/15–20cm long, are good for cutting, and they dry particularly well. Low tufts of rather pale greenery are formed by the soft, slim leaves. This grass grows best in fertile, well-drained soil that retains moisture, but it is adaptable and can withstand short periods of drought.

Phlox paniculata
e.g. "White Admiral"
○ ◐

type of plant: hardy perennial [4–8]
flowering time: late summer to early autumn
flower color: white
height: 36in/90cm

This vigorous and usually healthy variety of border phlox bears large, domed heads of sweetly and spicily scented flowers. Individual blooms are at least 1in/2.5cm wide. Bright green, pointed leaves clothe the strong stems. *P. paniculata* "Mount Fuji" (syn. "Fujiyama") is another, widely available, rather later-flowering border phlox with white flowers. There are also numerous varieties with richly colored blooms. They include dark-leaved *P.p.* "Starfire" (illustrated below), *P.p.* "Prince of Orange" (salmon-orange flowers), and *P.p.* "Brigadier" (orange-tinted, deep pink flowers). *P.p.* "Eventide" is a popular lavender-mauve variety; for a particularly fragrant variety, see p.310. All these plants perform best in moist, fertile soil with good drainage. Grown in these conditions, mildew—to which these perennials are prone—is unlikely to be a significant problem. For a variegated border phlox, see p.173.
also for: ■ Fragrant flowers (particularly *P.p.* "White Admiral")

Phlox paniculata
e.g. "Starfire"
○ ◐

type of plant: hardy perennial [4–8]
flowering time: mid- to late summer
flower color: deep cerise-red
height: 30–36in/75–90cm

See preceding plant.

Francoa sonchifolia
[bridal wreath]
○ ◐

type of plant: slightly tender perennial [7–9]
flowering time: mid- to late summer
flower color: pink or white + red
height: 24–36in/60–90cm
Evergreen/Deciduous

In mild areas, the rich green, deeply lobed leaves of *F. sonchifolia* are evergreen. Elsewhere, the foliage is herbaceous, and if the plant is grown outdoors it needs a warm, sheltered site with some winter protection. The cup-shaped flowers, each ½in/1cm or so across, are long-lasting when cut. They are held, well clear of the rosettes of foliage, on unbranched stems that are usually upright but that may lean and curve—particularly if the plant is grown in some shade. Fertile, moisture-retentive soil with good drainage is most suitable for this plant.

Lilium "Enchantment"
[lily]
○ ◐

type of plant: hardy bulb [5–9]
flowering time: early summer
flower color: reddish orange
height: 24–36in/60–90cm

L. "Enchantment" is one of the easiest lilies to grow. It is healthy and vigorous, and it thrives—and increases—in most soils with good drainage. It grows particularly well in a position where its flowers are in sun and its roots are cool and shaded. As well as being a very good cut flower, it is suitable for naturalizing. Lustrous, upward-facing blooms, each 5–6in/12–15cm wide, are arranged in generous clusters on strong, upright stems. The stems are clothed in narrow leaves that are rich green and pointed. *L.* "Enchantment" is an Asiatic hybrid lily. Other popular lilies of this type include *L.* "Connecticut King" (yellow) and *L.* "Côte d"Azur" (deep rosy red); they, too, have upward-facing flowers.

Ranunculus acris "Flore Pleno"
[tall buttercup]
○◐

type of plant: hardy perennial [4–9]
flowering time: late spring to midsummer
flower color: yellow
height: 24–36in/60–90cm

The shiny little "buttons" that this well-behaved buttercup produces are densely petalled and long-lasting. They are carried on slender, wide-branching stems above lowish clumps of lobed and toothed, rich green leaves. Each flower is about ½in/1cm across. Most fertile, moisture-retentive soils are suitable, including those that are quite damp and heavy.
also for: ■ Heavy, clay soils ■ Damp and wet soils ■ Long, continuous flowering period

Iris "Holden Clough"
○◐

type of plant: hardy perennial [5–8]
flowering time: early to midsummer
flower color: soft yellow + purple-brown
height: 24–30in/60–75cm
Evergreen/Deciduous

So subtly colored are these flowers that they can easily get overlooked in a garden. But when cut and brought indoors, their delicate markings and moody coloring can be fully appreciated. Each elegant flower is about 3in/8cm across, and there are several blooms on every branched stem. The narrow, light green leaves are rather lax and often slightly taller than the flowers. In mild regions the foliage is evergreen. As long as they are fertile, most garden soils are suitable for *I.* "Holden Clough"; it thrives in damp and wet positions.
also for: ■ Damp and wet soils

Paeonia officinalis
e.g. "Rubra Plena"
[peony]
○◐

type of plant: hardy perennial [3–9]
flowering time: early summer
flower color: bright rich crimson
height: 24–30in/60–75cm

The large, fully double flowers of this plant look lavish and splendidly opulent in flower arrangements. Each bloom is 5–6in/12–15cm wide. In spring, the plant's emerging shoots are, briefly, deep red. They develop into handsome, rich green leaves that are divided into broad-fingered leaflets. The foliage remains decorative long after the flowers have faded. Deep, fertile, moisture-retentive soil is most suitable for this long-lived, clump-forming plant. Other varieties of *P. officinalis* are available but not widely so. They include *P.o.* "Rosea Plena," which has double flowers of rich mid-pink.
also for: ■ Decorative, green foliage

Astrantia major "Rubra"
[masterwort, Hattie's pincushion]
○◐

type of plant: hardy perennial [5–9]
flowering time: early to late summer
flower color: dusky wine-red
height: 24in/60cm
Dr

Just as good for cutting and drying as *A. maxima* (see p.292) and *A. major* itself (see p.326), this plant is distinguished by its rich, deep coloring. Its papery flowers, each ¼–1in/2–2.5cm across, are decorative and long-lasting both in the garden and when used in arrangements indoors. They also dry well. They are held on branched stems, above clumps of lobed and toothed, mid-green leaves. In the fertile, moisture-retentive soils it likes best, the plant makes good ground-cover. It self-sows. The seedlings vary considerably in flower color and usually include pale pinks as well as much darker shades. *A. major* "Ruby Wedding" and *A.* "Hadspen Blood" are two further examples of good, dark red varieties.
also for: ■ Damp and wet soils
■ Ground cover ■ Long, continuous flowering period

Astrantia maxima
[masterwort, Hattie's pincushion]
○◐

type of plant: hardy perennial [5–9]
flowering time: early to late summer
flower color: pink
height: 24in/60cm
Dr

Only when grown in well-drained, fertile soil that is at least reasonably moisture-retentive does *A. maxima* form a really dense, spreading clump of ground-covering growth. When flourishing, this attractive plant also produces large quantities of long-lasting, papery flowers in branching heads. These charming, fruitily colored flowers, each about 1½in/4cm across, are excellent for cutting and drying and its mid-green, tripartite, lobed leaves make a pleasing background for the flowers.
also for: ■ Damp and wet soils ■ Ground cover ■ Long, continuous flowering period

Physostegia virginiana
e.g. "Vivid"
[obedient plant]
○◐

type of plant: hardy perennial [4–8]
flowering time: late summer to early autumn
flower color: bright mauve-pink
height: 18–24in/45–60cm

The flowers of this variety of obedient plant may be compliant (in so far as each small bloom, on its own little hinged stalk, stays "put" in whatever position it has been turned to) but the roots are occasionally less biddable. With a reliable supply of moisture in summer and fertile soil, *P. virginiana* "Vivid" can spread quite rapidly into dense patches of upright stems and slender, mid-green leaves. However, these conditions also insure that there are plenty of flowers for cutting. The tubular blooms, each about 1in/2.5cm long, are closely packed into spike-like clusters. *P.v.* "Summer Snow" is white flowered. A variety with cream-edged leaves is shown on p.173.

Narcissus e.g. "Carlton"
(Large-cupped)
[daffodil]
○◐

type of plant: hardy bulb [4–9]
flowering time: mid-spring
flower color: yellow
height: 18in/45cm

Its large flower size (each bloom is about 3½in/9cm wide), its vigor and its reliability have all made this hybrid daffodil popular as a cut flower. It is also a good garden plant that is easily grown, and it flowers freely in most soils provided that they remain moist throughout spring. *N.* "Carlton" is suitable for naturalizing and a popular choice for mass planting—as is another, vigorous and reliable, Large-cupped daffodil, *N.* "Ice Follies," which bears white flowers. For a pink-cupped daffodil of this type, see below. All these plants have strap-shaped, usually grayish green, basal leaves.
also for: ■ Heavy, clay soils

Narcissus e.g. "Salome"
(Large-cupped)
[daffodil]
○◐

type of plant: hardy bulb [4–9]
flowering time: mid-spring
flower color: palest cream + peach
height: 15in/38cm

Pink-cupped daffodils with white or pale cream petals make pretty material for flower arrangements. As well as the variety illustrated here, there is also—for example—the very similarly colored *N.* "Passionale." Both varieties are easily grown in most soils that remain moist during the growing season. Both have large flowers (3½–4in/9–10cm wide) and strap-shaped, grayish green basal leaves. Richer-colored daffodils with contrasting cups include *N.* "Jetfire" (a Cyclamineus variety with golden yellow petals and bright orange cups; zones 6–9) and *N.* "Suzy" (a scented, primrose-yellow Jonquilla daffodil with orange cups; zones 4–9). *N.* "Salome" is listed under Trumpet daffodils in some catalogs.
also for: ■ Heavy, clay soils

Camassia quamash
(syn. *C. esculenta*)
[quamash]
○◐

type of plant: hardy bulb [5–10]
flowering time: late spring to early summer
flower color: pale blue or dark blue or white
height: 12–30in/30–75cm

The very large bulbs of *C. quamash* should, ideally, be planted in humus-rich soil that is reliably moisture-retentive. Both the height and the flower color of this plant vary considerably, but there are always numerous, elegantly star-shaped flowers, up to 2in/5cm across. These are arranged in spikes that rise above rather untidy tufts of long, thin, bright green leaves. The flowers are good for cutting. Plants often increase rapidly, and they are suitable for naturalizing in grass. They die down toward the end of summer. For a white-flowered camassia, see p.43.
also for: ■ Heavy, clay soils

Narcissus
e.g. "February Gold"
(Cyclamineus)
[daffodil]
○◑

type of plant: hardy bulb [6–9]
flowering time: early to mid-spring
flower color: yellow
height: 12in/30cm

Despite its name, this daffodil seldom flowers in late winter. However, it does start to flower very early in spring and it continues to produce its 3in/8cm-wide blooms for several weeks. Its backswept petals and elegantly elongated trumpets look attractive both in the garden and in flower arrangements. It is popular for mass planting. Other popular Cyclamineus daffodils include *N.* "February Silver" (which is a white-petalled, primrose-trumpeted version of *N.* "February Gold"), *N.* "Peeping Tom" (which has yellow flowers with exceptionally long, slim trumpets), and white-and-yellow flowered *N.* "Jack Snipe" (which is particularly good for naturalizing). All these plants are early-flowering and robust and all can be naturalized in grass. Although they grow in most soils, they prefer soil that is both well drained and moist. Their leaves rise from the base of the plant and are strap-shaped and often grayish green. For *N. cyclamineus* itself, see p.32.

Primula Polyanthus Group
e.g. Crescendo Series
[polyanthus]
○◑

type of plant: hardy perennial/biennial [6–9]
flowering time: early to late spring
(see description)
flower color: mixed—red, pink, yellow, blue, white + contrasting central zones
height: 12in/30cm
Semi-evergreen

Mixtures of polyanthus are often treated as biennials and grown from seed for spring bedding or to provide early-flowering plants for containers. When grown from seed, their flowering period depends on sowing times. Plants in *P.* Crescendo Series are winter-hardy. They grow best in moist, humus-rich, fertile soil. Their heads of stalked, 2in/5cm-wide flowers are richly and brightly colored, and they last well in water. They are held on fairly thick stems above veined, dark green leaves. Seed catalogs may list some separate colors, too. Blue-flowered *P.* Crescendo Series plants are often fragrant.

Narcissus e.g. "Rip van Winkle"
(syn. *N. minor* var. *pumilus*
"Plenus") (Double)
[daffodil]
○◑

type of plant: hardy bulb [4–9]
flowering time: early spring
flower color: green-tinged yellow
height: 8in/20cm

The quill-like petals of this little daffodil are of uneven length and this gives the 2in/5cm-wide flowers a certain informal charm. The leaves are strap-shaped and bluish green. *N.* "Rip van Winkle" is best when grown in cool, moist conditions, and it is suitable for naturalizing in grass. For a paler, Double daffodil which has fragrant flowers, see p.287. The flowers of both these varieties last well in water.

ADDITIONAL DECORATIVE PLANTS, featured elsewhere in this book, that have flowers suitable for cutting

† = mainly suitable for drying

○◑ sun or partial shade

A very few of the plants in the unillustrated section below will also grow in full shade, but in <u>such</u> conditions of very limited light they produce fewer flowers. For plants that flower satisfactorily in full shade see the ◑● "partial or full shade" sections on p.295.

minimum height 10ft/3m or more
Cornus mas, see p.318
Magnolia x *soulangeana*, see p.28
Magnolia x *soulangeana* "Lennei," see p.100

minimum height between 3ft/90cm and 10ft/3m
Chaenomeles speciosa "Nivalis," see p.101
Chaenomeles x *superba* "Knap Hill Scarlet," see p.345
Chaenomeles x *superba* "Pink Lady," see p.45

†*Dipsacus fullonum*, see p.259
Forsythia x *intermedia* "Lynwood Variety," see p.21
Forsythia ovata, see p.319
Garrya elliptica, see p.325
†*Hydrangea macrophylla* "Générale Vicomtesse de Vibraye," see p.30
†*Hydrangea macrophylla* "Madame Emile Mouillère," see p.150
Itea ilicifolia, see p.325
Jasminum nudiflorum, see p.318
Pieris japonica "Valley Rose," see p.30
Rosa "Danse du Feu," see p.134
Rosa Iceberg, see p.346

minimum height 3ft/90cm or less
Alchemilla mollis, see p.114
Astrantia major, see p.326
Euphorbia amygdaloides var. *robbiae*, see p.86
Euphorbia polychroma, see p.114
Heuchera cylindrica "Greenfinch, see p.326

†*Hydrangea* "Preziosa," see p.346
Iris graminea, see p.311
Jasminum nudiflorum, see p.318
†*Luzula nivea*, see p.31
Lysimachia clethroides, see p.73
Narcissus poeticus var. *recurvus*, see p.311
Nectaroscordum siculum, see p.325
Nicotiana "Lime Green," see p.326
Paeonia lactiflora "Festiva Maxima," see p.309
Paeonia lactiflora "Sarah Bernhardt," see p.309
Phlox maculata "Omega," see p.310
Phlox paniculata "Mother of Pearl," see p.310
Phlox paniculata "Norah Leigh," see p.173
†*Physalis alkekengi* var. *franchetii*, see p.260
Physostegia virginiana subsp. *speciosa* "Variegata," see p.173
Thalictrum aquilegiifolium, see p.195
Trollius chinensis "Golden Queen," see p.74
Trollius europaeus, see p.75
†*Typha minima*, see p.76

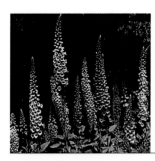

Digitalis purpurea
e.g. Excelsior Group
[common foxglove]
◐[○]

type of plant: hardy biennial [5–8]
flowering time: early to midsummer
flower color: mixed—purple, pink, white, cream
height: 5ft/1.5m

Some flower arrangers like the way the flowers of these particular foxgloves surround the stems of the plant, rather than hang from one side (as they do on *D. purpurea* itself and, for instance, its white-flowered form—for which, see p.48). Stout flower stalks rise from rosettes of large, pointed, deep green leaves, and are closely packed with almost horizontally held blooms, up to 3in/8cm long. Although easily grown in quite a wide range of soils and situations, these plants are at their best in a cool, shaded place and moist, humus-rich soil. *D.p.* "Sutton's Apricot" is another popular variety of common foxglove; it produces one-sided spikes of creamy apricot-pink flowers.
also for: ■ Heavy, clay soils

Aconitum e.g. "Ivorine"
[monkshood, aconite]
◐[○]

type of plant: hardy perennial [5–9]
flowering time: late spring to early summer
flower color: white or pale cream
height: 30–36in/75–90cm

As well as being denser and bushier than most of the dark blue- or purple-flowered monkshoods, this hybrid is also earlier-flowering. Its strong, upright flower stems rise just above clumps of deeply cut, dark green, lobed leaves. Slender, hooded flowers, each about 1in/2.5cm long, are arranged in narrow spires. To grow well, *A.* "Ivorine" needs moisture and fertile soil. It is only suitable for growing in full sun if it is planted in reliably moist soil; otherwise it may require watering. *A.* x *cammarum* "Bicolor" is another popular, pale-flowered monkshood; it produces its white-and-violet flowers from mid- to late summer. All parts of these plants are very poisonous and contact with their foliage can irritate skin.
also for: ■ Heavy, clay soils

Dicentra spectabilis "Alba"
[bleeding heart, lyre flower]
◐[○]

type of plant: hardy perennial [3–8]
flowering time: late spring to midsummer
flower color: white
height: 30in/75cm

With its arching sprays of heart-shaped flowers, this elegant plant is attractive both to gardeners and to flower arrangers. The little, dangling "lockets," each about 1in/2.5cm or so long, look especially graceful against the clumps of pale green foliage. Appearing early in spring, these lovely, ferny leaves have normally started to die back by midsummer. *D. spectabilis* "Alba" thrives in a cool, sheltered place and in moisture-retentive, open-textured soil that is fertile and not too alkaline. For *D. spectabilis* itself, see below.
also for: ■ Decorative, green foliage

Dicentra spectabilis
[bleeding heart, lyre flower]
◐[○]

type of plant: hardy perennial [3–8]
flowering time: late spring to early summer
flower color: pink + white
height: 24–30in/60–75cm

Just as attractive as its white-flowered variety (see above), *D. spectabilis* has equally graceful, arching sprays of flowers but, in its case, the dangling, heart-shaped "lockets" are of altogether brighter, sweeter coloring. The sprays, each about 9in/23cm long, are complemented by quantities of handsome, ferny, light green foliage. (Although the foliage appears early in spring, it has usually died down by midsummer.) *D. spectabilis* should be grown in a cool, sheltered site and in moist, humus-rich soil that has good drainage. Very alkaline soil is not suitable. The plant forms clumps of growth.
also for: ■ Decorative, green foliage

Digitalis x *mertonensis*
[foxglove]
◐[○]

type of plant: hardy perennial [5–9]
flowering time: early to midsummer
flower color: coppery rose
height: 24–30in/60–75cm
Evergreen

Luscious coloring and the large size of these foxglove flowers make them appealing to flower arrangers. *D.* x *mertonensis* is short-lived unless it is divided every year. Ideally, it should be grown in moist, well-drained soil, but it is tolerant of quite a wide range of soils and some sun. The flower stalks are sturdy and generously hung with pendent bells, each up to 2½in/6cm long. They rise from clumps of large, glossy leaves that are deep green and pointed.
also for: ■ Heavy, clay soils

Doronicum orientale
(syn. *D. caucasicum*)
"Magnificum"
[leopard's bane]
◐[○]

type of plant: hardy perennial [5–8]
flowering time: mid- to late spring
flower color: yellow
height: 18–24in/45–60cm

The yellow daisies of *Doronicum* bring a foretaste of summer to the spring garden. The particular variety illustrated here has flowers which are large—often up to 2in/5cm wide. They are inclined to fade in strong sun. *D. orientale* "Magnificum" is easy to grow, as long as it has moisture-retentive soil that is also well drained. (If it becomes too wet—in heavy soils and in regions of high rainfall, for instance—there may be root rot.) Flowering is often particularly good in areas with cool nights. The light green, heart-shaped leaves tend to die down in summer, especially in dry conditions.

x *Heucherella alba* "Rosalie"
◐[○]

type of plant: hardy perennial [4–8]
flowering time: late spring to midsummer (but see description)
flower color: pink
height: 12–15in/30–38cm
Evergreen

The light green, lobed leaves of this plant are heavily suffused with red-bronze along their veins when young and they often become bronzed again in autumn. They form clumps of ground-covering growth throughout the year. The main flowering season is noted left but, occasionally, more blooms appear as autumn approaches. Elongated sprays of tiny, bell-shaped flowers rise erectly above the foliage. They last well when cut. Each little bell is about ¼in/0.5cm long. To grow well and to flower freely, x *H. alba* "Rosalie" needs reliably moist, rather light soil with good drainage. It has a preference for neutral to slightly acid conditions. x *H.a.* "Bridget Bloom" produces pale pink flowers.
also for: ■ Ground cover ■ Variegated leaves (young leaves only) ■ Colorful, autumn foliage

ADDITIONAL DECORATIVE PLANTS, featured elsewhere in this book, that have flowers suitable for cutting

◐[○] **partial shade (or sun)**

minimum height between 3ft/90cm and 10ft/3m
Digitalis purpurea f. *albiflora*, see p.48
Enkianthus campanulatus, see p.243

minimum height 3ft/90cm or less
Aconitum "Bressingham Spire," see p.49
Gillenia trifoliata, see p.34

Helleborus argutifolius, see p.327
Helleborus foetidus, see p.82
Lilium speciosum var. *rubrum*, see p.33

◐ **partial shade**

minimum height between 3ft/90cm and 10ft/3m
Pieris floribunda, see p.49

Pieris "Forest Flame," see p.208

minimum height 3ft/90cm or less
Galanthus elwesii, see p.320
Galanthus nivalis, see p.320
Lunaria rediviva, see p.261

Polygonatum x *hybridum*
[David's harp, Solomon's seal]
◐●

type of plant: hardy perennial [4–9]
flowering time: late spring to early summer
flower color: white + green
height: 30–36in/75–90cm

This beautiful and accommodating, elegant plant grows anywhere there is sufficient shade. It is at its best, however, in cool, moist, humus-rich soil, where its gently arching stems form thickets of growth. Pointed, bright green leaves, 4in/10cm or more long, are poised almost horizontally on the stems. If sawfly have not decimated these leaves by late summer, then they and the stems turn butter-yellow in mid-autumn. From the undersides of the stems dangle modest but attractive, little flowers, each only about ¾in/2cm long. Flowers, leaves and stems all combine to make a graceful plant both indoors and outdoors. *P.* x *hybridum* "Striatum" (see p.180) has striped leaves.
also for: ■ Heavy, clay soils ■ Dry shade ■ Dense shade ■ Decorative, green foliage ■ Colorful, autumn foliage (see above)

ADDITIONAL DECORATIVE PLANTS, featured elsewhere in this book, that have flowers suitable for cutting

◐● **partial or full shade**

minimum height 90cm/3ft or less: *Convallaria majalis*, see p.314; *Helleborus foetidus*, see p.82; *Helleborus niger*, see p.321

PLANTS WITH

Fragrant flowers

AFTER LOOKING BRIEFLY at an unfamiliar flower, the next reaction of many people is to smell it, and to express some disappointment if it has no scent. Among familiar flowers, those that are sweetly perfumed enjoy a special popularity. The names alone of well-loved plants such as lily-of-the-valley (*Convallaria*), honeysuckle (*Lonicera*), and lilac (*Syringa*) are redolent of distinctive and delicious fragrances.

The range of floral scents is so large that there is surely a fragrance to suit every nose. There are flowers that give off invigorating, citrus-like smells, those that are warmly and spicily scented, and flowers that are richly and fruitily fragrant. Even among roses alone, there is a wide variety of scents, ranging from the exotically musk- and tea-scented to the lemon-fresh, with all sorts of clove, violet, and apple fragrances in between.

However, the perception of any particular scent does vary considerably from person to person. Not everyone agrees that, for example, *Cosmos atrosanguineus'* velvety blooms are chocolate-scented or that the flowers of pineapple broom (*Cytisus battandieri*) smell like pineapple. Privet (*Ligustrum*) flowers are generally regarded as having a rather unpleasant scent, yet a few people enjoy this and other unpopular smells. Some people find that certain flowers, such as those of the old pheasant's eye narcissus (*N. poeticus* var. *recurvus*) and of Japanese pittosporum (*P. tobira*), possess a fragrance that is so sweet and heavy that it is almost nauseating.

To maximize the perception of favorite fragrances, in cool climates particularly, it is worth giving plants fairly protected or enclosed sites in which scents can be "trapped" and thereby intensified. It is always important to place fragrant flowers where their scent can be easily enjoyed: beside a garden seat, near a window or doorway that is often left open during warm weather, or alongside a path that is used every day. Not many people linger in their garden in the coldest months, so the scented plants of winter—*Mahonia japonica*, *Sarcococca hookeriana* var.

humilis, and *Lonicera* x *purpusii* "Winter Beauty," for example—can all be appreciated if they are placed close to the house. Finally, plants with flowers that are at their most fragrant in the evening—many honeysuckles and ornamental tobacco plants (*Nicotiana*), for example—also need to be planted where it is easy to enjoy their fragrance late in the day.

Of the various plants featured in this list, relatively few have flowers that are richly or deeply colored. There are exceptions: for example, *Cosmos atrosanguineus*, *Heliotropium arborescens* "Marine," and *Iris graminea* in this list, and, elsewhere in the book, varieties of *Buddleja davidii*, such as "Royal Red," and the very dark-flowered lavender *Lavandula angustifolia* "Hidcote." However, the best sources of good scent combined with rich flower color are roses such as crimson-purple *Rosa* "Roseraie de l'Haÿ," red *R.* Fragrant Cloud, and rich cerise-pink *R.* Gertrude Jeykll.

The majority of scented blooms may lack deep color, but many plants with fragrant flowers have additional, decorative features. Several plants described below produce exceptionally good-looking, green foliage (examples include *Hosta* "Royal Standard" and *Mahonia japonica*), and the various lists featuring plants with variegated or unusually colored leaves also feature a number of fragrant plants, such as *Jasminum officinale* "Argenteovariegatum," *Buddleja davidii* "Harlequin," and *Philadelphus coronarius* "Aureus."

A few plants with fragrant flowers produce foliage that colors well during autumn (see, for example, *Fothergilla major* and *Rhododendron luteum*), and most lavenders, for example, have aromatic leaves as well as fragrant flowers.

As a considerable bonus, many flowers that are fragrant also last well when cut for indoor arrangements, and there are numerous plants in this list, from sweet peas (*Lathyrus*) and roses to lilacs and lilies (*Lilium*), that give at least as much pleasure indoors as outside.

Clematis rehderiana
○

type of plant: hardy climber [6–9]
flowering time: late summer to mid-autumn
flower color: pale yellow
height: 18–22ft/5.4–6.6m

The small but numerous, ¾in/2cm-long flowers of this very vigorous, twining clematis have a fresh, fruity fragrance. These bell-shaped blooms dangle prettily, in open clusters, and contrast pleasingly with the dense, fairly bright green mass of downy, veined leaflets. *C. rehderiana* is not particular about soil but it needs a warm position to flower really profusely. Other vigorous species of clematis with late-season, fragrant flowers include *C. flammula*; its profusion of small, white blooms has a sweet, rather heavy scent, reminiscent of the smell of hawthorn blossom. For the popular, very early-flowering *C. armandii*, see below.
also for: ■ Climbing plants

Acacia dealbata
[mimosa, silver wattle]
○ ✱

type of plant: half-hardy shrub [9–10]
flowering time: early to mid-spring
flower color: bright yellow
height: 15–25ft/4.5–7.5m
Evergreen

Where the necessary warmth and shelter can be provided, mimosa grows quickly into an upright, open shrub that spreads as it matures. In the warmest regions it grows very tall and tree-like. The full, sweet fragrance of its numerous, fluffy flowers is, perhaps, its main attraction, but its feathery, blue-green foliage is a source of additional, delicate beauty throughout the year. Spherical flowers, ¼in/0.5cm in diameter, are carried in generous clusters, 4–6in/10–15cm long. They are popular for cutting. Neutral to acid soil that is fertile and well drained is most suitable for this plant.
also for: ■ Acid soils ■ Gray, blue-gray, or silver leaves ■ Flowers suitable for cutting

Magnolia grandiflora
e.g. "Exmouth"
[bull bay, southern magnolia]
○

type of plant: hardy/slightly tender shrub/ tree [7–9]
flowering time: midsummer to mid-autumn
flower color: creamy white
height: 15–25ft/4.5–7.5m
Evergreen

This magnolia produces its sculptural, lemon-scented flowers from an early age. Individual blooms can be more than 8in/20cm across. The plant forms a dense pyramid of glossy, leathery, bright green foliage. Each leaf, gingery-felted beneath, is about 8in/20cm long. In cooler areas, *M. grandiflora* "Exmouth" is usually grown against a warm wall; in hotter climates, it needs no protection and forms a large tree. Tolerant of alkaline conditions and some dryness, the plant is at its best in deep, rich, moisture-retentive soil. *M.g* "Saint Mary" is compact; *M.g.* "Samuel Sommer" has very large flowers.
also for: ■ Atmospheric pollution ■ Decorative, green foliage ■ Flowers suitable for cutting ■ Long, continuous flowering period

Clematis armandii
○

type of plant: slightly tender climber [7–9]
flowering time: early to mid-spring
flower color: white
height: 15ft/4.5m
Evergreen

The vanilla-scented flowers on this vigorous clematis are carried in bold clusters among slender, leathery leaves. The foliage is bronze on first emerging and dark, glossy green when mature. Starry flowers, up to 2in/5cm wide, open from buds tinged with a soft "old rose" color. *C. armandii* climbs by means of twining leaf-stalks. It needs a sunny position and shelter, too—its brittle stems are liable to damage in a windy site. *C.* "Apple Blossom" is very similar; it has pink-tinged flowers that fade to white as they age. Both plants need well-drained but moisture-retentive soil. For a late-blooming, fragrant clematis, see above.
also for: ■ Climbing plants

Cytisus battandieri
[pineapple broom]
○

type of plant: slightly tender shrub [7–9]
flowering time: early to midsummer
flower color: yellow
height: 10–15ft/3–4.5m

As well as copious quantities of pineapple-scented flowers, this open, upright, fast-growing shrub produces very attractive foliage. The leaves, each composed of three, rounded leaflets, about 2½in/6cm long, are covered in silky, silvery hairs, giving a gray-green appearance overall. The flowers are arranged in dense, upright clusters. Most well-drained soils are suitable for *C. battandieri*, although it does not prosper on shallow soils that are chalky. It thrives in dry and infertile conditions. The protection of a sheltered wall is advisable in cooler regions. With age, the plant tends to become leggy and rather untidy.
also for: ■ Dry soils in hot, sunny sites ■ Gray, blue-gray, or silver leaves

Syringa vulgaris
e.g. "Katherine Havemeyer"
[common lilac, French lilac]
○

type of plant: hardy shrub [4–8]
flowering time: late spring to early summer
flower color: lavender-blue fading to mauve-pink
height: 10–12ft/3–3.6m

This lilac's exceptionally fragrant, double flowers are produced in broad, dense heads, each about 5in/12cm long. Individual blooms are purplish in bud. Like most varieties of common lilac, *S. vulgaris* "Katherine Havemeyer" has a rather limited flowering season. Each fresh green leaf is heart-shaped, smooth, and up to 4in/10cm long. Fertile, well-drained soils of most sorts are suitable for this robust, rather open and spreading shrub. It takes longer to become established on chalky clays. Single-flowered *S.v.* "Firmament" is often considered the bluest of the lilacs.
also for: ■ Shallow soils over chalk ■ Heavy, clay soils (see above) ■ Atmospheric pollution ■ Flowers suitable for cutting

Pittosporum tobira
[Japanese mock orange]
○

type of plant: slightly tender/half-hardy shrub [8–10]

flowering time: late spring to early summer

flower color: white turning to cream

height: 8–15ft/2.4–4.5m

Evergreen

P. tobira is usually a rounded, erectly branched shrub that thrives and may be very tall and tree-like in climates with warm winters; elsewhere, it needs a warm, sheltered site. It requires well-drained soil and tolerates periods of drought. Its glossy, deep green, leathery leaves withstand salt-laden winds, and *P. tobira* can be used for hedging in seaside and in warm gardens (plants should be about 30in/75cm apart). its clusters of bell-shaped, 1in/2.5cm-wide blooms are very sweetly scented. The leaves of *P.t.* "Variegatum" are irregularly edged and marked with creamy white.

also for: ■ Dry soils in hot, sunny sites ■ Windswept, seaside gardens ■ Decorative, green foliage ■ Growing in containers

Escallonia "Iveyi"
○

type of plant: slightly tender shrub [8–9]

flowering time: mid- to late summer

flower color: white

height: 8–10ft/2.4–3m

Evergreen

This escallonia's sweetly fragrant flowers are arranged in upright clusters. Each flower is bell-shaped and about ¾in/2cm across. The numerous blooms shine out against the rich dark green of glossy, rounded leaves. In cold weather the slightly aromatic and almost succulent foliage sometimes become bronze tinged. This dense and fairly upright plant is not fussy about soil, as long as it is reasonably well drained. *E.* "Iveyi" grows well in a coastal garden, but for an example of a particularly wind- and salt-resistant escallonia, see p.90. Escallonia flowers are attractive to butterflies.

also for: ■ Atmospheric pollution ■ Windswept, seaside gardens ■ Flowers suitable for cutting

Myrtus communis
[common myrtle]
○

type of plant: slightly tender/half-hardy shrub [8–9]

flowering time: midsummer to early autumn

flower color: white

height: 8–10ft/2.4–3m

Evergreen

Common myrtle is a dense, upright to rounded shrub with spicily aromatic foliage and an abundance of very sweetly scented, saucer-shaped, tufted flowers, each ¾in/2cm across. They are often followed by small, purple-black berries. The glossy, deep green foliage can be closely clipped for topiary and hedging (plants for hedging should be 18–24in/45–60cm apart). All well-drained soils are suitable. The plant needs a warm position and thrives in a seaside garden. For a smaller myrtle, see p.146. *M. communis* "Variegata" has gray-green leaves with creamy white edges.

also for: ■ Windswept, seaside gardens ■ Hedging plants ■ Growing in containers ■ Aromatic foliage ■ Ornamental fruit

Buddleja davidii
e.g. "White Profusion"
[butterfly bush, summer lilac]
○

type of plant: hardy shrub [6–9]

flowering time: mid- to late summer

flower color: white

height: 7–10ft/2.1–3m

As well as dark-colored varieties of *B. davidii* (for an example of which, see p.96), there are cultivars with pale flowers and they include the exceptionally free-flowering *B.d.* "White Profusion." All these plants grow quickly and have richly and sweetly scented flowers that are very attractive to butterflies. Their leaves are long and pointed and either mid-green or grayish green. All well-drained soils—including shallow, chalky soils—are suitable, and these shrubs tolerate fairly dry conditions. *B.d.* "White Profusion" creates a rounded mass of more or less erect growths. Its dense flower spikes may be up to 15in/38cm long.

also for: ■ Shallow soils over chalk ■ Atmospheric pollution

Buddleja "Lochinch"
○

type of plant: slightly tender shrub [7–9]

flowering time: late summer

flower color: lavender-blue

height: 7–9ft/2.1–2.7m

The very sweetly scented flower spikes on this fast-growing shrub are each about 8in/20cm long. They are carried at the tips of pale shoots and, compared to the flowers of *davidii* varieties (see above), they turn brown quite slowly. Most well-drained soils are suitable, but growth is especially good on deep, fertile soil. *B.* "Lochinch" produces branching growth on numerous, upright stems. As summer progresses, its gray-green, tapering leaves, each 6–8in/15–20cm long, become greener. The foliage of white-flowered *B. fallowiana* var. *alba* remains pale gray throughout the growing season. The flowers of both these plants are very attractive to butterflies.

also for: ■ Gray, blue-gray, or silver leaves (see above)

Carpenteria californica
○

type of plant: slightly tender shrub [8–9]

flowering time: early to midsummer

flower color: white + yellow

height: 6–8ft/1.8–2.4m

Evergreen

This shrub's gleaming, anemone-like flowers have a light, sweet fragrance. In the center of each lovely, 2½in/6cm-wide bloom is a haze of yellow stamens. In contrast to the pale flowers, the slender leaves are a rather somber, dark green. Growing quite loosely, the plant forms a rounded, bushy mass of growth on upright stems. Older specimens can become rather thin. Unless *C. californica* is given a really sheltered site, moderate to heavy frosts cause considerable superficial damage (although this is usually rectified quite quickly, once new growth starts). Good drainage is essential, but very dry soil is not suitable.

Lathyrus odoratus
e.g. "Noel Sutton"
[sweet pea]
○

type of plant: hardy annual climber [7–9]
flowering time: early summer to early autumn
flower color: mauve-tinged blue
height: 6–8ft/1.8–2.4m

The rich yet fresh fragrance of sweet peas is many people's favorite flower scent. Like most blue or blue-tinged sweet peas, *L. odoratus* "Noel Sutton" is very fragrant. This vigorous, tendrilled climber is a Spencer cultivar. These sweet peas carry four or five, 1½in/4cm-wide flowers on each long, strong stem. They are excellent for cutting and available in reds (including dark maroons like *L.o.* "Beaujolais"), pinks, creams, and whites (such as *L.o.* "White Leamington"), as well as blues and lavenders. All these plants need well-cultivated, fertile soil. Their foliage consists of pairs of pointed, oval leaflets. "Old-fashioned" sweet peas bear small, exceptionally fragrant flowers.
also for: ■ Climbing plants ■ Flowers suitable for cutting

Ozothamnus rosmarinifolius
(syn. *Helichrysum rosmarinifolium*)
○

type of plant: slightly tender/half-hardy shrub [9–10]
flowering time: early to midsummer
flower color: white (reddish rose in bud)
height: 6ft/1.8m
Evergreen

The pale, very upright stems of this free-flowering shrub are densely clothed in small, narrow, dark green leaves. ALthough the foliage is rosemary-like in appearance, it is not aromatic. However, the 1½in/4cm-wide clusters of crowded, daisy-like flowers smell sweetly of vanilla. These little flowers emerge from conspicuous, colorful buds. *O. rosmarinifolius* requires a warm, sheltered site and well-drained soil. The stems and young leaves of *O.r.* "Silver Jubilee" are pale silvery gray and the flowers are pinkish in bud. Even after flowering, these are both attractive plants with fine-textured foliage and almost white stems. They are excellent shrubs for gardens beside the sea.
also for: ■ Windswept, seaside gardens

Rosa e.g. "Fritz Nobis" (Shrub)
[rose]
○

type of plant: hardy shrub [5–9]
flowering time: early to midsummer
flower color: salmon-pink fading to pale pink
height: 5–6ft/1.5–1.8m

Numerous, beautifully scrolled buds on this rose open out into shapely, double blooms, 3in/8cm across. The flowers have a warm, clove-like fragrance and are followed by quantities of small, orange-red hips. *R.* "Fritz Nobis" is vigorous and bushy and often almost as wide as it is tall. It grows well in most soils but performs particularly well in moist, fertile, humus-rich soil. Its large, broad leaves—many are nearly 3in/8cm long—are leathery and a rich slightly grayish green. For another modern, pink rose with good scent and flowers of an "old rose" shape, see *R.* Gertrude Jekyll on the following page.
also for: ■ Ornamental fruit

Syringa pubescens subsp.
microphylla "Superba"
(syn. *S. microphylla* "Superba")
[lilac]   ○

type of plant: hardy shrub [6–8]
flowering time: late spring to early summer and early to mid-autumn/North America: late spring, with occasional repeats
flower color: rose-pink
height: 5–6ft/1.5–1.8m

Where varieties of common lilac (*S. vulgaris*) would be too large and have too short a flowering season, this lilac might be more suitable. Its sweetly fragrant blossom is attractive to butterflies and it is good for cutting. Rich pink buds open into tiny, tubular flowers that are carried in numerous, conical, slender-stemmed heads, to 5in/12cm long. The pointed leaves are deep green. This slow-growing, erectly branched shrub grows well in most reasonably well-drained, fertile soils, including chalky and clay soils. When used for informal hedging, plants should be about 24in/60cm apart.
also for: ■ Shallow soils over chalk ■ Heavy, clay soils ■ Hedging plants ■ Flowers suitable for cutting

Rosa e.g. "Madame Pierre Oger"
(Bourbon)
[rose]
○

type of plant: hardy shrub [5–10]
flowering time: mainly early to midsummer (see description)
flower color: pale silvery pink changing to rose-pink
height: 5ft/1.5m

The richly fragrant and voluptuously cup-shaped, double blooms of *R.* "Madame Pierre Oger" deepen in color when warmed by the sun. They are each about 2½in/6cm across and produced, in lavish clusters, early in the season and then, almost continuously but in smaller quantities, until early autumn. The slender, upright stems, which are clothed with light green, toothed and pointed leaves, are rather lax, and the plant grows loosely and openly. Moisture-retentive, well-drained, fertile soil gives the best results. Other popular Bourbon roses, all with excellent fragrance, include *R.* "Zéphirine Drouhin" (see p.307), white-flowered *R.* "Boule de Neige," and *R.* "Madame Isaac Pereire," which has large, crimson-pink flowers.

Romneya coulteri
[tree poppy, matilija poppy]
○

type of plant: slightly tender perennial/shrub [7–10]
flowering time: midsummer to early autumn
flower color: white + yellow
height: 4–6ft/1.2–1.8m

Bristly buds on this upright, often suckering subshrub open out into spectacular flowers, 5in/12cm or more across. The dazzlingly white, crinkled petals surround large, central domes of yellow stamens, and the flowers have a pronounced, sweet fragrance. The foliage is also attractive: bluish gray-green and deeply divided, with slender, pointed leaflets and lobes. Once established, in a suitably sunny site and well-drained soil, *R. coulteri* can spread invasively, by means of underground stems, and it needs careful positioning.
also for: ■ Gray, blue-gray, or silver leaves ■ Long, continuous flowering period

**Rosa e.g. Gertrude Jekyll =
"Ausbord" (Shrub)**
[rose]
○
type of plant: hardy shrub [5–9]
flowering time: early summer to mid-autumn
(see description)
flower color: rich cerise-pink
height: 4–5ft/1.2–1.5m

Little, rounded buds on this so-called English rose open out into 4in/10cm-wide, double blooms that are sweetly and spicily fragrant, and good for cutting. The main flush of flowers appears early in summer but some flowers are produced right through to mid-autumn. R. Gertrude Jekyll has a rather open habit of growth with strong, upright stems. It can be trained to grow as a short climber (6–8ft/1.8–2.4m high). The leaves are broad, pointed ovals of deep green. Pale pink R. Heritage is another fragrant shrub rose of this type, and see also p.270. Although these healthy plants can cope with poor soil, they grow best in well-cultivated, fertile, moisture-retentive soil.
also for: ■ Climbing plants (see above) ■ Flowers suitable for cutting

Lilium candidum
[Madonna lily]
○
type of plant: hardy bulb [5–9]
flowering time: midsummer
flower color: pure white
height: 3–5ft/0.9–1.5m

Madonna lily's erect buds—and there may be as many as fifteen on each dark, upright stem—open out into elegant, slender-petalled trumpets. These glistening white, 4in/10cm-wide blooms exude a delicious fragrance that is both sweet and fresh. Whorls of narrow, shiny leaves appear after the flowers. Unfortunately, Madonna lily is sometimes difficult to establish, and viral and fungal diseases may also pose problems. The plant needs good drainage, fertile soil and plenty of sunshine. It has a preference for alkaline soil and is suitable for hot, dry conditions.
also for: ■ Shallow soils over chalk ■ Dry soils in hot, sunny sites

**Clematis tubulosa "Wyevale"
(syn. C. heracleifolia var.
davidiana "Wyevale")**
○
type of plant: hardy perennial [4–9]
flowering time: late summer to early autumn
flower color: mid-blue
height: 36in/90cm

The 1¼in/3cm-wide flowers produced by this non-climbing clematis have a rich, heavy fragrance. They are arranged in dense clusters on stalks that are only a little taller than the main, leafy mass of the plant. Each flower has a tubular base that opens out into splayed, slightly crimped lobes. C. tubulosa "Wyevale" forms a rather open clump of herbaceous stems and numerous, fairly large (up to 6in/15cm long), three-lobed, light green leaves. If much of this foliage is stripped off, then the flowers make attractive material for cutting. There is some yellow autumn leaf color. Well-drained, fertile soil is most suitable for this plant, which usually needs support.
also for: ■ Flowers suitable for cutting

Crinum x powellii
○
type of plant: slightly tender/hardy bulb [7–10]
flowering time: late summer to mid-autumn
flower color: variable—pale pink to rose-pink
height: 36in/90cm
Semi-evergreen

By flowering time, the great, long, glistening leaves of C. x powellii form rather untidy masses of bright greenery. However, the trumpet-shaped blooms, up to 6in/15cm long, are so beautifully shaped and so sweetly fragrant that this shortcoming seems unimportant. There are up to ten of these spectacular, flared flowers on top of each thick stem. They open in succession over a long period. To perform really well, the plant needs a sheltered position in full sun and deep, fertile soil that remains moist during the growing season. C. x powellii "Album" has pure white flowers.
also for: ■ Long, continuous flowering period

Hedysarum coronarium
[French honeysuckle]
○
type of plant: hardy perennial/biennial [4–9]
flowering time: early to late summer
flower color: variable—purple-red to deep red
height: 36in/90cm

The glowing pea-flowers of French honeysuckle are borne on thick, branching stems and arranged in dense spikes. Not only are they very sweetly scented, with a clover-like fragrance, but they are also decorative over a long period. Each little pea-flower is about ¾in/2cm long, rich in nectar and therefore attractive to bees. The succulent leaflets, rounded and mid-green, are hairy beneath. The plant is normally a short-lived perennial; occasionally, it is biennial. Really well-drained soil produces the densest and most floriferous specimens, which cope admirably with infertile and shallow, alkaline soils.
also for: ■ Shallow soils over chalk ■ Flowers suitable for cutting ■ Long, continuous flowering period

**Rosa e.g. Fragrant Cloud =
"Tanellis" (Hybrid Tea or
Large-flowered)**
[rose]
○
type of plant: hardy shrub [6–9]
flowering time: early summer to mid-autumn
flower color: coral-red to geranium-red
height: 30–36in/75–90cm

The rich and exceptionally strong scent of R. Fragrant Cloud has insured its continued popularity, even though, in general, Hybrid Tea or Large-flowered roses are now rather out of favor. This well-branched, bushy plant blooms very freely, in a series of flushes, over a long season. The flowers, which are good for cutting, are neatly formed, double and about 4½in/11cm across. Those produced in autumn are often particularly fragrant. Black spot may sometimes mar the large, glossy, dark green leaves, but otherwise this is usually a healthy and vigorous plant. For plenty of flowers and disease-free growth, this rose should be given fertile, humus-rich, moisture-retentive soil.
also for: ■ Flowers suitable for cutting

Rosa Whisky Mac = "Tanky"
(Hybrid Tea or Large-flowered)
[rose]
○

type of plant: hardy shrub [6–9]
flowering time: early summer to mid-autumn
flower color: amber-yellow
height: 30–36in/75–90cm

The almost caramelized coloring of this free-flowering rose is best in cooler regions. Richly fragrant, double blooms, about 4in/10cm across, are produced in a series of flushes; they are excellent for cutting. Their lovely color is enhanced by plenty of dark green leaves that are tinged with bronze when young. Unfortunately, this prickly, rather open plant is prone to mildew. Growing it in humus-rich, moisture-retentive, fertile soil should insure that it is as healthy as possible and therefore less likely to become diseased. The Floribunda or Cluster-flowered *R.* Amber Queen is another modern, well-scented rose of approximately this coloring.
also for: ■ Atmospheric pollution ■ Flowers suitable for cutting

Saponaria officinalis
e.g. "Rosea Plena"
[soapwort]
○

type of plant: hardy perennial [4–8]
flowering time: late summer to early autumn
flower color: soft light pink
height: 24–30in/60–75cm

Since it is vigorous enough to become invasive, this prettily colored but rather untidy perennial is, perhaps, best suited to a wild or informal garden. Its sprays of long, slim buds open, in succession, into double or—as in the specimen shown here—semi-double flowers, ¾in/2cm across. These charming blooms have a delicious, light, sweet fragrance. The plant is easily grown in most soils with reasonable drainage. *S. officinalis* itself has variably colored, single flowers; it spreads and self-sows very freely. *S.o.* "Alba Plena" is double-flowered and white. All these plants have upright stems and smooth, pointed, rich green leaves. They form substantial patches of growth.

Cosmos atrosanguineus
○

type of plant: slightly tender/half-hardy tuber [8–10]
flowering time: midsummer to mid-autumn
flower color: deep maroon-crimson
height: 24in/60cm

Smelling deliciously—although not very strongly—of chocolate, these deeply colored, velvety flowers are produced over a long period. They are carried on long, clear stems, well above the low mound of rich green, pointed leaflets. Each saucer-shaped bloom is about 1½in/4cm across. *C. atrosanguineus* needs a sheltered site and moderately fertile, well-drained soil that retains moisture. In colder regions, it may be most convenient to treat the plant like a dahlia and to lift the tuberous roots and store them in a cool, frost-free place during winter.
also for: ■ Long, continuous flowering period

Mentzelia lindleyi
(syn. Bartonia aurea)
[blazing star]
○

type of plant: slightly tender/hardy annual [8–10]
flowering time: early summer to early autumn
flower color: golden yellow
height: 18–24in/45–60cm

In early evening the slender, pointed buds of this erect-stemmed plant open out into bright, shining flowers, each with a tuft of showy stamens. The flowers, 2½–3in/6–8cm across, exude a strong, sweet fragrance. They close during the following morning. Since they do not open in shady or overcast conditions, blazing star must have a position in full sun. Well-drained soils of all sorts, including sandy soils, are suitable; by the time it has reached flowering stage, this is a drought-tolerant plant. Narrow, dandelion-like leaves are mid-green to gray-green and often rather sparsely produced.
also for: ■ Dry soils in hot, sunny sites

Heliotropium arborescens
"Marine"
[cherry pie, heliotrope]
○

type of plant: grown as half-hardy annual [10–11]
flowering time: early to late summer
flower color: deep violet-blue
height: 18in/45cm

This bushy, spreading variety of *H. arborescens* has the characteristic, sweet and rich, "cherry pie" fragrance of the species, but its conspicuously wrinkled, pointed leaves are an especially dark green. The 4in/10cm-wide flower heads are made up of tiny, tubular flowers arranged in dense sprays. Some seed catalogs list the lower-growing *H.a.* "Mini Marine." These plants need well-drained, fertile soil that retains moisture. Their flowers are attractive to butterflies.
also for: ■ Decorative, green foliage

Lathyrus odoratus
e.g. Bijou Group
[sweet pea]
○

type of plant: hardy annual [7–9]
flowering time: early summer to early autumn
flower color: mixed—pink, salmon, red, mauve, blue, white
height: 12–15in/30–38cm

Bushy, non-climbing sweet peas, such as *L. odoratus* Bijou Group cultivars, usually need no support and are attractive for bedding and, for instance, for planting in a window box. Their flowers are about 1½in/4cm wide and arranged in clusters of three or four blooms per stem. The paler-colored flowers are fragrant. Sweet peas that are even lower-growing include *L.o.* Patio Group plants (which are about 12in/30cm high) and also *L.o.* Jet Set Group cultivars (which are about 36in/90cm high); both these Groups need some support, especially if they are to be used for cutting. Some of their flowers are fragrant. They all need fertile, well-drained soil. Their mid-green leaflets are arranged in pairs.

Erysimum cheiri
(syn. Cheiranthus cheiri)
"Harpur Crewe"
[wallflower]
○

type of plant: hardy perennial [7–10]
flowering time: late spring to midsummer
flower color: deep yellow
height: 12in/30cm
Evergreen

The semi-double to double flowers of this bushy perennial exude a rich, sweet scent. Arranged in short spikes, they open in succession over many weeks. Each little bloom is ¾in/2cm or so wide. In a sheltered site, flowering may begin quite early in spring. The plant is not especially long-lived, but its life is prolonged when it is grown in really well-drained, rather poor, and preferably alkaline soil. Its upright stems are clothed in narrow, grayish green leaves. Most other perennial wallflowers tend to be much less fragrant than E. cheiri "Harpur Crewe" (although recently developed E. "Walberton's Fragrant Sunshine" has good scent). For an example of the familiar, very fragrant, biennial wallflowers, see p.16.
also for: ■ Shallow soils over chalk ■ Long, continuous flowering period

Dianthus e.g. "Inchmery"
[carnation, pink]
○

type of plant: hardy perennial [4–8]
flowering time: early summer
flower color: pale pink fading to near white
height: 10–12in/25–30cm
Evergreen

The flowers of this old-fashioned pink are deliciously and heavily clove-scented. They are produced over a rather brief period—usually about two to three weeks—but their wonderful fragrance makes up for this shortcoming. Each gently colored, semi-double flower is about 1¼in/3cm across. Narrow, pointed leaves form a mound of neatly tufted, gray growth. Old-fashioned pinks thrive in full sun and really well-drained, preferably alkaline soil. They tolerate drought. Specialist suppliers list dozens of varieties of these plants, including some that have flowers with a deeper-colored "eye" and many very attractive "laced" varieties (laced pinks have petals edged in a contrasting color and an "eye" of that color, too). For another old-fashioned pink with excellent scent, see below.
also for: ■ Shallow soils over chalk ■ Dry soils in hot, sunny sites ■ Gray, blue-gray, or silver leaves ■ Flowers suitable for cutting

Narcissus
e.g. "Pipit" (Jonquilla)
[daffodil]
○

type of plant: hardy bulb [5–9]
flowering time: mid- to late spring
flower color: lemon-yellow + cream
height: 10–12in/25–30cm

As they age, the very sweetly, rather heavily scented flowers of N. "Pipit" lose most of their lemon-yellow coloring and become progressively creamier. Each stem carries two or three 3in/8cm-across blooms. The leaves are slender and bluish green. Other popular, scented daffodils of this type include the vigorous N. "Trevithian" (short-cupped flowers of soft lemon-yellow) and N. "Quail" (rich yellow blooms with larger trumpets). All these varieties do best in a sunny site and well-drained soil. They make attractive cut flowers.
also for: ■ Flowers suitable for cutting

Dianthus e.g. "Mrs Sinkins"
[carnation, pink]
○

type of plant: hardy perennial [5–8]
flowering time: early summer
flower color: creamy white
height: 9in/23cm
Evergreen

D. "Mrs Sinkins" is a mess but a much-loved mess. The flowers of this old-fashioned pink exude a wonderful, heavy, clove-like fragrance that, for many gardeners, more than compensates for the jumble of fringed petals, and for the flowering period of only two to three weeks. The flowers are double and up to 1½in/4cm across. The foliage consists of tufts of narrow, pale gray leaves. The plant thrives in really well-drained, preferably alkaline soil and full sun. It is drought-tolerant. Other richly fragrant, old-fashioned pinks include D. "Inchmery" (see above), D. "Dad's Favorite" (white with dark purple "eyes" and red-edged petals), and D. "Brympton Red" (deep crimson with deeper crimson edgings). Specialist suppliers list dozens more.
also for: ■ Shallow soils over chalk ■ Dry soils in hot, sunny sites ■ Gray, blue-gray, or silver leaves ■ Flowers suitable for cutting

Lilium formosanum var. pricei
[lily]
○

type of plant: hardy bulb [6–9]
flowering time: midsummer
flower color: white + purple
height: 8–12in/20–30cm

Considering how short their stems are, these flowers are very large as well as very fragrant. Each elegantly slim-tubed trumpet—striped and flushed plum-purple on the outside, glistening white inside—is about 6in/15cm long. There are between one and three flowers to each grassy-leaved stem, and their fragrance is full and sweet without being cloying. Although L. formosanum var. pricei is a good deal hardier than L. formosanum itself, it should be given a warm, sheltered site. Ideally, the base of the plant should be shaded. Neutral to acid soil that is moist and well drained is most suitable for this lily, which often increases quite quickly into sizable clumps.
also for: ■ Acid soils

Brachyscome iberidifolia
e.g. Blue Star
[Swan River daisy]
○

type of plant: half-hardy annual [9–11]
flowering time: early summer to early autumn
flower color: blue
height: 6–9in/15–23cm

In sunny weather, the finely cut, light green foliage of this well-branched plant is almost completely obscured by blue blooms; in prolonged periods of rain, there are far fewer flowers and the rather weak stems are easily damaged. Each daisy-like bloom is 1in/2.5cm or so across and has a delicate, sweet scent. Light, well-drained soil is most suitable for B. iberidifolia Blue Star and, to flower really well, it needs a warm, sheltered site in full sun. Swan River daisies are also available as mixtures that include flowers that are white, purple, and violet as well as blue.

Dianthus barbatus
e.g. "Indian Carpet"
[sweet William]
○

type of plant: grown as hardy biennial [6–9]
flowering time: late spring to early summer
flower color: mixed—crimson, red, pink, white + contrasting zones
height: 6–9in/15–23cm

Taller sweet Williams (for examples of which, see pp.279 and 330) make good cut flowers, but where a much lower-growing plant is needed—in a windy site, for instance—short-stemmed varieties such as D. barbatus "Indian Carpet" are preferable. The clove-scented flowers on these bushy, little plants are arranged in dense, slightly domed heads, about 2½in/6cm across. The stems are strong and upright and clothed in slender, pointed, mid-green leaves. All varieties of sweet William appreciate a sunny site and well-drained, slightly alkaline soil.

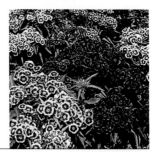

Nymphaea
e.g. "Odorata Sulphurea Grandiflora" (syn. N. "Sunrise")
[waterlily]
○

type of plant: hardy perennial (aquatic) [5–10]
flowering time: mid- to late summer
flower color: bright yellow
height: 4–6in/10–15cm

The elegant, many-petalled blooms of this waterlily are about 5in/12cm across and deliciously sweet-scented. They are raised slightly above the dark olive-green leaves, which are mottled with maroon and purple. Although N. "Odorata Sulphurea Grandiflora" is hardy, it flowers best in warmer regions. It should be planted in water 18–24in/45–60cm deep, with its roots in rich, loamy mud. This waterlily is moderately vigorous and spreads about 36in/90cm wide. N. "Marliacea Albida" is another readily available, sweetly scented waterlily; its 6in/15cm-wide flowers are white.
also for: ■ Variegated leaves

Jasminum officinale
[common jasmine]
○[◐]

type of plant: slightly tender climber [7–10]
flowering time: midsummer to early autumn
flower color: white
height: 30ft/9m
Deciduous/Semi-evergreen

Common jasmine's intensely sweet fragrance is one of the most popular of all scents; it is particularly strong and pervasive in the evening and at night. Trumpet-shaped flowers, about ¾in/2cm across, are carried in clusters at the ends of numerous, green stems. They are most profuse when this very vigorous, twining plant is allowed to grow freely in a warm, sheltered site. A warm position is especially important in cooler regions, where flowering can be disappointing (although the plants there usually produce copious amounts of deep green, tapering leaflets). All well-drained, reasonably fertile soils are suitable. For a variegated form of common jasmine, see p.168.
also for: ■ Atmospheric pollution ■ Climbing plants

Trachelospermum jasminoides
[Chinese jasmine, Confederate jasmine, star jasmine]
○[◐]

type of plant: slightly tender/half-hardy climber [8–9]
flowering time: mid- to late summer
flower color: white fading to cream
height: 20ft/6m
Evergreen

The starry flowers on this twining climber exude a rich, sweet fragrance that scents the surrounding air for a considerable distance. Plants need to be mature before they produce large quantities of the loosely clustered blooms, each about 1in/2.5cm across. The glossy, rich green, pointed leaves darken during summer and turn deep bronze and crimson in winter. *T. jasminoides* "Variegatum" has white-margined, gray-green leaves that become tinged with crimson and pink in cold weather. Both the species and its variety need warmth, shelter and well-drained, fertile soil to grow well. *T. asiaticum* is similar, though reputedly rather hardier than *T. jasminoides*.
also for: ■ Climbing plants ■ Colorful, autumn foliage (winter color, too)

Osmanthus delavayi
○[◐]

type of plant: slightly tender shrub [7–9]
flowering time: mid- to late spring
flower color: white
height: 6–9ft/1.8–2.7m
Evergreen

The small, but abundant and very sweetly scented flowers of this slow-growing shrub are arranged in bunches. Each trumpet-shaped bloom is about ½in/1cm long. Little, pointed leaves and stiff, arching stems eventually form a wide-spreading, dark grayish green mound. Given protection from cold winds, *O. delavayi* does well in almost any reasonably fertile soil, though it is not particularly long-lived on shallow, chalky soils. *O.* x *burkwoodii* is more tolerant of these conditions and also slightly hardier. Both these shrubs can be used for hedging (plants should be 18–24in/45–60cm apart).
also for: ■ Shallow soils over chalk (see above) ■ Atmospheric pollution ■ Hedging plants

Jasminum humile "Revolutum"
(syn. *J. reevesii*)
[jasmine]
○[◐]

type of plant: slightly tender shrub [8–10]
flowering time: late spring to early autumn
flower color: yellow
height: 6–8ft/1.8–2.4m
Semi-evergreen

This jasmine's clusters of starry flowers exude a very sweet, slightly heavy fragrance. There are about ten flowers to a cluster and each bloom is up to 1in/2.5cm across. Although flowering takes place over many months, at times there is no more than a substantial sprinkling of flowers. However, the yellow blooms are always conspicuous against the plant's bushy mass of bright green, tapering, slightly leathery leaflets. Most fertile, well-drained soils are suitable for this shrub, which grows very successfully on shallow, chalky soil. *J. humile* "Revolutum" flowers best in a warm, sheltered position.
also for: ■ Shallow soils over chalk ■ Atmospheric pollution ■ Long, continuous flowering period

Rosa e.g. "Frühlingsgold"
(Pimpinellifolia hybrid)
[rose]
○[◐]

type of plant: hardy shrub [4–9]
flowering time: late spring to early summer
flower color: creamy yellow
height: 6–8ft/1.8–2.4m

During its rather short flowering season, *R.* "Frühlingsgold" produces a mass of richly but freshly fragrant blooms on its long and gracefully arching stems. Each semi-double flower is about 4in/10cm across. Leaves are light green and slightly wrinkled. Most soils, including light soils, are suitable for this vigorous, healthy rose. It can be used for informal hedging (plants should be about 36in/90cm apart). Other roses with early, yellow blooms include single-flowered *R. xanthina* "Canary Bird" and double-flowered *R. banksiae* "Lutea" [zones 8–10]. Both plants are virtually scentless. Fragrant, yellow roses include climbing *R.* "Gloire de Dijon"; see also pp.269 and 301.
also for: ■ Hedging plants

Rosa e.g. "Penelope"
(Hybrid Musk)
[rose]
○[◐]

type of plant: hardy shrub [6–9]
flowering time: early summer to early autumn
flower color: creamy pink fading to cream
height: 6ft/1.8m

The sweet fragrance of this rose can be perceived some distance from the plant. Its semi-double flowers, up to 3½in/9cm across, are carried in large sprays. The main flowering season is midsummer. Little, pink hips ripen in autumn and remain decorative through winter. *R.* "Penelope" is rather bushier and more densely branched than many Hybrid Musk roses, and it can be used for hedging (plants should be about 36in/90cm apart). Its foliage is dark and slightly gray. Apricot-pink *R.* "Cornelia" is another popular Hybrid Musk; see also p.269. They all perform best in fertile, moisture-retentive soil.
also for: ■ Hedging plants ■ Ornamental fruit ■ Long, continuous flowering period

Ribes odoratum (syn. R. aureum)
[Buffalo currant, clove currant]
○[◐]

type of plant: hardy shrub [5–8]
flowering time: mid- to late spring
flower color: yellow
height: 5–6ft/1.5–1.8m

This prickle-free currant has an open, rather spreading habit of growth. Its little, tubular flowers, which have a clove-like fragrance, hang in clusters from the upright stems. Each cluster is about 2in/5cm long. As well as these scented flowers, this shrub has good autumn leaf color. Before they fall, the small, lobed and toothed leaves turn from bright, shiny green to rich shades of red and purple. In autumn, too, there are often purple-black berries and, though these are not particularly decorative, they are attractive to birds. Buffalo currant flowers more freely and grows more compactly in sun. Most soils are suitable, as long as they are reasonably moisture-retentive.
also for: ■ Colorful, autumn foliage

Philadelphus e.g. "Silberregen" (syn. P. Silver Showers)
[mock orange]
○[◐]

type of plant: hardy shrub [5–8]
flowering time: late spring to early summer
flower color: white
height: 4ft/1.2m

The arching growths of this upright plant create a dense, rounded mass of tapering, light green leaves and fragrant, cup-shaped flowers. Each of the numerous, strawberry-scented blooms is about 1½in/4cm across. The slightly taller P. "Avalanche" also has an arching habit of growth; its richly fragrant flowers are carried in clusters, whereas the flowers of P. "Silberregen" are borne singly. Neither of these plants is demanding, but they prefer well-drained, fertile soil and they are usually very successful on shallow, chalky soils.
also for: ■ Shallow soils over chalk ■ Atmospheric pollution ■ Flowers suitable for cutting

Lilium regale
[regal lily]
○[◐]

type of plant: hardy bulb [5–9]
flowering time: midsummer
flower color: white + pinkish purple
height: 3–5ft/0.9–1.5m

This is one of the easiest and one of the loveliest lilies. Its long, pinkish purple buds open to elegant, flared, yellow-throated trumpets that exude a rich and pervasive fragrance. The scent is especially pronounced in the evening. Each flower is 5–6in/12–15cm long, and there are, typically, between eight and twenty flowers to every stem. The erect to arching, dark stems are clothed in narrow, deep green leaves. Most well-drained soils are suitable, though extremely alkaline conditions should be avoided. L. regale "Album" has almost pure white flowers. Other popular lilies with very fragrant, trumpet-shaped flowers include L. Pink Perfection Group (rich purple-pink flowers) and L. African Queen Group (yellow or orange blooms).

Daphne x burkwoodii "Somerset"
○[◐]

type of plant: hardy shrub [5–8]
flowering time: late spring to early summer
flower color: rose-pink + pale pink
height: 3–4ft/0.9–1.2m
Semi-evergreen

Faster-growing than many daphnes, this vigorous plant has upright branches and is wider at the top than the base. It is free-flowering and blooms particularly profusely in sun, although in a sunny site it is especially important to provide consistently moist soil. D. x burkwoodii "Somerset" also needs good drainage. Fully open, the flowers, just over ¼in/0.5cm across, are starry and pale. They are arranged in thick clusters at the ends of the shoots. The mid-green leaves are small, neat and narrow with rounded ends. There are various cream- and yellow-variegated forms of D. x burkwoodii.

Reseda odorata
[mignonette]
○[◐]

type of plant: hardy annual [7–10]
flowering time: midsummer to early autumn
flower color: yellowish green + orange-brown
height: 18in/45cm

The open, cone-shaped heads of tiny flowers produced by this upright annual are not much to look at, but they have an intensely sweet fragrance reminiscent of crystallized violets. The flowers are attractive to bees. Some varieties have red-tinged flowers that are more colorful but less fragrant than those of R. odorata itself. Well-drained, fairly fertile soil is most suitable. Growth is not good on very acid soil. When cut, the flowers are exceptionally long-lasting and they retain their fragrance even when dried. The spoon-shaped leaves of R. odorata are bright mid-green, fleshy and each up to 4in/10cm long.
also for: ■ Flowers suitable for cutting

Matthiola longipetala subsp. bicornis (syn. M. bicornis)
[night-scented stock]
○[◐]

type of plant: hardy annual [7–10]
flowering time: mid- to late summer
flower color: lilac-pink
height: 12–15in/30–38cm

This untidy, small-flowered plant makes up for its inadequate appearance by being powerfully and deliciously scented. The flowers open only in the evening and at night, and on overcast days, when they release their rich fragrance. Slim-petalled flowers, each about ¾in/2cm across, are carried in little sprays on slender, branching stems. The leaves are long and narrow and gray-green. Night-scented stocks are easily grown in any well-drained soil, but have a preference for neutral to slightly alkaline conditions.

Hyacinthus orientalis
e.g. "City of Haarlem"
[hyacinth]
○[◐]

type of plant: hardy bulb [5–8]
flowering time: late spring
flower color: pale creamy yellow
height: 9in/23cm

The popular hyacinths used for spring bedding (and for growing in bowls indoors, too) have a pervasive, very rich, sweet fragrance. H. orientalis "City of Haarlem" makes a good garden plant. It is late-flowering; many other varieties flower in mid-spring. These widely grown hyacinths produce erect, stiff-stemmed, rather solid flower spikes in blue, pink, red, violet or white. Individual flowers, about 1in/2.5cm across, are usually bell-shaped. The leaves are strap-shaped and often bright green. Some bulb specialists also sell the less formal-looking Multiflora hyacinths; these plants have several stems per bulb and their fragrant flowers are loosely arranged. All these hyacinths are easily grown in most soils with reasonable drainage.

Matthiola
e.g. Cinderella Series
[stock]
○[◐]

type of plant: grown as hardy/half-hardy annual [7–10]
flowering time: late spring to early summer
flower color: mixed—red, pink, lavender-blue, yellow, purple, white
height: 8–10in/20–25cm

The numerous, richly and spicily fragrant, double flowers of these stocks are packed into dense, 6in/15cm-long spikes. These are carried on sturdy, branching stems clothed with grayish leaves that are slender and felted. Although the flowers last well in water, taller varieties of stock are more versatile for cutting (see, for example, the biennial mixture shown on p.287). M. Cinderella Series plants are so-called Ten Week stocks, which are always grown as annuals. Seed catalogs list tall- as well as lower-growing varieties of these plants, too. They all thrive in warm, sheltered sites and fairly fertile, moist but well-drained soil.

Primula veris
[cowslip]
○[◐]

type of plant: hardy perennial [5–8]
flowering time: mid- to late spring
flower color: variable—pale to rich yellow
height: 8–10in/20–25cm
Semi-evergreen

Cowslips have a very attractive and distinctive, clean, sweet fragrance. Little, nodding flowers—each about ¾in/2cm across—are arranged in one-sided clusters at the top of upright, often rather pale stems. The stems rise from tidy rosettes of crinkled, blunt-nosed leaves that are usually mid-green. This charming, very variable plant is at home in damp but well-drained, humus-rich soil. However, as long as conditions are consistently moist and there is at least reasonably good drainage, it will prosper. It is suitable for naturalizing in grass.
also for: ■ Damp and wet soils

Muscari armeniacum
[grape hyacinth]
○[◐]

type of plant: hardy bulb [6–9]
flowering time: mid-spring
flower color: bright mid-blue
height: 8in/20cm

M. armeniacum is very easy to grow in any soil that is at least fairly well drained. Indeed, the plant can increase so rapidly that it becomes a nuisance. It is suitable for naturalizing in short grass, where some of its vigor is curbed. When warmed by the sun, the dense, upright flower heads, to 3in/8cm long and composed of numerous, tubular flowers, give off a sweet, soft scent. Unfortunately, as the flowers open, the narrow, strap-shaped, mid-green leaves become straggly and rather unsightly. (Some of the foliage starts to appear in autumn.) The less readily available, yellow-flowered M. macrocarpum [zones 7–10] has a stronger, richer fragrance; it needs a warm, sheltered site and sharply drained soil.

Narcissus e.g. "Hawera"
(Triandrus)
[daffodil]
○[◐]

type of plant: hardy bulb [4–9]
flowering time: mid- to late spring
flower color: lemon-yellow
height: 8in/20cm

This popular little daffodil carries up to six very elegant, small-cupped, nodding blooms, about 1½in/4cm across, on each slender stem; every bulb produces several stems. The flowers are lightly and sweetly scented with a slightly fruity fragrance. They are accompanied by very slender, rich green leaves that are a good deal less obtrusive than the leaves of most hybrid daffodils. N. "Hawera" grows best in rich, well-drained soil in full sun. It is suitable for naturalizing. N. "Thalia" is another popular Triandrus daffodil, just over 12in/30cm high; its exceptionally graceful, white flowers are lightly scented.

Ipheion uniflorum
(syn. Tristagma uniflorum, Triteleia uniflora)
[spring starflower]
○[◐]

type of plant: slightly tender bulb [8–9]
flowering time: usually early to mid-spring
flower color: lilac-tinged white
height: 6in/15cm

When planted in a sunny site, spring starflower produces its lightly honey-scented flowers in particularly large numbers. The plant does well in partial shade, too—beneath a deciduous shrub or herbaceous perennial, for instance. Its slim, bright green and rather lax leaves smell of onions when bruised. In sunshine the slender-stemmed flowers spread open to a star shape and are about 1½in/4cm wide. Spring starflower needs fertile, well-drained soil that does not become too dry in summer. Readily available varieties of this plant include I. uniflorum "Charlotte Bishop" (lilac-pink flowers), I.u. "Froyle Mill" (rich violet), and I.u. "Wisley Blue" (lilac-blue).

Aponogeton distachyos
[Cape pondweed, water hawthorn]
○【◐

type of plant: slightly tender perennial
(aquatic) [8–10]
flowering time: late spring to mid-autumn
flower color: white fading to green
height: 3–4in/8–10cm

A. distachyos produces flowers that have a hawthorn-like fragrance, but theirs is a beautifully rich and sweet version of the hawthorn's scent, with none of its fishier overtones. The forked blooms, up to 4in/10cm long, consist of double rows of "petals" enclosing dark-tipped stamens. Full sun encourages the production of plenty of flowers. The bright green, almost lozenge-shaped leaves, which float on the surface of the water, are also attractive. *A. distachyos* is suitable for growing in still or very slow-moving water up to 30in/75cm deep. It is a vigorous plant and spreads to about 4ft/1.2m wide.

also for: ■ Decorative, green foliage ■ Long, continuous flowering period

ADDITIONAL PLANTS, featured elsewhere in this book, that have fragrant flowers

○【◐ sun (or partial shade)

minimum height 10ft/3m or more
Cordyline australis, see p.223
Jasminum officinale "Argenteovariegatum,"
    see p.168
Pittosporum tenuifolium,
    see p.222
Rosa "New Dawn," see p.130
Rosa "Wedding Day," see p.129
Tilia "Petiolaris," see p.98

minimum height between 3ft/90cm and 10ft/3m
Abeliophyllum distichum, see p.317
Corokia cotoneaster, see p.265
Elaeagnus pungens "Maculata," see p.169
Fothergilla major, see p.238
Galega officinalis, see p.343
Osmanthus heterophyllus "Goshiki," see p.169
Philadelphus "Virginal," see p.99
Rhododendron luteum, see p.238
Rosa "Blanche Double de Coubert," see p.142
Rosa "Roseraie de l'Haÿ," see p.343

minimum height 3ft/90cm or less
Dictamnus albus, see p.20
Dictamnus albus var. *purpureus,* see p.249
Malcolmia maritima Mixed, see p.157
Matthiola "Brompton Stocks Mixed," see p.287
Narcissus "Cheerfulness," see p.287
Narcissus "Geranium," see p.288
Philadelphus "Manteau d'Hermine," see p.19
Phlox carolina "Miss Lingard," see p.285
Phuopsis stylosa, see p.344
Rosa "Fru Dagmar Hastrup," see p.92

Lonicera japonica "Halliana"
[Japanese honeysuckle]
○◐

type of plant: hardy climber [5–9]
flowering time: midsummer to early autumn
flower color: white changing to buff-yellow
height: 25–30ft/7.5–9m
Evergreen/Semi-evergreen

This variety of Japanese honeysuckle is a very vigorous, twining plant that can be invasive. Although its tubular flowers, up to 1½in/4cm long, are not especially conspicuous among the bright green, pointed leaves, they have an intensely sweet fragrance that is strongest in the evening. When pegged down, the long, slender shoots root where they touch the soil and the plant forms a bushy carpet of ground-covering greenery (about 12in/30cm high). In moist, fertile, humus-rich soil and with its roots cool and shaded, this plant should not be troubled by aphids and mildew. *L. japonica* "Hall's Prolific" is especially free-flowering. For a less hardy, variegated form of Japanese honeysuckle, see p.171.

also for: ■ Ground cover ■ Climbing plants

Akebia quinata
[chocolate vine]
○◐

type of plant: hardy climber [5–9]
flowering time: mid- to late spring
flower color: maroon-purple
height: 20–30ft/6–9m
Semi-evergreen/Deciduous

The vanilla-scented flowers of this very vigorous climber hang among attractive, lobed foliage. Each cluster of blooms is made up several showy, 1in/2.5cm-wide female flowers and numerous paler, smaller male flowers. Strings of black-seeded fruits, shaped like sausages, appear regularly only in regions with long, hot summers. Slender, twining stems carry quantities of rounded, pale green leaflets, each about 2½in/6cm long. Most soils are suitable for this climber, as long as they are reasonably well drained and moisture-retentive. A sheltered site gives the flowers protection from damage by late frosts. *A. quinata* is suitable for growing into a tree.

also for: ■ Climbing plants ■ Decorative, green foliage

Rosa e.g. "Zéphirine Drouhin"
(Bourbon)
[rose]
○◐

type of plant: hardy shrub/climber [5–9]
flowering time: early summer to early autumn
flower color: cerise-pink fading to paler pink
height: 8–10ft/2.4–3m

These loosely double, 3in/8cm-wide blooms, which smell deliciously of ripe raspberries, are produced in particularly generous quantities early and late in the long flowering season. The plant's upright rather lax stems are virtually prickle-free and they are clothed in matt, light green leaves. *R.* "Zéphirine Drouhin" makes a good hedge (young plants should be about 36in/90cm apart) and it is an excellent climber for a north-facing wall. It can also be grown as a large, free-standing shrub (5–6ft/1.5–1.8m high x 6ft/1.8m wide) and, treated like this, mildew—which is sometimes a problem—is less likely to infect the plant. Although this rose tolerates poor soils, it is most floriferous in fertile, moisture-retentive soil.

also for: ■ Climbing plants ■ Hedging plants
■ Long, continuous flowering period

Viburnum x *carlcephalum*
○◐

type of plant: hardy shrub [5–8]
flowering time: late spring
flower color: white
height: 8–10ft/2.4–3m

This is one of a number of popular, fragrant, spring-flowering viburnums (for another example, see below). Its dense, domed flower clusters are exceptionally large (4–5in/10–12cm across). Shiny, soft pink buds open to numerous, trumpet-shaped flowers that exude a sweet, slightly spicy fragrance. The broad, dark green, 5in/12cm-long leaves often turn rich red and purple in autumn. This substantial, rounded, upright plant grows well in all moisture-retentive soils. Chalk soils are also suitable, as long as they are not too shallow and fast-draining. *V.* x *carlcephalum* may become rather leggy in maturity.
also for: ■ Heavy, clay soils ■ Colorful, autumn foliage

Azara serrata
○◐

type of plant: slightly tender shrub [8–10]
flowering time: early to midsummer
flower color: golden yellow
height: 8–12ft/2.4–3.6m
Evergreen

Especially when planted in a warm, sunny position, this dense, rather upright shrub produces numerous, pompom-like clusters of tiny flowers. Each little pompom is about ¼in/2cm across. The flowers have a sweet, slightly fruity scent. Although they are not as fragrant as the flowers of *A. microphylla* (see p.317), they are larger and much more conspicuous. Their rich coloring is enhanced by oval to rounded leaves that are a deep, glossy green. In cooler regions, *A. serrata* needs the protection of a warm, sheltered wall if it is to flower well. It is happy in any moist, humus-rich soil.

Viburnum x *burkwoodii*
○◐

type of plant: hardy shrub [5–8]
flowering time: mid- to late spring
flower color: white
height: 8ft/2.4m
Semi-evergreen/Deciduous

Although this broadly rounded plant grows well in a little shade, it is often given a sunny position to induce early flowering. Against a warm wall, *V.* x *burkwoodii* will exceed the height given here. Its pink-budded, tubular flowers have a full, sweet fragrance. They are carried in domed heads, about 3½in/9cm across, and are followed by clusters of small, black berries. Oval, pointed leaves, up to 4in/10cm long, are deep green and glossy. In autumn, the older leaves turn red and orange before falling. Almost any moisture-retentive soil is suitable. *V.* x *b.* "Anne Russell" is slightly lower-growing; it has very pale pink, dark-budded flowers.
also for: ■ Heavy, clay soils ■ Colorful, autumn foliage ■ Ornamental fruit

Clethra alnifolia
[sweet pepper bush]
○◐ ✳

type of plant: hardy shrub [4–9]
flowering time: late summer to early autumn
flower color: white
height: 6–8ft/1.8–2.4m

These flower spikes, 3–5in/8–12cm long, are spicily sweet-scented and attractive to bees and butterflies. Each spike consists of numerous, bowl-shaped flowers. The upright stems and brittle, twiggy growths of sweet pepper bush are clothed in pointed, deep green leaves that emerge late in spring. Autumn color comes late; it is usually clear yellow. Moisture—as well as acid soil—is essential for good growth. Provided conditions are moist enough, a sunny position is suitable, and sun encourages profuse flowering and good autumn color. *C. alnifolia* "Ruby Spice" has pink or pink-tinged blooms. Free-flowering *C.a.* "Hummingbird" is 3–4ft/0.9–1.2m high.
also for: ■ Acid soils ■ Damp and wet soils ■ Colorful, autumn foliage

Lonicera x *purpusii*
"Winter Beauty"
[shrubby honeysuckle]
○◐

type of plant: hardy shrub [5–9]
flowering time: midwinter to early spring
flower color: pale cream
height: 6–8ft/1.8–2.4m
Deciduous/Semi-evergreen

The bare, red-brown twigs of this shrubby honeysuckle carry dense clusters of ¼in/2cm-long, tubular flowers that exude an exceptionally sweet but fresh fragrance. The rounded, spreading mass of weaving twigs and dark to mid-green, pointed leaves is rather dull during the rest of the year. Although the flowers are reasonably weatherproof, a site with some shelter insures that the blooms remain undamaged by frosts or icy winds. This vigorous and floriferous plant can be grown in any well-drained soil. It is sometimes used for informal hedging (plants should be about 30in/75cm apart).
also for: ■ Hedging plants ■ Winter-flowering plants ■ Long, continuous flowering period

Nicotiana sylvestris
[tobacco plant]
○◐

type of plant: grown as half-hardy annual [9–10]
flowering time: late summer to early autumn
flower color: white
height: 5ft/1.5m

For sheer style, this towering annual takes some beating. Great, stout stems rise above rich green leaves, each of which may be more than 12in/30cm long. The exceptionally long-tubed flowers, clustered around the tops of the stems and drooping elegantly, exude a sweet, strong fragrance that is especially pronounced in the evening. The flowers, each about 4in/10cm long, close in full sun. *N. alata* (syn. *N. affinis*) is a lower-growing, fragrant, white-flowered tobacco plant (it is about 36in/90cm high). Both these plants need a warm, sheltered site and rich, moisture-retentive soil to do really well. In mild regions and with a dry, winter mulch to protect its roots, *N. sylvestris* is perennial.

Zenobia pulverulenta
○◐ ✳

type of plant: hardy shrub [6–9]
flowering time: early to midsummer
flower color: white
height: 4–6ft/1.2–1.8m
Deciduous/Semi-evergreen

These pendent, bell-shaped flowers, each only about ½in/1cm long, are distinctly aniseed-scented. They are carried in upright clusters on slender, almost wispy growths. When young, the plant is erect; as it matures, it becomes more arching and spreading. It tends to sucker. The immature leaves are covered with a blue-gray bloom, particularly on their undersides, that makes them appear bluish gray; they mature to rich mid-green. *Z. pulverulenta* needs humus-rich, acid soil that remains cool and moist in summer. In warmer regions some shade is advisable.
also for: ■ Acid soils

Rhododendron
e.g. "Daviesii"
[azalea]
○◐ ✳

type of plant: hardy shrub [5–9]
flowering time: late spring to early summer
flower color: pale yellow fading to cream
height: 4–5ft/1.2–1.5m

The graceful, long-tubed flowers of *R.* "Daviesii" are very sweetly scented. From buds tipped with soft pink, they unfurl to form flared trumpets about 2in/5cm across. They are arranged in loose clusters. The plant is upright and rather open with medium-sized, deep green, pointed leaves that take on rich tints of crimson, bronze and orange in autumn. *R.* "Daviesii" is normally classified as a Ghent azalea. These plants are noted for their pretty and often sweet-scented flowers. Other deciduous azaleas with fragrant flowers include pink-flowered *R.* "Irene Koster" [zones 6–9], and *R. luteum* (see p.238). Cool, moist, lime-free soil with good drainage is most suitable for all these plants.
also for: ■ Acid soils ■ Colorful, autumn foliage

Hesperis matronalis
[dame's violet, sweet rocket, wild phlox]
○◐

type of plant: hardy biennial/perennial [5–9]
flowering time: late spring to midsummer
flower color: lilac or purple or white
height: 36in/90cm

Although modest in appearance, this traditional, cottage garden plant is outstandingly fragrant. Branched heads of four-petalled, ¾in/2cm-wide flowers exude a rich, sweet perfume that has undertones of clove. The scent is most pronounced in the evening. *H. matronalis* is easily grown in any well-drained soil, though it has a preference for moist, neutral to alkaline conditions. This short-lived perennial is best treated as a biennial. Double-flowered forms of this plant last well when cut; they need moister, more fertile soil than the species. All these plants grow erectly. Their leaves are pale to mid-green and usually narrow, pointed and oval.
also for: ■ Shallow soils over chalk (species only)

Hosta "Royal Standard"
[plantain lily]
○◐

type of plant: hardy perennial [3–9]
flowering time: late summer to early autumn
flower color: white
height: 36in/90cm

In climates with cool summers, the sweetly scented flowers of this vigorous hosta may not be very freely produced. There are more flowers in a sunny position, and this is one of the best hostas for full sun—as long as the soil is reliably moist or damp (as well as fertile and, preferably, well drained). Its light green leaves, 8in/20cm long, are pointed, veined and puckered. They form a dense mound of weed-excluding growth, 24in/60cm high, 4ft/1.2m wide. Funnel-shaped flowers are arranged in long, one-sided spikes; they are most fragrant in the evening. *H. plantaginea* has exceptionally fragrant, white flowers; *H.* "Sugar and Cream" produces cream-edged leaves.
also for: ■ Damp and wet soils ■ Ground cover ■ Decorative, green foliage

Paeonia lactiflora
e.g. "Festiva Maxima"
[peony]
○◐

type of plant: hardy perennial [3–9]
flowering time: early summer
flower color: white
height: 36in/90cm

After a slow start, the herbaceous peonies make magnificent, very long-lived plants. They thrive when left undisturbed in deep, rich soil. The strong-stemmed, crimson-flecked flowers of *P.l.* "Festiva Maxima" have a sweet, fresh fragrance. These large, double blooms are 6–8in/15–20cm across. Leaf shoots emerge a deep, maroon-red in spring and soon expand into clumps of handsome, rich green growth. Each leaf is divided into elegant, pointed lobes. Like most double whites, *P.l.* "Festiva Maxima" lasts particularly well when cut (so too does *P.l.* "Duchesse de Nemours," another popular, double white that is fragrant). See also the following peony.
also for: ■ Decorative, green foliage ■ Flowers suitable for cutting

Paeonia lactiflora
e.g. "Sarah Bernhardt"
[peony]
○◐

type of plant: hardy perennial [3–9]
flowering time: early summer
flower color: pale pink
height: 36in/90cm

Most *P. lactiflora* varieties have fragrant flowers, especially the popular pale-flowered ones. The frilly, double blooms of *P.l.* "Sarah Bernhardt" are at least 8in/20cm across, and they exude a full, rich scent. They are excellent for cutting. This long-lived plant thrives in deep, rich soil, and dislikes being moved. Its rich green, lobed leaves are at first maroon-red. They form a clump of growth. A few varieties (for instance, the fragrant, single-flowered *P.l.* "White Wings") have foliage that becomes rich red and wine-purple in autumn. For another fragrant peony, see the preceding plant.
also for: ■ Decorative, green foliage ■ Flowers suitable for cutting

Phlox paniculata
e.g. "Mother of Pearl"
○◑

type of plant: hardy perennial [4–8]
flowering time: late summer to early autumn
flower color: pink-flushed white
height: 36in/90cm

Many modern varieties of *P. paniculata* are not nearly so well scented as the species. However, *P.p.* "Mother of Pearl" has a sweet, nutty fragrance that is pronounced and most attractive. The strong stems of this plant, which are clothed in mid-green, pointed leaves, support large, dense, domed heads of flowers. Each flower is 1¼in/3cm or more wide. Other readily available varieties of *P. paniculata* with good scent include *P.p.* "White Admiral" (see p.290) and lilac-flowered *P.p.* "Franz Schubert." The healthiest specimens of all these plants are grown in moist, fertile soil with good drainage. Some shade helps to conserve moisture on light soils.
also for: ■ Flowers suitable for cutting

Skimmia x confusa "Kew Green"
○◐●

type of plant: hardy shrub [7–9]
flowering time: early to mid-spring
flower color: greenish cream
height: 36in/90cm
Evergreen

Male skimmias do not produce berries but their flowers are very fragrant. Mound-forming, male *S. x confusa* "Kew Green" bears sweetly scented, starry flowers in dense trusses, up to 6in/15cm long. It flowers most freely in partial shade or sun. The rather sharply aromatic foliage is smooth and shiny. In bud, the flowers are pale green (the illustration shows *S. x c.* "Kew Green" in very early spring) and, at this stage, they look particularly pleasing with the rich bright green of the pointed leaves. Cool, moist, humus-rich soil with good drainage is most suitable for this skimmia. It does not grow well in very alkaline conditions. For a berrying skimmia, see p.260.
also for: ■ Atmospheric pollution ■ Ground cover ■ Growing in containers ■ Aromatic foliage

Daphne tangutica
○◑

type of plant: slightly tender shrub [7–9]
flowering time: mid- to late spring
flower color: rose-purple + palest pink
height: 30–36in/75–90cm
Evergreen

This neat shrub has stout, upright branches that are embellished with leathery leaves and dense clusters of richly fragrant flowers. It has a rather open and rounded habit of growth overall. The flowers, to ½in/1cm across, are purple in bud; when fully open they are pale and star-shaped, and conspicuous against the dark green of the narrow, pointed leaves.
D. tangutica thrives in fertile, humus-rich, moisture-retentive soil but, even in ideal conditions, it is slow-growing. Plants in *D.t.* Retusa Group are smaller and flower slightly later. *D. cneorum* is another small, fragrant daphne that is readily available; its pink flowers appear in spring, and the plant forms a spreading mound of growth about 9in/23cm high.

Phlox maculata
e.g. "Omega"
[meadow phlox]
○◑

type of plant: hardy perennial [4–8]
flowering time: mid- to late summer
flower color: white + lilac-purple
height: 30–36in/75–90cm

When fully expanded, the sweetly scented flower heads of meadow phlox varieties are slimmer, more cylindrical and less rotund than those of the *P. paniculata* cultivars (for an example of which, see above). The lilac-eyed blooms of *P. maculata* "Omega" are each about ¼in/2cm across. They are carried on strong, upright stems that are covered in smooth, pointed, rich green leaves. Although varieties of meadow phlox are not so prone to mildew as *paniculata* phlox, they still need soil that is consistently moist in order to perform well. Conditions should also be fertile and reasonably well drained, and some shade is beneficial on lighter soils. Other popular varieties of meadow phlox include the rose-pink *P. maculata* "Alpha" and the pink-and-white *P.m.* "Natascha."
also for: ■ Flowers suitable for cutting

Hemerocallis lilioasphodelus
(syn. H. flava)
[daylily]
○◑

type of plant: hardy perennial [3–9]
flowering time: early to midsummer
flower color: lemon-yellow
height: 30in/75cm
Semi-evergreen

The rather heavily scented flowers of this daylily are individually short-lived but plenty of flowers are produced in succession over several weeks, especially in not too shady a site. The elegantly trumpet-shaped blooms, each about 3½in/9cm wide, are carried on slender stems above a clump of narrow, arching, bright green leaves. *H.* "Marion Vaughn" is another daylily with shapely, lemon-yellow flowers that are sweetly fragrant. Both plants are easily grown in any moisture-retentive soil but they perform particularly well in fertile and damp conditions. They are suitable for ground cover.
also for: ■ Heavy, clay soils ■ Damp and wet soils ■ Ground cover ■ Decorative, green foliage

Narcissus poeticus var. recurvus
[old pheasant's eye]
○◑

type of plant: hardy bulb [4–8]
flowering time: late spring
flower color: white + yellow + red
height: 15in/38cm

The fragrance of old pheasant's eye is so rich that some people find it overwhelming, especially if the flowers are brought indoors. Outdoors, however, where some of the cloying undertones can be dispersed, the scent is usually perceived as wonderfully deep and spicy. Each graceful flower, with its back-swept petals and its "eye" of greenish yellow and red, is about 1½in/4cm across. Once established, this daffodil grows well in grass, although the closely related, larger-flowered, and more vigorous N. "Actaea" tends to be more successful; it, too, has richly fragrant flowers. Both plants do well in dry conditions in summer but need moisture in spring. Their leaves are narrow, grayish green and strap-shaped.
also for: ■ Flowers suitable for cutting (see above)

Tulipa sylvestris
[tulip]
○◑

type of plant: hardy bulb [5–9]
flowering time: mid-spring
flower color: yellow
height: 15in/38cm

Getting this graceful tulip established can be difficult sometimes but, once growing well, it may increase rapidly, spreading by underground stems. It can be grown in most well-drained soils, and it tolerates a certain amount of dryness in shade—beneath a deciduous shrub, for instance. It is suitable for naturalizing. In bud, the flowers are greenish and pendent, but when fully open they are erect. Each flower is about 2½in/6cm across and sweetly scented. T. sylvestris is not always free-flowering. Its leaves are pale bluish green and mostly slender.

Iris graminea
○◑

type of plant: hardy perennial [5–9]
flowering time: late spring to early summer
flower color: purple-violet
height: 2–18in/30–45cm foliage height; 9in/3cm flower height

The flowers of I. graminea, each to 3in/8cm across, emit a delicious, fruity scent reminiscent of newly cooked plums, which is why this plant is sometimes nicknamed the "plum tart iris." They nestle among narrow, pointed leaves that are erect to arching, and that form ground-covering clumps of glossy, bright green growth. This iris is easily grown in any reasonably moisture-retentive and well-drained soil. It dislikes being lifted and transplanted and so is best left undisturbed.
also for: ■ Ground cover ■ Flowers suitable for cutting

Nicotiana x sanderae
e.g. Domino Series
[tobacco plant]
○◑

type of plant: grown as half-hardy annual [8–10]
flowering time: midsummer to early autumn
flower color: mixed—red, pink, white, pale green, purple + bicolors
height: 12–15in/30–38cm

Although these five-pointed, tubular flowers are sweetly scented—most strongly so in the evening—they do not match species such as N. sylvestris (see p.308) for fragrance. The plants are, however, dense and bushy and considerably more weatherproof than some of the taller tobacco plants. Numerous, upward-tilted flowers, each 1–1½in/2.5–4cm wide, are open throughout the day. They are carried in clusters on erect stems. Both the stems and the mid-green, pointed or rounded leaves are hairy and sticky. Some seed catalogs also offer separate colors of N. x sanderae Domino Series plants: the white and pale green varieties tend to have the best scent, and N. x s. Domino Series "Salmon Pink" is popular. All these plants thrive in rich, moisture-retentive soil and a warm site.

Viola e.g. "Maggie Mott"
[violet]
○◑

type of plant: hardy perennial [5–8]
flowering time: late spring to late summer
flower color: pale mauve + cream
height: 6in/15cm
Evergreen

This bushy and vigorous violet, with its rounded, sweetly scented flowers (each nearly 2in/5cm across), has remained popular over many decades. Numerous blooms are produced over a period of many weeks, especially if V. "Maggie Mott" is cut back quite hard in midsummer, after the first flush of flowers, and if it is regularly dead-headed. The ideal growing conditions are a cool root run in soil that is fertile, moisture-retentive and well drained. V. "Columbine" (white flowers with violet-blue stripes) and V. "Rebecca" (ivory flowers edged and flecked with violet) are two further examples of free-flowering, fragrant hybrids. The rounded to pointed, toothed leaves of all these plants form tufts of mid-green growth.
also for: ■ Crevices in paving ■ Long, continuous flowering period

Lonicera periclymenum
e.g. "Serotina"
[common honeysuckle, woodbine]
◑[○]

type of plant: hardy climber [5–9]
flowering time: midsummer to early autumn
flower color: cream turning to yellow + red
or purple-red
height: 15–20ft/4.5–6m

Long, twining growths on this vigorous honeysuckle carry pointed, deep green leaves and clusters of tubular, 2in/5cm-long, lipped flowers. These flowers are very sweetly and spicily fragrant, especially in the evening. In cooler climates particularly, shiny crimson berries often ripen alongside the later flowers. *L. periclymenum* "Belgica" bears deep pink-and-yellow flowers in late spring and early summer; for a cream-colored variety, see p.344. All these plants need moisture-retentive, fertile soil and, ideally, a position where their roots are in shade and their upper growths receive more light.
also for: ■ Climbing plants ■ Ornamental fruit (see above) ■ Long, continuous flowering period

Mahonia japonica
◑[○]

type of plant: hardy shrub [7–9]
flowering time: late autumn to early spring
flower color: pale yellow
height: 6–8ft/1.8–2.4m
Evergreen

Many gardeners associate *M. japonica* with sprays of winter flowers exuding a lily-of-the-valley fragrance. However, its large whorls of rich green, gleaming foliage are also remarkable. *M. japonica* should be grown in moisture-retentive soil and it prefers a little shade. Some shelter from cold winds benefits both the cup-shaped flowers, each about ½in/1cm across, and the leaves, which are up to 18in/45cm long. In an exposed, sunny site, the spiny, usually oblong leaflets often turn red and bronze in winter. *M. japonica* forms a wide, spreading mass of stems and arching growths.
also for: ■ Atmospheric pollution ■ Decorative, green foliage ■ Winter-flowering ■ Long, continuous flowering period

Primula sikkimensis
[Himalayan cowslip]
◑[○]

type of plant: hardy perennial [5–8]
flowering time: late spring to early summer
flower color: variable—yellow or cream
height: 18–30in/45–75cm

When planted in really damp and wet soil that is humus-rich and, preferably, neutral to acid, Himalayan cowslip thrives. It produces clusters of sweetly scented, pendent, funnel-shaped blooms, each about 1in/2.5cm across, that are dusted inside with white powder. As the flowers fade and the seed ripens, the individual flower stalks become upright rather than pendent. The main flower stems rise from rosettes of light green, gleaming, wrinkled leaves, up to 12in/30cm long and variable in shape but always toothed. *P. alpicola* also has pendent blooms that are fragrant; it is about 12in/30cm tall and its flowers are white, cream, yellow or violet. It needs moist. well-drained soil.
also for: ■ Damp and wet soils

Arisaema candidissimum
◑[○]

type of plant: hardy/slightly tender tuber [7–9]
flowering time: early to midsummer
flower color: pink + pale green
height: 12–15in/30–38cm

The elegantly striped, deliciously sweet-scented flowers of *A. candidissimum* are, at first, unaccompanied by leaves. However, as the hooded flowers lengthen—usually to 4–5in/10–12cm—handsome, three-lobed leaves begin to expand. Each of the leaflets is broad and pointed. Sometimes, in late summer, spikes of poisonous, orange-red berries follow the flowers. Fertile, humus-rich, moisture-retentive soil with good drainage is most suitable for this plant, which seems to be most at home in a cool, woodland setting with some shelter.
also for: ■ Decorative, green foliage

Magnolia wilsonii
◐

type of plant: hardy shrub/tree [7–9]
flowering time: late spring to early summer
flower color: white + pink-purple
height: 20ft/6m

M. wilsonii forms a large, wide-spreading shrub or small tree. Its open network of branches creates a light canopy of growth. The pendent, cup-shaped flowers, 3–4in/5–8cm across, are beautifully fragrant, with a rich and fruity scent. There is a substantial and decorative boss of stamens in each flower. The leaves, when mature, are deep green, about 5in/12cm long and felted red-brown beneath. They are variably shaped but often quite slender. Although the plant is lime-tolerant, it needs soil that is moist and rich in humus; it is, therefore, not suitable for shallow, chalky conditions. It should be given a site sheltered from cold winds. For an evergreen magnolia with fragrant flowers, see p.297.

Rhododendron
e.g. "Loderi King George"
◐ ✳

type of plant: hardy/slightly tender shrub [7–9]
flowering time: late spring to early summer
flower color: pale pink changing to white
height: 10–15ft/3–4.5m
Evergreen

The huge flower trusses on this magnificent rhododendron are richly and sweetly fragrant, and they are borne in large numbers. Individual blooms can be more than 4in/10cm across. The leaves are large, pointed ovals of rich green. This vigorous, fairly open and spreading shrub needs a sheltered site—in light woodland, for instance—to protect it from the damaging effects of cold, dry winds. It also requires moist, well-drained, lime-free soil. Many of the most fragrant rhododendrons are a good deal less hardy than *R.* "Loderi King George." Some of the hardiest, most sweetly scented are to be found among the deciduous azaleas. For examples, see pp.238 and 309.
also for: ■ Acid soils

Cardiocrinum giganteum
[giant lily]
◐

type of plant: hardy/slightly tender bulb [7–9]
flowering time: mid- to late summer
flower color: white
height: 6–10ft/1.8–3m

The superb, maroon-throated flowers of this stately plant have a deep, sweet fragrance. They peer down from great, thick flower-stalks that rise erectly from basal rosettes of foliage. There are up to twenty magnificent trumpets, each 6–8in/15–20cm long, per stem. They are followed by big, smooth seed pods that ripen from light green to yellow. After flowering, *C. giganteum* dies but it produces quantities of seed and offset bulbs. It needs really fertile soil that both is well drained and moisture-retentive. The broad, dark green, glossy leaves can be 18in/45cm long.
also for: ■ Ornamental fruit (seed pods)

Corylopsis pauciflora
[buttercup winter hazel]
◐ ✳

type of plant: hardy shrub [6–8]
flowering time: early to mid-spring
flower color: pale yellow
height: 4–6ft/1.2–1.8m

C. pauciflora is a wide but graceful mass of spreading branches. Clustered all along the branches are pendent, bell-shaped flowers, each about 1in/2.5cm long, that appear before the leaves unfurl. They have a sweet, nutty fragrance (that not everyone can detect). The small, rounded leaves are, at first, pink-tinged; they mature to bright green. The plant needs a site that is sheltered from cold winds and frosts, and where it can remain cool during the summer months. A woodland setting is ideal. The soil should be fertile, moist but well drained, and acid to neutral.
also for: ■ Acid soils

Trillium luteum
(syn. *T. sessile* var. *luteum*)
[trinity flower, wood lily]
◐

type of plant: hardy perennial [4–9]
flowering time: mid- to late spring
flower color: variable—yellow to green-yellow
height: 12–15in/30–38cm

The upright flowers of this plant are stalkless and they "sit" directly on the marbled foliage. They are 2–3in/5–8cm long and sweetly and freshly fragrant. The mid-green leaves, perched on erect stems and attractively mottled with paler green markings, are usually very broad and sometimes almost circular. They die down during summer. *T. luteum* is most at home in moist, humus-rich soil that is, preferably, acid to neutral.
also for: ■ Variegated leaves

Hyacinthoides non-scripta
(syn. *Endymion non-scriptus*,
Scilla non-scripta, *S. nutans*)
[English bluebell]
◐

type of plant: hardy bulb [6–9]
flowering time: mid- to late spring
flower color: violet-blue
height: 9–15in/23–38cm

Ideally, English bluebells should be grown in fairly moist soil, but their presence near large, mature trees with extensive root systems shows their tolerance of quite dry conditions. On sunny days particularly, the pendent, bell-shaped flowers, to ¾in/2cm long, exude a soft, almost aromatic fragrance. The flowers are carried on nodding stems that rise above clumps of slim, glossy, rich green leaves. Some plants produce white or pink flowers. English bluebell is vigorous and can be invasive. Spanish bluebell (*H. hispanica*) is even more vigorous; its flowers are unscented and it hybridizes freely with English bluebell.
also for: ■ Dry shade

Cyclamen purpurascens
(syn. C. europaeum)
◑

type of plant: hardy tuber [6–9]
flowering time: mid- to late summer
flower color: variable—often carmine-pink
height: 3–4in/8–10cm

Among the cyclamen suitable for growing outdoors, this species is exceptionally fragrant. Its little, backswept flowers, no more than ¾in/2cm long, exude a strong, sweet scent. They are carried well above the rounded to heart-shaped leaves. Flowers and leaves appear at approximately the same time and the foliage persists through the winter months. The leaves, to 3in/8cm long, have attractive silvery green markings, although often only faintly so. Generally, *C. purpurascens* flowers profusely when given a lightly shaded, sheltered site and moist, well-drained, preferably alkaline soil. *C. repandum* [zones 7–9] flowers in spring; its pink-magenta blooms are sweetly fragrant.
also for: ■ Variegated leaves (see above)

Viola odorata
e.g. "Alba"
[sweet violet]
◑

type of plant: hardy perennial [6–9]
flowering time: mainly early to mid-spring
flower color: white
height: 3–4in/8–10cm
Semi-evergreen

As well as being sweetly scented, *V. odorata* and some of its varieties—including the example shown here—make good, small-scale ground cover. They form creeping, rooting carpets of tufted, fresh green foliage. Their leaves are conspicuously veined and generally heart- or kidney-shaped. The plants usually spread about 12in/30cm or so wide. Each charming, little flower is about ¾in/2cm across. *V. odorata* itself is also readily available; its fragrant flowers are violet-blue. There are also varieties with pink, purple, red, and lavender flowers. All these plants like a cool place and well-drained, humus-rich soil that remains moist in summer. In mild areas and a sheltered position, sweet violets may flower from the end of winter.
also for: ■ Ground cover ■ Crevices in paving

ADDITIONAL PLANTS, featured elsewhere in this book, that have fragrant flowers

◑ partial shade

minimum height between 3ft/90cm and 10ft/3m
Philadelphus coronarius "Aureus," see p.217

Philadelphus coronarius "Variegatus," see p.179

minimum height 3ft/90cm or less
Galanthus elwesii, see p.320

Galanthus nivalis, see p.320
Leucojum vernum, see p.50
Lunaria rediviva, see p.261
Smilacina racemosa, see p.231

Sarcococca hookeriana
var. humilis
[Christmas box, sweet box]
◑●[◯]

type of plant: hardy shrub [6–9]
height: 18–24in/45–60cm
Evergreen

The inconspicuous, white, tassel-like flowers of *S. hookeriana* var. *humilis* are only about ¼in/0.5cm long but their rich, vanilla fragrance is strong—and particularly welcome during mid- and late winter. They are followed by black berries. The plant is dense and suckering, although not invasive. Its upright stems and slender, pointed leaves slowly form spreading hummocks of tidy growth. Each glossy, dark green leaf is 2–3in/5–8cm long. All reasonably fertile soils are suitable, and the plant copes well with a variety of difficult circumstances, including dense shade and dry shade. If grown in sun, it needs moisture-retentive soil to prevent its foliage from becoming yellowish.
also for: ■ Shallow soils over chalk ■ Dry shade ■ Dense shade ■ Atmospheric pollution ■ Ground cover ■ Ornamental fruit ■ Winter-flowering plants

Convallaria majalis
[lily-of-the-valley]
◑●

type of plant: hardy perennial [4–9]
flowering time: late spring
flower color: white
height: 6–9in/15–23cm

When well established, lily-of-the-valley may become invasive and its creeping roots and shapely, pointed leaves may form large patches of dense growth. The foliage remains a rich fresh green over a long period, often right through autumn. Cool shade and moist, well-drained, humus-rich soil provide the ideal conditions, but this plant grows in almost any soil, and it tolerates both dry and dense shade. Bell-shaped flowers, to ½in/1cm across, are carried in arching sprays. They emit a sweet, clean fragrance. *C. majalis* var. *rosea* has pink flowers. The leaves of *C.m.* "Albostriata" are longitudinally striped in palest cream and bright green.
also for: ■ Dry shade ■ Dense shade ■ Ground cover ■ Decorative, green foliage ■ Flowers suitable for cutting

---

ADDITIONAL PLANTS, featured elsewhere in this book, that have fragrant flowers

◑● partial or full shade

minimum height between 3ft/90cm and 10ft/3m: *Sarcococca confusa*, see p.321

Winter-flowering plants

PERHAPS SURPRISINGLY, some of the most successful winter gardens have no winter-flowering plants. Many of these gardens rely on the natural or topiarized shapes of evergreens to create geometric drama in low, wintry light. Yet few gardeners are able to resist completely the pleasure of at least some flowers during the coldest months of the year.

The range of winter-flowering plants is quite large: in the following list there are trees, shrubs, perennials, bulbs, and tubers, and these plants vary in height, flower color, and the amount of sun or shade they need. However, even if a garden contained every one of the plants in this list, winter would not necessarily be a time of prolific blossom. Many of the plants that flower during winter, including, for example, winter jasmine (*Jasminum nudiflorum*) and laurustinus (*Viburnum tinus*), need the encouragement of a rise in temperature for there to be more than just a few blooms at any one time. Other plants such as heathers (*Erica*) and snowdrops (*Galanthus*) seem to keep on flowering bravely through remarkably chilly weather. A rise in temperature can, of course, be an artificial one, and picking winter flowers in bud and bringing them into the warmth of the house is one of the surest ways of enjoying winter flowers. Indoors, there is no danger of frosts or icy winds reducing potential blooms to sad, brown lumps.

Enjoying winter-flowering plants outdoors depends partly on careful positioning. Cold-weather blooms tend to be quite small, and they require either a contrasting background to make them really conspicuous or the presence of other flattering plants to highlight their decorative features and give them added impact. If fragrance is the main attraction of a winter-flowering plant, then it needs to be planted where its delicious scent is easily appreciated, and not where a special trip has to be made to savor its sweetness.

All winter-flowering plants have to contend with low temperatures, and, in an exposed garden particularly, some of them need the protection of a wall or of an evergreen hedge or screen to insure the production of plenty of undamaged blooms. In frost-prone areas, aspect is important. Positions in which frozen blooms thaw rapidly in the morning sun need to be avoided, since rapid thawing often destroys flowers completely. For this reason, plants grown in east-facing positions in the northern hemisphere are vulnerable.

The special charms and the relative rarity of winter flowers can make it all too tempting to choose lots of winter-flowering plants for the garden. However, especially where space is limited, it is important to think carefully about how these plants look during the rest of the year. Some of the shrubby honeysuckles, for example, have wonderfully fragrant winter flowers but their other attractions are few. On the other hand, many *Mahonia* produce strings of lovely, fragrant flowers in winter and they are bold, handsome foliage plants all the year round too, and witch hazels (various *Hamamelis*) have colorful autumn foliage as well as very attractively scented, winter flowers.

An alternative strategy, where space is limited, is to grow generous quantities of plants that complete their production of flowers and foliage early in the year and then rest, invisible above ground, during summer and autumn. Plants of this sort include most of the lovely early irises, as well as favorites such as winter aconites (*Eranthis hyemalis*) and snowdrops. Combined with, for example, polished bark, interestingly shaped twigs, good seedheads, or decorative foliage, these small plants can create garden pictures just as appealing, in their own quiet, midwinter way, as the lusher and more brilliant blooms of summer.

For additional winter interest, see also: "Plants with ornamental fruit," pp.252–61; "Plants with ornamental bark or twigs," pp.262–7; and all the lists of plants with decorative foliage (noting the evergreens).

Prunus x subhirtella
"Autumnalis"
[Higan cherry, rosebud cherry]
○

type of plant: hardy tree [5–9]
flowering time: late winter to early spring
flower color: white or pink-tinged white
height: 15–20ft/4.5–6m

Whenever the weather is mild during winter, the slender, spreading branches of this round-headed tree become decorated with clusters of semi-double flowers. Each pink-budded, bowl-shaped bloom is slightly almond-scented and about ¾in/2cm wide. Most of the blossom has faded by the time the tapering leaves appear. The foliage is deep green when mature, and in autumn it is predominantly yellow with some red. *P.* x *subhirtella* "Autumnalis Rosea" bears pink flowers, mainly from late winter. Most soils are suitable but well-drained, moisture-retentive ones of moderate fertility give the best results.
also for: ■ Atmospheric pollution ■ Colorful, autumn foliage ■ Flowers suitable for cutting

Clematis cirrhosa var. balearica
○

type of plant: slightly tender/hardy climber [7–9]
flowering time: late winter to early spring
flower color: cream + red-brown
height: 8–10ft/2.4–3m
Evergreen

The numerous, bell-shaped flowers on *C. cirrhosa* var. *balearica* are variably spotted within. The toothed leaflets are also small, and they are often bronze-tinged in cold weather. At other times they are a glossy, rich green. If the 2in/5cm-long flowers are brought indoors, their sweet, fresh fragrance becomes much more noticeable. To grow well, this vigorous, twining clematis needs a sheltered site in a sunny place (especially in cooler regions) and fertile soil that is well drained. The flowers of *C.c.* var. *purpurascens* "Freckles" are heavily speckled and they are larger than those of *C.c.* var. *balearica*.
also for: ■ Climbing plants ■ Fragrant flowers (see above)

Chimonanthus praecox
(syn. C. fragrans)
[wintersweet]
○

type of plant: hardy shrub [6–9]
flowering time: early to midwinter
flower color: pale yellow + purplish red
height: 7–10ft/2.1–3m

C. praecox makes an upright, twiggy shrub that flowers best and matures quickest when grown against a sheltered wall. Only plants that are several years old produce flowers in any quantity. The waxy-petalled blooms, about 1in/2.5cm wide, are rather like tiny tassels. They are deliciously scented—their fragrance being rich, sweet, and fruity. Large leaves, which are light green and willow-like, appear well after the flowering season is over. They are generally regarded as rather dull. Most soils are suitable for this shrub, as long as the drainage is reasonably good, and the plant does well in shallow, chalky soils.
also for: ■ Shallow soils over chalk ■ Fragrant flowers

Erica x darleyensis
e.g. "Silberschmelze"
(syn. E. x d. Molten Silver,
E. x d. "Silver Beads")
[heath]   ○

type of plant: hardy/slightly tender shrub [7–9]
flowering time: early winter to late spring
flower color: white
height: 12–18in/30–45cm
Evergreen

Most varieties of *E.* x *darleyensis* make good ground cover, with their bushy hummocks of rather upright growth, but the example shown here is particularly effective. Although some alkalinity is tolerated by these plants, they need soil that is moisture-retentive and well drained (and, ideally, acid to neutral). The tiny, tubular flowers produced by *E.* x *d.* "Silberschmelze" are arranged in 4in/10cm spikes. They are delicately honey-scented and very attractive to bees. The leaves are dark green and needle-like. For an example of a pink-flowered variety of *E.* x *darleyensis*, see p.106.
also for: ■ Acid soils ■ Ground cover ■ Fragrant flowers ■ Long, continuous flowering period

Iris unguicularis
(syn. I. stylosa)
○

type of plant: hardy perennial [7–9]
flowering time: mainly late winter to early spring
flower color: lavender-blue + white + yellow
height: 12–18in/30–45cm
Evergreen

The delicately marked flowers of *I. unguicularis* are 2–3in/5–8cm wide and lightly honeysuckle-scented. They are, perhaps, best appreciated indoors, where frost and wind cannot spoil them. Some flowers may open from late autumn onward, especially after a hot summer. *I.u.* "Mary Barnard" produces rich violet flowers; *I.u.* "Walter Butt" has very fragrant, pale violet blooms. Poor, preferably alkaline soil is most suitable for these irises, and they need really sharp drainage and plenty of sun to succeed. Their narrow, mid-green leaves form rather untidy clumps of growth that overtop the flowers.
also for: ■ Shallow soils over chalk ■ Dry soils in hot, sunny sites ■ Flowers suitable for cutting ■ Fragrant flowers

Iris "Harmony" (Reticulata)
○

type of plant: hardy bulb [4–8]
flowering time: late winter to early spring
flower color: rich sky-blue + royal blue + yellow
height: 6in/15cm at flowering time

I. "Harmony" is generally more robust than its relative, *I. reticulata* (see p.18), and its flowers, each 2–3in/5–8cm wide, are of a brighter color. However, these bright flowers lack the violet-like fragrance of *I. reticulata*. When given good drainage and full sun, *I.* "Harmony" is easy to grow. It has a preference for—but does not require—alkaline conditions. A dry summer period is generally beneficial and, in particular, it helps to insure that the bulbs do not dwindle away completely after a few years. The long, narrow, slightly gray, green leaves lengthen considerably after flowering is over, but they then die away quite quickly.
also for: ■ Shallow soils over chalk

Crocus chrysanthus
e.g. "Cream Beauty"
○

type of plant: hardy corm [4–9]
flowering time: late winter to early spring
flower color: rich cream
height: 3–4in/8–10cm

A warm, really sunny site encourages the flowers of this vigorous, little crocus to open early. Each long-tubed, globular bloom, about 1in/2.5cm across, has bright orange stigmas. The narrow, dark green leaves lengthen during and after flowering time. They are grass-like and have pale, central stripes. *C. chrysanthus* and its related varieties need good drainage. They thrive in dry soil in full sun. For a blue-flowered crocus of this type, see p.61.

also for: ■ Dry soils in hot, sunny sites

ADDITIONAL WINTER-FLOWERING PLANTS that are featured elsewhere in this book

○ **sun**

minimum height 10ft/3m or more
Alnus cordata, see p.40
Corylus maxima "Purpurea,"
see p.199

minimum height between 3ft/90cm and 10ft/3m
Daphne odora "Aureomarginata," see p.163

minimum height 3ft/90cm or less
Coronilla valentina subsp. *glauca* "Citrina,"
see p.335

Coronilla valentina subsp. *glauca* "Variegata,"
see p.164
Crocus chrysanthus "Blue Pearl," see p.61
Erica x darleyensis "Darley Dale," see p.106
Iris "Katharine Hodgkin," see p.18
Iris reticulata, see p.18

Abeliophyllum distichum
[white forsythia]
○[◖]

type of plant: hardy shrub [6–9]
flowering time: late winter to early spring
flower color: white
height: 4–6ft/1.2–1.8m

In cooler climates, this open and rather upright shrub usually flowers most freely either after hot summers or when it is grown against a warm, sunny wall; in warmer climates, white forsythia flowers well even when grown in a partially shaded site. The forsythia-like blossom is sweetly fragrant and carried on arching twigs. Each four-petalled flower is about ½in/1cm wide. Pointed, oval leaves do not emerge fully until after the flowers have faded. The mature foliage is dark green. Plants in the *A. distichum* Roseum Group produce pink flowers. Most soils with reasonable drainage are suitable for these plants.

also for: ■ Fragrant flowers

Erica carnea
e.g. "King George"
[heath, heather]
○[◖]

type of plant: hardy shrub [5–8]
flowering time: early to late winter
flower color: bright pink
height: 6–9in/15–23cm
Evergreen

The plant shown here is a particularly neat and early-flowering variety of *E. carnea*. Its tiny, dark green, linear leaves cover its spreading stems densely, and the plant soon forms a carpet of growth about 12in/30cm wide. The ¼in/0.5cm-long, bell-shaped flowers are freely borne at the ends of the little branches. Since it is so neat and flowers for such a long period, *E.c.* "King George" is a good choice for a container. Although *E. carnea* and its dozens of varieties tolerate mild alkalinity and very light shade, they prefer an open position and acid to neutral soil that is humus-rich and well drained. For further varieties of this heath, see pp.111 and 344. *E.c.* "Foxhollow" has yellow leaves that turn orange-red in cold weather.

also for: ■ Acid soils ■ Ground cover ■ Growing in containers
■ Long, continuous flowering period

ADDITIONAL WINTER-FLOWERING PLANTS that are featured elsewhere in this book

○[◖] **sun (or partial shade)**

minimum height 3ft/90cm or less: *Erica carnea* "Springwood White," see p.111; *Erica carnea* "Vivellii," see p.344

Azara microphylla
○◖

type of plant: slightly tender shrub [7–9]
flowering time: late winter to early spring
flower color: yellow
height: 12–15ft/3.6–4.5m
Evergreen

Except in warm gardens, this gracefully branched, rather upright and open plant needs the protection of a wall. In really mild areas it forms a tree about 25ft/7.5m high. Its clusters of tiny, tufted flowers are not very conspicuously displayed among the fans of foliage, but they have a delicious fragrance—a mixture of chocolate and vanilla scents. The leaves, too, are small, usually less than 1in/2.5cm long, and they create an airy, filigree pattern of glossy, dark green. *A. microphylla* is not particular about soil but it grows best in humus-rich, moisture-retentive conditions. *A.m.* "Variegata" is much slower-growing than the species; its leaves are edged in creamy white. *A. serrata* is shown on p.308.

also for: ■ Decorative, green foliage ■ Fragrant flowers

Cornus mas
[cornelian cherry]
○◐

type of plant: hardy shrub/tree [6–9]
flowering time: late winter
flower color: yellow
height: 10–15ft/3–4.5m

Tiny flowers in tufts less than 1in/2.5cm wide decorate the naked branches of this vigorous plant. In cooler areas, the bright red, edible, cherry-like fruits do not ripen reliably. *C. mas* is upright when young but, with age, it spreads to create a rounded mass of rather stiff growth. In warm regions, it may be up to 25ft/7.5m high and tree-like. The glossy, pointed, oval leaves take on bronze or purplish tints after a hot summer, particularly if the plant has been grown on light soil. *C.m.* "Variegata" is slower-growing; its leaves are white-edged. Most soils are suitable for these plants, which thrive on chalk.
also for: ■ Shallow soils over chalk ■ Colorful, autumn foliage (see above) ■ Ornamental fruit (see above) ■ Flowers suitable for cutting

Stachyurus praecox
○◐

type of plant: hardy shrub [6–9]
flowering time: late winter to early spring
flower color: pale greenish yellow
height: 10–12ft/3–3.6m

The catkin-like flower clusters of *S. praecox* hang from dark wine-red twigs. Each rigid, little tassel of bell-shaped blooms is 3in/8cm or more long, and the plant usually produces large numbers of flowers. Tapering, oval leaves, up to 6in/15cm long, expand after the flowers have faded. The foliage is often purple-tinged. When young, the plant is fairly upright but it becomes more arching and spreading as it matures. Most soils are suitable for this plant but those that are well-drained, moisture-retentive and, ideally, acid seem to give particularly good results. Although the flowers are remarkably frost-resistant, a position exposed to cold winds does not suit this plant.
also for: ■ Acid soils

Hamamelis x intermedia
e.g. "Pallida"
[witch hazel]
○◐

type of plant: hardy shrub/tree [5–9]
flowering time: mid- to late winter
flower color: yellow
height: 9–12ft/2.7–3.6m

This spreading, vase-shaped shrub or small tree produces masses of fragrant flowers on its bare branches. The remarkably weather-resistant, 1½in/4cm-wide clusters of spidery petals have a scent that is both sharp and sweet. In autumn, the large, almost circular leaves turn from bright green to rich yellow. The numerous witch hazel cultivars include some with orange or red flowers and good autumn leaf color (for example, *H. x intermedia* "Jelena" and *H. x i.* "Diane"). However, *H. x i.* "Pallida" and the smaller- and darker-flowered *H. mollis* have better fragrance. All these slow-growing plants are best in moist, neutral to acid soil with good drainage.
also for: ■ Acid soils ■ Colorful, autumn foliage ■ Fragrant flowers

Jasminum nudiflorum
[winter jasmine, hardy jasmine]
○◐●

type of plant: hardy shrub [7–10]
flowering time: early to late winter/North America late winter to early spring
flower color: yellow
height: 8–10ft/2.4–3m; 24in/60cm when grown unsupported

Winter jasmine is a cheering sight in winter. This reliable, very undemanding plant produces a profusion of 1in/2.5cm-long trumpets on its bright green, leafless shoots. The flowers appear in a series of flushes that coincide with mild spells; they can be cut often for arrangements since pruning encourages plenty of blooms the following year. Little, rich green, tripartite leaves appear after flowering. This scandent plant requires support to grow upright. Walls of all aspects—except those that face east—are suitable. Unsupported, the plant forms a spiky mass of rooting twigs, about 6ft/1.8m wide. Virtually any soil is suitable.
also for: ■ Ground cover ■ Climbing plants ■ Flowers suitable for cutting

Mahonia x media
e.g. "Charity"
○◐

type of plant: hardy/slightly tender shrub [7–9]
flowering time: late autumn to midwinter
flower color: yellow
height: 8–10ft/2.4–3m
Evergreen

The globular flowers of this plant are carried in 12in/30cm-long wands that are erect at first, then spreading. The flower stems rise from whorls of deep green, spiny leaflets. *M. x media* "Charity" is sweetly scented, but less strongly so than one of its parents, *M. japonica* (see p.312). Although quite a range of soils and sites are suitable for this stiff, upright plant, in cold areas it is best with some shade and shelter. In warmer regions, it can be given a sunny position. It enjoys moist, humus-rich, well-drained soil. Other varieties include *M. x media* "Winter Sun" (bright yellow flowers in arching spikes).
also for: ■ Atmospheric pollution ■ Decorative, green foliage ■ Fragrant flowers ■ Long, continuous flowering period

Viburnum tinus
[laurustinus]
○◐

type of plant: slightly tender shrub [7–10]
flowering time: late autumn to early spring
flower color: white
height: 8–10ft/2.4–3m
Evergreen

The pink-budded flowers of laurustinus open in large numbers whenever there is a mild spell. The five-petalled blooms are arranged in flattish heads about 4in/10cm across. Most moisture-retentive soils are suitable for this fast-growing, rounded shrub. Cold winds can scorch the fairly slender, dark green, pointed leaves, but in mild areas the plant may grow very large. It does well even in exposed, coastal gardens. It can be used for hedging (plants should be about 24in/60cm apart). Varieties of *V. tinus* include *V.t.* "Eve Price" (rich rose-pink buds) and *V.t.* "Variegatum" (for which, see p.172).
also for: ■ Heavy, clay soils ■ Windswept, seaside gardens ■ Atmospheric pollution ■ Hedging plants ■ Long, continuous flowering period

Viburnum x *bodnantense* "Dawn"
○ ◑

type of plant: hardy shrub [6–9]
flowering time: late autumn to early spring (see description)
flower color: pink fading to pinkish white
height: 6–8ft/1.8–2.4m

From rich pink buds, the tubular flowers of this popular shrub open out and form dense clusters about 3in/8cm wide. In very cold weather flowers that are still in bud remain closed, but they open and exude their sweet, heavy fragrance in warmer spells. The plant has an upright, somewhat gaunt habit of growth. Dark green, pointed, oval leaves begin to emerge as flowering finishes. Although this vigorous shrub does well on a wide range of soils, including shallow soils over chalk, it is best in fairly moist conditions. *V.* x *bodnantense* "Charles Lamont" has deeper pink flowers, while the those of *V.* x *b.* "Deben" are almost white.
also for: ■ Shallow soils over chalk ■ Heavy, clay soils ■ Fragrant flowers

Forsythia ovata
[early forsythia, Korean forsythia]
○ ◑

type of plant: hardy shrub [5–8]
flowering time: late winter to early spring
flower color: yellow
height: 4–5ft/1.2–1.5m

In the colder parts of the US, where varieties of *F.* x *intermedia* do not flower dependably, this hardier species can be relied on. *F. ovata* slowly makes a dense, rounded mass of grayish twigs. The flowers are small—about ½in/1cm wide—and short-petaled compared with those of *F.* x *intermedia* varieties. They are not always particularly numerous. The leaves are broad, pointed ovals of deep green. *F. ovata* "Tetragold" has larger flowers than the species, and it is more richly colored; *F.o.* "Ottawa" is especially hardy. Almost any soil is suitable for these tough, very easily grown plants.
also for: ■ Shallow soils over chalk ■ Heavy, clay soils ■ Atmospheric pollution ■ Flowers suitable for cutting

Rhododendron "Praecox"
(syn. *R.* x *praecox*)
○ ◑ ✱

type of plant: hardy/slightly tender shrub [7–9]
flowering time: late winter to early spring
flower color: rose-lilac
height: 4–5ft/1.2–1.5m
Evergreen/Semi-evergreen

Delicate, little clusters of blossom are liberally sprinkled over this bushy, twiggy, and rather open rhododendron. The early flowering season means that the 1½in/4cm-wide, open-faced flowers are susceptible to frost damage. A site that is sheltered—from cold winds in particular—is therefore necessary. The plant needs lime-free soil that is moist and well drained. Its small, dark leaves are glossy and pointed. They emit a refreshing scent when bruised. *R.* "Praecox" can be used for informal hedging (plants should be 24–36in/60–90cm apart).
also for: ■ Acid soils ■ Hedging plants ■ Aromatic foliage

Daphne mezereum
[mezereon, February daphne]
○ ◑

type of plant: hardy shrub [5–9]
flowering time: late winter to early spring
flower color: rich purple-pink or pink or purple-lilac
height: 3–4ft/0.9–1.2m

The stiff, upright branches of this slow-growing plant are closely set with clusters of ½in/1cm-wide, trumpet-shaped flowers. These richly and sweetly fragrant flowers open before the slender, pale green leaves expand; they are followed, in summer, by poisonous, red berries. *D. mezereum* f. *alba* has white blooms and yellow berries. Both plants do well in alkaline soil, but they resent dryness and grow best in deep, humus-rich soil. *D. bholua* "Jacqueline Postill" [zones 8–9] is another winter-flowering daphne with very fragrant flowers (the blooms are purple-pink and white, in this case); it is evergreen, vigorous, and very upright.
also for: ■ Ornamental fruit ■ Fragrant flowers

Viola e.g. Universal Series
[pansy]
○ ◑

type of plant: grown as hardy annual/biennial [6–9]
flowering time: early winter to late spring
flower color: mixed—red, yellow, white, blue, orange, purple + bicolors
height: 6–9in/15–23cm

At intervals throughout the winter months, these bushy, little plants open their rounded, 2–2½in/5–6cm flowers. Flowering is most profuse in mild spells and in the warmer weather of spring, and it can be prolonged by dead-heading, which also keeps the plants tidy. There is a wide range of colors in most mixtures. Some seedsmen offer winter-flowering pansies in separate colors. Fertile, well-drained soil that is rather dry seems to encourage the largest number of blooms. The leaves of these plants are mid-green, shallow-toothed, and approximately oval.

Scilla mischtschenkoana
(syn. *S.* "Tubergeniana")
○ ◑

type of plant: hardy bulb [6–9]
flowering time: late winter to early spring
flower color: pale blue
height: 4in/10cm

At close quarters, a tiny stripe of deeper blue can be seen on each of this plant's delicately colored petals. The ½in/1cm-long, bowl-shaped flowers begin to open almost as soon as the stems emerge from the ground. They are soon followed by slender, bright green leaves, and then both flower stems and leaves gradually elongate. A site that is sunny in winter but shaded in summer—beneath a deciduous shrub or tree, for instance—is ideal, as is moist but well-drained, fertile soil. However, this is an easily grown plant that can be naturalized in grass and that often self-sows.

ADDITIONAL WINTER-FLOWERING PLANTS that are featured elsewhere in this book

○◑ sun or partial shade

minimum height 10ft/3m or more
Parrotia persica,
   see p.241

minimum height between 3ft/90cm and 10ft/3m
Corylus avellana "Contorta," see p.267
Garrya elliptica, see p.325
Lonicera x purpusii "Winter Beauty," see p.308
Viburnum tinus "Variegatum," see p.172

minimum height 3ft/90cm or less
Crocus tommasinianus,
   see p.23
Jasminum nudiflorum,
   see p.318

Galanthus elwesii
[snowdrop]
◑

type of plant: hardy bulb [6–9]
flowering time: mid- to late winter
(see description)
flower color: white + green
height: 6–10in/15–25cm

G. elwesii resembles a larger and more substantial version of common snowdrop (see below). It has honey-scented flowers that are often 1in/2.5cm or more long, and its blue-gray, strap-shaped leaves are quite broad. The exact flowering season of G. elwesii is variable. Some forms may flower as early as Christmastime, while others may not begin to open until early spring.
G. "S. Arnott" is another, readily available, large-flowered snowdrop. It flowers late in winter or in early spring; it is vigorous and has a strong, sweet scent. Both plants like well-drained soil, and they seem to prosper in slightly drier conditions than common snowdrop. Specialist suppliers list dozens of different snowdrops for the enthusiast.
also for: ■ Flowers suitable for cutting ■ Fragrant flowers

Galanthus nivalis
[common snowdrop]
◑

type of plant: hardy bulb [4–9]
flowering time: mid- to late winter
flower color: white + green
height: 4–6in/10–15cm

Common snowdrop is the quintessential winter-flowering plant. Once established—beneath deciduous trees and shrubs, for instance—it can form large colonies. Bulb specialists' catalogs often list numerous varieties of G. nivalis, including the double-flowered G.n. f. pleniflorus "Flore Pleno." The attractively simple, single flowers of the species are ½–¾in/1–2cm long. Some of these snowdrops are more strongly honey-scented than others, although the fragrance is not always perceptible outdoors. Both the species and its varieties thrive in any cool, moisture-retentive soil, but they are especially good in humus-rich, open-textured soil. Their narrow, grayish leaves lengthen after the flowers have faded.
also for: ■ Heavy, clay soils ■ Flowers suitable for cutting ■ Fragrant flowers (see above)

Hepatica nobilis
(syn. Anemone hepatica,
H. triloba)
◑

type of plant: hardy perennial [5–8]
flowering time: usually late winter to mid-spring
flower color: usually mauve-blue (see description)
height: 4in/10cm
Semi-evergreen

The precise and dainty blooms of this little woodland plant are, on average, 1in/2.5cm wide. They have conspicuous tufts of white stamens. The flowers start to appear before the foliage has fully developed. Each leaf has three rounded lobes, and the plant forms a mound of fairly bright, mid-green foliage. Catalogs of specialists in rock-garden plants list varieties with white, pink, and deep purplish red flowers, as well as double-flowered forms and the more usual mauve-blue form. H. nobilis is most likely to thrive in well-drained, preferably neutral to alkaline, humus-rich soil and lightly shaded, woodland conditions. It takes a year or two to settle down after transplanting.

Cyclamen coum
◑[◯]

type of plant: hardy tuber [6–9]
flowering time: midwinter to early spring
flower color: pink or carmine-red or white
height: 3in/8cm

Both the flowers and the leaves of C. coum vary a good deal: shades—often bright—of pink and carmine-red are the most usual flower colors, while the glossy, rounded leaves are commonly dark green but they may be marked, to a greater or lesser extent, with pale silvery green. The ½in/1cm-long, backswept flowers appear at approximately the same time as the foliage. They are held, on red-brown stalks, well above the leaves. Humus-rich soil with good drainage, and a partially shaded position under deciduous trees or shrubs provide the ideal growing conditions for these cyclamen.
also for: ■ Variegated leaves (see above) ■ Decorative, green foliage (see above)

ADDITIONAL WINTER-FLOWERING PLANTS that are featured elsewhere in this book

◑[◯] partial shade (or sun)

minimum height between 3ft/90cm and 10ft/ 3m
Mahonia japonica, see p.312
Sarcococca confusa, see p.321

minimum height 90cm/3ft or less
Eranthis hyemalis, see p.49
Helleborus argutifolius, see p.327
Helleborus foetidus, see p.82
Sarcococca hookeriana var. humilis, see p.314

◑ partial shade

minimum height 3ft/90cm or less
Leucojum vernum,
   see p.50

Sarcococca confusa
[Christmas box, sweet box]
◐●◑

type of plant: hardy shrub [6–9]
height: 5–6ft/1.5–1.8m
Evergreen

More or less hidden among the leaves of this dense and bushy shrub are clusters of tiny flowers, which exude an intensely sweet fragrance. These creamy white, tassel-like inflorescences open from midwinter. They are followed by numerous, ¼in/0.5cm-wide, black berries that become shiny when fully ripe in late autumn and winter. The tapered leaves are glossy and bright green. *S. confusa* is at its best in a sheltered, shaded place and fertile, moisture-retentive soil. In shade, it tolerates dryness; in sun it needs moist soil. *S. hookeriana* var. *digyna* is similar but it suckers, is more open in habit of growth, and it is usually 4ft/1.2m high.
also for: ■ Shallow soils over chalk ■ Dry shade ■ Dense shade ■ Atmospheric pollution ■ Ornamental fruit ■ Fragrant flowers

Helleborus x hybridus
[hellebore]
◐●

type of plant: hardy perennial [5–9]
flowering time: late winter to mid-spring
flower color: pink or purple or pale green or pale purple or mixed
height: 15–18in/38–45cm
Evergreen/Semi-evergreen

H. x hybridus varies considerably in the color and shape of its flowers but most plants produce slightly cupped blooms that are 2–3in/5–8cm wide. Nurseries specializing in perennials usually sell selected color forms (for forms with very dark, almost black flowers, see p.332), as well as mixtures and some double-flowered variants. Although some of the richer colors may fade a little over time, the flowers of these plants remain decorative for many weeks. All these hybrid hellebores are easily grown in most soils that are reasonably fertile. They are at their best, however, in fertile, moisture-retentive, humus-rich soil and, when well suited, their deeply lobed leaves form thick, ground covering clumps of growth.
also for: ■ Dense shade ■ Ground cover ■ Long, continuous flowering period

Helleborus niger
[Christmas rose]
◐●

type of plant: hardy perennial [4–8]
flowering time: midwinter to early spring
flower color: white, sometimes pink-tinged
height: 12in/30cm
Evergreen

Christmas rose is much admired for the purity and simplicity of its flowers, but these do not always appear on 25 December. Each slightly pendent bloom is a shallow bowl, about 2in/5cm wide, with a thick, dark stem. Lance-shaped, rich green leaflets form a clump of leathery growth. This plant appreciates fertile, preferably neutral to alkaline soil that is both moist and well drained; shelter from cold winds is advisable. It can be difficult to establish, however. Cut flowers last longest if their stems are split lengthwise and then immersed in water for several hours before arranging.
also for: ■ Flowers suitable for cutting

Pulmonaria rubra "Redstart"
[lungwort]
◐●

type of plant: hardy perennial [5–8]
flowering time: midwinter to early spring
flower color: coral-pink
height: 12in/30cm
Evergreen

This cultivar is an especially early-flowering variety of *P. rubra*; other varieties and the species itself tend to start flowering in late winter. The ½in/1cm-wide, funnel-shaped blooms of *P.r.* "Redstart" are held in clusters above pointed, oval leaves. Although the clumps of light green, hairy foliage make good ground cover, the older leaves are inclined to look rather "tired" and untidy after the plant has flowered. Other popular varieties include pink-and-white flowered *P.r.* "Barfield Park," and *P.r.* "David Ward" (see p.181), which has variegated foliage. All these plants like cool, moist soil in shaded places.
also for: ■ Heavy, clay soils ■ Ground cover

ADDITIONAL WINTER-FLOWERING PLANTS that are featured elsewhere in this book

◐● **partial or full shade**

minimum height between 3ft/90cm and 10ft/3m
Jasminum nudiflorum, see p.318

minimum height 3ft/90cm or less
Helleborus foetidus, see p.82
Jasminum nudiflorum, see p.318

Pulmonaria rubra "David Ward," see p.181
Sarcococca hookeriana var. *humilis*, see p.314

Green flowers

GREEN FLOWERS ENJOY a special popularity. Their subtle shades make them easy to place in the garden, and they combine flatteringly with a wide range of other material in flower arrangements. One of the most useful of all plants for creating attractive combinations—indoors and outside—is lady's mantle (*Alchemilla mollis*). The foamy, yellowish green flower heads of this stylish but undemanding plant can be seen in thousands of gardens, where it seems to be the perfect companion for a multitude of other plants.

Although all the plants in the following list produce green flowers, there is quite a variety of shades: *Nicotiana* "Lime Green," for example, has flowers of a bright yellowish green, while the outer petals of *Fritillaria acmopetala*'s bell-shaped blooms are a very gentle, jade-green. Just how green some yellowish green flowers look depends, in part, on the color of surrounding materials. A background of "pure" yellow or of warm, orange-tinged yellow—either from flowers or foliage—heightens the greenness of flowers that are on the borderline of yellow and green.

Many plants in this list have subtly colored flowers, but this does not mean that most green flowers are dull and unobtrusive. Neither the midwinter catkins on silk-tassel bush (*Garrya elliptica*) nor the "pineapples" on pineapple flower (*Eucomis bicolor*) are a particularly conspicuous color, yet in shape and size they are outstanding. Even more striking perhaps are archangel's (*Angelica archangelica*) great domed clusters of tiny, green flowers and the large, cylindrical heads of yellow-green flowers produced by *Euphorbia characias* subsp. *wulfenii*.

Green flowers are, in a way, a compromise between flowers and foliage—being flowers in form, and foliage in color. While this makes them unusual and interesting, it also means that, in some multicolored mixtures of flowers and leaves, they have a tendency to merge with the foliage. This problem can be overcome either by using flowers of similarly subtle or pale colors—green-and-white partnerships are often particularly successful – or by using only green flowers and leaves. All-green combinations can be very elegant and, in the garden especially, they create a serene and sophisticated atmosphere. In these monochrome plantings and arrangements, where there are no distracting "extra" colors, the eye is concentrated on differences in form and texture that are so easily overlooked in multicolored compositions.

The range of flowers that are both decorative and green is not large, but it can be expanded if some flowers that are only temporarily green are admitted. Certain *Sedum*, such as *S.* "Herbstfreude" and *S. spectabile* "Iceberg," are striking even when their wide flower heads are still pale green, and the large, bell-shaped flowers of cup and saucer vine (*Cobaea scandens*) are very decorative in their greenish white, immature state. In addition, the flowering panicles of many grasses are almost as attractive when they are green as when they ripen to more mellow hues. Later in the gardening year, the fading blooms of some varieties of *Hydrangea macrophylla* become distinctly green-tinged during autumn (see *H.m.* "Générale Vicomtesse de Vibraye" and *H.m.* "Madame Emile Mouillère," for example).

For gardeners who become smitten with green flowers, there are various less readily available plants to track down. Some suppliers specialize in the more unusual stock plants such as *Veratrum viride*, a stylish perennial with pale green flower spikes and beautifully pleated foliage, and *Ribes laurifolium*, a flowering currant that produces hanging clusters of pale green flowers in late winter and early spring. Some rose specialists list the green rose (*Rosa* x *odorata* "Viridiflora") and, although they do not look at ease in most mixed plantings, florists' gladioli, such as the yellowish green *Gladiolus* "Green Woodpecker," can be obtained from bulb suppliers.

Kniphofia
e.g. "Percy's Pride"
[red hot poker, torch flower]
○

type of plant: hardy perennial [6–9]
flowering time: late summer to early autumn
flower color: yellow-green becoming yellower
height: 3½–4ft/1.05–1.20m

As well as the familiar bicolored red hot pokers, there are single-colored varieties with flower heads of red, orange, cream, or—as here—yellow-green. The dense flower spikes produced by K. "Percy's Pride" are each about 8in/20cm long and they rise, on thick, upright stems, above clumps of slender, bluish green, arching leaves. K. "Green Jade" is another readily available variety with green flowers; it is evergreen and a little taller than "Percy's Pride." Kniphofia hybrids need well-drained soil that remains moist during summer. In very cold areas, the roots of these plants should be given the protection of a heavy mulch during winter.

Amaranthus caudatus var. viridis
[love-lies-bleeding, tassel flower]
○

type of plant: half-hardy annual [10–11]
flowering time: midsummer to early autumn
flower color: pale green fading to cream
height: 3–4ft/0.9–1.2m

The thick, drooping tassels produced by this bushy plant can be more than 18in/45cm long, and they often touch the ground. They are carried on fairly erect stems that are clothed with large, conspicuously veined, light green leaves. The long clusters of tiny flowers dry well. A. caudatus itself has tassels of rich red. It and the green-flowered variant shown here should be given a sheltered site and soil that is well drained, moisture-retentive and, ideally, fertile.
also for: ■ Flowers suitable for cutting (and drying)

Zantedeschia aethiopica
"Green Goddess"
[calla lily]
○

type of plant: hardy/slightly tender perennial [8–11]
flowering time: late spring to midsummer
flower color: white + bright green
height: 3–4ft/0.9–1.2m

When grown in full sun and in fertile soil that is moist or wet, this intriguingly colored plant produces plenty of its 8in/20cm-long, trumpet-like "flowers" and generous clumps of its big, handsome leaves. From a distance, the flowers, with their green markings, and the arrow-shaped, slightly glaucous green leaves tend to "blend" and become almost indistinguishable from one another. The sculptural, pointed flowers last well when cut. In cold regions and especially when young, the plant needs protection. It can be grown in water up to 12in/30cm deep.
also for: ■ Damp and wet soils ■ Decorative, green foliage ■ Flowers suitable for cutting

Galtonia viridiflora
○

type of plant: slightly tender bulb [8–10]
flowering time: late summer
flower color: pale jade-green
height: 36in/90cm

The nodding, trumpet-shaped flowers of G. viridiflora are carried well above tufts of big, broad, grayish leaves. The individual flowers are 1¼in/3cm or so long, and well spaced along the strong, slightly arching stems. Moisture-retentive, fertile soil with good drainage is most suitable for this plant. In regions with cold winters, the bulbs should be lifted and stored in a frost-free place until replanted in spring. G. princeps is a smaller, earlier-flowering species that also has green flowers.

Moluccella laevis
[bells of Ireland, shell flower]
○

type of plant: slightly tender/half-hardy annual [8–10]
flowering time: late summer to early autumn
flower color: pale green + white
height: 24–36in/60–90cm

The true flowers of M. laevis are tiny and white (and balm-scented on first opening). But the "bells" or "shells" that surround each cluster of flowers are conspicuous, decorative, and green. The flowers and their surrounding outer parts are carried in spikes up to 12in/30cm long. They make good material for cutting, as the "bells" or "shells" are persistent when dried. This upright annual needs light soil that retains moisture. Its rounded, scalloped leaves are lime-green.
also for: ■ Flowers suitable for cutting (and drying)

Eucomis bicolor
[pineapple lily, pineapple flower]
○

type of plant: slightly tender/half-hardy bulb [8–10]
flowering time: late summer to early autumn
flower color: green + maroon
height: 18–24in/45–60cm

Although the broadly strap-shaped, basal leaves of this plant can look rather untidy, the heads of densely packed, starry flowers are an eye-catching distraction. These "pineapples," with their jaunty topknots of leaf-like bracts, are about 6in/15cm long; they are carried on stout, brown-spotted stems. The maroon-margined flowers are unpleasantly scented but the smell, which is reminiscent of stale vegetable soup, is not pervasive. The flower heads ripen into decorative, long-lasting, yellowish seedheads. E. bicolor needs a warm, sheltered site and fertile, well-drained soil.
also for: ■ Ornamental fruit (seedheads)

Tulipa e.g. "Spring Green" (Viridiflora Group)
[tulip]
○

type of plant: hardy bulb [5–9]
flowering time: late spring
flower color: green + cream
height: 15–18in/38–45cm

Specialist bulb nurseries offer quite a large number of tulips that have green markings on their petals, including T. "Spring Green," which is one of the most readily available varieties. Its exceptionally fresh combination of gentle colors means that it is an easy tulip to place in the garden, and it is attractive in flower arrangements, too. Additional tulips with green markings include T. "Artist" (salmon pink and green flowers) and T. "Groenland" (pale pink and green). Good drainage is important for all these tulips, which flower best in fertile soil. The bulbs may need lifting and storing after flowering if they are not to dwindle away rather quickly. The flowers of all these tulips are 3–4in/8–10cm wide, and their leaves are long, quite broad and grayish.
also for: ■ Flowers suitable for cutting

Fritillaria acmopetala
[fritillary]
○

type of plant: hardy bulb [7–9]
flowering time: mid- to late spring
flower color: pale jade-green + purple-brown
height: 12–15in/30–38cm

Its rather sophisticated coloring and its graceful shape might suggest otherwise, but this is one of the easiest fritillaries to grow (in regions with cold winters at least). The pendent, bell-shaped flowers, with their flared edges, are about 1½in/4cm long. They hang from slender stems that also bear long, slim, bluish green leaves. F. acmopetala thrives in light, rich soil that has sufficient organic matter to insure that the roots of the plant remain moist during the growing season.

Hermodactylus tuberosus (syn. Iris tuberosa)
[snake's-head iris, widow iris]
○

type of plant: hardy tuber [7–10]
flowering time: mid- to late spring
flower color: yellowish green + black
height: 12–15in/30–38cm

Flowers, like those of H. tuberosus, that are a combination of one subtle and one very dark color are interesting, but they need careful positioning to insure that such understated coloring is not overlooked in the garden. The sweetly scented, iris-like blooms of this plant are each about 2in/5cm wide; they open among rather untidy-looking, long, thin, blue-green leaves. H. tuberosus is at its best in regions with dry summers. It requires sharply drained, preferably alkaline soil and a warm, sunny site. When well suited, it self-sows.
also for: ■ Shallow soils over chalk ■ Dry soils in hot, sunny sites ■ Fragrant flowers

Iris e.g. "Green Spot" (Standard Dwarf Bearded)
○

type of plant: hardy perennial [4–9]
flowering time: late spring
flower color: white + green
height: 12in/30cm

Bearded irises of all sizes—dwarf, intermediate, and tall—are available in an enormous range of colors. This dwarf bearded hybrid is a popular, greenish flowered variety. However, specialist nurseries list hundreds of bearded irises and, particularly among the smaller plants, there will be other choices. These small irises, including I. "Green Spot," often make good garden plants that increase well when given free-draining soil and an open, sunny position. Their leaves are usually grayish and sword-shaped. The flowers of "Green Spot" are about 3in/8cm wide. For other standard dwarf bearded irises, see pp.57 and 58.

Petunia Surfina Lime = "Keiyeul"
○

type of plant: half-hardy annual [9–11]
flowering time: late spring to mid-autumn
flower color: white + green
height: 9–15in/23–38cm

Surfina petunias are vigorous, trailing plants that flower very freely. The blooms are 2–3in/5–8cm wide and shaped like fluted trumpets; they are less susceptible to rain damage than the flowers of some other types of petunia. The plants grow quite densely and there is a fairly good covering of small, pointed leaves. Surfina petunias cannot be grown from seed and must be bought as young plants. They need good drainage and flower best on light, rather poor soil.

ADDITIONAL PLANTS, featured elsewhere in this book, that have green flowers

○ sun

minimum height 10ft/3m or more
Liriodendron tulipifera, see p.219
Liriodendron tulipifera "Aureomarginata," see p.161

minimum height 3ft/90cm or less
Euphorbia characias subsp. wulfenii, see p.184
Euphorbia cyparissias "Fens Ruby," see p.203

Plantago major "Rosularis"
(syn. *P. rosea*)
[rose plantain]
○◐

type of plant: hardy perennial [4–9]
flowering time: mid- to late summer
flower color: green
height: 9–12in/23–30cm

Above a rosette of conspicuously veined leaves rise these curious "flower" heads on their strong stems. The "flowers," which consist of tightly packed bracts, are variable in shape: they may be conical or quite flat. Size, too, varies but, on average, each head is 2–3in/5–8cm wide. Even when flowering is finished, this is quite a decorative plant since its broad, oval leaves are fairly large—up to 6in/15cm long. *P. major* "Rosularis" is an easily grown plant and most soils are suitable.
also for: ■ Decorative, green foliage

Trochodendron aralioides
○◐

type of plant: slightly tender shrub/tree [8–9]
flowering time: late spring to early summer
flower color: bright green
height: 10–25ft/3–7.5m (see description)
Evergreen

Each of this shrub's tapered, leathery leaves grows on a long stalk. The rich green, gleaming foliage is arranged, at the tips of the branches, in bold whorls, usually at least 12in/30cm wide. At the centre of each whorl is a dense cluster of up to twenty, petal-less but many-stamened flowers. The plant thrives in moist, neutral soil in a sheltered site, and it is at its best in mild areas with high rainfall. In ideal conditions, *T. aralioides* eventually forms a wide, columnar tree with horizontally layered branches. However, it grows slowly and for many years is rounded and shrub-like.
also for: ■ Decorative, green foliage

Garrya elliptica
[silk tassel bush]
○◐

type of plant: slightly tender shrub [8–9]
flowering time: late autumn to late winter
flower color: pale silvery green
height: 8–15ft/2.4–4.5m
Evergreen

Male plants of *G. elliptica* produce the longest catkins. On varieties such as *G.e.* "James Roof," the pendent clusters of flowers may be more than 8in/20cm long. Flower production is best when plants are grown in sheltered sites, which also protect the leathery, dark green, oval leaves from becoming "burned" by cold winds. Untidy, faded flowers remain on plants until late spring at least. In their prime, however, they make striking cut flowers for winter arrangements. Female plants have much shorter tassels but, if fertilized, the flowers are followed by strings of purplish berries. Most well-drained soils are suitable for these dense, bushy, rather upright plants, which are quick-growing. They tolerate salt-laden winds and polluted air.
also for: ■ Windswept, seaside gardens ■ Atmospheric pollution
■ Ornamental fruit (see above) ■ Flowers suitable for cutting ■ Winter-flowering plants ■ Long, continuous flowering period

Itea ilicifolia
○◐

type of plant: slightly tender shrub [8–9]
flowering time: late summer to early autumn
flower color: pale green
height: 8–10ft/2.4–3m
Evergreen

The slender, dangling tassels of this shrub look impressive against glossy, rich green, holly-like foliage; in the evening they exude a honey-like scent. The strings of tiny flowers can be up to 12in/30cm long on mature plants. They remain decorative for many weeks, and make interesting material for cutting. The plant is upright when young; in maturity it is fairly lax with long, arching shoots. In cooler climates the shelter of a wall is needed, and there the plant may grow up to 15ft/4.5m tall. Well-drained soil that is reliably moisture-retentive is most suitable for *I. ilicifolia*, but it succeeds in most soils.
also for: ■ Decorative, green foliage ■ Flowers suitable for cutting ■ Fragrant flowers ■ Long, continuous flowering period

Nectaroscordum siculum
(syn. *Allium siculum*)
○◐

type of plant: hardy bulb [6–10]
flowering time: late spring to early summer
flower color: green + pink
height: 3–4ft/0.9–1.2m

Both the coloring of this plant and the arrangement of its flowers contribute to its stylish good looks. The green-flushed flowers, each on its own slender, green stalk, are upright in bud; when they open out into bells ½–1in/1–2.5cm long, they become pendent. Some of the stout-stemmed flower heads may consists of as many as thirty individual flowers. The ripe seed pods point upward. *N. siculum* grows well and usually increases quickly in all well-drained, fairly fertile soils. There are often numerous, self-sown seedlings and the bulbs produce offsets, too. The narrow, mid-green leaves of this plant smell of garlic.
also for: ■ Ornamental fruit (seed pods)
■ Flowers suitable for cutting (and drying)

Heuchera cylindrica "Greenfinch"
○◑

type of plant: hardy perennial [4–9]
flowering time: late spring to midsummer
flower color: yellowish green
height: 24–36in/60–90cm
Evergreen

The long flower stems of *H. cylindrica* "Greenfinch" rise, clear and erect, above ground-covering clumps of shining leaves. Tubular flowers, each about ½in/1cm wide, are carried in neat, rather slender heads. They are good for cutting. The rounded to heart-shaped, scalloped leaves are rich green with some silvery green mottling. *H.* "Green Ivory" is a somewhat similar, slightly shorter plant; it has green-tipped, cream flowers. Both these heucheras appreciate fertile, well-drained soil that retains moisture, but they are easily grown in most soils.
also for: ■ Ground cover ■ Decorative, green foliage ■ Flowers suitable for cutting

Astrantia major
[masterwort]
○◑

type of plant: hardy perennial [5–9]
flowering time: early to late summer
flower color: white + pale green, often tinged pink
height: 24in/60cm

The flower color of *A. major* and its varieties ranges from green-and-white, as shown here, through pink to dark red (see p.291). Tiny flowers are arranged in central "pincushions" and surrounded by papery ruffs. Each flower head is about 1in/2.5cm wide. Lobed and toothed, mid-green leaves form clumps of growth and, especially in moisture-retentive soil, they make good ground-cover. This self-sowing plant is easy to grow in most soils with reasonable drainage, but it is at its best in fertile, moisture-retentive conditions. *A. m.* subsp. *involucrata* "Shaggy" (syn. "Margery Fish") produces long, green-tipped bracts. *A. major* and all its variants are good for cutting and drying.
also for: ■ Damp and wet soils ■ Ground cover ■ Flowers suitable for cutting (and drying) ■ Long, continuous flowering period

Nicotiana
e.g. "Lime Green"
[tobacco plant]
○

type of plant: grown as half-hardy annual [8–10]
flowering time: midsummer to early autumn
flower color: sharp yellowish green
height: 24in/60cm

This upright, fairly open plant produces its flowers in profusion. In the evening these trumpet-shaped blooms emit a sweet, although not very pronounced, fragrance. Each flower consists of a long, elegant tube that opens out into a five-lobed "mouth," 1–1½in/2.5–4cm wide. Every stem carries numerous flowers and some fairly slender, pointed, light green leaves. Basal leaves are larger and rounded. *N. langsdorffii* also produces green flowers; these are slender-tubed bells of apple-green that hang from branching, 3–4ft/0.9–1.2m stems. This tobacco plant, too, is grown as a half-hardy annual.
also for: ■ Flowers suitable for cutting ■ Fragrant flowers (see above)

Ornithogalum nutans
[star-of-Bethlehem]
○◑

type of plant: hardy bulb [6–10]
flowering time: mid- to late spring
flower color: gray-green + white
height: 12–15in/30–38cm

This undemanding and pretty plant normally increases quickly in any well-drained soil. It self-sows freely and is suitable for naturalizing in grass. Nodding flowers—a dozen or so on each stem—are each about 1in/2.5cm long and shaped like flared trumpets. There is a conspicuous green stripe on the back of each petal. The bright green leaves of *O. nutans* are long, slim and rather untidy. *O. umbellatum* is a smaller plant with starry, white flowers which are marked green on the outside of the petals; it is often invasive and is best suited to a wild or informal garden.

Alchemilla conjuncta
○◑

type of plant: hardy perennial [5–9]
flowering time: early to late summer
flower color: yellowish green
height: 9–12in/23–30cm

Each of this plant's deeply lobed, prettily shaped leaves is covered, on the reverse, with pale, silky-smooth hairs. From above, these hairs appear as a very thin, white margin along the leaf edge. The foliage forms a dense clump of bright green growth about 12in/30cm across. *A. conjuncta* flowers over many weeks in summer, producing masses of clusters, each about ½in/1cm wide, arranged in branched heads. Like its larger relative, *A. mollis* (see p.114), this plant is easily grown in most soils; but, unlike *A. mollis*, it self-sows only very modestly. *A. alpina* is considerably smaller than *A. conjuncta*.
also for: ■ Heavy, clay soils ■ Ground cover ■ Decorative, green foliage ■ Long, continuous flowering period

ADDITIONAL PLANTS, featured elsewhere in this book, that have green flowers

○◐ sun or partial shade

minimum height 10ft/3m or more	minimum height 3ft/90cm or less	Euphorbia amygdaloides var. robbiae,
Decaisnea fargesii, see p.258	*Alchemilla mollis*, see p.114	see p.86

Angelica archangelica
[archangel]
◐ [○]

type of plant: hardy biennial/perennial
(herb) [4–9]
flowering time: early to midsummer
flower color: yellowish green
height: 6ft/1.8m

A. archangelica makes an imposing, upright plant with stout purplish stems and it looks good in borders and near streams, as well as in herb gardens. It lives longest if its emerging flower heads are removed. However, many gardeners appreciate the rounded, 9in/23cm-wide heads of tiny, green flowers just as much as the bold, divided leaves. The foliage is bright green and some of the lower leaves can be up to 24in/60cm long. This plant thrives in moist loam, and in a damp—but not wet—place. It self-sows prolifically. Young, crystallized stems of angelica are used to decorate cakes and other sweet foods.
also for: ■ Damp and wet soils ■ Decorative, green foliage

Helleborus argutifolius
(syn. *H. lividus* subsp. *corsicus*)
[Corsican hellebore]
◐ [○]

type of plant: hardy perennial [7–9]
flowering time: late winter to late spring
flower color: pale green
height: 24–30in/60–75cm
Evergreen

As well as beautifully colored, long-lasting flowers very early in the gardening year, this plant has handsome, tripartite leaves of soft rich green. The 1½in/4cm-wide, cup-shaped flowers are carried in generous clusters and they make good cut flowers. (Splitting the thick flower stems almost their entire length helps to make the flowers last well in water.) A wide range of soils is suitable for this shrubby, rather lax plant, but well-drained, moisture-retentive conditions and a cool site seem to give the best results. The plant often self-sows. In colder regions, some shelter and warmth may be needed. Another green-flowered hellebore is shown on p.82; specialist nurseries list other species.
also for: ■ Decorative, green foliage ■ Flowers suitable for cutting ■ Winter-flowering plants ■ Long, continuous flowering period

ADDITIONAL PLANTS, featured elsewhere in this book, that have green flowers

◐ [○] / ◐ partial shade (or sun)/partial shade

minimum height 3ft/90cm or less	*Helleborus foetidus*, see p.82	*Tellima grandiflora* Rubra Group,
Hacquetia epipactis, see p.349	*Tellima grandiflora*, see p.119	see p.243

Fritillaria pontica
[fritillary]
◐

type of plant: hardy bulb [6–9]
flowering time: mid- to late spring
flower color: pale green + maroon
height: 8–12in/20–30cm

F. pontica is nearly as easy to grow as *F. acmopetala* (see p.324), although it does require a cooler position. Any light, rich, well-drained soil is suitable, but it is most at home in soils with plenty of leaf mold. Each broad, pendent bell is about 1½in/4cm long and has a topknot of three pointed, gray-green leaves. There are sometimes two flowers to each leafy, grayish stem. (The specimens shown here have flowers that are not yet fully expanded.) *F. pallidiflora* enjoys similar growing conditions to *F. pontica*; it has pale, greenish cream, pendent flowers.

ADDITIONAL PLANTS, featured elsewhere in this book, that have green flowers

◐● partial or full shade

minimum height 3ft/90cm or less: *Euphorbia amygdaloides* var. *robbiae*, see p.86; *Helleborus foetidus*, see p.82

"Black" plants

DEPENDING ON HOW and where they are used, "black" plants can be formal and sophisticated or mysterious and alluring, or even jokey and fun. And, of course, they can be somber and serious. Most of the flowers, leaves, and other parts of plants that are described as "black" are, in fact, either very dark purple or very dark maroon. However, a few plants are exceptionally dark: in this list, the canes of the bamboo *Phyllostachys nigra*, the berries of *Phytolacca polyandra*, and the little flowers of *Viola* "Molly Sanderson" are all so dark-toned that they are, in effect, black. Other such plants include the very dark-leaved, grass-like *Ophiopogon planiscapus* "Nigrescens" and also the darkest forms of *Iris chrysographes* and *Fritillaria camschatcensis*.

Although there are relatively few flowers, leaves, and other decorative features that are dark enough to be described as "black," they are produced by plants that vary quite considerably in size, longevity, and growing requirements. As well as perennial and woody plants, this list contains various annuals and biennials, and the height of these plants ranges from a few inches to several yards. Many of the plants in the following list need sun in order to thrive, but some are equally happy in sun or partial shade; a few require shaded conditions.

The exceptionally deep tones of "black" plants are what make these plants so intriguing and desirable. Yet these very dark tones can also create problems. It is all too easy for "black" flowers or leaves to get lost among plants of brighter and livelier coloring and, from a distance, clumps of very dark leaves can create what look like plant-less "holes" in beds and borders.

The light-absorbing quality of black does mean that, even in the case of "black"-flowered plants that have green or gray leaves, it is the leaves that are immediately conspicuous, while the very dark flowers become apparent only on closer inspection. Interestingly, one way of making "black" flowers more noticeable is to boost their color by adding another plant of similar shade—a shrub or perennial with deep purple foliage, for instance. Alternatively a very strongly contrasting background, such as a white-washed wall or a mass of very pale leaves, can be used to pick "black" flowers from possible obscurity.

The larger masses of "black" created by very dark foliage can also be set against light backgrounds. Additional ways of enlivening such foliage and making it more conspicuous include growing pale-flowered climbers over or through it (some of the late-season, small-flowered clematis are ideal plant companions of this sort). Another option is to let low-growing, dark-leaved plants intermingle with, for instance, small, yellow-leaved grasses and herbs (see "Plants with yellow or yellow-green leaves," pp.209–217, for suggestions).

Gardeners who delight in the strangeness of "black" plants will want to grow a wider range of them than appears in this list. Some of the more readily available "black" plants include foliage perennials such as *Phormium* "Platt's Black" and the tender [zones 9–11], succulent *Aeonium* "Zwartkop." There are also some intriguing oddities, such as *Salix gracilistyla* "Melanostachys," a willow that has "black" catkins. *Hedera helix* "Atropurpurea" and *H.h.* "Glymii" turn such a dark purple in winter that they appear "black"-leaved.

Finally, some plants have flowers that are exceptionally dark maroon-red or red-purple, and, although these blooms are not "black," they can add rich, deep notes to very dark planting schemes. Suitable roses include *Rosa* "Guinée" and *R.* "Souvenir du Docteur Jamain," while *Clematis* "Romantika" has small, late-season flowers of very deep maroon-purple. Similar, deep purplish or maroon shades can be found in "Plants with purple, bronze or red leaves," pp.197–208.

Plants in this list are arranged in order of height alone.

Sambucus nigra
f. porphyrophylla "Gerda"
(syn. S.n. "Black Beauty")
[elder]
○

type of plant: hardy shrub [4–8]
flowering time: early summer
flower color: pink
height: 6–10ft/1.8–3m

Although the older, purple-leaved *S. nigra* f. *porphyrophylla* "Guincho Purple" is attractive, this newer cultivar has even darker—almost black—brown-purple foliage. This remarkable coloring is retained over a long period, but the pointed leaflets do not turn red in autumn as they do on *S.n.* f. *p.* "Guincho Purple." *S.n.* f. *p.* "Gerda" is vigorous and it soon forms a substantial, bushy plant with fairly upright branches. Its heads of foamy flowers are about 6in/15cm across and have a lemony scent with musk undertones. Birds find the very dark purple berries attractive. An extremely wide range of soils is suitable for this plant, which needs a sunny site for the best foliage color. An even newer variety, *S.n.* f. *p.* "Eva" (syn. *S.n.* "Black Lace") has very finely cut, nearly black leaves.
also for: ■ Shallow soils over chalk ■ Heavy, clay soils ■ Damp and wet soils ■ Atmospheric pollution ■ Fragrant flowers

Alcea rosea (syn. Althaea rosea)
"Nigra"
[hollyhock]
○

type of plant: grown as hardy biennial or annual [4–9]
flowering time: midsummer to early autumn
flower color: darkest maroon
height: 5–6ft/1.5–1.8m

Since they are set on pale, thick stems among light, grayish green foliage, these very deeply colored flowers look especially dark. Each saucer-shaped bloom is about 3in/8cm across. The leaves are rounded and shallowly lobed; those near the base of the impressively tall and erect stems are about 9in/23cm long. Hollyhocks need good drainage and, to perform well, they should have a fertile soil. A sunny, sheltered site is most suitable. In an exposed position, the tall, upright stems require staking.

Iris e.g. "Sable" (Tall Bearded)
○

type of plant: hardy perennial [4–9]
flowering time: late spring to early summer
flower color: very deep purple-violet
height: 36in/90cm

Some specialist nurseries offer hundreds of varieties of bearded irises, among which there will be several plants with "black" flowers. When sunlight shines through the petals of these flowers it is evident that they are, in fact, very dark purple, violet, or maroon. But, from a distance, and especially in overcast conditions, they are, in effect, black—and certainly dark and dramatic. As well as the elegantly curvaceous variety shown here, the vigorous, large-flowered, deep purple *I.* "Dusky Challenger" and the very dark maroon *I.* "Black Swan" are further examples of popular Tall Bearded irises with "black" flowers. (Irises of this type have flowers about 4–6in/10–15cm across.) *I.* "Little Black Belt" is a Standard Dwarf Bearded variety, 10in/25cm tall, with very deep violet flowers, each about 2½in/6cm across. All these plants need full sun and really well-drained, preferably neutral soil. Their leaves are sword-shaped and arranged in fan-like sheaves; they are usually a grayish green.
also for: ■ Flowers suitable for cutting

Papaver somniferum
"Black Paeony"
[opium poppy]
○

type of plant: hardy annual [7–9]
flowering time: early to midsummer
flower color: dark maroon-purple
height: 30–36in/75–90cm

The luxuriously colored and extravagantly frilled, fully double blooms of *P. somniferum* "Black Paeony" can be as much as 5in/12cm across. They are carried on erect stems above pale blue-green, lobed leaves. The flowers are followed by sea-green seed pods, about 1¼in/3cm long (for an illustration of opium poppy seed pods, see p.253). Both the flowers and seed pods are popular for cutting and the pods can be dried. This poppy is easily grown in most well-drained soils but deep, fertile soil is ideal.
also for: ■ Gray, blue-gray, or silver leaves ■ Ornamental fruit (seed pods) ■ Flowers suitable for cutting (and drying)

Scabiosa atropurpurea "Chile Black"
(syn. S. "Chile Black")
[pincushion flower, scabious]
○

type of plant: slightly tender/hardy annual/biennial/perennial [8–9]
flowering time: midsummer to early autumn
flower color: dark maroon-purple
height: 24in/60cm

The very dark, domed flower heads of this plant are freely borne on branching stems that rise above grayish green, basal leaves. Individual flower heads are up to 1¼in/3cm across, and they are attractive to bees and butterflies. The plant is often annual or biennial, but it may persist for several seasons. S. atropurpurea "Ace of Spades" has similarly colored, double flowers, about 2in/5cm wide, that are fragrant; it is annual or biennial and about 36in/90cm tall. Mixtures of S. atropurpurea, which include white, pink and blue as well as dark purple flowers, are also available. All these plants thrive in well-drained, slightly alkaline soil but do not live long in areas with damp winters. They make good material for cutting.
also for: ■ Shallow soils over chalk ■ Flowers suitable for cutting

Tulipa e.g. "Queen of Night"
(Single Late Group)
[tulip]
○

type of plant: hardy bulb [5–9]
flowering time: late spring
flower color: very dark maroon-purple
height: 24in/60cm

Flower arrangers like tulips of unusual coloring, such as varieties that produce green flowers (see, for instance, the green-and-cream tulip on p.324) or very deep—almost black—purple or maroon blooms, such as T. "Queen of Night." Tulips such as T. "Queen of Night" are classified as Single Late Group, and they have neat, often cup-shaped flowers, up to 3in/8cm across, on long stems. Their leaves are broad, pointed and grayish green. There is a wide range of colors— mainly shades of red, purple, pink, and yellow, and also white. Single Late Group tulips are popular for bedding as well as cutting. They need fertile, well-drained soil, plenty of sun, and some shelter from wind. They are short-lived on heavier soils and, in any case, tend to decrease in size from season to season, unless lifted and stored after flowering each year. T. "Black Parrot" (Parrot Group) has deep purple flowers with frilly, fringed edges to its petals.
also for: ■ Flowers suitable for cutting

Dianthus barbatus
Nigrescens Group
[sweet William]
○

type of plant: grown as hardy biennial [6–9]
flowering time: late spring to early summer
flower color: dark crimson-maroon
height: 15–18in/38–45cm

Dark-leaved, dark-flowered, and often dark-stemmed sweet Williams such as these Nigrescens Group plants need careful placing if they are not to "disappear" in mixed beds and borders. The dense, slightly domed flower heads, each 2–3in/5–8cm wide, have a sweet, spicy scent and are excellent for cutting. They are carried on stiff, upright stems. The leaves are slender and bronze-purple. D. barbatus "Sooty" is slightly smaller and produces very dark maroon flowers. Although these plants are short-lived perennials, they are nearly always treated as biennials. They thrive in well-drained, slightly alkaline soil and full sun.
also for: ■ Purple, bronze or red leaves ■ Flowers suitable for cutting ■ Fragrant flowers

Phyllostachys nigra
[black bamboo]
○[◐]

type of plant: hardy perennial (bamboo) [6–11]
height: 10–12ft/3–3.6m
Evergreen

In a sunny site the upright canes of this bamboo become a wonderful, polished jet-black in their second or third year. As the canes mature they arch at their tips. Black bamboo produces a luxuriant, airy mass of elegantly slender, pointed leaves, each about 5in/12cm long. The foliage is a bright rich green. In cool climates, the plant is clump-forming and non-invasive. It grows well in sites sheltered from cold winds and thrives in fertile soil that is both moist and well drained.
also for: ■ Decorative, green foliage ■ Ornamental bark or twigs

Cornus alba "Kesselringii"
[black-stemmed dogwood]
○ ◖◗

type of plant: hardy shrub [3–8]
height: 6–7ft/1.8–2.1m

Black-stemmed dogwood is easily grown in a wide range of soils, and it thrives in damp or wet ground. It produces a thicket of upright, very dark black-purple stems that are most deeply colored when the plant is grown in sun and when it is pruned really hard every other year. The stems look particularly striking alongside red- or yellow-stemmed dogwoods (for which, see pp.68, 169, 265). The dark green, oval, pointed leaves, each about 4in/10cm long, are tinged with purple, especially in spring. They turn red and reddish purple in autumn. The foliage provides a good background for the 2in/5cm-wide clusters of white berries that develop on the more mature wood after the less conspicuous, late spring to early summer flowers have faded.

also for: ■ Heavy, clay soils ■ Damp and wet soils ■ Atmospheric pollution ■ Colorful, autumn foliage ■ Ornamental fruit (see above) ■ Ornamental bark or twigs

Iris chrysographes
black-flowered iris
○ ◖◗

type of plant: hardy perennial [7–9]
flowering time: early summer
flower color: inky purple
height: 20in/50cm

The sheaves of narrow leaves produced by this iris are of a sufficiently light, grayish green to accentuate the very dark flowers. Each slender stem carries two gold-marked blooms, each 2½in/6cm across. The plant flowers freely, although for a fairly brief period. Black-flowered forms of *I. chrysographes* vary in just how dark their flowers are; named varieties, such as *I.c.* "Black Knight," are a more consistent source of very deep color. All these plants thrive in moisture-retentive to damp soils. They make very striking and graceful cut flowers.

also for: ■ Damp and wet soils ■ Flowers suitable for cutting

Phytolacca polyandra
(syn. *P. clavigera*)
[pokeweed]
○ ◐

type of plant: hardy perennial [6–9]
flowering time: late summer to early autumn
flower color: pink
height: 4–5ft/1.2–1.5m

Dense spikes, up to 12in/30cm long, of shiny, black berries are produced by this robust plant that is, perhaps, best suited to an area of fairly informal planting. The fruits are borne on erect, crimson, branching stems that become increasingly vividly colored as winter approaches. The preceding flowers are saucer-shaped. In autumn, the big, pointed leaves often turn yellow. *P. americana* flowers slightly earlier than *P. polyandra*; it produces dark maroon berries and its foliage takes on purplish tints in autumn. Any moisture-retentive soil is suitable for these poisonous plants, both of which tend to self-sow freely. *P. americana*'s berries, in particular, are highly toxic.

also for: ■ Colorful, autumn foliage

Aquilegia vulgaris
"William Guiness"
(syn. *A.v.* "Magpie")
[columbine, granny's bonnet]
○ ◐

type of plant: hardy perennial [5–9]
flowering time: late spring to early summer
flower color: deep black-purple + white
height: 24in/60cm

The very dark blooms on *A. vulgaris* "William Guiness" appear in large numbers on slender, dusky stems and are carried high above a clump of ferny foliage. The flowers—seen here, shining, after a recent shower—are each like a little hat and about 1½in/4cm across. The large, soft mid-green leaves are divided into many, lobed leaflets. This is an easily pleased plant that grows in a wide range of soils, though it is at its best in moist, well-drained conditions. Suppliers specializing in perennials often stock numerous different forms of *A. vulgaris*, including some very dark, double-flowered varieties.

Ophiopogon planiscapus "Nigrescens"
(syn. *O.p.* "Black Dragon")
[lilyturf]
○◑

type of plant: hardy perennial [6–10]
flowering time: mid- to late summer
flower color: pale pink-mauve
height: 6–8in/15–20cm
Evergreen

This perennial's clumps of narrow, arching leaves increase and spread slowly; they make good ground cover in all well-drained, reasonably moisture-retentive soils. Each leaf is up to 1ft/30cm long. If the very dark purple-black of the foliage is not to "disappear" in mixed plantings, then a contrastingly light background is needed. Sprays of tiny, bell-shaped flowers are followed by bunches of shiny, black berries that persist into winter. Although *O. planiscapus* "Nigrescens" grows best in retentive, slightly acid soils, it is tolerant of drier and more alkaline conditions.
also for: ■ Ground cover ■ Ornamental fruit

Viola e.g. "Molly Sanderson"
[pansy, violet]
○◑

type of plant: hardy perennial [5–8]
flowering time: late spring to late summer
flower color: nearly black + yellow
height: 4–6in/10–15cm

The flowers of *V.* "Molly Sanderson" are so small (about 1in/2.5cm wide) and so dark that they might easily be overlooked. However, the bright green foliage provides a good, contrasting background, and the flowers can be made still more conspicuous by combining them with paler plants (such as the yellow-leaved lamium—for details of which, see p.217—also shown in this illustration). Further examples of small-flowered, intriguingly colored violets and pansies include *V.* "Bowles' Black" (another "black"-flowered variety), *V.* "Jackanapes" (upper petals darkest maroon, lower petals yellow), and *V.* "Irish Molly" (yellow overlaid with bronze and khaki). All these plants flower over a long period if they are regularly dead-headed and if they are given a cool root-run in well-drained, moisture-retentive soil. Their leaves tend to form loose mats.
also for: ■ Crevices in paving ■ Long, continuous flowering period

Helleborus x hybridus
black-flowered
[hellebore]
◑●

type of plant: hardy perennial [5–9]
flowering time: late winter to mid-spring
flower color: very dark purple
height: 15–18in/38–45cm
Evergreen/Semi-evergreen

The flower color of *H. x hybridus* varies considerably, from white and yellow, through shades of pink, to purples and maroons that are so dark that they are almost black. Though the very deep coloring of "black" hellebores may fade a little over time, the flowers remain decorative for many weeks. Usually the flowers are single, 2–3in/5–8cm wide and slightly cupped. All these hellebores are easy to grow in most reasonably fertile soils. They are especially successful in fertile, moisture-retentive, humus-rich soil and, under these conditions, their clumps of deeply lobed leaves make good ground cover.
also for: ■ Dense shade ■ Ground cover ■ Long, continuous flowering period

Fritillaria camschatcensis
[black sarana]
◑

type of plant: hardy bulb [4–9]
flowering time: late spring to early summer
flower color: variable—gray-purple to purplish black
height: 12in/30cm (see description)

Black sarana is variable both in height (it can range from half to double the height given here) and in color (usually very dark with a grayish bloom, but occasionally green). This striking plant produces a cluster of dusky bells, each 1in/2.5cm or so long, at the top of bright green, upright stems. The glossy, ribbed leaves are bright green, too, and are arranged in whorls. Black sarana needs rich, moist, peaty soil and a cool position. *F. persica* "Adiyaman" also has very dark, plum-colored flowers; it is about 5ft/1.5m tall and needs deep, fertile soil in a sunny, sheltered site.
also for: ■ Acid soils

ADDITIONAL "BLACK" PLANTS that are featured elsewhere in this book

◑● partial or full shade

minimum height 3ft/90cm or less
Geranium phaeum, see p.86

The following plants regularly produce generous crops of conspicuous, black, or near-black fruit:
Fatsia japonica, see p.149
Lotus hirsutus, see p.187

Sambucus nigra f. *laciniata*, see p.226
Sarcococca confusa, see p.321
Viburnum rhytidophyllum, see p.226
Vitis vinifera "Purpurea," see p.203

A long, continuous flowering period

PART OF THE ATTRACTION of plants is their ephemeral nature. The gloriously abundant floral display produced by Japanese cherries is very short-lived but it is also, for numerous gardeners, one of the delights of spring. Certainly there are situations that require a definite preponderance of long-flowering plants, but perhaps the most satisfying gardens are those that have a small nucleus of plants that flower for many weeks and a wider range of short-season plants that add variety.

All the plants in this list normally bloom over a period of at least two months. Some of them produce flowers that are long-lasting because of their structure or their texture. *Hydrangea* "Preziosa," for example, has rounded flower heads that change gradually and decoratively into "dried" flowers, and these extend still further the plant's season of interest.

On a much smaller scale, the flowers of *Hacquetia epipactis* are constructed in such a way as to remain decorative almost all spring long. Various masterworts (*Astrantia*) and sea hollies (*Eryngium*) are examples of plants that produce conspicuously shaped blooms, which are decorative even before they color fully. Since parts of these flowers are of a papery or stiff texture, and therefore persistent, the flower heads manage to look attractive for a while after the flowers themselves have faded.

Other plants have relatively short-lived flowers but, as the first blooms fade, new flowers appear and this process continues over many weeks. Plants that produce a long succession of short-lived flowers include shrubs, such as *Hibiscus syriacus* "Oiseau Bleu" and x *Halimiocistus sahucii*, and numerous perennials, including various sundrops (*Oenothera*), flaxes (*Linum*), and spiderworts (*Tradescantia*). Plants that flower over a long period during winter are a special case. Their flowering season is prolonged by low temperatures, which slow down both the production and subsequent aging of their flowers.

In order to flower over a long period, a plant has to expend a considerable amount of energy and it is therefore not surprising to find that many long-flowering perennial and woody plants are fairly short-lived. Quite a few of the shrubs in the following list are subshrubby plants with woody bases and rather soft stems. Plants of this sort in the list include two Cape figworts (*Phygelius*) and also *Lavatera* x *clementii* "Barnsley" and *Erysimum* "Bowles' Mauve."

However, this list also includes shrubs that are both long-flowering and at least reasonably long-lived. These include many familiar plants: famous roses such as *Rosa* Iceberg; easy-going plants such as the shrubby potentillas (*Potentilla fruticosa* "Tangerine," for example); flowering quinces (*Chaenomeles* x *superba* "Knap Hill Scarlet"), and St John's worts (see *Hypericum* "Hidcote"); as well as various heaths and heathers (such as *Erica carnea* "Vivellii").

Some short-lived plants obligingly perpetuate themselves by self-sowing: *Verbena bonariensis*, *Gaura lindheimeri* and, for shadier places, *Corydalis lutea* and Welsh poppy (*Meconopsis cambrica*) are all examples of generous self-sowers featured in this list. Certain plants that flower very freely over a long period do so only if they are regularly rejuvenated by division: *Geum* hybrids, such as *G.* "Lady Stratheden," and *Achillea* "Moonshine" are two examples of plants that benefit significantly from this treatment. A few long-flowering but short-lived perennials (*Anthemis tinctoria* "Wargrave Variety," for instance) need to be cut back hard after flowering if they are to continue performing well.

Finally, if any plant is to flower well over a long period, its growing needs—whatever they are—should be carefully attended to. No plant that requires, for example, fertile and moisture-retentive soil is going to flower for long if it is struggling to survive in dry, infertile conditions. As a general observation, the regular removal of faded blooms persuades many plants to continue flowering for longer than they would naturally.

Solanum laxum
(syn. *S. jasminoides*) "Album"
[potato vine]
○

type of plant: half-hardy/slightly tender
climber/shrub [9–11]
flowering time: midsummer to mid-autumn
flower color: white
height: 15–20ft/4.5–6m
Semi-evergreen

The numerous clusters of starry flowers produced by this scrambling, twining shrub shine out from among dark foliage. Each flower, 1in/2.5cm across, has five pure white petals that surround rich yellow anthers. The leaves are about 2in/5cm long, and mostly rather slender and pointed. *S. laxum* needs a sheltered position and well-drained soil. In cold weather, its slender-stemmed, upper growth may die back to ground level but it usually regenerates, provided the roots have had some protection. Not everyone can detect the flowers' sweet fragrance.
also for: ■ Climbing plants ■ Fragrant flowers (see above)

Ceanothus "Autumnal Blue"
[California lilac]
○

type of plant: slightly tender shrub [8–10]
flowering time: late summer to mid-autumn
flower color: soft sky-blue
height: 7–10ft/2.1–3m
Evergreen

A rather loose, open habit of growth typifies this vigorous, upright shrub that is sometimes still in flower in late autumn and early winter. Its tiny flowers are arranged in branched heads, 3in/8cm long. The soft coloring of these flowers is enhanced and enlivened by the glossy, rich bright green of the oval leaves. *C.* "Autumnal Blue" grows quickly, but it is fairly short-lived. It needs a sheltered site, and good drainage is important, too. Hot, dry conditions are tolerated only by established plants. The plant does not do well in very alkaline conditions. .

Clematis e.g. "Etoile Rose"
○

type of plant: hardy perennial climber [5–9]
flowering time: midsummer to mid-autumn
flower color: deep rose-pink + palest pink
height: 7–8ft/2.1–2.4m

C. "Etoile Rose" produces its dark-stemmed, little bells over a period of several months. Each fluted flower, prettily edged in very pale pink, is about 2in/5cm long. Growth is normally vigorous, and especially so in ideal conditions of cool, fertile, well-drained soil for the roots and a sunny position for the upper parts of the plant. The weaving, scrambling stems, which are more or less herbaceous (depending on climate), carry rounded, rather light green leaflets. *C.* "Etoile Rose" is a *texensis* hybrid with nodding flowers. Some other related hybrids—including *C.* "Gravetye Beauty" (crimson) and *C.* "Duchess of Albany" (pink)—have upright, tulip-like flowers.
also for: ■ Climbing plants

Hibiscus syriacus
e.g. "Oiseau Bleu"
(syn. *H.s.* Blue Bird)
[rose of Sharon
○

type of plant: hardy shrub [6–9]
flowering time: late summer to mid-autumn
flower color: violet-blue
height: 6–8ft/1.8–2.4m

Varieties of *H. syriacus* prosper in fertile, acid to slightly alkaline soils with good drainage. They are tolerant of hot, dry conditions. To flower well, they need a warm, sheltered site. Their large and showy blooms—which are 3in/8cm wide on vigorous *H.s.* "Oiseau Bleu"—open in succession over a long period. (For a red-flowered variety, see p.145.) Their deep green, lobed and toothed leaves do not develop until late spring or early summer, and newly planted specimens may produce very few leaves. The flowers of all these upright, bushy plants are susceptible to damage by prolonged rain.
also for: ■ Dry soils in hot, sunny sites ■ Atmospheric pollution ■ Growing in containers

Lavatera x clementii
e.g. "Barnsley"
[tree mallow]
○

type of plant: slightly tender shrub/
perennial [7–10]
flowering time: early summer to mid-autumn
flower color: pale pink + red
height: 6–8ft/1.8–2.4m

This popular plant flowers prolifically over many weeks, producing its 3in/8cm-wide, cup-shaped blooms on upright stems. Its lobed leaves are of a soft sage-green. *L. x clementii* "Barnsley" is quick-growing but short-lived. In periods of prolonged cold weather, the openly branched top growth may die, and a warm position, as well as good drainage, are needed if the plant is to perform well. Other popular shrubby *Lavatera* include *L. x c.* "Rosea" (see p.90) and the still darker pink *L. x c.* "Burgundy Wine." All these plants do well in gardens near the sea, but they are not suitable for positions that are fully exposed to salt-laden winds.
also for: ■ Windswept, seaside gardens

Indigofera heterantha
(syn. *I. gerardiana*)
○

type of plant: slightly tender shrub [7–9]
flowering time: midsummer to early autumn
flower color: mauve-pink
height: 5–8ft/1.5–2.4m

I. heterantha grows best in light soils that drain quickly and it tolerates short periods of drought very well. During cold winters its slightly arching top growths may be killed, but this is a shrub that readily produces new shoots from the base. Whatever the weather in the preceding winter, the ferny, grayish green foliage does not appear until late spring. Pea-like flowers are produced over many weeks; they are clustered on more or less upright stalks, each about 4in/10cm long. The plant is usually as wide as it is tall.
also for: ■ Dry soils in hot, sunny sites ■ Decorative, green foliage

Verbena bonariensis
(syn. *V. patagonica*)
○

type of plant: slightly tender perennial [7–10]
flowering time: midsummer to mid-autumn
flower color: light lilac-purple
height: 5–6ft/1.5–1.8m

Even in the light soils where it is at its best, this long-flowering perennial tends to be rather short-lived. However, it usually self-sows freely. Its tiny, five-petalled blooms are arranged in dense clusters, up to 2in/5cm wide, that are carried on wiry, branching stems. There are only a few long, thin, dark green leaves. As well as good drainage, this most attractively light and airy plant needs soil that is fairly fertile and reasonably moisture-retentive.

Chamerion angustifolium
(syn. *Epilobium angustifolium*)
"Album"
[white fireweed]
○

type of plant: hardy perennial [3–7]
flowering time: midsummer to early autumn
flower color: white
height: 5ft/1.5m

This is the white-flowered form of *C. angustifolium*—the weed commonly known as rose bay willow herb or fireweed. Although it is not as invasive as the species, *C.a.* "Album" sows itself and spreads vigorously and so it is best given plenty of room and grown in informal parts of a garden. Its spires of pure white blooms open, in succession, over many weeks. Each saucer-shaped flower is about ½in/1cm across. The flowers are carried on upright stems that are clothed with narrow, slightly gray-tinged leaves. Growth is best on soils that are well drained and moisture-retentive but poor, rather dry conditions are also suitable (although here the underground stems may spread very widely).

Dahlia merckii
○

type of plant: slightly tender tuber [8–10]
flowering time: early summer to mid-autumn
flower color: lilac
height: 3–5ft/0.9–1.5m

In colder areas, the tuberous roots of *D. merckii* need to be lifted and stored in a dry, frost-free place during winter; in warmer gardens, they survive all but the coldest weather, as long as they are planted deeply in well-drained soil. Each charming, simple, often slightly nodding flower, about 2in/5cm across, has a yellow and maroon, central disk. The flowers are carried on branching stems, usually well above the fresh green, much-divided foliage. Since the stems are very slender, the plant is best given a position sheltered from wind.

Gaura lindheimeri
○

type of plant: hardy perennial [6–9]
flowering time: midsummer to mid-autumn
flower color: white fading to palest pink
height: 3–4ft/0.9–1.2m

Although this is a short-lived, sometimes rather untidy plant, *G. lindheimeri* makes up for these shortcomings by self-sowing readily and flowering over a period of many weeks. (It often flowers especially well in early autumn.) The willowy, branched stems are set with little, narrow, mid-green leaves, and there are masses of slim, pink buds that open out into starry flowers, each about 1in/2.5cm across. Varieties of this plant include *G.l.* "Siskiyou Pink," which has deep pink blooms, and *G.l.* "Corrie's Gold," which has gold-edged leaves. All these plants like a warm site with some shelter, and well-drained soil. In cool, damp climates they tend to flop and to produce relatively few flowers.

Delphinium x ruysii
"Pink Sensation"
(syn. *D.* Belladonna Group
"Pink Sensation")
○

type of plant: hardy perennial [5–8]
flowering time: midsummer to early autumn
flower color: pink
height: 36–42in/90–105cm

The classic, very tall delphiniums, with their dense flower spikes, are short-lived plants that require very careful cultivation in order to perform well. *D. x ruysii* "Pink Sensation," and the similar Belladonna delphiniums, are neither so demanding nor quite so short-lived. They have a branching habit and deeply cut, slim-lobed leaves. Most of them produce upright spikes of "pixie hat" flowers, in succession, over a period of many weeks (especially if they are dead-headed regularly). Individual flowers are, typically, single and about ¾in/2cm across. All these plants need deep, fertile soil with really good drainage. *D.* Belladonna Group "Cliveden Beauty" has sky-blue flowers.
also for: ■ Flowers suitable for cutting

Coronilla valentina subsp.
glauca (syn. *C. glauca*) "Citrina"
○

type of plant: slightly tender shrub [8–9]
flowering time: mainly midwinter to late spring
(see description)
flower color: pale yellow
height: 36in/90cm
Evergreen

The very sweetly scented pea-flowers of this rounded, bushy shrub are freely produced over many weeks, usually from midwinter onward. There are also some blooms through the summer months and into autumn. The flowers, about ½in/1cm long, are arranged in clusters and offset by rounded, bluish gray-green leaflets. *C. valentina* subsp. *glauca* itself has brighter yellow flowers and is slightly hardier than *C.v.* subsp. *glauca* "Citrina." A variegated form is shown on p.164. All these plants may be short-lived. They need really well-drained soil and a warm, sunny site. They thrive in alkaline soils.
also for: ■ Shallow soils over chalk ■ Growing in containers ■ Gray, blue-gray, or silver leaves ■ Fragrant flowers ■ Winter-flowering plants

Linaria purpurea
e.g. "Canon Went"
[toadflax]
○

type of plant: hardy perennial [5–8]
flowering time: early summer to early autumn
flower color: light pink
height: 36in/90cm

Although individual specimens are short-lived, *L. purpurea* "Canon Went" persists because it self-sows, usually freely. It comes true from seed (as long as it is not grown near the species, which has violet-purple flowers). Its snapdragon-like flowers, which are about ½in/1cm long, are arranged in long, slim spires, and the whole plant, including the thin, grayish leaves, is slender. *L.p.* "Springside White" is white flowered. *L. triornithophora* [zones 7–10] is another long-flowering toadflax; its pink or purplish, spurred flowers—which resemble little birds—are held in whorled clusters on 3–4ft/0.9–1.2m stems. All these plants thrive in light, well-drained soil.
also for: ■ Dry soils in hot, sunny sites

Phygelius aequalis
"Yellow Trumpet"
[Cape figwort]
○

type of plant: slightly tender shrub/perennial [8–9]
flowering time: midsummer to mid-autumn
flower color: pale greenish yellow
height: 36in/90cm
Evergreen/Semi-evergreen in mild regions

Throughout its long flowering season, this bushy, upright, suckering plant looks handsome. It carries its pendent flowers in conspicuous clusters; each slender, tubular bloom is about 1½in/4cm long. The leaves are mid-green and pointed. In regions with cold winters, it is probably best to regard *P. aequalis* "Yellow Trumpet" as an herbaceous perennial and to cut it to ground level in spring, even if the top growth has not been killed by frosts; in mild areas, it develops a woody base and grows taller. A warm, sheltered site is advisable in any case. The plant grows well in soil that has good drainage but it does not like being continually dry in summer. The following illustration shows a popular, pink-flowered hybrid.

Phygelius x rectus
e.g. "Winchester Fanfare"
[Cape figwort]
○

type of plant: slightly tender shrub/perennial [8–9]
flowering time: midsummer to mid-autumn
flower color: dusky pink
height: 36in/90cm
Evergreen/Semi-evergreen in mild regions

The more recent phygelius hybrids include this upright variety with its numerous, pendent, tubular flowers, each about 1½in/4cm long. The loose spikes of blooms rise above plenty of glossy, rich green, pointed leaves. Other readily available *P. x rectus* hybrids include *P. x r.* "African Queen" (red flowers) and *P. x r.* "Devil's Tears" (rich red-pink). The flowers of *P. capensis*, one of the parents of *P. x rectus*, are orange. A yellow-flowered variety is shown in the preceding illustration. All these suckering plants are best treated as herbaceous perennials in regions with cold winters; in mild areas they become woody and grow taller. They prosper in warm, sheltered sites and in soil that is well drained, but not continually dry in summer.

Verbascum
e.g. "Helen Johnson"
[mullein]
○

type of plant: hardy perennial [5–9]
flowering time: early to late summer
flower color: soft dusty pink-beige + dark chocolate-purple
height: 36in/90cm
Evergreen

Many hybrid mulleins, including *V.* "Helen Johnson," are rather short-lived, but they do give a long floral display. The saucer-shaped blooms produced by *V.* "Helen Johnson" are each about 1¼in/3cm across. They are carried in upright spires above rosettes of downy, gray-green, pointed leaves, up to 9in/23cm long. *V.* "Jackie" has flowers of similar coloring and is only 15–18in/38–45cm high. *V.* (Cotswold Group) "Pink Domino" is taller, with rose-pink flowers. All these plants thrive in light, rather poor, alkaline soil. They are drought-tolerant. For a yellow-flowered, hybrid mullein, see p.15.
also for: ■ Shallow soils over chalk ■ Dry soils in hot, sunny sites ■ Gray, blue-gray, or silver leaves

Anthemis tinctoria
e.g. "Wargrave Variety"
[ox-eye chamomile, golden marguerite]
○

type of plant: hardy perennial [4–8]
flowering time: early to late summer
flower color: pale yellow
height: 30–36in/75–90cm

The neatly shaped daisies, to 1½in/4cm across, of *A. tinctoria* "Wargrave Variety" are produced in large quantities over many weeks. They are very good for cutting. *A. tinctoria* and its varieties tend to be rather short-lived but their lives can be prolonged by giving them really well-drained soil that is not too rich and by cutting them back hard after flowering. Other popular varieties include *A.t.* "Sauce Hollandaise" (palest cream flowers) and *A.t.* "E.C. Buxton" (lemony cream; about 24in/60cm high). *A.* "Grallagh Gold" produces bright golden yellow blooms. The branching stems of all these plants rise above clumps of feathery, usually mid-green foliage.
also for: ■ Flowers suitable for cutting

Aster x frikartii "Mönch"
○

type of plant: hardy perennial [5–9]
flowering time: late summer to mid-autumn
flower color: lavender-blue + yellow
height: 30–36in/75–90cm

This healthy and elegant aster produces its slim-petaled flowers, each about 2½in/6cm across, in large numbers, over a remarkably long period. These blooms are carried in loose heads on strong, rather slender, upright stems that are clothed with small, pointed, deep green leaves. *A. x frikartii* "Mönch" is an outstanding variety, but *A. x frikartii* itself and *A. x f.* "Wunder von Stäfa" are very similar and also excellent. All these flowers are attractive to bees and butterflies, and they are good for cutting. Well-drained soils of most sorts are suitable but those that are moisture-retentive and fertile give much the best results.
also for: ■ Flowers suitable for cutting

Penstemon
e.g. "Alice Hindley"
○

type of plant: slightly tender perennial [8–10]
flowering time: midsummer to early autumn
flower color: pale mauve + white
height: 30–36in/75–90cm

The erect stems of P. "Alice Hindley" are clothed in fairly large, pointed, rich green leaves and wide-mouthed, tubular blooms. The flowers, 1½in/4cm long, are arranged in spires. They emerge from mauve-purple buds and, when fully expanded, their white throats are revealed. The long flowering season may well continue into mid-autumn. Other popular penstemons with this sort of coloring include P. "Stapleford Gem" [zones 7–10], which has purplish blue flowers, and the rather paler mauve P. "Mother of Pearl" [zones 7–10]. For examples of red- and white-flowered penstemons, see below. All these plants do best in well-drained, fertile soil and full sun.

Erysimum "Bowles' Mauve"
[wallflower]
○

type of plant: slightly tender perennial/ shrub [8–10]
flowering time: late spring to late summer
flower color: mauve
height: 30in/75cm
Evergreen/Semi-evergreen

This quick-growing but fairly short-lived subshrub has an exceptionally long flowering season. Indeed, there are usually a few flowers early in spring and in autumn, too. The dark gray-green of the slender leaves provides a very flattering background for these ½in/1cm-wide, virtually unscented blooms. (The illustration shows the plant before the flower spikes have lengthened fully; they are usually about 12in/30cm long.) E. "Bowles' Mauve" needs a sheltered site and good drainage. It is hardiest and most floriferous in light, rather poor soil and, in these conditions, the upright stems form a neat, dense mound of growth. It thrives on shallow, chalky soils.
also for: ■ Shallow soils over chalk ■ Gray, blue-gray, or silver leaves

Malva moschata f. alba
[musk mallow]
○

type of plant: hardy perennial [4–8]
flowering time: early summer to early autumn
flower color: white, sometimes tinged pink
height: 30in/75cm

The charming flowers of M. moschata f. alba emerge, in succession, from clusters of neat little buds. They open over a period of many weeks. Each saucer-shaped bloom is about 2in/5cm across. The foliage is finely cut, light green, and slightly musk-scented. In rich soils, the plant can be quite lax; in poor soils it is more upright. Flowering is best on fertile, fairly moisture-retentive soil with good drainage. M. moschata itself has pink flowers. Both the species and the white-flowered form are short-lived plants that self-sow, often freely.
also for: ■ Decorative, green foliage

Penstemon
e.g. "Andenken an Friedrich Hahn" (syn. P. "Garnet")
○

type of plant: hardy perennial [6–10]
flowering time: midsummer to early autumn
flower color: purplish red
height: 30in/75cm

Of the readily available penstemons with fairly large flowers, P. "Andenken an Friedrich Hahn" is one of the hardiest. Its tubular blooms, about 1¼in/3cm long, are carried on upright, russet-colored stems. The plant is bushy and vigorous with narrow, pointed, green leaves. P. "Schoenholzeri" (syn. "Firebird") and P. "King George V" are popular, bright red varieties [zones 6–10 and 8–10, respectively]. Other readily available, richly colored varieties include deep purple P. "Blackbird" and P. "Raven" [both zones 8–10]. All these plants flower for many weeks and are often still in bloom in mid-autumn. They all require well-drained, fertile soil and full sun. For a mauve penstemon, see above. The following illustration shows a white variety.

Penstemon
e.g. "White Bedder" (syn. P. "Burford White," P. "Royal White," P. "Snow Storm")
○

type of plant: slightly tender perennial [8–10]
flowering time: midsummer to early autumn
flower color: white
height: 30in/75cm

Popular penstemons with pale, delicately colored flowers include this cream-budded, white-flowered variety, which has erect stems with large, pointed, rich green leaves and 1½in/4cm-long, wide-mouthed, tubular flowers. Further possible examples are P. "Osprey" and P. "Thorn," which have pink-and-white flowers, and P. "Evelyn" [zones 7–10] and P. "Apple Blossom," which produce soft pink blooms. A red variety is shown in the previous illustration; for a mauve variety, see the top of this page. All these plants may continue to flower into mid-autumn. They need fertile soil, sunshine and good drainage to perform well.

Ceratostigma willmottianum
[Chinese plumbago]
○

type of plant: slightly tender shrub [7–10]
flowering time: late summer to mid-autumn
flower color: bright blue
height: 24–36in/60–90cm

The clear blue flowers of this late-flowering shrub are a treat worth waiting for. Each flat-faced, five-petalled flower is about 1in/2.5cm wide. As an extra autumn attraction, the bristly, almost diamond-shaped leaves take on red-bronze tints. Even the russety seed heads are quite pleasing. The plant has a rounded, spreading habit of growth. Light soils are most suitable, and they help to insure that the plant survives low winter temperatures. (In frost-prone areas, the upper growth often dies back each winter.) C. griffithii is similar to C. willmottianum; it is evergreen or semi-evergreen and slightly less hardy [zones 8–10].
also for: ■ Atmospheric pollution ■ Colorful, autumn foliage

Scabiosa columbaria subsp. *ochroleuca* (syn. *S. ochroleuca*) [pincushion flower, scabious]
○

type of plant: hardy perennial [5–8]
flowering time: midsummer to early autumn
flower color: primrose-yellow
height: 24–36in/60–90cm

The mass of wiry stems produced by this long-flowering plant are sparsely clothed with feathery, grayish green leaves. The stems branch above small, dense clumps of simpler, basal leaves. Particularly if *S. columbaria* subsp. *ochroleuca* is regularly dead-headed, its pretty, "pincushion" flower heads, each about 1in/2.5cm across, appear in large numbers. These flowers are attractive to bees and butterflies. Light soils and full sun are most suitable for this plant, which usually self-sows freely.

Erodium manescaui [heron's bill, stork's bill]
○

type of plant: hardy perennial [6–8]
flowering time: early summer to early autumn
flower color: magenta-pink
height: 20in/50cm

The flowers of this plant are borne profusely, over many weeks, above clumps of deeply divided, toothed, ferny. Individual leaves can be as much as 12in/30cm long. The combination of bright mid-green foliage and almost shocking-pink flowers is striking and stylish. The five-petalled blooms, each about 1¼in/3cm across, are arranged in heads of up to twenty flowers. *E. manescaui* is a vigorous, self-sowing plant that is easily grown in most soils with good drainage but, if conditions are too dry, the attractive foliage is rather sparse. It has a preference for alkaline conditions.
also for: ■ Shallow soils over chalk ■ Decorative, green foliage

Salvia verticillata "Purple Rain"
○

type of plant: hardy perennial [5–9]
flowering time: midsummer to early autumn
flower color: violet + deep purple
height: 20in/50cm

Even when the tiny, hooded flowers of this erect and leafy plant have faded, their conspicuous, deep violet-purple surrounds persist. However, at least some of the spent flower stems should be removed to encourage the production of plenty of blooms over a long period. The flowers are arranged in a series of whorls, creating richly colored spikes, each about 10in/25cm long. *S. verticillata* "Purple Rain" forms a generous clump of oval to oblong, mid-green leaves and slightly curved and arching stems.

Coreopsis verticillata [tickseed]
○

type of plant: hardy perennial [4–9]
flowering time: midsummer to early autumn
flower color: yellow
height: 18–24in/45–60cm

C. verticillata is one of the prettiest of the readily available tickseeds and longer-lived than most of them, too. It produces a mass of bright, starry, 2in/5cm-wide flowers and quantities of very finely divided, mid-green foliage. The whole plant is neat and bushy and needs no support. It prefers light, moderately fertile soil. There are a number of attractive varieties: *C.v.* "Moonbeam" has very pale yellow flowers and dark foliage, but it is not always easy to grow well in cool-summer climates; *C.v.* "Grandiflora" has large, deep yellow flowers; *C.v.* "Zagreb" is smaller (up to 12in/30cm).
also for: ■ Flowers suitable for cutting

Geum e.g. "Lady Stratheden" [avens]
○

type of plant: hardy perennial [5–9]
flowering time: early summer to early autumn
flower color: yellow
height: 18–24in/45–60cm
Evergreen

Like many geum hybrids, *G.* "Lady Stratheden" produces large quantities of flowers over many weeks—but only if it is divided every other year. Each flower is 1½–2in/4–5cm across, semi-double and attractively ruffled in appearance. The long, branched flower stems rise well above clumps of bright green foliage. The leaves are divided into mostly oval-shaped leaflets that are hairy and conspicuously veined. *G.* "Mrs J. Bradshaw" is another popular hybrid with a long flowering season; its semi-double flowers are rich scarlet. These plants perform best in fertile, well-drained soil that does not dry out in summer.

Salvia patens e.g. "Cambridge Blue"
○

type of plant: slightly tender/half-hardy perennial [8–10]
flowering time: late summer to mid-autumn
flower color: sky blue
height: 18–24in/45–60cm

Both *S. patens* itself, with its gentian-blue flowers, and this paler but still gloriously colored variety are upright, leafy plants with exceptionally long flowering periods. Their gaping, hooded flowers, each about 2in/5cm long, are arranged in pairs above hairy, mid-green leaves. In cooler regions, these salvias are either treated as annuals or their tuberous roots are lifted and stored under cover during winter. (If they are left in the garden in winter in frost-prone areas, they need some protection.) Both plants should be grown in a warm site and fertile, well-drained soil. In very mild areas they may be more than 4ft/1.2m high and, in maturity, rather straggly.

x *Halimiocistus sahucii*
(syn. *Cistus sahucii*)
○

type of plant: slightly tender/hardy shrub [8–9]
flowering time: early summer to early autumn
flower color: white
height: 18in/45cm
Evergreen

To do well, this wide-spreading, hummocky plant must have really good drainage and a position in full sun. It thrives in hot, dry conditions. Individually, the saucer-shaped, yellow-stamened flowers, 1¼in/3cm across, are short-lived, but numerous buds open in succession. Flowering is particularly profuse during the earlier part of summer. The dark green leaves are narrow and slightly resinous.
also for: ■ Dry soils in hot, sunny sites

Linum narbonense
[blue flax]
○

type of plant: hardy perennial [5–8]
flowering time: early to late summer
flower color: azure-blue
height: 18in/45cm

Provided the soil is light and the site is sunny, this willowy plant will be covered in flowers throughout the summer months. Each flower is a shallow funnel, about 1½in/4cm wide. Individually, the blooms are short-lived but numerous buds open in succession. The many slender, wiry stems and very narrow, slightly glaucous leaves form an airy clump of growth. *L. perenne* [zones 7–10] is another short-lived flax; its flowers fade from deep blue to sky-blue as the day progresses. The popular, yellow-flowered flaxes, such as *L. flavum* "Gemmell's Hybrid," are much lower-growing plants but they, too, flower for many weeks in summer

Nepeta sibirica
(syn. *Dracocephalum sibiricum*,
N. macrantha*)
"Souvenir d"André Chaudron"
(syn. *N.* "Blue Beauty")
[catmint] ○

type of plant: hardy perennial [5–9]
flowering time: early to late summer
flower color: soft lavender-blue
height: 18in/45cm

The more or less upright stems of *N. sibirica* "Souvenir d'André Chaudron" may need support. They are clothed in pointed, bright green leaves and topped with loose, branched spikes of flowers. Each tubular bloom is about 1½in/4cm long. The foliage has a not especially attractive, mint-like scent when bruised. *N. sibirica* itself is similar, but its flowering season is slightly shorter and it grows about 36in/90cm tall. Both these plants need well-drained soil. Their running rootstocks tend to spread very freely. *N. nervosa*, which is about 12in/30cm high, has denser spikes of blue flowers throughout summer.

***Oenothera fruticosa* "Fyrverkeri"**
(syn. *O.f.* Fireworks)
[sundrops, evening primrose]
○

type of plant: hardy perennial [4–9]
flowering time: early to late summer
flower color: yellow
height: 18in/45cm

Unusually, this *Oenothera* blooms during the day, rather than in the evening. Individually, its bowl-shaped flowers, each about 1½in/4cm wide, are short-lived, but numerous, slim buds unfurl in succession almost all summer long. The flowers are carried on upright, leafy stems and these—and often the flower buds too—are tinged with red. *O. fruticosa* "Fyrverkeri" forms clumps of growth. Its rosettes of slender, pointed leaves are suffused with reddish purple when young; the mature foliage is rich green. *O.f.* subsp. *glauca* "Erica Robin" has young leaves that are a bronzed apricot color. Both plants need fertile soil with good drainage.
also for: ■ Purple, bronze, or red leaves (young leaves only)

Osteospermum
e.g. "Buttermilk"
○

type of plant: slightly tender/half-hardy perennial [9–10]
flowering time: early summer to mid-autumn
flower color: pale yellow + white
height: 18in/45cm
Evergreen

Osteospermum produce their large, daisy-like flowers over several months. They are popular plants for bedding and for growing in containers. The range of *Osteospermum* continues to widen but there are only a few of these generally rather tender plants that are even moderately hardy (for an example, see the pink-flowered species on p.57). *O.* "Buttermilk," shown here, is a rather upright variety with slender, mid-green leaves that have an unpleasant, sweet scent when bruised. Its dark-centered, bronze-backed flowers are about 2in/5cm across. All these plants do best—and are hardiest—in light soil in warm, sheltered sites; they cope well with hot, dry conditions. They are especially floriferous in coastal gardens. Their flowers only open completely in full sun. For a variegated *Osteospermum*, see p.166.
also for: ■ Dry soils in hot, sunny sites

Potentilla "Gibson's Scarlet"
[cinquefoil]
○

type of plant: hardy perennial [5–8]
flowering time: early to late summer
flower color: bright scarlet
height: 18in/45cm

Throughout the summer, this herbaceous cinquefoil produces numerous, dazzling flowers. Each dark-centered saucer of brilliant scarlet is about 1¼in/3cm across. P. "Gibson's Scarlet" forms clumps of fairly upright stems that rise above attractive, veined and toothed leaflets. The foliage is a fairly bright mid-green. Other long-flowering herbaceous cinquefoils include P. atrosanguinea, which is usually some shade of bright red, and orange-red P. "William Rollison"; those with less vividly colored blooms include pink-flowered P. nepalensis "Miss Willmott." All these plants are easily grown in any well-drained soil.
also for: ■ Decorative, green foliage

Coreopsis rosea "American Dream"
[tickseed]
○

type of plant: hardy perennial [3–9]
flowering time: midsummer to early autumn
flower color: pink
height: 12–18in/30–45cm

All the familiar tickseeds have yellow blooms (see, for example, the long-flowering species on p.338), but this pink-flowered variety is increasingly popular. Like most of its yellow-flowered counterparts, C. rosea "American Dream" flowers over many weeks and tends to be rather short-lived. Its numerous, starry blooms, up to 1in/2.5cm across, cover tussocks of very fine, needle-like, bright green leaflets. The plant grows well in most soils with good drainage and thrives in moist, sandy soil. It is not drought-tolerant.

Buphthalmum salicifolium
○

type of plant: hardy perennial [4–9]
flowering time: early summer to early autumn
flower color: yellow
height: 12–15in/30–38cm

When planted in poor soil with good drainage, the slender, branching stems of B. salicifolium are upright and the mass of narrow, dark green leaves is quite dense. In richer, moister soils, general growth is much laxer and the flower stems flop and curve unless staked. In both types of soil, however, the slender-petaled daisies—each about 1in/2.5cm wide—are produced over a long period. They last very well as cut flowers. B. salicifolium is shown here with Alchemilla mollis (for details of which, see p.114).
also for: ■ Flowers suitable for cutting

Diascia rigescens
○

type of plant: slightly tender perennial [8–9]
flowering time: early summer to early autumn
flower color: dusky pink
height: 12–15in/30–38cm

In light soils and full sun many Diascia are very nearly hardy. They bloom for several months and the readily available species and varieties have flowers in particularly attractive shades of pink. The example shown here has strong stems, erect or semi-trailing, that are clothed with neat, pointed leaves of soft rich green and topped with dense spikes of tubular flowers. Each spike is 6–8in/15–20cm long. Although Diascia need good drainage, they require moisture, too, and they are not suitable for hot, dry positions. Other popular plants in this genus include D. barberae "Blackthorn Apricot" (apricot-pink flowers), D. vigilis (clear pink flowers and a creeping, wide-spreading habit of growth), and lower-growing D. barberae "Ruby Field" (rich rose-pink flowers).

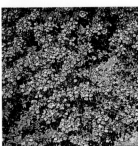

Nemesia denticulata
(syn. N.d. "Confetti")
○

type of plant: slightly tender perennial [8–10]
flowering time: early summer to early autumn
flower color: mauve-pink
height: 12–15in/30–38cm

N. denticulata is an exceptionally free-flowering plant that, in mild areas, can be left outdoors during the winter. It produces its mass of frilly flowers over a period of several months. The blooms, each less than ½in/1cm wide, have a slight, sugary, confectionery-like scent (the pale pink flowers of N. "Fragrant Cloud" have a more pronounced fragrance). The leaves are light green and narrow. As the rather brittle flowering shoots gradually lengthen, they may become lanky enough to benefit from cutting back hard from about midsummer onward; this rejuvenates the whole plant. A sheltered site and medium to light, well-drained soil that remains moist during summer suit N. denticulata best.

Malva sylvestris
e.g. "Primley Blue"
[mallow]
○

type of plant: hardy perennial/biennial [5–9]
flowering time: early summer to mid-autumn
flower color: pale violet-blue + dark violet-blue
height: 10–20in/25–50cm

The stiff stems of this rather short-lived mallow are mainly prostrate and spreading, and they often create a tangle of growth. They are decorated with numerous clusters of dark-veined flowers that open, in succession, over a long period. Each flower is shallowly funnel-shaped and 1½–2in/4–5cm across. The neat, lobed leaves are a slightly grayish green. Most soils with reasonable drainage are suitable for M. sylvestris "Primley Blue," which tends to live longest when conditions are neither very fertile nor very moist. The taller and more upright M.s. "Zebrina" has purple-veined, white flowers.

Parahebe cataractae
e.g. "Delight"
○

type of plant: slightly tender shrub/perennial [8–10]
flowering time: early summer to early autumn
flower color: blue-violet + red
height: 10–12in/25–30cm
Evergreen

P. cataractae and its varieties are attractive, sprawling to erect subshrubs for well-drained soil and a sunny site. They produce masses of little, red-eyed flowers over a long period. The funnel-shaped blooms, each about ½in/1cm across, are arranged in sprays. P.c. "Delight" forms a cushion of slender stems and neat, pointed, rich green leaves. As well as varieties with blue or purplish flowers, there are white- and pink-flowered varieties of P. cataractae.

Geranium x riversleaianum
"Russell Prichard"
[cranesbill]
○

type of plant: hardy perennial [6–8]
flowering time: early summer to mid-autumn
flower color: magenta-pink
height: 9in/23cm
Semi-evergreen

The prostrate flower stems of this cranesbill sprawl out, from a central crown, over a dense carpet of foliage, 24in/60cm or more wide. The stems end in erectly held, branched heads of 1¼in/3cm-wide, funnel-shaped blooms that are produced over an unusually long season. There is a definite grayish cast to the fairly bright green foliage, and the leaves are attractively lobed, toothed and veined. The plant retains its basal leaves in winter. For those gardeners who find the searing magenta-pink of these flowers too overpowering, there are the light pink blooms of G. x riversleaianum "Mavis Simpson." Most soils are suitable, as long as they are well drained.
also for: ■ Ground cover ■ Decorative, green foliage

Silene schafta
[campion, catchfly]
○

type of plant: hardy perennial [6–9]
flowering time: late summer to mid-autumn
flower color: bright magenta-pink
height: 6–9in/15–23cm
Semi-evergreen

S. schafta produces a mass of long flower buds over its clump of semi-prostrate stems and little, lance-shaped leaves. The foliage is bright green and softly hairy. Each flower has five notched petals, and individual blooms are usually less than 1in/2.5cm wide. In many years, S. schafta continues flowering until late autumn. Light, slightly alkaline soil is most suitable for this plant, but it is easily grown as long as it has good drainage.

Oenothera macrocarpa
(syn. O. missouriensis)
[Ozark sundrops]
○

type of plant: hardy perennial [5–8]
flowering time: early summer to early autumn
flower color: yellow
height: 6–8in/15–20cm

The reddish stems of Ozark sundrops sprawl outwards from a central point. They are clothed in slim, fresh green leaves, among which are borne goblet-shaped blooms, 4–5in/10–12cm wide. These open, in succession, from long, pointed buds, over a period of several months. Each short-lived flower begins to expand fully towards midday. In hot summers, huge seed pods develop. Most soils with good drainage are suitable, and the plant copes well with hot, dry conditions.
also for: ■ Dry soils in hot, sunny sites

Convolvulus sabatius
(syn. C. mauritanicus)
○

type of plant: half-hardy/slightly tender perennial [8–9]
flowering time: early to late summer
flower color: variable—bright purplish blue to mauve-blue
height: 6in/15cm

Although they look like miniature versions of morning glory flowers, these funnel-shaped blooms stay open all day. They are produced, in succession, throughout the summer. Each pretty flower is ¾–1½in/2–4cm across. The slender, trailing stems and rounded, sometimes grayish leaves create a neat, spreading mass of growth that is usually at least 18in/45cm wide. C. sabatius needs full sun and light, well-drained, rather gritty soil. It is particularly happy in a position where its roots can remain cool—in the crevices of a wall or between paving stones, for instance. It is increasingly popular for use in a hanging basket.
also for: ■ Crevices in paving

Sedum kamtschaticum var. floriferum "Weihenstephaner Gold"
[stonecrop]
○

type of plant: hardy perennial [4–8]
flowering time: midsummer to mid-autumn
flower color: golden yellow
height: 4in/10cm
Semi-evergreen

From a central clump, this plant produces numerous, prostrate, trailing stems that are clothed in rosette-like arrangements of spoon-shaped, glossy, olive-green leaves. In autumn, the foliage often becomes tinged with crimson. Large quantities of starry flowers appear, in clusters, over a period of many weeks. As each ½in/1cm-wide flower ages, it turns orange-bronze, then deep bronze. *S. kamtschaticum* var. *kamtschaticum* "Variegatum" has creamy white edges to its pink-tinged, light green leaves; its yellow flowers are borne over a slightly shorter season than those of *S.k.* var. *floriferum* "Weihenstephaner Gold." Both plants grow densely in really well-drained soil and full sun.
also for: ■ Dry soils in hot, sunny sites ■ Ground cover ■ Crevices in paving

Rhodohypoxis baurii
○

type of plant: slightly tender perennial [8–9]
flowering time: late spring to early autumn
flower color: deep pink
height: 3–4in/8–10cm

When given moisture-retentive soil that is also light and well drained, this plant survives most winters in milder areas. A combination of coldness and wetness is more damaging than low temperatures alone. In areas with hot summers, *R. baurii* needs some shade in order to conserve moisture—the flowering period is considerably shorter if conditions are dry. Cultivars of *R. baurii* with crimson, white or pale pink flowers can be obtained from nurseries specializing in rock plants or dwarf bulbs. Both the species and its varieties form clumps of usually narrow, hairy leaves from corm-like rootstocks. They are all very free-flowering plants. Their six-petaled blooms are normally not much more than ½in/1cm wide.

ADDITIONAL PERENNIAL PLANTS, featured elsewhere in this book, that have a long, continuous flowering period

○ sun

minimum height 10ft/3m or more
Clerodendrum trichotomum, see p.253
Eccremocarpus scaber, see p.128
Fremontodendron "California Glory,"
 see p.13
Magnolia grandiflora "Exmouth," see p.297
Solanum crispum "Glasnevin," see p.127

minimum height between 3ft/90cm and 10ft/3m
Abutilon megapotamicum, see p.145
Abutilon megapotamicum "Variegatum,"
 see p.163
Ceanothus x delileanus "Gloire de Versailles,"
 see p.52
Clerodendrum trichotomum, see p.253
Colutea arborescens, see p.253
Cortaderia selloana "Pumila," see p.269
Hibiscus syriacus "Woodbridge," see p.145
Lavatera x clementii "Rosea," see p.90
Lupinus arboreus, see p.91
Romneya coulteri, see p.299
Rosa Peace, see p.97
Rosa Warm Welcome, see p.128
Salvia uliginosa, see p.65
Spartium junceum, see p.52
Verbascum olympicum, see p.183

minimum height 3ft/90cm or less
Achillea "Moonshine," see p.186
Armeria maritima "Alba," see p.109
Calamintha nepeta subsp. *nepeta,* see p.247
Calluna vulgaris "H.E. Beale," see p.106
Catananche caerulea, see p.276
Centranthus ruber, see p.15
Ceratostigma plumbaginoides, see p.237
Cichorium intybus, see p.14
Convolvulus cneorum, see p.188
Coronilla valentina subsp. *glauca* "Variegata,"
 see p.164
Cosmos atrosanguineus, see p.301
Crinum x powellii, see p.300
Dianthus alpinus, see p.156
Echinacea purpurea, see p.271
Echinacea purpurea "White Swan," see p.277
Erica cinerea "C.D. Eason," see p.26
Erica x darleyensis "Darley Dale," see p.106
Erica x darleyensis "Silberschmelze," see p.316
Erica erigena "Brightness," see p.138
Erica tetralix "Alba Mollis," see p.26
Erica vagans "Mrs D.F. Maxwell," see p.26
Erigeron "Dunkelste Aller," see p.277
Erigeron karvinskianus, see p.154
Erigeron "Quakeress," see p.277
Eryngium alpinum, see p.274
Erysimum cheiri "Harpur Crewe," see p.302

Euphorbia characias subsp. *wulfenii,* see p.184
Fuchsia magellanica "Versicolor," see p.163
Gaillardia "Burgunder," see p.277
Geranium "Ann Folkard," see p.213
Geranium "Ballerina," see p.60
Gypsophila repens "Rosea," see p.60
Hedysarum coronarium, see p.300
Lobelia "Queen Victoria," see p.66
Lotus hirsutus, see p.187
Lychnis flos-jovis "Hort's Variety," see p.189
Lythrum salicaria "Blush," see p.42
Lythrum salicaria "Robert," see p.66
Mimulus aurantiacus, see p.146
Osteospermum jucundum, see p.57
Osteospermum "Silver Sparkler," see p.166
Penstemon pinifolius, see p.58
Rosa Blue Moon, see p.273
Rosa Sweet Dream, see p.147
Salvia microphylla var. *microphylla,* see p.146
Satureja montana, see p.247
Scabiosa caucasica "Clive Greaves," see p.15
Sisyrinchium idahoense "Album," see p.156
Stokesia laevis, see p.282
Trifolium repens "Purpurascens Quadrifolium,"
 see p.168
Ulex europaeus "Flore Pleno," see p.54
Verbascum "Gainsborough," see p.15
Zauschneria californica "Dublin," see p.58

Rosa e.g. "Golden Showers" (Climbing)
[rose]
○ [◐]

type of plant: hardy climber [5–9]
flowering time: early summer to mid-autumn
flower color: rich yellow fading to cream
height: 8–10ft/2.4–3m

A long and continuous succession of semi-double, loosely formed flowers emerge from the red-tinged buds of *R.* "Golden Showers." Individual blooms are often 4in/10cm across, and they are only slightly fragrant. The nearly prickle-free stems are rather stiff and upright but, since flowering is good even when the plant is grown erectly, this feature is an asset in a small garden and other confined spaces. The glossy, dark green foliage is rather sparse. This generally healthy rose performs well on a north-facing wall, and it is tolerant of fairly poor soils (although a sunny site and fertile, well-drained, moisture-retentive soil give better results). See pp.133 and 134 for two further examples of climbing roses with long flowering seasons.
also for: ■ Climbing plants

Rosa e.g. "Roseraie de l'Hay" (Rugosa)
[rose]
○[◐]

type of plant: hardy shrub [5–9]
flowering time: early summer to early autumn
flower color: crimson-purple
height: 6ft/1.8m

The opulently colored, double blooms of this vigorous rose are produced continuously throughout the summer months and into autumn. The flowers, each about 4in/10cm across, exude a warm, sweet, almost nutty fragrance. There are no hips, but in autumn the light green, crinkly leaves turn deep yellow. This prickly-stemmed plant is dense and bushy, and it is a good rose for hedging (young plants should be about 36in/90cm apart). It is wind- and salt-resistant. Most soils, including quite light and poor ones, are suitable. For another fragrant Rugosa rose that flowers almost continuously, see p.142.
also for: ■ Windswept, seaside gardens ■ Atmospheric pollution ■ Hedging plants ■ Colorful, autumn foliage ■ Flowers suitable for cutting ■ Fragrant flowers

Galega officinalis
[goat's rue]
○[◐]

type of plant: hardy perennial [4–9]
flowering time: early to late summer
flower color: variable—lilac, white, purple, sometimes bicolored with white
height: 4–5ft/1.2–1.5m

G. officinalis is easily pleased in most soils but it has a preference for fairly moist conditions. In rich soil particularly, the plant grows strongly and its clump of growth is liable to sprawl—often widely, and in any case to about 36in/90cm across. The pea-flowers are numerous and arranged in loose spikes approximately 6in/15cm long; they have a sweet, coconut-like scent. Quantities of slender, mid-green leaflets clothe the erect but rather lax stems.
also for: ■ Fragrant flowers

Lobelia x gerardii "Vedrariensis"
○[◐]

type of plant: hardy perennial [5–8]
flowering time: midsummer to mid-autumn
flower color: violet-purple
height: 36in/90cm

Many lobelias have a flowering period of several months (see also the example shown on p.66). The hybrid shown here has rosettes of dark green, often red-tinged, pointed leaves to complement its opulently colored, lipped flowers. Individual blooms are only about 1in/2.5cm across but each spike, up to 18in/45cm long, bears numerous flowers. The stout, upright, leafy stems form clumps of growth. L. x gerardii "Vedrariensis" grows best in rich, damp soil, but it is happy in most soils that are fertile and reliably moist. L. "Tania" bears redder flowers that are produced from midsummer until early autumn.
also for: ■ Damp and wet soils

Potentilla fruticosa e.g. "Tangerine"
[shrubby cinquefoil]
○[◐]

type of plant: hardy shrub [3–7]
flowering time: early summer to mid-autumn
flower color: copper-tinged yellow in sun; pale orange in shade
height: 30in/75cm

Shrubby cinquefoils are easily grown plants with long flowering seasons. Many varieties have yellow flowers (for an example, see p.110), others have flowers that are pink (e.g. P. fruticosa Princess), white (e.g. P.f. "Abbotswood"), or cream (see p.142), or the flowers may be more warmly colored, like those of P.f. "Tangerine." These numerous, 1¼in/3cm-wide, saucer-shaped blooms fade in strong sun and under dry conditions (as do, for instance, the red flowers of P.f. "Red Ace" and the blooms of other, deeply colored varieties). P.f. "Tangerine" is a dense, bushy, ground-covering mass of small twigs and soft mid-green, little leaflets. P. fruticosa and its varieties are happy in most soils, as long as they are not either wet or very dry.
also for: ■ Heavy, clay soils ■ Ground cover

Rudbeckia fulgida var. sullivantii "Goldsturm"
[black-eyed Susan, coneflower]
○[◐]

type of plant: hardy perennial [4–9]
flowering time: midsummer to mid-autumn
flower color: deep yellow + dark brown
height: 30in/75cm

The flowers of R. fulgida var. sullivantii "Goldsturm" are up to 5in/12cm wide and freely borne on upright stems above clumps of broad, basal leaves. These substantial daisies appear over a very long period. Their prominent, central cones are dark, contrasting well with the rich yellow of the petals and contributing to the sprightly air of the whole plant. R. fulgida var. deamii has slightly narrower, lighter yellow petals, while R. laciniata "Goldquelle" bears double, lemon-yellow flowers. Any moderately fertile garden soil that is moisture-retentive is suitable for these plants. They all make good cut flowers.
also for: ■ Heavy, clay soils ■ Flowers suitable for cutting

Tradescantia Andersoniana Group e.g. "Osprey"
[spiderwort]
○[◐]

type of plant: hardy perennial [5–9]
flowering time: early summer to early autumn
flower color: white + lilac
height: 20–24in/50–60cm

Although many spiderworts produce rather untidy clumps of long, slim leaves and fleshy stems, their three-petalled blooms are pretty and they open, in succession, throughout the summer months and into autumn. The flowers are usually held just above the foliage. T. Andersoniana Group "Osprey" creates a vase-shaped clump of arching, mid-green leaves. Its lilac-centered blooms are each 1½–2in/4–5cm across. Other popular T. Andersoniana Group varieties include "Innocence" (pure white), "Isis" (blue) and "Purple Dome" (rich purple). All these plants are easy to grow in most soils, as long as conditions are reasonably moisture-retentive. A position in full sun encourages the production of plenty of flowers.

Phuopsis stylosa
(syn. *Crucianella stylosa*)
○[◐]

type of plant: hardy perennial [6–9]
flowering time: early to late summer
flower color: pink
height: 10in/25cm

The numerous, sticky stems and the whorls of tiny, bright green leaves produced by P. stylosa are sharply and rather unpleasantly scented. However, they form efficient, weed-smothering carpets of growth (especially if the plant is cut back after flowering, to prevent it from becoming straggly). The dense, 2½in/6cm-wide heads of tubular flowers have a sweet scent and are attractive to butterflies. This vigorous, sometimes invasive plant needs good drainage, but really dry conditions are not suitable.
also for: ■ Ground cover ■ Fragrant flowers

Erica carnea
e.g. "Vivellii"
[heath, heather]
○[◐]

type of plant: hardy shrub [5–8]
flowering time: late winter to mid-spring
flower color: mauve-pink turning to magenta
height: 6–8in/15–20cm
Evergreen

In cold weather, the tiny, dark green, needle-like leaves of E. carnea "Vivellii" become tinged with deep bronze. Against this background, the dense spikes of ¼in/0.5cm-long, bell-shaped flowers look especially vivid. This floriferous plant blooms for many weeks and, particularly because it grows fairly slowly, it is a good choice for a container. It spreads about 15in/38cm wide. Some varieties of E. carnea grow much more vigorously (for an example, see p.111). All these plants create dense, carpeting ground cover. Although they tolerate alkaline conditions and a little shade, they prefer acid to neutral soils that are both humus-rich and well drained, and an open position.
also for: ■ Acid soils ■ Ground cover ■ Growing in containers ■ Winter-flowering plants

---

ADDITIONAL PERENNIAL PLANTS, featured elsewhere in this book, that have a long, continuous flowering period

○[◐] sun (or partial shade)

minimum height 10ft/3m or more
Clematis "Bill MacKenzie," see p.256
Rosa "New Dawn," see p.130

minimum height between 3ft/90cm and 10ft/3m
Acanthus spinosus, see p.223
Artemisia lactiflora, see p.284
Jasminum humile "Revolutum," see p.304
Lathyrus latifolius "White Pearl," see p.130

Potentilla fruticosa "Vilmoriniana," see p.142
Rosa "Penelope," see p.304
Rudbeckia laciniata "Herbstsonne," see p.43
Tropaeolum tuberosum var. *lineamaculatum* "Ken Aslet," see p.130

minimum height 3ft/90cm or less
Anaphalis triplinervis, see p.194
Aponogeton distachyos, see p.307
Astrantia major "Sunningdale Variegated," see p.169

Caltha palustris var. *alba*, see p.71
Erica carnea "King George," see p.317
Erica carnea "Springwood White," see p.111
Fuchsia magellanica var. *gracilis* "Aurea," see p.214
Geranium sanguineum, see p.111
Monarda "Cambridge Scarlet," see p.249
Monarda "Croftway Pink," see p.69
Potentilla fruticosa "Elizabeth," see p.110
Tradescantia Andersoniana Group "Blue and Gold," see p.215

Lonicera periclymenum
"Graham Thomas"
[honeysuckle]
○◑

type of plant: hardy climber [5–9]
flowering time: midsummer to early autumn
flower color: pale cream turning to yellow
height: 15–20ft/4.5–6m

For gardeners who dislike the pinks and purples of many honeysuckle flowers, there are the cream, then yellow blooms of this very long-flowering variety (and see also L. japonica "Halliana," p.307). The numerous, tubular, lipped flowers, each 1½–2in/4–5cm long, are arranged in clusters; they are sweetly and spicily fragrant, especially in the evening. In cooler climates particularly, shiny, red berries often ripen alongside the later flowers. The leaves are fresh green, oval, and pointed. This vigorous, twining honeysuckle should be given moisture-retentive, fertile soil and, ideally, a position where its roots are in shade and its upper growths are in sun.
also for: ■ Climbing plants ■ Ornamental fruit (see above) ■ Fragrant flowers

Clematis e.g. "Perle d'Azur"
◯◑

type of plant: hardy climber [5–9]
flowering time: midsummer to early autumn
flower color: light blue + mauve
height: 10–15ft/3–4.5m

Vigorous and reliably free-flowering C. "Perle d'Azur" produces 4in/10cm-wide, slightly nodding flowers over many weeks (indeed, there are often considerable numbers of blooms in mid-autumn). Its broad, pointed, mid-green leaves are fairly large. The plant likes its roots to be cool and moist in fertile soil, while its upper growths receive a reasonable amount of sun. Walls of any aspect are suitable, as long as they are not very exposed. In order to climb, the plant must be given a support for its twining leaf-stalks to clasp. Other popular, blue clematis include mauve-blue C. "Prince Charles" and double, purplish blue C. "Multi Blue"; both varieties flower throughout summer.
also for: ■ Climbing plants

Clematis e.g. "Niobe"
◯◑

type of plant: hardy climber [6–9]
flowering time: early to late summer
flower color: dark wine-red
height: 7–10ft/2.1–3m

The sumptuously colored, velvety blooms of C. "Niobe" open in succession over many weeks. Each flower is up to 6in/15cm across. The dark "petals," which surround clusters of contrastingly pale yellowish green stamens, show up well against the plant's fairly large, light green, pointed leaves. As the flowers fade, the purplish undertones in their coloring become more prominent. To perform well, larger-flowered hybrid clematis, such as C. "Niobe," need fertile, humus-rich, moisture-retentive soil with good drainage. Ideally, their roots should be cool and shaded and their top growth should be in sun. They climb by means of twining leaf-stalks. C. "Niobe" can be grown on walls of any aspect. C. "Madame Julia Correvon" has bright red, narrow-"petalled" flowers, 3in/8cm wide, from midsummer into autumn.
also for: ■ Growing in containers (C. "Niobe") ■ Climbing plants

Salvia guaranitica
◯◑

type of plant: slightly tender/half-hardy perennial [9–11]
flowering time: late summer to mid-autumn
flower color: bright rich blue
height: 4–6ft/1.2–1.8m

S. guaranitica produces its strikingly colored flowers over a period of several months late in the gardening year. It is, perhaps, at its very best in autumn. Its upright stems bear largish, pointed leaves of bright mid-green. At the ends of these stems are spikes of gaping, tubular flowers, each flower up to 2in/5cm long. In really mild areas this subshrubby perennial does not need winter protection; elsewhere protection is usually essential (and in cooler regions this salvia is quite often grown as an annual). In any case, a warm, sheltered site and fertile, well-drained soil are required. S. guaranitica "Blue Enigma" produces numerous, clear blue flowers over an exceptionally long period.

Chaenomeles × superba
e.g. "Knap Hill Scarlet"
[flowering quince]
◯◑

type of plant: hardy shrub [5–9]
flowering time: early spring to early summer
flower color: orange-red
height: 4–5ft/1.2–1.5m

Although a sunny position encourages the production of particularly large numbers of blooms, this open, bushy shrub flowers almost anywhere and in a wide variety of soils (although extreme alkalinity is best avoided). When trained against a wall, C. x superba "Knap Hill Scarlet" exceeds the maximum height given here and flowering may begin in late winter. The earliest flowers open before the oval, glossy, mid-green leaves emerge. Each bowl-shaped bloom, 2in/5cm or more across, is filled with golden stamens. Cut sprays last well indoors. In autumn, yellow, apple-like fruits ripen; they are fragrant and edible. For a pink-flowered variety of C. x superba, see p.45.
also for: ■ Heavy, clay soils ■ Atmospheric pollution ■ Ornamental fruit ■ Flowers suitable for cutting

Hypericum "Hidcote"
[St John's wort]
◯◑

type of plant: hardy shrub [7–9]
flowering time: midsummer to mid-autumn
flower color: bright yellow
height: 4–5ft/1.2–1.5m
Semi-evergreen

This dense, bushy, rounded shrub covers itself in 2in/5cm-wide, saucer-shaped flowers for several months each year. The plant, with its fairly upright branches and numerous red-brown twigs, is usually rather wider than it is tall. Even in cold regions the deep green, pointed leaves are retained until early winter. They emit an "oranges-and-lemons" fragrance when crushed. H. "Hidcote" grows in any reasonably well-drained soil. Although it is a robust and tolerant plant, it is not at its best in very dry conditions. It makes a floriferous, informal hedge (young plants should be about 30in/75cm apart).
also for: ■ Atmospheric pollution ■ Hedging plants ■ Aromatic foliage

Rosa e.g. Iceberg = "Korbin" (Floribunda or Cluster-flowered) [rose]
○◐

type of plant: hardy shrub [5–9]
flowering time: early summer to mid-autumn
flower color: palest cream
height: 4–5ft/1.2–1.5m

R. Iceberg is vigorous, free-flowering and generally healthy. Its slightly fragrant, double blooms are carried, in generous sprays, on virtually prickle-free stems. These almost pure white flowers, each about 3in/8cm across, are weather-resistant and excellent for cutting. The foliage is light green. In most soils, *R.* Iceberg grows strongly. Its rather upright shape makes it suitable for hedging (young plants should be about 24in/60cm apart) and it is very good as a standard. Other popular Floribunda or Cluster-flowered roses include *R.* Mountbatten (yellow), *R.* "The Queen Elizabeth" (pink), and very fragrant, white-flowered *R.* Margaret Merril. Like many roses of this type, these plants flower continuously over a long period. In mild areas, *R.* Iceberg may still be in bloom in early winter.
also for: ■ Atmospheric pollution ■ Hedging plants ■ Flowers suitable for cutting

Hydrangea e.g. "Preziosa" (syn. *H. serrata* "Preziosa")
○◐

type of plant: hardy/slightly tender shrub [6–9]
flowering time: midsummer to early autumn
flower color: pink changing to crimson or deep red
height: 3–5ft/0.9–1.5m

Good autumn foliage as well as a long flowering season make this one of the most effective hydrangeas. Its broad, pointed leaves are purplish when young, rich green in maturity and deep bronze-purple in autumn. Rounded flower heads, 4–5in/10–12cm across, are carried on dark, upright, rather slender stems; they dry well. The plant grows best in fertile, moisture-retentive soil that is rich in humus. It thrives in urban gardens. In cold climates, a sheltered site is often needed, since frost and cold winds can damage the buds. Some shade is usually needed in regions with hot summers.
also for: ■ Atmospheric pollution ■ Growing in containers ■ Colorful, autumn foliage ■ Ornamental fruit ("seed" heads) ■ Flowers suitable for cutting (mainly drying)

Fuchsia e.g. "Mrs Popple"
○◐

type of plant: slightly tender shrub [8–11]
flowering time: midsummer to mid-autumn
flower color: crimson-red + violet
height: 3–4ft/0.9–1.2m (see description)

This vigorous, free-flowering fuchsia produces masses of pendent flowers over a long period. Its neat, dark, often purple-tinged leaves enhance the rich coloring of the bell-shaped blooms, each of which is about 2in/5cm across. In mild regions, where its top growth is retained during winter, *F.* "Mrs Popple" is shrubby and a good deal taller than indicated here, with arching growths; elsewhere, it is herbaceous and rather upright. Well-drained soil in which the plant's roots remain cool and moist is ideal. The numerous, so-called hardy, hybrid fuchsias [zones 8–11] include *F.* "Lady Thumb" (red-and-white flowers), *F.* "Tom Thumb" (see p.151) and trailing *F.* "Lena" (white-and-magenta).
also for: ■ Windswept, seaside gardens

Amsonia tabernaemontana
○◐

type of plant: hardy perennial [4–9]
flowering time: late spring to midsummer
flower color: pale blue
height: 18–24in/45–60cm

A. tabernaemontana is an appealing plant that is in flower for many weeks. Its numerous, stiff, upright stems are topped with loose, rounded clusters of starry flowers. Each delicately shaped "star" is up to ¼in/2cm across. This long-lived plant forms clumps of leafy growth. The leaves are smooth, slender and rich mid-green. Although it prefers fairly moist conditions, *A. tabernaemontana* is adaptable, and most soils are suitable.

Aster thomsonii "Nanus"
○◐

type of plant: hardy perennial [4–9]
flowering time: late summer to mid-autumn
flower color: lilac-blue
height: 15–18in/38–45cm

This excellent, little plant looks like a miniature, rather wispier version of *A.* x *frikartii* "Mönch" (see p.336). It produces numerous, small sprays of slim-petalled daisies, for many weeks, late in the gardening year. Each yellow-centered flower is 1½–2in/4–5cm across. As well as these neat and simple blooms, there is good, leafy growth on the erect stems. The foliage has an attractively soft, grayish cast to it. To grow and flower well, *A. thomsonii* "Nanus" needs fertile soil that does not dry out in summer.

Calamintha grandiflora
[calamint]
○◐

type of plant: hardy perennial [6–9]
flowering time: early summer to early autumn
flower color: lilac-pink
height: 15–18in/38–45cm

All through summer and into autumn this bushy, spreading plant produces its bright, tubular blooms on upright stems. The flowers, up to 1½in/4cm long, are very attractive to bees. The little, pointed leaves smell of mint when bruised. They are conspicuously veined and toothed and are usually a rather light green. The foliage of *C. grandiflora* "Variegata" is flecked and speckled with greenish cream. Both these plants have a preference for alkaline soil that is well-drained but not dry.

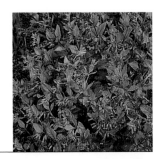

Geranium endressii
[cranesbill]
○◐

type of plant: hardy perennial [4–8]
flowering time: early summer to early autumn
flower color: bright rose-pink
height: 15–18in/38–45cm
Evergreen

G. endressii spreads, by means of underground stems, into dense patches of light green, toothed and lobed leaves. It is usually about 24in/60cm wide. Its small clusters of flowers open in succession over many weeks. Each flower is trumpet-shaped, about 1¼in/3cm across, and is held more or less upright, well clear of the foliage. Any soil with reasonable drainage is suitable and the plant can cope with dry shade (although not as well as *G. nodosum* and *G. macrorrhizum*, for details of which see pp.82 and 251).
also for: ■ Ground cover ■ Decorative, green foliage

Geranium wallichianum "Buxton's Variety"
(syn. *G.* "Buxton's Blue")
[cranesbill]
○◐

type of plant: hardy perennial [5–8]
flowering time: midsummer to mid-autumn
flower color: lavender-blue + white
height: 12in/30cm

As well as clear-colored flowers produced over a very long period, this sprawling cranesbill has neatly lobed, faintly marbled leaves of rich green. In autumn, the leaf edges become red-tinged. Most well-drained soils are suitable but *G. wallichianum* "Buxton's Variety" is at its best when it has a cool root-run. Especially in sun, the plant is usually dense enough to provide good ground cover. However, there are always long, trailing stems—which sometimes clamber into other plants—as well as the more compact, central, carpeting growths. Each saucer-shaped flower is up to 1¼in/3cm across.
also for: ■ Ground cover ■ Decorative, green foliage ■ Colorful, autumn foliage.

Corydalis lutea
○◐

type of plant: hardy perennial [5–8]
flowering time: late spring to early autumn
flower color: yellow
height: 9–12in/23–30cm
Evergreen

Although this prolific self-sower thrives in alkaline conditions, it is very easy to please in a wide variety of soils and sites. Its seedlings often establish themselves in shady walls. The tubular flowers, up to ¾in/2cm long, are arranged in elongated clusters that are held just above the mound of light green, ferny foliage. Flowering takes place over an exceptionally long period, especially in a shaded position.
also for: ■ Shallow soils over chalk ■ Ground cover ■ Decorative, green foliage

ADDITIONAL PERENNIAL PLANTS, featured elsewhere in this book, that have a long, continuous flowering period

Tricyrtis formosana
[toad lily]
◑[○]

type of plant: hardy perennial [7–9]
flowering time: early to mid-autumn
flower color: pale mauve or white + red-purple
height: 24–36in/60–90cm

T. formosana needs careful positioning if its airy heads of delicately marked and subtly colored flowers are not to be overlooked. It thrives in a cool, shady place and in rich, moist soil with good drainage. In cold regions especially, it requires some shelter in order to flower well. The flowering season is long and late, and each star-shaped bloom is about 1½in/4cm wide. When growing well, the plant may be as much as 4ft/1.2m tall and its erect stems and shining, veined leaves create sizeable clumps. *T. hirta* [zones 5–9] has similarly shaped and colored flowers, most of which are borne close to the stems of the plant.

Meconopsis cambrica
[Welsh poppy]
◑[○]

type of plant: hardy perennial [6–9]
flowering time: mainly late spring to late summer
flower color: yellow or orange
height: 12–18in/30–45cm

Ferny foliage and lovely, simple flowers give this prolific self-sower considerable charm, but it can be a nuisance in a small garden where there is not enough space for its offspring. Nearly all plants of the genus *Meconopsis* need moist, acid soil. It is especially at home in a cool, shady place and it is excellent for naturalizing in an informal, woodland garden. It tolerates some dryness and competition from other plants. Its 2in/5cm-wide, thin-stemmed flowers open, in succession, over many weeks, above little tufts of light green, lobed or divided foliage. Some double-flowered varieties are available and, being sterile, they do not produce the tenacious, tap-rooted seedlings of the species.

Epilobium glabellum
[willow herb]
◑[○]

type of plant: slightly tender perennial [7–9]
flowering time: early summer to early autumn
flower color: creamy white or pink
height: 8in/20cm
Semi-evergreen

Unlike its relative, the very invasive rose bay willow herb, this little plant forms either a neat mat or a clump of growth, and it makes good ground-cover. The leaves are a rich, slightly olive green, and they are often suffused with bronze-red. Funnel-shaped flowers, each about ¾in/2cm across, are arranged in short, dark-stemmed spikes. They open over a period of several months. *E. glabellum* thrives in a cool place and in moist, well-drained soil.
also for: ■ Ground cover

Asarina procumbens
(syn. *Antirrhinum asarina*)
◑[○]

type of plant: slightly tender perennial [7–9]
flowering time: early summer to early autumn
flower color: cream
height: 3–4in/8–10cm
Evergreen/Semi-evergreen

The trailing stems of *A. procumbens* are clothed in rounded leaves that are soft and velvety but also rather sticky. The sage-green coloring on these leaves makes a flattering background for the snapdragon-like flowers, up to 1½in/4cm long, which appear over many weeks. This plant needs good drainage; it is susceptible to damage if its roots are wet in winter. *A. procumbens* is particularly at home in lightly shaded crevices and crannies and, as this illustration shows, it looks pretty trailing down a wall.
also for: ■ Ground cover ■ Crevices in paving

ADDITIONAL PERENNIAL PLANTS, featured elsewhere in this book, that have a long, continuous flowering period

◑[○] **partial shade (or sun)**

minimum height 10ft/3m or more
Lonicera x *brownii* "Dropmore Scarlet," see p.135
Lonicera x *heckrottii* "Gold Flame," see p.135
Lonicera periclymenum "Serotina," see p.312

minimum height between 3ft/90cm and 10ft/3m
Clematis "Hagley Hybrid," see p.136
Hydrangea macrophylla "Ayesha," see p.103
Hydrangea macrophylla "Mariesii Perfecta,"
  see p.33
Mahonia japonica, see p.312

minimum height 3ft/90cm or less
Helleborus argutifolius, see p.327
Helleborus foetidus, see p.82
Omphalodes cappadocica,
  see p.120

Nepeta govaniana
[catmint]
◐

type of plant: hardy perennial [5–9]
flowering time: midsummer to early autumn
flower color: light yellow
height: 36in/90cm

In contrast to many catmints, *N. govaniana* appreciates moisture as well as good drainage and it grows best in a cool position. Its delightfully airy spikes of 1in/2.5cm-long, tubular flowers are held on upright, branched stems. When bruised, the tapering, light green leaves, to 4in/10cm long, give off a not particularly pleasant, rather nutty scent. The plant forms a clump of slender growth. For an example of a catmint that produces blue flowers over a long season, see p.339.

Dicentra "Bacchanal"
◐

type of plant: hardy perennial [4–8]
flowering time: mid-spring to midsummer (see description)
flower color: dark crimson
height: 12–15in/30–38cm

D. "Bacchanal" produces abundant clumps of lovely, pale green, ferny foliage from mid-spring onward. The tinge of gray-blue present in the leaves and the charming way in which the locket-shaped flowers dangle above the foliage add to the general impression of light laciness. Each little spray of flowers is about 1in/2.5cm long. Given moist, humus-rich soil and some shade, *D.* "Bacchanal" is an exceptionally long-flowering plant. In ideal conditions there may still be some flowers at the beginning of autumn.
also for: ■ Gray, blue-gray, or silver leaves

Corydalis flexuosa "China Blue"
◐

type of plant: hardy perennial [5–8]
flowering time: mid-spring to early summer (see description)
flower color: bright blue
height: 12in/30cm

The intense flower color of *C. flexuosa* "China Blue" is its most arresting feature, although the finely divided, olive-green leaves are also attractive. The foliage, which may be purple-tinged, forms loose mounds of growth, above which rise erect stems carrying slender, tubular blooms, each 1in/2.5cm long. Ideally, moist, open-textured soil and a cool site should be provided. In these conditions, the flowering period may well extend into the middle of summer. After flowering, the plant tends to die back, particularly if growing conditions are dryish. Varieties of this plant include *C.f.* "Purple Leaf," which has flowers, stems and leaves tinged with purple.
also for: ■ Decorative, green foliage

Phlox divaricata subsp. laphamii "Chattahoochee" (syn. P. "Chattahoochee") [blue phlox, woodland phlox]
◐

type of plant: hardy perennial [5–9]
flowering time: late spring to midsummer
flower color: lavender-blue
height: 6–9in/15–23cm
Semi-evergreen

The slim, little leaves of this lax-stemmed, prostrate plant are covered, for weeks on end, with a mass of flowers. Each five-petalled bloom, about ¾in/2cm across, has a conspicuous, purplish red eye. The flowers are held in branched heads. This short-lived plant is happiest in cool, moist conditions. It thrives in moisture-retentive soil that is rich in humus. *P. divaricata* subsp. *laphamii* "Chattahoochee" is usually about twice as wide as it is tall.

Hacquetia epipactis (syn. Dondia epipactis)
◐

type of plant: hardy perennial [5–7]
flowering time: early to late spring
flower color: yellow + lime-green
height: 4in/10cm

The minute, yellow flowers of this slow-growing plant are surrounded by much larger, bright lime-green bracts. This arrangement produces an overall effect of yellow-centered, green flowers. These charming blooms, each up to 1½in/4cm across, are very long-lasting—although the color of the bracts does soften as the weeks pass. In early spring, the plant is simply a dome of flower heads and the just-emerging foliage is more or less obscured. After flowering is finished, the glossy, bright green, three-lobed leaves develop fully. They too are decorative. *H. epipactis* is most at home in cool, moist, humus-rich soil.
also for: ■ Decorative, green foliage ■ Green flowers

ADDITIONAL PERENNIAL PLANTS, featured elsewhere in this book, that have a long, continuous flowering period

◐ partial shade

minimum height between 3ft/90cm and 10ft/3m
Desfontainia spinosa, see p.36

◐● partial or full shade

minimum height 3ft/90cm or less
Geranium nodosum, see p.82
Helleborus foetidus, see p.82
Helleborus x *hybridus*, see p.321

Helleborus x *hybridus* black-flowered, see p.332
Hypericum calycinum, see p.82
Liriope muscari, see p.83
Pratia pedunculata, see p.159
Pulmonaria angustifolia, see p.50

Indexes

Index of botanical names

Numbers in **bold** indicate the main description and photograph for each plant. Numbers in *italic* indicate synonyms.

Plant sources, acknowledgements and credits

Plant sources

The most popular plants in this book will be readily available from nurseries and garden centers. Slightly less usual and rare plants, and popular plants too, can be obtained by consulting *The Andersen Horticultural Library's Source List of Plants and Seeds* (compiled by Richard Isaacson and published by Andersen Horticultural Library). Although this list is available in book form, a frequently revised and therefore much more up-to-date version of the information is available on subscription via the Andersen Horticultural Library's Plant Information Online website, at http://plantinfo.umn.edu. The website's Sources for Plants and Seeds section, compiled by Richard Isaacson and Katherine Allen, currently lists more than 88,000 plants and 2,000 suppliers.

Author's acknowledgments

There can be very few authors who, once their book is completed, can pat themselves on the back and say "All my own work;" like most writers, I am indebted to many people. My agent, Uli Rushby-Smith, has been not only perceptive and tenacious, but also kind and patient – as always.
Although Camilla Stoddart no longer works for Cassell, it was she who understood, right from the beginning, that *Right Plant, Right Place* needed a comprehensive overhaul. Anna Cheifetz, publishing manager at Cassell, was an outstandingly capable, clear-sighted, and charming administrator of what were often rather complex affairs. Joanne Wilson, editor at Cassell, worked long and hard over the administration of the pictures for the book. Joanna Chisholm was an impressively incisive and thorough editor, and I have very much appreciated all Helen Taylor's design skills. Finally, I owe a special debt of gratitude to my family, particularly my husband and children, who encouraged me and, most generously, helped me in all sorts of ways throughout the long gestation period of this book.

Author's picture acknowledgements

The author is most grateful to the numerous gardeners, garden and nursery owners, and gardening organizations who gave her permission to take photographs and who were so helpful in many ways. She is especially grateful to the following:

Macplants, Berrybank Nursery, East Lothian.
The National Trust for Scotland (photographs taken at the following properties: Arduaine Garden, Branklyn Garden, Crathes Castle, Culzean Castle, Falkland Palace, Geilston Garden, Greenbank Garden, Hill of Tarvit, Inveresk Lodge Garden, Inverewe Garden, Kellie Castle, Malleny Garden, Priorwood Garden and Threave Garden).
The Royal Horticultural Society for permission to photograph plants at RHS Garden Wisley.

She is very grateful to the following individuals and organizations whose gardens or nurseries are, at the time of writing, open to the public on a regular basis for more than just one or two days a year: Belfast City Council (International Rose Garden, Belfast); Blair Charitable Trust (Blair Castle, Perth and Kinross); Mr and Mrs C.H.A Bott (Benington Lordship, Hertfordshire); Lady Buchan-Hepburn (Kailzie Gardens, Scottish Borders); Vanessa Cook (Stillingfleet Lodge Nurseries, North Yorkshire); The Dowager Countess Cawdor (Cawdor Castle, Highland); Mr and Mrs J.G. Chambers (Kiftsgate Court, Gloucestershire); Beth Chatto (The Beth Chatto Gardens, Essex); R.E.J. Compton (Newby Hall, North Yorkshire); Teyl de Bordes (Lilliesleaf Nursery, Scottish Borders); Mr and Mrs Graham Buchanan-Dunlop (Broughton Place, Scottish Borders); Mr and Mrs Peter Cox (Glendoick Garden Centre, Perth and Kinross); Dobbies Garden World (Melville Nursery, Midlothian); East Durham and Houghall Community College (Houghall Gardens, Co Durham); Edinburgh City Council (Inch Nursery, Princes Street Gardens, Saughton Park, Edinburgh); Fife Council (St Andrews Botanic Garden, Fife); Fingal County Council (Ardgillan Demesne Gardens, Co Dublin); Forest Service, Department of Agriculture for Northern Ireland (Castlewellan National Arboretum, Co Down); Sir Charles and Lady Fraser (Shepherd House, East Lothian); Furzey Gardens Charitable Trust, (Furzey Gardens, Hampshire); M. Patrice Fustier (Domaine de Courson, Ile-de-France, France); Glasgow City Council (Glasgow Botanic Garden, Glasgow); Mrs W.T. Gray (Eggleston Hall Gardens, Co Durham); Kerry Hamer (The Dingle, Powys); Hampshire County Council (The Sir Harold Hillier Gardens and Arboretum, Hampshire); Miss

M.G. Heslip (MGH Nurseries, Co Down); Howick Trustees Ltd (Howick Hall, Northumberland); Coen Jansen (Vaste Planten, Dalfsen, The Netherlands); Mr and Mrs John Jenkins (Wollerton Old Hall, Shropshire); Lakeland Horticultural Society (Holehird, Cumbria); Leeds Castle Foundation (Leeds Castle and Culpeper Gardens, Kent); Judith Lockey (Halls of Heddon, Northumberland); Mr and Mrs Hugh Montgomery (Benvarden, Co Antrim); The National Trust, Northern Ireland Region (Mount Stewart, Co Down; Rowallane Garden, Co Down); Northern Horticultural Society – now merged with the Royal Horticultural Society (Harlow Carr Botanical Gardens, North Yorkshire); North Lanarkshire Council (Colzium Walled Garden, North Lanarkshire); The Duke of Northumberland (Alnwick Castle, Northumberland); Oatridge Agricultural College (Suntrap Horticultural and Gardening Centre, Edinburgh); Office of Public Works, Republic of Ireland (National Botanic Gardens, Glasnevin); Mrs Farquhar Ogilvie (House of Pitmuies, Angus); Wendy and Michael Perry (Bosvigo House, Cornwall); Dougal Philip (New Hopetoun Gardens, West Lothian); Nori and Sandra Pope (Hadspen Garden, Somerset); Mary Pring (Lower Severalls Gardens and Nursery, Somerset); Sir William and Lady Proby (Elton Hall, Cambridgeshire); Mark Robson (Bide-a-Wee Cottage, Northumberland); The Royal Zoological Society of Scotland (Edinburgh Zoo, Edinburgh); The School of Economic Science (Waterperry Gardens, Oxfordshire); Malcolm and Carol Skinner (Eastgrove Cottage Garden, Worcestershire); Mrs Hilda Spray (Pentland Plants, Midlothian); Ann and Mervyn, Ann and Nigel Steele-Mortimer (Golden Grove, Clwyd); Trustees of the National Galleries of Scotland (Scottish National Gallery of Modern Art, Edinburgh); Trustees of the Royal Botanic Gardens (Royal Botanic Gardens, Kew, Surrey); UDV UK (Bell's Cherrybank Gardens, Perth and Kinross; gardens now administered by The Trustees, Scotland's Garden Trust); University of Cambridge (University Botanic Garden, Cambridgeshire); University of Dundee (Dundee Botanic Garden, Dundee); University of Edinburgh (King's Buildings and Pollock Halls, Edinburgh); Michael Wickenden (Cally Gardens Nursery, Dumfries and Galloway); Susie White (Chesters Walled Garden, Northumberland); Anne Wilson (Teviot Water Gardens, Scottish Borders).

The author is also indebted to the following gardeners, owners of nurseries, and owners and administrators of gardens: Mrs L.G. Allgood; Mr and Mrs David Barnes; Lt Col. and Mrs M.D. Blacklock; Mr and Mrs A.J. Bowen; Mr Nick Burrowes; Mr and Mrs James Buxton; The Commissioners, Queen Street Gardens West; Mrs Evelyn Carruthers; The Headmaster, Gordonstoun School; Professor and Mrs Gordon Graig; Mr and Mrs Malcolm Gordon; The Hon. Peregrine and Mrs Fairfax; Mr and Mrs Chris Fletcher; Mr and Mrs Anthony Foyle; Mr and Mrs Michael Kennedy; Ms Laura Mackenzie; Mr and Mrs Jacek Makowski; Mr and Mrs Ron Mason; Lady Nicholson; Mrs Margaret Owen; Mr and Mrs E. Pickard; Mr and Mrs D.H.L. Reid; Mrs David Skinner; Mr and Mrs Michael Maxwell Stuart; Mr Simon Toynbee; Mr and Mrs Giles Weaver; Mrs Gavin Younger.

Publisher's acknowledgements

Cassell Illustrated would like to thank Robert Herman for his advice on plant availability in the USA, Richard Sanford at the RHS; Jo Knowles for illustrating the Zone maps; Sophie Delpech, Vickie Walters, and Christine Junemann at Hamlyn for their help in picture research; Jackie Strachan, Kathy Fahey and Chris Bell for all their assistance with Americanization.

Photography credits

Special Photography by © Nicola Ferguson
All other photography:

Andrew Lawson 236 bottom center, 240 bottom left, 241 bottom center right, 256 bottom left. **dk images** 238 top left. **Edward Shepherd** 13 bottom right, 15 center, 19 bottom right, 25 top center right, 26 bottom left, 28 bottom center, 31 center, 32 bottom left, 34 top left, 40 top left, 46 bottom center left, 49 bottom center right, 50 center, 54 bottom center left, 55 top center right, 57 bottom center right, 58 bottom center left, 63 center, 63 bottom right, 66 bottom center left, 66 top center left, 71 top center right, 72 center, 72 bottom center left, 74 top left, 77 top right, 77 top center right, 78 top left, 81 bottom center right, 86 center, 86 bottom left, 95 bottom right, 99 top center right, 101 center, 101 bottom right, 103 top right, 110 center, 110 bottom left, 111 bottom center right, 116 top left, 117 bottom center right, 123 top right, 128 top center left, 130 top left, 135 bottom right, 136 bottom center left, 138 bottom center, 146 top center left, 147 top right, 147 top center right, 149 bottom right, 151 top right, 156 top left, 157 bottom center right, 163 center, 165 center, 166 center, 167 bottom right, 168 top center left, 172 bottom center, 179 bottom center right, 183 top right, 186 bottom center left, 187 center, 187 bottom right, 189 top center right, 191 bottom right, 193 bottom right, 194 bottom left, 199 center, 203 bottom right, 205 bottom right, 210 bottom center, 211 bottom center right, 212 bottom center, 215 bottom right, 215 bottom center right, 222 bottom left, 224 top left, 225 top center right, 232 bottom center left, 233 bottom right, 237 bottom center right, 250 top left, 264 bottom center left, 265 bottom center right, 265 top center right, 266 bottom center left, 266 top center left, 267 top right, 273 bottom right, 275 top center right, 276 bottom left, 278 bottom center, 280 bottom center left, 281 bottom center right, 290 bottom left, 299 center, 299 bottom right, 299 bottom center right, 300 bottom center, 301 bottom center right, 302 bottom center left, 304 center, 308 bottom center left, 310 top left, 313 bottom center, 313 bottom center right, 316 bottom left, 319 top right, 320 top left, 334 bottom left, 335 bottom center right, 336 top left, 338 bottom center left, 343 center, 343 bottom center right, 346 top left. **Garden World Images** 14 top left, 14 top center left, 16 top left, 17 bottom right, 18 top left, 20 top left, 22 bottom center left, 25 bottom center right, 29 top right, 31 bottom center, 31 top center right, 34 center, 41 bottom right, 41 bottom center, 41 bottom center right, 42 bottom left, 44 top right, 49 top right, 50 bottom left, 53 top right, 54 top center left, 57 center, 57 top center right, 59 top right, 59 bottom center right, 60 bottom center left, 61 top center right, 62 bottom left, 63 bottom center right, 65 top center right, 69 top right, 78 bottom left, 82 bottom left, 83 top center right, 89 center, 89 top right, 89 bottom center right, 94 bottom left, 95 bottom center right, 96 center, 98 bottom left, 99 top right, 99 bottom right, 100 center, 105 center, 105 bottom right, 108 top left, 108 center, 108 bottom center left, 109 bottom center, 110 top left, 125 center, 127 top center right, 128 top left, 128 bottom left, 129 bottom center right, 130 bottom center left, 131 top right, 132 top left, 132 center, 138 top center left, 143 top center right, 145 top right, 146 top left, 150 center, 152 bottom left, 154 bottom center left, 155 top right, 156 bottom left, 156 bottom center, 157 top center right, 158 top left, 158 bottom left, 166 bottom center left, 166 top center left, 167 center, 171 top center right, 176 top left, 177 center, 177 top center right, 179 top center right, 180 center, 183 bottom center right, 188 top center left, 198 top left, 202 bottom left, 207 bottom center right, 208 bottom left, 210 bottom center left, 212 top center left, 217 bottom center, 223 top right, 224 bottom center left, 228 bottom center left, 235 top right, 235 bottom right, 236 center, 236 top center left, 237 top right, 238 top center left, 239 bottom center right, 239 top center right, 246 center, 249 bottom right, 249 bottom, 255 top right, 255 bottom center right, 256 top left, 257 top center right, 258 top left, 261 bottom right, 261 bottom center right, 263 top center right, 269 top center right, 270 top left, 270 top center left, 271 center, 271 top right, 271 bottom right, 271 bottom center right, 273 bottom center, 273 bottom center right, 274 bottom left, 275 bottom center right, 276 bottom center left, 276 top center left, 279 center, 282 center, 282 top center left, 283 bottom right, 283 center, 285 bottom center right, 286 top center left, 287 top right, 287 bottom center right, 292 bottom left, 292 top center left, 297 center, 297 bottom right, 299 bottom center, 300 center, 301 bottom center, 303 top right, 303 center right, 305 bottom right, 305 top center right, 307 top center right, 309 center, 313 center, 314 top center left, 318 top left, 319 bottom center right, 324 bottom center left, 325 top right, 329 bottom right, 340 bottom left, 341 bottom center, 345 bottom right, 345 bottom center right, 346 center, 346 top center left. **Global Publishing Pty Ltd** 17 center, 21 top right, 22 top center left, 23 bottom right, 26 bottom center left, 27 bottom center right, 28 top left, 30 center, 31 top right, 32 top left, 33 center, 37 top center right, 40 bottom center left, 40 top center left, 45 top right, 52 center, 53 bottom right, 53 top center right, 55 top right, 60 top center left, 82 center, 83 bottom right, 89 bottom right, 92 top left, 94 bottom center left, 94 top center left, 96 top left, 96 top center left, 97 center, 99 bottom center right, 100 top left, 106 top center left, 107 bottom center right, 112 bottom center left, 114 bottom center left, 120 bottom left, 121 bottom center right, 122 center, 125 top right, 127 center, 127 bottom right, 133 top center right, 136 bottom left, 139 top right, 140 top left, 140 center, 142 center, 145 bottom center, 149 top right, 154 bottom left, 154 bottom center, 155 center, 157 bottom right, 158 bottom center left, 165 top right, 170 bottom left, 173 top right, 184 bottom left, 186 center, 187 bottom center, 190 bottom center, 191 bottom center right, 192 top left, 193 top center right, 198 bottom left, 203 bottom center right, 210 top center left, 217 top center right, 219 center, 219 bottom right, 222 center, 225 bottom right, 233 top center right, 235 bottom center, 237 bottom right, 238 bottom center, 240 top center left, 241 top center right, 249 center, 253 bottom center, 254 bottom right, 257 top right, 269 bottom right, 270 bottom center left, 279 top right, 280 center, 281 bottom right, 281 top center right, 282 top left, 282 bottom left, 283 top right, 289 top right, 294 bottom left, 295 center, 300 bottom left, 306 top left, 307 bottom right, 308 center, 312 top left, 313 top center right, 314 bottom left, 321 bottom center right, 324 center, 324 top center left, 325 bottom right, 326 bottom center left, 329 bottom center right, 330 top left, 342 center. **Harpur Garden Library** 184 bottom center, 235 center. **John Glover** 89 top center right, 159 bottom center right, 188 bottom center left, 243 center, 253 center, 304 top left. **Fothergill's Seeds** 129 top center. **Octopus Publishing Group Limited** 30 bottom center left, 30 top center left, 36 top center left, 47 top right, 79 top right, 91 bottom center right, 95 top center right, 107 top center right, 109 bottom center right, 113 center, 129 bottom right, 136 top left, 149 bottom center right, 175 center, 194 center, 202 bottom center left, 240 top left, 240 bottom center left, 255 bottom right, 257 bottom right, 260 top left, 304 bottom center left, 311 top right, 323 bottom center right, 326 center. **Peter Stiles Photography** 13 top center right, 13 top right, 28 center, 33 top right, 33 top center right, 53 center, 65 bottom center right, 65 bottom right, 66 top left, 67 top right, 69 center, 70 center, 83 center, 95 top right, 97 bottom right, 122 bottom left, 128 center, 134 center, 152 top, 161 bottom center, 178 bottom left, 179 bottom right, 185 bottom center right, 185 center, 191 top right, 192 bottom left, 195 top right, 208 top center right, 235 bottom center right, 241 top right, 246 bottom left, 247 bottom right, 253 top center right, 258 bottom left, 269 top right, 284 top right, 286 bottom left, 292 center, 297 bottom center right, 305 center, 305 bottom center, 306 bottom center, 309 bottom right, 316 center, 319 bottom right, 323 top center right, 338 bottom center. **Photos Horticultural** 46 bottom left, 58 top left, 302 top center left. **Ray Cox Photography** 318 bottom left. **Science Photo Library** 16 bottom center right, 116 bottom center, 303 bottom right. **Sutton's Seeds** 306 top right. **British Iris Society** 57 bottom right. **Thompsons** 301 bottom right, 306 top center left.

Hardiness zones

Temperature ranges		
°F	Zone	°C
below -50	1	below -45
-50 to -40	2	-45 to -40
-40 to -30	3	-40 to -34
-30 to -20	4	-34 to -29
-20 to -10	5	-29 to -23
-10 to 0	6	-23 to -17
0 to 10	7	-17 to -12
10 to 20	8	-12 to -7
20 to 30	9	-7 to -1
30 to 40	10	-1 to 5

Each of the plants illustrated in this book has been given a hardiness rating in figures – [4–9] for example. These figures refer to the hardiness zones devised by the United States Department of Agriculture. The zones are based on average annual minimum temperatures. Temperature ranges for the various zones appear in the key. The lower the zone figure, the colder the zone. It is important to remember that there are many factors that can alter considerably a map reading of a zone. Such factors include light levels, shelter and drainage in a particular site.

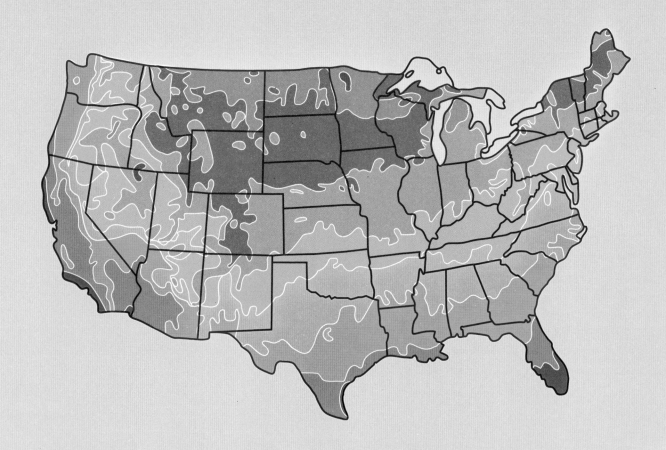